Paths to War: New Essays on the Orig

C000262540

Paths to War

New Essays on the Origins of the Second
World War

EDITED BY
ROBERT BOYCE
AND
ESMONDE M. ROBERTSON

MACMILLAN

First published 1989

Published by
MACMILLAN EDUCATION LTD
Houndmills, Basingstoke, Hampshire RG21 2XS
and London
Companies and representatives
throughout the world

Printed in the People's Republic of China

ISBN 0–333–37517–3 (hardcover)
ISBN 0–333–37518–1 (paperback)

Contents

viii   CONTENTS

Preface

This volume was originally intended to appear as a second edition of *The Origins of the Second World War* edited by Esmonde Robertson. As the first edition is now seen as something of a classic in the debate about the Second World War, we have decided to bring out this volume of essays as a new book, as indeed it is a completely new collection of essays by different authors on different subjects. *The Origins of the Second World War* will continue to be kept in print, and this new volume has been given the title *Paths to War: New Essays on the Origins of the Second World War*.

ROBERT BOYCE

Introduction

ROBERT BOYCE

The origins of the Second World War, like other major conflicts in history, are amenable to both a simple and an infinitely complex explanation. As the decision actually to commit troops in an aggressive act requires human agency, primary responsibility for the war rests with the leaders of the aggressor states, Hitler, Mussolini, and Tojo, along with their immediate *entourages*, who took the crucial decisions. This was the verdict of the war crimes tribunals at Nuremburg and Tokyo, and over 40 years of reinvestigation and reconsideration have done little to shake the validity of that judgment.[1] But this is a jurist's approach; the explanation sought by the historian is of a completely different order. It embraces the actions not only of those who directly participated in decisions for aggressive war, but of all the individuals, groups, interests, and classes who were capable of materially affecting the course of events that led to war. Moreover, it seeks to comprehend not only what they did or failed to do, but the reasons for their behaviour. Since, as A.J.P. Taylor has suggested, the Second World War may be said to have begun in September 1931 and gradually expanded until December 1941 when it involved every major power, the historian's range of subject matter is obviously extremely wide.[2] The unceasing proliferation of publications that has resulted must seem to the casual observer an obstacle to agreement on a coherent explanation. But it is wrong to expect that historical research will, or indeed should, eventually yield such an agreement: the number of historical actors and the number of component scenes are too great for a consensus ever to be reached even on the broad lines of explanation. Since no one decision or action can be regarded as altogether decisive, they are better examined as discrete issues; their relative importance must remain a matter of individual judgment.

1

I

In 1971, when Macmillan published a volume of essays edited by
Esmonde Robertson on the origins of the Second World War, histori-
cal interest was still dominated by the controversies raised in A.J.P.
Taylor's book of the same title, which had appeared ten years earlier.
In 'A Reply to Critics', printed as an afterward to the second edition,
Taylor wrote, 'My book has really little to do with Hitler.'[3] This was a
typical Taylorism: his book in fact had everything to do with Hitler.
Two generations of historians had seen in Hitler the embodiment of
brutal aggression, a dictator driven by grotesque racial theories to
pursue the goal of world power. Taylor insouciantly and inconoclasti-
cally dismissed this view. Hitler, he affirmed, was nothing like so
grandiose in his vision nor so grotesque in his commitment to global
race war. On the contrary, he was a rather ordinary statesman with a
rather ordinary mission – that of increasing his nation's standing
among competing nation-states – whose only novelty perhaps was to
exaggerate his nation's military power rather than understating it. At
all events, he simply took advantage of situations as they arose,
scarcely ever taking the initiative himself. And while Allied statesmen must share responsibility for the war because of the confusing
signals they gave by their hesitations and concessions, the principle
of appeasement underlying their policies corresponded with broad
popular opinion among their own electorates.[4]

It must be said that the intensity of reaction to Taylor's account
was due largely to its author's delight in paradox and his proneness to
overstatement. For what is to be made of the claim that 'it was never
Hitler's method to take the initiative,' when it appears immediately
after an account of his sudden and daring reoccupation of the
Rhineland[5]; or the assertion that 'in principle and doctrine, Hitler
was no more wicked and unscrupulous than many other statesmen,'
when it is juxtaposed with an acknowledgment that Hitler took
German talk of dominating Europe with 'a terrifying literalism,' and
was prepared to risk the lives of millions – the final reckoning was at
least 45 million casualties – in his pursuit of a greater Germany?[6] But
to his credit, the issues Taylor raised were of such importance that
historians of the stature of Hugh Trevor-Roper, Alan Bullock, James
Joll, and Tim Mason joined issue with him in Robertson's collection
of essays.

The same issues remain even today at the centre of historical
debate. The ordinariness or extraordinariness of Hitler's statesman-

ship has in fact become a chapter in the larger controversy over the peculiarities of modern German history. Throughout the nineteenth century publicists for German nationalism promoted belief in the distinctiveness of the German historical experience and increasingly in the superiority of German *Kultur* over French *civilisation*.[7] With the rise of Hitler, historians came close to agreement on the central importance of Germany's failure to establish liberal democracy in explaining the resort to aggression in 1914 and from 1936 onwards. To summarise in a few words a very elaborate thesis, largely owing to the weakness of the liberal tradition in Germany, the frustrations arising from rapid industrialisation were not alleviated by the agency of democratic institutions, and hence the state became exposed to constant challenge from the emerging industrial classes. The old élites, increasingly beleaguered, sought to resist change by forging new alliances with emerging élites and by redirecting the aggression of the lower classes outwards, that is by employing a policy of social imperialism, with the result that European stability was twice under-mined by German action. As Fritz Stern has explained in a singularly eloquent essay, Europe fell victim to the failure of illiberalism in Germany.[8]

The publication of Fritz Fischer's *Griff nach der Weltmacht*, pub-lished in English as *Germany's Aims in the First World War* in 1967, added a new dimension to debate over German history[9]: from cul-tural and political history, the focus shifted to social and economic history, with sociological theory contributing far more than before. This has led to intense controversy over the responsibility of the old order of Wilhelminian Germany in promoting social imperialism, the autonomy of the middle classes, and the more problematic claims of a German *Sonderweg*, that is a departure from the historical path taken by Britain, France and the other western powers until conflict led to defeat in 1945 and made 'normal' progress again possible.

No student of modern history could fail to appreciate the brilliance of the recent debate on German history – much of it stimulated by the work of British scholars – and the importance of the issues raised.[10] But there remains the original question as to Hitler's ordinariness as a national leader even within the extraordinary context of develop-ments since the formation of the second Reich (1871) or beginning of the Wilhelmine period (1895). Enough ink has been spilled by now to accept that on present evidence it is impossible to prove conclusively that Hitler intended to follow European conquest with a struggle for world domination.[11] All the same it is evident that by 1922, if not earlier, his vision had become fixed upon the realisation of an Aryan world order. This led him to demand the transformation of Germany by revolutionary methods, in order to mobilise the necessary force for conflict on a massive scale. Social Darwinism, racism, and even an element of madness may be detected in the diplomatic calculations of some of his predecessors, but none was driven with the same intensity by these demons, whose exorcising threatened limitless rather than merely domestic or even continental conflict. It is thus difficult to accept Hitler's repeated references to global conflict as idle daydreams, when his ideological fixation was bound sooner or later to drive him into just such a conflict.[12]

As for the closely related question of the existence of a coherent programme or timetable of aggression, supporters of the sceptical Taylorite view continue to amass evidence that Hitler proved inconsistent in word and deed, that he hesitated at crucial moments, that he was indeed often without military plans until shortly before major confrontations, and to argue that Hitler was driven along by the chaotic or competing forces within the Nazi state rather than proceeding in a manner of his own choosing. In *Mein Kampf*, for instance, he ruled out conflict with Britain and deplored the decision of German leaders in 1914 to engage in a two-front war, yet in 1941 he found himself repeating the same blunders.[13] At the meeting with senior advisors on 5 November 1937 he dilated upon situations which would justify striking against Czechoslovakia and Austria before rearmament was completed in 1943, though in 1938 he acted against these countries in quite unanticipated circumstances. In March 1938 he evidently chose to annex Austria outright only after confrontation with Schuschnigg, the Austrian Prime Minister, led to a show of strength. In August 1939 he set aside his seemingly implacable ideological hostility towards Bolshevism in order to obtain a non-aggression pact with Soviet Russia. Then, having wrongly assumed that the pact would deter the West from intervening and that Italy would stand by the Pact of Steel of 22 May 1939, and hesitating for five days, he invaded Poland despite the risk of war with both Britain and France. For another month he had no definite plans to attack France.[14] And as late July 1940, as Esmonde Robertson points out in an essay in the present volume, he still had no plan for the invasion of Russia and was even reducing the divisional strength of the *Wehrmacht*.[15]

On this evidence it is difficult in the extreme to claim that Hitler proceeded according to a *detailed* programme of any kind. It is also true that the Nazi state functioned in a near anarchical way, with institutions in brutal competition with one another, that senior officials including Schacht and Hitler's own choice for foreign minister, Ribbentrop, differed sharply over external policy, and that much of the drive for rearmament came not from Hitler but from industrialists, admirals, generals, diplomats, and other members of the traditional élite. But it is also obvious that – as Alan Bullock has pointed out – the argument for the existence of a programme is not undermined by evidence of opportunism or of miscalculation in carrying it out. Hitler's capacity to focus upon one issue to the exclusion of everything was as notorious as the intensity of his racial vision.[16] The Hossbach memorandum, whose literal importance Taylor dismissed and authenticity Hans Koch and others have disputed,[17] was almost certainly an accurate record of a crucial meeting: as Jonathan Wright and Paul Stafford have described it, 'a vital landmark in the history of the Third Reich', when *Lebensraum* ceased to be a dream and became the basis of actual plans for foreign conquest.[18] The following month Hitler issued the high command a directive mentioning a 'war of attack on Czechoslovakia'.[19] Advisors who opposed his plans were dismissed or cowed into submission. Austria and Czechoslovakia, having been singled out as the next targets for aggression, were soon overwhelmed. And shortly thereafter plans were devised for the conquest of further territory in the east. Of course, the process of *Gleichschaltung* or regimentation was not without its casualties and failures. But Hitler clearly retained his grip on foreign policy and exploited the imperialist ambitions of the industrial, military and other interests within Germany without allowing them to constrain or divert him from his goals. In the words of Ian Kershaw, 'Hitler's foreign policy was . . . in no way independent of structural determinants' of different kinds. These, however, pushed him if anything still faster on the path he was in any case determined to tread.[20]

But there remains the question of Germany's preparations for war, which Taylor presented as the bedrock argument against claims that Hitler actually intended to embark upon a major war in 1939. Relying upon the investigations of Burton Klein, an American economist, Taylor wrote that German rearmament was so modest that it could only have served as an adjunct to diplomatic bluff or finesse, or at most for limited *Blitzkrieg* war. It was undertaken in breadth, not in depth. Having barely begun in 1935, Hitler cut armament plans by 30 percent after Munich, cut them again after the defeat of France in 1940, and proceeded to cut them again after the initial victories against the Soviet Union in June 1941.[21] Thus, Taylor triumphantly declared,

> In considering German armament we escape from the mystic regions of Hitler's psychology and find an answer in the realm of fact. The answer is clear. The state of German armament in 1939 gives the decisive proof that Hitler was not contemplating general war, and probably not intending general war at all.[22]

This assertion was soon challenged. Tim Mason, in a perceptive analysis, explained the apparent contradiction by disputing the accuracy of Klein's evidence, in particular its estimate of the Nazi regime's commitment to rearmament, and by arguing that if Hitler resorted to war before armament levels justified the risk it was to escape from the insoluble economic and institutional dilemmas that the regime had created.

> The only 'solution' open to this regime of the structural tensions and crises produced by dictatorship and rearmament was more dictatorship and more rearmament, then expansion, then war and terror, then plunder and enslavement. The stark, ever present alternative was collapse and chaos, and so all solutions were temporary, hectic, hand-to-mouth affairs, increasingly barbaric improvisations around a brutal theme.[23]

Alan Bullock and others took up the theme of *Blitzkrieg* strategy, mentioned by Mason, and argued that the elaboration of the doctrine of *Blitzkrieg*, or lightning wars, during the 1930s enabled Hitler to contemplate aggression without incurring the massive economic and human costs of the First World War. A kind of *Blitzkrieg* diplomatic offensive, relying upon surprise and speed to divide opponents and overwhelm them one at a time, had proven remarkably successful in the years leading up to 1939. Thereafter Hitler pursued a *Blitzkrieg* military strategy, bringing to bear military forces in short concentrated blows, causing maximum damage to the enemy with minimum disruption to the national economy. Thus freed from the necessity of choosing guns or butter, his Nazi regime was able to maintain its mass support.[24]

This thesis, with Hitler acting either from desperation or cleverness, has gained wide acceptance. But in recent years the case for the military component has been effectively challenged. Despite appearances, it is clear that Hitler and his generals had by no means recognised the potentiality of a *Blitzkrieg* strategy when they embarked upon hostilities in 1939. Careful planning and the ability to concentrate vastly superior forces upon a single enemy produced rapid victories. But it was only under the pressure of Hitler's orders that the *Wehrmacht* and *Lufwaffe* found themselves employing *Blitzkrieg* tactics, from which strategic lessons belatedly followed.[25] It is now clear that the concept of a *Blitzkrieg* economy is also belied by the evidence. As Richard Overy in his contribution to the present volume shows, neither Hitler nor his generals drew the lesson from the First World War that another war on this scale was unsustainable and must be avoided, but rather that next time the German economy and society must not be allowed to let the military down. From 1933 onwards great efforts were therefore made to mobilise them both. Although it is evident that, for reasons inherent in the Nazi régime, the practical result was much less impressive than might have been expected, the inferences to be drawn can hardly be exaggerated. They confirm that Nazi leaders expected to fight not merely an aggressive war but a large-scale war – and very likely an intercontinental war as well.

The third major issue made controversial by Taylor's book was that of appeasement. For 20 years after the war scarcely a single independent voice was raised in defence of the British appeasers, who were portrayed either as cynical defenders of the capitalist system who hoped to drive Germany and Russia into mutual destruction, or as the embodiment of insularity, timidity and cowardice. It thus came as a tremendous shock to find an eminent historian affirming that appeasement was not necessarily wrong, merely badly handled. After initial bad-tempered reactions a debate got under way, which continues as lively as ever without a new consensus yet apparent.[26]

Early critics of appeasement, as Donald Cameron Watt has observed, wrote from a standpoint 'too exclusively European and concerned with central Europe rather than the Mediterranean.'[27] Their works betrayed little appreciation of Britain's global commitments and its diminishing capacity to defend them. This has been largely remedied by the appearance of monographs such as Lawrence Pratt's account of British policy in the eastern Mediterranean, studies of Britain and the Ethiopian and Spanish conflicts, a host of studies on British policy in the Far East by William Roger Louis, Bradford Lee, Anne Trotter, Peter Lowe, James Neidpath, Paul Haggie and others, the massive and undeviatingly sympathetic biography of Baldwin by Keith Middlemas and John Barnes, the excellent account of British naval policy between the wars by Stephen Roskill, the volume on inter-war British defence policy by Norman Gibbs in the official history of the Second World War, the essays edited by David Dilks, and the concise but invaluable survey of Britain's strategic dilemmas between the wars by Michael Howard.[28] Due emphasis has now been given to the fact that Britain, possessed of an empire larger than ever before, faced three potential enemies after 1935 as well as increased difficulties created by the nationalist movements within its dependent possessions. Equally, domestic public opinion until the Munich conference in September 1938 leaned towards appeasement, the most strenuous anti-appeasers within the government's ranks having little impact on acccount of their reputation for bellicosity or political extremism. Appeasement was similarly encouraged by the uncertainty of support from Britain's 'Anglo-Saxon' allies overseas.[29]

Britain had come within weeks of collapse during the First World War when its sources of credit threatened to run out, and was saved only when the United States entered the conflict.[30] Having severely depleted its international financial assets on that occasion, Britain was all the more reluctant to become involved in a continental conflict without the assurance of American support. The support of the British Dominions was scarcely less important. The First World War had offered a salutary reminder of their potential contribution of manpower and resources: as just one illustration, Canada, involved from the outset, suffered as many casualties in the conflict as the United States. Moreover, the importance of empire solidarity had become all the greater since the early 1930s when Britain, abandoning hope of internationalist solutions to the world depression, turned hopefully to the Dominions to form a preferential trade system. But as Ritchie Ovendale explains in his essay in the present volume, the Dominions required a great deal of persuading that appeasement was futile before conceding their support for a British policy of resistance to Fascist aggression.

Besides strategic problems, Britain in the 1930s also faced serious economic and financial inhibitions on rearmament, problems better understood today than they were to a generation of historians unused to the idea of Britain's long-run decline. These have been minimised by reference to the reluctance of Conservative-dominated governments in the 1930s to adopt Keynesian schemes for reflation, but as Ross McKibbin, R.A.C. Parker, George Peden, and others have pointed out, this is too simple.[31] Radical policy changes to be effectively applied, required a measure of understanding among

Treasury advisors and the business community, which was slow in coming. Besides, bottlenecks caused by shortages of skilled labour for the airframe and machine tool industries diminished the importance of aggregate spending levels. This raises the different question, whether accelerating the pace of rearmament before 1939 would have strengthened Britain's hand, given that much of the equipment produced would have been obsolete almost from the moment it came out of the factory. After all, it was only in the 12 months before the war began that effective radar and anti-aircraft gun systems were developed and the new generation of fighter aircraft (Hurricanes and Spitfires) came into production.[32]

But if Britain's leaders had strong reasons for hesitating before confronting the country's potential enemies, there are also strong grounds for doubting the quality of the decisions they actually took. Official and private records offer abundant insight into their deliberations, yet one looks in vain for a clear recognition of the destructive dynamic of Nazism and Fascism, or of the dangers to Europe's balance of power attendant upon their concession of Germany's 'natural' frontiers.[33] The strategic value of the east European countries, Czechoslovakia in particular, was largely ignored until it was too late.[34] Accumulated grievances led them similarly to leave France all but completely out of their strategic calculations as well, thereby undermining France's security and intensifying its domestic instability which in a self-fulfilling way provided justification for their policy.[35] They also chose to disdain co-operation with the Soviet Union and ignore the increasing indications that in the absence of a western alliance Stalin would come to terms with Hitler.[36] They were ill-served by their military intelligence and senior military advisors who from the mid-1930s consistently exaggerated the external threat.[37] None of them, it seems, was capable of dealing rationally with the fear that 'the bomber will always get through':either to subject it to serious question or to draw the proper strategic conclusions.[38] Arguably, therefore, they allowed the European balance of power to turn decisively against them before choosing to make a stand.[39]

Too much has been made of the Eden–Chamberlain feud and claims – fostered after the outbreak of the war when Eden was again foreign secretary – that Eden could have saved the situation by handling the Italians more firmly and the United States more tactfully.[40] Differences over policy there were, but they were not of fundamental importance. Eden had been a member of the cabinet that approved the Hoare – Laval pact, had resisted oil sanctions against Italy, appeased both the Germans and the French after the Rhineland crisis, and promoted a policy of neutrality and non-intervention in Spain. No amount of skilful diplomacy was likely to transform Italy from a potential enemy to a British ally.[41] As for the United States, there was precious little that a British statesman could do to persuade American opinion of the need for a firmer stand against Japan or Germany, and what little could be done was being attempted, albeit unskilfully, by Chamberlain.[42]

British leaders were probably also right to discount the appeals of the German conspirators whose emissaries, slipping through the garden door of No.10 Downing Street in 1938, encouraged hopes of a coup against Hitler if only the western powers stood firm against him at Munich.[43] On the other hand it is far more difficult to accord public opinion an important role in holding the government to appeasement. Recent research has confirmed that the government itself actively manipulated public opinion through a variety of propaganda techniques in order to sustain support for appeasement policies,[44] and long after public and parliamentary opinion turned decisively against appeasement, Chamberlain continued to look for a nego-tiated settlement, abandoning the quest only in February 1940.[45]

What then of the now common view that Chamberlain had a clear-headed appreciation of the Nazi threat by the time he became Prime Minister in May 1937 and was simply playing for time in order to re-earm?[46] Indeed, what of the judgment to be passed on British policy itself? The availability of massive official documentation has encouraged historians to dwell upon the viewpoints, the experiences, and the sheer complexity of the challenge facing British policy-makers, and to treat their record with sympathy. But as Sidney Aster suggests in his essay on the 'Guilty Men' in this volume, historical revisionism is in danger of becoming apology and obscuring the moral compromises that beset British policy.

II

It would be wrong, however, to encourage the impression that the origins question revolves solely around Britain, Germany, and Anglo–German relations. Historiography has moved on, and as Europe's displacement from the centre of world affairs has become acknowl-edged the tendency has been to place the war in a broader historical and global perspective. The relationship between the First and Sec-

ond World War is a case in point. So catastrophic was the Second
World War and so manifold were its connections with the First that,
inevitably perhaps, historians have given short shrift to the statesmen
responsible for the 1919 settlement. Nothing of course could be
easier. As J.M. Keynes demonstrated in his influential polemic on
The Economic Consequences of the Peace – written in disillusionment
after attending the Paris peace conference – Lloyd George,
Clemenceau and Woodrow Wilson almost begged to be caricatured.
Since then many tracts have been written crudely schematising their
work as examples of realist or idealist policy. But as Sir Michael
Howard reminds readers in his essay in this volume, this is to obscure
the magnitude of the challenge that faced them at the end of the war
and the range of immediate, practical decisions they were forced to
make. Never in modern times had Europe's social and political order
been so severely dislocated. In the circumstances, a peace conference
could scarcely be expected to have resolved even the most prominent
issues to the satisfaction of all the countries concerned, and, as in the
aftermath of the Second World War, there was bound to be a
prolonged period of uncertainty while pressures for revision and
stabilisation were accommodated. Probably this could only have
ended in a breakdown of the settlement and renewed war, in the
absence of a remarkable conjuncture of forces including economic
conditions that favoured peace.

The international relations of the 1920s, so long out of fashion with
historians, who have preferred the more sharply delineated crises of
the 1930s, are now receiving the attention they deserve.[47] As a result
it is clearer than ever that this is no mere interlude between the two
great armed conflicts of the century, but instead a period when
important initiatives were taken in an effort to reorganise the international order and forestall renewed resort to war. The operation of the
League of Nations, the beginnings of a disarmament campaign and
the resumption of conventional alliance diplomacy are familiar aspects of the period, but this was also a time of competing approaches
to international order.

Britain, with largely unofficial US support, promoted the reconstruction of the international trade and payments system on the
Cobdenite assumption that prosperity was the surest means of discouraging conflict in the world. Thus Britain turned away from the
wartime trend towards protectionism, and took the lead in settling its
war debt with the United States, in returning to the gold standard,
and in developing the economic agencies of the League of Nations,

while the Federal Reserve Bank of New York and certain American investment bankers co-operated so far as they were able to offset the economic nationalism of their own government.[48] The French meanwhile pondered the problem of controlling the warmaking potential of the vast industrial concentration in the Rhine region, and toyed with the idea of promoting more radical, supranational solutions to forestall another major conflict.[49] Briefly, during the years 1926–31, the success of Anglo–American economic diplomacy and the combination of French prosperity and German weakness encouraged co-operation among the European powers. But opposition came not only from nationalist elements within Germany and France but also liberals in Britain who feared that a continental economic bloc would undermine internationalism, and both French and British initiatives foundered with the onset of the world depression.[50] The untimely end of prosperity in the autumn of 1929 was not due merely to bad luck – structural weaknesses in the international balance of payments system made a breakdown virtually inevitable in the absence of collective action on a major scale, as contemporary observers recognised as early as 1927 – but it was certainly a misfortune that it should have coincided with the death of the German foreign minister Gustav Stresemann, whose successors possessed none of his vivion.

Historians, in tune with the present age, have recently demonstrated very considerable interest in the economic aspects of the war's origins: the role of industrialists, bankers, and other economic interest groups in supporting – or not supporting – extremist forces bent on aggression; economic factors in rearmament and defence; and the question of economic motives behind decisions for appeasement or war. By now practically every account of war origins acknowledges the importance of the world depression – the most prolonged and severe depression in modern history – in creating the conditions for war,[51] but there is probably much more to be learned from a careful and above all imaginative analysis of evidence on this subject, though less in terms of crude economic motives or pressure group politics, than within the realm of ideas. While extreme doctrines of nationalism, imperialism, and racism gave shape to the aggressive policies of the period, their popularity derived largely from fears of economic destitution or national collapse. As the present writer explains in Chapter 2, such fears fed the misunderstandings that existed among leaders of the western liberal powers and resulted in a serious deterioration in their relations, indeed into a virtual capitalist war, which tended to obscure the threat posed by the Axis powers until at least 1938. The evidence suggests that liberal statesmen not only misunderstood the motives behind one another's economic policies but also wrongly assumed that economic motives governed the behaviour of the aggressor powers – an assumption held with only somewhat more justification by Hitler, Mussolini, and the Japanese of the liberal powers themselves. The economic policies of the powers are becoming better understood, but the heavily technical jargon in which economic issues are usually presented still tends to discourage historians from the task of identifying the elements that unite or create divisions between the thought processes of the élite groups in the various powers.

III

Of all the countries hit by the depression none was worse affected than France, although the impact was due less to the actual severity of the economic blow than to its timing. The depression in Germany and Britain reached its nadir in 1932, at which time France had only begun to experience its grievous impact. For the next four years, as the French economy declined, its chief enemy across the Rhine swiftly recovered, while its principal ally across the Channel similarly regained its capacity for independent action. This left France in a desperate situation, its internal divisions aggravated by the increasing external threat and a frustrating dependence upon Anglo-Saxon support.

The publication of archivally-based studies of French policy in the 1930s have been as belated as was France's recovery from the slump. However, with the appearance of works by Anthony Adamthwaite, Jean-Noel Jeannenay, Robert Young, Jean-Baptiste Duroselle, Robert Frankenstein and others, the debate on France's response to the international crisis has at last been fully joined.[52] Duroselle, the *doyen* of modern French diplomatic history, presents a magisterial but perhaps also broadly conventional view in a survey appropriately entitled *La décadence*.[53] France slid towards humiliating defeat, he suggests, largely because its institutions permitted only weak government and its politicians betrayed a *manque de sérieux*, a lack of vision and commitment to the national interest, which contributed to a kind of moral decay. This image of France, riven by class conflict, tainted by Fascism and anti-semitism, weakened by a venial *burgeoisie*, and governed by unstable, usually ineffectual coalitions, is, if familiar, scarcely wrong on that account.[54] But as Frankenstein has shown in a pathbreaking work, the picture can be overdrawn.[55] Despite a commitment to long-overdue industrial and social reform, Léon Blum, leader of the Popular Front government in 1936–37, placed country over class and party by giving priority to national defence. Between 1936 and 1938 the burden of national defence consumed upwards of a third of the national budget, and more than twice the fraction of national income as in 1913. In 1939 the arms industry underwent major reorganisation, and by the eve of the German invasion in 1940 France was actually producing more military aircraft than either Germany or Britain. Unfortunately, rearmament had begun very late in the day, and for a time at least aggravated social conflict.

If Blum made his contribution to the nation's defence, what of the other political leaders whose names became synonymous with appeasement and defeatism? Pierre Laval, who was executed after the liberation for his involvement in the Vichy regime, was Prime Minister at the time Italy broke the Stresa front by embarking upon its Ethiopian adventure and co-author of the Anglo – French proposal for appeasing Mussolini at this time. The cruel dilemmas that he faced in the mid- 1930s have been the subject of judicious reviews by Geoffrey Warner and Robert Young, who accord him respectable motives if little success.[56] Edouard Daladier, the Radical party leader and Prime Minister from April 1938 to March 1940, has recently been the subject of even greater controversy. The portait presented by several leading French authorities is that of a statesman yielding ground to Hitler with evident reluctance, because of France's as yet incomplete rearmament and Britain's refusal to join in a firmer policy.[57] But as Adamthwaite has pointed out, there are still strong reasons for doubting Daladier's realism in view of his dogged pursuit of an agreement with Hitler and Mussolini months after Munich. Nor does reference to public opinion or dependence upon Britain necessarily justify his appeasement policy. As in the case of Britain, it was not the government that was constrained by public opinion so much as public opinion manipulated by the government to acquiesce in appeasement. Similarly, while France was clearly in acute need of British financial and military support and thus sensitive to British foreign policy, it is not so obvious that Daladier (or his predecessors in office) wished to pursue a different policy, given their unrelieved fear of social upheaval.[58] Georges Bonnet, Daladier's foreign minister, has fared less well by this exercise in rehabilitation. His preference for appeasement *à tout prix* has been distinguished from Daladier's more circumspect policy, although even here a few voices have been raised in mitigation of the charges. Adamthwaite regards him as at least consistent by his own misguided lights and no worse than Daladier, while other writers, Duroselle included, have acknowledged that once the depression in France lifted and rearmament strengthened their hand, both Daladier and Bonnet displayed markedly greater firmness towards Germany.[59]

Re-evaluation of political leaders has been paralleled by a re-examination of the French military establishment. Two recent studies of the high command by Robert Young and Jeffrey Gunsberg have been broadly sympathetic, and a third study by Martin Alexander is expected to be so as well.[60] There are nevertheless strong objections to this view expressed by Williamson Murray, who gives failing grades to military leaders for their failure to revise strategic doctrine or take the difficult decisions needed from 1936 onwards. By this account, decadence was all-pervasive. In Murray's words, 'To a great extent the French army reflected the paralysis and crisis in leadership that seems to have gripped French society in the 1930s.[61] Perhaps the greatest enigma is General Gamelin, the commander-in-chief. As Nicole Jordan explains in Chapter 4, Gamelin was possessed of a strategic vision that corresponded with French national sentiment but increasingly proved fatally flawed.

Perhaps nowhere in this history does the term decadence apply better than in the case of Italian foreign policy. During the first decade of power, Mussolini's Fascist regime contented itself with occasional displays of *machismo* but otherwise sought prestige by participating in international organisations and generally remaining within the bounds of international society. During the early 1930s Mussolini developed plans for a colonial empire. This was of itself scarcely a departure from the course followed by earlier governments. But the scope of Mussolini's plans became grandiose. He boasted of his intention to turn the Mediterranean into an Italian lake, which was wholly unacceptable to France and Britain, and when he persisted in this quest his previous policy of 'equidistance' – playing the other powers off against each other for Italian national advantage – collapsed, leaving him to drift into a subordinate relationship with Hitler's Germany.

The familiar portrait of Mussolini as a grotesquely self-important figure, as ignorant of conditions within his own country as within others, and mesmerised by his own propaganda, receives detailed corroboration in the works of Giampiero Carocci and Denis Mack Smith.[62] The trend of recent historical writing has been, however, to accord Mussolini rather more calculation and consistency, either insofar as his foreign policy was concerned, as presented in the works of C.J. Lowe and Frank Marzari, John F. Coverdale, Esmonde Robertson, and Rosaria Quartarero, or in his pursuit of ideological objectives through foreign policy, as described in the works of Renzo de Felice and MacGregor Knox.[63]

The evidence is by no means straightforward. Mack Smith himself points to elements of consistency in Mussolini's foreign policy such as his hankering after a German partnership as far back as the 1920s, well before the collapse of equidistance led him into it, and also credits him with a measure of commitment to his Fascist ideology of Darwinian struggle. De Felice and Knox, authors of two of the most important books on the subject, go much further in according Mussolini the consistency of a true revolutionary bent upon transforming Italy and Italians through the experience of war. This being the case, it is perhaps remarkable that Galeazzo Ciano, Mussolini's son-in-law and foreign minister, succeeded in deflecting him from his commitment to Germany in August 1939. (And ironically, had Ciano not been successful, as Mack Smith has pointed out, it is conceivable that Britain would not have signed its treaty with Poland, leaving Hitler to undertake his conquest without a general war.[64]) At all events a wide gap persists between current historiographical approaches, for whereas those who accord Mussolini the qualities of a *Realpolitiker*, albeit in severely flawed form, leave open the possibility that he might have been constrained further by domestic interests or foreign powers, those who stress ideology present a Mussolini far less amenable to constraint.

IV

For many years the Soviet Union constituted the black hole of diplomatic history for the 1930s, its archives closed, its policies the object of speculation based upon conjecture, anecdote, and a few uncorroborated collections of documents. But since 1969 the situation has considerably improved. For Russian readers the series *Dukumenty neshnei politiki SSSR* has been extended to cover the 1930s. Further evidence of Soviet decision-making is now available from the opened Belgian, French, and Italian archives, and for convenience two volumes of documents in English have been published on the crucial 12 month period leading to the German–Soviet Pact of 23 August 1939.[65] We can hope that *perestroika* has put an end to the Soviet practice of presenting the 1930s as pure apologetics.[66] However, in the meantime Jonathan Haslam has made use of evidence from practically every available archive to produce a four-volume history of Soviet foreign relations in the 1930s, which when completed will constitute one of the major achievements in modern diplomatic historiography.[67]

Haslam's *Narkomindel*, or foreign office, is not the monolithic centre or Stalinist cipher of earlier accounts, but one in which foreign policy remained the subject of almost constant dispute. Litvinov, the architect of collective security, faced recurrent challenge from more nationalist or isolationist elements within the ministry who deprecated his hopes for collaboration with the western powers and suspected them of harbouring greater anti-Communism than anti-Fascism. As interesting as the precariousness of the collective security policy is the intensity and apparent sincerity with which it was pursued, and the frustrations caused by the refusal of the western powers to grasp the outstretched Soviet hand. If A.J.P. Taylor is right that the Second World War was the unnecessary war, he is also right in pointing to the failure to create an Anglo–French–Soviet alliance as one of the missed opportunities for averting it. Haslam indicates that anti-Communism, discounted in most studies of British (but not French) appeasement, indeed was a major obstacle to agreement. By the same token, Soviet suspicion of western as well as German intentions puts Soviet behaviour in hacking out a *glacis* through eastern Poland, the Baltic countries and southern Finland in 1939 in a new light.

V

The origins of the Pacific war and the role of its two chief antagonists, Japan and the United States, have been the subject of revision along remarkably similar lines to their European counterparts. No longer is Japan represented as engaged in a premeditated policy of aggression between 1931 and 1941. Instead, historians have come to emphasise the internal divisions within its governing circles, the doubts and hesitations, the mistakes and the ultimate breakdown of policy evaluation. Although to contemporary western observers Japan's aggression appeared to be of a piece, to the Japanese there was not one war but several, the Manchurian 'affair', the China war, the war for

South-East Asia, and the Pacific war, each one for limited ends but each one leading in unforeseen ways to the next.

This sinuous path, carefully mapped out by Ian Nish, Akira Iriye, and the indispensable selections of documents edited by James Morley,[68] reveals that, for example, the Marco Polo Bridge incident of July 1937, which led to the extension of the war into the centre of China, was triggered by Chiang Kai-shek's forces and not by the Japanese. In fact, the Japanese army was unprepared for a new campaign, but the expansion of the incident into a full-blown conflict was nonetheless due, it seems, to a failure of Japanese military intelligence which led to the Chinese being provoked into a serious challenge.[69] Although the Japanese military and particularly middle-ranking officers had played a vital role in sustaining pressure for aggressive solutions to the nation's problems since 1931, army commanders were soon prepared to accept a compromise peace with China; leading civilian members of the cabinet, however, posed an obstacle by seeking extreme conditions. Similar cases are described in recent accounts, which make the old assumption that Japan was divided between moderate civilians and extremist military men no longer acceptable without severe qualification. As Professor Nish points out, the foreign ministry itself was closely associated with the military by this time.[70] The involvement of the Emperor in militarist plans has not however been established. The question of his general responsibility for the drift towards the militarisation of politics raises complicated political and ethical issues,[71] but the sensational work of David Bergamini charging Hirohito with leading the Japanese conspiracy for war has met with scepticism by practically every scholar who has examined the often opaque documentation on which his charges are based.[72]

The improvisational character of Japanese decision-making invites speculation about the inevitability of war, although as might be expected, recent studies offer no clear answer. Even General Tojo Hideki, the former chief of staff of the Kwantung army in Manchuria who became Prime Minister on 17 October 1941 and was eventually executed as a war criminal, supported a final attempt to negotiate a compromise settlement with the United States. From the Japanese side it is clear that the United States' China policy throughout the 1930s must have seemed to consist of loudly proclaimed principles and threats which were not to be taken seriously. Only very late in the day did the threats become unmistakably serious. Unfortunately, as Hatano and Asada point out in Chapter 12, Japanese naval officers on whom the decision for war rested were prone to disregard realities in the predicament they had created for themselves. Miscalculation on both sides appears strikingly evident. While the US misconstrued many of Japan's deterrent actions as signs of aggression, and in a practical-minded way assumed that tightening sanctions on the Japanese economy would eventually bring a climbdown, the Japanese chose to believe that their own unbending will would prevail over their much more powerful but supposedly weak-willed opponent.

The firmness with which US public opinion supported sanctions against Japan is indicative of the difficulties faced in analysing America's role in the events leading to war. In 1933, when Franklin Roosevelt entered the White House , the country was in a strongly isolationist mood. Some, like Robert Dallek, author of one of the best accounts of American foreign policy in the 1930s, treat Roosevelt as an internationalist who made only a tactical retreat towards isolationism in his first years in office to ensure support for domestic recovery programmes, but then proceeded as fast as opinion would allow towards an active role in international affairs.[73] This is also the view of William Kinsella as well as an older generation of liberal historians such as Basil Rauch, Arthur Schlesinger Jr., and Frank Freidel, who evidently sympathise with the President's efforts, and Wayne Cole, an authority on isolationism who has recently claimed that Roosevelt pursued a mean-spirited vendetta against the isolationists.[74] For all the abundance of evidence there is however still no agreement among historians as to whether Roosevelt led public opinion or timidly followed behind it. Robert Divine, Arnold Offner, David Reynolds and Frederick Marks regard his record as one of excessive caution and inconsistency – Marks's Roosevelt is duplicitous *and* incompetent.[75] The difficulty arises largely from the fact that Roosevelt seldom proceeded in a straightforward manner and tended to put on a different face for different audiences. It is also easy to forget the bitterness that isolationism aroused in the 1930s, how it threatened Roosevelt's consensus-building on domestic recovery programmes, and how isolationist the United States remained even on the very eve of war. Only four months before Pearl Harbor the House of Representatives passed a draft-extension bill by a single vote and 64 Democrats voted against the President. In November 1941 more Congressmen voted against neutrality than had voted against Lend-Lease in February. But whether Roosevelt could have done more to change opinion is another matter.

Since the early 1950s, when William Appleman Williams published his essay on 'The Legend of Isolationism in the 1920s'[76] and particularly after the escalation of the war in Vietnam in the mid-1960s raised large questions about America's global ambitions, the greater part of American writing on the inter-war period has adopted the Williams thesis. Briefly stated, it asserts that the impetus to escape domestic dilemmas by outward expansion governed US foreign policy in the 1920s much as it had since the birth of the nation, and that after the brief hiatus caused by the economic crisis of 1932–33 the United States again moved to resolve its internal contradictions by aggressively seeking overseas markets. From this has followed a kind of Hagelian transvaluation of values. Herbert Hoover becomes in the new history an 'independent internationalist', notwithstanding an increase in in trade protection to record levels, a rundown of military strength and an acute reluctance to concert with any other powers on security or economic issues.[77] Similarly, under Roosevelt the New Deal is chiefly a programme for export expansion: his intervention in the domestic economy which so enraged American businessmen becomes little more than a detour from the main thrust of policy.[78]

There are, it must be said, problems with this thesis. Isolationism traditionally meant no entangling alliances; it by no means ruled out foreign commerce, finance or cultural relations. The fact that the United States engaged in foreign commerce and finance on a larger scale than before in the 1920s therefore scarcely explodes the myth of isolationism. Careful examination of the evidence has also left unaltered earlier claims that for most of his first two terms of office Roosevelt displayed little interest in foreign commerce and privately mocked Cordell Hull, his secretary of state, whose faith in freer trade as a panacea verged on fanaticism. Moreover, the organisations such as the Export-Import Bank that revisionist historians point to as evidence of commitment to the Open Door policy, restricted their activities almost exclusively to Latin America, which is consistent with 'hemispheric' isolationism.[79] One feature of this revisionism has been, however, to highlight Anglo – American rivalry, a phenomenon predating independence but intensified by the British Ottawa agreements on trade, which helped to keep the two countries at arm's length.[80] Roosevelt's position was, as Callum MacDonald describes in Chapter 8, exceedingly difficult, and if he failed in his deterrence policy against the aggressor states it was largely because of the constraints imposed upon him by traditional anglophobe isolationism.

VI

Every generation brings to bear its own preoccupations on the past. At present one of these is the role of intelligence, studies of which have lately become a growth industry. The contribution they make to an understanding of international relations in the 1930s is on occasion dizzying, as if nothing is what it seems to be, whereas that the true reasons for decisions and events are hidden in files of coded reports. It is well known that Mussolini had daily access to the cables of the British embassy in Rome, which enabled him to flout cautionary advice on his foreign adventures, knowing British intentions with a certainty. It is now known as well that Hitler was able to read much if not most of the British diplomatic traffic to chanceries in central Europe, including Prague, which he put to good use at the Munich conference.[81] Of equal importance, after Munich anti-Nazi conspirators, among them Carl Goerdeler, planted information on Britain of an imminent German invasion of the Low Countries, which led directly to the decision to build up a continental army, initiate staff talks with the French, double the Territorial Army and introduce conscription. Subsequently 'black propaganda' by anti-Nazis in the *Abwehr* warning of a German attack on Poland led Britain to issue a unilateral guarantee to that country on 31 January 1939.[82] In Tokyo two and a half years later Richard Sorge, the Soviet spy in the German embassy, learned that the Japanese did not intend to exploit Operation Barbarossa by attacking Russia, which enabled 200,000 soldiers of the Red Army's Far Eastern forces to be speedily redeployed to the beleaguered western front.[83]

Others examples of intelligence affecting the course of events could be cited. But far more often it is a case of interesting information wasted because it is incompatible with the existing assumptions about the foreign power concerned or does not fit conveniently into existing strategy. Wesley Wark, in a valuable account of British military intelligence in the 1930s, describes how estimates of German rearmament veered from optimistic to pessimistic in 1936, and in 1939 back to optimistic, each time due to dubious assumptions or expectations.[84] Robert Young describes how the French disregarded inconvenient intelligence in order to persuade themselves of Russia's and Czechoslovakia's military weakness and the unimportance of German experiments with tactical air support for armoured formations during the Spanish civil war where, it seems, only the Germans learned anything from this rehearsal for the world war.[85] The British failed to heed the defector Krivitsky's warnings of a Soviet – German *rapprochement* in 1938 because it did not fit into their preconceptions.[86] The Americans, despite their code-breaking device MAGIC, failed to assess Japanese intentions in 1941, with tragic results at Pearl Harbor. And the Russians, as John Erickson has explained, allowed a faulty threat assessment framework turn valuable intelligence into noise, with nearly fatal results to the regime in June 1941.[87]

It will take some time before the new findings are fully integrated into the broader interpretations of the war's origins. Meanwhile changing circumstances are likely to draw scholars to other aspects of the subject which will thereby gain new prominence. No doubt every advance requires both the speculative mind to sketch grand patterns on the past, and the careful investigator who is prepared to follow the trail of evidence alert to every clue as to its meaning. Taylor has been the master speculator in this field; his stimulus, so evident in the earlier volume of essays from Macmillan, remains with us. Sadly, Esmonde Robertson, the editor of that volume and exemplar of the other approach to history, died in the midst of preparing the present volume. Several of the contributors were his students at the LSE or academic friends, who remember his generosity and endless curiosity about the past. These essays are accordingly dedicated to his memory.

NOTES AND REFERENCES

1. Which is not to say that all aspects of the tribunals' findings, including the existence of a conspiracy involving the Axis powers to engage in war, are correct.
2. A.J.P. Taylor, 'The Second World War', *The Creighton Lecture in History, 1973* (London, 1974), pp. 1–2. Never one to stand still, intellectually speaking, Taylor subsequently argued that the World War did not actually begin until June 1944 and lasted only 11 months. Before that there was merely a series of related but separate small wars. Taylor, '1939 Revisited', *German Historical Institute, London, 1981 Annual Lecture* (London, 1981), Addendum.
3. Taylor, *The Origins of the Second World War*, 2nd ed. with 'A Reply to Critics' (New York, 1966), p. 279. All subsequent references are to the US paperback edition.
4. As Taylor explained to his US readers, 'The general moral of this book, so far as it has one, is that Great Britain and France dithered between

resistance and appeasement, and so helped to make war more likely.'
Ibid., p. 102.

5. *Ibid.*, p. 107.

6. *Ibid.*, p. 72. Detailed assessments of Taylor's analysis are presented in William Roger Louis (ed.), *The Origins of the Second World War: A.J.P. Taylor and his Critics* (New York, 1972), and more recently Gordon Martel (ed.), *'The Origins of the Second World War' Reconsidered. The A.J.P. Taylor debate after twenty-five years* (London, 1986).

7. See for instance Rohan D'O. Butler, *The Roots of National Socialism, 1783–1933* (London, 1941), Peter Viereck, *Metapolitics. From the Romantics to Hitler* (New York, 1941), Leonard Krieger, *The German Idea of Freedom: The History of a Political Tradition* (Boston, 1957), Hans Kohn, *The Mind of Germany* (London, 1960).

8. Fritz Stern, *The Failure of Illiberalism. Essays on the Political Culture of Modern Germany* (London, 1972). Other major works with a similar theme include, A.J.P. Taylor, *The Course of German History: A Survey of the Development of German History since 1815* (London, 1945), Hajo Holborn, *A History of Modern Germany*, vol. 3 (London, 1969), Karl Dietrich Bracher, *The German Dictatorship. The Origins, Structure, and Consequences of National Socialism* (Harmondsworth, 1973), Gordon A. Craig, *Germany, 1866–1945* (Oxford, 1978).

9. Fischer continued his debate with German critics in *World Power or Collapse* (New York, 1970). See also the useful summary of the Fischer controversy in J.A. Moses, *The Politics of Illusion* (London, 1975).

10. For historiographical surveys by some of the major contributors see David Blackbourn and Geoff Eley, *The Peculiarities of German History* (Oxford, 1984); Geoff Eley, *From Unification to Nazism. Reinterpreting the German Past* (London, 1986); Richard J. Evans, *Rethinking German History. Nineteenth-Century Germany and the Origins of the Third Reich* (London, 1987); and *idem*, 'The New Nationalism and the Old History: Perspectives on the West German *Historikerstreit*', *Journal of Modern History*, vol. 59 (December 1987), pp. 761–797.

11. See for instance the affirmative view presented in Milan Hauner, 'Did Hitler want a World Dominion?' *Journal of Contemporary History*, vol. 13 (1978), pp. 15–32; and the sceptical view presented in Dietrich Aigner, 'Hitler's Aims – A Program of World Dominion?' in *Aspects of the Third Reich,* ed. H.W. Koch (London, 1985), pp. 251–66. The thesis that Hitler possessed coherent plans for world domination is also advanced in Klaus Hildebrand, *The Foreign Policy of the Third Reich* (Berkeley CA, 1973), and Andreas Hillgruber, *Germany and the Two World Wars* (London, 1981).

12. Among the best recent restatements of this argument are Eberhard Jäckel, *Hitler's Weltanschauung. A Blueprint for Power* (Westport CN, 1972), and MacGregor Knox, 'Conquest, Foreign and Domestic, in Fascist Italy and Nazi Germany', *Journal of Modern History*, vol. 56

(March 1984), pp. 1–57. See also Woodruff D. Smith, *The Ideological Origins of Nazi Imperialism* (Oxford, 1986), ch. 10.

13. H.W. Koch, 'Hitler and the Origins of the Second World War: Second Thoughts on the Status of Some of the Documents', *Historical Journal,* vol. 11 (1968), reprinted as ch. 8 of Robertson (ed.) *The Origins of the Second World War*. One of the most enthusiastic supporters of the Taylorite view has been Norman Stone. In his *Hitler* (London, 1980), he describes the notion that Hitler 'had some kind of concrete plan worked out in the early 1920s' as 'farfetched' (p. 67). Nevertheless, two pages later he states: 'Hitler's first task would be to overthrow the Versailles order . . . His next step would be to re-establish the kind of Middle-European empire . . . that had, fleetingly, existed in 1918'.

14. E.M. Robertson, *Hitler's Pre-War Policy and Military Plans, 1933–1939* (London, 1963), p. 193.

15. See ch. 11 this volume; also H.W. Koch, 'Hitler's "Programme" and the Genesis of Operation "Barbarossa"', *The Historical Journal*, vol. 26 (1983), pp. 891–920, which places principal responsibility upon Stalin for prompting Hitler to resume his aggression in the east.

16. Alan Bullock, 'Hitler and the Origins of the Second World War', *Proceedings of the British Academy*, 53 (1967), reprinted as ch. 9 of Robertson (ed.), *The Origins of the Second World War*.

17. Taylor, *The Origins of the Second World War*, pp. 128–31, 287–89; Koch, 'Hitler and the Origins of the Second World War: Second Thoughts on the Status of Some Documents'.

18. Jonathan Wright and Paul Stafford, 'A Blueprint for War? Hitler and the Hossbach Memorandum', *History Today*, vol. 38 (March 1988), pp. 11–17. See also the discussion in Gerhard Weinberg, *The Foreign Policy of Hitler's Germany*, vol. 2: *Starting World War Two* (London, 1980), pp. 34–43; and in the brief but excellent study, William Carr, *Arms, Autarky, and Aggression: A Study in German Foreign Policy, 1933–1939*, 2nd ed. (London, 1979), pp. 71–80.

19. Documents on German Foreign Policy (D.G.F.P.), Series D, vol. II, doc. 221, quoted in D.C. Watt, 'Appeasement. The Rise of a Revisionist School?' *Political Quarterly*, vol. 36 (1965), p. 205.

20. Ian Kershaw, *The Nazi Dictatorship. Problems and Perspectives of Interpretation* (London, 1985), p. 119. See also the valuable collection of essays, *Das Deutsche Reich und der Zweite Weltkrieg*, vol. 1, *Ursachen und Voraussetzungen der Deutschen Kriegspolitik*, ed. Wilhelm Deist, Manfred Messerschmidt, *et al* (Stuttgart, 1979).

21. Taylor, 'War Origins Again', *Past and Present* (April 1965), reprinted in Robertson (ed.), *The Origins of the Second World War*, p. 137.

22. Taylor, *The Origins of the Second World War*, p. 211.

23. T.W. Mason, 'Some Origins of the Second World War', *Past and Present* (December 1964), reprinted in Robertson (ed.), *The Origins of the Second World War*, pp. 124–25. Mason's argument is further elaborated

in 'Intention and Explanation: a Current Controversy about the Interpretation of National Socialism', in Gerhard Hirschfeld and Lothar Kettenacker (eds.), *The 'Fuhrer State': Myth and Reality* (Stuttgart, 1981), pp. 23–42.

24. Bullock, 'Hitler and the Origins of the Second World War', p. 220; Alan S. Milward, 'Hitlers Conzept des Blitzkrieges', in Andreas Hilgruber (ed.), *Probleme des Zweiten Welkrieges* (Köln, 1967), pp. 19–40; *idem*, *The German Economy at War* (London, 1965).

25. Jost Dülffer, *Weimar, Hitler und die Marine: Reichspolitik und Flottenbau 1920–1939* (Düsseldorf, 1973); Wilhelm Deist, *The Wehrmacht and German Rearmament* (London, 1981); Williamson Murray, *The Change in the European Balance of Power, 1938–1939. The Path to Ruin* (Princetone NJ, 1984), pp. 32–38.

26. Watt, 'Appeasement. The Rise of a Revisionist School?', pp. 192, 199–200.

27. D.C. Watt, 'The Historiography of Appeasement', in *Crisis and Controversy. Essays in Honour of A.J.P. Taylor*, ed. Alan Sked and Chris Cook (London, 1976), p. 113. For a careful attempt to synthesise the old and the new views emphasising the role of domestic public opinion, see Lothar Kettenacker, 'Die Diplomatie der Ohnmacht. Die gescheiterte Friedensstrategie der britischen Regierung vor Ausbruch des Zweiten Weltkrieges', in *Sommer 1939. Die Grossmächte und der Europaische Krieg*, ed. Wolfgang Benz and Hermann Graml (Stuttgart, 1979), pp. 223–79.

28. Lawrence R. Pratt, *East of Malta, West of Suez: Britain's Mediterranean Crisis, 1936–1939* (Cambridge, 1975); Frank M. Hardie, *The Abyssinian Crisis* (London, 1974); Jill Edwards, *The British Government and the Spanish Civil War, 1936–1939* (London, 1979); William Roger Louis, *British Strategy in the Far East, 1919–1939* (Oxford, 1971); Bradford A. Lee, *Britain and the Sino – Japanese War, 1937–1939: A Study in the Dilemmas of British Decline* (Stanford, 1973); Anne Trotter, *Britain and East Asia, 1933–1937* (Cambridge, 1975); Peter Lowe, *Great Britain and the Origins of the Pacific War: A Study of British Policy in East Asia, 1937–1941* (Oxford, 1981); James Neidpath, *The Singapore Naval Base and the Defence of Britain's Eastern Empire, 1919–1941* (Oxford, 1981); Paul Haggie, *Britannia at Bay: The Defence of the British Empire against Japan, 1931–1941* (Oxford, 1981); Keith Middlemas and John Barnes, *Baldwin, a Biography* (1969); Stephen Roskill, *Naval Policy between the Wars*, 2 vols. (London, 1968 and 1976); Norman H. Gibbs, *Grand Strategy*, vol. 1: *Rearmament Policy* (London, 1976); David Dilks, *Retreat from Power: Studies in Britain's Foreign Policy of the Twentieth Century*, vol. 1, *1906–1939* (London, 1981); Michael Howard, *The Continental Commitment: The Dilemma of British Defence Policy in the Era of the Two World Wars* (London, 1972). Wolfgang Mommsen and Lothar Kettenacker (eds.), *The Fascist Challenge and the Policy of Appeasement*

(London, 1983) provides a very useful introduction to the subject.

29. Ritchie Ovendale, *'Appeasement' and the English Speaking World. Britain, the United States, the Dominions, and the Policy of 'Appeasement' 1937–1939* (Cardiff, 1975).

30. Kathleen Burk, *Britain, America and the Sinews of War, 1914–1918* (London, 1985).

31. Ross McKibbin, 'The Economic Policy of the Second Labour Government, 1929–1931', *Past and Present*, no. 68 (August 1975); R.A.C. Parker, 'Economics, rearmament and foreign policy: the United Kingdom before 1939 – a preliminary study', *Journal of Contemporary History*, vol. 10 (1975), pp. 637–47; Parker, 'British rearmament 1936–9: Treasury, trade unions and skilled labour', *English Historical Review*, vol. 96 (1981), pp. 306–43; George Peden, *British Rearmament and the Treasury, 1932–1939* (Edinburgh, 1979). On Keynes's views in their relationship to rearmament, see Peden, 'Keynes, the Economics of Rearmament and Appeasement', in *The Fascist Challenge and the Policy of Appeasement*, ch. 10. Robert P. Shay, Jr., *British Rearmament in the Thirties: Politics and Profits* (Princeton NJ, 1977), finds less excuse for the pace of rearmament. See also the elaborate but sometimes obscure analysis of British politico-economic policy-making by the political scientist Gustav Schmidt, *England in der Krise. Grundlagen and Grundsüge der britischen Appeasement-Politik (1930–1937)* (Wiesbaden, 1981) translated as *The Politics and Economics of Appeasement: British Foreign Policy in the 1930s* (London, 1986).

32. D.C. Watt, *Too Serious a Business. European Armed Forces and the approach to the Second World War* (London, 1975), pp. 72–74; Paul Kennedy, *The Realities Behind Diplomacy. Background Influences on British External Policy, 1865–1980* (London, 1981), p. 292.

33. Kennedy, *The Realities Behind Diplomacy*, pp. 292–93; Corelli Barnett, *The Collapse of British Power* (London, 1972), pp. 505 and *passim*; Murray, *The Change in the European Balance of Power*, ch. 2.

34. Milan Hauner, 'Czechoslovakia as a Military Factor in British Considerations of 1938', *Journal of Strategic Studies*, vol. 1 (1978), pp. 194–222; and more generally, David E. Kaiser, *Economic Diplomacy and the Origins of the Second World War. Germany, Britain, France, and Eastern Europe, 1930–1939* (Princeton NJ, 1980).

35. Nicholas Rostow, *Anglo-French Relations, 1934–36* (London, 1984); Anthony Adamthwaite, *France and the Coming of the Second World War, 1936–1939* (London, 1977), pp. xv and *passim*; Adamthwaite, 'War Origins Again', *Journal of Modern History*, vol. 56 (1984), p. 113.

36. Jonathan Haslam, *The Soviet Union and the Struggle for Collective Security in Europe, 1933–39* (London, 1984), pp. 46, 157, 165, 167, 205, 210 and *passim*.

37. Brian Bond, *British Military Policy between Two World Wars* (Oxford, 1980), p. 284ff.

38. Uri Bialer, *The Shadow of the Bomber: The Fear of Air Attack and British Politics, 1932–1939* (London, 1980); Watt, *Too Serious a Business*, pp. 72–77; Murray, *The Change in the European Balance of Power*, pp. 80–84. For an interesting account of similarly exaggerated hopes and fears of airborne attack in more recent years, see Michael S. Sherry, *The Rise of American Air Power: The Creation of Armageddon* (New Haven CN, 1987).

39. This is the thesis of Murray, *The Change in the European Balance of Power*. Professor Cameron Watt takes issue with this view in *Too Serious a Business*, and in his forthcoming book on 1939.

40. The importance of Eden's diplomatic initiatives is accepted in Robert Rhodes James, *Anthony Eden* (London, 1986), treated sceptically in Sidney Aster, *Anthony Eden* (London, 1976), and A.R. Peters, *Anthony Eden at the Foreign Office* (Aldershot, 1986), and disputed in David Carlton, *Anthony Eden, a Biography* (London, 1981).

41. The argument that Britain missed a chance over Italy is advanced in Cedric J. Lowe and Frank Marzari, *Italian Foreign Policy, 1870–1940* (London, 1970), pp. 264, 325, and revived by Richard Lamb, *The Ghosts of Peace, 1935–1945* (London, 1987). But see the review by Christopher Seton-Watson, in *Association for the Study of Modern Italy Newsletter*, no. 12 (Autumn 1987). On the negative strategic value of Italy see Murray, *The Change in the European Balance of Power*, pp. 317, 319–20.

42. Callum MacDonald, *The United States, Britain and Appeasement, 1936–1939* (London, 1981), ch. 5; David Reynolds, *The Creation of the Anglo–American Alliance, 1937–41: A Study in Competitive Co-operation* (London, 1981), pp. 16–23; Gillian Bennett, 'The Roosevelt Peace Plan of January 1938', *Foreign and Commonwealth Historical Branch Occasional Papers*, no. 1 (November 1987), pp. 27–38.

43. Lamb, *The Ghosts of Peace*; Sidney Aster, *1939. The Making of the Second World War* (London, 1973), pp. 43, 230 and *passim*; Klaus-Jürgen Müller, 'The German Military Opposition before the Second World War, in *The Fascist Challenge and the Policy of Appeasement*, eds. Mommsen and Kettenacker, ch. 5; Christopher Andrew, *Secret Service. The Making of the British Intelligence Community* (London, 1985), p. 395; D.C. Watt, 'British Intelligence and the coming of the Second World War in Europe', in *Knowing One's Enemies: Intelligence Assessment before the Two World Wars*, ed. Ernest R. May (Princeton NJ, 1984), p. 263.

44. Anthony Adamthwaite, 'The British Government and the Media, 1937–1938', *Journal of Contemporary History*, vol. 18 (April 1983), pp. 281–97. See also the introduction to Frances Thorpe and Nicholas Pronay, *British Official Films in the Second World War: A Descriptive Catalogue* (Oxford, 1980); Bryan Haworth, 'The British Broadcasting Corporation, Nazi Germany and the Foreign Office, 1933–1936', *Historical Journal of Film, Radio and Television*, vol. 1 (March 1981); Nicholas

Pronay, 'The First Reality: Film Censorship in Liberal England', in *Feature Films as History*, ed. K.R.M. Short (London, 1981), ch. 6; Nicholas Pronay and D.W. Spring (eds.), *Propaganda, Politics and Films, 1918–1945* (London, 1982).

45. Peter Ludlow, 'The Unwinding of Appeasement', in *The 'Other Germany' in the Second World War*, ed. Lothar Kettenacker (Stuttgart, 1977), p. 39.

46. This view is most clearly presented in David Dilks, 'Appeasement Revisited', *University of Leeds Review*, vol. 15 (1972), pp. 38–49; and David Dilks (ed.), *Retreat from Power*, vol. 1, Introduction.

47. The literature is summarised in Walter A. McDougall, 'Political Economy versus National Sovereignty: French Structures for German Economic Integration after Versailles', and Marc Trachtenberg, 'Reparation at the Paris Peace Conference', with Comments by Charles S. Maier, Klaus Schwabe, and Gordon Wright, in *Journal of Modern History*, vol. 51 (1979), pp. 4–85; Peter Krüger, 'Das Reparations-problem der Weimarer Republik in Fragwürdiger Sicht: Kritische Über legungen zur neuesten Forschung', *Vierteljahrshefte für Zeitgeschichte*, vol. 29 (1981), pp. 21–47; Jon Jacobson, 'The Strategies of French Foreign Policy after World War I', *Journal of Modern History*, vol. 55 (1983), pp. 78–95; idem, 'Is There a New International History of the 1920s?', *The American Historical Review*, vol. 88 (June 1983), pp. 617–45.

48. Robert Boyce, *British Capitalism at the Crossroads, 1919–1932: A Study in Politics, Economics, and International Relations* (Cambridge, 1987). On the (generally exaggerated) American role, see Werner Link, *Die amerikanische Stabilisierungspolitik in Deutschland 1921–32* (Dusseldorf, 1970); Stephen A. Schuker, *The End of French Predominance in Europe: The Financial Crisis of 1924 and the Adoption of the Dawes Plan* (Chapel Hill NC, 1976); Melvyn P. Leffler, *The Elusive Quest: America's Pursuit of European Stability and French Security, 1919–1932* (Chapel Hill NC, 1979); Frank Costigliola, *Awkward Dominion. American Political, Economic and Cultural Relations with Europe, 1919–1933* (Ithaca NY, 1984).

49. Marc Trachtenberg, *Reparation in World Politics. France and European Diplomacy, 1916–1923* (New York, 1980); Jacques Bariéty, *Les relations franco-allemandes après la première guerre mondiale (Paris, 1977);* Walter A. McDougall, *France's Rhineland Policy, 1914–24: The Last Bid for a Balance of Power in Europe* (Princeton NJ, 1978); Georges Soutou, 'Une autre politique? Les tentatives francaises d'entente économique avec l'Allemagne', *Revue d'Allemagne*, vol. 8 (1976), 21–34; Edward D. Keeton, 'Economics and Politics in Briand's German Policy, 1925–1931', in *German Nationalism and the European Response, 1890–1945*, eds. Carole Fink, Isabel V. Hull, and MacGregor Knox (London, 1985), pp. 157–80.

50. Boyce, *British Capitalism at the Crossroads*, chs. 7, 8, 10.

51. Economic factors receive close attention in P.M.H. Bell, *The Origins of the Second World War* (London, 1986). More typical is Robert Ferrell, *American Diplomacy in the Great Depression: Hoover-Stimson Foreign Policy, 1929–1933* (New Haven CN, 1957), which, despite the title, has nothing to say about the great depression.

52. Robert J. Young, *French Foreign Policy, 1918–1945. A Guide to Research and Research Materials* (Wilmington, Del., 1981), is helpful but needs updating.

53. J-B. Duroselle, *La politique étrangère de la France: La décadence, 1932–1939* (Paris, 1979). Support for this thesis also comes from René Girault, Duroselle's successor at the Sorbonne: 'Les décideurs français et la puissance française en 1938–1939', *La puissance en Europe, 1938–1940*, eds. René Girault and Robert Frank (Paris, 1984), p. 39.

54. Still unrivalled for their flavour of the period for English readers are Denis Brogan, *France under the Republic: The Development of Modern France (1870–1939)*, (London, 1942), the several works by the Manchester Guardian's Paris correspondent Alexander Werth, particularly *France in Ferment* (London, 1935), *The Destiny of France* (London, 1937), and *France and Munich: Before and After the Surrender* (London, 1939), and Jean-Paul Sartre's fictional trilogy, *Roads to Freedom*.

55. Robert Frankenstein, *Le prix du réarmament français (1935–1939)*, (Paris, 1982); also his 'The Decline of France and French Appeasement Policies, 1936–9', in *The Fascist Challenge and the Policy of Appeasement*, eds. Mommsen and Kettenacker, ch. 16.

56. Geoffrey Warner, *Pierre Laval and the Eclipse of France* (London, 1968); R.J. Young, *In Command of France: French Foreign Policy and Military Planning, 1933–40* (Cambridge MA, 1978); Frankenstein, *Le prix du réarmement français*, ch. 2.

57. René Rémond and Jean Bourdin (eds.), *Édouard Daladier, chef de gouvernement (avril 1938 – septembre 1939)*, (Paris, 1977); R.J. Young, 'A.J.P. Taylor and the Problem with France', in *The Origins of the Second World War Reconsidered*, ed. Martel, pp. 105–06; Frankenstein, *Le prix du réarmement français*, chs. 8, 9. Daladier the politician is also treated with some sympathy in Serge Berstein, *Histoire du Parti Radical: crise du radicalisme (1926–1939)* (Paris, 1982). From an examination of British records, Callum MacDonald, 'Britain, France and the April Crisis of, 1939', *European Studies Review*, vol. 2 (1972), pp. 151–69, underlined Daladier's independence from British policy and called for a reappraisal of the Anglo – French relationship.

58. Anthony Adamthwaite, *France and the Coming of the Second World War, 1936–1939* (London, 1977), pp. 106–07 and *passim*; Adamthwaite, 'France and the Coming of War', in *The Fascist Challenge and the Policy of Appeasement*, ch. 17.

59. Adamthwaite, *France and the Coming of War, pp. 104–05*; Adamthwaite, 'France and the Coming of War', p. 249; Duroselle, *La*

décadence, chs. 12–15. See also Douglas Johnson, 'The French View', in *1939. A Retrospective Forty Years After*, ed. Roy Douglas (London, 1983), pp. 56–57.

60. Robert Young, *In Command of France*; Jeffrey A. Gunsberg, *Divided and Conquered: The French High Command and the Defeat of the West, 1940* (Westport CN, 1979).

61. Williamson Murray, *The Change in the European Balance of Power, 1938–1939*, p. 97ff.

62. Denis Mack Smith, *Mussolini's Roman Empire* (London, 1976); *idem*, *Mussolini* (London, 1981). See also Giampiero Carocci, *Italian Fascism* (Harmondsworth, 1974).

63. C.J. Lowe and Frank Marzari, *Italian Foreign Policy, 1970–1940* (London, 1975); John F. Coverdale, *Italian Intervention in the Spanish Civil War* (Princeton NJ, 1975); Esmonde M. Roberston, *Mussolini as Empire-Builder: Europe and Africa, 1932–36* (London, 1976); Rosaria Quartarero, *Roma tra Londra e Berlino: Politica estera fascista dal 1930 al 1940* (Roma, 1980); Renzo de Felice, *Mussolini il Duce*, vol. 1, *Gli anni del consenso 1929–1936*, vol. 2, *Lo Stato totalitario 1936–1940* (Turin, 1974, 1981); Quartarero, 'Imperial Defence in the Mediterranean on the Eve of the Ethiopian Crisis (July–October 1935), *The Historical Journal*, vol. 20 (1977), pp. 185–220; B.M. Knox, *Mussolini Unleashed, 1939–1941* (New York, 1982); *idem*, 'Conquest, Foreign and Domestic, in Fascist Italy and Nazi Germany', *Journal of Modern History*, vol. 56 (March 1984), pp. 1–57.

64. Denis Mack Smith, 'Appeasement as a Factor in Mussolini's Foreign Policy', in *The Fascist Challenge and the Policy of Appeasement*, eds. Wolfgang Mommsen and Lothar Kettenacker (London, 1983), pp. 264–65.

65. V.M. Falin et al (eds.), *Soviet Peace Efforts on the Eve of World War II (September 1938 – August 1939): Documents and Records*, 2 vols. (Moscow, 1973). For a discussion of the contents of these volumes and alterations in the second one-volume edition which appeared in 1976, see John Hermon, 'Soviet Peace Efforts on the Eve of World War Two: A Review of the Soviet Documents', *Journal of Contemporary History*, vol. 15 (1980), pp. 577–602.

66. Margot Light, 'The Soviet View', in *1939. A Retrospect Forty Years After*, ed. Roy Douglas (London, 1983), pp. 74–89. A few critics have braved censure by speaking out, see Teddy J. Uldricks, 'A.J.P. Taylor and the Russians', in *The Origins of the Second World War Reconsidered*, ed. Gordon Martel (London, 1986), pp. 178–79.

67. Jonathan Haslam, *Soviet Foreign Policy, 1930–1933: The Impact of the Depression* (London, 1983); *idem*, *The Soviet Union and the Struggle for Collective Security in Europe, 1933–1939* (London, 1984); *The Soviet Union and the Threat from the East, 1933–41* (forthcoming); *Soviet Foreign Policy, 1939–41: Isolation and Expansion* (forthcoming).

68. Ian Nish, *Japanese Foreign Policy, 1869–1942* (London, 1977); Akira

Iriye, *The Origins of the Second World War in Asia and the Pacific* (London, 1987); James William Morley (ed.), *The China Quagmire: Japan's Expansion on the Asian Continent* (New York, 1974); *idem, Deterrent Diplomacy: Japan, Germany and the USSR, 1935–1940* (New York, 1976); *idem, The Fateful Choice: Japan's Advance into South-east Asia, 1939–1941* (New York, 1980), and the essays in *idem, Dilemmas of Growth in Pre-war Japan* (Princeton NJ, 1971). See also William Carr, *Poland to Pearl Harbor. The Making of the Second World War* (London, 1985), a lucid account that sets the Far Eastern crisis into its international context; and Kyozo Sato, *Japan and Britain at the Crossroads, 1939–1941. A Study in the Dilemmas of Japanese Diplomacy* (Tokyo, 1986).

69. Michael A. Barnhart, 'Japanese intelligence Before the Second World War: "Best Case" Analysis', in *Knowing One's Enemies*, E.R. May (ed.), pp. 432–35.

70. Ian Nish, 'Japan and the Outbreak of War in 1941', in *Crisis and Controversy*, eds. Alan Sked and Chris Cook, p. 142.

71. Hans H. Baerwald, *The Purge of Japanese Leaders under the Occupation* (Berkeley CA, 1959); Richard H. Minear, *Victor's Justice: The Tokyo War Crimes Trial* (Princeton NJ, 1971); David A. Titus, *Palace and Politics in Prewar Japan* (New York, 1974).

72. David Bergamini, *Japan's Imperial Conspiracy: How Emperor Hirohito led Japan into War against the West* (London, 1971). For a detailed criticism, see C.D. Sheldon, 'Japanese Aggression and the Emperor, 1931–41, from Contemporary Diaries', *Modern Asian Studies*, vol. 10 (February 1976), pp. 1–40.

73. Robert Dallek, *Franklin D. Roosevelt and American Foreign Policy, 1932–1945* (Oxford, 1979).

74. William E. Kinsella Jr., *Leadership in Isolation: FDR and the Origins of the Second World War* (Cambridge, MA, 1978; Basil Rauch, *Roosevelt. Munich to Pearl Harbor* (New York, 1962); Arthur Schlesinger Jr., *The Age of Roosevelt*, vol. 3 (New York, 1966); Frank Freidel, *Franklin D. Roosevelt*, vol. IV (Boston, 1973); Wayne S. Cole, *Roosevelt and the Isolationists, 1932–45* (Lincoln NB, 1983).

75. Robert A. Divine, *The Reluctant Belligerent: American Entry into World War II* (New York, 1965); Arnold A. Offner, *The Origins of the Second World War: American Foreign Policy and World Politics, 1917–1941* (New York, 1975); *idem, American Appeasement: United States Foreign Policy and Germany, 1933–1938* (New York, 1976); David Reynolds, *The Creation of the Anglo – American Alliance*; Frederick W. Marks III, *Wind over Sand: The Diplomacy of Franklin Roosevelt* (Athens GA, 1988).

76. *Science and Society*, vol. 18 (Winter, 1954), pp. 1–20. The same thesis is advanced in many of Williams's publications including 'The Frontier Thesis and American Foreign Policy', *Pacific Historical Review*, vol. 24 (1955), pp. 379–95, and *The Contours of American History* (Chicago, 1961). For an acute criticism of the Williams thesis, see J.A. Thompson,

'William Appleman Williams and the "American Empire"', *Journal of American Studies*, vol. 7 (1973), pp. 91–104.

77. The phrase is coined by Joan Hoff Wilson in *American Business and Foreign Policy, 1920–1933* (Lexington KY, 1971), p. xvi, a work acknowledging Williams's influence. Wilson's biography, *Herbert Hoover: Forgotten Progressive* (Boston, 1975), which also uses it to characterise foreign policy in the 1920s (ch. 6), received almost universal praise in the United States when it appeared. David Burner, *Herbert Hoover: a Public Life* (New York, 1979), ch. 13, borrows uncritically Wilson's argument: see especially ch. 13. See also her 'A Re-evaluation of Herbert Hoover's Foreign Policy', in *The Hoover Presidency: A Reapparaisal*, Martin L. Fausold and George T. Mazuzan, eds. (Albany NY, 1974), pp. 164–86.

78. Lloyd Gardner, *Economic Aspects of New Deal Diplomacy* (Madison WI, 1964); James R. Moore, 'Sources of New Deal Economic Policy: The International Dimension', *The Journal of American History*, vol. 61 (December 1974), pp. 728–44. Vestiges of the same thesis are apparent in Patrick J. Hearden, *Roosevelt Confronts Hitler*.

79. Dick Steward, *Trade and Hemisphere: The Good Neighbour Policy and Reciprocal Trade* (Columbia MO, 1975); Frederick C. Adams, *Economic Diplomacy: The Export-Import Bank and American Foreign Foreign Policy, 1934–1939* (Columbia MO, 1976).

80. Recent literature on the Anglo – American relationship is examined in D. Cameron Watt, *Succeeding John Bull. America in Britain's Place, 1900–1975. A Study of the Anglo – American Relationship and World Politics in the Context of British and American Foreign Policy-making in the Twentieth Century* (Cambridge, 1984).

81. Christopher Andrew, *Secret Service. The Making of the British Intelligence Community* (London, 1985), p. 400.

82. D.C. Watt, 'British Intelligence and the Coming of the Second World War in Europe, in *Knowing One's Enemies*, ed. E.R. May, p. 248.

83. F.W. Deakin and G.R. Storry, *The Case of Richard Sorge* (London, 1966), p. 233; Gordon W. Prance, *Target Tokyo: The Story of the Sorge Spy Ring* (New York, 1984), ch. 56.

84. Wesley K. Wark, *The Ultimate Enemy: British Intelligence and Nazi Germany, 1933–1939* (London, 1985).

85. Robert J. Young, 'French Military Intelligence and Nazi Germany', in *Knowing One's Enemies,* ed. E.R. May, pp. 297, 308; Wesley K. Wark, 'British Intelligence and Small Wars in the 1930's, *Intelligence and National Security*, vol. 3 (1988), pp. 67–87.

86. Watt, 'British Intelligence and the Coming of the Second World in Europe', in *Knowing One's Enemies*, ed. E.R. May, p. 248.

87. John Erickson, 'Threat identification and Strategic Appreciation by the Soviet Union, 1930–1941', in *Knowing One's Enemies,* ed. E.R. May, p. 409 and *passim*.

1. The Legacy of the First World War

MICHAEL HOWARD

Before 1914 the peoples of Europe had looked on the prospect of war with very mixed feelings. Older Men like the British foreign secretary Sir Edward Grey watched 'the lights going out in Europe' with anguished apprehension, but many of their juniors welcomed war as a liberation or at least an adventure and, like Rupert Brooke, thanked the 'God who had matched them with His hour.' Even the eloquent minority of pacifist liberals and socialists, in Britain and elsewhere, soon, with few exceptions, ceased their opposition to a conflict in which their nations were fighting either to defend their territory or to assert principles of international justice, and rationalised their change of heart by declaring this to be a 'a war to end wars'.

Insofar as the governing classes of Europe did dread the prospect of war before 1914, their fears were less of the slaughter it would involve on the battlefield than of the stress it would impose on the already strained fabric of their societies. The growth of the political and social expectations of the urban working classes had long been manifesting itself in increasing strikes and disorders. In Russia in 1905 war had produced actual revolution. Both in Germany and in Britain, hopes that war might be an instrument of social cohesion were balanced if not outweighed by fears that it would result in revolutionary upheaval. The dislocation of agriculture and industry through shortage of manpower, the impact of massive military demands on civil transportation, the rise in insurance rates, the run on the banks – all would, it was feared, result in catastrophic increases in the prices of essential commodities. This would lead to bread riots, which would be all too easily fomented by agitators into revolution.

The only hope was that the war could be kept short. All the belligerents planned for a short war – in which victory was to be achieved by
the immediate commitment of all available forces – because they
could not conceive how they could survive a long one.

In the short run these fears proved groundless. The governing
classes under-rated both the cohesive effect of national feeling in
overcoming class antagonisms, and the capacity of their bureaucrats
to create and manage a war economy. Everywhere there was an
increase in state intervention of a kind unimaginable before 1914,
and judicious concessions were made to the working classes in terms
both of wages and political power. The problem was eased for France
and Britain by the unrestricted access they enjoyed to the resources
of the United States; access which left them, however, with a moun-
tainous burden of debt. But in the long run the pessimists proved
right. Russia, whose political system was too arthritic to make the
necessary adjustments and whose bureaucracy too incompetent to
run a successful war economy, did collapse as a result of urban
insurrection in 1917. In the cities of central Europe, from 1916
onward, strikes and demonstrations provoked by food shortages
were increasingly frequent. In August 1918 it was the spectre of
revolution at home as much as setbacks in the field that led the
German high command to seek a negotiated end to the war.

This decision was rapidly transformed by the collapse of their allies
and the pressure of the enemy offensive on the western front into a
quest for an immediate armistice. The consequent disintegration of
domestic order in Germany – the mutiny of the fleet at Kiel, the
seizure of power by soldiers' and workers' councils in every major
city, the erosion of discipline in the rear echelons of the army –
placed her at the mercy of her adversaries, who imposed armistice
terms designed to make it impossible for her to start fighting again.
By the terms of the armistice German troops were to abandon all
their conquests in eastern Europe, withdrawing to their frontiers of
1914, and evacuate the territory they still occupied in France and
Belgium. Allied forces were to occupy German territory west of the
Rhine and hold bridgeheads at Cologne, Coblenz and Mainz. There
was to be a massive surrender of German military and naval material,
on a scale effectively to disarm the German army and navy. With
their country in flames behind them, the German delegates had no
alternative but to sign the armistice, which they did on the evening of
10 November 1918. At 11 am next morning it came into effect along
the entire western front, and the nations of Europe began to count
the cost.

The generally agreed total of losses during the First World War is some 13 million dead, missing or crippled by wounds. Demographically this was not unacceptably high; the costs of the Thirty Years' War had probably been, comparatively speaking, even higher. But apart from the personal tragedies implied by every one of these figures, the experience of suffering and deprivation had a profound effect on the peoples of Europe. In Britain the reluctance of the electorate to participate in such another war was to set strict limits to the conduct of British foreign policy for the next 25 years. In France, whose static population of 40 million confronted Germany with its buoyant 65 million, peace led to an obsessive quest for security in which the demand for immediate guarantees against the revival of German power was to make reconciliation in the long run very difficult. In Germany and Italy, the memory of the losses which their armies had endured embittered resentment at what was generally seen as an intolerably unjust peace, and groups of demobilised soldiers, unable or unwilling to adjust to a civil society which they believed had shamefully betrayed them, set about creating their own kind of new order.

These popular attitudes were the more significant since the war allegedly fought to make the world safe for democracy had in the short run actually done so. In France universal suffrage had existed in one form or other since the Revolution. In Britain the wartime erosion of class and sex barriers resulted in a reform of the franchise in 1918 which increased the electorate from seven to 20 million. In Germany the Weimar Republic swept away the unequal voting rights which had been so anachronistic a feature of the old Prussian monarchy and gave the vote to adults of both sexes above the age of 20. In Italy universal suffrage had been introduced in 1912, but it is fair to assume that the elections of November 1919, which returned a chamber dominated by the left, were the first in which the new electorate made its presence felt. As for the successor states in eastern Europe, their constitutions at least paid lip service to constitutional processes, and in none could public opinion be totally ignored. In Russia a brief glimpse of 'bourgeois democracy' in 1917 had been replaced by a totalitarian regime under a party *apparat* which relieved their people of the need to think for themselves; in this as in so many other ways the Soviet Union was to turn its back on western Europe for the next 20 years.

The Allied leaders who assembled in Paris in January 1919 to make the peace settlement were thus in a very different situation from their predecessors at the Congress of Vienna in 1814. They did not have a free hand to reshape the world in conformity with the principles of order and justice, or of national self-determination, or even of the traditional balance of power. They were responsible to electorates still in the grip of war fever, whose passions and prejudices could not be ignored. In any case the mounting chaos in central Europe made it at times appear doubtful whether any stable regime would survive east of the Rhine with which the victorious Allies could make peace at all. President Woodrow Wilson of the United States was able to enunciate, and attempt to apply, the '14 Points' which he had laid down a year earlier as the basic principles for future peace, only because by coming to Europe he insulated himself from his own electorate. That electorate, in the form of a jealous and suspicious Congress, was to take a terrible revenge by rejecting the settlement which Wilson had so painfully worked out and washing its hands of all responsibility for maintaining it.

Wilson's 14 Points none the less set the agenda for discussion in Paris, as principles to be either applied or circumvented. They were no less important for the defeated Germans, who hoped that Wilson would be prepared to implement them even if his European associates were not. It is important therefore to recall what these points were.[1]

The first five points dealt in generalities which embodied the pure doctrine of nineteenth century Cobdenism. First, there were to be 'open covenants of peace openly arrived at': no more secret agreements whereby diplomats bargained away the destinies of peoples behind their backs and over their heads. Second, there was to be 'absolute freedom of the seas in peace and war': no more infringement of neutral rights by a powerful British navy or lurking German submarines. Third, all economic barriers were to be repealed: in future European nations could not put up protective tariffs against the flow of – among others – American goods and services. Fourth, armaments should be reduced to 'the lowest point consistent with national safety'. Finally, in the adjustment of colonial claims, 'the interests of the populations concerned must have equal weight with the equitable claims of the government whose interest is to be determined'.

The next eight points focussed on particular issues. All Russian and Belgian territory occupied by the defeated powers was to be restored. The provinces of Alsace and Lorraine, annexed by Germany in 1871, should be returned to France. Italian frontiers were to be adjusted 'along clearly recognisable lines of nationality': the century-old process of Italian unification should thus at last be completed. In eastern Europe and the Balkans the peoples of the Habsburg and Ottoman Empires were to be accorded 'the freest opportunities for autonomous development', and frontiers were to be determined 'along historically established lines of allegiance and nationality'; a convenient phrase which fudged a large number of complex if not insoluble problems. Finally, an independent Polish state was to be re-established for the first time since 1791, enjoying uninterrupted access to the sea.

The last and fourteenth point was that to which Wilson himself attached greatest importance. 'A general association of nations must be formed under specific covenants for the purpose of affording mutual guarantees of political independence and sovereignty to great and small powers alike'. This was the League of Nations. It was to this that Wilson looked for the long term viability of the peace settlement: this, and popular opinion in favour of peace, to which he believed he could appeal over the heads of governments to support the establishment of his new order. In this belief he was strengthened by the frenzied enthusiasm which greeted him on his arrival in Europe in December 1918. No matter that the British government stuck to their traditional opposition to freedom of the seas in time of war; that the Italians wanted – and had been promised by the secret Treaty of London in 1915 – a great deal more territory than they could obtain under 'clearly recognisable lines of nationality'; that the French had no intention of disarming and entrusting their security to any League of Nations; or that Poland could obtain access to the sea only by annexing territories with clearly Germanic populations and cutting eastern Germany in two. If the League could be established, so Wilson believed, it would gradually resolved these problems. So it was on the drafting of the Covenant of the League that the peace conference concentrated when it assembled in Paris in January 1919, before it turned its attention to the peace settlement with the defeated powers.

There was some enthusiasm for the League in Europe, especially in those British liberal circles where the idea had originated in the early months of the war. But on the whole European statesmen accepted the idea to humour President Wilson, and to use a bargaining counter to extract concessions from him on other matters, rather than out of any belief that it would introduce a brave new world. The French in particular saw it merely as a continued alliance of the victors to maintain the peace settlement against the *revanchism* of Germany and her allies. Had the United States Senate ratified the

Covenant the League might effectively have fulfilled this role, and gone on to act as the instrument of revision that Wilson intended. But the Senate's rejection of the Covenant in November 1919, together with the exclusion of Germany and the self-isolation of Communist Russia, reduced it initially to a rump capable of dealing only with marginal disputes. Its increased effectiveness in the mid-1920s and the enlargement of its membership to involve Germany and the Soviet Union was the result of improved relations among the powers of Europe rather than the cause. When those relations began to deteriorate during the following decade the League could do nothing to prevent it.

There was in any case no question in 1919 of Germany yet being admitted to the League, as it was still regarded by its victorious adversaries not as a potential partner but as an adversary to be punished. In Britain Lloyd George's coalition government had in November 1918 campaigned and been returned to power, in the first British election to be fought under conditions of quasi-universal suffrage, on the slogan, 'Make Germany Pay'. In France there were no immediate elections but in his 'horizon-blue' Chamber of Deputies (the French equivalent of the British military khaki) the Premier Georges Clemenceau obtained a 75 per cent majority for his hard line policy. After all the French had lost, out of the 8.5 million men who had served with their armies during the war, 1.3 million dead and – a yet grimmer reminder of their sufferings – 600 000 severely disabled, *grands mutilés de la guerre*. Thanks to German wartime occupation of its industrial north-eastern provinces, France's industrial production in 1919 was only 60 per cent of pre-war and agrarian production 70 per cent. Both Britain and France had disinvested heavily to pay for the war, raising huge internal and external loans. With the withdrawal of the American support on which, during the last year of the war, both had become completely dependent, they looked forward to a bleak economic future. This determination of both nations to recoup their losses at the expense of Germany was, if primitive, understandable.

To this determination the French added no less understandable fears for their own security. As we have seen they faced with a static population of 40 million a Germany 65 million strong with far greater industrial power and potential than France could command. The counterweight on which France had relied before 1914 – the Russian Empire – had vanished, taking billions of francs' worth of investment with it. Anything that could possibly be done to weaken Germany therefore, in the French view, had to be done. The maximum territory should be taken from it on her eastern frontiers to build up new nations in a *cordon sanitaire* under French influence which would both ward off the encroachments of Bolshevism from the east and replace the old Dual Alliance as an instrument for the containment of German power. In the west, not only must Alsace and Lorraine with its valuable iron ores be restored to France, but the coal-rich valley of the Saar should be added to them. Further, the Rhineland, the old territories of the Palatinate lying on the left bank of the Rhine, should if possible be detached from Germany altogether and constitute an autonomous state or group of states under French protection.

This entire region was seen, especially by the Allied supreme commander Marshal Foch, as vital to French security. If it remained in German hands not only would the industrial balance remain tilted in Germany's favour, but France would be deprived of all forward defences. Next time there would be no Russian steam-roller to distract the German armies. In an interview with a British newspaper in April 1919 Foch outlined what the strategic consequences were likely to be.

What was it that saved the Allies at the beginning of the war? Russia. Well, on whose side will Russia be in future? The Allied Armies – where will the Allied Armies be? The British Army will be in Canada, in Australia, in New Zealand. The American Army will be in the United States . . . And next time, remember, the Germans will make no mistake. They will break through into Northern France and will seize the Channel ports as a base of operations against England.[2]

It has to be admitted that Foch had a point, but it was not one that was accepted by either Wilson or Lloyd George. Both took the principle of national self-determination seriously; the latter if only for pragmatic reasons. A French-ruled Rhineland, Lloyd George insisted, would be simply an Alsace-Lorraine in reverse, a cause of constant friction that would be effectively uncontrollable. When Foch promised that precautions would be taken 'to conciliate the feelings and interests of the people', Arthur Balfour, the British foreign secretary, replied bitterly that that was precisely what the British had been trying to do with the Irish for years. Wilson and Lloyd George therefore formally told Clemenceau that they could not consent to any occupation of the left bank of the Rhine except a short occupation as provisional guarantee for Germany's debt. They were however prepared to offer a military guarantee against any unprovoked aggression on the part of Germany against France.

This of course was an offer which neither Wilson nor Lloyd George was entitled to make without consulting their respective legislatures. The British Parliament endorsed it but the United States Congress refused, which enabled the British government to renounce its obligation as well. Clemenceau however accepted the assurances of his allies as the best solution he was likely to get, thereby setting himself against only Foch but the even more *revanchiste* President of the Republic, Raymond Poincaré, who decided to take independent action. With their encouragement the French occupation authorities in the Rhineland identified and supported a group of local separatists, who saw the advantages which a collaborationist Rhenish Republic might enjoy in escaping from the hardships likely to be imposed on the rest of Germany. In June 1919 this group attempted a *putsch*, which the French military authorities declared to be representative of popular demand. No one believed them. The Allies were hostile, Clemenceau disowned their activities, and the whole enterprise collapsed.

After the failure of this effort the French government agreed to demand only the total demilitarisation of the left bank of the Rhine, and of the right bank to a depth of 50 km. An Allied military presence would remain on the Rhine itself, to be phased out over 15 years against payment of reparations; and 'adequate guarantees' would be provided against German aggression. In addition, Germany was to cede ownership of the Saar coalfields to France. The region itself was to be administered under the auspices of the League of Nations for 15 years, and its destiny was then to be determined by plebiscite. In addition (and without plebiscite) Alsace and Lorraine were returned to French sovereignty. In the short term at least, France did not do too badly. The settlement of Germany's western frontiers was realistic, and not unfair.

British security demands were more easily solved – again in the short run – by the surrender of the German fleet, and the imposition of stringent limitations on future naval building. The British also took their traditional perquisite, the colonies of their defeated adversaries; not so much because they wanted them as because the self-governing Dominions of the Empire did, in recompense for their own participation in the war. New Zealand acquired Samoa, Australia Papua – New Guinea (Japan acquiring German Pacific possessions north of the Equator) and South Africa took over German South-West Africa. Britain itself took only the German territory of Tanganyika to complete what was now an unbroken chain of British dominance from the Cape to Cairo; a chain extended by acquisitions from the disintegrating Ottoman Empire through Palestine, Arabia, Iraq and the Gulf States to the borders of India.

This transfer of colonial territory without any concern for the wishes of the indigenous population, in apparent disregard for the fifth of the 14 Points, was justified on the grounds, first that the Germans had shown themselves – through their brutal suppression of revolt in South-West Africa – unfitted for colonial responsibilities, and second by the device of the 'mandate'. The territories were nominally allocated to their new possessors by the League of Nations to be held in trust for the international community and administered so as to prepare the native populations for self-government. In fact the British were to get little joy out of their new possessions, especially those in the Middle East. Occupied for the traditional reason that they protected the route to India, as well as the new one that they provided access to oil, they provided more problems than profit, and were increasingly to distract Britain from playing its part in maintaining the stability of the European settlement.

In 1919, however, the British public were less concerned about imperial acquisitions than they were about 'reparations'. Over this there was initially no attempt to mitigate French demands. 'Make Germany Pay' was the popular mood of the country. President Wilson had set his face against 'indemnities', as he had against 'annexations', but as annexations could be camouflaged as 'mandates', so indemnities could be disguised as 'reparations' for 'damage done to civilian populations of the Allies and their property.' Initially this definition was intended to apply primarily to the populations of the occupied and devastated areas of France and Belgium, but the French and British rapidly extended it to cover not only such marginal expenses as interest charges on war loans and general cost of reconstruction, but severance allowances, pensions to disabled ex-soldiers, and to the orphans and widows of the dead in perpetuity; a sum so huge that it could not even be computed. The peace conference referred the whole matter to a Reparations Commission that was to report in 1921. Meanwhile the Germans were to pledge themselves in advance to accepting its findings and to pay an advance of 20 million marks. The Allies would keep their military forces on the Rhine to enforce payment, and have the right to reoccupy German territory in the event of default.

By fixing reparations at an impossibly high figure, the French could thus hope to maintain their control over the Rhineland without using the clumsy expedient of a puppet regime. But this did not solve their fundamental problem, which Balfour defined in a prescient memorandum in March 1919:

> If there is a renewal of German world politics, it is towards the East rather than towards the West that her ambitions will probably be directed . . . The collapse of Russia and the substitution of a number of small and jealous states will increase the opportunities for German diplomatic intrigue and diminish the resisting power of anti-German forces in the East . . . No manipulation of the Rhine frontier is going to make France anything more than a second-rate power trembling at the nod of its great neighbours in the East and depending from day to day on the changes and chances of shifting diplomacy and uncertain alliances.[3]

For it was eastern Europe that presented the peacemakers with their most complex problems. On the Rhine the situation was a familiar one; after all, the French had simply won one more round in a contest which had been going on for over 200 years. But in eastern Europe the entire framework of international politics had disintegrated with the disappearance of the three empires which had upheld it since the eighteenth century – the Habsburg, the Hohenzollern and the Romanov. Their disappearance left power to be contested not so much between their successor regimes as by the dozens of aspirants to national statehood which had been breeding there during the past 50 years, and whose representatives thronged the corridors of the peace conference pleading their respective cases.

As happens in the aftermath of the fall of all political regimes, there immediately followed a period not so much of *sauve qui peut* as of *saise qui peut*, on the all too justifiable assumption that possession is nine points of the law. The capacity of the western Allies to influence events was limited by the reluctance of their peoples to become militarily involved, but in so far as they could intervene at all they were influenced by three considerations. One was the belief in national self-determination, passionately held by President Wilson and Lloyd George and their supporting delegations in Paris. 'It was' wrote the British diplomat Harold Nicolson, 'the thought of the new Serbia, the new Greece, the new Bohemia, the new Poland which made our hearts sing hymns at heaven's gate . . . the Paris Conference will never be properly understood unless this emotional impulse is emphasised at every stage'.[4] The 'Utopianism' later to be condemned by E.H. Carr in the *The Twenty Years Crisis* dominated the thinking of both Anglo-Saxon delegations – except where their own immediate interests were concerned. A second factor was the fear of the spread of 'Bolshevism' from Russia, a concern strongly felt by the French and Bristish high commands. And the third, common to all Frenchmen virtually without exception, was the desire to weaken Germany, economically, territorially and politically.

These three factors were particularly influential in shaping the future of Poland. The independence of Poland was the only explicit war aim in eastern Europe which found a place in Wilson's 14 Points. It was a matter on which all the belligerents had anyhow virtually agreed. In August 1914 the Czar had given a guarded promise of Polish autonomy after the war. In 1916 the Germans, having effectively expelled the Russians from the old Grand Duchy of Warsaw, also promised Polish independence, and set up a puppet 'Regency Council' to administer the region. France and Britain endorsed President Wilson's 13th point in June 1918. As for the Austrians, they had created a fully formed Polish army, the Polish Legion, whose leader Josef Pilsudski was the generally recognised leader of the Polish national resistance. Pilsudski had refused to allow his troops to take the oath of allegiance to the Regency Council and had therefore been imprisoned by the Germans. On the collapse of the Hohenzollern regime in November 1918 he was sent back to Warsaw. There he received a tumultuous welcome, was appointed commander-in-chief and head of the new Polish state, created an army out of troops who had served under three warring flags, and set about seizing every scrap of territory that he could lay hands on.

The armistice terms signed by Germany had said little about the eastern front, and what they did say was contradictory. On the one hand German forces were to withdraw to the frontiers of August 1914. On the other they were not to evacuate the territory they occupied (which included most of western Russia) until 'the Allies think the moment suitable, having regard to the internal situation of these territories.'[5] The allies in fact hoped to use the German forces to police the area and maintain order there until the new settlement could be established. With the new German government itself struggling for survival in Berlin, decisions about what to do with German forces in the east devolved on the German high command in that theatre. For them the area fell into three clearly defined sections. There were the old German territories claimed by Poland – Posen, Silesia and West Prussia – which they had no intention of abandoning and which under the terms of the armistice they had no obligation to evacuate. There was the former Russian province of Poland which they had occupied during the war, whose independence Germany had already recognised and from which German troops were now withdrawn in defiance of Allied requirements. And there were the occupied lands of Russsia itself, which German forces were leaving as fast as they could and intended to do so whatever orders they received to the contrary. As it was, the high command saw nothing to be gained in attempting to maintain control of territories over which the forces of the new Poland and the new Russia were bound to come to blows. They would serve German interests very well by so doing.

The core of the new Poland was the old 'Congress Poland' or Grand Duchy of Warsaw whose frontiers had been established in 1814: ethnically predominantly Polish, but recognised as part of the Russian Empire until 1917. There was no problem about adding to this the former Austrian lands of Galicia to the south, where the Habsburgs had always given the Polish gentry a free hand to rule their Ruthenian and Ukrainian peasants. To the west, as we shall see, the Germans were to be forced to yield up most of the territory acquired by Prussia in the eighteenth century. But eastward from Congress Poland lay the extensive, indeterminate lands of 'The Borders'. In past centuries this region had been ruled by the Grand Duchy of Lithuania, which had shared with Poland the same kind of dynastic link that the Scots shared with the English and whose sway had ebbed and flowed over Lettish, Livonian, Byelorussian and Ukrainian territory between the Baltic and the Black Sea. In this region the Poles had been a conquering and colonising aristocracy, and wherever they had left their traces the leaders of the new Poland felt justified in staking a claim.

In Paris the Allies agreed on a line which marked the ethnically indisputable eastern limit of Poland, called, after Balfour's successor as Britain's foreign secretary, 'the Curzon line'. Neither the Poles nor the Russians were prepared to accept this as their frontier for a single moment. The revolutionary government in Moscow was unwilling to abandon any former Russian territory to what they regarded as a reactionary White Guardist regime supported, if not manipulated, by western counter-revolutionary forces. In spite of his impeccable revolutionary background Pilsudski appeared to them simply as another reactionary general like Denikin or Wrangel. As for Pilsudski, who had been born in them, these eastern territories were the true heartland of Poland and it was inconceivable that they should be abandoned. So when early in 1919 the Germans withdrew their forces from the region, Poles and Russians raced to fill the vacuum with armies that had to be created as they went along. Polish bravura took them as far as the historic Lithuanian capital of Vilno in the north; to Minsk in the east; and in May 1920 to Kiev in the Ukraine. But they over-reached themselves, the Russians counter-attacked, and in August 1920 the Red Army reached the outskirts of Warsaw.

The western Allies were appalled by these developments but there was little they could do about them. They sent a commission to Warsaw to observe the situation, a very little money, and a military advisory commission under Foch's former chief of staff General Weygand. None of Poland's neighbours had either the desire or the capacity to help. The new Czechoslovak Republic was sympathetic to Russia and had anyway been alienated by the Polish attempt to seize the disputed territory of Teschen, while the Germans declared their neutrality and watched the discomfiture of the new Polish state with sardonic amusement. Poland was saved by its own exertions and the mistakes of its enemy. The Red Army had greatly over-extended itself in the mistaken belief that its appearance would trigger a rising by the Polish peasants and proletariat – a rising which would give the signal for the German workers to revolt in their turn. Once their spearheads were halted the Soviet forces had no logistical or oper-ational support and Pilsudski was able to bundle them back as fast as they had come. With both sides exhausted, peace was signed at Riga in March 1921 and Poland took possession of the area now occupied by its armies, extending well east of the Curzon line. The Soviet government accepted the settlement *de facto*, as they accepted the independence of the new Baltic Republics of Latvia, Estonia and Lithuania, because they were too weak to do anything else. But these lands remained *irredenta*, and the Soviet Union had no intention of abandoning them for ever.

The Germans meanwhile had to accept a settlement of their Polish frontiers which they resented no less strongly. The problem here was complicated both by the confused ethnic mixture of the region and by the Allied pledge, enshrined in the 14 Points, to give Poland secure access to the sea. This access could be provided only by making over to Poland the valley of the Lower Vistula; and although the river flowed for most of its course through ethnically Polish territory, at its mouth it did not; while the port of Danzig which gave access to the valley was unmistakably 90 per cent German. Moreover, to make over to Poland these lands of 'western Prussia' was to isolate the province of East Prussia – a totally German enclave to which not even Pilsudski laid claim.

The Germans felt as strongly about these eastern territories as the Poles felt about their Borderlands. They had possessed them since the eighteenth century, investing heavily both in the industries of Upper Silesia and in the farmlands of Posen and West Prussia, where they had bought out or expropriated Polish landowners and installed German settlers. By doing so they had raised the standard of living far above that of the neighbouring Polish territories and thus attracted considerable Polish immigration. Largely to control this, the German government had since the 1880s carried out a vigorous programme of cultural Germanisation, forbidding the use of Polish in schools or for official purposes. The Poles they regarded as a servile race, *Untermensch*, to be treated firmly but kindly. As German industrialisation attracted Polish peasants as a *Lumpenproletariat* to every city in Germany, this attitude became generalised throughout the Reich. The German attitude towards the Poles lay somewhere between than of the English towards the Irish in the nineteenth century and that of white South Africans towards blacks in the twentieth. The idea of putting German settlers and landlords under Polish rule was profoundly offensive to German national pride.

The Poles did not help their case in Paris by the megalomaniac nature of their claims. They demanded territory even where Poles were in a minority, on the grounds that the statistics emanated from German sources and had therefore been fudged, and rejected the test of a plebiscite lest the Polish population should be intimidated by their German neighbours. The French supported their claims to the hilt, for understandable strategic reasons. The stronger the new Poland could be made, the more effectively would it fulfil the dual role of containing the Germans to the west and checking the tide of red Bolshevism from the east. The Americans, with their strong domestic Polish electorate, were also sympathetic. The British were not – for bad reasons as well as good ones. First, their colonial and Irish experience gave the British ruling classes some sympathy with the German view of the Poles as *Untermensch*. An indiscreet witticism by Lloyd George, that to put the industries of Silesia into the hands of the Poles was like putting a watch into the paws of a monkey, enjoyed wide circulation. Moreover such fighting as the Poles had done during the war – as Lloyd George unkindly reminded the Polish President Paderewski – had been against the Allies, unlike the Czechs who had deserted to the Russians *en masse*. But more important, it seemed crazy to present the Germans with a whole seedbed of grievances on their eastern frontiers which they would seek to redress as soon as they were strong enough, without the west being able to do anything to prevent them. Lloyd George's closest advisor, the South African Jan Christian Smuts, summarised these two reasons in a memorandum of 22 May 1919:

> The new Poland will contain millions of Germans and Russians. It is reasonably certain that both Germany and Russia will again be great powers and that sandwiched between them the new Poland can only be a success with their good will. How, under the circumstances, can we expect Poland to be other than a failure even if she had that ruling and administrative capacity which history shows she has not?[6]

Lloyd George was able to make some impression on his allies. Danzig was not given over to the Poles, as they had demanded, but was made a 'free city' under a High Commissioner responsible to the League of Nations. The Poles got their corridor to the sea, cutting off East Prussia from the rest of Germany, but it contained few undisputably German areas. Plebiscites were held in the two most contentious regions, Mazuria (the southern part of East Prussia) and Upper Silesia. Both votes went in Germany's favour, but in Silesia it did not settle the matter. The presence of Allied forces could not prevent savage inter-communal fighting. The region was ultimately divided along communal lines, but was administered as an economic unit by a complex mixed commission until Hitler imposed a draconic solution in 1939. Altogether Germany lost on its eastern frontier about 5 per cent of its population and 15 per cent of its agricultural land. But its enduring resentment at these losses was not to be measured in terms of statistics alone.

Much less contentious was the settlement of the frontiers of the new state of Czechoslovakia, which contained three million Germans within its borders; about a quarter of the total population. In view of the fuss that was to be made about these *Sudentendeutsch* 20 years later this absence of protest may seem surprising, but these provinces had never been part of Germany, and there were none of the personal and historic connections which were so strong in the cases of Silesia, Posen and West Prussia. The *moral* argument – that such a settlement, in view of the clearly-expressed desire of these Germans not to be ruled by their traditional Czech antagonists, was contrary to the principle of national self-determination – was unanswerable; but it was urged more strongly by Austro–Germans (like Adolf Hitler) than by natives of the old Second Reich. Not even Lloyd George had much time for it. The Czech lobby in London, thanks to the skill of Jan Masaryk and the support of influential publicists such as R.W. Seton Watson and Wickham Steed, was highly effective. The Czechs, unlike the Poles, were considered by the British to be a stable and responsible people. To separate out the German territories which surrounded the Czech core of Bohemia would leave the new state impoverished and vulnerable, and its western patrons did not contemplate doing this for a moment. On the contrary, Czechoslovakia was to be strengthened as a bastion of democracy in the centre of Europe.

There was also, at the time, little protest against the veto imposed by the Allies on any union, or *Anschluss*, between Germany and the Austro–German provinces which were all that remained of the old Habsburg Empire. Both parties declared themselves in favour. The National Assembly of German Austria declared itself, on 12 November 1918, to be an integral part of the new German Republic, and the following February the German Constituent Assembly at Weimar said the same: 'German-Austria must be united with the mother country for all time'. But the French imposed an absolute veto on any such accretion to the power of Germany. The British were worried (rightly, as it turned out) about the threat which such an *Anschluss* would pose to their *protégés*, the Czechs. Moreover neither the Germans nor the Austrians were whole-hearted about the *Anschluss*. Northern Germans did not welcome the prospect of the influx of some seven million southern Catholics to upset the delicate regional and confessional balance established under the Second Reich. Besides, after what was seen as their abysmal military performance during the war, the reputation of the Austrians throughout Germany stood very low indeed. In Austria this wartime dislike was heartily reciprocated, – the Germans had not made themselves popular with their allies — and in Catholic rural areas the largely urban phenomenon of pan–Germanism was not widely shared. For the time being at least, the new Germany and the new Austria were content to go their separate ways.

The peacemakers of Versailles have come under much criticism for breaking up the Habsburg Empire and thus creating a political vacuum in the centre of Europe which they had no capacity to fill. In fact the empire was in a state of terminal disintegration long before the war ended; disintegration only marginally affected by Communist propaganda from the east and nationalistic from the west. The Versailles settlement did no more than recognise a *fait accompli*. The last Emperor of Austria and King of Hungary, Charles VIII, abdicated at noon on 11 November 1918, an hour after the armistice between Germany and its adversaries came into effect on the western front. The Austrian armies had already collapsed after the belated Italian victory at Vittorio Veneto and an armistice had been signed on 31 October. The disintegration of the Habsburg armies precipitated that of the Habsburg Empire itself. The threat of revolution gave the *bourgeois* leaders of the various nationalist communities a strong incentive for pre-emptively seizing power and bureaucrats of the old regime for co-operating to ease the transition. On 12 November in Vienna the German members of the old Imperial Parliament proclaimed the Republic of Austria and two days later their Czech colleagues did the same for Czechoslovak Republic in Prague. After the protracted quarrels between Germans and Czechs which had paralysed government in Vienna for the past 25 years, the parting was relatively amicable.

In the Hungarian lands of the empire, things did not go so smoothly. A liberal government in Budapest under Count Michael Karolyi acquiesced in the secession of the Slav provinces which the Magyars had held in subjection for so long. The Slovaks joined their Czech cousins, the Transylvanians accepted annexation to Rumania, the Croatians joined the Slovenes and Serbs to transform the old Kingdom of Serbia into the new state of Yugoslavia. All that was left was a rump Magyar state, and the territory even of that was threatened by a Rumania who, with French support, was prepared to press its territorial demands to the maximum. The advance of the Rumanian armies in March 1919 provoked in Budapest a mood of desperation which led to the overthrow of the moderate Karolyi government with its links to the west, and the advent to power of the Bolshevik leader Bela Kun. Kun proclaimed the dictatorship of the proletariat, looked eastward to the Russsians for help, mounted a campaign not only against the Rumanians but also the Slovaks, and set up a reign of terror under workers' commissars. A combination of Allied economic blockade and Rumanian military pressure brought down the Kun regime and installed in its place a classic counter-revolutionary government under Admiral Horthy, which extirpated the revolutionaries with great savagery.

Thereafter Hungary was a 'pariah state' in Europe. Its reactionary regime made it unacceptable to western liberals, who channelled

their economic support into the more respectable *bourgeois* democratic republic of Austria. The nostalgia of its ruling classes for the
Habsburg monarchy – Horthy declared himself regent for the former
King Charles, who made one or two comic-opera attempts to return –
deepened the mistrust of the successor states Czechoslovakia, Rumania and Yugoslavia. These three states were thus easily bound
together under French influence in a 'Little *Entente*'; designed as
much as a *cordon sanitaire* (together with Poland) against Soviet
penetration as to maintain the *status quo* against Hungary. There still
remained many ragged edges, especially on the frontiers of Poland;
but on the whole, in stabilising central and eastern Europe along lines
of national self-determination, the Allies could congratulate themselves that they had not done too badly. Certainly the states established by the settlement have remained viable ever since.

That left Italy, which took part in the peace conference as one of
the Big Four. By the secret Treaty of London of 1915, Italy had been
persuaded to join the Allies by promises of Austrian territory which
ran flatly contradictory to all principles of national self-determination
In the north its frontier was to be extended to the defensible
frontier of the Brenner pass, which placed a sizeable community
of German-speaking Tyrolese under its rule. In the north-east
it was to receive Trieste, which had an Italian population, but also its
hinterland of Venezia Giulia, which was largely Croatian and
Slovene. In addition it was to receive the northern part of
Dalmatia; Valona and its hinterland in Albania; and various Adriatic
islands. From Turkey Italy was to obtain full sovereignty over the
Dodecanese, which had been occupied after the Italo – Turkish War
of 1912, and the province of Adalia in Asia Minor.

There would have been less problem about all this if Yugoslavia
had not come into existence: the Allies made no trouble about Italy
annexing German lands from a defeated Austria, but to put Slovene
provinces under rule of Italians instead of granting them independence within the new Slav state – an independence which they had
been explicitly promised by Allied wartime propaganda – was out of
the question. As for Adalia, the revived nationalist government of
Turkey under Mustapha Kemal was to make it impossible for either
Italy or Greece to obtain the territories in Asia Minor they were
allocated by the peace settlement and which their forces attempted to
seize as soon as the Ottoman Empire surrendered.

Italy had suffered, comparatively speaking, more than any of its
allies in the war with the exception of Russia and Serbia. Three years
of fruitless battering against Austrian defences on the Isonzo had left

it with 1 400 000 wounded and dead. The Italian economy was in a state of chaos – less than half its budget of 1919 could be covered by revenue and its industries were dependent on imported raw materials for which it had no means of paying. Its industrial proletariat appeared to be on the verge of revolution, and Italy could not, like its allies, claim reparations from its defeated enemy, because that enemy, the Habsburg Empire, had ceased to exist. Annexation of territory alone could provide compensation, and the promised territory was no longer available. A combination of right-wing indignation, ex-servicemen's discontent and fear of revolution produced in April 1919 the first *Fasci di Combattimento*, paramilitary groups with a programme of counter-revolution at home and expansion abroad. In September a group of volunteers under the romantic poet Gabriele D'Annunzio seized the port of Fiume, which even under the Treaty of London had been promised, not to Italy, but to the notional state of 'Croatia' whose hinterland it served. Fiume became both the touchstone of Italian patriotism and a good excuse for Italy's allies to denounce its claims and abjure the Treaty of London. Isolated and unpopular, the Italian government had to abandon those claims, to the fury of their right wing supporters. Under fire from both left and right, saddled with an unmanagable economy and a deeply divided country, the parliamentary regime in Italy lasted only for two more years before being overthrown by a Fascist *coup d'etat* in October 1922. Thereafter, 'Fascism' was to be seen as an increasingly popular solution to political, economic and social problems which parliamentary regimes seemed powerless to solve.

It says much for the stability of German society that it was ten years before it turned in the same direction. The survival of democracy in Germany was due largely to the existence of a Social Democratic party which was able to retain the allegiance of the industrial working classes, and with whom, largely for that reason, other elements in the state – in particular the bureaucracy and the army – were prepared to co-operate. The army supported the seizure of power by the Social Democratic leaders on the collapse of the Hohenzollern regime in November 1918, and volunteer paramilitary units, the *Freikorps*, smashed the attempts of the Communists to overthrow them in Berlin and elsewhere during the ensuing winter. This made it possible for a Constituent Assembly to meet at Weimar in 1919 and create a *bourgeois* democratic regime, enjoying broad if in some quarters reluctant support. It was this regime that had to sign the Treaty of Versailles.

The Treaty was not negotiated. Its terms were formulated by the

Allies and presented to the German delegation on 7 May 1919. With its armed forces effectively demolished and the Allies continuing the full rigour of the wartime blockade the Germans had no option but to sign, though those who did so were never forgiven by the men of the extreme right. The frontier revisions we have already considered. In addition Germany was required to run down its army to 100 000 men deprived of 'offensive' weapons such as tanks, to disband its general staff, to abolish its air force and to confine its naval building to ships of less than 10 000 tons displacement. This, it was maintained, would 'render possible the initiation of a general limitation of the armaments of all nations'. It did not, and its failure to do so was to be used by the Germans to excuse their denunciation of these restrictions and begin rearming 15 years later. Reparations we have also considered. In order to provide a legal basis for them, Article 231 of the treaty stated that 'The Allied and Associate Governments affirm and Germany accepts the responsibility of Germany and her Allies for causing all the loss and damage to which the Allied and Associate Governments have been subjected as a consequence of the war imposed on them by the aggression of Germany and her Allies'.[7]

Not all these clauses were equally resented in Germany. The loss of the navy and the colonial empire affected only minority interests, and the restraints on military power found much support on the left. The prohibition of the *Anschluss* with Austria and the treatment of the Sudeten Germans were resented in principle but roused no strong feelings, for the reasons already indicated. The demilitarisation of the Rhineland and the temporary loss of the Saar were naturally unwelcome but not unacceptable. The deepest feelings were aroused by the loss of German lands in the east, the open-ended obligations to reparations – on which the German government was able to blame all its economic ills for the next six years – and, most widespread of all, the acceptance of 'war guilt' by a people who genuinely believed that the war had been imposed upon *them*, and that their sacrifices over the past four and a half terrible years had been in a noble cause. Further, many Germans felt that they had not been defeated at all. Their armies, after all, had been continuously victorious until the last few months of the war. They had, it was plausibly argued, been deprived of the victory which was their due only because they had been cheated by the Allies over the armistice terms and 'stabbed in the back' by socialists who had exploited the difficulties of the moment in order to seize power. Even for those who did not accept this *Dolchstoss* legend, the continuing legitimacy of any German government would depend on its success in modifying the servitudes imposed by the treaty, if not abrogating them altogether.

And what in the long run was to prevent Germany from doing so? Of the adversaries whose combined efforts had been necessary to defeat her, the United States had returned to its traditional posture of self-isolation from European affairs. The new Soviet Union was itself a revisionist power, as hostile to Britain and France and as interested in overturning the peace settlement as was Germany itself. As for the British, their wartime fever rapidly cooled. John Maynard Keynes's brilliant phillipic *The Economic Consequences of the Peace*, directed primarily against the reparations clauses of the settlement, persuaded many of his countrymen that the treaty as a whole was inequitable, and created in liberal and left wing circles a wave of sympathy in favour of Germany. British military leadership distracted by a new obligations in the Middle East as well as old ones in Ireland and India, was at one with public opinion in its determination not to become involved in continental warfare again. British business interests pressed for the rehabilitation of Germany as a major trading partner. By 1922, when Lloyd George fell from power, there was a general consensus among all parties that, since German recovery neither could nor should be prevented, German grievances must be redressed. 'Appeasement' was not yet a dirty word.

That left France with the impossible task of enforcing the peace terms virtually on its own. After four years of German prevarication over reparations payments the French government in 1923 exercised their rights under the settlement and occupied the Ruhr. German non-co-operation ensured that this brought them no financial gain; French public opinion regarded the exercise as a failure and replaced Raymond Poincare's hard line government with a conciliatory regime of Edward Herriot. But the crisis forced the Germans also to accept that there was no future in continuing confrontation with their former enemies, and brought to power a statesman, Gustav Stresemann, who saw that the only way to revise the treaty lay in co-operating with the Allies, not in opposing them. By this time the United States was prepared to be more accommodating over their war debt policy *vis-à-vis* the Allies, which made the latter ready to treat the Germans more generously. So in 1924–5 the Dawes Plan and the Locarno agreements laid the foundations for a new system of economic and political co-operation which appeared to have fair prospects of success.

Were these prospects illusory, or was the system inherently unstable? Could a Germany readmitted as a full partner in the system have ever reconciled herself to the loss of its eastern territories? Or could its new partners have accepted a revision of the settlement which would have given Germany a hegemonial position in central Europe from which it might be able to dominate Europe as whole? Given time, could the Locarno settlement of Germany's western borders have been peacefully extended to the east? Or was it the domestic situation in Germany that was inherently unstable, and likely sooner or later to produce a regime that would force revisions *so oder so*, on the model of Mussolini rather than Stresemann? Or finally, did the instability lie in the economic system which supported the whole edifice, and which was to disintegrate over the next two decades? In the absence of a satisfactory solution to these questions, it was perhaps inevitable that there would one day be another war.

NOTES AND REFERENCES

1. See Louis L. Snyder, *Historic Documents of World War I* (Van Nostrand, New York 1958) p. 164.
2. Quoted in Jere C. King, *Foch versus Clemenceau*, (Harvard UP 1960) p. 57.
3. Quoted in Arno J. Mayer, *Politics and Diplomacy of Peacemaking* (London 1968) p. 516.
4. Harold Nicolson, *Peacemaking 1919* (Universal Library edn. 1965) p. 33.
5. Harry R. Rudin, *Armistice 1918* (Yale U P 1944) p. 428.
6. Quoted in Arno J. Mayer, *op.cit.* p. 797.
7. Louis L. Snyder, *Historic Documents*, p. 188.

2. 'World Depression, World War: Some Economic Origins of the Second World War'

ROBERT BOYCE

So dramatic and complex are the events surrounding the two World Wars that, perhaps inevitably, they tend to obscure the impact on international affairs of the third global catastrophe of the century – the world economic depression which occurred midway between the wars. Beginning in 1929, the depression wreaked havoc on currencies, trade and employment throughout the world, brought down governments, undermined political systems and scarred the lives of nearly everyone who survived its depredations. Its consequences were so pervasive that simple reference to it possesses almost no explanatory value. Yet without minimising sources of conflict existing before the depression, any study of war origins must take account of the fact that the watershed between the two wars – the point at which the post-war era gave way to another pre-war era – coincided with the onset of the depression. It is not too much to say, indeed, that the course of events leading to the war cannot be understood without due recognition of the fact that the international economic and political order broke down simultaneously.

The most obvious way in which the depression contributed to the

55

making of the Second World War was by undermining support for moderate, reformist governments in Japan, Germany and elsewhere, and creating a climate of desperation that favoured extremist parties and policies. In May 1928 Hitler's National Socialist party obtained a mere 12 of the 463 seats in the *Reichstag* elections, while the Nationalist party declined from 103 to 76 seats and was left financially embarrassed. In July 1929 Shidehara Kijuro returned to the Japanese foreign ministry in the new business-minded government of Hamaguchi Yuko, and soon confirmed his readiness to collaborate with western powers on further naval arms limitation. In August 1928 Italy signed a treaty of friendship and arbitration with Ethiopia. In the spring of 1930 the British ambassador in Rome reported that Mussolini was casting about for new alliances or alignments, perhaps with Germany, perhaps even with the Soviet Union, though he wanted nothing more than co-operation with Britain in a policy of peaceful European reconstruction if only Britain would offer a lead.[1] In short, until at least the end of the 1920s there was no compelling reason to anticipate aggression by any of the future Axis powers, but thereafter, as the economic slump worsened, the prospects swiftly dimmed.

In Germany the last coalition of centre-left parties fell in March 1930, unable to resolve the dilemma of choosing between 'sound finance' and assistance for the growing army of unemployed. This ended government by consent of the *Reichstag*, and after a campaign devoted to the crushing burden of foreign reparation demands, the Nazis saw their representation leap from 12 to 107 seats in the September 1930 *Reichstag* elections. In November 1930, with economic conditions also at crisis stage in Japan, Hamaguchi, the Prime Minister, was shot and nearly assassinated by a right wing fanatic. Plans for a military *coup* in Tokyo reached an advanced stage in March 1931 before the conspirators broke ranks. Barely six months later extremist elements of the Kwantung army staged an incident that triggered off the occupation of Manchuria and Jehol.[2] Italy, already under Fascist dictatorship, did not experience a decisive break in domestic politics or foreign relations at this time. Nevertheless, the process of 'Fascistisation' intensified. Corporativism was formally instituted in 1932, and when this did nothing to reduce unemployment or revive the depressed economy extremists within the Fascist party demanded a 'second revolution'. Already in 1931 Fascist politicians had begun to turn their attention towards colonial adventures as a possible means of dealing with the crisis.[3] Until 1936 Mussolini continued to defend the Versailles settlement. But in 1932 he dismissed the pro-British Dino Grandi from the foreign ministry, took personal control himself, and that same year initiated plans for the conquest of Ethiopia. Meanwhile he used the threat of a German nationalist revival to squeeze concessions from France. It was a very dangerous game, as events were to prove.

The effect of the depression in fostering a climate for Fascist or militarist adventurism is reasonably well understood, but this is only one side of the coin. The other, less familiar side is the effect of the depression in undermining the capacity of the liberal-democratic powers to unite in forestalling or resisting aggression. The one way this occurred that has already been treated at length by historians, was in delaying national rearmament.[4] At a time when budgetary deficits were held to be tantamount to inflation, a serious decline in revenue was bound to discourage democratic governments from increasing defence spending and encourage them to appease their potential enemies. This was so in the case of both Britain and France during the 1930s. Yet rearmament was a problem of the second order, for it would not have become such a crucial issue in the late 1930s had the democratic powers *either* combined to halt the depression before it drove other countries to extremism and aggression *or* combined to resist the aggression. Of course they did neither, and one of the main reasons they did not was because the depression also drove them apart from one another.

The three great democratic powers, Britain, France and the United States, were also the three great creditor powers of the world; it was their financial resources and leadership as well as their commodity markets on which the world depended for its stability after the First World War. But from the outset economic issues constantly prejudiced relations between them, and from 1929 the depression drove them into a Hobbesian condition of each against all. In the midst of this crisis the danger of militarist aggression paled before the much more immediate danger of domestic economic and social collapse. And for each of the creditor powers the main source of difficulty appeared to be not Japan or Germany or Italy, but the aggressive and irresponsible actions of the other creditor powers. The result was to obscure the threat posed by the Fascist or militarist states and practically remove the possibility of collaboration among the creditor powers during the crucial years, 1929–34. By the time the animosity generated in this period was overcome and *rapprochement* begun, it was almost too late. With the aggressor states virtually beyond control, the path led straight to war.

I

In purely economic or statistical terms the experience of the three great democratic powers in the 1920s stands in sharp contrast to their experience in the decade that followed. After the severe post-war slump of 1920–21, the 1920s were a time of sustained economic growth and increasing price and currency stability, whereas the 1930s began with several years of renewed instability, a serious decline in domestic economic activity, and a prolonged slump in international trade and commerce. Leaving the statistics aside and turning to contemporary perceptions of the economic situation, it is noteworthy that statesmen in two of the three countries, Britain and France, regarded their economic situation in the 1920s virtually as unsatisfactory as they were to find it in the 1930s, albeit for different reasons.

In the case of Britain, contemporary observers regarded the country as economically depressed throughout the 1920s. It is true that gross domestic product was increasing, structural changes were being implemented and productivity was improving, but the indicators on which contemporaries focussed their attention were not these but instead visible trade and unemployment, along with certain financial indicators such as gold reserves and foreign loans; and by all these criteria Britain seemed in decline.[5] The one major source of pride was the restoration of the pound sterling to the gold standard at the pre-war parity of $4.86 in April 1925, but despite this (or rather because of it), industry continued to face difficulties, unemployment remained abnormally high, the pound remained precarious, and the Bank of England was forced to maintain high interest rates, discourage foreign lending and appeal for increased co-operation from central bankers in the other major financial centres, New York and Paris.[6] Thus even in May 1929, that is before the world slump began, the general election was dominated by the unemployment question.

The French experience in the 1920s was quite different. The French economy recovered swiftly from the war and continued to expand until 1930; recorded unemployment fell to nearly zero by the latter years of the decade, and industrial and agricultural demand drew in perhaps as many as two million additional foreign workers.

Like the pound sterling the franc was restored to the gold standard, but unlike the Bank of England the *Banque de France* succeeded in accumulating a massive gold and foreign exchange reserve in order to defend the currency against the vagaries of international demand. Yet for a variety of reasons the French economic experience in the 1920s was also a profoundly unhappy one.

In the first place hopes of meeting the heavy cost of reconstruction through reparation claims on Germany proved illusory, and accumulating budget deficits contributed to inflation and currency depreciation that eventually threatened to get completely out of control. Briefly in 1926 the franc fell to 250 to the pound or one-tenth of its pre-war value, and even the Poincaré 'miracle' of restoring confidence in the franc left it depreciated by four-fifths.[7] The sizeable element of the population that depended upon income from government securities or pensions was thus left shaken and disappointed when the franc was formally restored to the gold standard in 1928. Moreover, despite the appearance of strength, officials were grimly aware that the franc was bound to come under pressure again if French price levels continued to move upwards while world commodity prices continued to decline. The dissatisfaction of the *rentier* class was matched by that of the very numerous peasant population which was confronted with policies favouring town over country and a downward drift of agricultural prices. Despite the appearance of strength, therefore, few Frenchmen could wholly believe the claim made after the depression struck that France was an *île heureux*, its economy uniquely balanced between industry and agriculture and thus invulnerable to the storm blowing all around it. Indeed, as early as the summer of 1930 Paris officials recognised the statistical signs that France too was heading for trouble.[8]

The establishments in Britain and France thus entered the 1930s in a common mood of dissatifaction. But that was not all. They also shared the belief that each was the author of much of the other's difficulties and, combined with the economic challenge posed by the United States, regarded each other as a threat to their very survival as great powers. So different were their recent economic experiences that what seemed a solution to one was usually seen by the other as part of the problem.

Within Britain, confrontation over reparation demands upon Germany had firmly established France as the main target for criticism as early as 1920. Having quickly abandoned wartime ideas of imperial protection and state-led export expansion, Britain looked once more

to international commerce and finance as the key to renewed prosperity. French efforts to extract reparations from an impoverished
Germany thus became, as J.M. Keynes so vividly described them, the
chief obstacle to Europe's and Britain's recovery.[9] The Franco–Belgian occupation of the Ruhr in 1923, although eventually self-
defeating for France, confirmed France in British eyes as a militarist
power bent on dominating Europe. For a time the spectacle of
French governments persisting in huge budget deficits and fumbling
in their efforts to halt the slide of the franc confirmed British opinion
that France was also a morally inferior nation, and even after the
Poincaré miracle this view was sustained by French resort to allegedly
sharp practices in their economic behaviour. One instance was the
French delay in ratifying the Churchill–Caillaux war debt agreement
of 1926 from one year to the next. Another was France's adherence
to tariff protection, its continued use of non-tariff protection introduced during the war, and its decision in 1927 to revise import duties
for the benefit of German trade at a time when the British deficit on
Anglo–French trade was more one-sided than ever.[10] A third was
France's alleged manipulation of international finance for political
ends.

The idea that the French state could and did control the disposition
of vast financial assets to reward friends and punish enemies became
a firmly held conviction in British governing circles in the 1920s, and
strongly coloured attitudes towards France. Knowledge that France
had cemented its alliance with Russia before the First World War by
helping to arrange huge loans lent credence to the idea, as did the
occasional flight of capital from London to Paris at times of diplomatic tension after the war. To judge by the paucity of loans to France's
eastern allies during the 1920s, however, it seems that French commercial bankers were as jealous of their independence as were their
British counterparts, and that French officials were seldom willing or
able to influence their judgment on foreign lending.[11] Manipulation
of assets held by the French Treasury and *Banque de France* was a
somewhat different matter. In 1927–28, when British and French
central banks disputed control of reconstruction loans to Rumania
and Yugoslavia, and again in 1929 when Britain demanded substantial modification of the Young plan for German reparations, French
authorities threatened to destabilise the pound sterling by withdrawing official balances on deposit in London.[12] These threats could not
be ignored because French sterling balances exceeded the Bank of
England's gold reserves. But on neither occasion was the threat

carried out, and at other times when British observers imputed a political motive to gold or capital movements, French official balances were not involved. Nevertheless the combination of vast French assets in London, a precarious pound, recurrent Anglo–French political differences and the new and mysterious phenomenon of 'hot' money moving nervously from one financial capital to another in search of safety was almost bound to give rise to dark suspicions.

From Paris, however, the prospect could not have been more different. Reparations promised by the Versailles treaty and counted on to finance the rebuilding of the ten northern *départements* devastated by the war, were not forthcoming apparently because Britain and the United States had connived at repeated German non-payment. All the while the Anglo–Saxon powers maintained their own demands for war debt repayment. Thus, from Paris it seemed that Germany was to be revived for the sake of Anglo–Saxon commercial interests while the French people shouldered the cost of the war. French and Belgian troops had occupied the Ruhr in 1923 not to flaunt their power, but in a desperate attempt to force Germany to accept its obligations and persuade the Anglo–Saxon powers to join in a reasonable settlement of the reparation issue.[13] The latter powers did reluctantly join in negotiations, but in 1924 the French felt themselves again to be the victims when British and American financiers withheld assistance for the declining franc until French statesmen acceded to the Dawes reparation plan.[14] If the franc had been stabilised at all, it was no thanks to the Anglo–Saxon powers. The American authorities had insisted upon acceptance of a war debt settlement before allowing access to its capital markets. Montagu Norman, Governor of the Bank of England, had similarly refused help in 1926 when the franc was in near free fall, and meanwhile he persisted in attempts to extend his influence in eastern Europe among countries belonging to the French alliance system.

On the commercial front French authorities could point to the fact that their import duties, if higher in money terms, were only slightly more protectionist than in pre-war times, and had little to do with the deterioration in Britain's trade balance with France. In addition they had removed most quantitative trade controls introduced during the war, accepted the principle of conditional most-favoured-nation treatment, and taken other steps to assist in the liberalisation of European trade. Britain, on the other hand, had introduced a number of protective measures and extended the application of empire preference on articles of some importance to French trade, all the while criticising the European countries for not allowing greater access to their markets.[15] Who then was the imperialist power? From Paris the answer was Britain and – above all the United States.

Until the 1970s, when Japan's emergence as the world's second industrial power became the subject of worried speculation, no country has aroused so much apprehension on account of its economic dynamism as did the United States in the 1920s. The basic reason was of course the remarkable scale of American mass production industry. This was the age of assembly line production at Detroit, where the Ford Motor Company produced its model Ts by the million. It was also the first great age of Hollywood, whose films extolling the blessings of the American way of life reached cinemas in practically every town and village of Europe. The Dawes Plan, which ended the confrontation between Germany and France, had been devised with unofficial American assistance, and thereafter American commercial lending to Europe had quickly revived, enabling countries to stabilise their currencies and support trade liberalisation initiatives. All this was widely welcomed, but the speed with which Europe declined into a dependent economic relationship with the United Sates soon aroused strong reactions.

The United States, despite its position as major creditor in the post-war world, continued to act the role of a debtor. It reduced but refused to write off Europe's war debts and maintained the fiction that they were unrelated to reparations. Moreover, instead of lowering import duties, it adopted the Fordney–McCumber tariff in 1922, raising duties to the highest level in the country's history. Thereafter, Herbert Hoover, the secretary of commerce, saw to it that private exporters received strong backing from the state. The result was truly awesome. Between 1919 and 1929 the United States more than doubled its industrial exports; by the latter part of the decade it had surpassed Britain as the world's largest exporter of manufactured goods. Meanwhile, serious questions had begun to be raised about Germany's ability to service its massive and ever-growing dollar debt. Even more ominously, doubts arose about the United States' capacity to absorb more of its own mass produced goods, which led to predictions of a global trade war once the American domestic market was 'saturated'.[16]

A further cause of anxiety was the way the United States used its surplus on international payments to penetrate European markets. The 1920s were a time of extraordinary expansion both for American exporters and for American multinational industry. Available statistics are not very precise, but it seems probable that American firms expanded abroad at a faster rate in the six years after the adoption of the Dawes Plan than at any time before or since.[17] Much of this expansion was concentrated in the new and most dynamic sectors of industry, such as motor vehicles, electrical goods, office machinery, communications, and chemicals, with American firms taking over foreign competitors or erecting branch plants, and much of the activity was concentrated in western Europe. To this was added the difficulties caused by the Wall Street boom which got underway in earnest in 1928, severely disrupting the flow of dollars to Europe. Dollar loans – hitherto increasing – sharply declined, and European funds were similarly drawn to the high interest rates offered by New York banks, threatening Europe with renewed financial instability. The final stroke came when Herbert Hoover's victory in the presidential election of November 1928 was followed by indications that the United States would soon intensify its protectionism. Hoover, as secretary of commerce for six years, had become the embodiment of America's globalist economic ambitions. During the election campaign he had appealed to the farm vote by assuring farmers the protection of the home market. In itself this was scarcely significant, since the domestic agricultural market was already secure from extensive foreign competition, but in January 1929, when Congress took up the tariff question, a log-rolling process began that threatened to end in a general increase in the already massive American tariff. Academic economists and international bankers, anticipating serious consequences for overseas debtors, warned against a tariff hike. Unfortunately their warnings went unheeded. Whatever economists and Wall Street bankers might think, most Americans were indifferent to developments abroad and saw no reason to consider foreign reactions to domestic legislation. Once Congress confirmed its readiness to proceed with the protectionist bill, however, nearly every foreign country issued protests and none more loudly than France.

In April the Paris press reported suggestions of an alliance among European car manufacturers to resist the 'transatlantic enemy'.[18] In May the Socialist party appealed to the American government

to consider whether it is possible, wise and without danger to civilisation and the economic life of the world to compel Europe to export for a long period of years large quantities of gold, while it is subjected by the United States to the competition of an output having lighter charges and protected by higher tariff walls.[19]

In June a letter jointly issued by the presidents of the *Confédération générale de la production française* and the *Association nationale de l'expansion économique* raised the spectre of conflict in its condemnation of further American trade protection.

> the increase of the proposed new tariff rates is in many cases so great that it must render imports impossible . . . It is proposed, for instance, to increase to 90 per cent the duty on French dresses . . . Will such methods, which will inevitably call for reprisals, help to consolidate peace?[20]

That same month the 500 presidents of the semi-official French chambers of commerce adopted a resolution denouncing the United States for the absurdity of claiming full advantage of its position as Europe's chief creditor while barring entry to European exports, practically the only means by which dollars could be earned abroad. Since the United States was evidently rejecting 'all economic solidarity with other nations' and 'forcing Europe into an *impasse* in which it cannot allow itself to be imprisoned,' the resolution continued,

> in spite of what it may cost French industry and commerce to speak to the United States in a manner to which we are not accustomed, it is necessary in the interest even of the economic future of the world to raise an alarm and to demand that the French government shall emerge from its neutrality and enter into such negotiations with other European nations as may be necessary to defend Europe from the economic point of view and thus form the indispensable barrier against the imminent danger that threatens it.[21]

France, its nationalism intensified by the war, its security interests battered throughout the 1920s by the Anglo–Saxon powers, and only just recovered from financial chaos, confronted a larger, potentially stronger and barely subdued Germany without a single large ally. Negotiations were proceeding in the spring of 1929 for a permanent settlement of the German reparations issue, and once again France seemed destined to sacrifice military sanctions in order to be assured of future payments. The deadline for ratification of the Mellon-Bérenger war debt agreement with the United States, signed in 1926 but not yet approved by the French Parliament, was also approaching. French statesmen thus experienced acute insecurity before the world depression began.

In Britain public expression of annoyance at American economic expansion was much more restrained than in France or elsewhere in

Europe. Britain, after all, was still the world's greatest trading and creditor nation and depended for its survival upon access to global markets. It could not happily contemplate international commercial conflict or the break up of the world economy into separate and hostile commercial *blocs*. In 1927 the breakdown of the Geneva naval disarmament conference resulted in the exchange of bitter recriminations between London and Washington, and both in public and private British observers expressed fears that relations with the United States would break down completely. However, once the impossibility of surviving such a conflict became clear, talk of actual war subsided, and shortly after the US presidential election the British government took steps to settle the naval arms limitation dispute.[22] In the spring of 1929 the British General Electric Company's efforts to forestall an attempted take-over by discriminating against American shareholders were abandoned when the City press raised a storm of protest against such a dangerous precedent.[23] A few months later Britain officially remained silent while nearly every other country in the developed world issued formal protests against the decision of the US Congress to endorse plans for a major increase in tariff protection.[24]

Anxiety about American economic domination was nevertheless evident. In 1928, with a minimum of publicity, the British government amalgamated the various elements of the commercially controlled network of imperial communications into Cable and Wireless, in part at least to ensure that the United States did not gain monopoly control over the industry.[25] At about the same time a number of firms of strategic importance altered their articles of association to ensure continued British control; among them Fairey Aviation, Imperial Airways, Marconi International Marine, Rolls Royce, and the Rubber Plantation Investment Trust.[26] During the winter of 1928 Sir Philip Cunliffe-Lister, president of the Board of Trade, voiced his anxiety about the threat of American economic domination. Sir Austen Chamberlain, the foreign secretary, circulated a paper to the cabinet about the need to co-ordinate British commercial and financial resources in order to avoid being squeezed out completely by American competition in overseas markets.[27] Stanley Baldwin, the Prime Minister, shared his own anxiety with Ramsay MacDonald, his successor in the event of a Labour victory at the forthcoming general election,[28] and all the while Montagu Norman at the Bank of England worked behind the scenes to resist the American take-over of British overseas assets and persuade American bankers to relieve pressure on the rest of the world by bringing the Wall Street boom under control.

From this brief survey of developments in the 1920s, two points deserve underlining. The first is that political relations among the major democratic powers were profoundly affected by their economic relations. By and large this was a decade of increasing prosperity for all three powers, but from the political standpoint the crude statistics tell the wrong story. Not only did contemporary statesmen base their judgments of performance on a different set of criteria than is commonly used today, they also tempered their judgment by an acute – and generally accurate – awareness of the profound shift in global power that accompanied the economic changes. As a result, what in retrospect appears to have been a relatively satisfactory period in world economic history left contemporary leaders uncomprehending of each other's predicament, alienated from one another and increasingly willing to contemplate economic, if not military, conflict.

The second point is that the breakdown in international economic relations, usually identified with the Wall Street crash of October 1929, is more accurately identified with the Wall Street *boom* that got underway in earnest in the autumn of 1928, some 12 months earlier. The boom led to borrowing rates in New York that far exceeded rates elsewhere, discouraged American foreign lending, drew in European deposits and disrupted the recycling of dollars on which European stability depended. In Germany the banks relied on foreign deposits for some 40 per cent of their resources, and therefore faced immediate difficulties. By the spring of 1929 Germany began to experience sharply rising unemployment, a slump on the Berlin *bourse* and a looming crisis over the budget which threatened the breakdown of the recently reformed Weimar coalition government.[29] Meanwhile central bankers in several other European capitals were driven to appeal for support from the Bank of England, while Montagu Norman appealed to his American colleagues for help in increasingly shrill tones.[30] The economic crisis thus began a full year before the Wall Street crash and the depression itself. This helps to explain the remarkable deterioration in international relations that began almost before the depression and thus at first glance appears unconnected with economic difficulties. It also makes it easier to understand why the liberal democratic powers found it so difficult to establish any basis for co-operation once the depression struck with full force.

II

The history of relations among the democratic powers in the early years of the economic crisis is crowded with initiatives, some British, some French, a few American, each one intended to alleviate the crisis but merely contributing to further misunderstanding. The first formal initiative was the Young Plan negotiations in 1929, to devise a final solution to the German reparations issue. The story of the negotiations is too familiar to require retelling here.[31] The outstanding feature for the present account was the way the new British Labour government used the diplomatic conference convened to ratify the plan to demonstrate its ability to defend British interests. Philip Snowden, the Chancellor of the Exchequer, shared the frustration of the British public, which had come to believe that Britain had made sacrifices enough for the sake of European reconstruction. He engaged in a prolonged, ill-tempered confrontation with the French, Belgians and Italians, which, if it accomplished anything, served to demonstrate to his countrymen how selfish, narrow-minded and even corrupt the Europeans were.

Besides Snowden's performance, perhaps the most significant was Hoover's in Washington. Hoover, a hard-working but essentially parochial nationalist, was a westerner with the westerner's ingrained suspicion of Wall Street and Europe. He was also, by the summer of 1929, deeply disturbed by the behaviour of the stock markets in New York and indications that Wall Street men like Owen D. Young and Thomas W. Lamont were falling in with European plans to use American resources to overcome their common problems. As Hoover saw it, the Young Plan was nothing less than an elaborate plot to embarrass the American people into further sacrifices to Europe, and he was not going to be taken in. He repeatedly complained to Young about the expert's plan to align future German reparation payments to the Allies with Allied debt payments to the United States, which gave the appearance that America was the ultimate recipient of all the funds, and displayed such intense suspicion that Young was forced to consider resigning from the expert committee.[32] Subsequently he announced that the Federal Reserve System would have nothing to do with the proposed Bank for International Settlements (BIS), which formed an integral part of the Young Plan. The BIS was intended as a means of cushioning the impact of large reparation transfers across the international exchanges and creating new liquidity to forestall a major international credit crisis. But Hoover would have no part of a 'reparations' bank.[31] Already the crisis was thus having an important effect on American–European relations. In 1927, without publicity, an American citizen had joined the League Financial Committee on the nomination of the Federal Reserve Bank of New York. Now, even informal co-operation with Europe was being shunned.

Meanwhile the French found themselves in an embarrassing position. They had accepted the Young Plan, then ratified the American war debt agreement, only to find that the British insisted upon major concessions at The Hague conference. The value of the plan for France derived mainly from the opportunity it presented for the pre-payment of reparations by means of one or more international loans issued on the security of Germany's 'unconditional' reparation obligations. By issuing such loans, the French hoped to make Germany's commercial creditors their allies in seeing to it that Germany continued full reparation payments, and after their financial troubles earlier in the decade, pre-payment of reparations offered the tremendous attraction of ensuring a balanced budget for years to come. But even the unmodified plan required French agreement on the early evacuation of all remaining Allied troops from the Rhineland. This removed an important constraint upon German foreign relations and was strongly resisted in certain conservative circles in France. When, on top of this, French negotiators gave way to British demands for a redivision of the unconditional reparations, right wing criticism of Aristide Briand, the foreign minister, increased.[34]

The logical next step for Briand was to proceed rapidly with *rapprochement* with Germany. This he did by announcing at the tenth assembly of the League of Nations in September 1929 his support for the federation of Europe. The primary motive was undoubtedly to submerge the German problem within a multilateral framework, but equally important was Briand's fear of American economic domination, which he had harboured since the war, and the hope that other Europeans were also sufficiently worried to join France in a European-wide initiative, if only to forestall a wholesale resort to protectionism. He could not say this publicly, of course, but it was scarcely necessary to spell it out. As he explained to the assembly, 'I think that among peoples constituting geographical groups, like the peoples of Europe, there should be some kind of federal bond. . . Obviously [the federation] would be primarily economic, for that is the most urgent aspect of the question.'[35]

Briand's proposal for European federation was also the parting of the ways for Britain and France in their efforts to surmount the world depression. The British government launched a series of attempts to halt the growth of protectionism and maintain the principles of multilateralism. In December 1929 they took the lead at the third prohibitions conference, which sought agreement on the complete removal of quantitative trade controls, such as quotas, embargoes and barter and trade licensing agreements. In February 1930 they took the lead in promoting a conference on concerted economic action, aiming first at the organisation of a general tariff truce, then at concerted measures for reversing the trend towards tariff protection. They used League of Nations agencies, and continued their efforts at two more sessions of the conference on concerted economic action in late 1930 and early 1931.

Meanwhile the French took the lead in promoting European – that is regional – economic co-operation and trade liberalisation: through the Briand plan, which was formally launched in May 1930, at the eleventh League assembly in September 1930, at a succession of cereals conferences attended by the east European countries and in their attempt to diffuse the crisis that arose over the Austro–German customs union scheme in March 1931. The French opposed the British free trade approach, which seemed hopeless in face of American non-co-operation and general fears of balance of payments difficulties. But the British as firmly opposed the French approach, which threatened to divide the world into separate, warring *blocs*, and used their economic and political influence to discourage other countries from following the French lead. Thus the two powers continued their destructive struggle until the financial crisis in central Europe erupted later in the spring.

On 11 May 1931 news reached foreign capitals that the *Osterreich-ische Kreditanstalt*, the largest commercial lending institution in the Danube region, was virtually insolvent. British financial houses, with a crucially large stake in the bank, sought to steady the situation, and the Austrian government quickly extended assistance. But already the Austrian schilling had come under pressure, forcing the Austrian National Bank to seek support in Paris, the one financial market with ample liquid resources for a loan. French commercial banks were not averse to lending to Austria, but nervously insisted upon their government underwriting the risk, which placed the French government in a position to set terms for its support. This it did in the form of a virtual ultimatum to Austria formally to renounce the customs union scheme. The Austrian government chose to resign rather than be humiliated at the hands of the French, but in the meantime the Austrian National Bank had obtained a short term loan from Montagu Norman of the Bank of England to tide it over the month end.[36] The upshot of these developments was intense annoyance in both Paris and London. British bankers and statesmen were infuriated with the French for using their financial resources to bully Austria and wantonly undermine the financial stability of Europe. Their French counterparts were only slightly less offended at Norman's initiative which they interpreted as yet another instance of his imperialist ambition to undercut French influence in central Europe and force the whole of the continent into a position of dependence upon the London financial markets.[37]

By this time investor nervousness had begun to shift to Germany and threatened to destroy the Reichsmark. British statesmen were initially cool to German warnings of the necessity to reopen the reparations question but their attitude abruptly changed when it became apparent that the flight from the mark could end in catastrophe. Hurried consultations with American bankers and Hoover's secretary of state, Henry Stimson, followed, and on 20 June Hoover announced this support for a one-year moratorium on all intergovernmental debt payments. News of the proposal was greeted with tremendous enthusiasm in London. City institutions were heavily committed in Germany, indeed so heavily that many of them faced insolvency if something was not done to avert a German default.[38] Members of the government shared their enthusiasm not only or even mainly out of concern with the threat to the British banking system, which had not yet been fully brought home to them, but rather because the moratorium proposal appeared to herald acceptance by the United States of a major responsibility for world stability.[39]

The obstacle soon proved to be France. The Anglo – Saxon powers had huge commercial credits tied up in Germany, far more than was at stake on reparations account, whereas France had little in the way of commercial credits in Germany but the largest claim for reparations. Not surprisingly, therefore, French statesmen regarded Hoover's moratorium offer with an extremely jaundiced eye. To them it seemed not a great and generous initiative but a cynical manoeuvre designed to save British and American commercial creditors at France's expense. The proposal thus added to the difficulties already facing the French government. Domestic criticism of Briand's policy of Franco – German *rapprochement* had become increasingly strident in the summer of 1930, when the departure of the last French troops from the Rhineland was followed by crude Nazi celebrations, renewed complaints about reparations and spectacular Nazi gains in the September *Reichstag* elections. After the virtual rejection of his European plan, Briand had suffered a further blow to his prestige when the Austro – German customs union scheme was revealed in March 1931, barely two weeks after he had publicly discounted the possibility of an *Anschluss*. Thus when Hoover sprang his moratorium proposal upon France without consultation, Briand had no choice but to demand concessions from Germany before conceding French support. Two weeks of strenuous bargaining were required before British and American statesmen were able to persuade the French to acquiesce. All the while, tempers became more frayed as the flight from the Reichsmark continued, draining the reserves of the *Reichsbank,* and threatening to cause the complete breakdown of Germany.[40]

During the week of 7–14 July, Hans Luther, president of the *Reichsbank*, flew from Berlin to Paris, to London, and finally to Basle, headquarters of the BIS, in a desperate attempt to organise international support for the Reichsmark. His efforts brought little result. The following week the pound suddenly came under pressure. Several factors doubtless come into play, including Britain's own worsening balance of payments, the rundown of London balances by institutions in other financial centres which were themselves facing difficulties, and a flight of British and foreign capital from sterling into the franc and the dollar in search of greater safety. Once again British observers chose to interpret the massive outflow of capital as part of a French design to force British acquiescence in a French solution to the German problem. As on nearly every other occasion, these suspicions were totally unfounded: the French authorities, so far from orchestrating a movement of gold from London, were actually doing everything they could to shore up sterling.[41] Tom Johnston, the secretary of state for Scotland, travelled to Paris in August 1931 to confront Pierre Laval, the French Prime Minister, and Pierre-Etienne Flandin, the minister of finance, with the accusation of financial manipulation. He himself returned to London convinced of French goodwill[42], but there was no convincing his colleagues in the cabinet or many of the bankers of the City.[43]

On 21 September 1931 the pound sterling was forced off the gold standard and left to float on the foreign exchanges. British banking authorities had obtained the full co-operation of their American and French counterparts, and the money markets of London, New York and Paris remained calm. But the downfall of the gold standard was nevertheless a source of deep humiliation for Britain. The nation's stature as a great power rested largely upon its financial and commercial strength, which depended upon a stable and respected currency. Thus along with the decline of the pound the nation's very status seemed diminished. Moreover, the stability of its social order, which had come under threat in the months following the armistice in 1918 and again during the General Strike of 1926, once again seemed seriously threatened. The attempt to reduce public sector wages in September had led to a mutiny in the North Sea fleet; meanwhile the Labour party and the TUC planned to mount strenuous opposition to retrenchment at the next general election. British authorities persuaded themselves that, having imposed savage retrenchment measures on the country and restored a balanced budget, they had done everything possible to maintain international economic stability: it was the other creditor powers who had refused to play by the rules of the game, by their protectionism, their accumulation of huge gold reserves, and their refusal to participate in world reflationary action. As Snowden explained to the House of Commons on 21 September 1931, Britain had repeatedly sought an international solution to the problem created by the concentration of monetary gold in the coffers of France and the United States. Now that sterling had been forced off the gold standard, perhaps it would

> bring home to those who have hitherto been reluctant to enter into a discussion on the matter the pressing necessity of concerted action. . . I think we are entitled to look for some recognition on the part of other creditor nations of their responsibility for the present situation. . . . Much more could be said, but I will only add this: America and France taken together have now acquired three-quarters of the entire gold in the world and have buried it in their vaults, where it is largely sterilised and useless for the purpose of promoting international trade.[44]

Faced with the threat of class conflict and national decline, British hostility towards the ostensible authors of this predicament was intense. American bankers found this when they contacted City colleagues.[45] Aimé-Joseph de Fleuriau, the French ambassador, reported that it was stronger than at any time since the occupation of the Ruhr, and found it undiminished six weeks later.[46]

If the bankers of the City and the officials of the Board of Trade and Treasury were among those mostly deeply annoyed by the 'betrayal' of the other creditor powers, the least affected were perhaps the officials of the Foreign Office, who took relatively little interest in economic affairs. Senior Foreign Office officials now argued for a policy of close co-operation with France in an effort to halt the crisis before Germany became wholly dominated by extremists. As they warned the cabinet,

> People in this country seem to be unaware of the extent to which the future of 'civilisation' depends on what happens in Germany in the course of the next six months and of the grave doubt as to whether the upshot will be peace or war, recovery or collapse.[47]

The only practical approach, according to the same officials, was to recognise that the political, security and economic problems were bound up together, and accept that Britain must use every instrument available to break the deadlock. At present, Britain possessed three effective instruments: the power to grant continued access to the world's largest import market, the decision over whether or when to stabilise the pound, and the means of providing France with the reassurance of support it craved by signing the Geneva protocol. It was possible that, left to its own devices, France might turn to Germany and form an industrial *bloc* based on iron, steel, coal and finance that would enable it to dominate the continent. More likely, Germany would emerge from the present economic crisis as the dominant power of Europe, and if allied to Italy and the Soviet Union could over-awe France and its remaining allies. Britain had the means of forestalling these outcomes, if it was prepared to adapt its economic policy to the larger strategic imperatives. But time was short. The economic crisis made sweeping initiatives imperative.

> Unless a solution can be found for these problems, and that very soon, we may very possibly be faced with a world crisis in which country after country will be plunged into political and economic crises with considerable risk to the whole structure of civilisation . . . What we must try to do is to assemble and assess all our bargaining counters and utilise them *en bloc* in order to achieve as substantial an advance towards world recovery as possible. On no account ought we allow them to be frittered away in return for only subsidiary advantages.[48]

Just how right the Foreign Office officials were in their predictions was to become grimly evident over the next eight years but their appeal to the cabinet was a vain effort, as they undoubtedly appreciated at the time. The crisis had exhausted the politicians' patience with the economic behaviour of the other democratic powers and spurred them into a decisive abandonment of economic internationalism in favour of closer state regulation of external economic relations. The assertion of economic priorities over international political and strategic goals meant a much greater role for the Board of Trade and the Treasury, and the virtual eclipse of the Foreign Office in the decision-making process. After Lord Reading, foreign secretary in the shortlived first National government, the office was held by Sir John Simon, a Liberal with few friends in the cabinet and precious little in the way of vision. Ramsay MacDonald, the Prime Minister, betrayed signs of senility and was a spent force. Neville Chamberlain, the Chancellor of the Exchequer, and Walter Runciman, the president of the Board of Trade, thus easily dominated deliberations. Both were men of commanding presence and confident of their grasp of economic issues, a subject on which most of their colleagues felt out of their depth. Faced with an unprecedented crisis, both men judged other countries in terms of their presumed contribution to economic stabilisation. And while both became aware of the threat posed by the Fascist powers in the next few years, they tended to see it as a product of the economic crisis and responsive to economic remedies. Hence they dwelled upon the shortcomings of the liberal capitalist powers whose role was undeniably crucial in the search for agreement on a new international order. The irony was that much of what they did to appease the Fascist powers and safeguard Britain's economic position actually reduced the possibility of agreement.

The situation was only slightly different in the other democratic powers. On 22 September 1931 French banks reacted to the sudden collapse of sterling by trying to dispose of their sizeable dollar balances. That day the Federal Reserve Bank of New York lost a record amount of gold.[49] The tightening of credit and spreading nervousness forced hundreds of small banks to close their doors in the next few weeks. Hoover, faced with an ominous crisis, called upon American banks to defend themselves through collective action. The National Credit Corporation was established in October 1931. When this proved unavailing, he reluctantly set aside his free market principles and created the Reconstruction Finance Corporation early in the new year. This succeeded for the time being in stemming the banking crisis, but Hoover was clearly annoyed at the necessity to increase government intervention in the private sector.

He was barely civil to Laval when the French leader visited him in October 1931, and on several occasions he encouraged Americans to believe that their economic difficulties would have been alleviated by now had it not been for the way Europe mismanaged its affairs.[50]

Unprepared to help further on the economic front and faced with a hostile Congress and public, Hoover and Henry Stimson, his secretary of state, were all the more annoyed when Japan seized the initiative by overrunning Manchuria and in January 1932 extending the conflict by a violent aerial bombardment of Shanghai. Hoover was unwilling to take direct action against Japan, but he authorised Stimson to announce that the United States would not recognise any territorial change in China brought about by force. This attempt to apply moral pressure merely aggravated Anglo – American relations without fundamentally altering Japanese behaviour. The Stimson doctrine of non-recognition, as it came to be known, embarrassed British statesmen, who were more anxious than ever for American support in the Far East but were reluctant to endorse the doctrine so long as Britain, with its extensive holdings in China, was left to face Japanese retaliation alone. American critics, however, scarcely appreciated Britain's predicament. Britain was suspected of willingness to connive at an imperialist carve-up of East Asia, perhaps of hankering after a revival of the Anglo – Japanese Alliance, and despite the emptiness of Stimson's threat, the myth arose that the United States had been ready to stop Japan in 1932, and would have done so if Britain had not dragged its feet.[51] In May 1932 Stimson, a man who found war planning more congenial than disarmament, advanced a proposal for a one-third reduction in arms at the disarmament conference at Geneva. The proposal, albeit attractive from a cheeseparing budgetary standpoint, was made without reference to the security requirements of any of the major powers affected. France was placed in the acutely embarrassing position of having to reject it and once again appear as a militarist and imperialist power in the eyes of the entire Anglo – Saxon world.[52] Thus instead of contributing to European security, the only result was to fuel the Fascists' propaganda machine and alienate the democratic powers still further from one another.

In the case of France, all efforts to re-establish working relations with Britain and the United States were ignored, misinterpreted or rebuffed. In early October 1931 Sir Frederick Leith Ross of the British Treasury accompanied the foreign secretary, Lord Reading, to Paris to discuss international monetary reform. There, Clément

Moret, governor of the *Banque de France*, pointed out to Leith Ross that his institution had tied up huge balances in London throughout the summer to support the pound sterling, and had suffered massive losses when the pound depreciated. As a result, the *Banque* was bankrupt, and he therefore sought compensation from Britain. The French case deserved sympathy because both the Bank of England and the British government had called upon the *Banque de France* for assistance during the crisis. The *Banque* could not in good faith have rendered assistance while at the same time driving down the pound by selling off its sterling balances. Leith Ross, however, would not consider Moret's case, and dismissed it so abruptly that Moret, hitherto very friendly disposed towards Britain, bitterly threatened to dump his sterling balances without further regard to the consequences. This was a serious threat since the *Banque* held enough sterling practically to destroy the exchanges. But once again France could not afford to take such foolhardy action, and after Flandin gave assurances of a state indemnity Moret returned to the path of reasonableness.[53]

A few weeks later, Laval risked his standing in French political circles by crossing the Atlantic for conversations with President Hoover. Laval was anxious to undo the damage to Franco – American relations caused by French obstruction of the Hoover debt moratorium in June, and had halted official dollar sales before his departure. Nevertheless, it seems that he underestimated the intensity of anti-French feeling in Washington. Discussing the intergovernmental debt crisis, Hoover offered him a vague assurance that the United States would consider a further easing of war debt demands once Europe put its own house in order and that he would resurrect the World War Foreign Debt Committee to examine requests for debt reduction. This was scarcely an advance from earlier statements that America had played its part by participating in the moratorium and that it was up to Europe to make the next move. Nevertheless Laval hopefully took it to mean that European agreement on reduced reparation demands on Germany would be matched by reduced American war demands on Europe.[54] How wrong he was to look for help in this direction soon became apparent.

In December, urged on by the State Department, Hoover accompanied his request for Congressional ratification of the moratorium with a cautious recommendation that the World War Foreign Debt Committee should be reconstituted, to consider 'in some cases. . . still further temporary adjustments. . . during the present emergency'.[55] But Hoover was by now a lame duck president. Moreover, only two days before he had repeated his complaint that American recovery was being held back by the quarrelsome Europeans, and assured Congress that the United States could afford to isolate itself from a total European breakdown and recover independently from the rest of the world.[56] American business opinion was strongly opposed to concessions to Europe when overseas markets were being closed and the federal deficit threatened to drive up taxes, and particularly hostile to France now that its coffers bulged with gold and it apparently grew rich while other countries slumped. Suspicious politicians imagined they saw in Hoover's recommendation the hand of Wall Street financiers who allegedly sought to safeguard their overseas investments at the expense of the American taxpayer. By a large majority, therefore, the Senate banking committee rejected the initiative.[57]

Progress towards a solution to the reparations problem was agonisingly slow. In January 1932 negotiations broke down when the French blamed Britain for further encouraging the Germans to expect a complete end to reparations after the Hoover moratorium year ended. Finally in July of that year Édouard Herriot, Prime Minister in the new centre-left French government, joined Neville Chamberlain, the British Chancellor of the Exchequer, and Franz von Papen, the German Chancellor, at Lausanne for formal negotiations. Chamberlain, for whom this was the first international conference, had become convinced that the survival of capitalism demanded an end to reparations, and that a firm British lead at the conference was imperative. 'The foreigner,' he wrote, 'could not be expected to be far-sighted on this matter, so it was Britain's duty to make him see reason.'[58] British inflexibility and von Papen's manoeuverings briefly threatened to realise Foreign Office fears of the French being drawn into a continental *bloc*. Stern British warnings served to pull Herriot back from von Papen's embrace, and after further negotiations Herriot agreed virtually to abandon reparations on the assurance of British consultation in future on matters affecting the issue.[59] But the British assurance was as vaguely worded as the assurance Hoover had given Laval the previous October, as the French were soon to discover.

That summer British efforts to salvage its commercial interests in face of unprecedented economic storms led to a serious worsening of relations with the United States. At Ottawa British efforts to unite the Commonwealth by reducing internal trade barriers ended with agreement instead to maintain existing protection within the Commonwealth and raising barriers against the external world. British statesmen, although disappointed with the result, regarded this as a necessary response to the protectionist policies of the United States, France and other foreign powers, but as the Foreign Office had warned, it was interpreted by Americans as a deliberate attempt to exclude them from a large part of world markets by improper, discriminatory measures, and aroused the strongest criticism.[60] Meanwhile, within a few days of the end of the Lausanne conference, British statesmen confirmed the existence of a so-called 'gentlemen's agreement', which made the reparations settlement dependent upon American acceptance of an end to war debts. This revelation raised a storm of protest in the United States, directed mainly against France. Now that the presidential election campaign had begun, American political leaders were anxious to avoid the subject and annoyed at the way the Europeans had put them on the spot.[61] When it became clear that the United States would demand a further instalment of war debt payments on 15 December, French Treasury officials advocated payment. Since Britain was sure to pay, they believed France also must also continue paying to avoid a break with Britain and jeopardising access to the American capital market at a time when the growing threat of war from Germany made access an absolute necessity. But so strong was public resentment at American non-cooperation that Herriot stood no chance of securing parliamentary approval for a further payment.[62] To make matters worse, it became apparent that, despite earlier assurances of consultation, Britain had no intention of collaborating with France in a joint effort to secure relief from further payments to the United States.

Chamberlain, whose already strong dislike of the United States had been intensified by its response to Lausanne, favoured consultation with the French and firm opposition to further payments, but MacDonald, as hostile to the French as he was ignorant of their predicament, argued strenuously against any association with them. The American authorities, he was sure, recognised the injustice of the 1923 Anglo – American debt funding agreement, whose terms were more onerous than those imposed on other debtors, and could be expected to offer Britain much greater concessions on a bilateral basis than if Britain aligned herself with France.[63] Chamberlain, anxious about the renewed weakness of the pound, acquiesced as did other ministers. Frustrated as they were by America's insistence upon continued payments, they found the prospect of repudiation too awful to contemplate. Stanley Baldwin, Lord President of the Council, warned that Britain's default would almost certainly lead other countries, including important British debtors in Latin America and Asia, to follow suit. The British working class would lose its respect for the law. Thus 'repudiation might bring the world within sight of the end of capitalism.'[64] On 15 December, therefore, Britain paid her war debt instalment while France defaulted. French default was accompanied by the downfall of the Herriot government and the beginnings of a prolonged budget crisis. For the first time since 1926 the franc displayed marked weakness on the international exchanges.[65]

Briefly, with Hoover on the verge of retirement and Franklin D. Roosevelt poised to take over the American presidency, the crisis among the democratic powers seemed to be at an end. At the time of the presidential election, both the British and the French ambassadors in Washington encouraged hopes of improved relations. Paul Claudel reported that after 12 years of Republican government marked by 'contradictory [economic] restraint and imprudent expansion, isolation and megalomania,' and by 'self-interested and mean-spirited conservatism,' France could look forward to a new Democratic administration inspired by international-minded liberalism. Sir Ronald Lindsay, his British counterpart, reported to London in similar term,[66] but it soon became evident that Roosevelt was if anything more ignorant of international affairs than his predecessor and shared his prejudices against Wall Street and Britain.

For the first six months of 1933 relations among the three creditor powers were dominated by the uncertainty surrounding Roosevelt's intentions as he grappled with the domestic financial crisis. Shortly after his inauguration in March, he invited MacDonald to visit Washington for talks. Unbeknownst to MacDonald, however, he also invited Herriot, the French Prime Minister, Grandi of Italy, and several other foreign statesmen to make the same journey. Then, with several of his guests on the high seas, he announced the abandonment of the gold standard. MacDonald, although shaken, was prepared to believe that this action had been forced upon Roosevelt as a means of forestalling Congressional demands for more radical inflationary measures, and Roosevelt assured his guests of his undiminished support for international monetary and financial co-operation.[67] But a point had been reached when mutual incomprehension made every initiative the source of further antagonism.

France, left with a seriously overvalued franc after the departure of Britain and other countries of the sterling area from the gold standard in 1931, was now suffering acutely from the depression. Hitler's accession as Chancellor in Berlin on 30 January 1933 and Mussolini's increasingly belligerent gestures in Rome caused the French deep unease. If there was one thing more worrying than the foreign threat, however, it was the fear that the franc might be forced off the gold standard and plunge the nation into chaos, as had nearly happened in the mid-1920s. French leaders were therefore desperate to secure immediate British and American agreement on currency stabilisation,[68] but to their intense frustration the British were exceedingly reluctant to commit themselves. Montagu Norman at the Bank of England opposed any commitment to stabilise the pound, since to do so would again expose British currency management to the vagaries of American economic policy and risk a return to the same difficulties that had forced the Bank into such unpopular policies during the 1920s. Neville Chamberlain, the minister responsible, yielded only reluctantly from this position. To his tidy, rule-bound mind, Roosevelt was behaving with frightening irresponsibility if not downright hostility by deliberately abandoning the gold standard when there was no economic necessity to do so. To stabilise sterling in these conditions meant jeopardising everything he had accomplished since becoming Chancellor, in insulating the national economy from external deflationary pressures and fostering recovery through a policy of cheap money. He was prepared to consider currency stabilisation to restrain Roosevelt from causing even greater damage, but only on a tentative, *de facto* basis while the war debt issue remained unresolved.[69]

Everything that Britain did served to convince Roosevelt that he must avoid commitments with the British on currency policy. Like most of his countrymen he regarded Britain with some affection, but his view was coloured by a greatly exaggerated notion of British wealth, power and aggressiveness. To some extent he shared the view of his secretary of state, Cordell Hull, that the Ottawa agreements on empire trade were an act of economic aggression against the United States.[70] He also looked with deep suspicion upon Britain's creation of an exchange equalisation account in 1932. The ostensible purpose of the account was to smooth out short term fluctuations in the international value of sterling, but to suspicious Washington observers it seemed to be a device for keeping the pound artificially low in order to give British exporters an unfair edge over their American competition. The same motives were imputed to the decline of sterling towards the end of 1932. Roosevelt almost certainly abandoned the gold standard the following spring as much to strengthen his hand *vis-à-vis* Britain as to remove this potential constraint on domestic reflationary initiatives.[71]

The caution with which British authorities approached the question of currency stabilisation appeared to Roosevelt as confirmation of their determination to retain an exchange advantage over the dollar. Then when Britain accepted the need for an agreement, he began to suspect that it must be a trap.[72] Feeling his way towards a reflationary solution to the unprecedented domestic economic crisis within the United States and aware of strong opposition to monetary or financial innovation among members of the New York banking community – the 'economic royalists', as he called them – he became suspicious about the links between the Bank of England, the Federal Reserve Bank of New York and J.P. Morgan's, the most powerful investment bank in New York and fiscal agent for both the British and French governments in the United States. In his ignorance, he persisted in imagining that Chamberlain was an agent of the City of London, although in fact he was a career politician whose background was in manufacturing rather than finance, and whose outlook was more narrowly nationalist than was common among City bankers.[73] Roosevelt therefore kept the Federal Reserve Bank of New York almost completely in the dark about his intentions. According to one plausible account, he came to believe that stabilisation was being foisted upon him by a conspiracy of Wall Street and City bankers.[74] When currency stabilisation became the primary item on the agenda of the World Economic Conference, which convened in London in June 1933, the stage was set for another major crisis among the creditor powers.

The World Economic Conference was the last attempt to devise a comprehensive solution to the economic crisis before the war. After the succession of failures in the previous half-dozen years, the prospect of another conference was approached with scant enthusiasm, and indeed it owed its origin to somewhat disingenuous British efforts to draw the United States into a comprehensive reparations-war debt settlement in 1932. Nevertheless, such was the plight of the international economy and the uncertainty over Roosevelt's intentions that by the time the conference opened on 12 June 1933 it attracted greater interest than any other international gathering since Locarno. Delegates, convened in the sweltering heat of the auditorium in the Kensington geological museum, waited with increasing anxiety

for three weeks before he announced his decision. Fears of a decline
in the dollar led to increased pressure on the Swiss franc, the Dutch
florin and other currencies still attached to gold. On 22 June Georges
Bonnet, head of the French delegation, warned MacDonald that
there was little to be hoped for from Roosevelt, and appealed for
British co-operation.

> If agreement was not reached between America and other nations, a
> very serious situation threatened. All the European exchanges were
> threatened with collapse, and even in France which was better pro-
> tected, difficulties would be encountered. In the next month or so he
> apprehended very grave political, economic and social difficulties in
> Europe. . . . [E]verything would depend upon the co-operation of
> France, Italy and especially Great Britain. If public opinion got the
> idea that the pound was going to follow the dollar it could not tell how
> far things were going. If people thought that the United Kingdom,
> France and Italy would not maintain financial order, people would
> think that there was no chance of saving the situation.[75]

Bonnet proposed 'drastic measures' of retaliation against the United
States, and pressured British leaders to line up with the 'gold'
countries of Europe. A few days later, when the uncertainty of
British policy began to add to pressure on the remaining gold currencies, he accused them of driving Europe to virtual destruction. If
British authorities did not immediately discourage the impression
that the pound would be depreciated along with the dollar, he
warned MacDonald and Chamberlain on the morning of the 26th, the
result would be 'irreversible catastrophes'. It would open the door in
Europe to 'monetary anarchy' that could not fail to have 'the gravest
social and political consequences.' Made desperate by the prospect of
a currency collapse, Bonnet alternated between appeals and threats.
Once again he announced his intention of blaming Britain for the
breakdown of monetary relations and the failure of the conference if
British statesmen did not side with Europe.[76]

Meanwhile General Smuts led a Commonwealth delegation in an
endeavour to persuade Chamberlain to co-ordinate reflationary policy with Roosevelt. Chamberlain was appalled by the speculative
pressures that Roosevelt had aroused in the United States – 'the
source of the gravest possible danger to America herself, and to the
rest of the civilised world' – but confronted a painful dilemma. As he
told the delegation, he could not contemplate joining the French in

retaliation against the United States, nor of exposing Britain to another deflationary crisis similar to that of 1931 by linking the pound to the franc, the florin and the lira. But neither could he contemplate supporting Roosevelt's madcap actions, which threatened Europe with disaster. Britain had a strong interest in the welfare of the continent. If Roosevelt continued his present policy,

> the inevitable result must be that one by one the European countries remaining on the gold standard would be pitched off that standard in complete disorder and confusion. He did not know what would happen in that event, but it was quite certain that Europe would be filled with welter and chaos and might possibly be faced with social and political disorder of the gravest character. There was only one country, namely the United Kingdom, which could hold the position in this respect, and we must, so far as we were able to do so, ensure that the state of affairs that he had outlined never came to pass.[77]

Roosevelt's 'bombshell' message denouncing the very idea of currency stabilisation was released on 3 July. In the event it was so thoroughly anticipated that the immediate impact upon foreign currencies was less dire than seemed certain beforehand. But the experience of being lectured to by the American president while he proceeded recklessly to distort currency relations at a time when the world was already experiencing unprecedented economic difficulties, left an enduring legacy of bitterness in Paris and London which was to last until 1939. Lord Hailsham declared Roosevelt's economic policy 'a gross fraud'. Chamberlain described his message as 'arrogant' and hectoring 'in a manner and in circumstances which were hardly believable'. Walter Runciman described its rationale for non-stabilisation as 'not merely offensive, but also grossly untrue'. French statesmen used similar language in their condemnation.[78]

Chamberlain was almost as annoyed at Bonnet as he was at Roosevelt.[79] He managed to overcome Bonnet's attempt to embarrass Roosevelt by breaking up the conference, but although it continued for another three weeks little more was accomplished during its remaining sessions. Even before it closed, the divisions within the international economy widened, with the gold standard countries forming a gold *bloc* and the dominions forming a sterling *bloc*. The gold standard countries bolstered their exchange positions by increasing trade restrictions, and sterling, caught in the middle of this widening gulf, rose sharply on the foreign exchanges then abruptly slumped in the wake of a massive flight of capital to Paris, Amsterdam, and Zurich.[80] For Chamberlain and his colleagues, the result could hardly have been worse.

The final act of alienation began on 27 October 1933 when Roosevelt attempted to stimulate the domestic economy by massive purchases of gold. The effect on France was as disastrous – if not quite so swift – as had been predicted in the summer. The Daladier government had just been defeated in parliament after three days of intense and sometimes acrimonious debate on its retrenchment proposals, which included higher indirect taxes and a six per cent reduction in public sector pay.[81] Already that year two billion francs (£16.4 million) had been cut from the defence budget, and conservative critics such as Paul Reynaud and Ernest Mandel sternly warned of the folly of disarming when Germany was rapidly rearming.[82] But once Roosevelt's actions intensified speculation against the franc, French governments saw no alternative but to reduce civil *and* military spending. The tensions generated by the slump and evidence of political incompetence and veniality erupted in riots on 6 February 1934, when right wing extremists joined by Communists brought down Daladier's second government, though failing in what appears to have been an attempted *coup*.

The government of national unity under the former President, Gaston Doumergue, which took office on 9 February, restored order without however overcoming the basic dilemma facing France. Supported by most of the conservative elements in the country, Doumergue refused to contemplate devaluation. Instead, he used his decree powers to reduce public sector pay by ten per cent, state pensions by three per cent, and further reduce military spending. Funds for military equipment declined from francs 610 million to 200 million; officers on active duty were reduced by 1,200; fewer reservists were called up; and all idea of large scale manoeuvres was set aside for the year.[83] This, however, only compounded the national demoralisation without succeeding in eliminating the budget deficit, which grew steadily larger. Domestic hoarding now reached massive proportions, and the formation of the Popular Front, which united Socialists, Communists, and in 1935 also Radicals, marked a new stage in the polarisation of domestic politics.

The effect of Roosevelt's monetary experiments was equally serious for Anglo–American relations. In December 1933 the British government grudgingly paid another token instalment of war debts. But they did so on the understanding that Roosevelt would not declare them in default. They were therefore shocked to find in February 1934 that Congress intended to include Britain within the operation of the Johnson Bill, which on enactment would exclude defaulters from access to American capital markets, and that the administration was not prepared to put up serious resistance on their behalf.[84] This was an extremely serious situation in view of the fact that Britain had only been saved from collapse in the First World War by drawing upon American financial resources. But so angry were British statesmen at this ostensibly unjustified punishment that appeals from Sir Ronald Lindsay, the ambassador in Washington, not to lose sight of the larger issues were ignored.[85] Sir Robert Vansittart, the permanent secretary at the Foreign Office, angrily commented,

> this strengthens my conviction that we have been too tender, not to say subservient, with the U.S. for a long time past. It is we who have made all the advances, and received nothing in return. It is still necessary. . . that we should get on with this untrustworthy race; but I think our methods will obviously have to change. . . [Even then] we shall never get very far; they will always let us down.[86]

Vansittart thereupon proposed approaching Japan first, rather than the United States, to discuss preparations for the forthcoming naval conference. Two years earlier, at the Lausanne conference, Neville Chamberlain had denounced the suggestion of repudiation of war debt obligations as 'Langism and Bolshevism'[87], yet on 15 June 1934 Britain refused payment of the six monthly instalment. In the Treasury anti-American sentiment had reached almost pathological intensity. In the cabinet, ministers went so far as to claim that it was the Americans who would regret that the break had come.[88] Mainly as a result of this protracted financial conflict, Neville Chamberlain acquired what the diplomat Sir Alexander Cadogan described as 'an almost instinctive contempt for the Americans,' which was to remain with him throughout his term as Prime Minister.[89] Sadly for both, Roosevelt maintained the same attitude towards Chamberlain.[90]

This was not the limit of the damage, however. Frustrated by the turn of events in 1933, the British government reacted with unrestrained anger when the French government yielded to intensified pressures for protection and reneged on promises to remove the discriminatory duties on British exports. On 6 February 1934, the very day that the riots in Paris threatened to destroy the Third Republic, British Embassy officials were called upon to deliver Runciman's announcement of punitive action against France. The Foreign Office regarded it as folly to compound the difficulties already facing Daladier's recently formed second government, and hastily intervened to secure a brief postponement.[91] A few months later the feud over commercial relations was ended, with the French giving way on the major issues.[92] But the crisis not only heightened British disdain for French friendship, it also increased Britain's reluctance to defend the European balance of power.

Preoccupied with the threat from the large and shrilly anti-capitalist left within Britain, ministers found it hard to think of the Fascist states without crediting them with crushing their own left wing opposition, and since France appeared more obstructive and unreasonable than ever, they were prepared to excuse some of the most ominous initiatives by Germany and Italy as anti-French and not necessarily a threat to peace. Convinced that France had behaved immorally in its monetary, financial and commercial policies to the point of subverting the pound and the world economy itself, they now looked with equanimity upon France's domestic crisis as proof of its moral decadence, and almost welcomed it as an excuse to rule out France as a serious factor in the strategic balance. As Chamberlain commented during the trade war, 'The French have behaved like madmen. If they are going to quarrel with their best friends they will deserve what they will get.'[93] Two years later, after the Germans had flaunted their commitment under the Locarno Pact by remilitarising the Rhineland, MacDonald, now Lord President of the Council, recorded in his diary, 'France has again had a severe lesson and I hope it will take it this time. . . Hitler's stroke has been admirably bold. My old trouble: can we trust him? I am still doubtful.'[94] Later in 1936, after the upheavals following the election of the Popular Front government in France, Sir Maurice Hankey, the secretary to the cabinet and to the Committee of Imperial Defence, described Britain's most important ally as 'half rotted with discontent and Communism.'[95] Evidently there was little to be hoped for from this direction.

Feelings were very largely reciprocated. From their standpoint, French statesmen became progressively more annoyed by Chamberlain's exchange rate policy. Desperate about the fate of the franc, particularly after the severe gold reserve losses that followed the victory of the Popular Front parties in the May 1935 municipal elections, they looked for an assurance that devaluation of the franc would not become the signal for a currency war in which sterling was depreciated in order to maintain its exchange value, driving down the franc still further and shattering what remained of their domestic social order. But Chamberlain was once again unable to commit himself on account of American determination to keep the dollar seriously undervalued against other currencies. He felt annoyed by his helplessness, and in turn American and French statesmen interpreted his insistence upon allowing the pound to float almost as an unfriendly act.[96] Not until September 1936 were suspicions even partially allayed by the tripartite agreement, a modest arrangement among the democratic powers that enabled the French to devalue without fear of plunging the country into the abyss but left currency arrangements to continue on a day to day basis.

Besides renewed problems with the franc, however, trade relations among the democratic powers remained very strained during the next two years. Roosevelt was never as devoted to the goal of foreign trade expansion as was his secretary of state, Cordell Hull, but he shared in a limited way Hull's conviction that the Ottawa agreements were a malevolent anti-American design and moreover a major, perhaps *the* major, source of international frustration and tensions. Time and again American officials criticised British policy. 'The more it closes the Empire to outsiders, the more it is driving the "have-nots" to seek their place in the sun through unorthodox means,' J. Pierrepont Moffat, chief of the State Department's Division of European Affairs, wrote in June 1936. A few months later he affirmed, 'At present [Britain] thinks she can count on our help politically and yet hit us below the belt commercially all over the world.'[97] British authorities, holding American protectionism to be largely responsible for the general retreat into commercial *blocs*, treated these complaints as a gross impertinence. As a result this festering sore remained untreated until 1938, when a new trade treaty was finally signed. But it required prolonged negotiations which left both sides bruised, and neither side felt justice was obtained in the final result.[98]

IV

Of the many problems besetting world peace between the wars, none was more serious than the economic conflicts among the major democratic powers. The severity of the world depression is well known. But, as has been seen, the tension that marked relations among the democratic powers due to economic differences was both more protracted and more acute than is commonly appreciated. The

1920s, a time of increasing prosperity, was not a time of increasing harmony for the economic relations among these powers. At best it was a kind of armed truce. This explains the hasty resort to defensive weapons, such as tariffs, quotas, trade preference schemes, and currency depreciation, at the first sign of serious trouble early in 1929. Thereafter, in the period 1929–34, economic relations declined to a state of virtual war, wherein mutual incomprehension fuelled a downward spiral in relations which left the three powers alienated from one another and incapable of addressing the problems underlying the crisis.

In the United States Hoover and for at least a year after him Roosevelt encouraged Americans to believe that the catastrophe that had overtaken their country was largely due to Europe and that the economic salvation of the New World required isolation from the Old. In Britain the French problem, economic as well as political, was allowed to overshadow the German problem, at least until 1933, at which point the American problem temporarily overshadowed both. By then Neville Chamberlain had come to dominate the British cabinet by reason of his supposed expertise in economic matters, and to use his influence to promote a businessman's approach to international relations. In France political leaders were quicker than their British counterparts to recognise the emerging threat posed by Hitler in Germany, but found themselves unable to respond effectively on account of the more immediate threat of internal collapse due to the increasingly overvalued franc and accompanying deterioration in public finances. So grave was this threat that successive governments of the centre and the right were obliged to give first priority to restoring public confidence in the currency. As one authority has written, 'the simple, physical fact was that the energies of French statesmen were almost wholly absorbed by the fight to save the franc and the search for economic recovery.'[99] All of them accepted reductions in public expenditure, and even those who rejected the disarmament proposals raised at Geneva found themselves unilaterally disarming through reductions in military spending. For this they blamed Britain and the United States.[100]

The same period, and in particular the years between 1931 and 1933, which were the nadir of the world depression, can be seen also as a political turning point, when Japan took its first step towards the making of its so-called 'Greater East Asia Co-Prosperity Sphere' by seizing Manchuria and attacking Shanghai, when Italian imperialist ambitions in the Balkans and Africa became suddenly more prominent, and when Hitler exploited the collapse of *bourgeois* coalition government in Germany to manoeuvre his way into power. With these developments the post-war era gave way to another pre-war era. Tragically, statesmen in the principal democratic powers were aware of this turn of events. If they did virtually nothing to forestall or resist it, it was largely because they were themselves already immersed in what they saw as a struggle for national survival. Long run strategic interests gave way to ostensibly short run economic necessity. And from this vantage point the gravest threats came not from the Fascist or militarist power but the other democratic powers themselves.

NOTES AND REFERENCES

1. FO 371/14365, C2355/230/18, Graham to Henderson, no. 187, 14 March 1930.
2. 'Then came the world economic crisis of 1929–33, which shook the island economy to its foundations. It is not too much to say that it gave a decisive twist to Japanese foreign policy reviving old imperialist dreams and setting her on a road which ended in September 1945 with the formal surrender of the armed forces to General Douglas MacArthur on board the battleship *Missouri*.' William Carr, *Poland to Pearl Harbor: The Making of the Second World War* (London, 1985), p. 23.
3. Enzo Santarelli, 'The Economic and Political Background of Fascist Imperialism,' in *The Ax Within. Italian Fascism in Action*, ed. Roland Sarti (New York, 1974), pp. 167–68.
4. See for instance, G.C. Peden, *British Rearmament and the Treasury, 1933–1939* (Edinburgh, 1979); Robert Shay, *British Rearmament in the Thirties: Politics and Profits* (Princeton NJ, 1977); Robert Frankenstein, *Le Prix du réarmement français 1935–1939* (Paris, 1982).
5. Commenting on the recent experience of British industry, *The Times*, on 1 February 1927, spoke of 'five years of the most intense depression they had ever experienced' – before the year of the General Strike, 1926, 'the blackest of black years'.
6. On Norman's struggle to defend sterling and the international monetary system see Robert Boyce, *British Capitalism at the Crossroads, 1919–1932. A Study in Politics, Economics, and International Relations* (Cambridge, 1987), ch. 5.
7. The pre-war Germinal franc had a sterling parity of 25.22 francs to the pound. On 25 June 1928 the franc was formally restored to the gold standard at 124.21 francs to the pound.
8. France, Ministry of Finance, $F^{30}/141$, note by Lacour–Gayet, 23 October 1930. The finance minister, Louis Germain Martin, called for

retrenchment in September 1930 to cope with the looming crisis. See his *Le Problème financier 1930–1936* (Paris, 1936), p. 24.

9. J.M. Keynes, *The Economic Consequences of the Peace* (London, 1919).
10. André Mertens, 'L'Accord commercial franco–allemand du août 1927,' *Revenue Economique Internationale*, October 1927, pp. 23–45; Documents on British Foreign Policy (hereafter DBFP), Ser. 1A, Vol. 4, French note in Phipps to Chamberlain, 2 April 1928; Alfred Sauvy, *Histoire économique de la France entre les deux guerres*, iv (Paris, 1975), pp. 20, 23; Pierre Guillan, 'La politique douanière de la France dans les annés vingt,' *Relations Internationales*, 16 (Paris, 1978), pp. 315–31.
11. B. Michel, 'Aspects of western equity investment in the banking systems of East Central Europe: Commentary,' in *International Business and Central Europe, 1918–1939*, eds. Alice Teichova and P.L. Cottrell (Leicester, 1983), p. 351.
12. Emile Moreau, *Souvenirs d'un Gouverneur de la Banque de France* (Paris, 1954), pp. 488–89; Sir Frederick Leith Ross, *Money Talks, Fifty Years of International Finance* (London, 1969), p. 124.
13. W.A. McDougall, *France's Rhineland Diplomacy, 1914–1924: The Last Bid for a Balance of Power in Europe* (Princeton NJ, 1978), pp. 327, 350. On French hostility towards Britain's German policy, see W.M. Jordan, *Great Britain, France, and the German Problem, 1919–1939* (London, 1943), pp. 50–51 and *passim*.
14. Stephen Schuker, *The end of French Predominance in Europe. The Financial Crisis of 1924 and the Adoption of the Dawes Plan* (Chapel Hill NC, 1976), pp. 300–18.
15. On French tariff levels, see Sauvy, *Histoire économique*, iv, pp. 11, 25; League of Nations, *International Economic Conference. Tariff Level Indices* L.N. 1927.11.34 (Geneva, 1927), annex ii. On creeping British protectionism, see DBFP, ser. 1A, vol. 4, Phipps to Chamberlain, 29 March 1928.
16. For a vivid description of American expansion, see Ludwell Denny, *America Conquers Britain* (New York, 1930), and the more recent Frank Costigliola, *Awkward Dominion: American Political, Economic, and Cultural Relations with Europe, 1919–1933* (Ithaca NY, 1984).
17. Mira Wilkins, *The Maturing of Multinational Enterprise: American Business Abroad from 1914 to 1970* (Cambridge MA, 1974), ch. 7. The bulk of American foreign direct investment during the decade was concentrated in years 1924–1929.
18. *The Economist*, 20 April 1929, p. 848.
19. *Ibid*, 8 June 1929, p. 1279.
20. *Ibid*, 22 June 1929, p. 1393.
21. *Ibid*, 13 July 1929, p. 64. On other reactions, see André Siegfried, 'European Reactions to American Tariff Proposals,' *Foreign Affairs*, October 1929, pp. 13–19; Joseph M. Jones Jr., *Tariff Retaliation, Repercussions of the Hawley–Smoot Bill* (Philadelphia, 1934).

22. Boyce, *British Capitalism at the Crossroads*, pp. 147–48, 181–82.
23. R. Jones and O. Marriott, *Anatomy of a Merger. A History of GEC, AEI, and English Electric* (London, 1970), ch. 5–6; *The Manchester Guardian Commercial*, 21 March 1929, p. 342; *The Economist*, 8 June 1929, p. 1292, 15 June 1929, p. 1350, 22 June 1929, p. 1388.
24. Boyce, *British Capitalism at the Crossroads*, pp. 183–84.
25. CAB 32/67, I.W.C. (28)75, telegram to Dominions governments, 9 March 1928. For an analysis of the politics of imperial communications, see Robert Boyce, 'Canada and the Making of a City Giant: Cable and Wireless,' paper presented to the British Association of Canadian Studies conference, Birkbeck College, London, 1987 (mimeographed).
26. *The Manchester Guardian Commercial*, 16 May 1929, p. 578, and 30 May 1929, p. 632; *The Daily Telegraph*, 22 June 1929.
27. FO 371/14094, W1846/1846/50, Chamberlain memorandum, 16 February 1929; FO 371/13510, A1397/12/45, Cunliffe–Lister minute, 1 March 1929.
28. Thomas Jones, *Whitehall Diary*, vol. ii, *1926–30*, ed. Keith Middlemas (London, 1969), p. 177.
29. Harold James, *The Reichsbank and Public Finance in Germany, 1924–1933; A Study of the Politics of Economics during the Great Depression* (Frankfurt am Main, 1985), p. 105 and *passim*.
30. Federal Reserve Bank of New York papers, C261, Norman to Harrison, no. 108, 10 May 1929.
31. The most comprehensive account is in Jon Jacobson, *Locarno Diplomacy. Germany and the West, 1925–1929* (Princeton, 1972).
32. Owen D. Young papers, Crocker diary, 9 April 1929.
33. Owen D. Young papers, Young to Schneider, 17 May 1929.
34. John M. Sherwood, *Georges Mandel and the Third Republic* (Stanford CA, 1970), 111.
35. League of Nations, *Official Journal*, Records of the Tenth Assembly, 1929, Plenary Meetings, p. 36.
36. F^{30}/B12614, Rueff to Flandin, no. 58, 544, 18 June 1931. See also Foreign Relations of the United States, 1931, vol. 1 (hereafter FRUS. 1931.I, etc), Atherton (for Mellon) to Stimson, no. 191, 17 June 1931; Edward W. Bennett, *Germany and the Diplomacy of the Financial Crisis, 1931* (Cambridge MA 1962), pp. 151–52.
37. F^{30}/B12657, Berthelot to de Fleuriau, no. 70, 501, 20 June 1931.
38. Sir Charles Addis diary, 17, 18 July 1931; MacDonald papers, PRO 30/69/1/260, Keynes to MacDonald, 5 August 1931; T188/21, Leith Ross minute, 13 August 1931.
39. FO 800/284, Henderson to Briand, 23 June 1931.
40. FO 371/15182, C4391/172/62, Vansittart minute, 22 June 1931; FO 371/15182, C4455/172/62, Lindsay to Henderson, no. 351, 24 June 1931; PRO 30/69/8/1, MacDonald diary, 5 July 1931.
41. See for instance, the *Daily Mail*, 'New French Gold Raid,' 11 July 1931; *Financial Times*, *'Money Market Notes,'* 13 July 1931; *Evening*

Standard, 'French Taking Gold,' 14 July 1931. Tyrrell made inquiries in Paris about the alleged French gold raid: FO 371/15187, C5298/172/62, Tyrrell to Vansittart, no. 174, 16 July 1931.

42. Tom Johnston, *The Financiers and the Nation* (London, 1934), p. 198.
43. *Banque de France, délibérations du Conseil Général*, 18, 23, 27 July 1931.
44. HC Deb. 5s, vol. 256, col. 1291.
45. FO 371/15195, C6974/172/62, Law to O'Malley, 9 September 1931; Beaverbrook papers, C/27, Baxter (enclosure) to Beaverbrook, 30 April 1934.
46. FO 800/226, Selby to Vansittart, 2 October 1931; F^{30}/B 12625, de Fleuriau to Briand, no. 581, 18 November 1931.
47. CAB 24/225, C.P.–301(31), Foreign Office memorandum, 26 November 1931.
48. *Ibid.*
49. On 22 September 1931 the Federal Reserve lost $116 million, of which $50 million went to the *Banque de France*. This was 'the largest gold loss ever suffered by the United States in a single day,' Lester V. Chandler, *American Monetary Policy, 1928–1941* (London, 1971), pp. 167, 170.
50. Robert Ferrell, *American Diplomacy in the Great Depression: Hoover-Stimson Foreign Policy, 1929–1933* (New Haven CN, 1957), pp. 12, 204; FRUS, 1931.I, Hoover to Congress, 8 December 1931, p. xiv.
51. Christopher Thorne, *The Limits of Foreign Policy: The West, the League and the Far Eastern Crisis of 1931–1933* (London, 1972), pp. 210–11, 247–48, and *passim*.
52. Ferrell, *American Diplomacy in the Great Depression*, pp. 203, 214; PRO 30/69/8/1, MacDonald diary, 1 May 1932.
53. T160/403, F12666, Leith Ross minute, 7 October 1931.
54. Geoffrey Warner, *Pierre Laval and the Eclipse of France* (London, 1968), p. 48; Melvin Leffler, *The Elusive Quest: America's Pursuit of European Stability and French Security, 1919–1933* (Chapel Hill, 1979), p. 266.
55. FRUS. 1931.I, p. xxv.
56. FRUS. 1931.I, pp. xiii–xiv.
57. Leffler, *The Elusive Quest*, p. 266. See also Leffler, 'Laval's Visit to America: The Constraints on American Policy-making, 1931/32,' in *Konstellationen internationaler Politik 1924–1932*, ed. Gustav Schmidt (Bochum, 1983), pp. 281–91. Working both sides of the street, Leffler attests to Hoover's far-sightedness by quoting statements by him and his colleagues which indicate that they appreciated the 'interdependence' of the United States and Europe. But he then points out that the United States was *not* dependent upon Europe, in order to assert the reasonableness of Hoover's refusal to join in a sustained and consistent way in the search for international solutions to the world depression. This seems designed to prove that America's flight into isolationism began with Roosevelt and the Democrats rather than earlier with Hoover and

the Republicans. As Leffler explains in *The Elusive Quest*, pp. 360, 359, Roosevelt, after six months of dithering, in June 1933 'embarked upon a course of economic nationalism and political isolationism,' which 'signified a turning point in American foreign policy.'

58. Neville Chamberlain papers (hereafter NC), 18/1/789, Neville to Hilda Chamberlain, 26 June 1932.

59. Jacques Bariéty and Charles Bloch, 'Une tentative de reconciliation franco-allemande et son échec (1932–1933),' *Revue d'histoire moderne et contemporaine*, vol. xv (July to September 1968), pp. 452–53; Neville Waites, 'The Depression Years,' in *Troubled Neighbours: French–British Foreign Relations in the Twentieth Century*, ed. N. Waites (London, 1971), pp. 138–39.

60. CAB 27/475, O.C.(31)86, 'United Kingdom and Empire Tariffs in Relation to Foreign Countries', 30 June 1932.

61. *Documents diplomatiques français* (hereafter DDF), ler sér., vol. 1, Claudel to Herriot, nos. 474–79, 12 July 1932.

62. DDF, ler sér., vol. 1, Note de la direction du mouvement des fonds, 28 October 1932; Michel Soulié, *La Vie politique d'Édouard Herriot* (Paris, 1962), pp. 409–10; Walter Edge, *A Jerseyman's Journal: Fifty Years of American Business and Politics* (Princeton NJ, 1948), p. 224.

63. PRO 30/69/8/1, MacDonald diary, 27 November 1932.

64. CAB 23/73(32), 63(32) Appendix, 28 November 1932.

65. M. Coste, 'Movements of Capital in France from 1929 to 1933,' *BIS Monetary and Economic Department*, C.B. 76 (May 1934), p. 21.

66. DDF, ler sér., vol. 1, Claudel to Herriot, nos 794–96, 9 November 1932; T160/417, F6677/06/1, Osborne to Simon, 27 October 1932.

67. CAB 23/76, 33(33)2, Conclusions, 5 May 1933.

68. DDF, ler sér., vol. 3, Paul–Boncour circular telegram, no. 968, 25 April 1933.

69. CAB 21/374, Treasury to Lindsay, no. 208, 26 April 1933; T175/79, Hopkins minute, 3 May 1933.

70. Cordell Hull, *Memoirs* (New York, 1948), pp. 355, 518–30. See also David Reynolds, *The Creation of the Anglo–American Alliance, 1937–41: A Study in Competitive Cooperation* (London, 1981), pp. 24–25, 43.

71. F^{30}/1412, Monick to Bonnet, 19 April, 29 May 1933.

72. F^{30}/1416, de la Baume to Bonnet, 10 May 1933.

73. D.C. Watt, *Succeeding John Bull. America in Britain's Place, 1900–1975: A Study of the Anglo–American Relationship and World Politics in the Context of British and American Foreign Policymaking in the Twentieth Century* (Cambridge, 1984), p. 81.

74. Lloyd C. Gardner, *Economic Aspects of New Deal Diplomacy* (Madison WN, 1964), p. 273.

75. T172/1816, minute of conversation between MacDonald, Bonnet, and Bizot, 22 June 1933.

76. F^{30}/1416, Bonnet to Paul Boncour, 27 June 1933.

77. T172/1811, M.E. Conv. 23, 30 June 1933.
78. T172/1811, M.E. (U.K.) 18th mtg., 2 July 1933; T172/1810A, M.E.(U.K.) 19th mtg., 3 July 1933.
79. Sir Keith Feiling, *The Life of Neville Chamberlain* (London, 1946), p. 224.
80. Ferrell *American Diplomacy in the Great Depression*, p. 273; Georges Étienne Bonnet, *Vingt ans de vie politique 1918–1938* (Paris, 1969), p. 176; Sir Henry Clay, *Lord Norman* (London, 1957), p. 405.
81. Alexander Werth, *The Destiny of France* (London, 1937), p. 43; Julian Jackson, *The Politics of Depression in France, 1932–1936* (Cambridge, 1985), p. 76.
82. Sherwood, *Georges Mandel*, p. 136; Paul Reynaud, *La France a sauvé l'Europe*, vol. 1 (Paris, 1949), p. 286.
83. Reynaud, *La France a sauvé l'Europe*, i, pp. 297–300.
84. United Kingdom, Cmd. 4609, Papers Relating to the British War Debt, 15 June 1934.
85. FO 371/17567, A1061/15/45, Lindsay to Simon, no. 54K, 5 February 1934; FO 371/17568, A3229/15/45, Lindsay to Simon, no. 131, 24 April 1934, Vansittart minute, 27 April 1934, Fergusson to Clifford, 27 April 1934; FO 371/17585, A3513/383/45, Lindsay to Simon, no. 139, 3 May 1934.
86. FO 371/17593, A785/785/45, Vansittart minute, 5 February 1934.
87. Chamberlain papers, NC 18/786, Neville to Hilda Chamberlain, 11 June 1932. Langism refers to the head of the left-wing Australian government, which had accumulated an insupportable burden of overseas (mostly sterling) debt.
88. Watt, *Succeeding John Bull*, p. 82.
89. David Dilks (ed.), *The Diaries of Sir Alexander Cadogan, 1938–1945* (London, 1971), p. 53.
90. John M. Blum, *From the Morgenthau Diaries*, Vol. 1, *Years of Crisis, 1928–1938* (Boston, 1959), p. 141; Vol. 2, *Years of Urgency, 1938–41* (Boston, 1965), p. 95.
91. PRO 30/69/1/429, Campbell to Simon, no. 31, 6 February 1934; FO 371/17637, C865/10/17, Sargent minute, 7 February 1934.
92. This and other sources of Anglo–French friction are described in Robert Boyce, 'Insects and International Relations: Canada, France and British Agricultural "Sanitary" Restrictions between the Wars', *International History Review*, vol. 9, no. 1 (February 1987), 1–27.
93. NC, 18/1/868, Neville to Ida Chamberlain, 10 February 1934.
94. PRO 30/69/8/1, MacDonald diary, February 1936. See also diary entries of 10 February, 6 May, 15 December 1934, 12 July 1936.
95. Stephen Roskill, *Hankey, Man of Secrets* (London, 1973), p. 238.
96. NC, 2/23A, diary, 3 February 1935; T160/840, F13427/2, Phillips minute, 30 March 1935; T188/269, Leith Ross to Bewley, 14 May 1935; T160/845, F13640/1, Chamberlain minute, 21 May 1935; T160/840, F13427/4, Chamberlain to Monick, 12 September 1936.

97. J. Pierrepont Moffat to Norman Davis, 19 June 1936, and Moffat to George Messersmith, 15 October 1936, quoted in Patrick J. Hearden, *Roosevelt Confronts Hitler. America's Entry into World War II* (Dakalb Ill., 1987), pp. 85, 86. See also pp. 92–94.

98. T160/753, F14239/14, Lindsay telg. no. 106, 18 July 1938; FO371/21506, A7789/1/45, Cadogan minute, 11 October 1938: 'American methods [of negotiating on trade] are very galling, and in ordinary circumstances one would like to break with them.

99. Anthony Adamthwaite, *France and the Coming of the Second World War, 1936–1939* (London, 1977), p. xiii.

100. As the British financial *attaché* in Paris commented, 'it takes considerable argument to convince even intelligent people that the depression in France is due rather to internal deflation than to external pressure.' FO 371/18795, C2877/41/75, enclosure in Clerk to Hoare, no. 54OE, 4 April 1935.

3. Hitler's War Plans And The German Economy

RICHARD OVERY

Economic modernisation has created a vital link between military capability and economic strength. Modern technology and modern industry have transformed the nature of warfare and armaments. The larger the economy, and the more sophisticated its scientific and technical base, the greater its military strength. This has been a natural development, made explicit by the slow emergence of an international system dominated by the 'super powers'. Yet in Europe the nature of this relationship was only fully recognized during the First World War, with the coming of industrialised warfare and the strategies of blockade and attrition. The armies that marched to war in 1914 expected quick victories, with the weapons to hand. By 1918 the concept of total war, the mobilisation of all material and moral resources for the war effort, had replaced the traditional strategy, born in an age of agrarian states, of a quick, mobile campaign.

Nowhere was this shift more significant than in Germany, for the Germans blamed their defeat in 1918 on the failure to prepare the economy for war, or to maintain the home front once the war turned into a struggle of material resources. The lesson that the German military took from the First World War was that any future conflict would be a war of economies as well as armies, and that it was the responsibility of the armed forces to ensure that the economy was thoroughly prepared as an instrument for waging that war. The leading spokesman of this view was General Groener, who had signed the army pact with Ebert in 1918, and from 1928 was defence minister in the Weimar coalition governments. During the 1920s he laid down the guidelines for a fundamental shift in German strategy from the age of Moltke and Schlieffen to the age of industry. He argued that the German military had ignored the modern economy at their peril, and that it was now necessary to forge close links between the two. This meant not only industrial preparations, so clearly lacking before 1914, but the organisation of the entire labour force, the distribution of adequate resources for the home front, and the maintenance of high morale. 'It is necessary', Groener concluded, 'to organise the entire strength of the people for fighting and working'.[1] Such a strategy presupposed that if war came it would be another titanic struggle like the first, for the German military assumed that powerful modern states would not fight unless it were a matter of life and death. Colonel Georg Thomas, head of the army economic staff set up at Groener's inspiration, argued that 'modern war is no longer a clash of armies, but a struggle for the existence of the peoples involved. All resources of the nation must be made to serve the war'.[2] For Groener too, it was 'the future of the race' that was at stake.

During the 1920s the German army leadership laid the foundation for a strategy of total economic mobilisation. They called this conception *Wehrwirtschaft*, the defence based economy, capable of generating the resources necessary for the conduct of total war. Gradually during the inter-war years the linking of 'defence' and 'economy' became popularly accepted as a crucial component in national security. In Thomas' opinion 'the frontiers between war and peace, state and economy, politics and the conduct of war have disappeared and the defence based economy has become the definite economic trend of our time'.[3] *Wehrwirtschaft* was as such part of the intellectual apparatus of Germany's military leaders and officials as 'empire' was in Britain. Much recent research has shown that German military and economic preparations for war were not the product of Nazi planning alone, but conformed well with strategic conceptions developed before Hitler ever came to power.[4]

In 1924 the army established an economics staff (*Wirtschaftsstab*), whose job it was to plan for the time when Germany could embark on rearmament in earnest. A network of ex-officers working in business was set up to establish close links between industry and the military, a system that was considerably strengthened when the Allied Control Commission left Germany in 1926 and secret rearmament could be undertaken with fewer risks. In December 1925 the Army Armaments Office, together with a number of industrialists, founded a 'statistical society' (*Statistische Gesellschaft*), whose object beneath the innocent exterior was 'to underpin and promote the work of the defence ministry' and to establish contact with key firms not yet involved in military production. From 1928 onwards the scope of secret rearmament was enlarged, the economics office increased in size and significance, and with the support of Groener and the efforts of General Kurt von Schleicher, who became Chancellor in December 1932, the army began to reassert its traditional political role in Germany, endeavouring through its emphasis on the need for 'total mobilisation' to bring military affairs to bear on every area of public life.[5]

There can be no doubt that with Hitler's assumption of power in 1933, the new strategy of Germany's armed forces found an enthusiastic champion. Hitler's world view embraced entirely the link between war and economy. For Hitler no war could be fought, and certainly not a conflict for racial survival, without a strong economy. Like the armed forces he was obsessed with the lessons of 1914–1918, and believed that to wage a future war successfully it was necessary to prepare the economy for complete conversion in advance. It was essential to provide sufficient food for the home population to prevent another 'stab in the back'. But most of all Hitler's populist conception insisted that only the whole people, morally armed and materially prepared, could prosecute war in the struggle between the races.[6] Hence Nazi insistence during the war that everyone was a national 'fighter' – the soldier at the front, the miner and the factory hand. Hitler also recognised that war was in essence about economic resources. War would be fought to capture fresh resources and *Lebensraum*, living space for the German people, but it could only be won by mobilising all existing economic potential. This was almost exactly the argument used by Groener – that any war was about the future of a country's economic life, and that military victory could mean economic power and security.[7]

Hitler's priorities in 1933 thus served to reinforce and enlarge initiatives already undertaken. The Nazi government wanted economic recovery, greater economic self-sufficiency (autarky) to avoid the danger of blockade or boycott, and what Hitler called '*Wiederwehrhaftmachung*', or re-establishment of a broad military capability. This required not only the rebuilding of Germany's armed forces, but also the material and psychological preparation of the whole people for future conflict. There was little here for the army leaders to dispute. The new defence minister, Werner von Blomberg, was on good terms with Hitler before 1933, and the army as a whole at first welcomed the political stability brought about by the establishment of an authoritarian state, and the special role in it promised by Hitler for the armed forces. 'Never', claimed von Reichenau, Blomberg's chief of staff, 'were the armed forces more identical with the state than today'.[8] Under Blomberg the armed forces high command was content to leave the wider questions of foreign policy and economic recovery to the government. They concentrated instead on the rearmament programme promised by Hitler in February 1933 and officially launched in December of the same year.

I

In the early years of the Third Reich rearmament was left largely to the armed forces, who continued to build on the narrow foundation established before 1933. Between 1930 and 1932 the generals prepared a second Armaments Programme to succeed the first one of 1926, designed to expand the size and effectiveness of the armed forces beyond the level allowed under the Versailles Treaty. In December 1933 the new programme was finally authorised for a 21 division peacetime force, three times the size of the existing army, which was to be established between 1934 and 1938.[9] This was an army much smaller than that of France. The December programme was not expected to offer protection to Germany in the event of a major war. The first priority for the armed forces was to build up again the infrastructure of military power, and the trained men necessary to run the new forces, and to offer at least a limited defence against aggression.

The question of economic preparations was not forgotten either. The army economic office, which was absorbed into the defence ministry in 1933 under the title Economics and Armaments Office, continued the work begun in the 1920s, drawing up plans and schedules for mobilisation and building the network of economic officers into a national system of armaments inspectorates. At a national level the armed forces, through a new Reich defence council, composed of civilian and military leaders, hoped to create a forum in which to influence all major areas of policy in favour of military priorities. During 1934 the army pressed for the appointment of an 'economic dictator' who could centralise economic preparations for war under a single authority. Though the forces would have preferred a military candidate, the choice for the post fell on Hjalmar Schacht, the minister of economics, who had shown himself since 1933 to be sympathetic to the rearmament programmes and an ally of the military and business circles already active in military affairs. In May 1935 he was created plenipotentiary for war economy. In November von Blomberg published full 'Guidelines for the unitary preparation of the defence of the Reich', dividing up tasks between the armed forces and Schacht: the former to control all armaments and related production, the latter to supervise the co-ordination of the civilian areas of the economy.[10]

The achievements of the first years of military build-up were modest. (See Appendix for figures on military expenditure) Financed by a mixture of ordinary revenue and secret state bills (the Mefo Bills), military expenditure represented 1.9 per cent of GNP in 1933 and four per cent in 1934, only reaching economically significant levels in 1935–6.[11] Even Hitler felt the constraint of international opinion, and hesitated to arm too quickly or openly in the first years of Nazi power. Much of the initial expenditure was invested in building up equipment, accommodation and bases denied Germany under the Versailles Treaty, and which were essential to provide facilities for an extensive training programme. The rapid expansion of the forces had to wait until the infrastructure of military life was fully restored. This explains the slow initial growth of the new German air force. The early production plans were small scale and improvisatory. The first programme called for 294 aircraft in 1933 and 1934, most of them converted civilian types or trainers. The first full production schedule was drawn up in March 1934, a programme of 17 000 aircraft in five years. Though impressive on paper, 58 per cent of the aircraft were trainers, and only 18 per cent combat aircraft, many of which were obsolescent bi-planes or converted transport aircraft of doubtful usefulness.[12] Air force leaders in Germany called their force the *Risiko-Luftwaffe*, or 'risk air force', as an indication of its obvious weaknesses in the early years of expansion. It was, of course, very difficult to move more rapidly, for Germany possessed no significant aircraft industry in 1933. Large investments and labour retraining schemes were necessary to provide the industrial capacity as quickly as possible. In 1933 aircraft output was valued at 37 million marks, and the industry employed 12 000 people; in 1936 output had risen remarkably to 527 million marks, with 188 000 employed, and Germany was in the forefront of aviation technology.[13]

The navy, too, expanded slowly, along lines laid down in the Weimar period. Hitler was unenthusiastic at first about expanding

German naval power, and not until March 1934, after Admiral Raeder, the commander-in-chief, had persuaded him that there lay some diplomatic advantage in a more powerful navy, was a replacement shipbuilding programme authorised which promised to take German naval strength beyond the levels permitted by Versailles. However, shortages of construction capacity and skilled labour, a consequence of the more successful pressure of the army and air force for economic resources, produced a constant lag between the programme and its realisation. Naval spending from 1933 to 1936 totalled only 2.6 billion marks, or 13 per cent of total military expenditure.[14]

There is no doubt that Hitler intended, as did the individual heads of the three services, to build up much larger forces once the economic capacity was available, and once the early problems of organisation and expansion were overcome. Indeed the speed with which it was intended to make Germany defence-proof again, within the space of three or four years, was a tribute to the widespread support for rearmament in the civilian and military establishments. With the rapid fall in unemployment and the growth of industrial output, encouraged by government construction and motorisation policies, conditions were created that permitted a higher level of rearmament. From 1935–6 economic policy was directed much more at restructuring the economy to conform with the needs of future warfare.[15] Yet neither Hitler nor the war ministry imposed any overall plan for rearmament, relating service costs and requirements within a set budget on any long term basis. The three services were allowed to pursue their individual programmes regardless of the cost or of the impact made on each other. The subsequent lack of co-ordination brought increasing problems of competition for resources of labour and materials. By 1936 von Blomberg and Schacht began to look for ways of controlling the pace and scope of rearmament to ensure that it posed no danger to the stability of the economy in the early stages of recovery from the depression, while at the same time it fulfilled the wider aim of building a broad, total preparation for defence.[16]

II

For Hitler the conditions that made for a cautious programme of rearmament – fear of foreign intervention and the weaknesses of the German economy – gave way by 1936 to a quite different set of

conditions. In 1935 he declared Germany's rearmament in public,
overturning the Versailles settlement. In March 1936 German troops
reoccupied the demilitarised zone in the Rhineland. Neither action
provoked any significant reaction from the treaty powers. The Ethiopian crisis, the Spanish civil war and Russian rearmament suggested
the need for greater speed in the military build-up. The obvious
failure of the League to establish a system of collective security
provided the opportunity for action. The economy in 1936 was
nearing full employment and had recovered to a degree that made
the next stage of Hitler's foreign and military programme possible.
For Hitler the object was not merely to make Germany capable of
defending herself again, and to harness the economy to that end, or
even to reverse the territorial clauses of Versailles, but to use Germany's new economic and military strength to embark on a period of
active expansion in Europe, and eventually the achievement of
German world power status.

   This was a conception that went well beyond what the army or the
conservative politicians expected. Indeed Schacht was by 1936 anxious
lest the unco-ordinated expansion of German armament should
threaten the economy by denying opportunities to expand consumer
goods and exports. The armed forces also expressed concern about
the economy, though for different reasons. The army now believed
that the initial plan for a 300,000 man force could not guarantee the
defence of Germany. During the first half of 1936 the army staff
worked on a new plan, eventually published in August, for the
build-up of an 800,000 man army, whose equipment would make
even greater demands on the German economy. Calculations showed
that the new forces would cost 8 billion marks in each year 1937–9,
instead of the 3.6 billion originally scheduled.[17] To cope with these
new requirements, von Blomberg and the army leaders tried during
1936 to exert a greater degree of military control over the economy,
particularly of raw materials and trade, and to achieve the rational
defence economy first mooted in the 1920s. Absence of such control
would, they feared, endanger the whole military programme. According to the armed forces, uncontrolled civilian demands increased
pressure on imports and directed resources from exports, which were
essential to earn foreign exchange to buy raw materials for military
industries. Civilian demand created undesirable pressures on investment and finance as well. In August 1936 von Blomberg wrote to
Goering: 'Measures of the armed forces themselves will not suffice to
overcome the difficulties . . . Everything must be postponed that
does not serve export and expanded armaments. That includes the

work of the Labour Front, the *Autobahnen* and also house
construction . . . It also appears to be necessary to direct domestic
policy in such a way that damage to export prospects will be avoided'.
What the armed forces wanted was the 'right to instruct all the
highest offices of state for the unitary conduct of all preparations for
war'.[18]

Yet just at the point where the military leaders believed they could
create the new 'military economic' state, and would have support
from Hitler for doing so, the terms of the political situation changed
fundamentally; and they changed primarily because of rearmament.
During 1936 there was growing evidence of pressure in the economy
in certain sectors, brought about by rapid military expansion since
1934. Schacht and his supporters now argued that rearmament should
accordingly be slowed down; expanding rearmament further
threatened to create serious economic crisis, which in turn compromised the prospects for fulfilling existing rearmament plans. The
armed forces were caught in a dilemma. They did not want either to
provoke an economic crisis, nor to reverse the tempo of rearmament.
At first efforts were made to reconcile economic and military priorities. In April 1936 Hitler appointed Goering, with the qualified
approval of von Blomberg and Schacht, as commissioner for raw
materials and foreign exchange, responsible for extending state control over their use.

Despite Goering's appointment, the situation continued to worsen
over the summer. While the army pushed ahead with its vast new
plans for equipment, the air force launched a major phase of modernisation and expansion. It was impossible in the end for the armed
forces to agree to less rearmament, for this contradicted the whole
trend of military policy since 1932. The loose alliance between von
Blomberg and Schacht, between the military and civilian conservatives, was severed. To Hitler it was evident from the squabbling and
confusion between the two sides that to have both economic stability
and arms it was necessary to extend more government control over
the economy. Moreover, now that the economy had recovered and
unemployment was no longer a political issue, it was possible to
utilise industry more generally and deliberately for war. This meant
in the main a policy of greater economic self-sufficiency, and more
comprehensive controls over labour, raw materials and investment
and, of course, more arms. Hitler was no longer prepared to put such
an economic and military strategy at risk by leaving it to military or
financial experts critical of Nazi policy.

There remained nonetheless a close identity of interest between

Hitler and the military. Both wanted to gear economic development to military requirements, not just in the production of armaments, but in all areas of economic life, but who should bear responsibility for this was a political, not an economic, question. Hitler had to make sure that war preparations were in the hands of those who entirely shared his foreign policy ambitions, and who would be politically capable of overcoming domestic resistance to their achievement. Hitler revived the idea of an 'economic dictator', but instead of choosing an army officer, he decided to expand the powers already exercised by the air force leader, Goering. It was not in the end a surprising choice. Goering combined high military and civilian office, and was a major figure in the Nazi movement. He was a keen autarkist and rearmer: 'Carrying out of the armaments programme according to schedule and planned scale', he claimed in July 1936, 'is *the* task of German politics'.[19] Goering was, according to Hitler, 'the best man that I possess, a man of the greatest willpower, a man of decision who knows what is wanted and will get it done'.[20] No-one else was so uncompromisingly committed to large scale preparations for war. During August 1936 Hitler retired to his summer retreat where he worked on what was to form the basis of the second Four Year Plan. In September Goering was formally given the twin tasks of preparing the economy and the armed forces for war. When he described his new office to his cabinet colleagues he stated that 'all measures have to be taken just as if we were actually in the stage of imminent danger of war'.[21]

The creation of the Four Year Plan was a decisive step towards preparing Germany for total mobilisation. Goering later argued that the plan 'was a basic prerequisite for the entire building-up and expansion of the armament industry'. The plan was the instrument which was to enable the Nazis 'to determine the whole of Germany's economic and social policy'.[22] Although the plan was never in practice quite as far-reaching as this, Goering was never constrained by its terms of reference, but willingly trespassed in any area of economic policy if it furthered Hitler's aims. There is no doubt that it symbolised a major change of pace and direction in German war preparations. Indeed, it marked the point at which the armed forces' conception of a recovery of defensive strength gave way to Hitler's conception of large scale preparations for aggressive imperialism, over which the armed forces were to have less and less say.

The core of the Four Year Plan was the increase in the domestic production of vital raw materials: synthetic rubber, fuel oil and iron ore, all of which were resources essential for waging war. The synthetics programme dated from well before 1936, for the Nazis had favoured autarkist solutions from the start, but Hitler was dissatisfied with the slow rate of which the schemes were developing. During 1937 large-scale plans were adopted for the production of synthetic rubber, or 'Buna', and synthetic fuel produced from coal, as well as a whole range of other products. The plans were to be completed by the mid-1940s [details are set out in Appendix 5], but their expense and complexity made them difficult to accelerate, and much of the initial planning and development was finished only in 1938 and 1939. In the area of domestic iron ores, the Four Year Plan, in the face of considerable hostility from the iron and steel industry and from Schacht, insisted on exploiting the low yield ores of central and southern Germany to reduce dependence on Swedish and French supplies, neither of which could be guaranteed in wartime. To carry this policy out Goering founded a large state-owned concern, the *Reichswerke Hermann Goering*, which within a year was the third largest concern in Germany, and branched out from iron ore into the production of finished steel and armaments. The object was to turn the *Reichswerke* into 'the core of the whole of German rearmament, of supplies for the arms industry in peace and war'. By 1939 it was the largest concern in Europe, engrossing almost all the industrial and raw material supplies of the territories acquired in 1938 and 1939. The *Reichswerke* symbolised in a very literal sense the close connection in Hitler's strategy between economy and war.[23]

During the years between its inception and the outbreak of war the Four Year Plan encroached on all the major areas of economic policy-making, so much so that Schacht resigned as minister of economics in November 1937 in protest, and his place was taken by Walthèr Funk, a political nonentity, entirely subordinate to Goering. By 1938 Goering was 'economic distator' in all but name, with the ultimate say over all areas of the economy vital for war: agriculture, in order to expand food supply in case of blockade in wartime; labour, to be trained and distributed as the needs of rearmament dictated; trade and foreign exchange, in order to give priority to strategic imports; and control over prices, to ensure that rapid increases in armaments and strategic heavy industries should not run the risk of inflation. Though Schacht and other conservative economists predicted swift economic disaster as result of these policies, Goering was able to attract a large circle of officials, businessmen and officers sympathetic to the general drift of Hitler's strategy to implement the detailed industrial and financial policies. The army economic office continued its own work in loose association with the Four Year Plan organisations, sometimes duplicating, sometimes complementing, what Goering was doing.

During this period control over the economy gradually passed to the state, so that the armed forces found that their influence over the economic aspects of war production was much reduced. The army in particular regarded this as far from satisfactory. Even though Goering's policies were precisely those anticipated by the 'total war' strategists of the 1920s and 1930s, army leaders only very reluctantly accepted their reduced responsibility for *Wehrwirtschaft* within the changed political balance, and resented encroachment on what they saw as soldiers' work. Even the explosives programme was removed from army control and placed under a commissioner from the staff of the Four Year Plan. So too, in the summer of 1938, was the building of the fortifications along the western frontier, the so-called *Westwall*, which became the responsibility of Fritz Todt, head of the *Autobahn* project. Moreover, oil, motor vehicle and machinery production came under Four Year Plan supervision in order to integrate them into the overall plan for economic mobilisation.

These programmes were not pursued without difficulty. Shortages of skilled labour and raw materials were apparent as early as 1936, and the financing of the new schemes (the Four Year Plan took over 50 per cent of all industrial investment in 1938 and 1939) placed new demands on the brittle German financial system. Nevertheless strict regulation and state intervention prevented a serious crisis. 'Measures', Goering said, 'which in a state with a parliamentary government would probably bring about inflation, do not have the same results in a totalitarian system'.[24] Under state control interest rates were forced down, while prices and wages were maintained at the levels of the early 1930s, with only minor adjustments. Even by 1939 the state debt in Germany was lower than in Britain and the United States.

In a great many respects the extension of state power over the economy was a logical outcome of the rapid and unco-ordinated growth of armaments between 1933 and 1936. Though the armed forces carped at the loss of responsibility for areas that they regarded as properly military in nature, rearmament and economic stability were both safeguarded after 1936, and the economy was directed, through the Four Year Plan, much more specifically to the needs of defence.

Preparations for war dominated economic and political decisions in Germany after 1936. A momentum was given to German rearmament, fuelled by the protection it received from Hitler in state affairs, by the enthusiasm of the movement's leaders and the unwillingness of the armed forces to reduce the demand for more arms.

III

What increasingly worried financial and military authorities in Germany was the exact nature of Hitler's plans. The armed forces expected rearmament to peak in 1937–9 and then for the level of expenditure to be gradually reduced by two-thirds, leaving enough to maintain a large number of conscripts with modern weapons. Some civilian ministers and officials assumed that rearmament would be completed even earlier, in 1937–8, and thereafter progressively scaled down. Yet the whole tenor of Hitler's strategy from autumn 1936 onwards, when he talked privately about the need to solve the problem of *Lebensraum* through conflict in the east, was to prepare Germany for a large scale war at some date in the future. There were plenty of indications about what Hitler's aims were: the construction of *Mitteleuropa* (union with Austria, the return of the Sudetenland and Silesia, domination of the Balkans) was common knowledge by 1937 and was widely supported.[25] But in November 1937, talking to the service chiefs, Hitler gave formal notice that his ambitions were much greater than this. The first stage was to create a large, resource-rich area in central Europe, to be achieved without general war. This was to be followed 'by 1943–45' by major war with the great powers in order 'to solve Germany's problem of *Lebensraum*'. Hitler's strategic plan foresaw a conflict for continental hegemony, and war with Russia for a Eurasian empire. Beyond that lay imperial fantasies: world dominion, war with the United States and the British Empire.[26]

As Germany grew militarily and economically stronger, Hitler moved from consolidation to active expansion. He did so against the background of economic restructuring already described. Yet many historians have argued that before 1939 German rearmament was deliberately restricted, that Germany's leaders set out to pursue short, limited wars which would make the minimum of demands on the civilian economy. This was partly, it is argued, from fear of the political repurcussions of cutting living standards, partly because of the difficulties in mobilising resources inherent in the confused administrative jungle of the Nazi state. In 1961 A.J.P. Taylor, in an influential and controversial book, challenged the very idea that Hitler even planned to do more than build up limited armed strength in order to reverse the territorial clauses of Versailles, and that he had achieved all he wanted by 1939. The evidence that Hitler wished to go further than this is now overwhelming, but whether he sought to achieve this by total or limited war is still very much in dispute.[27]

Yet as more evidence comes to light on detailed service programmes, on economic preparations under the Four Year Plan, it seems clear that the Nazi leaders intended to establish the army vision of total mobilisation. How successfully they did so is another question. Much of the argument, of course, hinges on how rearmament or military preparations are defined. Though formal expenditure on armaments and military investment was higher than that of any power save Russia before 1939, the investment in the military infrastructure and the heavy industrial and engineering base of the economy for strategic purposes demonstrated the wider economic commitment to war. In 1939 Colonel Thomas noted: 'The *Führer* stands by the view that any mobilisation must be a total one, and that the three pillars, military, economy and party have their own great tasks in wartime'.[28] According to Goering: 'The Four Year Plan has the task of preparing the German economy for total war'.[29] The surviving documents from 1938 onwards are littered with references of this kind.

The point that is too often overlooked is that Hitler wanted total economic mobilisation in *any* war with other great powers, regardless of whether the conflict was a short one or a long drawn out affair. The outcome of military campaigns could not be planned in advance, as the failure of the Schlieffen plan in 1914 had shown. Hence the need for thorough economic preparation and conversion in case the worst happened. In May 1939 Hitler told his generals:

> Everybody's Armed Forces and Government must strive for a short war. But the government must, however, also prepare for a war of from ten to 15 years' duration. History shows that wars were always expected to be short. In 1914 it was still believed that long wars could not be financed. Even today this idea buzzes in a lot of heads. However, every state will hold out as long as it can . . .

Either way, to gamble with the economy was to court the disaster of the First World War again. 'The idea of getting out cheaply is dangerous', Hitler continued, 'there is no such possibility'.[30] This view was a central part of Groener's argument in 1928, that the economy should be adjusted in such a way that it could be quickly and completely converted to war in order to utilise, in one great campaign, all the resources of the nation. The object of German war preparations was to win the war next time, whatever its nature.

Limited war could be fought with stocks of weapons and raw materials (imported and home produced) while making very little additional claim on the civilian economy and labour force. The Four Year Plan involved quite a different strategy. Its programme of import substitution was expensive and long term. Investment in the *Reichswerke* at Salzgitter, Linz and Brüx (in the Sudetenland) totalled 800 million marks, more than all the investment in the aircraft industry from 1933 to 1937. The rubber, fuel and explosives plans called for sums of the same magnitude. The state invested 280 million marks directly in Buna production, out of a total investment of 940 millions. The explosives plan finalised in 1938, the so-called *Schnellplan* (accelerated programme) required a 40 per cent increase in the output of heavy machinery in Germany, and 480,000 additional tons of steel a year.[31] The programme for expanding food output was to enable Germany to withstand a long war of attrition. Controls over investment directed capital away from consumer industries to armaments and war-related tasks, which took well over 60 per cent of all capital invested between 1936 and 1939. The controls over labour, which took the form of compulsory retraining and civilian conscription, though used sparingly before 1939, anticipated the mobilisation of the entire working population for war tasks. Propaganda efforts were focused on preparing the population 'spiritually for total war'.[32] That many Germans found such a prospect unthinkable in the late 1930s only demonstrated the extent of the gulf which existed between popular perceptions of foreign policy and the extravagant war plans of their leaders.

The Four Year Plan provided the economic substructure which permitted the expansion of the superstructure of actual armaments production, the guns, aircraft and submarines. It was the very scale of these armament programmes that led to the growing economic commitment after 1936. During the course of 1938, with the original aircraft production plans coming to an end, and the army still struggling to complete the August 1936 programme on schedule, Hitler ordered the expansion of the armed forces to a scale well beyond anything that the services had asked for, or could reasonably cope with. Between the Hossbach conference on 5 November 1937 and the conference called with the commanders-in-chief on 28 May 1938, Hitler discussed at length prospects for a new level of arms output. Exact records of the May conference are missing, but the surviving evidence suggests that Hitler's purpose was to match military output with his now much enlarged foreign policy aims. Not only did this mean more weapons, it also meant more money. Hitler authorised a radical change in Reich financial policy, ending the system of Mefo bills which had helped to finance rearmament since 1934, and resorting instead to Reich loans, increasing the public debt by 30 per cent in the fiscal year 1938/9.[33]

The navy was a major beneficiary of this increased commitment to armaments. Because Britain and France were now potential enemies, it won a higher priority from Hitler. He called especially for more battleships, and a speeding up of construction on those already laid down, as well as an expanded programme of submarine building. During 1938 the navy worked out plans for a large battle fleet for war with Britain which formed the basis of the so-called 'Z-Plan', published in January 1939, for six battleships, four aircraft carriers, eight heavy cruisers, 233 submarines and numerous destroyers and smaller craft.[34] The air force won its share of the new spending too. During the summer of 1938 a new production programme, Plan 8, was drawn up which would take the *Luftwaffe* from the initial stage of training and establishment to the creation of a large fleet of combat aircraft, 16 000 aircraft in all, in two years. The new aircraft were among the most advanced air weapons in the world. On 14 October 1938 Hitler confirmed these plans with a commmitment to increase the size of the air force five-fold, including a large core of 4 300 medium and heavy bombers.[35] The army was told to speed up the activation of its forces, and to expand motorisation. Explosives production, which had lagged significantly behind the output of finished weapons, was now programmed to reach the levels of the last months of the First World War; and it was placed under the Four Year Plan with the publication in July of the '*Wehrwirtschaftliche neue Erzeugungsplan*' (new defense economy production plan).[36] In October Goering announced to his staff Hitler's general decision to raise 'the level of armament from 100 to 300 . . . a gigantic programme compared with which previous achievements are insignificant'.[37]

It is difficult to see how such programmes taken together can be regarded as limited rearmament. No area of the economy remained untouched by the demands of war. The effect on consumption was clear. Consumer industries were held back during the recovery period. Investment in the consumer industries failed to reach the level of 1928 where investment in heavy industry exceeded it by 72 per cent. Real earnings, after allowance for increased taxation and party levies, and declining quality of goods, failed to regain the levels of the late 1920s, even though real GNP per head was 31 per cent higher. Consumption as a share of national income declined from 71 per cent in 1928 to 59 per cent in 1938, while consumer industries came bottom of the list in the allocation of raw materials and capital. The deliberate containment of consumption encouraged higher levels of saving, which was then chanelled via the banks and savings institutions into government loans for the war economy. Nazi leaders were well aware that this was part of the price for the economic strategy pursued after 1936. For Hitler it was the necessary, if regrettable, outcome. When he was told bluntly about economic problems in June 1939 by Emil Puhl, deputy head of the *Reichsbank*, he responded by saying 'yes, he feared it might be so and he knew that the German housewife must be having a hard time to make both ends meet. But he wondered whether she does not sometimes consider that this is a relatively small price to pay for the great advantages which had been gained for Germany'.[38] As early as 1934 Thomas recorded that it was 'Hitler's own insistence that the people take deprivations and curtailments upon itself'. On the eve of the war in 1939 he told Birger Dahlerus, the envoy between Goering and the British government, 'War does not frighten me. If privation lies ahead of the German people, I shall be the first to starve and set my people a good example'.[39] The German people were expected to bear their part of the sacrifices during the period of German expansion. The scale of preparations made this unavoidable.

So extensive were the new plans from 1938 that the armed forces themselves began to question their feasibility. The rearmament programme was increasingly out of their control. Admiral Raeder tried to resign in January 1939 rather than attempt Hitler's extravagant naval programme. Hitler, though sometimes painted as a leader remote from the day to day workings of the economy and military affairs, played a central role in dictating not just the broad outlines of policy, but details of individual programmes. It is not clear that he himself ever seriously questioned how realistic his programmes were, although he did claim during the war that he exaggerated requirements in order to achieve more than his timid commanders would have asked for. He admired men like Erhard Milch, Goering's

deputy, for whom 'there was no such word as impossible'.[40] This
made it harder for those who wanted rearmament to take a more
modest course, or who could not understand what Hitler wanted the
forces for. During the summer of 1938 the army found it impossible
to meet its scheduled expansion on time, and find all the raw materials and labour to provide the weapons. By the second half of
the year the armed forces were taking almost one-third of all iron and
steel production, while future programmes promised to claim more
copper, tin, zinc and aluminium than Germany could produce or
import. In November the army, though still enthusiastic for a carefully prepared armament in depth, sent a long report to Hitler,
explaining that inflation appeared unavoidable, and that this would
threaten internal stability and the continuation of rearmament.[41] The
finance minister made the same point: expenditure would have to be
cut or German finances would face serious difficulties. At the *Reichsbank* Schacht made one more concerted effort to deny Hitler access
to the financial resources he needed to carry out the new programmes.

   Another political crisis, like that of 1936, appeared likely, but
Hitler was determined to maintain the tempo of military preparation
at all costs. He saw it as the responsibility of the state to take the
necessary measures to ensure that an economic crisis could be
avoided, a view briskly summed up by Goering the previous June:
'There is no place for the collapse of parts of the economy. Ways will
be found. The Reich will step into the breach to help'.[42] Rather than
cut back, Hitler sacked Schacht and other critics from the *Reichsbank*. Von Krosigk and Funk were authorised to work out new
financial arrangements, and in April 1939 a new finance plan was
made law, designed to accommodate the state's new expenditure
without inflation. Despite a major increase in the state debt, the price
index rose by less than one per cent in 1939. Serious planning was
initiated for wartime finance and rationing, and for current savings in
non-military expenditure. Goering embarked on a programme of
industrial and administrative rationalisation designed to free labour
and resources for war preparation at the expense of the 'inessential
industries'.[43] Ignoring all the warnings, Hitler permitted military
expenditure to rise sharply in 1939, consuming more in the first nine
months than in the whole of 1938, while avoiding serious economic
crisis.

   The purpose for which Hitler wanted such forces was far from clear
to the critics of rearmament, and has remained an area of controversy
ever since. They were certainly not designed, as Taylor argued, to

defeat Czechoslovakia and Poland and establish German domination of central Europe. The forces available to Germany by 1938 and 1939 were more than equal to such a task, as they showed in the rapid defeat of Poland. The new rearmament programmes only made sense in terms of a major war with other great powers; in the east to establish *Lebensraum*, and in the west, against Britain and the United States, in order to realise Germany's claim to world power status. The naval programme and the strategic bomber plans, including the *Amerikabomber* on which Messerschmitt began work in 1939, in addition to the range of advanced technological projects on which German research was engaged, all indicate clearly the drift of Hitler's strategy. The important question was one of timing. As Hitler indicated in November 1937, the major programmes would be completed by 1943–5. The air force plans would not be completed until 1942 at the earliest. The Z-Plan covered the whole period from 1939–49. The army motorisation and its training schedules for officers and technicians would run on to 1943. More important, the raw material programmes in oil, rubber, aluminium and iron and steel, including the incorporation of the captured resources of central Europe, would not be finished until the same date. The plans to modernise and strengthen the railway system, begun seriously only in 1939, would carry on until 1944.[44] Had Germany enjoyed a further four or five years of peace, the military forces and economic resources available would have made her, like the Soviet Union and the United States, one of the military super powers of the 1940s.

Hitler's problem was to avoid a major conflict until these programmes were complete, and it is here that his strategic competence and political judgement proved seriously flawed. Until late in August 1939 he expected that Britain and France would not fight for Poland. There were good grounds for this belief: Britain and France had been only too willing to sell out Czechoslovakia and were still talking of settlement and compromise in the summer of 1939; military intelligence in Germany suggested that western rearmament, particularly in the air, was still far behind Germany's and Hitler's political instincts told him that the western leaders would not risk plunging their countries into war for fear of political collapse at home (see Chapter 7). The strength of this conviction was recalled by a German official later in the war:

> When the German leadership decided on a final solution through force of the conflict with Poland in September 1939, they were firmly

convinced that it would only come to a war with Poland . . . On the basis of certain information from England and France, and despite numerous warnings, they had a fixed belief that these two countries would not stand by the obligations of their guarantee to Poland and at the very least would not enter into any serious war against Germany.[45]

The German non-aggression pact with the Soviet Union in August 1939 was expected to be a diplomatic *coup* of the greatest importance, for it would come at just the right psychological moment from Hitler's point of view, and seemed to remove once and for all the threat of a serious crisis in the west. He was soon to be disillusioned.

It is clear now that Hitler misjudged the political situation in both France and Britain. His intelligence on their war preparations was badly flawed, and his personal judgement of his adversaries, though in a great many respects correct, failed to account for the pressures for war with which both Daladier and Chamberlain were faced. To have deliberately sought a general war in 1939 runs against the whole nature of German economic preparations. On 21 August the German armed forces high command (OKW) was specifically instructed by Hitler only to prepare for a limited economic mobilisation against Poland, not general mobilisation. Not until after Britain and France had finally declared war on 3 September did Hitler order the total mobilisation of the economy.[46]

By September 1939, as Hitler and the Nazi leaders knew, German preparations were far from complete. Germany entered the war with no operational heavy bomber, only five battleships and 50 submarines, and only 300 of the most up to date Mark IV tank. The factories of the Four Year Plan were in some cases still on the drawing board. The large programme of armaments set in motion in 1938 was only in its early stages. Aircraft production plans were revised downwards during 1939 to achieve what the air ministry thought was a more realistic match between plan and industrial capacity. Of the new generation of advanced aircraft only 1,800 had been produced by April 1939 (11 per cent of the programme), while 15,500 remained to be produced.[47] The army faced the same problems. Motorisation was slow, so much so that a special commissioner was appointed under the Four Year Plan, General von Schell, to speed up the rationalisation of the motor industry and to adjust it more effectively to meet military needs. In 1939 the armed forces took only 8 per cent of the output of the vehicle industry. When war broke out stockpiles of weapons and munitions were low, and there was a serious shortage of bombs and shells. The horse remained the main form of traction for the German forces at the front throughout the war.

The most obvious difficulties for rearmament lay in the supply of labour and raw materials, and it was here that government efforts were directed in 1938 and 1939. After regular promptings from the army, Goering set up a comprehensive register of all workers so that less essential labour could be transferred to where it was most needed. The *Wehrarbeiter* (workers vital for the defence industries), were to be given protected status. Efforts were made to increase female labour, already at a high level by western standards. More foreign labour was recruited, reaching a level of 435,000 by the spring of 1939. The unemployed in Austria, the Sudetenland and Bohemia were rapidly absorbed into the German industrial effort. The Four Year Plan and the Labour Front also embarked on programmes of retraining and apprenticeships to produce more of the skilled workers needed by the armaments industry. By 1939 the supply of trained, skilled metalworkers, a bottleneck in the First World War, actually exceeded demand. In 1938–9 513,000 workers were retrained under the new schemes. In addition, industry retrained an estimated 500,000 itself and another 223,000 were retrained under other programmes. Labour was attracted away from consumer sectors to heavy industry and engineering by the prospect of fuller and more regular hours and higher earnings.[48]

Military claims on raw materials, and on machinery and equipment, were also a constant source of friction. Expansion of investment in armaments and strategic sectors starved other areas of the economy – the Ruhr coal and steel industry, the railways – of sufficient resources to cope with the high level of military demand or for renewal work on the West Wall in 1939; and the difficulties of finding sufficient foreign exchange to buy important materials abroad remained endemic, even more so with the growing demands in world markets for materials from other rearming powers. In the light of these problems, it is easy to see how important to German rearmament were the areas acquired in central Europe. Iron ore and engineering works in Austria, lignite in the Sudetenland for synthetic fuel production, coal, iron, steel and armaments in Bohemia. Austria became the site in 1939 for a huge new steel and armaments complex at Linz, and the industries of Bohemia were integrated at once into the programmes of the Four Year Plan. The occupation of western Czechoslovakia in March 1939 had been carried out, Goering told his staff in July, 'in order to increase German war potential by the exploitation of the industry there'. It also provided Germany with equipment from the Czech army.[49]

Such problems were made more difficult than they might have been through the failure to establish a satisfactory organisation for war production and mobilisation planning under the Four Year Plan. Although Goering was the ultimate authority on these questions, as head of the plan and chairman of the Reich defence council, formal central control was not exercised on any regular or systematic basis. As a result decisions at local level were often made by the armed forces' armaments inspectorate, which was relatively experienced and had a large organisation already in being. The armed forces abandoned their special powers in the economy only with great reluctance after the summer of 1938, when Goering and Hitler tried to confine their responsibility to 'armed combat' alone. The armed forces and the war ministry (which was converted into the OKW in February 1938) continued their work in preparing the necessary legislation and decrees for mobilisation, and did much of the groundwork for '*Mob. Plan Wirtschaft*', the technical schedules for economic mobilisation should war break out. The military thus retained much more influence than Hitler intended, and they were able, almost by default to reassert this when war came in September 1939.[50]

It would nevertheless be wrong to exaggerate the extent to which the rearmament effort was affected by organisational problems, any more than by shortages of raw materials. It should not be forgotten that a very great deal was achieved by 1939 in the space of only five or six years. Yet it is certainly true that Germany was not fully prepared for a general war in 1939. In some major industrial and research programmes work had only begun seriously in 1939, for a major war still assumed to be, if ever, some years ahead. The register of labour and of firms, the mobilisation plans for each major industrial sector, the preparations for war finance and rationing, only started during the course of that year. When war broke out the registers were barely two-thirds completed and nothing had been settled about how to finance a war. Many sectors, vital to any war effort, lacked any mobilisation plan at all. On 8 August, just three weeks before the war, OKW drew up the following list of industrial sectors for which mobilisation plans already existed, those in preparation, and those still to be produced. It is significant that the mobilisation plans that were complete were exclusively in the heavy industrial sectors, the foundations of the war economy, and were almost entirely lacking in the manufacturing sectors, reflecting closely the priorities established

MOBILIZATION PLANNING BY INDUSTRY, AUGUST 1939[51]

I completed	II in preparation	III no mobilisation plan

iron and steel
chemicals (in part)
 	
mineral oil
	mining (coal)
	semi-finished metal
	  goods
	machine tools
		motor vehicles
		aircraft industry
		
		precision instruments,
		  optical goods
		iron and steel
		  manufactures
		metal goods
		refining processes
		electrical industry
		construction industry

under the Four Year Plan in 1936.

Even in the heavy industrial sectors there was still much that needed to be done. On 3 September, at a meeting called by OKW for all three services, Colonel Thomas explained how much basic preparation was incomplete:

> The position is clear. The total mobilisation of the economy has been ordered . . . a whole number of programmes are still at this time in progress, which should actually have been ready by the outbreak of war: the giant explosive plan; the programme for munitions production; the substitution of scarce materials; the Ju-88 programme; the building up of the oil industry; the expansion of Buna, aluminium and magnesium production; the construction of fortified airfields; further necessary building on the West Wall and the construction of public air raid shelters.[52]

These were all projects due for completion during the following four or five years.

Given the nature and timing of the rearmament drive and the loose strategic guidelines from Hitler this situation should not surprise us. Yet much of the problem was self-inflicted. The whole strategy of 'armament in depth' was a counsel of perfection, reflecting the ambitions of highly trained and professional armed forces, but in many respects unrealisible at the optimum. Military planners insisted from the outset on the highest quality equipment, and on the right of the soldiers to interfere at every stage in the production process or in the development of weapons with little regard for productivity, industrial priorities or costs. According to a war academy lecture in 1936: 'Armament is for us a question of quality in every sense, but particularly in the technical sense . . . an armament that overemphasises quantity and speed of production is only to be achieved at the expense of material and individual quality'.[53] Hence the reluctance of the army to mobilise the mass-production car industry in Germany either before or after 1939, in stark contrast to the practice in Britain and the United States. From 1938 onwards the Four Year Plan initiated policies to achieve greater rationalisation and a simplification of weapons and production methods, but with little effect. Even in the most advanced sector – the aircraft industry – traditional work methods, excessive use of skilled labour and wasteful material policies undermined the drive to greater output started by Hitler in 1938.

In the end much of this problem stemmed from the excessive competition for resources and duplication of effort between the three services, which refused to co-ordinate their production, leading to a multiplicity of types of weapons and their components. There was far too little standardisation. Prospects for economies of scale and long term production, of which German industry was perfectly capable, were poor from the outset. The military preferred close links with small, specialised firms which were more responsive to individual requirements rather than with new mass-production industries. Not surprisingly, therefore, the armed forces found it difficult to win the confidence and co-operation of industry. This was partly because many businessmen hoped that economic recovery would result in more exports and greater consumer demand, where long term prospects for growth and profits seemed brighter. Many assumed that rearmament would soon slow down and hesitated to risk putting too many resources into military work in case the market collapsed, and they were left with unusable capacity. Businessmen, particularly in the private sector, resented the spread of state controls made necessary by rearmament and the subordinate role they were expected to play to the armed forces and the Four Year Plan. Manufacturers complained all the time about 'planlessness' and incompetent procurement policies but since in the end the marriage of military and industry, the dream of the total war strategists, was a military affair, businessmen and engineers were ignored.[54] The 'military-industrial' complex was a one-sided arrangement, creating through military priorities and technical ignorance a high cost, wasteful and poorly organised armaments economy. If Hitler's demands in 1938 were beyond what Germany could currently produce, they were not entirely beyond what a better organised and more rational productive system could have achieved with more years of preparation.

IV

Some historians have argued that it was precisely the contradictions, represented by this failure to match Hitler's exaggerated demands with economic reality, that created the pressure to go to war in 1939. The threat of inflation and the popular unrest which lurked behind it, is said to have produced a situation of economic chaos, a contradiction that could only be resolved by embarking on short wars of plunder to keep the German people quiet.[55] The evidence for such a view is slender. Hitler was much more concerned with the pressures of foreign rather than domestic policy. Economic pressures suggested that general war should be avoided until the programmes begun in 1937–8 could be completed, a view Hitler reiterated in May 1939, after the plan to defeat Poland had been drawn up. Nor is there any conclusive evidence that the working class was politically restive in 1939, and much evidence to the contrary. The state apparatus was more widespread and more effective by 1939 than at any previous stage in the Third Reich.[56] 'Revolution from within is impossible', Hitler told his commanders-in-chief in November 1939.[57] The propaganda of the regime was relatively more effective in creating nationalist support among the population in 1939 against the new 'encirclement' plans of Britain and France than had been the case during the Czech crisis. Local party and security reports in the summer show little sign of serious discontent and much support for Hitler's policies. 'Trust in the *Führer*', ran one report, 'and pride in German policy among the population is boundless. Everyone is sympathetic'.[58]

Nor is there compelling evidence that Hitler was worried about living standards to the extent that such fears forced him to choose war. A reasonable minimum was achieved by 1939 and would be guaranteed in wartime thanks to a thorough system of rationing and welfare payments designed to avoid the poverty and hardships of the First World War. Reports from Berlin suggested that there was 'plenty of minor grumbling, but no serious discontent'[59] as a result of rationing and mobilisation measures. Consumption had been delib-

erately suppressed and wages kept low well before 1939. Even after
the war Hitler's plans for the reconstruction of German cities on a
vast scale promised to take up whatever resources might have been
available for boosting living standards.[60] There was no effective way
this political situation could be reversed, as long as the state was
willing, forcefully, to impose economic regulations, including effective price and wage controls, and to repress any dissidence fiercely.
Moreover, as we have seen, great efforts were made in 1938 and 1939
to cope with the economic problems thrown up by rearmament – the
new finance plan, greater savings, labour retraining. In many respects
the German economy was stronger in 1939 than its enemies or critics
supposed, and very much more so than during the severe slump of
1929–33. It was the second largest industrial economy in the world,
with increasing domination of the smaller economies around it,
capable by 1939 not only of devoting 23 per cent of GNP to military
spending, but of building huge public projects and the *Autobahnen*,
as well as maintaining living standards at a level unlikely to provoke
serious political dissent. It was an economy which, far from collapsing
from 'over-heating' as British strategists hoped, or later cracking
under blockade and bombing, took the combined might of the other
three largest industrial economies to defeat during four years of bitter
conflict.

Of course rearmament did have political effects – it dominated the
political scene after 1933. Under Hitler pursuit of rearmament was a
means to political advancement, and any policy that promised to
enlarge or protect the defence capability of the state, however
tenuous, found all doors open. The major political changes in 1936–8
were concerned essentially with the economic consequences of rearmament. State policy was more and more concerned with promoting war
preparations at the expense of every other priority. Goering's rapid
rise to become 'economic dictator' can be attributed very largely to
his defence of rearmament and his promise to provide an alternative,
Nazi-led economy to the more conservative schemes of Schacht. The
seizure of the political initiative in directing resources to war
stemmed from the Nazis' own view of the role of the economy in the
state:' It is the duty of the leadership of the state politically to
develop and direct the economy, so that it may best serve the
preservation of the nation . . . the economy must conform itself with
defence, and defence with the economy, and politics must take care
that defence and economy correspond to one another and increase
each other's power.'[61] Rearmament was both a technical problem

and a political one. Hitler expected the forces and the Four Year Plan to solve the technical side, but only the Nazi movement itself, through a revival of national consciousness and political will, could be trusted to solve the ultimate questions about Germany's future. This view led logically and inexorably to that point in the war where Nazi appointees and the SS finally assumed control over the means of waging war.[62]

From the point of view of German military and economic preparations, the war that broke out in the autumn of 1939 was the wrong war. There was not even any serious planning for operations with the western powers, no Schlieffen Plan. When on 1 September Dahlerus warned Hitler of British firmness, his response was spontaneous: 'If necessary I will fight for ten years'.[63] When general war came on the 3rd a state of full economic mobilisation was declared at once, putting all the nation's resources at the service of the war. Widespread rationing was introduced, immediately cutting civilian consumption to low levels. Within two years 60 per cent of the German industrial workforce was engaged on military orders, a higher proportion than in Britain. Hitler himself, still closely involved in drawing up the production plans for the war economy, put his signature in the winter of 1939 to amrs programmes 'with the highest possible figures', that exceeded even the unrealistic schedules of 1938. 'We Germans', Hitler confided in what proved to be one of the last of his private audiences, in October 1939, 'have learnt much from our experiences in the First World War and are fully prepared, both militarily and economically, for a long war'.[64] The wheel had come full circle. Groener's 'total mobilisation' was finally realised in Hitler's 'struggle for national existence'.

NOTES AND REFERENCES

1. General W. Groener, 'Bedeutung der modernen Wirtschaft für die Strategie' reprinted in D. Fensch, O. Groehler, 'Imperialistische Ökonomie und militärische Strategie: eine Denkschrift Wilhelm Groeners', *Zeitschrift für Geschichtswissenschaft* 19 (1971) pp. 1167–77.
2. B.A. Carroll, *Design for Total War: Arms and Economics in the Third Reich* (The Hague, 1968) p. 40.
3. Bundesarchiv BA-R7 XVI/36, Colonel Thomas, Vortrag vor der Wehrmachtakadamie, 7.11.1935, p. 4.
4. W. Deist, *The Wehrmacht and German Rearmament* (London, 1981) esp. chs 1–2; M. Geyer, *Aufrüstung oder Sicherheit. Die Reichswehr in der Krise der Machtpolitik 1924–1936* (Wiesbaden, 1980); Carroll, *De-*

sign, chs. 2–3; W.M. Stern, 'Wehrwirtschaft: a German Contribution to Economics', *Economic History Review*, 2nd ser. 13 (1960/1) pp. 270–81.
5. Carroll, *Design*, pp. 54–7, 64–71; E.W. Hansen, *Reichswehr und Industrie. Rüstungswirtschaftliche Zusammenarbeit und wirtschaftliche Mobilmachungsvorbereitungen 1923–1932* (Boppard a Rhein, 1978); P. Hayes, 'Kurt von Schleicher and Weimar Politics', *Journal of Modern History*, 52 (1980) pp. 35–65.
6. T. Taylor (ed.), *Hitler's Secret Book* (New York, 1961), pp. 26–7, 46: 'in the future the enlargement of people's living space . . .' will require staking the whole strength of the people' (p. 96).
7. *Ibid.*, pp. 13–24: Groener, 'Bedeutung' pp. 1175–7.
8. K-J. Müller, *Das Heer und Hitler. Armee und nationalsozialistische Regime 1933–1940* (Stuttgart, 1969) p. 63.
9. H.J. Rautenberg, 'Drei Dokumente zur Planung eines 300 000 Mann-Friedenheeres aus dem Dezember 1933 *'Militärgeschichtliche Mitteilungen* 22 (1977) pp. 103–39; M. Geyer, 'Das Zweite Rüstungsprogramm (1930–1934)', *Ibid.* 17 (1975) pp. 25–72.
10. Carroll, pp. 91–2, 108–9, 120.
11. 'Mefo' – Metallurgische Forschungsgesellschaft, a holding company set up to handle additional secret Reich funds for rearmament.
12. R.J. Overy, 'German Air Strength 1933–1939: a Note', *Historical Journal* 27 (1984) pp. 466–9.
13. E. Homze, *Arming the Luftwaffe: the Reich Air Ministry and the German Aircraft Industry 1919–1939* (Lincoln, Nebraska, 1976) p. 184; National Archives, Washington D.C. (NA) T177 Roll 32, frames 3720919–36, 'Die Flugzeugindustrie 1933–36', Feb. 1938, pp. 1–5.
14. Deist, pp. 70–4. Figures from J. Dülffer, *Weimar, Hitler und die Marine: Reichspolitik und Flottenbau 1920–1939* (Düsseldorf, 1973) p. 563.
15. There is still much dispute about how extensive rearmament was in the early years of the regime. Much hinges on how rearmament is defined. Certainly a strong economy would make rearmament easier to achieve. This is the argument of A. Schweitzer, 'Die wirtschaftliche Wiederaufrüstung Deutschlands 1934–1936', *Zeitschrift für die gesamte Staatswissenschaft* 114 (1958) and H-E. Volkmann, 'Aspekte der ns "Wehrwirtschaft" 1933 bis 1936' *Francia 5* (1977). In the narrower sense of military direct expenditure and investment it is clear that in the first two years of the regime much state and private activity was in non-military areas. See M. Wolffsohn, 'Arbeitsbeschaffung und Rüstung im national-sozialistischen Deutschland 1933' *Militärgeschichtliche Mitteilungen* 22 (1977) pp. 9–19; R.J. Overy, 'Cars, Roads and Economic Recovery in Germany 1932–38' *Economic History Review* 2nd ser., 28 (1975) pp. 466–83.
16. Imperial War Museum (IWM), Wehrwirtschaftsstab papers, EDS Mi 14/317, German War Ministry 'Grundsätze für die wirtschaftliche Mobilmachung' 1.2.1936.

17. Deist, pp. 44–7.
18. Bundesarchiv–Militärarchiv (BA-MA), Wi I F5.203, von Blomberg to Goering, 31.8.1936; Wi I F5.3615, Jodl to von Blomberg, 'Vortragsnotiz über Vierjahresplan und Vorbereitung der Kriegswirtschaft 30.12.1936'.
19. *Ibid.*, Goering to von Blomberg, 19.6.1936.
20. E. Gritzbach, *Hermann Göring* (Berlin, 1938) p. 104.
21. International Military Tribunal, *Trial of the Major War Criminals*, vol. 36, p. 491, Council of Ministers, 4.9.1936.
22. *Ibid.*, vol. 9, p. 450. See too D. Petzina, *Autarkiepolitik im Dritten Reich* (Stuttgart, 1968).
23. G. Meinck, *Hitler und die deutsche Aufrüstung 1933–37* (Wiesbaden, 1959) pp. 159–69; R.J. Overy, 'Heavy Industry and the State in the Third Reich: the Reichswerke Crisis' *European History Quarterly* 15 (1985) pp. 316–23; M. Riedel, *Eisen und Kohle für das Dritte Reich* (Göttingen, 1973), esp. pp. 25–61; on synthetic fuel see W. Birkenfeld, *Der synthetische Treibstoff 1933–1945* (Göttingen, 1963) p. 77 ff.
24. *Nazi Conspiracy and Aggression* (NCA), (Washington, 1946) vol. 3, p. 883, Meeting of Council of Ministers, 12.5.1936.
25. R.J. Overy, *Goering: the 'Iron Man'* (London, 1984) pp. 76–8.
26. M. Hauner, 'Did Hitler want a World Dominion?' *Journal of Contemporary History* 13 (1978); M. Michaelis, 'World Power Status or World Dominion?' *Historical Journal* 15 (1972); G. Weinberg, *World in the Balance* (New England University Press, 1981), esp. ch. 3 on Hitler's attitude to the United States; *idem, Hitler's Foreign Policy 1937–39* (London, 1980); K. Hildebrand, 'La programme de Hitler et sa réalisation' *Revue d'histoire de la Deuxième Guerre Mondiale*, 21 (1971); W. Michalka, *Ribbentrop und die deutsche Weltpolitik 1933–1940* (Munich, 1980), esp. pp. 172–6, 220 ff; J. Thies, *Architekt der Weltherrschaft: die Endziele Hitlers* (Düsseldorf, 1980). There is interesting, if unreliable, testimony in H. Rauschning, *Hitler Speaks* (London, 1939). See too the recent discussion in E. Robertson, 'Hitler's Planning for War and the Response of the Great Powers 1938 to early 1939' in H. Koch (ed.) *Aspects of the Third Reich* (London, 1985) pp. 206–34.
27. A.J.P. Taylor, *The Origins of the Second World War* (London, 1961); *idem*, '1939 Revisited', German Historical Institute Annual Lecture, 1980; A.S. Milward, *The German Economy at War* (London, 1965) ch. 1; W. Carr, *Arms, Autarky and Aggression* (London, 1972).
28. IWM, EDS Mi 14/377 (file 2), Thomas memorandum, 28.3.1939 'Gesichtspunkte für die Änderung der Mob. Vorbereitungen der Wirtschaft', p. 2.
29. BA-MA, Wi IF 5.412, conference with Goering, 16.7.1938, p. 1.
30. *Documents on German Foreign Policy*, Ser D, vol 6 (HMSO, 1956), no. 433, p. 577.
31. For details see G. Plumpe, 'Industrie, technischer Fortschritt und Staat. Die Kautschuksynthese in Deutschland 1906–1944/5', *Geschichte und*

Gesellschaft 9 (1983) p. 594; on the Reichswerke IWM FD 264/46 'Konzernverzeichnis HGW Montanblock'; on the Schnellplan, A. Bagel-Bohlan, *Hitlers industrielle Kriegsvorbereitung 1936 bis 1939* (Koblenz, 1975) pp. 117–21.

32. Overy, *Goering*, p. 84. The place of propaganda in German war preparations is an important one. Both the army and Hitler put great value on morale – attitudes to authority, the willingness to accept sacrifices, psychological orientation to military goals. See J. Sywottek, *Mobilmachung für den totalen Krieg: die propagandistische Vorbereitung der deutschen Bevölkerung auf dem Zweiten Weltkrieg* (Opladen, 1976) pp. 94–103, 194–201; D. Aigner, *Das Ringen um England: die öffentliche Meinung 1933–1939* (Munich, 1969) pp. 349–53.

33. M. Geyer, 'Rüstungsbeschleunigung und Inflation: zur Inflations Denkschrift des OKW von November 1938' *Militärgeschichtliche Mitteilungen* 23 (1981); Graf Schwerin von Krosigk, *Staatsbankrott: Finanzpolitik des Deutschen Reiches 1920–1945* (Stuttgart, 1974), pp. 281–5.

34. Deist, pp. 82–4; Dülffer, pp. 488–504. At the time the German navy possessed only three small battleships, no heavy cruisers or aircraft carriers, and only 36 submarines.

35. NA T177 Roll 14, frames 3698585–8, letter from Luftwaffe General Staff to Generalluftzeugmeister, 9.8.1939; R.J. Overy, 'From "Uralbomber" to "Amerikabomber": the Luftwaffe and Strategic Bombing', *Journal of Strategic Studies*, 1 (1978), pp. 155–7.

36. Bagel-Bohlan, *Kriegsvorbereitung*, pp. 118–20.

37. NCA vol. 3, p. 901; IMT, vol. 32, p. 413, note on the meeting of the Reich Defence Council, 18.11.1938.

38. Bank of England, Central Bank Papers (Germany), OV34 vol. 9, Notes of a conversation with Dr Puhl in Basle, 12.6.1939.

39. Carroll, p. 89; see too BA-MA, Wi I F 5.114, 'Aufrüstung und Export', lecture by Thomas to Reichsgruppe Industrie, 10. 6.1937, p. 21: 'Everything that only serves to increase amenities or concerns the improvement of the living conditions of the people must take second place'.

40. D. Irving, *The Rise and Fall of the Luftwaffe* (London, 1973) p. 150.

41. Geyer, 'Rüstungsbeschleunigung', pp. 125–7.

42. *Ibid.*, p. 136.

43. NCA, vol. 3, pp. 902–3, 1301–PS, conference with Field Marshal Goering, 14.10.1938; BA-MA, Wi I F 5.560, Sitzung des Reichsverteidigungsrats 18.11.1938: 'not food but the increase in armaments is the most important thing . . . review of the economy must concern itself with which production units are really necessary. Those that are not essential must be converted'.

44. R.J. Overy, 'Hitler's War and the German Economy: a Reinterpretation', *Economic History Review*, 2nd ser. 35 (1982), pp. 276–7.

45. IWM EDS AL 2719, 'Deutschlands gegenwärtige Wehrwirtachftliche Lage, Juni 1944', Dr Tomberg, 7.8.1944, introduction p. 1.

46. IWM EDS Mi 14/328(d), OKW, minutes of meeting of Wehrwirtschaft inspectors, 21.8.1939; OKW, Wehrmachtteile Besprechung, 3.9.1939, p. 1; *Dokumente zur deutschen Politik*, vol. 7 (Berlin, 1941), pp. 403–4, Kriegswirtschaftsverordnung, 4.9.1939.

47. Overy, 'German Air Strength', p. 470.

48. J. Gillingham, 'The "Deproletarianization" of German Society: Vocational Training in the Third Reich' *Journal of Social History* 19 (1985/6), pp. 427–8; see too IWM Mi 14/478, Heereswaffenamt, 'Die personelle Leistungsfähigkeit Deutschlands im Mob. Fall', March 1939.

49. NCA, vol. 8, p. 202, R–133, note of a conference on July 25th 1939 with Field Marshal Goering.

50. IWM EDS Mi 14/294 (file 5), OKW, 'Die Munitionslage 1939', Nov. 1939; Mi 14/328 (d), OKW, Wehrmachtteile Besprechung 3.9.1939, p. 1: 'direction of the production plans obviously comes from the armed forces themselves as only they can judge what they need'; Carroll, *Design*, pp. 163–5.

51. IWM EDS Mi 14/294 (file 5), Major Neef, 'Grundlagen und Verfahren zur Schaffung von Mob. Erzeugungsplänen', 9.8.1939, p. 9.

52. IWM EDS Mi 14/328 (d), OKW Wehrmachtteile Besprechung, 3.9.1939, pp. 1–2.

53. BA-R7 XVI/36, Wehrwirtschaftsstab memorandum, 25.2.1936, p. 5.

54. A. Schröter, J. Bach, 'Zur Planung der wehrwirtschaftlichen Mobilmachung durch den deutschen faschistischen Imperialismus vor dem Beginn des Zweiten Weltkrieges' *Jahrbuch für Wirtschaftsgeschichte* 17 (1978), pp. 42–5; W. Treue, 'Die Einstellung einiger deutscher Grossindustriellen zu Hitlers Aussenpolitik' *Geschichte in Wissenschaft und Unterricht* 17 (1966), pp. 103–4. On the attitude of industry to mobilisation planning see IWM EDS Mi 14/294 (file 5), Wi Rü Amt 'Die mangelnde Vorbereitung der Industrie durch den GBW', 24.11.1939. On industry and the business cycle see Geyer 'Rüstungsbeschleunigung' pp. 134–6.

55. T.W. Mason, 'Innere Krise und Angriffskrieg' in F. Fortmeier, H-E. Volkmann (eds.), *Wirtschaft und Rüstung am Vorabend des Zweiten Weltkrieges* (Düsseldorf, 1975) pp. 158–88. See too C. Bloch, 'Die Wechselwirkung der Nationalsozialistischen Innen-und Aussenpolitik 1933–1939' in M. Funke (ed.) *Hitler, Deutschland und die Mächte* (Düsseldorf, 1976) pp. 205–21.

56. Something along these lines has already been argued by Mason himself. See T.W. Mason, 'Die Bändigung der Arbeiterklasse in Deutschland' in C. Sachse et al. (eds.), *Angst, Belohnung, Zucht und Ordnung: Herrschaftsmechanismus im Nationalsozialismus* (Düsseldorf, 1982) pp. 48–53.

57. NCA vol. 3, p. 578, 789–PS, Führer conference with heads of armed forces, 23.11.1939.

58. IWM, Foreign Office internal publication, n.d., *Aus deutschen Urkunden 1935–1945*, p. 211, Kreisleitung report, Kreis Darmstadt, August 1939.

59. Bank of England, Central Bank Papers (Germany), OV34 vol. 9, memorandum on the situation in Germany, 23.10.1939.
60. J. Thies, 'Hitler's European Building Programme', *Journal of Contemporary History* 13 (1978).
61. BA-R7 XVI/36, Wehrwirtschaftsstab memorandum, 25.2.1936, p. 1.
62. A Speer, *The Slave State* (London, 1981); E. Georg, *Die wirtschaftlichen Unternehmungen der SS* (Stuttgart, 1963).
63. B. Dahlerus, *Last Attempt* (London, 1948), p. 119.
64. Sven Hedin, *German Diary* (Dublin, 1951), pp. 46–7.

APPENDIX I

GERMAN MILITARY EXPENDITURE 1933/4 to 1938/9 (M RM)

| | Total | I Budget Expenditure | | | II | Total |
		Army	Air Force	Navy	Mefo Bills	I + II
1933/4	750	–	–	–	–	750
1934/5	1,953	815	642	496	2,140	4,093
1935/6	2,772	1,041	1,036	695	2,720	5,492
1936/7	5,821	2,435	2,225	1,161	4,450	10,271
1937/8	8,273	3,537	3,258	1,478	2,690	10,963
1938/9	17,247	9,465	6,026	1,756	–	17,247
Fiscal year April 1st–March 31st						

Source: Dülffer, *Marine*, p. 563; BA R2/21776-81, Reichsfinanzmin. 'Entwicklung der Ausgaben in der Rechnungsjahren 1934–1939' 17.7.1939; Schwerin von Krosigk, *Staatsbankrott*, pp. 230–1.

APPENDIX II

GERMAN AIRCRAFT PRODUCTION 1933–1939

	1933	1934	1935	1936	1937	1938	1939
total	368	1,968	3,183	5,112	5,606	5,235	8,295
Combat	–	840	1,823	1,530	2,651	3,350	4,733

Source: R. Wagenführ, *Die deutsche Industrie im Kriege* (Berlin, 1963), p. 74.

APPENDIX III

THE PRODUCTION PROGRAMMES OF THE FOUR YEAR PLAN

	Production in 1936	Production in 1942
	000 tons	
Mineral oil	1,714	4,920
Aviation fuel	76	1,200
Aluminium	98	255
Buna rubber	0.7	114
Artificial Fibres	26.7	142
Leather substitutes	14.5	70
Explosives	38	450
Basic chemicals	2,765	5,334
Synthetic textiles	88	395
Iron ore	7,570	20,932 *
Coal	158,300	264,500
Lignite **	161,400	248,900
Machinery and machine tools (bill.RM)	2.57	5.55

* figure for 1941 (excluding occupied areas)
** known in Germany as 'brown coal', lignite was a vital material in the production of synthetic fuel.

Source: Bundesarchiv Koblenz, R 26 I/18 'Ergebnisse der Vierjahresplan-Arbeit' pp. 20–40

4. The Cut Price War on the Peripheries: The French General Staff, The Rhineland And Czechoslovakia

NICOLE JORDAN

It was not the diplomats but the military in France who held most tightly to the Eastern allies. Treaty obligations which the diplomats had come to regard as 'charges' both 'morally and juridically embarrassing', the military still looked upon as assets. (Alexis Léger to an interviewer, 1951)[1]

I

In late January 1933, during the week in which Adolf Hitler took power in Germany, Maurice Gamelin, the heir apparent of the French defence establishment, met General Jan Syrový, chief of the Czechoslovak general staff, for unofficial talks in Paris. Since 1930, five years ahead of schedule, French troops had been withdrawn from the demilitarised Rhineland zone. An international disarmament conference had been in session in Geneva since 1932. German

128

demands for equality of rights at the disarmament conference, to which the French had recently made important concessions, signified to Gamelin and his Czech colleague in January 1933 that the Germans intended to remilitarise and fortify the Rhineland. The two agreed that Germany would then attack in the east. Walled in by German fortifications, France would be unable to force the barrier erected against it in order to aid an unspecified ally in the east.[2]

The sequence of events leading to the collapse of the French alliance system – the unopposed Rhineland reoccupation of March 1936 and the French abdication at Munich in 1938 – appears arrestingly mapped out in these candid, unofficial conversations between two generals, each destined to preside over the collapse of his nation's military establishment. Yet Gamelin did not meet with Syrový to pronouce a *post-mortem* on France's eastern alliance system. Traditional French strategy *vis-à-vis* Germany required an eastern counterweight in a two front war. France's pre-1914 alliance system, which bound it by a surgically precise accord to Czarist Russia, had been based on the assumption that France would bear the brunt of German force. The 1933 talks between Gamelin and Syrový, with their shared assumption that the next conflict would begin in the east, acknowledged that the chronic problem of an eastern counterweight had to be seen in a radically new light. For Gamelin, the attraction of the eastern alliances lay in averting a repetition of the Franco–German bloodletting of 1914–18 by a war of coalition in the east in which France might act as a secondary force against Germany.

This chapter will focus on how Gamelin constructed a strategy of an eastern counterweight upon his early anticipation of a Rhineland reoccupation. It will then consider how this highly defensive strategy came apart, with profound implications for Czechoslovakia and ultimately for France itself. To understand Gamelin's strategy and the prolonged crisis which it represented, it will be necessary briefly to explore two related themes: first, the evolution of the French alliance system before January 1933, its diplomatic discordance and strategic rationale; and second, the way in which the French military, confronted by a shrinking power base and a domestic climate hostile to arms expenditure, intensified their reliance on allies in the early 1930s.

In January 1933, the French alliance system consisted of a motley set of treaties, with Belgium (1920), and four eastern states, Poland (1921, 1925), Czechoslovakia (1924, 1925), Rumania (1926) and

Yugoslavia (1927). The seven eastern treaties had few common features.[3] The 1921 political and military agreements with Poland were concluded amidst intense fears of German–Soviet collusion against the Versailles settlement, and covered both a German and Soviet menace. After Prague refused French offers of a military alliance to consolidate the Polish agreements, France's subsequent eastern treaties, including its loosely constructed political and military arrangements with Czechoslovakia (1924), were less explicit and wide-ranging.

The pattern was of a progressive weakening of diplomatic obligation as the memory of the war's end receded. This diminution became dramatic after 1925 when, at Locarno, France guaranteed arbitration agreements which Poland and Czechoslovakia signed with the Weimar Republic. The German arbitration treaties in the east did not include territorial guarantees. Locarno thus created a formal distinction between the eastern and western territorial settlement, the latter being voluntarily accepted by Germany in 1925. By attaching France's guarantee to eastern arbitration treaties, Paris did not exclude limited, peaceable territorial revision. The 1925 treaties of guarantee with Poland and Czechoslovakia also subordinated French action to the League of Nations' designation of an aggressor.

Events at Locarno soon overtook negotiations for France's treaties with Rumania and Yugoslavia, states allied to Czechoslovakia in the 'Little Entente', a diplomatic and military organisation directed mainly against Hungary. The resulting treaties contained arbitration provisions modelled on the 1925 eastern treaties. This similarity lent the French system a semblance of juridical coherence, but at a price. The arbitration provisions and the meagre Rumanian and Yugoslav obligation of consultation in the event of a conflict were intended to establish Paris' distance from what French diplomats, in a reference to the antecedents of the First World War, called 'obscure Balkan quarrels'.

In the negotiations for the 1926 and 1927 treaties, the French foreign ministry, the Quai d'Orsay, promoted border pacification and *détente* between Italy, the Soviet Union and its new treaty partners. Its stress on arbitration was galling to the small powers, who sought French friendship as much to ward off Italian and Soviet predations in the Adriatic and Bessarabia as to parry a distant German menace. Locarno diplomacy also occasioned a series of French *démarches* designed to invalidate the anti-Soviet clauses of the 1921 agreements with Poland. The French justified the diplomacy of border pacification by the argument that it lessened the blurring in allied foreign policies caused by fear of Italy and the Soviet Union rather than Germany. The rub was that French diplomacy shaded imperceptibly into designs to involve regional great powers in the defence of central Europe against Germany. By implying a diminution of French loyalties, these designs aroused a deepening distrust of France and fear of abandonment, especially on the part of Poland and Yugoslavia, countries which were to become the nerve centre of central European neutralism.[4]

Another profound structural weakness in the French diplomatic system of the 1920s was Polish–Czech hostility. Its post-war virulence dated from competing border claims for Teschen, awarded to Czechoslovakia in 1920, and from the Polish–Soviet conflict of 1920–1, when Czech neutrality impeded French supplies to Poland. In the 1920s the Czechs envisioned themselves as a bridge between the Soviet Union and western Europe. They were also reluctant to estrange the Weimar Republic by establishing close treaty relations with Poland, the prime target of Weimar's territorial revisionism. In contrast, the Poles sought automatic security conventions against both the Soviet Union and Germany, a quest related to their yearning to create a central European power *bloc* between Berlin and Moscow. The tenacious Polish–Czech hostility expressed itself in festering border and minorities claims, as well as in tangled regional relationships. A Polish–Rumanian treaty (1922) directed against the Soviet Union co-existed alongside the allegedly Russophile Little *Entente*, a perennial object of Polish suspicions.

As opposed to the ragbag of diplomatic interests represented by the alliance system, the French general staff's interest in the alliances developed along highly rational lines. This outwardly Cartesian development was in fact inseparable from diplomatic concessions over the Rhineland and German rearmament.

With the cessation of hostilities in 1918, the French military had pressed for the pinioning of Germany: in the west, by a permanent occupation of the Rhineland; in the east, by the attachment of Danzig and Upper Silesia to Poland, and by the creation of a strong Czechoslovakia at the expense of Austria and Hungary. For the French general staff, peace and the consolidation of the new states could be assured as long as French troops were on the Rhine to deter Germany from attacking France or to crush Germany if it attacked one of France's eastern allies. At Versailles, however, Clemenceau abandoned military demands for a Rhineland zone permanently under allied control, in exchange for a stillborn Anglo–American guarantee of France. To the military's dismay, while the zone was theoretically to be demilitarised in perpetuity, the allied military occupation would be only temporary. It was to end at a particularly vulnerable point – in 1935 at the onset of *les années creuses*, the leanest years of French demographic growth – if it was not bartered away well before that date. After Clemenceau's concessions in 1919, the French military could have no confidence in the Rhineland buffer zone, and they restively searched for *espaces de manoeuvre* in Belgium, Poland and Czechoslovakia.[5]

The longterm strategic function conferred on the original members of the alliance system, Belgium, betwixt France and Germany, and Poland and Czechoslovakia, which ringed Germany in the east, was to enable France to fight outside her frontiers. This became the central imperative of French military planning between the World Wars. Grimly aware of the slaughter of the First World War, the French general staff were determined to avoid a repetition by ensuring the integral defence of France's frontiers. This strategic tenet commanded virtually automatic assent in a society with a debilitating awareness of its industrial and demographic inferiority and an abhorrence of war from which no segment of opinion was exempt. Eventually symbolised in the popular imagination by the Maginot line, the military's determination to shield France from war also induced a less conspicuous determination that any future war should be fought on foreign soil. The general staff's interest in France's eastern allies was governed by the latter objective. To the essential Polish–Czech–Belgian nucleus of 1920–4, later treaties with Rumania (possessed of valuable oil reserves) and Yugoslavia added concentric states without borders on Germany. One of their chief military attractions was communications: Rumania's position on the Black Sea, Yugoslavia's sure connections with the Adriatic and the route to Salonica, the base for a major French amphibious operation in the First World War.[6]

The disaster of the Ruhr occupation in 1923–4 definitively discredited unilateral French coercion in the Rhineland. Afterwards, French diplomacy under Aristide Briand sought to elaborate a durable European settlement resting on the formula 'Arbitration, Security, Disarmament'. Shortly after Locarno, Briand agreed to the first phase of allied evacuation of the Rhineland, despite German rearmament violations. In private talks at Thoiry, Briand and Stresemann went further, discussing complete evacuation of the Rhineland, the suspension of allied arms supervision, and arbitration of Polish –

German territorial disputes. The last of France's troops left the Rhineland in 1930 and within a year, during preliminary discussions on the disarmament conference, high-ranking members of the French government openly bruited Polish renunciation of Danzig and the Corridor. In conversations on Mussolini's proposed Four Power Pact in 1933, French interest in an arms limitation settlement further estranged the Poles.[7] Increasingly wary of French treachery, the Poles signed a non-aggression declaration with Hitler, the new Chancellor of Germany, in January 1934.[8]

For the general staff, Briandism posed divisive challenges: early evacuation of the Rhineland, territorial revisionism, and a dedication to arms limitation which made it a fixture of French diplomacy. Immediately after Locarno, Foch, as commander-in-chief of the Allied armies, had vehemently objected to premature 'abandonment' of the Rhineland bastion. Foch's outspoken letter to his government, however, lacked any trace of resolve to defend the zone's demilitarised status once allied troops were withdrawn. At that point, and he pleaded that it be as late as possible, Foch argued that French security would demand fortifications.[9] In the event, the advice of the military about the final evacuation of troops in 1930 was blatantly disregarded.[10] The erection of the Maginot line, however, was to accompany early French withdrawal, in order to parry France's worrisome demographic weakness and to protect France against surprise attack. As a corollary, construction of the Maginot line would invite German fortifications in the zone after it fell to Germany and indirectly, German attack in the east or through Belgium. The early evacuation of the Rhineland furnished the backdrop to the sisyphean task Gamelin undertook on the eve of Hitler's advent to power, the salvaging of France's security by a coalition effort in the east. After a Rhineland reoccupation, he recognised, an eastern counterweight could only be held together by the interested co-operation of other great powers who would provide conduits for French involvement. In the highly adverse but stimulating circumstances of the disarmament talks, he turned to the preparation of this coalition.

When Gamelin met with Syrový in January 1933, much of his strategic picture derived from the 1920s. He foresaw a two front war with initially quasi-autonomous fronts. The pressures of these fronts would open the way for a successful French offensive across southern Germany linking the two theatres of war. Both generals assumed that the bulk of the action would take place in the central European theatre. Gamelin counselled the broadening of the Little *Entente*'s war plans against Hungary, the most revisionist of the small ex-enemy states, in order to reckon with a general conflict with Germany. He also urged Syrový to join forces with the Poles so as to occupy German Silesia, an important industrial area and a bastion for the defence of Bohemia.[11] Of Italy and the Soviet Union, Gamelin said little. Italy was presumed to be hostile, but Gamelin pointed out to Syrový that Soviet neutrality would secure the Polish and Rumanian rear lines.

The association of the Soviet Union and Italy with an allied coalition was encouraged by a French interministerial study of 1932–3 which examined the adequacy of wartime supply lines to Poland and the Little *Entente*. The study underscored the extent to which such routes would be at the mercy of the regional great powers: the Soviet Union could block access to the Straits and the Black Sea ports; Italy, access to the eastern Mediterranean and Salonica, which, in Gamelin's view, was the most efficient supply route.[12]

In January 1934 conversations with the French disarmament delegation in Geneva encouraged Gamelin to extend typically prudent support for an *entente* with the Soviet Union and Italy. The prospect of arms limitation in itself spurred the search for great power allies to help maintain security. This logical point should not obscure the fact that for Gamelin the desire to integrate the Soviet Union and Italy into the French system had a decidedly eastern referent. Nor could these larger states supplant Czechoslovakia and particularly Poland, with their borders on Germany.

In a memorandum of January 1934 Gamelin wrote that Russia's benevolent neutrality would safeguard the Polish and Rumanian rear lines, and could be extended to include Soviet air attack against the Reich and Soviet material aid to France's allies. This last provision would largely satisfy France's 1921 obligation of direct aid to Poland. Significantly, Gamelin did not look beyond Soviet benevolent neutrality. Like the diplomats, the general staff was wary of close political collaboration with the Soviet Union, which was ideologically suspect and geographically remote.

Gamelin's ambitions for Franco–Soviet relations never rivalled those he nursed for Italy. While in January 1934 he still envisaged a hostile Italy, he recognised the attractiveness of Italian neutrality and an Italian guarantee of Austrian independence. Beyond this, 'Franco–Italian co-operation against Germany on Austrian territory would also be very interesting but at some future date'.[13] Mussolini's show of force at the Austrian frontier in July 1934, in protest against the assassination of the Austrian Chancellor Dollfuss by Austrian Nazis, allowed Gamelin to shelve the hypothesis of Italian hostility. The prospect of Franco–Italian co-operation against Germany in the defence of Austria and Czechoslovakia rapidly conditioned his allegiances to France's allies of the 1920s. His *penchant* for Italy met the necessity of having a staff plan that allowed for a broad variety of manoeuvres, including arms limitation negotiations, while avoiding the impression that France itself seriously contemplated making war.

The course of French arms limitation diplomacy resembled a hairpin curve from the spring of 1934. Early in the year, Hitler simultaneously accepted a British plan restricting the *Reichswehr* to 300 000 men and issued an ambitious arms budget. The French cabinet was at first paralysed. Prime Minister Doumergue and his abrasive *éminence grise*, André Tardieu, opposed the German offer to restrict the *Reichswehr*. The spirited minister of foreign affairs, Louis Barthou, and the man soon to succeed Barthou at the Quai d'Orsay, Pierre Laval, pleaded for acceptance of Hitler's offer. Barthou used ammunition from André François-Poncet, the French Ambassador in Berlin, to argue that limited, supervised German rearmament was preferable to uncontrollable German rearmament and an arms race. The stalemate within the cabinet was broken by Tardieu and Doumergue who prevailed on Barthou to refuse the German offer in a trenchant note of 17 April 1934. It proclaimed that France would henceforth give priority to its own security, which was inseparable from that of other interested powers. This stilted phrase, a sensation in its day, implied both France's severance from the Geneva conference and an audacious allied strategy. Within three days of the April note, Barthou approached Italy and the Soviet Union.[14]

Barthou, however, was no proponent of a classical alliance system which would have confirmed French intransigence by excluding Germany from collective security. Although his earlier support for Hitler's offer had been frustrated, Barthou's vigorous collective diplomacy represented an indirect means of reaching agreement with Germany by including it in large scale negotiations of which arms limitation would be a necessary part. In his 20 April approach to Mussolini, who fervently desired legalised German rearmament, he promised to approve the Italian thesis (no French disarmament, combined with legalised, limited German rearmament), provided that the German question could be settled outside the disarmament

conference, presumably in security negotiations.[15] In the opinion of
French disarmament experts, the security guarantees afforded by his
ambitious project for an eastern Locarno – the inclusion of Germany
not least – presented the surest way to remove the arms clauses of
Versailles. Barthou's Italian and Soviet diplomacy, which involved
Danubian and Eastern pacts to include Germany, and French spon-
sorship of Soviet entry into the League, should thus be placed in the
context of his disquiet at the decision to refuse Hitler's offer and his
obsessive desire to avert an arms race.[16]

For the general staff, the most significant fact about the April 1934
note was the lack of substantial French rearmament at a time when it
believed (incorrectly) that German rearmament was massively accelerating. From May 1934 the chief military deliberating body, the
Conseil Supérieur de la Guerre, warned that France was in danger of
losing its military edge over Germany.[17] Pessimistic general staff
estimates of the Franco–German balance included on the German
side the enormous reservoir of rapidly mobilisable paramilitary forces and police housed in barracks, which were set against reductions
in French strength between 1931 and 1934. Faced with the world
economic crisis, successive French governments of the centre-right and
centre-left alike had cut defence expenditure in an attempt to balance
the country's budget and avoid currency devaluation which was so
repugnant to French political opinion. The public mood of pacifism
also lent itself to deep defence cuts.

In these years, Gamelin's superior in the military hierarchy, Maxime Weygand, abrasively lobbied for the army's restoration to its
1931 strength. In contrast, Gamelin's nimble advancement in the
early 1930s amidst the mine field of French civil–military relations
testified to his readiness to adapt the command's requirements to the
domestic political climate. Gamelin, like Barthou, had favoured
acceptance of Hitler's 1934 arms limitation offer . His justification,
that civilian financial stringency would gravely handicap the already
diminished French army in an arms race with Germany, revealed his
pervasive sense of French inferiority.

On the politically sensitive topic of disarmament, Gamelin considered that ' . . . there are currents which one cannot resist
directly . . . I conceived in this realm not positions of principle to
formulate, but "particular cases to resolve." '[18] An obvious case was a
Rhineland reoccupation, at a time when arms cuts, tolerated by
Gamelin, ensured that the French army would not contemplate an
armed contest with Germany in the west.

On retirement Weygand left his successor a 'military testament' which voiced anguish at France's unpreparedness and the conviction that allies could do little for its security. Gamelin's response was to listen politely and remark evasively: 'All of this is very interesting, *mon Général* . . .But you know, I am a strategist'.[19] Gamelin's strategy was to obviate a French military response to a German reoccupation of the Rhineland by associating France with Italy and the Soviet Union on a principal front distant from France.

After his appointment as commander-in-chief designate, Gamelin elaborated the bases of his strategy in a new mobilisation plan, the so-called 'Plan D *bis*'. The plan incorporated the decision not to fight for the Rhineland zone, and carried with it the implication that the French offensive necessary for victory would be difficult unless the bulk of the German forces attacked elsewhere, in the east.[20] In effect it compensated for French weakness by making a French offensive dependent on the direction of the German attack. Germany could not attack in the west without reoccupying the Rhineland, but Gamelin reckoned that it would reoccupy the zone only in order to turn east. Gamelin thus wagered that the Franco–German balance, imperiled by France's *de facto* disarmament, could be redressed by an allied strategy unofficially resting on the eastern calculation voiced in his 1933 talks with Syrový.[21] The plan met the post-Rhineland contingency by its stipulation that France would not remain pinioned behind the Maginot line, although operations at that point would depend entirely upon the functioning of an expanded allied coalition.

Barthou provided political and diplomatic support for Gamelin's strategy, but after Barthou's assassination at Marseilles in October 1934 the realisation of the general system of security conceived in 1934 fell to Pierre Laval, his canny, unpolished successor. In the face of greater provocation, Laval found it as difficult as Barthou to divorce security from arms limitation.

Laval continued diplomatic efforts to browbeat and cajole Hitler into negotiations for a broad European settlement including arms limitation. When Laval went to Rome in January 1935 to sign the Rome accords, Mussolini told him: 'Either we make war with Germany or we negotiate with her'. Burning to conquer Ethiopia, Mussolini had little desire for a German war. Although he was shortly to make overtures for bilateral military talks on Austria, he and Laval actually agreed on certain conditions to legalise German rearmament and to obtain German participation in a Danubian pact for the security of Austria, which would supplant the Rome accords.[22] This determination to include Germany remained a factor in Franco–Italian relations even after the German declaration of conscription in March 1935 prompted the creation of a porous Anglo–Italo–French front at Stresa. As a Quai d'Orsay memorandum of June 1935 reflected:

> Perhaps by its attitude Germany will one day induce us to construct and organise a unilateral chain of resistance to its ambitions. For the moment at least, it is difficult to avoid exhausting – in Central as in Eastern Europe – the possibilities of a collective policy.

Accordingly, German refusal to participate in the Danubian and Eastern pacts would 'entirely modify the general conception of the Rome accords'.[23]

As with Barthou, Laval appears to have become enmeshed with the Soviet Union through the desire to prevent an arms race. In response to Hitler's declaration of German conscription, the Quai d'Orsay argued that France should interpose itself between Germany and Russia. A policy of collective security including Germany would then limit rearmament by pooling the forces of participating states. The alternative, abandoning Germany and the Soviet Union to a virulent ideological rivalry, would be the surest way to *surarmement*, an accelerated arms race.[24] At the same time, the Quai d'Orsay shied away from bilateral involvement with Russia, as did the general staff. Gamelin's appreciations of the value of Soviet support in 1934–5 were given exclusively in terms of an Eastern pact to include both Poland and Germany.[25]

The Russians, however, were stung by their exclusion from Stresa and threatened to terminate all negotiations unless a bilateral treaty was signed. This threat imperilled Laval's position within the French cabinet. Precipitously he agreed to a freestanding bilateral pact with the Soviet Union in late April 1935.[26] The Czechs promptly followed suit, concluding a bilateral treaty with Moscow, though making it conditional upon the operation of France's treaty with Russia. Laval promptly regretted his Franco–Soviet diplomacy. In the months after Stresa, he ostentatiously took up a British scheme for a general European non-aggression pact, a diluted form of the Eastern pact, in order to facilitate an arms limitation agreement with Germany. As the chances for such a pact slipped away, he was increasingly wary of being left in close quarters with the Russians. In particular, Laval fretted that Hitler would seize on ratification of the Franco–Soviet treaty to reoccupy the Rhineland before agreement on arms limitation could be achieved.[27]

While the unimpeded German resurgence made arms limitation a pressing subject for French politicians, Gamelin calmly received the news of German conscription. He told his colleagues, 'If the Germans have not reoccupied the Demilitarised Zone . . . it is because they are not ready'.[28] The reoccupation was imminent; the timing was a matter of German choosing and would signify German preparedness for a larger conflict.

When the topic of the Rhineland arose in intra-governmental exchanges before the Stresa conference which condemned German conscription, Laval asked Gamelin whether France could act militarily in the event of either a reoccupation or an *Anschluss*. In a remarkable letter to his old comrade, the minister of war, General Maurin, Gamelin skilfully turned the government's consideration of an effective *riposte* with Italy from the Rhineland to a central European theatre. He argued that the time for a reprisal operation in the Rhineland to force Germany to conform to the peace treaties was over. Certainly his letter contained ritual allusions to the danger of a sudden German attack on France: such allusions remained indispensable as a means of resisting further defence cuts. It also reiterated the general staff's orthodoxy that Germany might attack in any direction. But its bent was plain:

> It is certain that the interest for us is in a conflict beginning in Central Europe, so that we would act as a secondary force against a Germany already engaged in that region with its principal forces. Of course the condition of effective action in Central Europe is the collaboration of the Little *Entente* and *entails the possibility of using Austrian territory*.

Gamelin, the letter confirmed, was determined to have a reoccupation viewed not as an event putting at stake France's security, but through the distant optic of a war of coalition beginning in the east. He was careful not to rule out a more independent French response to German provocation, but he wrote that time worked for Germany as much as for France. Gamelin's reasoning implied that since France could not keep pace with Germany, rearmament would assure France of allies rather than providing it with the strength to counter German expansionism directly. In the event of questions being asked at Stresa about French readiness to parry German moves into the

Rhineland and Austria, he advocated reiterating a preparedness he knew to be critically flawed. Discretion for Gamelin had become the better part of valour.[29]

The French military regarded staff talks with Italy as vital. An opportunity arose shortly after Laval's visit to Rome when the Italians offered talks in order to tantalise Paris before Mussolini's invasion of Ethiopia, for which preparations were conspicuous from April 1935.[30] Its terms too good to be true, the Italian general staff offered to commit itself to action in Austria or to send nine divisions to France, while requiring France to dispatch only two divisions to the central European front which Gamelin was eager to designate the principal front of the next war. Gamelin was unconcerned by chronic Italo – Yugoslav hostility, which had been exacerbated by the murder of King Alexander of Yugoslavia by Italian-trained terrorists the preceding October. He observed to a hesitant Laval that bad relations between Italy and Yugoslavia would merely have the effect of making them dependent on French military liaison on the central European front.[31] He also glossed over the troubling ambivalence of Austro–Italian military relations. Doubtless he supposed that a reoccupation, by directly threatening Austria, would create a seamless front. By his letter to Maurin and cool persuasion in governmental meetings in spring 1935, he prodded Laval into accepting peacetime staff conversations with Italy.

The Gamelin–Badoglio staff talks of June 1935 conferred on Italy a central place in French strategy.[32] Italy was the *sine qua non* of the Austrian operation envisaged by Gamelin since January 1934. The timely dispatch of a French expeditionary force across Italy to the central European front would justify French claims to lead a war of coalition in the east, while the exorbitantly generous terms of the Italian military offer promised a cut price war on the peripheries.[33] Others, Italy and the Balkan states with their reservoirs of peasant soldiery, would do most of the fighting on the central European front. The French contribution would be political liaison and the timely dispatch of expeditionary forces across Italy and eventually via Salonica to provide heavy-duty *matériel* which could not be obtained from the Russians. The manpower for the expeditionary force could be drawn from French alpine units released from guarding the Franco–Italian frontier by the June 1935 accords. And by ensuring the safe transport of French troops from North Africa, Italian friendship would also free French troops for the Belgian theatre, into which Gamelin intended to move troops when the Germans invaded central

Europe after reoccupying the Rhineland. So brilliant were the strategic prospects held out by the June 1935 talks that he henceforth considered French involvement in central Europe without Italy as unthinkable.[34]

Given the strength of their reliance on Italy, it is difficult to exaggerate the French military's consternation at the international crisis over Ethiopia, which from late summer 1935 caught France squarely between Britain and Italy. Gamelin considered that France had every interest in supporting Italy, from both the European and colonial viewpoints. He thus fully supported Laval's tortuous personal diplomacy of innocuous sanctions and the promotion of peace negotiations with Italy.[35] The disastrous Hoare–Laval episode of December 1935, however, threw French diplomacy into disarray. Hitler's decision to reoccupy the Rhineland in 1936 was made in February, and was intimately connected with the diplomatic crisis over Ethiopia, which made his military foray virtually risk-free.[36]

In the same weeks, the general staff pressed for the implementation of a new arms programme in which a reoccupation was styled as 'a wave of force beating against the foot of the sea wall [the Maginot line]'. As this German recrudescence could only be hastened by negotiating away the zone, the general staff favoured leaving the water to rise, inexorably albeit as slowly as possible, until the tide of its own accord ran eastwards. Thus Gamelin repeated to a military audience as late as January 1936 his frayed wager that Germany would attack central Europe after neutralising France by fortifications, adding, 'the Demilitarised Zone will be reoccupied with this aim as soon as possible'.[37] Ironically, when Hitler reoccupied the Rhineland at daybreak on 7 March 1936, the exact timing surprised Gamelin, whose strategy of default had for years been predicated on the event. He had waited so long for the reoccupation that on 3 March he wondered aloud whether the next German menace would not be against Czechoslovakia after all.[38] His musings illustrate the deadening quality of Hitlerian 'surprise', which so far from being totally unexpected, encouraged the potential adversary to indulge in an overkill of anticipation.

II

Traditionally, the Rhineland reoccupation has been seen as nullifying at one stroke France's eastern strategy. To understand Gamelin's strategy in 1936–7 and its culmination in the diplomatic defeat of Munich, it is essential to consider the meaning of the Rhineland crisis for the French military. The general staff considered that the form of the reoccupation, a remilitarisation without an attack on France, validated Gamelin's conception of the conflict most advantageous for France, a war of coalition in which the brunt of German force would be concentrated against central Europe. For the military, the threat posed by the crisis arose less from Hitler's long anticipated action than from Italian estrangement over Ethiopia, and from the politicians' deep fear of isolation if France did not respond forcefully.

With regard to Hitler's action, the military viewpoint was sharply defined: to do nothing to provoke Germany into accompanying a reoccupation with an attack on France.[39] Six weeks from elections and fearful of destroying the franc, Albert Sarraut's caretaker French cabinet in March 1936 debated a range of collective action, some of which risked provoking Germany, but all of which were meant to facilitate negotiations.[40] This orientation towards negotiation, ideally to follow a German withdrawal from the zone, was epitomised by the foreign minister, Pierre-Etienne Flandin. Theatrical and evasive, Flandin engaged the military in a dialogue of the deaf, each side attempting to save face over the demilitarisation statutes, whose violation neither was ready to resist.[41] In emergency meetings on 9 March 1936, Flandin, with negotiations in mind, suggested mobilising two divisions to compel the Germans to evacuate the zone. Afraid of unleashing action against France, Maurin, the minister of war, gave the impression of knowing nothing of the army's mobilisation plans.[42] The upshot was a decision to confront the Locarno powers with the crisis at a special London meeting.

For Maurin and Gamelin the reoccupation signified that Hitler had crossed the Rubicon. (A true enough supposition in light of the *Wehrmacht's* actual orders on 7 March to fall back, but not flee, before an armed response.) The political compensation for the loss of the Rhenish 'no man's land' was to be a Franco–British–Belgian front, that is, security guarantees implying passage rights, rather than ineffective military action. The last pockets of civilian bellicosity vanished when a stunned French delegation found itself confronted by the menace of complete inaction at the London meetings of the Locarno powers and the League Council. Italy's role was limited to observation, on account of sanctions, and British opinion as represented by *The Times* was disarmed by Hitler's offer that Germany should rejoin the League of Nations. Led by Flandin, who in 1935 had foreseen Franco–British staff talks as a guarantee for a general European settlement, French diplomats rapidly drew the conclusion that honour could best be salvaged by giving them priority.[43]

The immediate French aim in the trilateral staff talks of April 1936 was to secure a British commitment to aid Belgium and so repair the Franco–Belgian *entente*, damaged by Belgium's denunciation in February 1936 of its 1920 military accord with France. The creation of a trilateral front would cut short the Belgians' flirtation with neutralism and so restore French rights of passage for a war in the east.[44] For as one of Gamelin's colleagues remarked, since Germany would soon turn eastwards, a Franco–British convention referring only to the French frontier would apply to an inoperative case. The British, still smarting from Laval's treatment in the early stages of the Ethiopian war, were non-commital. Gamelin therefore decided not to broach directly French planning involving Italy and the central European uses of the Belgian front.[45] Instead he relied on British protestations of weakness to incline London to improve the general strategic situation by ending the Ethiopian war. He also looked to the British to supplement French capability in the Belgian theatre with mechanised forces. His close attention to the development of German mechanised forces had convinced him that the ideal terrain for their operation would be Belgium and Poland.[46]

The French representative at the trilateral staff talks, General Schweisguth, diffidently acquainted the British with Gamelin's strategic agenda. Schweisguth hinted that because of German fortifications, operations should be mounted in the more open terrain of the Low Countries, where 'French and British interests had always been closely tied'. This military diplomacy met Belgian fears of a German irruption through Holland, a contingency for which the British military had already generated a 'paper plan'.[47] In a French governmental meeting several months after the reoccupation, Gamelin spoke of a manoeuvre into Belgium and Holland to circumvent anticipated German fortifications in the Rhineland. This strategic notion contained in germ the Breda variant of 1940, with its reckless dash to Holland to head off a German breakthrough. In 1936, however, his various Belgian proposals rested upon the premise that the main German attack would come in the east. Behind closed doors in Paris, Gamelin insisted on the need to solder the French and Belgian frontiers so that the French army could move into Belgium at a German aggression in central Europe.[48] The Belgian *porte de sortie* would assure France's eastern allies that it would not remain pinioned behind the Maginot line. Elliptical but vital assurances to this effect were dispensed to the central European military *attachés*.[49]

The defusing of the Rhineland crisis left Gamelin free to proceed to his next prediction, a German attack on Czechoslovakia. His calculations emerge clearly from a 7 April 1936 map exercise on the impact of the Rhineland affair. There he anticipated that German fortifications would make impossible a frontal French intervention on behalf of an ally, now explicitly identified as Czechoslovakia. As a result, the French offensive would be limited to Belgium. Poland and Italy were to save the Czechs.[50]

The issue of German fortifications also figured in an early April meeting between Gamelin and the cabinet. Given French passivity and the attractiveness of Hitler's peace offers for France's menaced eastern allies, the politicians voiced legitimate fears that these allies would be drawn into the German camp, thus leaving France isolated. In response, Gamelin imperturbably guided discussion away from the government's emphasis on preventing the construction of German fortifications to the French position once German fortifications matched the Maginot line in solidity. To the agitated politicians, he advocated an operation to Salonica as in the First World War, and in the following weeks he proliferated projects dependent on Italian goodwill: the dispatch of a French division to the Brenner in the event of a Nazi *putsch* in Austria, and the constitution of a French expeditionary force for action in central Europe.[51] As a consensus still existed in military and diplomatic circles on ending the Ethiopian war by a compromise peace, Flandin made a series of peace overtures to Rome aimed at inducing Mussolini to assume obligations towards Czechoslovakia as well as Austria.[52]

Untroubled by Mussolini's smooth evasiveness, Gamelin took steps to advance military co-operation with Italy and Poland.[53] In May 1936 he hastened to authorise the reorganisation of the alpine units designated for the central European expeditionary force. (An Italian military alert early in June against the continuation of sanctions caused him to demote his orders from implementation to study, but the study was meticulously executed, down to the testing of boats for Danubian transport.) Also in May 1936, with the promise of important arms aid to Poland, he attempted to foster Polish–Czech staff contacts and a Polish commitment to establish an East Prussian front against the Reich.[54] Like his anticipation of German fortifications in the west, Gamelin's fixation on Italy and Poland made planning for an eastern war of coalition, and warnings against unilateral French intervention on behalf of Czechoslovakia, virtually indistinguishable. He complacently assumed that the reoccupation, by creating an obvious German menace in the east, would unite the threatened states. But as the Nazis were already demonstrating domestically with resounding success, a blatant threat to a vulnerable segment of a community did not generate solidarity. Gamelin's strategic preference for a war in the east left Hitler with ample leeway to mark out Czechoslovakia and to pit against it other French allies whom the Reich could treat as less menaced so long as it served German purposes. The weapon for this selection process lay readily to hand: ideology.[55]

For the assemblage of his grand coalition, which required the liquidation of sanctions against Italy, Gamelin looked to new political masters. The parliamentary elections in the spring of 1936 gave victory to the Popular Front, a left wing coalition which had made an electoral issue of Laval's Ethiopian policy and which the military wrongly expected would reject closer ties with the authoritarian Polish regime. The new Popular Front government was headed by Léon Blum, a humanistic socialist and conditional pacifist in the tradition of Jaurès.[56] Ties between the new government and the Czech social democrat Beneš were strong, and the defence of Czechoslovakia was a vital concern for Blum, who personally was determined to play a major part in foreign policy. Blum immediately perceived the harm which the Rhineland reoccupation had done to France's relations with its traditional allies.[57] At the moment of the reoccupation, Poland and the Little *Entente* countries had not demanded a French military response.[58] The delayed effect of the crisis, however, was an outpouring of anxiety that had built up in central Europe since the Ethiopian war.[59] As organised Ethiopian military resistance to Italy collapsed in the spring of 1936, and as it became apparent that France could not eliminate German fortifications in the Rhineland, the Czechs accused Paris of destroying the League with its Italophile policies.[60] In the Czech view, these had paved the way for an unopposed German repudiation of Locarno, and estranged France from the Yugoslavs who were now paralysed by fear of an Italian attack. This resentment against France left the Czechs susceptible to Hitler's offers of non-aggression pacts *à la polonaise*.

Soon after Blum took office, the vulnerability of Czechoslovakia figured in high level discussion. In the newly formed *Comité Permanent de la Défense Nationale* (CPDN) the starting point was Blum's proposal to dispatch munitions and replacement parts to the Czech airfields. Behind the proposal, innocuous in itself, loomed the plan of the air minister, Pierre Cot, to link the Czech aviation infrastructure to the Soviet air force and industry. In the June meeting of the CPDN, Cot began his abrasive campaign for a Soviet military alliance, proferred by the Soviet foreign minister, Litvinov, with renewed vigour since the victory of the Popular Front.[61]

The French defence establishment reacted strongly to this pressure. Cot's enthusiasm for the Soviet Union was familiar to the military from his 1933 tour of duty at the air ministry, but in 1936 he represented a disturbing new constituency. Blum's governing coalition of Radicals and Socialists depended on Communist backing in the Chamber of Deputies. When the 1936 elections sparked spontaneous strikes, taking the trade unions and French Communist party by surprise, the military and defence minister Daladier saw the hand of the Comintern and predicted the extension of Communist-organised strikes to the French arms factories.[62] Externally as well, the general staff regarded the Franco–Soviet connection with increasing distrust. Fledgling Franco–Soviet association had provided Hitler with a highly effective pretext for reoccupying the Rhineland, and the Belgians with a motive for the repudiation of their domestically divisive treaty with France.

For the first time, in June 1936, government debate set Soviet air and military support, as advocated by Cot, against the Italo–Polish front advocated by Gamelin and Daladier. In keeping with Gamelin's position that the army should mute its opposition to the new government, the military mobilised behind the scenes against a Soviet military alliance while pressing their case for Italian indispensability to the 'rapid organisation of a coherent allied front and eventually for the salvation of Czechoslovakia'. In the June CPDN, Gamelin opposed the dispatch of a French mission to Soviet manoeuvres to be held on the Polish border, observing gruffly: 'The French problem depends essentially on alliances. . . and Poland will be able to come to the aid of Czechoslovakia quicker than anyone.' Indeed, it was Gamelin's redoubled attachment to Italy and Poland in the tense summer of 1936 which prompted Léger's later observation that the military had held most tightly to the eastern alliances. In the summer of 1936, the military lent two different values to the phrase 'encirclement of Germany'. If realised with Italy and Poland, an encircling coalition would provide 'the largest possibilities of manoeuvre', deter Hitler by its efficacy and preserve peace; if accomplished alongside a

Soviet military alliance, it would incite Hitler to aggression, possibly in the west.[63]

As its disaffection with Blum's government grew in 1936-7, the general staff's infatuation with Italy deepened. On 11 July 1936, a week before the outbreak of the Spanish civil war, Italy stood aside when Austria proclaimed itself an independent German state. The Austro–German accord was a critical step towards an *Anschluss*. It was immediately understood as heralding the formation of an anti-Czech *bloc* – Poland, Austria, Italy, Hungary, perhaps even Yugoslavia – the product of Germany's triumphant bilateral diplomacy and anti-Bolshevik propaganda. This propaganda, to which Mussolini was increasingly attuned, threatened to divide Europe into two ideological camps, a prospect as alarming to Blum as to French diplomats and military.[64]

Blum displayed a nuanced attitude towards Italy. Throughout the previous month his goverment had engaged in thankless diplomacy to co-ordinate with the British the end of sanctions and to persuade Italy to rejoin the League reformed along lines (regional military pacts) suggested by the Ethiopian disaster. Although Blum's political views made him less flexible than his predecessors, in June 1936 he had made it clear to Rome that he did not intend to behave as a doctrinaire anti-Fascist. Moreover, a fact often ignored by contemporaries as well as by historians, Blum's goverment met all of the demands formulated by Mussolini.[65] Italian acquiescence in the Austro–German accord, however, alerted Blum to Mussolini's abandonment of his central European interests and to a shift in his designs towards the Mediterranean, which threatened a clash with French and British interests.[66] The government's final experiment in reconciling Italy with Geneva failed miserably in September 1936. Recriminating only against France over the issue of recognition of his African conquest, Mussolini threatened to rupture diplomatic relations with Paris and noisily initiated a diplomatic partnership with Berlin.[67]

Disquieted by this diplomatic tempest and adamant that Italy was indispensable to any French opposition to Germany in central Europe, the general staff preferred to fault the Blum government for the state of Franco–Italian relations rather than to adapt its strategy to rapidly shifting central European events. Speaking to fellow staff officers, Schweisguth, Gamelin's representative to the Allied armies, flatly refused to predict Italy's alignment, and compared Italy with Poland as a capricious but indispensable element of victory.[68]

The signature of the Franco–Soviet mutual aid pact in May 1935 coincided with the death of the Polish ruler, Marshal Pilsudski, and initiated a period in which Pilsudski's successors cultivated Franco–German military rivalry for Poland's allegiance. The Poles intended to make the French pay for their Soviet pact, and in late 1935 they requested important French arms aid.[69] The general staff's response was governed by its apprehension about the unfolding of Franco–Soviet relations rather than by concern to use the Polish arms demands to harmonise France's Polish and Soviet treaties. Its recurrent nightmare in 1936–7 was that Franco–Soviet military negotiations would provoke the Poles into transforming their 1934 understanding with Germany into a Polono–German *bloc* against Russia, Poland's hereditary enemy. The military reasoned that such a *bloc* would not only neutralise Soviet aid to Czechoslovakia but speed the Germans westward.[70] These military anxieties shaped the Franco–Polish arms negotiations, into which the Blum government was drawn by the Poles' threat to purchase arms in Germany, and by its own quest for effective support for Czechoslovakia. The Blum government sent Gamelin to Warsaw in August 1936 to carry out the main negotiations *entre soldats* due to the untrustworthiness of the Polish foreign minister, Beck. It was largely on the strength of assurances given to Gamelin by his Polish counterpart, Rydz-Smigly, that France signed the Rambouillet accords, a two billion franc arms deal with Poland, in September 1936.[71]

In Warsaw, Gamelin cold-shouldered a Polish–Czech political *entente* – the most important issue for the Blum government in the negotiations – in favour of Polish–Czech military co-operation.[72] Since the reoccupation, Gamelin had promoted discreet Polish––Czech staff contacts in order to discourage the Czechs from relying upon the Russians. In the summer of 1936 Gamelin saw no advantage in pushing the Poles and Czechs into a provocative political *entente*, while a Soviet mortgage still hung over Czech policy and the Blum government's attitude to a Soviet military pact remained fluid. With Rydz-Smigly, Gamelin quietly broached the topic of eventual Polish–Czech military collaboration in Silesia and, very obliquely, that of Soviet material aid to Poland in a conflict. Rydz-Smigly's acceptance of French liaison in the event of a conflict seemed to promise Gamelin leverage to influence the Poles in a Czech–German crisis. In real terms, however, the general staff's dependence on the volatile Poles only obscured the hardening in 1936–7 of traditional Polish calculations regarding Czechoslovakia.[73]

In its search for guarantees for Czechoslovakia, the Blum government carried on parallel negotiations with the Little *Entente* states. The Russians loomed behind these negotiations from the start, and in their shadow central European neutralism assumed an acute and paralysing form. As the Little *Entente's* dismay at French inaction at the time of the reoccupation became increasingly evident in June and July 1936, the Soviet Union, seconded by Cot, pressed for the unification of France's obligations in central Europe into a single pact embracing the Soviet Union, Poland and the Little *Entente*. Soviet interest in such unified and strengthened French obligations was two-fold: Franco–Soviet military conversations to underwrite serious central European resistance, and French-mediated passage rights for the Red Army across Poland.[74]

The Soviets pursued this agenda with terrifying malatroitness. Initially, they encouraged proposals by Titulesco, the Rumanian foreign minister, for a French–Little *Entente* mutual aid pact accompanied by a Rumanian–Soviet accord. This encouragement alternated with Soviet threats in Bucharest to turn Rumania into a battlefield in a German–Soviet war, should Titulesco's diplomatic approaches to the Quai d'Orsay prove fruitless. To keen Soviet displeasure, the domestically unpopular Titulesco fell from power in August 1936. Further agitated by conversations on disarmament and security between Blum and Hjalmar Schacht, the head of the *Reichsbank*, the Soviet Union retaliated with a campaign in Paris which alternated rumours of imminent German attack in the west with threats of Soviet abandonment of collective security if France did not sign a military pact with Russia.[75]

This Soviet heavy-handedness acquired alarming connotations in the context of the Spanish civil war. Among France's conservative allies, Spain inspired fears of a general conflagration into which they would inexorably be drawn by the French and Czech–Soviet pacts. Fed by Soviet bluster and Hitler's strident rhetoric at Nuremberg in September 1936, fears of a German–Soviet war produced strong currents of central European neutralism. In case of a general conflict, Rumania and Yugoslavia implied that they would at all costs avoid taking sides. This neutralism was compounded by dread that any association with the Russians would bring havoc at the over-active hands of the Comintern, as it had to the Spanish Popular Front. Many central European conservatives also believed that the Spanish convulsion would soon extend to Blum's Popular Front.[76]

These indigenous fears were skilfully amplified by German propaganda which portrayed France as an advanced air base – in its hyperbole, a west European Czechoslovakia – for the Russians in the Spanish war. Such propaganda, which reached a crescendo in the anti-Comintern pact between Germany and Japan (November 1936), constituted an ideological barrage against European Popular Fronts, isolating the Russians and their French and Czech allies from the rest of Europe.[77] Predicting that France would soon suffer the fate of Spain, Hitler announced to the French ambassador that the Reich would not regard a Communist triumph in France as an internal French affair. He also whipped up the French military's anxiety, induced by the Spanish conflict, at being placed in the direct line of fire in a domestic insurrection. Hitler's feel for the pulse of his audience was as usual superb. Leading members of the general staff were soon reported to believe that a Communist general strike, accompanied by assassination of leading military figures, could be exploited by Hitler to stage a *coup de force* within France.[78]

The Spanish civil war which redoubled the military's worries about the French domestic situation also intensified its opposition to a Franco–Soviet military pact. In an influential report on the 1936 Soviet manoeuvres, Schweisguth judged the Soviet military unprepared for war against a great power and went on to draw highly politicised conclusions from Soviet attempts to prod France into intransigence towards Germany. Schweisguth argued that the Russians much preferred that the German *maelstrom* break over France, expecting to emerge as the revolutionary arbiter of a conflict devastating western Europe. This theory had been a staple of German propaganda for many months. In the autumn of 1936, Schweisguth adduced for its proof the Russians' intervention in Spain, Soviet insensitivity to German fears of encirclement by promoting Franco–Soviet military contacts and Comintern propagandising in the French army, which he presented as a Soviet snare to make France appear easy prey to the Reich.[79] The implication was clear: a Franco–Soviet military *entente* for the defence of Czechoslovakia would bring about a Franco–German war and revolution in the west. According to the general staff's lights, the Reich was preparing its attack on Czechoslovakia by fostering benevolent neutrality or complicity in Italy, Poland and Belgium, precisely those states on which Gamelin relied for a coalition effort in the east. The general staff's susceptibility to the politics of anti-Bolshevism obscured the fact that these states had never shown the slightest pro-Czech inclination.[80]

In November 1936, after the circulation of the Schweisguth report,

Gamelin and Daladier, joined by the foreign minister, Delbos, put an end to Cot and Litvinov's plan to unify France's obligations in central Europe. The cabinet postponed Franco–Soviet military contacts, while authorising immediate, separate negotiations for a French–Little *Entente* pact.[81] Blum apparently felt that Little *Entente* negotiations under French auspices would steady the Czechs, amid central European trepidation on the subject of the Soviets. The Quai d'Orsay half-heartedly pursued the French–Little *Entente* negotiations, while the general staff regarded Blum's attempt to provide diplomatic support for the Czechs as beside the point. As Schweisguth put it, '. . . the formulae so abundantly employed by statesmen and journalists,"collective security" and "mutual aid", are in reality of a difficult, slow and limited application.' Schweisguth's moral was the familiar one, with its implicit warning against unilateral involvements: a French policy in central Europe independent of 'geographical realities', such as Italian aid, was an illusion. On the basis of an exhaustive general staff study, he claimed to a select military audience in April 1937 that with Italy's friendship the first French troops would arrive on the Danube within three days, the entire expeditionary force within three weeks.[82] These were impressive figures but by the spring of 1937 they were scarcely realistic. An Italo–Yugoslav political treaty of March 1937, Mussolini's response to the Austro–German accord, indicated a clear shift in Italian policy, in which recent defeats in Spain played a part, from central Europe to the Mediterranean.[83]

Blum was, if anything, more anxious to find a way of helping the Czechs after the Italo–Yugoslav accord wrecked the French–Little *Entente* negotiations. Soviet military conversations still figured on the government's agenda. Blum had complex motives in turning to the Russians. He reckoned that technical military contacts were indispensable to the defence of Czechoslovakia, and feared the effects on French internal politics and security of increasingly vituperative Soviet threats to realign with Germany. Perhaps most importantly, Blum had come to see a tragic resemblance between the contemporary occlusion of diplomatic options and that of 1914, an analogy which carried with it a despairing acceptance of the possibility of war. He saw no alternative to an attempt to recreate the pre-1914 Anglo–Franco–Russian alliance. In practical terms, this meant staff talks with the Russians until Britain rearmed. The Blum government decided on unofficial Soviet talks in late May 1937.[84]

Gamelin and the general staff were vehemently opposed to staff talks. Their reaction was dramatised by Polish threats to appeal to Germany against the Russians, threats which elevated to blackmail the interallied ambiguities accepted by Gamelin in the Rambouillet accords. The military pleaded that to attach French security to Czech–Soviet force would engender a Polish–German *bloc* and invite a situation in which Germany could freely move westward. They were well aware that the alternative they advocated, a Polish–Czech combination, carried the risk of a German–Soviet *rapprochement*, but as Schweisguth told French diplomats, given the Russians' general duplicity, a signed agreement on whichever side would be no guarantee of their loyalty.[85]

The unleashing of the Soviet military purges and the fall of Blum's domestically embattled government in June 1937 ensured that the critical debate concerning the defence of Czechoslovakia, begun a year before and posed in its most extreme form by the general staff's opposition to Franco–Soviet military talks in May and June 1937, was never formally resolved. The Germans had every reason to be jubilant about the so-called 'Toukhatchevsky Affair', a successful intrigue to discredit the leadership of the Red Army, which was fabricated by the Gestapo but taken up by the Soviet Secret Police with Stalin's connivance. As always after one of their *coups*, they lost no time in quieting French fears. After the execution of Marshal Toukhatchevsky and other Soviet generals in June 1937, the cordial German military attaché assured members of the general staff that the Red Army was no longer to be feared. Kuhlenthal threw in a soldierly reminiscence. He had attended a lunch at the Kremlin in 1929 for 36 guests, of whom only two were still alive. In a deft allusion to Mussolini's 1933 proposals for territorial revision in central Europe, Kuhlenthal remarked that the only solution was a revival of the Italian conception by which the four powers would reach an understanding to assume the direction of Europe.[86]

The contours of Munich were also visible in the future French policy which Yvon Delbos, again foreign minister under Blum's lacklustre successor, Chautemps, outlined to the American ambassador in July 1937:

Insofar as he could foresee the future, the position that France would take would depend entirely on the position of England. France would not undertake to fight Germany and Italy. The position of France would be the same as her position in the Spanish affair [i.e. formal non-intervention]. If England should wish to stand firmly by the side of France against Germany and Italy, France would act. If England should continue to hold aloof, France could not act.France would never be caught in the position of having the Soviet Union as her only ally.[87]

Increasingly common in French political circles, the Czech–Spanish analogy had the connotation, soothing to many, of *non-intervention généralisée*. Delbos' observations also encapsulated the conclusion which the Quai d'Orsay had drawn from the failure of the French-Little *Entente* negotiations, that France should dispense with an active policy in central Europe without British backing.[88]

The Franco–British diplomatic tandem in central Europe, which dated from the failure of these negotiations (and not, as is usually argued, from the immediate aftermath of the Rhineland reoccupation), marked the passage of British involvement from implicitly to explicitly conditioning the Quai d'Orsay's commitment to a constructive French policy in central Europe. In this respect, it commenced the phase of Franco–Czech relations which ended in Munich. This phase was marked by the search for that elusive entity, an honourable Czech–German accord.[89] For some months this policy commanded considerable consensus in Anglo–French governing circles, including pro-Czech opposition circles led by Churchill and Blum.[90] Nevertheless, unofficial diplomacy, such as Halifax's visit to Hitler and private conversations between Chautemps, Georges Bonnet and Papen, all in the autumn of 1937, frankly betokened the sell-out that occurred at Munich. The international tide actually turned against Czechoslovakia from November 1937.[91]

Gamelin's active disassociation from the fate of Czechoslovakia began when Mussolini allowed Hitler to seize Austria in March 1938. In a series of memoranda after the *Anschluss*, Gamelin sought to ensure that the Czechs' surrender of Bohemia would be a diplomatic, not a military, defeat for France. He pressed for timely, limited negotiations, which would avert what he foresaw as the military disaster of a successful German *campagne d'été* in central Europe, followed directly by an onslaught against France. The core of his response was as usual anticipation, but at the *Anschluss*, anticipation far outpaced any regenerative strategic response on Gamelin's part. He wrote that Germany could very soon simultaneously wage a two front war, a panic-sticken assessment which called into question his calculation from 1933 onwards that a war in the east would forestall a German onslaught against France itself. Time remained for Gamelin the critical dimension, and in breathless pursuit, he made what can be seen as an insidious case for the centrality of the vanished Italian *entente*. His reflections on the pending Czech disaster were not without the vestigial hope that a rapid Italian *volte-face* might prevent a crisis of sweeping proportions.[92]

While ostensibly the ensuing debate was about the scant possibilities of defending Czechoslovakia, in fact it concerned protecting France from attack. When he conferred with Prime Minister Daladier at the height of the Munich crisis, Gamelin's reasoning had an almost surgical cleanness. He proceeded directly from his antiseptic position of April 1936, that Czechoslovakia could only be saved by Poland and Italy, to evoke adverse contemporary hypotheses–Italian mobilisation against France and Polish intervention against Czechoslovakia in agreement with Germany – which made French action unwarranted. To these he added warning of a recent deterioration in Franco–Belgian military relations, which precluded a French sprint through Belgium to aid Czechoslovakia. For the rest, Gamelin effaced himself before what he respectfully termed 'the importance of the air factor to the government's deliberations'.[93] In September 1938, neither Gamelin nor Daladier mentioned the Russians or their air force. Nor was there consideration of direct French intervention on the Czech's behalf. Dismissal of such intervention had been the one constant in Gamelin's planning between 1933 and 1938.

III.

This essay began with the argument that Gamelin long expected a Rhineland reoccupation, which he sought to parry by an anticipatory strategy. This strategy would at once obviate French resistance to a Rhineland reoccupation, which he believed would end in stalemate on the Franco–German frontier, in what he subsequently called *'une forme de bataille de la Somme modernisée'*; and it would ensure Germany's eastward movement after it fortified the zone. In the constructive phase of his strategy (1933–1935), Italy and more marginally the Soviet Union were added to the French diplomatic system of the 1920s whose most vulnerable point by 1935–6 was Czechoslovakia. Hitler reoccupied the Rhineland in the middle of the Ethiopian war in March 1936, using ratification of the Franco–Soviet pact as the pretext for action. Hitler's move appeared to confirm Gamelin's wager on the direction a German attack would take. But

Hitler's timing and pretext were well chosen to disrupt Gamelin's strategy, and brilliantly exploited the gap between his intention (a coalition among France's quarrelling allies catalysed by a clear German threat) and its effect (the high cost of French inaction).

Gamelin's unswerving gaze on the rising German danger had led him to brush aside the destabilising potential of Mussolini's ambitions for a Mediterranean empire in 1935–6. After the German reoccupation of the Rhineland, Mussolini allowed the Austro–German accord and Italian involvement in the Spanish war to influence him into joining the German camp, despite attempts by the new Blum government to liquidate the Ethiopian crisis and return Italy to a reformed League. The escalation of German anti-Bolshevism, together with Soviet nervousness, produced European-wide neutralist currents which isolated France and Czechoslovakia. These neutralist currents, along with social effervescence in France itself, excited French military fears that closer collaboration with the Russians would intensify the Polish–German *entente* and allow the Reich to turn on France. In a period in which Hitler's pressures were still not overtly expansionist, the French security system was corroded ideologically from within over the issue of Czechoslovakia. The general staff's exclusive reliance after 7 March 1936 on Italy and Poland for the defence of Czechoslovakia acquired independent existence only as a shield against Soviet 'duplicity' and against the other option, unilateral French initiative, to which Blum's government appeared dangerously inclined, and which technically would activate Soviet obligations to the Czechs. Under these ideological pressures, and with the *Anschluss* intensifying Gamelin's root fear of a confrontation in which France would bear the brunt of German force, the military joined the diplomats – long quizzical about the value of the eastern treaties – in disengaging themselves from Czechoslovakia.

Gamelin's response to the eastern crises of 1938 provides the best illustration of the self-defeating quality of his anticipation. At word of the *Anschluss*, he anticipated a huge increase in German force. Yet actual German war potential did not approach his estimates in the spring of 1938. It was Hitler's bloodless occupation of Prague (not Vienna) which underpinned subsequent German military victories. The evolution of the *Blitzkrieg*, initially an improvised form of warfare, against Poland and then against France itself relied significantly on the German seizure in March 1939 of Czech war materials produced by the Skoda works. These included highly prized Avia 534 fighters with French engines. In other equally devastating respects,

Hitler's resourcefulness maximised the profits to be had from Gamelin's anticipation. German fortifications in the west were still incomplete in the autumn of 1938. Thus a compelling case can be made that a determined French offensive on behalf of Czechoslovakia might have succeeded.[94] Gamelin, however, had long since 'completed' the Siegfried line in anticipation, and from 1933 written off unilateral French intervention in central Europe. Hitler's construction of western fortifications *en trompe l'oeil* was entirely successful. Indeed, Gamelin did nothing to alter his conclusion that Czechoslovakia could not be saved when he learned in 1938 that the Siegfried line was in fact far from complete.

Both Gamelin's defensive attachment to the eastern front and its provisional abandonment in 1938 were inextricable from domestic constraints. His strategy was originally evolved to compensate for the political pressures generated by fiscal cuts and a diplomacy avid for arms limitation. It mirrored these pressures in its awareness of French weakness and vulnerability, as in his fear of provoking Germany whose strength he believed had attained military parity with France. The peculiarly debilitating quality of this French weakness arose less from the particular constraints of the early 1930s which Gamelin after all tolerated, than from the military's anticipation of impotence caused by recent civilian concessions over the Rhineland.

In the aftermath of the reoccupation, the domestic constraints the general staff experienced under Blum were quite different from those of preceding goverments. Departing from the deflationary policies of the past, the Popular Front government began serious French rearmament, with defence expenditure exceeding the military's original estimates.[95] Civilian–military relations, however, were scarred by the government's attempts to implement a major arms programme alongside social reform and what the general staff regarded as outright Comintern sabotage of arms production. In strategic terms, the general staff blamed the Popular Front for what it considered the government's lamentable performance *vis-à-vis* allies, notably Italy.[96] It imputed this to ideological blindness and cavalier disregard of the geographical realities on which a land-based strategy should be based. The ideological decomposition of Gamelin's strategy for a war of coalition predicated on Italy, together with the military's acute anxiety about the launching of rearmament in the corrosive circumstances of 1936–7 – this conjunction has been central to a debate which has pitted rearmament against strategy in a pulverising series of recriminations over political *vs.* military responsibility for the 1940 defeat.

This chapter contends that strategy, far more than the flaws in French rearmament, was key to the military events leading to the armistice. In relation to Gamelin's strategy, as General Georges shrewdly suggested in late 1937, France's rearmament served principally to attract indispensable late comers to a coalition, not to meet the German danger head on or virtually alone. Gamelin, after the premature evacuation of the Rhineland, had fallen back on an allied strategy minute in its attention to 'modernising' the lessons of the last war. Chief among these lessons was not the advantage of a strictly defensive posture, in the contemporary context of being pinioned behind the Maginot line, but of fighting the war elsewhere. In the very nature of things the Rhineland reoccupation underscored Gamelin's strategic adaptation of his chief responsibility, namely the integral defence of France's frontiers. His strategy for a cut price war on the peripheries appears nowhere more starkly than in his insistence some months after Hitler's move into the Rhineland that the narrowness of the Franco–German frontier dictated its enlargement via Belgium and Holland or in central Europe 'if only by a rapid, symbolic force while awaiting the possibility of a large scale operation.'[97] Gamelin's reliance on Poland and the Low Countries, like that on Italy, rested on this single geographical imperative. The inescapable logic of his strategy, with its mixture of self-fulfilling prophecy and desire to economise French means, condemned him to an unending search for a defensive war beyond France's frontiers.

The turn of Poland offered the unexpected boon of a war in the east after the humiliation of Munich. With the stirrup of the British guarantee, France would not declare war alone, although as German force visibly accrued in war materials, power and prestige, Gamelin could never feel prepared. Chronic fears of unreadiness thus made inaction as compelling as ever. Gamelin gave almost no active aid to the Poles. The defensiveness of his attachment to the eastern theatre dictated his departure from the sound strategic principle of the two front war, although he publicly laid claim to it through the eve of the Polish campaign. As he informed his British counterpart in July 1939:'. . . we have every interest in the war beginning in the east and becoming a general conflict only little by little. We will thus have the time necessary to put on a war footing all Franco–British forces'.[98]

With the end of the *Blitzkrieg* in the east, Gamelin clung to the vestiges of his tattered strategy for a war elsewhere. Despite very adverse political circumstances, and again in the hope of economising French blood, he dispatched the elite of the army to northern Belgium and Holland in May 1940, while the Germans broke through the Ardennes, in the south.[99] It still seems amazing that the fall of France in 1940 came about not from lack of weapons nor until after Dunkirk from a lack of men, but from a complete absence of planning for a German breakthrough.[100] This fact resists explanation until placed in the context of Gamelin's calculations and his attachment to a cut price war on the peripheries.[101] These were the unifying strands in a strategy which more than any other single factor accounts for the armistice of June 1940. By attempting to fight the war elsewhere, Gamelin in effect made it impossible to fight at all. Ultimately, the blood of others was not a viable solution to the historical problem of the two front war.

NOTES AND REFERENCES

I am indebted to the Campus Research Board of the University of Illinois at Chicago for funding research in the National Archives, Washington D.C.

1. E. Cameron, 'Alexis Saint-Léger Léger,' in G. Craig, F. Gilbert, *The Diplomats* (N.Y., 1963), II, p. 393. Léger was secretary–general of the French Ministry of Foreign Affairs from 1933 until 1940.
2. Service Historique de l'Armée de l'Air, 2B98 'Conversations franco-tchécoslovaques,' 28–31 Jan. 1933.
3. The standard sources on the eastern network are J. Laroche, *La Pologne de Pilsudski* (Paris, 1953) and *Au Quai d'Orsay avec Briand et Poincaré* (Paris, 1957); P. Wandycz, *France & Her Eastern Allies, 1919–1925* (Minneapolis, 1962); W. Jedrzjewicz (ed.), *Diplomat in Berlin: The Papers of Joseph Lipski* (New York, 1968); G. Soutou, ' L' Impérialisme du pauvre', *Relations Internationales*, 7 (1976); and A. Toynbee, *Survey of International Affairs 1924* (Oxford, 1926), pp. 441–51; . . . *1927* (Oxford, 1929), pp. 161, 163.
4. For Warsaw, the multilateral negotiations of the mid-1930s for an Eastern pact scarcely concealed another campaign by France to revise the 1921 accords and diminish its obligations to Poland by including the Soviet Union in the security arrangements. Belgrade regarded the Italo–Yugoslav *entente* desired by Paris as a snare to allow the French to withdraw behind their frontiers while Italy succeeded France as the dominant power in the region.
5. Although Marshal Foch originally opposed extensive engagements to Poland, he was pleased by the new alliances with states bordering on Germany and saw in Belgium, Czechoslovakia and Poland 'a single front which constitutes the best safeguard of peace'. S.H.A., 'E.M.A./2 Tchécoslovaquie', 19 Mar. 1924.
6. It was symptomatic that both the polished, opaque Gamelin and his fiery colleague on the general staff, Maxime Weygand, would be drawn by farflung operations to Salonica. For Gamelin, the 1915 Salonica

expedition pointed to the neglected advantages of a strategy of extended fronts.

7. Jon Jacobson, *Locarno Diplomacy* (Princeton, 1972), pp. 83–90, 95, 156; Jedrzjewicz, pp. 7, 12–9; Laroche, *La Pologne*, p. 17; A. Cienciala, 'The Significance of the Declaration of Non-Aggression of January 26, 1934', *East European Quarterly* I, 1 (1967), pp. 7–11; Wandycz, pp. 312–368; M. Vaïsse, *Sécurité d'Abord: La Politique française en matière de désarmement* (Paris, 1981), pp. 360–2, 520. For Gamelin's favourable reflections on the Four Power Pact–arms limitation concept at the wartime Riom trial, see Papiers Blum, 3BL3 Dr1, M. Gamelin, 'La Politique Etrangère de la France 1930–9 au point de vue militaire', pp. 2–4.

8. Beck, the Polish foreign minister, believed that Hitler's advent furnished Poland with 'a unique opportunity to redress our situation in the European balance'. The Poles reasoned that the Austrian Hitler could be deflected southward into Austria and Czechoslovakia, as opposed to the due east direction, i.e. against Poland, advocated by traditional Prussian revisionism. J. Beck, *Dernier Rapport* (Neuchatel, 1951), pp. 28–9.

9. Foch, 8 Mar. 1926, in Adamthwaite, *The Lost Peace* (New York, 1981), pp. 79–82. The politicians' commitment to fixed fortifications soon surpassed that of the E.M.A. B.A. Lee, 'Strategy, arms and the collapse of France 1930–1940' in *Diplomacy & Intelligence during the Second World War*, ed. R. Langhorne (Cambridge, 1985), p. 64.

10. S. Schuker, 'France and the Remilitarization of the Rhineland, 1936', *French Historical Studies* 14 (1986), pp. 317–8.

11. Gamelin continued to insist on Czech–Polish collaboration in Silesia, even when the German–Polish Declaration led the Czechs to consider abandoning plans to defend their ethnically German Bohemian territories. S.H.A., 7N3444, Gamelin–Krejcí conversation, 11–12 July 1934.

12. Ibid., June 1932, 21 Jan. 1933; M.A.e., 'Tchécoslovaquie–Petite Entente', Gamelin letter 20 Jan. 1933; 20 Dec. 1932, 2, 3, Nov. 1933.

13. D.D.F. I, 4, nos. 3, 35; 5, nos. 28, 84, 120; S.H.A., 'Cabinet du Ministre', Gamelin Note, Jan. 1934.

14. Vaïsse, pp. 529–94.

15. D.D.F. I, 6, nos. 110, 164, 177, 191, 213; F. Piétri, 'Souvenir de Barthou', *Revue des Deux Mondes*, 1 March 1961, p. 67; P. Aloisi, *Journal 1932–1936* (Paris, 1957), pp. 189–96. Barthou's murder at Marseilles in October 1934 makes definitive assessment impossible; however his dispatches in September 1934 suggest that he had not ruled out an arms limitation agreement under Franco–Italian auspices. D.D.F. I, 7, nos.233, 566.

16. *Ibid.*, no. 180; W. d'Ormesson, *France* (London, 1939), pp. 126–9.

17. S.H.A., C.S.G. 9 May 1934, cited in H. Dutailly, *Les Problèmes de l'Armée de Terre Française 1935–1939* (Paris, 1980), p. 119.

18. M.Gamelin, *Servir* II (Paris, 1946), p. 56.

19. J. Weygand, *Weygand Mon Père* (Paris, 1970), p. 239; P.C.F. Bank-witz, *Maxime Weygand and Civil–Military Relations in Modern France* (Cambridge, Mass., 1967), p. 113.
20. Dutailly, pp. 19, 42, 70.
21. This wager also figured in an early 1935 interchange between Gamelin and the Prime Minister, P-E. Flandin. Flandin, enticed by British schemes to incorporate arms limitation into a general European settle-ment, pressed for figures on the Franco–German balance. Gamelin quietly insisted that such figures were less important than the German aim, namely action in the east. D.D.F. I, 9, no. 57.
22. *Ibid.*; see also G. Warner's classic study, *Pierre Laval & the Eclipse of France* (London, 1968), pp. 63–71.
23. Papiers Massigli, 'L'Europe centrale', 10 June 1935.
24. *Ibid.*, 'Pacte Franco–Soviétique,'29 Mar. 1935.
25. Papiers Schweisguth, henceforth Schw., 1SC2 Dr8, 24 Mar. 1936.
26. 'The Struggle of the USSR for Collective Security in Europe during 1933–1935', *International Affairs*, 10 (Moscow, 1963), pp. 112–4; J. Haslam, *The Soviet Union and the Struggle for Collective Security in Europe 1933–1939 (London, 1984), pp. 43–51;* Cameron in Craig & Gilbert, *The Diplomats* II, pp. 385–7. According to Léger, Laval even suggested bilateral military conversations to Stalin. P.R.O., F.O. 371, 19880, C/7267/92/62.
27. J. Szembek, *Journal 1933–1939* (Paris, 1952), pp. 70–6; S.H.A.A., 2B188, H.C.M., 21 Nov. 1935.
28. Schw. 1SC2 Dr1, 'Notes générales'; 1SC2 Dr3, 'Rapport,' 16 Apr. 1935.
29. D.D.F. I, 10, no. 155.
30. From the early stages of planning in 1932 for his Ethiopian enterprise, Mussolini spoke of the inescapability of *Anschluss* and the need to create a second line of defence by falling back on Yugoslavia. E.M. Robertson, *Mussolini as Empire Builder* (London, 1977), pp. 33, 42, 66.
31. D.D.F. I, 10, nos. 247, 495.
32. Leaving nothing to chance, the Italians had invited the French military operations section to submit its strategic desiderata before Gamelin's visit. The resulting Gamelin–Badoglio accords conformed closely to the French studies; see R. Young's useful article, 'French Military Intelli-gence and the Franco–Italian Alliance', *The Historical Journal*, 28 (1985), p. 159.
33. 3^e Bureau studies of this expeditionary force to central Europe counted on sending 300 military trains across Italy within a two week period. *Ibid.*, p. 161.
34. National Archives, Czech documents in T–120, henceforth Czech T–120, 1143/2028/444368–9. These prospects were most striking when set against the known weakness of the British army and the chariness of British support on the continent. Not until early 1939 did Britain offer a comparable presence.

35. Schw. 1SC2 Dr5, 6 Aug., 19, 21, Sept.; 1SC2 Dr6, 12 Dec. 1935; Papiers Fabry, 'Journal de Marche', 28 Aug. 1935.

36. J.T. Emmerson, *The Rhineland Crisis* (London, 1977), pp. 72–103.

37. Dutailly, p. 122; D.D.F. II, 1, no. 83.

38. Schw. 1SC2 Dr8, 'Rapport', 3 Mar. 1936.

39. D.D.F. II, 1, no. 170.

40. This debate ranged from action under League auspices, the bent of a rhetorically powerful speech to the country by Prime Minister Sarraut, to partial mobilisation (along with Poland). G. Sakwa, 'The Franco–Polish Alliance and the Remilitarisation of the Rhineland', *The Historical Journal*, 16, 1 (1973), pp. 135–6.

41. Just prior to Hitler's action, Flandin tried to extract simulated war planning (regarded by the general staff as a dangerous bluff), to back up a preventive collective *démarche* which would draw Hitler into negotiations on the zone, a prospect which the general staff firmly rejected in 1935–6. D.D.F. I, 9, no. 57; II, 1, nos. 105, 141, 170, 186, 196.

42. Schw. 1SC2 Dr8, 9, 10 Mar., 'Rapports', 9, 10 Mar. 1936.

43. *Ibid.*, & 17 Mar.; 2SC2 Dr11, 18 Mar. 1936; D.D.F. I, 9, no. 57 ; II, 1, nos. 202, 391, 425.

44. *Ibid.*, 2, no. 97; Schw. 2SC2 Dr12, Note, 17 Apr. 1936. Belgium's denunciation of the outmoded 1920 accord had been expected from the 1930 allied evacuation of the Rhineland. The Belgians worked from 1931–2 to steer their foreign relations towards a 'safer' position, independent of international obligations which would make the country one of the battlefields of the next war. Ratification of the Franco–Soviet pact in February 1936 added tinder to the already flammable Belgian domestic controversy over the French military connection. (I am indebted to Dr Martin Alexander for sharing his extensive knowledge of Franco–Belgian relations.)

In 1932–5, Gamelin had been disquieted by the risks attendant on the general staff's policy of a 'forward defence' of heavily industrialised northern France by advancing, even without adequate Belgian co-operation, into Belgian territory. It may well be that Belgian reticence originally predisposed Gamelin towards an eastern strategy as affording a greater chance of warding off overwhelming German blows.

45. *Ibid.*, 1SC2 Dr8, 31 Mar., 1 Apr. 1936; Papiers Flandin, 74, 29 Mar. 1936.

46. Gamelin's expectations of the British were tailored to reports that London assigned itself the role of purveyor of *matériel*, not men, in a future conflict. *Ibid.*, 1SC2 Dr7, 15 Jan.; 1SC2 Dr8, 1 Apr. 1936; 2SC2 Dr2, 2 Oct. 1935; 2SC2 Dr13, Note, 24 June 1936; S. H. A., C. S. G. 29 Apr. 1936; Papiers Flandin, 74, 29 Mar. 1936; D. D. F. II, 2, No. 375; M.S. Alexander, 'Maurice Gamelin and the Defence of France', Diss. University of Oxford 1982, pp. 207–8, 228–35; P. LeGoyet, *Le Mystère Gamelin* (Paris, 1976), p. 108.

47. Schw. 2SC2 Dr12, 17 Apr. 1936; M. Alexander, 'Gamelin', pp. 169–71.
48. S.H.A., C.P.D.N., 29 July; D.D.F. II, 2 no. 480; Schw. 'Rapport', 31 Mar., 1 Apr. 1936.
49. *Ibid.*, SC4 Dr3, 20 Apr. 1937; S.H.A., 'M.M.F. Prague', Circular, 13 Mar.; 'Roumanie A.M.', 1 May 1936.
50. Schw. 1SC2 Dr8, 7 Apr. 1936.
51. D.D.F. II, 2, nos. 23, 138; Schw. 1SC2 Dr8, 24 Mar., 22 Apr. 1936.
52. Having, to the dismay of the French and Czechs, peddled his Austrian interests in Berlin in January 1936, Mussolini told the French in April that once satisfied in Africa, Italy would 'defend the line of the Danube, particulary Austria, with all of its force'. Of Czechoslovakia, he made no mention. D.D.F. II, 1, no. 34; 2, nos. 46, 62, 90; Papiers Flandin, 'Conversation Cerruti fin avril 1936'; D.G.F.P. C, IV, no. 485; Czech T–120, 1041/1809/414080.
53. Observing the ill-feeling between French politicians and the military over the Rhineland affair, and the diplomats' lassitude at the prospect of a camouflaged German *coup* in Austria, Weygand's *protegé* on the general staff, General Georges, considered that Gamelin's strategic plans should be shelved until the politicians understood that all future governmental consideration of military action depended on Italian and Polish dispositions. Schw. 1SC2 Dr8, 4, 21, 22 Apr. 1936; D.D.F. II , 2, nos. 113, 138.
54. Schw. SC4 Dr3, C.H.E.D.N., 17, 20 Apr. 1937; Dutailly, pp. 51–2.
55. German military planning against Czechoslovakia was triggered by serious discussion of a bilateral Franco–Soviet pact from March 1935. E.M. Robertson, *Hitler's Pre-War Policy and Military Plans* (London, 1963), pp. 89–91.
56. J. Joll, *Europe Since 1870* (London, 1973), p. 64.
57. *L'Oeuvre de Léon Blum* (Paris, 1954–), IV–2, pp. 364–5.
58. After 7 March, the Polish foreign minister played a double game, offering mobilisation only when certain of French inaction. Prague, the most supportive of allied governments, merely promised to follow the French lead, whatever that might be. D.D.F. II, 1, *passim*; 2, nos. 71, 255; S.H.A., 'Pologne A.M.', 15 April 1936; D.G.F.P. C, V, nos. 61, 106, 173; Czech T–120, 1041/1809/414086–7, 414091–3, 414096.
59. D.D.F. I, 12, nos. 366, 390; II, 1, nos. 256, 270, 308, 424, 476, 495.
60. S.H.A., 7N3107, 18 Apr. 1936; M.A.e., 'Tchécoslovaquie', 20 Oct. 1935; D.D.F. II, 2, nos. 291, 304, 365. Czech identification with Ethiopia as a blameless victim of aggression extended to sending arms to Addis Ababa, a manifestation of League loyalty which rankled with Mussolini. Czech T–120, 1041/1809/414089.
61. D.D.F. II, 2, no. 369; Schw. 1SC2 Dr9, 24 June 1936.
62. *Ibid.*, 25 June. Gamelin does not figure among the vocally anti-Bolshevik generals of Schweisguth's journal. Faced with the social turbulence of early June, his only recorded comment was 'Give an

example of silence in all domains'. *Ibid.*, 'Rapport', 9 June 1936. At the Riom trial in 1941, however, Gamelin, characteristically refusing to speak out, circulated a memorandum in which he blasted 'the criminal demagoguery of the Popular Front. . . which dragged us to the bottom of the abyss.' Papiers Blum, 3BL3 Dr1, p. 21.

63. Schw. 1SC2 Dr9, 25, 27, 30 June; 1SC2 Dr10, 8 Oct. 1936; D.D.F. II, 2, nos. 357, 419.

64. *Ibid.*, I, no. 332, 2, nos. 254, 272, 432, 452; Commission des Affaires étrangères, 30 July; Schw., 1SC2 Dr10, 15 Oct. 1936.

65. Mussolini's demands in June 1936 included efforts to persuade England to lift its anti-Italian assurances to the Mediterranean states; a conciliatory ministerial declaration by the Popular Front; and action to spare Italy problems at Geneva over the recognition of its Ethiopian conquest. D.D.F. II, 2, nos. 289, 311, 324, 328, 329; Papiers Massigli, 'Violations de la Rhénanie' 2 July 1936; J. Barros, *Betrayal From Within* (New Haven, 1969), p. 120; G. Ciano, *Ciano's Diplomatic Papers*, ed. M. Muggeridge (London, 1948), p. 7.

66. *L'Oeuvre*. . . IV–2, p. 381.

67. Barros, pp. 126–40; D.D.F. II, 3, nos. 239, 277, 281, 286, 318, 329.

68. Schw. SC4 Dr2, C.H.E.D.N., 5 Nov. 1936.

69. S.H.A., 7N3032, 22 May 1935; Szembek, pp. 68–9.

70. M.A.e., 'Pologne', 26 Oct.; S.H.A., 'Pologne A.M.', 11 Dec. 1935; *ibid.*, 'Pologne Rambouillet', 29 Jan. 1936; *ibid.*, 7N3000, 3 Feb.; D.D.F. II, 1, no. 106; 2, no. 419.

71. *Ibid.*, nos. 349, 364; S.H.A. 7N3012, 1 July; *ibid.*, 7N3000, 2 July; *ibid.*, 7N3032, 20 July 1936; P.R.O., F.O. 371, 20764, C6144/981/55. The allegation made by the French Ambassador in Warsaw, Léon Noël, that the Blum government could have dismissed Beck as a precondition of its arms aid will be challenged in this author's forthcoming study.

72. Papiers Daladier, 1DA7 Dr2, 30 July, 13, 14 Aug. 1936; Czech T–120, 1041/1809/414109–10; *L'Oeuvre, IV–2, pp. 369–70.* A central political issue was Polish collusion in German propaganda falsely charging that Czechoslovakia was an aircraft carrier for the Soviet Union. The Czechs and Russians carried on sporadic talks about air co-operation, but did not proceed to the construction of enormous airfields for common use, as Goebbels' 'preventive journalism' claimed.

73. From late 1936, as Belgium accelerated its move into neutrality, Beck deemed the French alliance virtually useless. F.R.U.S., I (1937), pp. 77, 91. Powerful affinities developed in this period between Belgian, Polish and Roumanian neutralism on such issues as intensified Franco–Soviet relations and French/Soviet passage.

74. Papiers A. d'Ormesson, 14 July 1936; P.R.O., F.O. 371, 19880, C7507/92/62, C7102/92/62, C7262/92/62. Soviet defensive and offensive advantage coincided in the objective of Polish passage. The Russians reckoned that a German attack on the Soviet Union would only be

possible through Poland, while the most effective aid they could give to Czechoslovakia would be to attack eastern Germany through Poland. In terms of complementarity of railroad gauges, there was no question that the mass of the Red Army would have to pass through Poland rather than neighbouring Rumania. F.R.U.S. I(1936), p. 200; T. Taylor, *Munich: the Price of Peace* (N.Y., 1980), p. 453.

75. Papiers Massigli, 'Europe centrale', 27 June; Papiers A. d'Ormesson, 14 July 1936; P.R.O., F.O. 371, 19499, R4616/1/67; 19880, C6630/92/62.

76. *Ibid.*, 20436, R4727/1627/92; D.D.F. II, 2, nos. 238, 295; 3, nos. 174, 198, 428, 464. The Popular Front's acute dilemma in central Europe was articulated in a November 1936 warning to Moscow: 'A psychosis is being created according to which the Soviet *entente* leads to communism. This fear tends to neutralise the fear inspired by the German menace and to paralyse the. . . co-operation of peaceful powers at the very time that it should intensify.' *Ibid.*, no. 472.

   To similar Czech complaints, the Russians retorted: 'Bolshevistic propaganda in these countries if it exists is an absolute dwarf against the systematic and brilliant propaganda of Germany. It would be good if. . . [Rumania and Yugoslavia] concerned themselves with the German danger before it is too late.' Czech T–120, 1143/2028/444464.

77. D.D.F. II, 3, nos. 88, 100, 174, 232, 250, 254, 294, 306, 328, 469; Czech T–120, 1041/1809/414108–9.

78. D.D.F. II, 3, no. 334; Schw. 1SC2 Dr10, 22, 30 Oct.; 30 Nov.; for the German military *attaché's* anti-Bolshevik exertions *vis-à-vis* Gamelin's aide, Petitbon, *ibid.*, 6 Oct. 1936.

79. *Ibid.*, 2SC2 Dr7.

80. S.H.A., 7N1522–1. 9 Mar.1937.

81. Schw. 1SC2 Dr10, 20 Oct. 'Rapport,' 26, 27, 31 Oct., 7 Nov. 1936.

82. D.D.F. II, 2, no. 372; 3, no. 457; Papiers Massigli, 'L'Europe centrale,' 8 July 1936; Schw. SC4 Dr2, 20 Apr. 1937; Col. J. Delmas, 'Les exercises du Conseil supérieur de la Guerre 1936–7 et 1937–8,' *La Revue historique des armées,* 4 (1979).

83. Germany actually engineered the *rapprochement* between Italy and Yugoslavia, for which the French had tried since the mid-1920s, and this despite extreme Yugoslav fears of Italy as recently as June 1936. C. Macartney, A. Palmer, *Independent Eastern Europe* (London, 1962), p. 356; J. Hoptner, 'Yugoslavia as Neutralist,' *Journal of Central European Affairs*, 16 (1956); Papiers Massigli, 'Italo–Ethiopie,' 1 May 1937; and above, note 30.

84. Schw. 1SC2 Dr12, 19 Mar., 9, 13 Apr., 26 May 1937; P.R.O., F.O. 371, 20702, C3685/532/62; F.R.U.S. I (1937), pp. 94, 97.

85. Schw. 1SC2 Dr12, 8 Apr., 29 May 1937; D.D.F. II, 5, no. 480; 6, no. 35.

86. *Ibid.*, 1SC2 Dr13, 17 June 1937.

87. O. Bullitt, *For the President, Personal and Secret* (Boston, 1972), p. 222.

88. Papiers Massigli, 'L'Europe centrale', 12 February 1937.
89. During Blum's government, the Czechs twice tried unsuccessfully to reach agreement with Germany, secretly in late 1936, then with Paris' assent in the spring of 1937. G Weinberg, 'Secret Hitler–Beneš Negotiations in 1936–7,' *Journal of Central European Affairs* 19, no.4 (1960), pp. 366–74; F.R.U.S. I (1937), pp. 77–9; D.D.F. II, 5, nos. 217, 228.
90. The highly charged complexities of Blum's response to the Czechs' plight will be a major focus of the author's forthcoming study; for Churchill's contacts with Prague, Czech T–120, 1143/2028/444495–7.
91. D.G.F.P. D, 1, nos. 22, 63; Earl of Birkenhead, *Halifax* (London, 1965), pp. 368–70.
92. D.D.F. II, 8, no. 432; 9, no. 73; Delmas, p. 47; see also S.H.A., 5N579, Louis Buisson's impassioned note, 'L'Alliance France–Italie C'est du Point de Vue Militaire La Paix de l'Europe Assurée,' 13 Mar. and Gamelin's drier appraisal, *ibid.*, 27 Apr. 1938.

   In September 1938, before the staged Sudetendeutsch revolt provoked Chamberlain's personal diplomacy, Gamelin again pressed for negotiations, ostensibly to retain Czechoslovakia as a strategic piece in the French system. He envisioned a Czechoslovakia defensively reorganised like Belgium, with an elaborate system of national redoubts – his answer to minority problems within a rump Czech state. Gamelin in the fall of 1938 predicted an imminent German attack in the west, in which a reduced Czechoslovakia might still play a part in a water-siphoning system to contain the German inundation. D.D.F. II, 11, no. 65.
93. Papiers Daladier, 2DA1 Dr3, 'Munich', pp. 70, 95–7; Papiers Blum, 3BL3 Dr1, p. 16. The best account of France's policy at Munich is Anthony Adamthwaite's *France and the Coming of the Second War*. See also J-B. Duroselle, *La Décadence*, R.J. Young, *In Command of France* and Telford Taylor, *Munich: the Price of Peace*.
94. W. Deist, *The Wehrmacht and German Rearmament* (London, 1981), pp. 88–9; Adamthwaite, *France*, pp. 226–7, 234; see also the simulation of multilateral military options in 1938 in Williamson Murray's *The Change in the European Balance of Power 1938–9* (Princeton, 1984), pp. 217–263.
95. The Blum government's rapid adoption of the September 1936 rearmament programme was a direct, undoctrinaire response to the provocation of Hitler's extension of German conscription. R. Frankenstein, *Le prix du réarmement français* (Paris, 1982), pp. 72–7.
96. On the transition in 1938 from the Popular Front period to the Daladier government, a government 'free of socialist allegiance and soon opposed to Communism,' Gamelin asked rhetorically in his Riom memorandum: 'In the realm of foreign policy,. . . was not the damage already done in such a way that it could not be repaired?' Papiers Blum, 3BL3 Dr1, p. 14.
97. Georges, cited in Dutailly, p. 57; Schw. 1SC2 Dr11, 24 Feb. 1937.

98. Gamelin's calculations in 1939 have been brilliantly explored in an unpublished essay, 'La France devant l'Allemagne et la guerre au début de septembre 1939' by J-L. Crémieux–Brilhac. By 1939, cynicism was blatant in Gamelin's planning, e.g. in his May 1939 promise to the Poles of a bold French relief offensive within three weeks of a German attack.

99. The Breda variant, the French sprint to stem the German flood in Holland, was intended to pin down the German attack in northern Belgium. Gamelin thus continued to transfer precious tank divisions to the north even as German armoured divisions appeared on the Meuse. Jacques Minart, *P.C. Vincennes, Secteur 4* (Paris, 1945)', pp. 92–3; Don Alexander, 'Repercussions of the Breda Variant.' *French Historical Studies*, Spring 1974, p. 488.

Don Alexander argues that the disastrous Breda variant could have been separated from the Dyle manoeuvre, the French advance into Belgium, which he considers justified. He wrongly assumes, however, that the Breda variant was a 'new concept' in French strategic planning (pp. 464, 479). In fact, Breda and Dyle were inextricable for Gamelin who had projected the move into the Low Countries from the mid-1930s, see above p. 143 and cf. Minart, p. 157.

100. As Don Alexander explains in his seminal article, 'Gamelin squandered his strategic reserve in Holland, forcing Georges to replace these forces [originally situated within reach of the critical Ardennes hinge]. . . with France's remaining reserve units.' Crucial reserves then, including French tank units designated to repulse a German onslaught, were shifted northwards with execution of the Breda variant. It is true that sizeable reserves remained behind the Maginot line, but these troops were without any contingency planning for counterattack. D. Alexander, pp. 469, 472, 479, 485–7. Minart refers to a 'dead letter' order by Gamelin to reorganise the reserves behind the Maginot line into a usable strategic reserve. Minart, p. 80, n. 2.

101. Compare this passage from a fine recent article on France's collapse in 1940: 'There was a serious incongruity in the outlook of virtually all French generals. While committed to the strategic defence in the early stages of a war, they devoted the bulk of their attention to offensive tactics. For all their fear that Germany might achieve surprise and penetrate into France, they gave little thought to what operational manoeuvers, with what types of forces, would be necessary to rescue the situation in that case.' Lee, p. 61. From Gamelin's opening stamp on French defence planning, *Plan D bis*, through May 1940, his closefisted and reckless strategy for a cut price war on the peripheries expressed, repressed and sublimated a fear of not being able to hold the Germans again. I am indebted to Philip Bankwitz for this formulation in the language of depth psychology.

5. Anglo-Italian Rivalry in the Mediterranean and Middle East, 1935–1940

STEVEN MOREWOOD

'If for others the Mediterranean is a route, for us Italians it is life'

So, in November 1936, did Benito Mussolini capture the essence of Anglo – Italian rivalry. Italy, its shores totally enclosed by the Mediterranean, was yet denied the dominance of that sea by Britain, who controlled both exits, Gibraltar in the west, Suez in the east. This study will seek first to define Italian and British interests in the Mediterranean and Middle East; to examine how their rivalry developed, especially during the Italo – Ethiopian war; to explore the search for a *modus vivendi* in the later 1930s; to compare their opposing military strategies; and finally to summarize the events and reasons leading to the extension of the war in Europe to the Mediterranean and Middle East in the summer of 1940.

I

Following the First World War, Britain largely secured its territorial and strategic objectives in the Middle East. Egypt, although granted

167

nominal independence in February 1922, was still very much under British control; neighbouring Sudan, technically an Anglo – Egyptian condominium, was in reality a British protectorate. Palestine and Iraq were placed under British mandate – the former acted as a buffer against any attacks upon the Suez Canal from the east, the latter was important as a source of oil. Iraq became independent in 1932, but only after a treaty had provided for the maintenance of British land and air forces in the country and for their unimpeded movement through it. In addition, Egypt, Iraq and Palestine formed vital links in the developing imperial air routes connecting the empire. Although not under direct British tutelage, Iraq represented a further important source of oil with an annual production of seven million tons by 1936, which could be switched to meet deficits east or west provided the Mediterranean remained open to shipping. This little emphasized factor was to be one of the underlying reasons for Britain's appeasement of Italy.[1]

The beginning of the First World War saw Italy with only a limited colonial empire dating from the late nineteenth century and consisting of Eritrea and part of Somaliland in the Red Sea region and Libya in North Africa. Italy had hoped to enhance its empire considerably when it deserted Germany and sided with the Allies in 1915 – indeed, there were promises to this effect (see Chapter 1).[2] At the end of the conflict, however, the western powers refused to relinquish their Red Sea colonies despite making rich gains in other areas. The modest territorial concessions meted out to Italy caused considerable resentment which carried over into the Fascist era.

To maintain its position in the Middle East, Britain relied heavily on its prestige as a great power, recently victorious, backed, where required, by military force. Until the 1930s coercion normally took the form of air strikes supported by armoured cars, which provided a cheap and fast-acting means of suppressing insurgent natives. Local levies were also used. The army, based mainly in Egypt, was deployed to reinforce outlying territories (such as Palestine in 1929) while the navy exercised gunboat diplomacy – especially against troublesome Egyptian governments – and showed the flag. Provided no serious external threat arose, British hegemony could be maintained at a relatively low cost.

It was to be Fascist Italy who would provide the threat. Until recently Mussolini has been portrayed as an opportunist whose foreign policy had no consistent aims; a portrait largely derived from the writings of Gaetamo Salvamini, the anti-Fascist historian, and recently renewed by Denis Mack Smith.[3] Latter day commentators have largely rejected this view and stressed the similarities of his ambitions and those of his predecessors. Richard Bosworth maintains that the aims of liberal and Fascist Italy were essentially the same – to achieve great power status via an African empire – while recognising that the methods of diplomacy were different.[4] In the early 1970s Enzo Santorelli offered convincing evidence that Mussolini had consistently sought to dominate the Mediterranean and the more serious view of the dictator was epitomised by the start of a multi-volume biography. Another authority has suggested that Mussolini had a programme which was established in its essential details by the mid-1920s, including an interest in exploiting an eventual break-up of Ethiopia.[5]

At Fiume in 1919, three years before coming to power, Mussolini had declared that 'the first thing to be done is to banish foreigners from the Mediterranean, beginning with the English'. His short-lived occupation of Corfu in 1923, which he was compelled to call off because of the threat of decisive British naval action, showed the dictator that he was as yet in no position to pursue his ambition. He therefore instigated measures to strengthen his armed forces and meanwhile pursued a more cautious and ostensibly pro-western foreign policy, receiving in succeeding years several leading British statesmen in a friendly spirit. Britain did its best to foster this attitude. To curb Italian resentment at not being granted an African mandate at Versailles, it ceded Transjubaland and the Jarabub oasis, a stronghold of the rebellious Senussi, to Italy in 1924–5, and in the 1927 Rome Agreement attempted to demarcate respective spheres of interest in the Red Sea region.[6]

Italian co-operation over European issues – in particular its adhesion to the Locarno Treaty of 1925 and the Kellogg – Briand pact of 1928 – tended to blind successive British governments to the fact that Italy remained subjectively a 'have-not' power. As early as April 1926 the British Foreign Office recognised that, although the possibility of war with Italy was 'remote', it was already a 'disturbing element' in international relations.[7] Throughout 1933 and 1934 Mussolini had declared that the League of Nations and its principles were unworkable and he intimated that he might follow Japan and Germany in leaving the international peacekeeping organisation. Despite this in November 1933 the British cabinet characterized Italy (with France and the United States) as a friendly power against whom no major defence preparations were necessary. The development of Italy's air arm, the *Regia Aeronautica*, to the status of the world's largest air force, was ignored despite the pleadings of the commander-in-chief Mediterranean fleet, Admiral Sir William Fisher, who maintained that this made the position of Malta, his force's principal base, exceedingly vulnerable. The chiefs of staff, preoccupied with defence preparations against Germany and Japan, found it more convenient not to consider Italy as a likely threat which allowed them to tolerate the Committee of Imperial Defence's long and inconclusive deliberations as to how Malta might best be defended.[8]

The chiefs of staff would have been wiser to heed Fisher, more especially as Malta had already been the scene of Anglo – Italian rivalry. There were political reasons for concern. Although a British colony, the island had strong Italian links, particularly through the Roman Catholic Church. Indeed, Italian had survived as a rival language to English, and was used as a second language by the clergy, traders and members of the independent professions. Most of the islanders spoke the Punic language of their forebears. In 1929, Malta's new governor, Lord Strickland, tactlessly banned the use of Italian in all government offices. Following the Lateran agreements of February 1929 Mussolini came under considerable pressure from the Vatican to reverse this decision. Duting and after 1929 Italian educational establishments on Malta were opened or extended, where minimal fees were charged in a blatant attempt to compete with state schools. The Italian newspaper *La Tribuna* made personal attacks upon Strickland which were authorised by Mussolini. The campaign reached its height in the winter of 1931–32 with a series of pro-Italian demonstrations on Malta which culminated in the election of the pro-Italian Nationalist party the following summer. Despite Mussolini's assurances to the British government that 'no sane Italian cast an eye on Malta', the admiralty made apparent its concern over the island's future as the principal British naval base in the Mediter-ranean. Following this, in November 1933, London dismissed the Nationalist party from office and suspended the constitution. The deteriorating situation in Europe brought about by Hitler's rise to power and Anglo – French complicity over naval reductions discour-aged Mussolini from further antagonizing Britain over Malta, and until late 1934 he let the language issue drop. But thereafter British authorities had to provide against espionage and sabotage by Italian residents in Malta, some of whom belonged to the Fascist party. From autumn 1935 onwards the British also had to reckon with the possibility of disruptive action by the large Italian community in Egypt.[9]

Another area of potential Anglo–Italian rivalry was the Red Sea. Strategically vital to a Singapore-bound fleet using the Suez route, its sea lanes were also important for British army transports travelling to India or carrying Indian troops to Egypt or Iraq. British policy, therefore, dictated that no alien power must control any Red Sea islands or both its coastlines. It was at the southern end, where Italy had unsuccessfully claimed the Farasan Islands in 1919, that Britain appeared to be most vulnerable. The Yemen remained free of British influence and consequently became the subject of Italian penetration. In September 1926 the two powers concluded a treaty of amity and commerce and Italy began supplying the Yemen with arms which encouraged incursions into the Aden Protectorate, forcing the British air force, the RAF, to mount air attacks to repel Yemeni forces. Elsewhere in the region Britain was more secure against Italian penetration. A continuous chain of British-protected sheikdoms and sultanates stretched along the south and east coast of the Arabian peninsula from Aden to Kuwait.

The 1927 Rome agreement marked an attempt by Britain to stem Italian influence in the Red Sea and to diffuse a potentially explosive situation. Both powers agreed to respect the independence of the Arab states on the Red Sea coast of Arabia and to oppose the establishment of any European power there. As a further means of upholding the *status quo* Britain supported Ibn Saud, whose various territories were united to form Saudi Arabia in 1932. The Imam of the Yemen did not wish to fall under Italian dominance entirely and so, in February 1934, signed a treaty of friendship with Britain which saw the final evacuation of Yemeni forces from the Aden Protectorate. Unfortunately, this was the signal for the Imam to wage war with his arch rival, Ibn Saud, over disputed coastal territories. Britain gave Saudi Arabia financial aid during the conflict, which lasted between March and May 1934, while Italy supplied the Yemen with arms. Neither power, however, could intervene openly without risking similar action by the other. The victor, Ibn Saud, prudently refrained from attempting to conquer the Yemen and his peace terms were moderate due, it would seem, to his fear of Italy and uncertainly as to whether Britain would intervene.[10]

Italy had inherited from Turkey the dispute over the southern boundary of Libya. Despite Egypt's relinquishment – under British pressure – of the Jarabub oasis to Italy, this still left in dispute an area known as the Sarra Triangle between Libya and the Sudan, a desert waste which the Italians coveted as an aircraft staging post enabling them to reach East Africa from Libya without having to land on foreign territory. By May 1933 their forces had occupied Oweinat Well, an encroachment monitored by RAF reconnaissance missions. That November, at Britain's instigation, talks on the dispute were held in Rome. These collapsed when the Italians cheekily proposed that they should receive not only the Sarra Triangle but also a large adjacent strip of the Sudan. As this would place Italian forces within 18 hours of the Nile, the Sudan defence force was moved into position to forestall unilateral action. In July 1934 further negotiations took place. On this occasion the Italians conceded Britain's case for defining the Sudan's frontiers. The British Foreign Office's representative suspected an ulterior motive for this sudden change of face and suggested that Italian designs on Ethiopia were the reason.[11]

The issue of the undemarcated frontier between British and Italian Somaliland, which involved the grazing rights of British-protected tribes, appeared to be resolved by a joint boundary commission of 1931. The frontier agreement remained unratified, however, and the lingering dispute increasingly involved Ethiopia. The section of Ethiopian territory used by British-protected tribes was regarded by Italy as being within its sphere of influence under the Anglo – Italian Agreement of May 1894. In 1930 Italy occupied and fortified the Wal Wal wells and two years later demanded that local tribesmen, whether under British or Ethiopian protection, must seek permission to use the wells. This marked the start of a more overtly aggressive policy by Italy towards Ethiopia, with contingency plans to overwhelm that country by force being drawn up in November 1932. Haile Selassie, Ethiopia's Emperor since 1930, determined to check these Italian encroachments – which he feared might precede an invasion – by a show of strength. Thus a native force accompanied an Anglo – Ethiopian boundary commission to Wal Wal. Despite British notification to Rome of the commission's peaceful intentions, the Italian commander at the wells was left in ignorance, resulting in a skirmish, won by his superior forces, on 6 December 1934. The available evidence suggests that the incident was not staged by Rome, although it later provided Mussolini with a convenient excuse to invade Ethiopia. Orders were given later in the same month to prepare for an offensive to commence by the following October.[12]

II

All these incidents by themselves were not sufficient to imperil good Anglo – Italian relations, which continued to be governed by the European situation. In July 1934 Italy backed the western powers' opposition to a German *Anschluss* with Austria; in April 1935 at Stresa, Italy joined Britain and France in condemning Hitler's renunciation of the military restrictions of Versailles. Until the summer of 1935 Britain continued to treat African issues as secondary to European ones. Consequently Italy's growing dispute with Ethiopia, arising from the Wal Wal incident, was not discussed at ministerial level at Stresa. Contrary to the popular view, it was the British draft, and not changes suggested by Mussolini, which proposed that the agreement to oppose 'by all practical means any unilateral repudiation of treaties' should apply only to Europe. Again, the British authorities took months to define their strategic interests in Ethiopia following Italy's approach on the subject in January 1935. As many commentators have noted, Mussolini gained the impression from Britain's decision to postpone the League's examination of the Wal Wal incident and France's expression of 'disinterest' in Ethiopia in January 1935 that he could pursue his Ethiopian ambitions without fear of outside interference. More important still, this belief led him to deploy substantial forces in East Africa for the coming conquest of Ethiopia. To have backed down at the eleventh hour when Britain began to mobilise its forces in the Mediterranean, therefore, would have involved Mussolini in a tremendous loss of face and prestige. For the same reason, last ditch efforts by the western powers to appease Italy – the Zeila proposal of June 1935, the tripartite talks of August – were doomed to failure.

British policy, it should be emphasised, sought compromise rather than confrontation with Italy. Many factors underlay this approach including the desire not to weaken Italy's resolve to resist German revisionism; the wish to preserve existing armaments for possible use against Germany and Japan, who were identified as the more serious long term threats to British security; the belief that appeasement could reduce the number of potential enemies. Hardly less important was the fear that Italy's outright victory or defeat in Ethiopia would produce administrative problems as well as unrest for Britain throughout the Middle East and Africa, a view expressed by Sir Samuel Hoare, the foreign secretary, in July 1935.[13] A diplomatic solution therefore seemed essential, and accordingly both western powers maintained their ambassadors in Rome throughout the crisis which followed Italy's invasion of Ethiopia on 3 October 1935. Had the transparently ineffectual sanctions imposed on Italy at Geneva the following month been maintained unaltered then Mussolini would have had no need to threaten Britain with military reprisals. However, the Canadians, much to British embarrassment, proposed that oil should be added to the embargoed items. If this suggestion were implemented it threatened to bring Mussolini's campaign to a halt very quickly. To prevent such an eventuality the dictator used various diplomatic channels to threaten war with the western powers. Mussolini also dispatched an emissary, General Garibaldi, to London to demarcate his terms for a possible settlement. Garibaldi was soon joined by Dino Grandi, the Italian ambassador in London, who took over the later stages of the discussions which took place with Sir Robert Vansittart, permanent under-secretary at the Foreign Office, and Sir Maurice Hankey, secretary of the cabinet and Committee of Imperial Defence. These two influential figures were steadfast believers in the value of Italian friendship. Both strove to persuade Hoare (who initially favoured an oil sanction) and Stanley Baldwin, the Prime Minister, that an accommodation with Italy over Ethiopia was vital in view of the ever growing German threat.[14] Vansittart and Grandi produced proposals which were extremely favourable to Italy, including the control of Tigre province and the Chorcher highlands near Harar. The subsequent Hoare – Laval Plan of December 1935 so reduced these concessions that Mussolini hesitated to accept them, but in the event it was the British House of Commons that repudiated them, since even in their reduced form they strongly favoured the aggressor. The unfortunate Hoare was forced to accept responsibility and resign (though he was quickly back in the cabinet) from a government which only recently had won an overwhelming election victory on a pro-League platform.[15]

Despite Britain's public commitment to collective security through the League, Whitehall had in fact long doubted the efficacy of such a system. The admiralty especially disliked open-ended and unpredictable liabilities which threatened its carefully laid plans to reinforce Singapore. Nor did Britain consider Ethiopia sufficiently important to justify conflict with Italy, as the Maffey Report of June 1935 made clear.[16] Hoare admitted to the French that his government did not particularly sympathise with Ethiopia, which had caused Britain just as much trouble on the Sudanese frontier as the Italians had experienced in Eritrea. Ethiopia had 'no effective government' and 'was a bad neighbour'.[17] Ironically, this had been Britain's position when it had unsuccessfully opposed Ethiopia's entry into the League during 1923.

From late August 1935 Britain dispatched substantial reinforcements to the Mediterranean and Red Sea theatres, but the reluctance of military advisors to contemplate confronting Italy alone was enough to discourage a firm stand. As an excuse for inaction ministers raised the convenient argument that the British navy, impeded by years of disarmament and expenditure cutbacks, could not act. In October 1935 Baldwin broadcast that although the navy would 'in the long run bring . . . victory home . . . that victory would be won at a cost of life unnecessary and wanton'. Again, the same month Lord Hailsham rejected arguments for the closure of Suez to Italian ships because this would mean provoking a single-handed war with Italy which involved 'departing from the whole conception of collective security'.[18] Such pronouncements were designed to prepare the way for the soft sanctions which were implemented against Italy in November 1935. Britain was only prepared to support military (and quickly effective) sanctions, with their attendant risk of provoking war, if it were assured of the armed support of other Mediterranean powers, principally France, and this it failed to obtain because it refused the necessary *quid pro quo* of a practical guarantee of the demilitarisation of the Rhineland.[19] (See Chapter 4).

Not unnaturally, Hugh Dalton, Labour's foreign affairs spokesman, enquiring upon the lifting of sanctions in June 1936, asked why, if the government did not intend that a single ship be sunk in the cause of Ethiopia, such substantial reinforcements had been committed to the Mediterranean and Red Sea areas?[20] The answer lay in Britain's concern to protect its interests should Italy commit a 'mad dog' act against it. In the summer of 1935 Italian threats to obliterate Malta and to attack Egypt were taken seriously in London. And, following the implementation of economic sanctions by the League against Italy there always remained the possibility that, should Italian forces be thwarted in Ethiopia, Mussolini might assail British interests in revenge. So, despite the lack of crippling sanctions – the closure of Suez and an oil embargo – London judged that conflict with Italy remained a possibility as long as the Ethiopian dispute continued. The crisis for Britain was thus less an international emergency than an imperial one. Precautionary steps actually preceded any expected action by the League. Indeed, they began before Italy attacked Ethiopia.[21] Later, British ministers argued publicly that their government could not be expected to act alone in defence of collective security but avoided mentioning that British forces were prepared to take stern counter-measures should Italy assail British interests in the Mediterranean and Middle East.

For some years after 1945 the thesis developed that the failure to check Italian empire building in 1935–36 marked a decisive turning point towards world war. Contemporaries such as Churchill, Liddell Hart and Eden all took this view.[22] Their case rested on the assumption that Britain acting alone could have defeated Italy, bringing about the overthrow of Mussolini and the strengthening of collective security to combat German expansion. In recent years, this scenario has been seriously questioned. Professor Marder and Captain Roskill explained the British chiefs of staff's pusillanimity by reference to their concern that losses sustained in defeating Italy would adversely affect preparations against Germany and Japan.[23] Rosario Quartararo goes a stage further, alleging that the chiefs' strategy for war with Italy was 'chaotic and confused', with the implication that if it had been put to the test, the verdict of 1940 might have been reversed.[24]

The global over-extension thesis can certainly be upheld: the chiefs of staff warned before, during, and after the Ethiopian emergency that Britain could not afford to become engaged in a major war given the present state of rearmament and the uncertain attitude of the Dominions (see chapter 9). Moreover, none of the fighting services regarded the Mediterranean theatre as a suitable or desirable theatre for combat: the army and air force preferred to orientate their training towards European warfare; the admiralty for war in European waters and especially the Pacific. This emerged strikingly during the Rhineland crisis of March 1936 when the chiefs of staff protested at what they regarded as the dangerous concentration of forces in the Mediterranean.[25] Central to this reasoning was the view that Italy was not, nor could ever become, a serious enemy. The joke in service circles during 1935 was that Italy would have recourse to League intervention after suffering defeats by Ethiopia. As Quartararo notes, the chiefs' reports contain an inherent contradiction: on the one hand Italian military capabilities were disparaged; on the other they were magnified to the point where their air force and navy, much weaker than in 1940, were deemed capable of dominating the central Mediterranean.[26] Similarly, the British navy's shortage of anti-aircraft ammunition was presented by those opposing risking war with Italy, such as Hankey, as a fatal weakness when in fact the ability of anti-aircraft fire to destroy aircraft had yet to be proven.

The extreme claims of Italian strength and British weakness are however unsustainable. An examination of the views of the local British commanders responsible for helping devise and implement strategy shows that, in contrast to their superiors, they were willing, even anxious, to risk Italian wrath. In June 1936 *The Times'* editor found Admiral Fisher 'very insistent that the Italians would have had short shrift in the Mediterranean'.[27] Several constituent parts of the strategy, implemented successfully in 1940, were already present in 1935–36, including planned RAF bomber raids against Italian aerodromes and maintenance organisations and a carrier-launched air strike against Taranto naval base. Nor was Italy's newly developed long range bomber, the Savio Marchettie (SM) 81, the trump card that Quartararo supposes. In Spain it only proved effective when protected by close fighter escort. Yet Alexandria, the Mediterranean fleet's main base during the Ethiopian crisis, was beyond the range of Italian fighters operating from Libya. The SM 81's bomb mechanism did not facilitate accurate bombing and it was soon superceded by the SM 79. Moreover, Italy lacked an armour-piercing bomb or torpedo bombers, which make it improbable that any capital ships would have been lost as the admiralty feared.[28] The over-estimation of the SM 81's capabilities reflected a failure of intelligence. Even so, it is apparent that even when intelligence improved during the later stages of the emergency it had no impact on the stance of the chiefs of staff. By May 1936, for instance, they were aware of Italian difficulties in servicing their aircraft. The admiralty even refused to make use of intelligence related to Italian warships and forts in Libya and East Africa which it considered too secret to utilise.[29]

III

Britain's failure to uphold collective security brought about the collapse of the League's authority, for it enabled Hitler to advance by one year his plans to remilitarise the Rhineland. This act, carried out on 7 March 1936, helped to unite Germany and Italy, the very combination which British policy had sought to avoid. Worse was to follow. On 25 November 1936 Germany and Japan concluded the anti-Comintern pact; on 6 November 1937, having become thoroughly embroiled in the Spanish civil war, Italy joined the pact and the following month finally left the League. The British nightmare of a tri-power threat to its empire had become a reality. The chiefs of staff repeatedly made it clear that Britain singlehandedly could not hope to defeat such a combination; it therefore needed to cultivate allies and to reduce the threat through the appeasement of one or more of the anti-Comintern powers. Part of Britain's dilemma was that its domination of the Mediterranean, and especially of Suez, could equally be seen as a reason for Italy wanting peace or war with Britain. There thus emerged, from 1935, two opposing views on the best policy to pursue towards Italy. Some, including Anthony Eden, the foreign secretary, believed that Britain must stand firm against Mussolini, who would go to war if the opportunity presented itself to unite his African colonies. Others, notably Neville Chamberlain, who became Prime Minister in May 1937, and Hankey, were fully prepared to forgive Italian misdemeanours in the hope that the traditional Anglo – Italian friendship could be restored. The latter group fully appreciated that Italy would take some years to consoli-date its position in Ethiopia, while its increased reliance on Suez to keep its new colony supplied was likely to make it covet British friendship. Their case was strengthened by the state of overall British preparedness for war in relation to that of its potential adversaries. Thus, as Lawrence Pratt has demonstrated, the chiefs of staff, their ministers and the cost-conscious Treasury remained reluctant to sanction any policy which even hinted at possible confrontation with Italy.[30]

Some Foreign Office departments, especially the Egyptian and Eastern, with knowledge of Italian anti-British subversion in the Middle East, were sceptical of the prospects for procuring genuine Italian friendship. Their memoranda led Vansittart to conclude in October 1936 that Italy was 'a great menace to our future in the Near East', which marked a radical change from his earlier position.[31] Eden wanted to build up defences in the region to persuade Italy to come to terms, and he was supported by Sir Miles Lampson, the British ambassador in Egypt. On 27 November 1937 the latter warned that Italy was on its way to gaining a 'pincerlike hold over Egypt, the Sudan and the Red Sea' via ts African colonies. Lampson acknowledged that there were constraints against Italy making war, such as shortages of foreign exchange and oil and the dispersal of its colonial forces. But, he warned prophetically, these were not suf-ficient to deter Mussolini, provided that he could count on Germany and Japan 'to create diversions elsewhere'. Moreover, if French participation were in doubt, 'the chance of such a gamble would be increased'.[32]

The services exerted considerable pressure on the Foreign Office to improve relations with Italy, which would allow them to concentrate against Germany and Japan. Eden had to bow to the combined weight of service and ministerial opinion which favoured acceptance of Mussolini's offer of a 'gentleman's agreement'. Concluded on 2 January 1937, it put on record both parties' mutual interest in maintaining peace and affirmed that their respective interests in the Mediterranean were not incompatible. Eden had wanted the agreement to be less cosmetic but failed to win agreement to his proposal to ask Italy to conform to League procedures. Mussolini's reinforcements to General Franco, the very day that the agreement was signed, destroyed its value in Eden's eyes and coloured his attitude towards Italy thereafter.[33]

For Mussolini *detente* with Britain held several advantages: it increased his influence with Germany; it helped to isolate France; it afforded him time to build Italy's armed forces. Nonetheless, as Mack Smith argues, he was essentially a bully rather than a negotiator; Fascism, by its very nature, demanded that concessions be won through fear and force. Mussolini held the erroneous view that the British loathed land warfare. Consequently, he sought a diplomatic victory by massing forces on the Egyptian – Libyan border. This move, first employed during the Ethiopian crisis to deter British military intervention, was to be repeated in 1937, 1938 and 1939. Its apparent success persuaded him that he might treat Britain with impunity, and this was a central cause of the ensuing war in the Mediterranean. To him, Britain was a decadent power with a declining population, an excess of the aged over the young and of women over men, and an empire that was doomed.[34]

It was in Mussolini's interests to refrain from formal alliance with Germany as long as possible so that he might extract concessions from the western powers for his 'friendship'. He was therefore ready to speak the language of appeasement when it suited his purposes. After the conquest of Ethiopia in May 1936 he declared that Italy was now a 'satisfied power' which harboured no designs against the British Empire. Upon the conclusion of the Anglo – Italian agreement in April 1938 he wrote to Chamberlain to assure him that 'there can now be opened a new period of confidence and friendship . . . which accords with our traditional friendship'.[35] Such sentiments were insincere and derived partly from Mussolini's knowledge of British anxieties for peace which he had obtained from the regularly purloined contents of the British embassy's safe in Rome.[36] For

Mussolini no agreement was meant to be eternal. The problem for British diplomacy was, as Lord Halifax once remarked, that the dictators did not play the game. Only three months after the conclusion of the Anglo – Italian Agreement, Chamberlain complained to his sister that 'Musso is behaving just like a spoilt child and it is difficult to know just how to deal with him'.[37] Germany offered Mussolini the hope of realising his ambition of Mediterranean hegemony. The western powers, in contrast, could offer only small concessions. They were reluctant to do more out of fear that further concessions would undermine their prestige and position in the Middle East by impressing the Arab world with Italy's might.

The clash between the rival Whitehall factions as to the best methods by which Italy might be appeased reached its climax in February 1938 with Eden's resignation (see Chapter 8). Space does not permit a full explanation of this momentous event, but it is important to outline the broad issues. Eden believed, correctly, that given his current difficulties over Ethiopia (in a state of semi-revolt), Spain and Austria, Mussolini was anxious to bolster his flagging prestige by reaching an agreement with Britain. Intelligence reports accurately suggested that Italy had acquiesced in the efforts Germany was making to 'Nazify' Austria in exchange for Hitler's recognition of the Mediterranean as an exclusive Italian sphere of influence. Before entering negotiations, therefore, the foreign secretary wanted tangible proof of Italian sincerity in the form of a commitment to withdraw their forces from Spain. Chamberlain, however, was afraid that by stalling talks Britain's overall strategic position would worsen considerably if Italy were to be added to the already formidable list of potential enemies. Moreover, Hitler was due to visit Mussolini in May 1938 and, without a prior Anglo – Italian accord, the Rome – Berlin 'Axis' might become so cemented as to be unbreakable. On 18 February 1938 Chamberlain intervened personally when, with Eden, he spoke to Grandi at 10 Downing Street. At that time German – Austrian *Anschluss* seemed imminent. Chamberlain, whose emissary had been seeing the Italian ambassador secretly since October 1937 to reassure Italy of his desire for negotiations, chose to believe Grandi's denials of the truth of the intelligence reports. Chamberlain was further impressed by the Italian foreign minister, Count Ciano's, argument that it was ridiculous to expect Italy to move troops to the Brenner to prevent an *Anschluss* while it was being menaced by Britain in the Mediterranean. Chamberlain and Eden set out their respective positions in the four-hour cabinet meeting which took place the next day. A majority of ministers sided with the Prime Minister, leading Eden to tender his resignation on 20 February 1938, much to the relief of the Italians.[38]

The Anglo – Italian Agreement which followed brought a temporary relaxation of tension between the two signatories but it did not represent a genuine appeasement in the sense that Italy might again be reckoned as a friendly power by Britain. The agreement was dominated by promises which Italy had broken previously and could break again in the future.[39] Thus, had the rate of promised troop withdrawals from Libya been maintained, 50 000 would have left within a year. As it was, less than 10 000 had departed by September 1938 when they were sent back during the Sudeten crisis and at a time when Britain needed to maintain its troop levels in Palestine to contain the unrest there. Again, although Italian anti-British propaganda subsided temporarily, German propaganda in the Middle East immediately increased, suggesting collusion with Italy.[40] But unreliability was not due solely to Rome. From the Italian viewpoint, Britain's renewed adherence to the 1888 Constantinople Convention, which guaranteed the Suez Canal's use at all times irrespective of flag, could not be regarded as ensuring continued supplies to East Africa – for during the First World War Britain had flagrantly violated the convention.[41]

The climax of Mussolini's contribution to appeasement came at Munich, where his mediation won him western praise and persuaded him that Italy was now a great power. But the tremendous reception which he received upon his return to Rome did not transform him into a peacemaker. Rather, he determined to emulate German ways, ever more convinced that the west would give way under threat. Italian claims, raised on 30 November 1938 against France, called for the annexation of Nice, Corsica and Tunis and for Italian representation on the French-dominated Suez Canal company board of directors. This unwelcome heightening of international tension followed Britain's decision to ratify the Anglo – Italian Agreement which the Italians had requested. Although Italy began implementing certain clauses of the agreement from the date of its signature, the Chamberlain government, mindful of its parliamentary critics, had made the recognition of Italian sovereignty over Ethiopia dependent upon a satisfactory settlement of the Spanish question but following Mussolini's helpful role at Munich, it was prepared to accept that Italy's withdrawal of 10 000 volunteers from Spain was sufficient, even though this was actually less than half of the estimated Italian forces there and took no account of aircraft and technicians.[42]

At Munich Mussolini had invited Chamberlain to Rome for talks. During preparations for the meeting, the British ruled out the concession of an Italian seat on the board of the Suez Canal company on grounds of security; nor would they enter negotiations to delimit the frontiers of Italian East Africa and the surrounding British or British-protected territory, which would only invite Italian demands for transit rights.[43] Britain was not alone in having little tangible to offer. Mussolini himself had no agenda, a fact which belies a recent claim that he saw the visit as an important opportunity to gain British mediation in Italy's dispute with France and for increasing Anglo – Italian commercial ties to reduce Italian dependence on Germany.[44] The Chamberlain – Halifax visit to Rome in January 1939 marked a turning point in Britain's judgement of Italy's amenability to appeasement. Thereafter Britain could at most hope for Italian neutrality in a future conflict involving Germany. The two sides did not progress beyond expressions of loyalty towards their respective partners, France and Germany. Chamberlain warned Mussolini that in certain circumstances the democracies would fight. Unfortunately, he issued the warning at a reception where its meaning was lost. Mussolini, contemptuous of his guests' umbrellas and their craving for peace, decided to reinforce Libya still further, this time in an effort to pressure the French into making colonial concessions.[45] On 30 January 1939 Hitler pledged that any attack upon Italy would bring German intervention in its support. The upshot was that on 6 February Chamberlain publicly and unequivocally pledged British support for France if its vital interests were threatened. In fact, following intelligence which suggested (incorrectly) that Rome had accepted Berlin's proposal for a formal alliance, the British cabinet's Foreign Policy Committee had approved staff talks with France on the basis of war with Germany and Italy, and authorised the discussion of combined operations in the Mediterranean and Middle East.[46]

V

With the greatest reluctance the Chamberlain government recognised that the appeasement of Italy might not succeed. Italy's designated status slowly deteriorated from that of a friendly power (November 1933–July 1937) to that of a potentially unfriendly power against whom limited defensive preparations must be made. Not until

October 1938, however, was Italy classified as a prospective enemy, and French overtures for joint staff conversations on the possibility of war with Italy were rejected throughout 1938 and not pursued until March 1939. Indeed, before 1939 the defence of the Mediterranean and Middle East was considered to be last but one in order of priority. Although in 1938 the Egyptian theatre was made the British army's first overseas commitment, in practice the field force remained in Britain, a reflection of the general staff's determination that western Europe was where it should serve.[47]

The chiefs of staff's 'Review of Imperial Defence' of February 1937 recognised that the 'dispatch of a fleet to the Far East remains the operation upon which the security of the eastern half of the empire depends'. The fleet was to be composed largely of units from the Mediterranean fleet which would mean abandoning the eastern Mediterranean and leaving British interests in the Middle East exposed to Italian attack. The chiefs of staff realised that the ideal would be to make their air and land forces in Egypt self-sufficient for an extended period to deter Italian aggression. However, such a policy would entail major increases to British forces in the region, which the chiefs of staff hoped to avoid through the appeasement of Italy. They were convinced that Italy would not attack British interests unless London was already at war with another major power and unless its intervention might bring about Britain's defeat.[48] As a result, Middle Eastern defences were not strengthened and when Italy began reinforcing Libya in the autumn of 1937, Britain had no anti-aircraft or fighter units in Egypt. Lampson and the local commanders made their alarm apparent to Whitehall. This marked the beginnings of an unremitting campaign by the ambassador for reinforcements, which won the full backing of the Foreign Office. Eventually, Lampson's name became repugnant to the chiefs of staff who dubbed him an interfering alarmist. His warnings might have been without effect had they not been accompanied by the expressed alarm of successive Egyptian governments at Britain's seeming inability to defend them as it had undertaken to do in the Anglo-Egyptian Treaty of August 1936. There was an increasing recognition by the chiefs of staff that, although Italian resources were insufficient for a sustained conflict, Mussolini might attempt a 'lightning war'. The multiplication of Italian aircraft and submarine bases in the Mediterranean after 1937 and the concentration of Italian forces in north and east Africa all suggested such a strategy. British forces in the region were progressively increased, and in March 1939 the service chiefs received approval to accumulate sufficient reserves to hold Egypt for 90 days, while reinforcements were brought in via the safer Cape of Good Hope route. An overland route from Basra was also prepared in case the Red Sea were closed in the early stages of war.[49]

Although formally British strategy, even after Munich, gave precedence to the dispatch of a fleet to Singapore in the event of trouble with Japan, the need for Britain to ensure the support of its Mediterranean allies and potential allies (France, Turkey, Greece, Rumania, Egypt) had effectively altered priorities by 1939. In March of that year Winston Churchill had suggested that 'England's first battlefield is the Mediterranean'.[50] This theme was taken up by the French in the joint staff talks which belatedly opened at the end of the month. The French insisted that the Mediterranean must take precedence over the Far East; otherwise, they threatened to dissociate themselves from any schemes to contain German aggression in central and eastern Europe (see Chapter 4). Momentarily, the staff talks veered towards the idea of delivering an early 'knock-out' blow against Italy in a war with the Axis powers. The French soon got cold feet about their own proposal to attack Libya from Tunisia, however, while the British military planners concluded pessimistically that in the early stages of conflict no decisive military measures could be taken. But paradoxically the Tientsin crisis of June – July 1939 brought home to British planners that Mediterranean defence must assume a greater importance than that of the Far East. The delicate European situation made Chamberlain and the chiefs of staff fear that the dispatch of a major fleet to Singapore as planned would tempt Mussolini into joining Hitler in a war against the western powers. The situation in the Far East was ironically saved by the Nazi – Soviet non-aggression pact which resulted in the installation of a moderately pro-western government in Tokyo[51] (see Chapter 7).

VI

Italian grand strategy was profoundly influenced by the Ethiopian crisis which showed that Mussolini's future ambitions might be met with British armed opposition. Notwithstanding the prestige of his Ethiopian victory, Marshal Badoglio, chief of the supreme general staff, exercised little influence upon strategy until 1939. This allowed General Pariani, chief of the army general staff since October 1936, to orientate planning towards a future conflict with the democracies in Africa. In December 1937 Pariani set out the premises for future strategy at a meeting of heads of the general staff. When the Germans attacked France, Italy would descend upon Egypt, which seemed 'an easy prey', while remaining on the defensive in the Alps. Because of the difficulty of reinforcing Libya by sea in wartime, the colony was to be stocked with reserves of men and materials beforehand. The plan, agreed between the army and air force, foresaw the dispatch of 178 000 men and 10 000 vehicles. The concept of a 'lightning war' against Egypt and the Sudan found support from Marshal Balbo and the Duke of Aosta, respectively governors of Libya and Ethiopia. Count Ciano was also intoxicated by the idea.[52]

The sheer size of the infantry force intended for north Africa demonstrated the Italians' lack of understanding of the requirements for successful desert warfare. The Italian army planned to wage its 'war of rapid course' with truck-borne infantry rather than heavy mobile armour, which was to prove a costly mistake. It tended to make its assessments in terms of numerical strength alone. On this basis it had been the only branch of the armed forces confident of victory over Britain if battle had been joined during the crisis over Ethiopia. Later, despite being aware of the establishment of a British armoured division in Egypt from September 1938, the Italian army high command remained convinced that Britain's position there was weak. In fact, the Italian army itself suffered from a number of paralysing defects. Its re-equipment was relegated behind that of the other services, thereby depriving it of necessary tanks and vehicles. The wars in Ethiopia and Spain and the enormous number of troops needed to crush revolts in Ethiopia proved further drains. Experience gained in Spain showed that existing light armoured fighting vehicles were inadequate for use against modern forces. Moreover, no Italian tank was designed specifically for desert operations. Although the British suffered from the same handicap, in 1940 the Matilda would prove vastly superior to its Italian counterpart, the Fiat L3.

In January 1939 Badoglio reasserted his authority and opposed plans for war with Britain. He had already warned Mussolini in August 1935 that such a contingency would reduce Italy to the level of a Balkan state. Since Mussolini foresaw a long period of peace with Britain following Munich, Badoglio ordered the planned Egyptian offensive to be abandoned. Visits to Libya in February and June of 1939 convinced him that reinforcements could only support defensive operations. Even so, Pariani and Balbo continued to plan unrealistic offensive operations. In October 1939 Pariani and General Valle, under-secretary of the air force, were dismissed by Mussolini for deceiving him as to their forces' readiness for war. The Libyan and east African offensives were then definitely cancelled by Badoglio in favour of holding operations.[53]

Overall, the Italian armed forces were unco-ordinated, a fact which would prove a decisive weakness. As minister for all three fighting services, Mussolini had insufficient time to devote to any one of them. This unsatisfactory position was compounded by inter-service rivalries. In March 1938 Admiral Cavagnari, chief of the naval general staff, officially rejected proposals for the construction of aircraft carriers – instead the navy was to rely on the *Regia Aeronautica* for air support. Yet fighter and bomber aircraft were not even provided with radio contact with the navy. This farcical situation arose from the air force's conviction that it could successfully pursue a separate strategy, based on Douhet's theory that a single high level bombing attack could so devastate ships and population centres as to win a war single-handed. In reality, Italian bombs remained of such low calibre and Italian aircraft of such poor design for precision bombing that this policy was a non-starter. Although on Badoglio's intervention torpedo installations were fitted to SM 79s, they were never truly torpedo bombers, which were essential if the British navy's dominance of the Mediterranean was to be seriously challenged. While several long range bombers were eventually developed, all the fighters remained of short range which proved a major impediment to operations when war came. Again, although Italy boasted, on paper, of possessing a considerable air force, in November 1939 it was found that only 650 bombers and 190 fighters were actually combat-worthy. Similarly, the inexplicable failure to fit dust filters to aircraft in Libya led to more being grounded than were destroyed by the RAF in 1940.[54] The *Regia Aeronautica* was truly a paper tiger, albeit one which the British had to take seriously in view of their own lack of air strength in the Mediterranean region.

The Italian submarine fleet was another example of quantity without quality. Italy could boast the largest such fleet in the world, yet the boats lacked attack computers and their slowness to submerge made them exceedingly vulnerable. Moreover, British plans to close the Mediterranean to merchant traffic in the event of hostilities with Italy would deprive its submarines of easy targets. Although head of the most efficient armed service, Admiral Cavagnari was prepared to do battle with the British navy only if his force was superior in numbers and equipment. He hoped, not without reason, that the German and Japanese threats would so weaken the British Mediter-

ranean fleet as to allow his own to dominate the eastern Mediterranean.[55] Despite their weaknesses, Italian forces ought to have
proved capable of capturing Malta, of penetrating further into Egypt
than they did, and of occupying a Balkan state. That they did not do
so was a reflection of the inefficiencies of the Fascist regime. As John
Whittam comments: 'Propaganda replaced realistic planning, bombastic speeches and slogans the careful evaluation of strategies.'[56]

VII

Fascist Italy did not only pose a military threat to Britain and France
but systematically attempted to subvert their respective empires by
means of propaganda and bribery. Throughout the Middle East there
was by the 1930s a strong undercurrent of nationalism which the
Italians sought to harness to their advantage. Radio Bari, a propaganda wireless station, was launched in 1934 after Mussolini's 'Second Quinquennial' speech of 18 March in which he declared that
Italy's main interests lay in Asia and Africa. Its Arabic broadcasts
were not at first particularly anti-British, but once the Ethiopian crisis
began it seized on and exaggerated every British difficulty. In
November 1935, at a time of anti-British riots in Egypt, Bari high-
lighted the contradiction between Britain's efforts to uphold the
independence of the 'savage' Ethiopians and her policy of suppressing the civilised Egyptians. Similarly, the outbreak of the Palestine
rebellion in April 1936 provided Bari with the opportunity falsely to
accuse the British of committing atrocities against Muslims.[57] For
several years the British preferred to limit their response to diplomatic protests. By 1937, however, the station's almost incessant anti-
British tirades had persuaded the cabinet to respond in kind. The
BBC reluctantly agreed to undertake broadcasts in Arabic from
Daventry which provided straight news rather than propaganda.[58]

Neither side was as effective with its propaganda as was hoped:
both were regarded by the Arab world as imperialist powers. But for
a time Mussolini proved successful. By November 1936 he had
abandoned plans to invade the Yemen, which apart from risking war
with Britain would have upset his developing pro-Arab policy. During March 1937 the dictator visited Libya to open a new coastal road,
the 'Via Balbo'. There he received the Florence-made 'Sword of
Islam'. The effect of this gesture was not helped by its incorrect shape
and Egyptians ridiculed Mussolini's newly bestowed title of 'Protec-

tor of Islam', since a Christian power could transparently not be a defender of the Muslim faith. Nonetheless, in Libya Italy had done much to dispel Arab mistrust arising from its past treatment of the Senussi, but in October 1938 this benevolent policy was reversed disastrously when, as part of Italy's policy of making Libya a 'fourth shore' of the mainland, 20 000 peasant migrants were sent to the colony amid a blaze of publicity. These were the first annual intake of Balbo's projected Five Year Plan which aimed to ease Italy's problems of *Lebensraum* at home, strengthen the military position in Libya, and convert peasants into landowners. The upshot was that local Arabs were displaced from their best grazing land to accommodate Italian farmers. Not only did this cause great resentment locally, it also provoked violent demonstrations as far away as Baghdad and the French were able to stir up anti-Italian feeling among their Arab populations in Tunisia and Algeria. Mussolini ordered that future emigration must take place quietly, but the damage had been done.[59] Mussolini further alienated Muslim opinion when he attacked the one European state with a Muslim majority.

VIII

The Italian invasion of Albania formed part of the grand strategy which Mussolini outlined before the Fascist Grand Council in February 1939. He declared that Italy, whom he portrayed as a prisoner of Anglo-French predominance in the Mediterranean, must 'march to the ocean': either the Indian Ocean by linking Libya with Ethiopia through the Sudan, or the Atlantic via French North Africa to Cameroon. The timing was influenced by Hitler's unannounced take-over of rump Czechoslovakia, which flaunted the Munich agreement to which Mussolini had been a major party. He ordered the invasion on 2 April in the hope of restoring his influence with Hitler, to forestall any German move in the Balkans, and in the belief that Britain would not take umbrage. While the British had received reports of a possible Italian move against Albania, the actual landing on Good Friday, 7 April, caught them unawares with two battleships and half a flotilla actually in Italian harbours on courtesy visits. They were quickly ordered to sea and the question was raised as to what the British response should be. Albania had been acknowledged as a virtual Italian protectorate since 1919 and, in contrast to conditions in 1935, its membership of the now discredited League of Nations was of no consequence. By 10 April the cabinet had accepted that the Italian *coup* was not part of a co-ordinated Axis plan to launch offensives from the North Sea to Egypt (as the panic-stricken French had suggested), and that it seemed unlikely that Mussolini had decided on war with Britian. At the same time, the cabinet resolved that Italian reassurances were no longer enough and that, as with Germany, a line must be drawn beyond which Italy could not go without risk of war with the western powers. On 13 April Britain and France guaranteed Greece and Rumania against unprovoked aggression and the following month added Turkey to this list. Incensed at what he regarded as western encirclement, Mussolini finally felt provoked into concluding an alliance with Germany, the 'Pact of Steel' of 22 May 1939.[60]

The British government was sensitive to the Axis powers' charges of encirclement, especially as such a perception on the part of its adversaries was held to have been a major cause of the First World War. Moreover, despite recent events, Chamberlain continued to believe that Mussolini could restrain Hitler if only he were convinced that the west did not intend to attack him. In order to secure the *Duce's* good offices the Foreign Office felt that France must first make some of the concessions that Italy had demanded of it the previous November, but the French could not be persuaded that such a policy was in their best interests. In April 1938 Duff Cooper had found great scepticism among French ministers as to the value of the recent Anglo–Italian accord in view of Italy's past betrayal of agreements and allies.[61] In May 1939 Halifax encountered much the same attitude when he saw Edouard Daladier, the French Prime Minister, in Paris. Whitehall believed that he was too amenable to the advice of the anti-Italian Quai d'Orsay. Accordingly, in June Britain's ambassador, Sir Eric Phipps, was recalled from France to discuss the lines of a personal appeal from Chamberlain to his French counterpart. It was agreed, for security reasons, that Britain should continue to oppose the appointment of an Italian director to the board of the Suez Canal company, but if the issue were to be discussed by France and Italy, and if the latter's attitude towards the west became one of genuine friendship, then this concession could be made.[62] Chamberlain's letter of 13 July 1939 failed to move Daladier, who insisted that any concessions to Italy would only make it 'crow loudly and . . . interpret such concessions as a sign of weakness and as an indication that France had no intention of supporting Poland in the matter of Danzig'. During a lengthy interview between Daladier and Phipps, the latter pointed to such recent British concessions to the French viewpoint as conscription and the postponement of the general election (to justify delaying the French elections until 1941), but Daladier maintained his position. With heavy irony he suggested that if Britain wished to mollify Italy it should give them Egypt. The only concession Britain obtained from France was its agreement to return to Madrid gold transferred by the Republicans for safekeeping, in an effort to secure General Franco's neutrality.[63]

IX

Mussolini rushed headlong into an alliance with the Germans, allowing them to draft a treaty which resulted in Italy being committed to support Germany even in a war provoked by them. Only belatedly, on 30 May 1939, did the Germans receive the now infamous Cavallero memorandum which stressed that Italy did not want war for at least three years. Among the reasons given for the delay were the need to create a black army in Ethiopia, to move vulnerable industries from northern to southern Italy, and to incite the Arabs, Indians and Irish against the British. In staff conversations with the Italian high command between April and June, the Germans only discussed conflict against the democracies as a distant objective and gave no indication of their immediate designs on Poland. Yet the day following the conclusion of the 'pact of steel', Hitler had ordered preparations for war against Poland to begin (see Chapter 7).

Throughout the early summer Mussolini resisted Hitler's invitations to visit Berlin to co-ordinate strategy despite his ambassador's warning that otherwise the Germans would act alone. Not until German plans for war with Poland were well advanced was Ciano dispatched to Salzburg where, between 11 and 13 August, he impressed on Hitler the present vulnerability of Italian colonies: Libya's fortifications against French Tunisia were inadequate; Ethiopia was fertile for revolt; the British, because of their control of Suez, could sever Italian communications with East Africa; Turkey threatened the Dodecanese. Hitler, however, was only at this stage envisaging war against Poland, for which purpose Italian belligerency was unnecessary.[64]

A crucial factor in Hitler's calculations was his belief that Britain would be prevented from taking action on behalf of Poland because of its strained relations with Italy in the Mediterranean, with Japan in the Far East, and with the Arab world. Provided this pressure was maintained, he did not believe that Britain's leaders would dare risk losing their empire over Poland.[65] At the end of July Mussolini had foolishly assured Hitler that whenever he decided on war Italy would back him to the hilt and was ready to mobilise at a moment's notice. Hitler maintained his confidence in Mussolini's support until 25 August when he was hit by two bombshells which made him postpone the imminent attack on Poland: first, reports that Britain intended to ratify its pact with Poland, and, soon afterwards, the warning that Italy could not participate in a general war without immediate German material support. A colossal list of Italian requirements arrived the next day which Germany could not possibly meet in full. With the relief of Japanese pressure on Britain in the Far East following the fall of the pro-Axis Hiranuma regime, Hitler feared that a public declaration of Italian neutrality would make British intervention certain and might require him to cancel the invasion of Poland. Hitler engaged in a frantic series of exchanges with his fellow dictator, following which Mussolini promised to continue his military posturing to keep the west guessing as to his real intentions to the very last moment. Italy had begun reinforcing Libya on 16 August; on the 27th, Mussolini undertook to send two further divisions there shortly. These measures had indeed forced the British to initiate preparatory steps in case of an Italian attack. At the same time, the Italians dreaded provoking a concerted Anglo–French onslaught, for which they were unprepared, and by 31 August dared to keep them guessing no longer; that day Ciano secretly assured Britain that Italy would never start a war with the west. The next day, following the start of German military operations against Poland, Italy officially declared its 'non-belligerency' but it was by then too late to stop Hitler, who could now ignore Mussolini's constant offers of mediation in the Polish dispute.[66]

The wisdom of the allied decision to allow Italy to remain neutral and yet continue to strengthen military resources in its colonies has long been debated. According to one authority, since the blockade of Germany was essential to allied strategy, the Italian gap should have been closed. Hitler had indeed come to appreciate the economic value of benevolent Italian neutrality by late August 1939.[67] Even so, the prospect of defeating Germany economically was wildly exaggerated, especially after Germany began to obtain food and raw materials from the Soviet Union and additional resources through territorial conquest. It is true that Italian belligerency in September 1939 might have forced Germany to divert resources to Italy, but had there been an earlier Italian collapse in the Mediterranean theatre, this would almost certainly have prompted German military intervention and with it the exposure of the lack of adequate air and ground defences in Egypt. Italian 'neutrality' did at least allow the British to keep open their normal supply lines to the Mediterranean and Far East. It should also be remembered that British strategy assumed the continued participation of France in the war. Only in the knowledge of the French collapse in June 1940, which led to Italian belligerency, can it be contended that an allied offensive against Italy should have been undertaken earlier. Without this Italy might well have remained sitting on the fence in the knowledge that its intervention would probably result in the collapse of its empire at the hands of British and French forces.

XI

The story of the months preceding Italian entry into the war is largely one of Mussolini's irritation and embarrassment at having to remain neutral together with the efforts of Ciano, decidedly anti-German after his frosty reception at Salzburg, to restrain his leader. Until the spring of 1940, when the German offensive in the west began, Ciano, backed by the king and several key military leaders, including the cautious Badoglio, was successful. The unpreparedness of Italian forces for war, so dramatically revealed by the investigation into military readiness of November 1939, itself acted as a temporary restraint upon Mussolini. That autumn he ordered the armament industries to increase their output as much as shortages of raw materials, machine tools and skilled workers would allow. Badoglio's aversion to war meant that he was able to institute a defensive strategy aimed at securing one year's self-sufficiency in the colonies.[68]

Mussolini had expected a negotiated peace to follow Germany's rapid conquest of Poland. When this did not materialise and Hitler failed to attack in the west until May 1940, Italian leaders ceased to be sure of the war's outcome. In November 1939 Ciano recorded his belief that 'England is growing stronger every day'. The following month, when Mussolini suggested a renewed campaign for Corsica and Tunisia, his son-in-law rejoined that 'in the event we must be ready, because this would inevitably mean war'.[69] The combined

Anglo–French naval forces dominated the Mediterranean and Italy was only too well aware that its industrial centres in the north were vulnerable to bombing raids launched from southern France. On 3 January 1940 Mussolini wrote to Hitler urging caution. Remembering the First World War, the *Duce* predicted a stalemate in the west. Besides, American intevention was likely to prevent a defeat of the democracies. Nevertheless, he assured Hitler that Italy constituted Germany's political, diplomatic and military reserve.[70]

While the British were anxious that Italy remained out of the conflict, their blockade of Germany increasingly affected the Italians. On 10 December 1939 Mussolini threatened to institute countermeasures but was dissuaded by Ciano, who underlined Italy's present inability to oppose them.[71] Three months later Mussolini rejected Britain's offer to supply most of Italy's coal requirements because in return it would be required to provide arms and ammunition. The dictator was neither willing to see Italian war capacity reduced nor to alienate his German ally, who offered to send coal overland to Italy. On 5 March 1940 the British navy impounded 13 Italian vessels carrying German coal. Although they were released following Rome's protests, the incident only served to heighten Mussolini's sense of impotency while Italy remained out of the conflict.[72]

Between December 1939 and March 1940 Mussolini spoke of various dates for Italy's entry into the conflict, the earliest being the latter part of 1940. He conceded to Ciano on 16 March 1940, 'a great deal will depend upon how the war goes'.[73] Thus, when he met Hitler at the Brenner Pass that month, the *Duce* could only promise intervention when Germany began to be victorious against the west. On 31 March he issued a directive which made clear his determination to wage a parallel war to that of Germany in pursuit of Italian ambitions in the Mediterranean. He proposed a broadly defensive strategy save for general naval action in the Mediterranean and attacks against Jibouti and Kenya from Ethiopia. It seems that at this point he was trying to overcome opposition to intervention by showing cognisance of Italy's military unpreparedness, but once in the war, he became immediately more aggressive.[74]

The British were acutely aware that if the war went badly for them, Italian intervention was more likely. On 23 April 1940, in the light of the German occupation of Norway, the Chamberlain government decided to reinforce the eastern Mediterranean to deter Italy. Four days later the admiralty initiated precautionary measures, including the partial closure of the Mediterranean, while in the same month its Operational Intelligence Centre at Malta began remitting daily reports on Italy, whose reinforcements to Libya between February and March 1940 had brought its garrison close to war strength.[75] The allies feared that Italy might be tempted to attack Yugoslavia, which they had not guaranteed against aggression and they did not know how to assist. Mussolini did indeed plan to make such an attack, but he felt that the German offensive in Norway was too far removed from the decisive European theatre of operations and awaited Hitler's attack in the west before comitting himself.[76]

The devastating German onslaught against Holland and Belgium so impressed Rome that the day after its commencement thousands of anti-British posters appeared all over Italy. By 13 May Mussolini had concluded that the Allies had 'lost the war'; he now contemplated intervention within a month and Ciano no longer felt able to oppose him.[77] By 17 May Paris itself was under threat after the Maginot line had been outflanked via the Ardennes and a bridgehead established at Sedan. Badoglio, who had predicted that a German assault on the fortified line would take months and cost a million lives, now began reluctantly preparing for war. Mussolini overcame the king's resistance by wrestling the command of the armed forces in battle from him, and on 29 May an Italian high command was created with the *Duce* as supreme commander.[78] On 10 June Italy declared war on Britain and France.

XII

Britain and Italy had been on a collision course since 1935; whether war broke out depended on the overall European situation. Underlying their rivalry in the Mediterranean and Middle East was Britain's determination to retain its interests there and Mussolini's equal resolve to develop a new Roman Empire in the same region. Clearly, Britain treated Italy as a friendly power for too long, often giving it the benefit of the doubt when a more robust response was required. This was due largely to the hope, which did not vanish entirely until 10 June 1940, that Mussolini might restrain Hitler, though perhaps equally to Britain's global over-extension. Chamberlain and Lord Chatfield (First Lord of the Admiralty, 1933–38), among others, indicated that they would have answered Mussolini's impudence very differently had Italy represented Britain's only threat. In the event, as the German and Japanese menace grew, so did the Italian. Indeed, Mussolini's ambitions in the Mediterranean led him to rely increasingly on Germany to protect his flank in Europe and on Japan's tying down a part of the British fleet. This doomed to failure British efforts to break up the Axis partnership. Once Germany had all but defeated France and Britain in Europe, Mussolini felt able to unleash the ambitious programme he had expounded to the Fascist Grand Council in February 1939. He pressed for access to the Atlantic via French North Africa, an idea soon to be vetoed by Hitler. He sought free access to the Indian Ocean through the military conquest of Egypt, British Somaliland, the Sudan and Aden. In October 1940 he also gave vent to his long cherished ambitions of expansion in the Balkans when he invaded Greece. But his 'parallel war' proved to be a failure due to military incompetence, inadequate equipment and inspired British and Greek resistance. As a result Germany was to intervene to save its ally from total collapse, and in the process extended the Anglo–German conflict in Europe to the Mediterranean.

NOTES AND REFERENCES

1. See S. Morewood, 'The British Defence of Egypt, 1935–September 1939', unpublished Ph.D thesis (University of Bristol, 1985), ch. 1.
2. See R. L. Hess, 'Italy and Africa: Colonial Ambitions in the First World War', *Journal of Contemporary History* vol. IV (1963).
3. G. Salvamini, *Mussolini Diplomatico* rev. ed. (Rome, 1945); D. Mack Smith, *Mussolini* (London, 1981).
4. R. J. Bosworth, *Italy: The Least of the Great Powers* (London, 1979).
5. E. Santorelli, *Storia del Fascismo*, 3 vols (Rome, 1973); B. M. Knox 'Conquest, Foreign and Domestic, in Fascist Italy and Germany', *Journal of Modern History* vol. 56 (1984), p. 14.
6. See P. Edwards, 'Britain, Mussolini and the Locarno–Geneva System', *European Studies Review*, vol. 10 (1980).
7. Foreign Office memorandum, 10 Apr. 1926, *DBFP* (I), vol. II, Appendix.
8. See S. Roskill, *British Naval Policy Between the Wars*, vol. II (London, 1976), ch. IX.
9. See E. M. Robertson, *Mussolini as Empire-Builder. Europe and Africa 1932–1936* (London, 1977), pp. 18–20; P. Kent, *The Pope and the Duce. The Lateran Agreements* (London, 1981).
10. C. Leatherdale, *Britain and Saudi Arabia, 1925–1939* (London, 1983), ch. 6. For Italian policy see R. Quartararo, 'L' Italia e lo Yemen Uno

studio politicita di expansione Italiana nel Mar Rosso (1923–1937)', *Storia Contemporania*, vol. X (1979).

11. Morewood, 'Defence of Egypt', ch. 3; M. Peterson, *Both Sides of the Curtain* (London, 1950), p. 96.
12. See Robertson, *Mussolini as Empire-Builder*, pp. 104–13.
13. Hoare to Clerk (Paris), 29 July 1935, *DBFP* (2), vol. XIV, no. 403.
14. For their efforts see S. Roskill, *Hankey: Man of Secrets*, vol. III (London, 1974), pp. 186–91; A. Goldman, 'Sir Robert Vansittart's Search for Italian Co-operation against Hitler, 1935–1936', *Journal of Contemporary History*, vol. VIII (1974).
15. See R. Quartararo, 'Le origini del piano Hoare-Laval', *Storia Contemporanea* vol. VIII (1977); D. Waley, *British Public Opinion and the Abyssinian War, 1935–1936* (London, 1976).
16. The Maffey Report, 18 June 1935, *DBFP* (2), vol. XIV, App. I.
17. Edmund to Vansittart, 11 Sept. 1935, *Ibid*, no. 553.
18. *The Times*, 26 Oct. 1935.
19. See R. A. C. Parker, 'Great Britain, France and the Ethiopian Crisis of 1935–1936', *English Historical Review*, vol. LXXXIX (1974).
20. Dalton, 23 June 1936, *Hansard Parliamentary Debates*, House of Commons, 5th Series, vol. 313, c. 1711.
21. R. Quartararo, 'Imperial Defence in the Mediterranean on the Eve of the Ethiopian Crisis: July–October 1935', *Historical Journal*, vol. XX (1977).
22. See W. S. Churchill, *History of the Second World War: The Gathering Storm* (London, 1948), pp. 153–4; B. Liddell Hart, *The Memoirs of Captain Liddell Hart* (London, 1965), p. 289; Lord Avon, *Memoirs: Facing the Dictators* (London, 1962), p. 388.
23. Roskill, *British Naval Strategy*, vol. II ch. IX; A. Marder, *From the Dreadnought to Scapa Flow* (London, 1974), ch. 3.
24. Quartararo, 'Imperial Defence', p. 220.
25. For the chiefs of staff's views see *DBFP* (2), vol. XVI, no. 134.
26. Quartararo, 'Imperial Defence', p. 212.
27. Dawson Diary, 26 June 1936, Dawson Papers.
28. For Italian weaknesses see B. M. Knox, *Mussolini Unleashed, 1939–41. Politics and Strategy in fascist Italy's Last War* (Cambridge, 1982), ch. 1.
29. C. M. Andrew, *Secret Service. The Making of the British Intelligence Community* (London, 1985), p. 401.
30. L. Pratt, *East of Malta, West of Suez. Britain's Mediterranean Crisis, 1936–1939* (Cambridge, 1975).
31. Vansittart minute, 15 Oct. 1936. PRO FO 395/536.
32. Lampson to Eden, 27 No. 1937, *DBFP* (2), vol. XIX, no. 350.
33. See C. Seton-Watson, 'The Anglo–Italian Gentleman's Agreement of January 1937 and its Aftermath', in J. Mommsen, L. Kettenacker (eds.), *The Fascist Challenge and the Policy of Appeasement* (London, 1983).

34. D. Mack Smith, 'Appeasement as a Factor in Mussolini's Foreign Policy', *ibid*.

35. Mussolini to Chamberlain, 16 Apr. 1938, PRO PREM 1/ 276.

36. See D. N. Dilks, 'Flashes of Intelligence: The Foreign Ofice, the SIS and Security before the Second World War' in D. N. Dilks, C. M. Andrew (eds.), *The Missing Dimension: Governments and Intelligence Communities in the Twentieth Century* (London, 1984).

37. Neville to Ida Chamberlain, 4 July 1938, Neville Chamberlain Papers, NC/ 18/ 1/ 1058.

38. See R. Douglas, 'Chamberlain and Eden, 1937–1938', *Journal of Contemporary History*, vol. XIII (1978); R. Rhodes James, *Anthony Eden* (London, 1986), pp. 176–95.

39. For details of negotiations see DBFP (2), vol. XIX.

40. See F. R. Nicosia, *The Third Reich and the Palestine Question* (London, 1985), pp. 174–80.

41. See D. Bolech, '"L' accordi di due imperi". L'accordi Italo–Inglese del 16 Aprile 1938', *Politico*, vol. 39 (1975).

42. See. D. C. Watt, 'Britain, France and the Italian Problem, 1937–1939' in *Les Relations Franco–Britanniques, 1935–1939* (Paris, 1975).

43. Cabinet 57(38), 30 Nov. 1938, PRO CAB 23/ 95.

44. R. Quartararo, *Roma tra Londra e Berlino: La Politica estera fascista dal 1930 al 1940* (Rome, 1980), pp. 404–23. For the opposite view see P. Stafford, 'The Chamberlain–Halifax Visit to Rome: A Reappraisal', *English Historical Review*, vol. XCVIII (1983).

45. For details of the Italian attitude see M. Muggeridge (ed.), *Ciano's Diary, 1939–43* (London, 1947) and *Idem* (ed.), *Ciano's Diplomatic Papers* (London, 1948).

46. Morewood, 'Defence of Egypt', ch. x.

47. See G. C. Peden, 'The Burden of Imperial Defence and the Continental Commitment Reconsidered', *Historical Journal*, vol. XXVII (1984).

48. Chiefs of staff's Review of Imperial Defence, 29 Feb. 1937, *DBFP* (2), vol. XVIII, app. 1.

49. Morewood, 'Defence of Egypt', chs. 7–8.

50. W. S. Churchill, 'Memorandum on Sea Power, 1939', 25 Mar. 1939, PRO PREM 1/ 345.

51. See *DBFP* (3), vol. V.

52. See L. Ceva, *Storia della societa Italiana: Le Forze Armate* (Torise, 1981), ch. 13.

53. See Historical Dictionary of Italian Fascism (New York, 1982).

54. Knox, *Mussolini Unleashed*, ch. 1.

55. See B. M. Knox, 'Fascist Italy Assesses Its Enemies, 1935–1940', in E. R. May (ed.), *Knowing One's Enemies. Intelligence Assessments Before the Two World Wars* (London, 1984).

56. J. R. Whittam, 'The Italian General Staff and the Coming of the Second

World War' in A. Preston (ed.), *General Staffs and Diplomacy before the Second World War* (London, 1978), p. 84.

57. See J. Grange, 'Structures et techniques d'une Radio-Bari', *Relatione Internationales*, vol. II (1974).
58. See C. A. MacDonald, 'Radio Bari: Italian Wireless Propaganda in the Middle East and British Counter Measures, 1934–1938', *Middle Eastern Studies*, vol. 13 (1977).
59. C. G. Segre, 'Italo Balbo and the Colonisation of Libya', *Journal of Contemporary History*, vol. 7 (1972).
60. D. Mack Smith, *Mussolini's Roman Empire* (London, 1976), ch. 11; Cabinet 19 (39), 10 Apr. 1939, PRO CAB 23/ 98; C. A. MacDonald, 'Britain, France and the April Crisis of 1939', *European Studies Review*, vol. 2 (1972).
61. A. Diff Cooper, *Old Men Forget* (London, 1953), p. 219.
62. Anglo–French Conversations, 20 May 1939, *DBFP* (3), vol. V, no. 370; Neville to Ida Chamberlain, 10 June 1939, Neville Chamberlain Papers, NC 18/ 1/ 1102.
63. Bullitt (Paris) to Cordell Hull (Washington), 18 July 1939, Franklin D. Roosevelt Library, File 25. On the Spanish gold, see below, p. 266.
64. Mack Smith, *Roman Empire*, ch. 14; Knox, *Mussolini Unleashed*, ch. 1; Foreign Ministry's Secretariat, 12 Aug. 1939, *DGFP* (D), no. 43.
65. *DGFP* (D), vol. VII, app. 1.
66. *Ibid*; D. Irving, *The War Path. Hitler's Germany 1933–9* (London, 1978), pp. 246–52.
67. W. Murray, *The Change in the European Balance of Power, 1938–9. The Path to Ruin* (Princeton, 1984), ch. X.
68. Knox, *Mussolini Unleashed*, ch. 2.
69. Ciano Diary, 30 Nov., 9 Dec. 1939.
70. Mussolini to Hitler, 3 Jan. 1950, *DGFP* (D), vol. VIII, no. 504.
71. Ciano Diary, 10 Dec. 1939.
72. Knox, *Mussolini Unleashed*, ch. 2; Ciano Diary, 6 Mar. 1940.
73. Ciano Diary, 16 Mar. 1940.
74. Knox, *Mussolini Unleashed*, ch. 2.
75. Cadogan Diary, 23 Apr. 1940; F. H. Hinsley *et al*, *British Intelligence in the Second World War*, vol. I (London, 1979), ch. 6.
76. L. Woodward, *British Foreign Policy in the Second World War* (London, 1962), ch. 1; Ciano Diary, 22 Apr. 1940.
77. Ciano Diary, 13 Mar. 1940.
78. Ciano Diary, 29 May 1940.

6. The European Great Powers and The Spanish Civil War, 1936–1939

GLYN STONE

Historians now accept, contrary to the contemporary propagandist claims of Communists and Fascists, that the Spanish civil war was initially a domestic affair, and that foreign interference before the outbreak on 17 July 1936 was negligible.[1] The effect of foreign intervention or deliberate non-intervention after 17 July is another matter. While the ultimate consequences remain a matter of disagreement there is no disputing that it had a major impact on the course of the war. It was, for example, only through the provision of transport aircraft by Italy and especially Germany that General Franco was able to transfer Spanish Moroccan forces to southern Spain during the crucial early weeks of the conflict. And it was only as a consequence of the Soviet Union's provision of arms and aircraft, coupled with the arrival of the International Brigades, that Madrid was saved for republican Spain in November 1936 and the war prolonged for another two years.[2] The present essay examines the motives which led the European Great Powers to intervene or remain aloof and the impact of the war on their relations. As will be seen, the Spanish civil war, while not a direct cause of the subsequent World War, critically influenced the shaping of Great Power alignments in the years before September 1939.

INTERVENTION AGAINST THE REPUBLIC – NAZI GERMANY AND FASCIST ITALY

The response of Germany and Italy to the failed insurrection of the Spanish military was neither spontaneous nor immediate. It was not until 25 July and foreign minister Ciano's meeting in Rome with Antonio Goicoechea, a leader of *Renovación española*, a Spanish monarchist group founded in 1932, that the decision to intervene was taken; Mussolini having previously, on 20 July, rejected a request from the Spanish rebels for aircraft.[3] Hitler's decision to intervene was taken almost simultaneously, in the early hours of 26 July, independently of Italy. Against the advice of his foreign and war ministries the *Führer* responded positively to a request from General Franco for armaments and aircraft which had been presented to him personally at Bayreuth by Joannes Bernhardt, a member of the Nazi *Auslandsorganisation* and formerly director in Morocco of its economics section.[4]

For both Germany and Italy the limited commitment of July 1936 was to expand considerably by the end of the civil war. Throughout its duration more than 16 000 Germans helped the Nationalist forces, although the maximum at any one time was 10 000. These forces included the Condor Legion which consisted of 5 000 tank and air personnel. At their maximum Italian forces in Spain numbered between 40 000 and 50 000 troops including air personnel. German casualties were very slight, amounting to no more than 300 dead. Italian losses were far heavier with around 4 000 dead and 11 000–12 000 wounded. German military hardware consisted essentially of tanks, aircraft and anti-aircraft guns plus a substantial quantity of small arms – machine guns, rifles and revolvers – transported via Portugal. Italy's contribution in this sphere was even more impressive including aircraft, tanks, motor vehicles, artillery and small arms.[5] It is estimated that the total cost of Italian war *matériel* amounted to 6 billion lire (£64 million) while for Germany the cost is variously estimated at between 412 million and 540 million Reichmarks (£35 million and £46 million).[6]

The expenditure of such large resources was clearly a measure of the determination of the two dictator powers to ensure the victory of the Nationalist forces in Spain despite the risks of a further deterioration in their relations with Britain and France and even of a wider European conflagration. In the initial stages of the civil war ideological considerations figured prominently both in Rome and Berlin and continued to exert an influence throughout the conflict. Contrary to the views of certain historians, Italian claims that they were fighting against the forces of Communism in Spain were not mere façade or disguise but were genuinely held.[7] Nor were Fascist fears of a red revolution in Spain and its possible effects misplaced, in view of the increasing popularisation of the Spanish Republican defence including the establishment of revolutionary committees. In this connection the Italian government was not inclined to make a distinction between libertarian anarchists in Spain, of whom there were many, and Soviet orientated Communists of whom there were few in July and August 1936. A victory for the left in Spain held considerable dangers elsewhere since it might encourage revolutionaries in France and all of western Europe including Italy. As Mussolini told his wife, Rachele: 'Bolshevism in Spain would mean Bolshevism in France, Bolshevism at Italy's back, and danger of Bolshevisation of Europe'. The *Duce* and Ciano continued throughout the civil war to regard their intervention in Spain as safeguarding Fascism in Italy. However, the ideological motive remained essentially a negative one. With the possible exception of the Farinacci mission to Spain early in 1937 there was no serious or sustained attempt to convert Franco's regime to Fascism during the civil war.[8]

The ideological motive was also prominent in Germany's decision to intervene in Spain, and also, as in the Italian case, essentially a negative one. Despite the involvement of the German ambassador, General Wilhelm Faupel, with the one genuine Spanish Fascist movement, the *Falange*, there was no intention of seeking to establish a National Socialist regime in Spain; an exercise which Hitler himself believed would be 'totally impossible not to mention superfluous and absurd'.[9] What mattered was the dangerous contagion of Bolshevism. Hitler, referring to his decision of 26 July 1936, five years afterwards, explained that 'if there had not been the danger of the Red Peril's overwhelming Europe' he would not have intervened.[10] The *Führer's* memory was not at fault. Sir Robert Vansittart, the permanent under-secretary of state at the Foreign Office, visited Germany in August 1936 and found Nazi ruling circles obsessed with events in Spain and the threat of Bolshevism: 'this is the constant theme of every man and woman in Berlin; indeed they can think and talk of little else. The obsession [with Communism] is in any case endemic, but Spanish events have reinforced their thesis'.[11] In fact, on 26 July Hitler had warned Joachim von Ribbentrop that a victory for Communism in Spain would in a short time result in the Bolshevisation of France in view of the current situation in that country; by which he probably meant the advent of the Popular Front Government of Léon Blum and their declared sympathy for the Spanish Republicans. The German foreign minister, Constantin von Neurath, was equally apprehensive about the Bolshevik contagion spreading from the Iberian Peninsula to the rest of western Europe.[12] Hitler, sharing the fears that arose from the civil war, also exploited them by extending conscription from one to two years and introducing the Four Year Plan.[13]

This ideological preoccupation was linked in German minds with strategical considerations to produce what Denis Smyth refers to as 'a geo-ideological conception of the international system'.[14] Vansittart, for one, had no doubts but that it was the international strategical dimension of Bolshevism that concerned the Nazi leadership. They had little to fear from 'an internal [Communist] recrudescence which would be ruthlessly crushed'. What they did fear was 'an external convergence, that Communism will extend in Europe and round on, if not encircle, Germany'.[15] The Nazis had no illusions concerning their strategic position. The possibility of a further strengthening of links between France, Soviet Russia and Czechoslovakia, following on from their mutual assistance pacts of 1935 and the victory of the Popular Front in France in the elections of May 1936, was all too real. No doubt they were also alarmed by the more than doubling of Soviet Russia's defence budget in 1936 from 6.5 billion to 14.8 billion roubles.[16] Apart from posing an external threat the strategic consequences of a victory for Communism in Spain would bode ill for the long term racial-imperialist ambitions of the Third Reich in eastern Europe and Soviet Russia; not least because, as Hitler himself revealed in April 1937, at a time of potential military co-operation between the French Popular Front and Soviet Russia, the establishment of a 'Bolshevik state' in Spain would 'constitute a land bridge for France to North Africa' which would safeguard the passage of French colonial troops to the northern frontier of France.[17] On the other hand, a victory for the militarists in Spain would weaken Germany's potential adversaries, in particular France, improve the Reich's strategic defence and enhance its prospects for the conquest of *Lebensraum* in the East; whether as an end in itself or merely a staging post in a phased programme (*Stufenplan*) for world dominion.[18]

Both Germany and Italy recognised the strategic benefits, especially in the naval sphere, which might accrue to them as a consequence of co-operation with a grateful Nationalist Spain; benefits which would clearly be to the detriment of adversaries such as Britain and France. In the summer of 1938 the Nazi general, Walter von Reichenau, outlined them to an audience of National Socialist leaders:

> A state like ours, not being in a position to acquire the necessary *points d'appui* by direct action must fill in the gaps thanks to its alliances. This we have done by means of our Italian agreement embodied in the Berlin–Rome axis, and by means of our intervention on General Franco's behalf. From the point of view of military strategy, we have got at the most vital lines both of England and France. Therein lies the paramount importance of our intervention in Spain.

Reichenau also advised that a victory for Franco in the civil war would provide the opportunity to transform Portugal into a willing satellite of the Axis and thereby secure considerable strategic benefits in the western Atlantic and western Mediterranean with dire consequences for Britain's own naval strategy. Significantly, at the time Reichenau made his speech Hitler was planning a giant battlefleet for war in the Atlantic where he needed bases.[19] Reichenau's observations on Portugal, although officially denied as authentic, were not isolated ones but reflected official thinking in Berlin and also Rome. Indeed, from the outset of the civil war in Spain the German and Italian governments sought to exploit Anglo–Portuguese differences over Spanish policy.[20]

Italy's intervention in Spain was certainly influenced by its strategic interest in the western Mediterranean. According to John Coverdale, from the outset of his regime in 1922 Mussolini thought of Spain primarily in terms of strengthening Italy's position *vis-à-vis* France by denying the latter the possibility of transporting troops across Spain from its north African empire, and that he might also have hoped to obtain bases in the Balearic Islands which intersected the routes between north Africa and France's Mediterranean ports.[21] In taking his decision to intervene Mussolini was aware that a Republican victory obtained with French support implied closer Franco–Spanish relations and the loss of Italian influence in the western Mediterranean. The reverse might be the case if the Spanish military succeeded in their rebellion. To ensure this outcome Ciano insisted in his conversation with Goicoechea of 25 July that in return for Italian support the rebels would adhere to the terms of the 1934 agreement, signed by Mussolini and Spanish monarchists, which bound Spain to denounce a supposed secret Hispano–French pact.[22]

Apart from acquiring the general support and collaboration of a victorious rebel government, the Italians hoped to establish naval and air bases in the Balearic Islands, which would weaken both the French and British strategic position in the western Mediterranean. Indeed, the British authorities were extremely concerned about the presence of an increasingly large number of Italian air force personnel on Majorca between August and December 1936.[23] It is unlikely that in pursuing strategic objectives Mussolini believed he could establish a complete Italian ascendancy in the Mediterranean basin and in the process revive the old Roman Empire, nonetheless a successful intervention in Spain would strengthen Italy's security and that of its African empire while providing some scope for the further advance of imperial ambitions.[24]

The initial expectation of Hitler and Mussolini that the civil war would be of short duration precluded any expectation that intervention in Spain would yield actual military benefits, as opposed to strategic gains. However, as a by-product of the extension of the conflict from a matter of weeks to a matter of years, the Axis powers were able to test their weapons and to train personnel in their use under combat conditions. Indeed, many of Hitler's future wartime military commanders were present in Spain at various times including Generals Janecke and Sperrle of the *Luftwaffe*, Admiral Wilhelm Canaris, head of German Military Intelligence, General von Thomas of the future *Afrika Korps*, General Guderian and General Richtofen.[25] The Germans learned a number of valuable military lessons in Spain which were to be applied during the Second World War. In his address to National Socialist leaders, alluded to previously, Reichenau referred to some of these lessons which included the organisation of defence against air attacks; the superiority of the heavily armed tank as opposed to lighter models (such as the Italian Fiat Ansaldos or the German Panzer Mark I) which had proved ineffective against heavier Russian tanks in 1936 and 1937; the use of motor vehicles in war; the vital importance of spare parts, oil and fuel; and the use of boldness in the conduct of operations in a war of movement. Reichenau also recognised the significance of the civil war for the development of tactical air strikes in support of ground forces. Later, a member of the *Luftwaffe*, General Karl Dunn, was to emphasise that of all the experience gained by the Condor Legion in Spain it was 'that pertaining to the methods of tactical air employment which was most significant and most far reaching in its effects'.[26] While such lessons were indeed learned, others were missed; not least the *Luftwaffe's* assumption that high-performance and well-armed bombers in mass formation could protect themselves against enemy fighters in daylight missions. The result was the very high losses sustained by *Luftwaffe*-trained bomber crews during 1940. The Italians also failed to learn lessons from the Spanish conflict such as the inadequacies of light tanks armed only with machine guns. In 1939 Italy manufactured only 194 tanks armed with cannon.[27]

Connected with their military operations in Spain was the prestige of the Italian and German governments. In the summer of 1936 neither Hitler nor Mussolini required a victory in Spain as a distraction from internal complications; a consideration which certainly figured prominently in Mussolini's decision a year earlier to wage war in Ethiopia.[28] Nonetheless, having committed themselves to the cause of the Nationalists in Spain through their military and economic support and by their *de jure* recognition of Franco's administration in November 1936, it would have been difficult for the two dictators to save face in the event of defeat. Certainly, Italy's determination to maintain its forces in Spain until Franco's final victory, despite mounting costs and casualties, was connected to the prestige of the Fascist regime; and this was true particularly after the Italian defeat at Guadalajara in March 1937.[29]

While it is probably correct to regard actual military considerations as a by-product of Italian and German intervention, it is a mistake, at least in the German case, to view economic considerations in a similar light.[30] If Hitler's initial decision to intervene was motivated by geo-ideological considerations, it soon became clear that the war *matériel* provided from German sources would not be given *gratis* but that the Germans would exact a price in the form of Spanish raw materials in lieu of gold and foreign currency, which were in short supply on the rebels' side owing partly to the success of the Republican government in maintaining control of Spain's gold reserves. In any case the Germans preferred the compensation to be paid in this form because these materials included iron ore, copper, pyrites and sulphur which were vital to Germany's second Four Year Plan, the inception of which coincided with the initial build-up of German aid to Franco's forces. The organisation charged with the task of obtaining and shipping these materials to Germany was the HISMA (*Compāñía Hispano–Marroquí de Transportes*) trading company which worked in concert with another company called ROWAK

(*Rohstoffe–und–Waren–Einkaufsgesellschaft*) which was set up simultaneously in Berlin and which performed the task of distribution within Germany itself.

By exacting such compensation the German government was able to overcome the chronic shortage of foreign currency which limited their ability to purchase essential raw materials on the open market. Also, the Germans anticipated that in the event of a Nationalist victory supplies of such materials would be continued in the event of a general European war.[31] In this last connection the German economic ministry acknowledged Britain's lead in Spain in terms of foreign investment and called for greater German direct investment in order to ensure continuity of supply of essential raw materials. Consequently, in 1937 and 1938 the Reich government sought to create a German owned network of enterprises to extract and acquire Spanish raw materials but the project, code-name MONTANA, was strenuously resisted by the Nationalist authorities and was only partly successful. Moreover, it alerted Franco to the danger of being drawn too closely into the German economic orbit and led him to give a more sympathetic reception to British requirements than might otherwise have been the case.[32]

In contrast to Germany Italy made no concerted or sustained effort to advance its economic interests in Spain by exploiting Franco's dependence on Italian war *matériel*. While it is true that bilateral agreements were signed which provided for partial repayment in the form of Spanish raw materials – notably iron ore, pyrites, cocoa, olive oil, raw wool and coal – the Italians allowed postponement of repayment of a substantial proportion of Nationalist debts for the duration of the civil war. According to a leading authority on the finances of the Spanish civil war, Angel Viñas, the generosity of the Italians was 'the principal way in which the Burgos government could manage to make the international payments necessary to strengthen the war sector of its economy'. Indeed, the relatively harmonious nature of Italo–Nationalist economic and financial relations provided a stark contrast to the ruthless and opportunistic economic policies of the Third Reich in Spain. Later, the Italians lamented their generosity. On 26 August 1939 Mussolini complained to the German ambassador that his country had been 'bled white' by the Spanish civil war which had made enormous inroads on Italian foreign exchange reserves, thereby greatly increasing the problem of obtaining raw materials.[33]

It would appear then that ideological and strategical considerations were uppermost in the minds of Hitler and Mussolini when taking their respective decisions to intervene in Spain in July 1936, and with respect to their subsequent action. Early in the civil war economic considerations acted as a further incentive for German intervention which provided the opportunity to overcome problems of supply of important raw materials for the Four Year Plan. The decision to intervene by both Germany and Italy would have been taken even if the civil war had not provided the opportunity to test new weapons and to train personnel under wartime conditions. Military considerations of this kind should be regarded as a welcome by-product of the Spanish conflagration rather than as a motivation for intervention.

INTERVENTION ON BEHALF OF THE SPANISH REPUBLIC – SOVIET RUSSIA

Unlike the German and Italian cases it is not possible as yet to pinpoint precisely when the Soviet government decided to intervene in Spain on behalf of the Spanish Republic. The initial response of the Soviets towards the outbreak of the war revealed little immediate concern. Confidence was expressed as to the capacity of the Republicans to quell the military uprising. In late July 1936 while individual Communist parties, such as those in Britain, the United States, Poland and France declared their support and solidarity for the struggle against Fascism in Spain, the Comintern remained as unmoved as its Soviet masters in Moscow.[34] During the first three weeks of August the Soviet response was confined to providing financial support derived from collections – in reality deductions from wages at source – amongst Soviet workers. Then, on 22 August, the Soviet government adhered to the Franco–British sponsored non-intervention agreement. By this agreement the export of arms to the Republic was prohibited on 28 August and a non-intervention committee was established in London to ensure compliance. The same day, however, the first Soviet ambassador to be accredited to a Spanish government, Marcel Rosenberg, arrived in Madrid accompanied by a Soviet military delegation headed by General Jan Berzin. A few days previously Vladimir Antonov-Ovsëenko, a hero of the Russian civil war, had been appointed as Soviet consul-general in Barcelona. However, a further month elapsed before the fall of Toledo to the rebels, which left Madrid open to attack, compelled the Soviet authorities to risk a breach with the non-intervention committee by sending large scale military aid to Republican Spain. On 7 October the Soviet representative, Samuel Cahan, warned the non-intervention committee that unless breaches of the non-intervention agreement by Germany, Italy and Portugal ceased immediately the Soviet government would 'consider itself free from the obligations arising out of the [non-intervention] agreement'. That same day the first consignment of Soviet armaments probably left Odessa on board the Soviet vessel *Komsomol* which arrived at Cartagena, Republican Spain's main naval base, on 15 October. The Soviet naval *attaché*, Kuznetsov, was instructed officially to meet the vessel on arrival, and the same day an exchange of telegrams took place and was reported in *Izvestia*.[35]

From October 1936 until the summer of 1938 Soviet military aid to the Republicans was extensive, and included aircraft, tanks, armoured cars, artillery pieces, lorries, machine guns, rifles and mortars. The Soviets also provided most of the Spanish government's imports of oil. During the civil war between 2 000 and 3 000 Russians were present in Spain with 700 as the maximum at any one time. Soviet personnel, with the exception of some pilots and tank crews, did not engage directly in combat; rather they acted in the capacity of specialist advisors and included amongst their number agents of the Soviet secret police, the NKVD, who were active late in 1936 and during 1937 in helping their Republican counterparts to expose and liquidate anarchist and Trotskyist 'subversives'.[36] As a direct consequence of Soviet aid, and in contrast to the limited influence which Germany and Italy wielded within the political counsels of the Francoist authorities, Soviet influence on the political and military organisation of Republican Spain was profound. Increasingly, Republican policies were subordinated to directives emanating from Moscow. Moreover, while Soviet advisors were penetrating many institutions of the Spanish government the membership of the *Partido Comunista de España* (PCE) expanded rapidly. In April 1936 the PCE claimed 50 000 members, by the end of the year the party general Secretary, Jose Díaz, estimated its membership at 250 000. The increase in numbers was accompanied by a rapid extension of the PCE's prestige and authority.[37] However, the change in the fortunes of the PCE, as a direct consequence of Soviet aid, did not presage a Soviet revolution within Republican Spain. Contrary to German and Italian expectations, the Soviet authorities had no intention of 'Bolshevising' the Iberian Peninsula and western Europe. On the defensive, they too approached the conflict from a 'geo-ideological' perspective, which led them to pursue collective security and, through the Comintern, a Popular Front strategy in the mid-1930s.

Prior to 1933 Soviet foreign policy, reflecting the triumph of the doctrine of 'socialism in one country' over that of 'world revolution', was essentially isolationist. The only Communist state in the world, the bastion and supposed hope for further Communist advance at a distant date, the Soviet Union needed time to develop the fundamental industrial and technological capacity so essential for its security in a hostile capitalist world. From 1928 until 1933 rapid and forced industrialisation at home was accompanied by a Soviet search for security through 'the exploitation of friction and antagonism within the capitalist camp'; an approach which ruled out entangling alliances.[38] In 1933 the advent of the Nazi regime in Germany, with its virulent anti-Communist rhetoric, its suppression of the German Communist party, its exit from the disarmament conference and League of Nations and its *rapprochement* with Poland towards the end of the year, created considerable apprehension in Moscow and encouraged the alternative foreign policy approach of collective security, which was favoured by the Soviet foreign minister, Maxim Litvinov, and the *Narkomindel* (Russian foreign ministry). To this end Soviet Russia entered the League of Nations in 1934 and in 1935 signed separate pacts with France and Czechoslovakia.[39]

The adoption of collective security by the Soviet government was not followed immediately by a change in direction on the part of Comintern, many of whose members remained critical of the change in Soviet policy. At its seventh and final congress during July–August 1935, however, the Comintern adopted a Popular Front strategy which involved co-operation and collaboration between Communists, Socialists (the former Social Fascists of the sixth congress), and liberal progressives.[40] The Popular Front was intended to facilitate and complement the policy of collective security. Unfortunately for the Soviets the very governments earmarked for collaboration in an alliance against German Fascism, namely Britain and France, viewed the Popular Front with alarm and suspicion. These apprehensions appeared to be borne out by the decisive election victories of Popular Front coalitions in Spain and France in February and May 1936 respectively and by the sit-ins and demonstrations of French factory workers in June.

This contradiction notwithstanding, Soviet leaders continued to pin their faith on collective security and the Popular Front strategy after the intervention of Germany and Italy in Spain in July 1936.

They recognised that a victory for the militarists in Spain, backed by Hitler and Mussolini, would leave France, Russia's new partner, surrounded on three sides by hostile neighbours, while the collapse of the Popular Front in Madrid would have serious consequences for its French counterpart, but they faced an acute dilemma when the French Popular Front government proved reluctant to intervene. Soviet intervention was required to save France from encirclement, but any attempt to intervene would upset the delicate balance in France and jeopardise the Franco–Soviet alliance. Accordingly, in the absence of French or British intervention in Spain during August 1936 the Soviets restricted their activities to propaganda support for the Republic accompanied by demonstrations and collections in the cities of Russia. In order to keep in step with the development of Anglo–French policy the Soviets reluctantly acceded to the French proposal for a non-intervention agreement on Spain and accepted membership of the non-intervention committee. However, continued intervention by Italy, Germany and Portugal, despite adherence to the non-intervention agreement, and the uproar this created in left wing circles in Europe, including Britain and France, compelled Moscow to alter its policy during September and October to one of covert intervention in Spain combined with active participation in the work of the non-intervention committee.[41]

Soviet intervention helped to reinforce the Italo–German relationship, which was consolidated in the declaration of the Rome–Berlin Axis during October 1936, and encouraged Germany to sign an anti-Comintern pact with Japan in November. Relations with France and Britain were also impaired. However, with Soviet assistance Madrid was saved from Franco's forces and the Spanish struggle prolonged. Soviet leaders still hoped to persuade the western democracies to help save the Spanish Republic and themselves from the consequences of Fascist aggression. To this end they used their increasingly vital intervention to pressure the Spanish authorities into creating a conventional Republican army in place of the anarchist and Trotskyist POUM (*Partido Obrero de Unificación Marxista*) militia system and to suppress radical social experiments within the Republican territories. In order to strengthen the Republic's military resistance, to neutralise the possibility of a *bourgeois* secession to the Spanish Fascists and to make the French and British governments more amenable the Soviet leaders were prepared to sacrifice the Spanish revolution. Indeed, at their insistence the Spanish government espoused the cause of *bourgeois* parliamentary democracy and refused to condone 'any action against the property rights and legitimate interests of those foreigners in Spain who were citizens of states which did not support the rebels'.[42]

From October 1936 until the summer of 1938 the Soviets, in their pursuit of collective security, sought in vain to use the Spanish conflagration as a means of persuading the British and French governments to forsake their appeasement of the Fascist dictators. Moscow's patient commitment to collective security during this period was not a product of illusion but of the absence of a viable alternative policy other than a return to isolationism. A *rapprochement* with Berlin, despite tentative feelers on the Soviet side, was ruled out by Hitler's continued hostility and his ambitions in central Europe.[43] Meanwhile, Japanese aggression in northern China, especially in August 1938, imposed further problems for Soviet defence in the Far East.[44]

The exclusion of Soviet Russia from the Munich conference signalled the collapse of the policy of collective security and a return to isolationism. It was now clear, if it had not been before, that Republican Spain could not expect a concerted Anglo–French–Soviet intervention on its behalf. As E.H. Carr notes, the Munich agreement showed that Spain had been relegated 'to an insignificant place' in the preoccupations of the European powers and that 'no future efforts to sustain the democratic cause in Spain could be expected from those who had so easily abandoned it elsewhere'.[45]

The Soviet failure to win the western powers to collective security through Spain did not mean that Soviet intervention was entirely fruitless from the point of Soviet interests. As with Germany and Italy, as a by-product of her intervention Soviet Russia was able, in the words of the Spanish socialist Indalecio Prieto, to use Spain as 'a real life military academy' to test some of its latest weapons and to provide battle experience for ground and air personnel. Many of the leading Soviet army commanders of the Second World War visited Spain including Marshals Zhukov, Voronov and Malinovsky, Generals Rokossovsky, Krivoshein, Meretskov, Yakushin, Koniev and Butov, and Admiral Kuznetsov, commander of the Soviet fleet throughout the Second World War. Other ex-Spanish veterans such as Antonov-Ovsëenko, Berzin, Kolzov and Goriev were not so fortunate, suffering execution or slow death in concentration camps on their return to Russia.[46] Moreover, although the Soviet Union failed to obtain short term or long term economic concessions in Spain, the financial cost of its intervention was defrayed to a large extent by the deposit of Spanish gold, amounting to $518 million, in Moscow early in 1937.[47]

THE NON-INTERVENTION POWERS: BRITAIN AND FRANCE

The policy of non-intervention in the Spanish civil war was the invention of the French authorities. The British government, however, was already committed in thought and deed to non-intervention before the French made their proposal for a non-intervention agreement on 1 August 1936, and adhered strictly to the agreement throughout the 32 months of the civil war. Yet France was not entirely strict in its neutrality, while Britain chose to interpret non-intervention in politico–military terms which did not preclude economic intervention. During the civil war the French sold between 100 and 150 aircraft to the Republicans. Facilities were provided for the export of gold from the Bank of Madrid between July 1936 and March 1937 while the Soviet *Banque Commerciale pour l'Europe de Nord*, operating in Paris under French laws, was able to facilitate international payments for war *matériel* on behalf of the Spanish Republic. At various times during the war the French Pyrenean frontier was opened for the transportation of arms to Spain, notably during July and August 1936, October 1937–January 1938, March–June 1938, and January–February 1939. The largest contingent of foreign combatants in the International Brigades was composed of Frenchmen, some 10 000 in all.[48] In the economic sphere the British authorities deliberately sought to curry favour with the Spanish Nationalists in order to counter German influence which threatened established British economic interests in Spain, notably those of the Rio Tinto and Tharsis Sulphur and Copper companies. In November 1937 they went so far as to concede *de facto* recognition by appointing a special agent, Sir Robert Hodgson, to the Nationalist authorities and receiving the Anglophile Duke of Alba in return. The French government studiously avoided following the British example despite their own economic interests in Nationalist Spain which were, admittedly, less extensive.[49]

Ideological influences figured prominently in the French and British decisions to pursue non-intervention in Spain. The initial, and natural, response of the French Popular Front government was to provide military assistance to the Popular Front government in

Spain. But fears of a right wing backlash in France creating further civil disorder and ideological division and possibly civil war, following the occupation of the factories in June, prompted a more cautious response, not least to preserve the social reform programme of the Popular Front as enshrined in the Matignon agreements which had brought the occupations to an end.[50] The French government itself was divided over allowing the export of French arms and aircraft, though not entirely along Radical–Socialist party lines. As a compromise the government proposed the non-intervention agreement in the hope that, starved of outside assistance, the rebellion would be short-lived. For most members of the government and the Quai d'Orsay there appeared to be little alternative since it was clear within days of the Generals' revolt that Britain intended to pursue a strictly neutral policy which would leave France dangerously isolated if it intervened in the Spanish conflagration. French efforts to persuade the British to change their position, such as the visit to London of Jules Moch, assistant to the French leader, Léon Blum, on 30 July and the mission of Admiral Darlan to London on 5 August, proved unavailing despite growing evidence of Italian and German intervention in Spain.[51]

In order to overcome the increasing opposition to non-intervention within the Popular Front, which resulted from an increased awareness of German and Italian intervention, Yvon Delbos, the foreign minister, and his officials at the Quai d'Orsay, deemed it essential to win full backing from Britain for their non-intervention proposals. Eden, Halifax and the Foreign Office proved only too willing to support French requests for assistance. This collaboration between the two foreign ministries ensured the survival of the non-intervention policy. Without Britain's full backing it is probable that the moderates in the Popular Front, including Delbos, Edouard Daladier, the minister of war and Blum himself, would have been unable to restrain those elements which incessantly demanded French intervention on behalf of the Spanish Republic.[52]

In contrast to the French the ideological predilections of the British government in July and August 1936 were clearly anti-Republican and pro-insurgent. Within days of the rebellion Conservative politicians such as Sir Henry Channon and the government Chief Whip, David Margesson, were lamenting its failure while the Prime Minister, Stanley Baldwin, was adamant that 'on no account French or other' should the government enter the civil war 'on the side of the Russians'. The expropriation by armed workers of British companies in Republican Spain, such as the Barcelona Power Light and Traction Company, in late July and early August 1936 strengthened the anti-Republican sentiment in Whitehall. In addition, the failure of the Madrid authorities to control the extreme elements in the Spanish Popular Front and to restore law and order within their territory earned the contempt of senior Foreign Office officials, including Vansittart, his deputy Sir Alexander Cadogan, and Sir George Mounsey, the superintending assistant under-secretary of the League of Nations and Western Department which was responsible for Spanish matters. These same officials remained convinced that Soviet–Comintern influence had been active in Spain long before the revolt of 17 July. During the early weeks of the civil war, in spiritual unison with Hitler and Mussolini, they continued to fear the spread of the Bolshevik contagion to France. The only dissentient voice at the Foreign Office was Lawrence Collier, head of the Northern Department.[53]

The British Admiralty shared these misgivings. At various times during 1936 and 1937 senior naval officers, such as Admiral Sir Ernle Chatfield, the First Sea Lord, his successor, Sir Roger Backhouse, and Admiral Geoffrey Blake, Commander of the Home Fleet, expressed strong anti-Republican and pro-Franco sentiments. After May 1937 Alfred Duff Cooper, as First Lord of the Admiralty, was no less sympathetic to Franco than his senior naval advisors or his predecessor, Sir Samuel Hoare. All, with Invergordon probably in mind, continued to condemn unreservedly the killing of Spanish naval officers by Republican sailors during the early weeks of the civil war despite the fact that these officers were in open revolt against the democratically elected government of Spain.[54] Although Eden and Vansittart were converted during 1937 to the view that the survival of Republican Spain was in Britain's best political and strategic interests the passage of time converted few others. Indeed, Neville Chamberlain, the Prime Minister, was compelled to warn his cabinet colleagues in January 1939 that the government 'should avoid showing any satisfaction at the prospect of a Franco victory'.[55]

While there was a strong ideological antipathy towards the Spanish Republic and sympathy for Franco's cause in British ruling circles it was hardly possible for the British government to assist actively a rebellion against a legitimate and democratically elected government, particularly when such action would alienate the French and arouse the fury of the political opposition at home. British statesmen recognised that the best means of containing the Bolshevik contagion was to support Blum's non-intervention proposals. Failure to provide such support would undermine the moderate elements in the French government and make French intervention a certainty.[56]

The French government's persistence in pursuing non-intervention in face of increasing hostility within the Popular Front cannot be explained merely in terms of their fear of civil disturbances at home and the need to keep in step with London. Blum, Delbos, Daladier and other ministers genuinely feared a general European war if intervention in Spain proceeded unchecked. Nor could this danger be discounted. When Blum referred to the possibility in a major speech at Luna Park in Paris on 6 September 1936, and urged that non-intervention was the best means of preventing such a calamity, there was little dissent, and he was able to maintain Socialist party support for the non-intervention policy.[57] During July and August 1936 Eden and his Foreign Office advisors, who had a horror of a European war based on ideological divisions, similarly insisted that it was essential to confine the conflict to Spain.[58] Like Blum they also feared that any intervention in Spain by either Britain or France might irretrievably jeopardise their efforts to reach a general European settlement, based on a new Locarno, which had been proceeding since Hitler's reoccupation of the Rhineland in March.[59] Indeed, especially after Chamberlain became Prime Minister in May 1937, the British government was determined not to allow the civil war to interfere with its efforts to appease both Hitler and Mussolini despite their constant breaches of non-intervention.[60]

Both Paris and London recognised that the civil war held serious strategic consequences. As early as 24 August 1936 the British chiefs of staff advised that in a war with a European power it would be essential for British interests that Spain should be friendly or at worst strictly neutral. A hostile Spain or the occupation of Spanish territory by a hostile power would make Britain's control of the Straits of Gibraltar and the use of Gibraltar itself as a naval and air base extremely difficult if not impossible, and would accordingly endanger imperial communications through the Mediterranean. Similarly, the possession by a hostile power of the harbours of the Spanish Atlantic seaboard would imperil Britain's communications across the Atlantic. The chiefs emphasised that Britain's interests in the Spanish crisis were first, the maintenance of the territorial integrity of Spain and its possessions (Balearics, Morocco, Canaries and Rio de Oro); and second, to secure the benevolent neutrality of a future Spanish government in the event of Britain being engaged in any European war. They shared the Foreign Office view that the best means of securing these objectives was by promoting non-intervention. They repeated this advice in July 1938, and in the course of a major appreciation of Britain's strategic position during February 1939 they could not emphasise too strongly 'the strategic need of pursuing a policy which will ensure at least the neutrality of Spain, whatever the outcome of the civil war'.[61] The decision to exchange agents with Franco in November 1937 was due as much to the need to safeguard Britain's strategic position in the western Mediterranean as to concern for British economic interests in Spain, since his government controlled all Spanish territory in proximity to Gibraltar and the Straits.[62]

The French high command regarded the strategic implications of a Franco victory in co-operation with Germany and Italy as extremely serious for France. In that case the Iberian Peninsula would become a third unsympathetic if not hostile front which could only be defended at the expense of the Rhine and Alpine theatres. A Franco victory might also result in a tightening of Spain's stranglehold on the Straits of Gibraltar by means of Italian and German air and naval bases on the Spanish coast or in the Balearics or Canaries which could seriously impair the co-ordination of Franco–British naval operations in the western Mediterranean and western Atlantic. The exploitation of Spanish bases by pro-rebel forces, whether nationalist or foreign, could jeopardise troop and munition transports between France and north Africa with grave consequences for the operation of the French mobilisation plan. The dilemma was that these strategic dangers could come to pass if France intervened unsuccessfully in the civil war just as much, if not more than, if it remained neutral. In particular there was a risk of escalating the war into a major European conflict, which might have as one of its theatres the Pyrenees, the least fortified of French frontiers. Moreover, intervention might prejudice Franco's supposed resolve to remove his civil war partners once his victory was assured. At the same time, any military intervention was certain to be expensive in financial, material and human resources which would necessarily be diverted from the more acute dangers on the Rhine and Alpine frontiers. The French high command therefore favoured non-intervention, but to understand fully this preference it is important to recognise that they expected the rebels to win in Spain and that their sympathies, as General Gamelin later admitted, were always with Franco.[63]

For the French governments of the period intervention in Spain was considered an extremely high risk policy and both the army high command and the Quai d'Orsay counselled against such a venture. As late as March 1938, in the immediate aftermath of the *Anschluss*, during the short lived second ministry of Léon Blum, Gamelin advised against intervention on the grounds that France had insufficient forces to risk war, while the secretary general of the Quai d'Orsay, Alexis Léger, expressed his conviction that both Italy and Germany would regard French intervention in Spain as a *casus belli*.[64] In view of these risks the Blum, Chautemps, and Daladier administrations, at various times between August 1936 and February 1939, used non-intervention as a cover for assisting the Republican forces in Spain, though on nothing like the same scale as Soviet aid to the Republic or Italian and German assistance to the rebels. In this way their consciences were eased to some degree and the non-intervention policy was made more palatable to the rank and file of the Popular Front.[65]

The British authorities were not prepared at any point during the civil war to risk a European conflagration by intervening in Spain, and especially not on the side of the Spanish Republic. Nonetheless, they recognised that despite the exchange of agents there was a clear danger that British influence in Spain might be eclipsed in the event of an Axis backed victory for Franco, which seemed increasingly likely as time went by. In order to justify this risk, which was inherent in non-intervention, the British government fell back on two superficially attractive arguments. The first was that by pursuing a politically non-partisan policy Britain would receive favourable treatment from whichever side emerged victorious because it alone among the European powers had not intervened to kill Spaniards. The second argument emphasised the financial superiority of Britain in that whoever won in Spain would have to seek British financial assistance in the task of reconstruction, particularly as it was widely believed that neither Germany nor Italy could provide such assistance.[66] The aftermath of the civil war was to demonstrate the emptiness of these assertions.

THE IMPACT OF THE CIVIL WAR ON EUROPEAN GREAT POWER RELATIONS

From the ideological standpoint the outcome of the Spanish civil war represented a notable success for both Germany and Italy. Although

Franco's Spain was not transformed into a Fascist state on the German or Italian model it was ardently anti-Communist, as its adherence to the anti-Comintern pact on 27 March 1939 demonstrated. The threat of the Bolshevik contagion which figured so prominently in the calculations of Mussolini and Hitler in July and August 1936 was completely eradicated. The removal of this threat alone justified Axis intervention in Spain, as Ciano, for one, recognised: 'At Malaga, at Guadalajara, at Santander, we were fighting in defence of our civilisation and our Revolution'.[67] It was particularly important that the possible spread of the Bolshevik contagion to France should be neutralised. In fact the Spanish civil war contributed to the eclipse of the Popular Front. The ideological divisions within French society, so clearly apparent in February 1934 and June 1936, were, if anything, exacerbated by the civil war and this in itself probably weakened France's resolve to resist Hitler's ambitions for European hegemony.

Aside from these unanticipated gains, the Axis powers benefited from the fact that France and Britain could no longer take for granted Spain's benevolent neutrality in any future European war, and more specifically that France would be preoccupied in making contingency plans for the defence of its Pyrenean frontier. No doubt they were relieved to find that the war had not strengthened the Franco–Soviet relationship, and they also gained from the heightened fear of Bolshevism, engendered by the Comintern's involvement in Spain, which led right wing governments in the Baltic states and eastern Europe, Poland excepted, to look to Germany for deliverance.[68] Otherwise, the Axis powers gained little in the way of positive strategic benefits from their involvement in the Spanish conflict. In September 1938, at the height of the Czech crisis, Franco declared Spain's neutrality in the event of war, and in late August 1939, encouraged by Portugal's Salazar, the Spanish dictator confirmed his intention to remain neutral.[69] Franco's declaration contributed to Mussolini's decision to remain a non-belligerent, and in September 1939 Salazar, encouraged by London, adopted a policy of benevolent neutrality towards Britain and France.[70] Franco also refused the Axis powers the use of the Canaries or Balearics as strategic bases. Hitler, who in January 1939 initiated his Z-Plan for the construction of a giant battlefleet, found his naval ambitions delayed by the Polish crisis and obstructed by Franco's neutrality. The only concession Franco made, in strictest secrecy, was to permit German submarines to refuel at Spanish bases while engaged in attacking British Atlantic shipping.[71]

The economic benefits which Germany derived from its intervention in Spain continued after the civil war, and indeed after September 1939, in so far as it was able to obtain a range of important minerals such as iron ore, copper, pyrites, wolfram, zinc, tin, mercury and lithium. At the same time, German imports of Spanish minerals during the civil war had fallen short of targets set under the Four Year Plan. Pyrites stocks, for example, were equal to only six months' consumption at the beginning of 1939. Moreover, no doubt with the experience of the Montana project in mind, Franco was determined to limit the amount of long term economic concessions to the Axis powers and to control strictly the operations of foreign mining concern in Spain, including British ones such as Rio Tinto.[72]

Despite their independent decisions to intervene in the conflict there can be few doubts that the civil war in Spain, by providing an arena in which they could co-operate on a common project, contributed significantly to the *rapprochement* between Germany and Italy which had been set in train previously by Germany's benevolent neutrality in the later stages of the Italo–Ethiopian war and by Italy's decision to adopt a passive attitude to Hitler's remilitarisation of the Rhineland. Significantly, it was after the outbreak of the war that Mussolini abandoned support for the Zionists and went over to a policy of anti-semitism.[73] At the same time, British efforts to improve relations with Italy after the Ethiopian *débâcle* foundered over the Spanish problem, not least because of the increasing hostility, arising from the civil war, in Franco–Italian relations. That this benefited Nazi Germany cannot be denied. However, it does not follow, as some historians claim, that Hitler deliberately limited the extent of German intervention in Spain (in particular his refusal to send ground forces) in order to prolong the conflict and thereby keep alive the tensions engendered by it as a distraction from Nazi political and military expansion in central and eastern Europe.[74] Although the *Führer* told his military advisors at the Hossbach conference of 5 November 1937 that Germany was more interested in a continuation of the war with all the tensions arising from it between Italy and France in the Mediterranean, his decision to limit the scale of German support for Franco was influenced by a more vital consideration. The dispatch of a large expeditionary force to Spain would have incurred the real risk of provoking a general conflagration. Any illusions that this might not be the case must have been dispelled by Delbos' warning of 23 December 1936 that if Germany sent further troop transports, in addition to the Condor Legion, such action 'would necessarily lead to war'. Moreover, the dispatch of such a force carried the further risk of fulfilling the primary objective of Soviet intervention in Spain, namely the crystallising of an anti-Nazi coalition comprising themselves and the western democracies. By limiting the scale of German intervention in Spain Hitler was able to contribute towards the neutralisation of Bolshevik influence without unduly antagonising Britain and France.[75]

There can be little doubt that the defeat of the Spanish Republic was a painful and bitter experience for the Popular Front including the Radical Socialists as well as the Socialist and Communist parties, when they found that they could not save their Spanish comrades. Nevertheless, the adoption of non-intervention probably prevented a socio-political crisis in France. Despite occasional breaches of the non-intervention agreement by the French authorities the French right was mollified by the policy of non-intervention, especially as it appeared to benefit Franco rather than the Republicans and because it was consistent with British policy. Although sympathetic to the Spanish Republicans, when their cause appeared hopeless in February 1939 French political leaders were quick to repair relations with the victorious Nationalists through the granting of *de jure* recognition to the Franco regime and the signing of the Bérard–Jordana agreement.[76] Clearly, from the ideological point of view Franco's victory was satisfactory for the British government and their official advisors: but while, unlike the Labour party, they did not mourn the passing of the Spanish Republic it is to their credit that in February 1939 they tried to achieve safeguards against reprisals as a condition for granting *de jure* recognition to Franco's regime.[77]

The decision of Britain and France to adhere to a policy of non-intervention did not safeguard their strategic position in the western Mediterranean and along the western Atlantic seaboard. British military authorities had hoped at best to secure a benevolently neutral Spain in any future European conflict; at worst a strictly neutral Spain. In March 1939 the joint planning staff were compelled to recognise that, in view of German and Italian armed assistance Franco's Spain might be hostile or at any rate afford facilities to the Axis powers. This led them to take a serious view of the broader strategic implications:

If Spain were hostile there would be a threat not only to Gibraltar, but also to Portuguese territory, and this might involve us in further commitments in this area. The use of Spanish harbours, including those in the Balearic and Canary Islands, by German and Italian naval forces, especially submarines, would add considerably to our difficulties, particularly in the Atlantic and of France's communications in the Western Mediterranean.[78]

Hence, they considered it imperative to secure Spain's neutrality. The French authorities were no less concerned to ensure a neutral Spain. During the second stage of the Anglo–French military talks in late April–early May 1939, they admitted the vulnerability of south and south-western France to air attack from aerodromes in Spanish territory and the grave disadvantage of having a third frontier to defend. They also took into account Spain's importance as a supplier of strategic materials, notably iron ore, copper, pyrites, mercury, lead and zinc.[79]

Strategic issues alone made it imperative for the two western powers to improve their relations with the new Spain. Britain was only too willing to try, and enlisted the full support of Portugal. However, despite the Bérard–Jordana agreement France made little headway in its promotion of a Franco–Spanish *rapprochement*. On 8 April 1939 Franco's adhesion to the anti-Comintern pact was made public, fortifications were erected on the Spanish side of the frontier between the French and Spanish zones in Morocco, and the Spanish authorities refused to take back 400 000 refugees who had fled over the frontier during the last days of the civil war and its immediate aftermath.[80] British and Portuguese efforts during May and June to persuade the French to make concessions to Franco's Spain proved unavailing owing to French insistence that they would not return the remaining Spanish gold, deposited in France by the Republicans and not sent to Moscow, unless there was substantial progress on the refugee question. However, in view of the increased possibility of war and the need of France's expanding economy for Spanish Republican labour, Paris relented in July and returned the gold to Madrid.[81] Despite their best efforts, the Allies could not stop Spain from adopting a policy of benevolent neutrality towards Germany in September 1939 or, after France's collapse and Italy's entry into the war in June 1940, a more threatening policy of non-belligerency.

Some consolation was, however, obtained through Britain's success in preserving the Anglo–Portuguese Alliance. The Salazar regime's abhorrence of non-intervention and ardent support of Franco's cause throughout the civil war had presented Germany and Italy with a golden opportunity to undermine Anglo–Portuguese relations, but though they sought strenuously to win Portugal to their side, they failed owing to the intensive counter efforts of the British authorities.[82] The British achieved further success in the economic sphere, not least because of the limited success of German policy. The sovereignty of British companies, in the pyrites trade for example, was preserved; supplies to Britain were not restricted during or after the civil war while as early as May 1939 the Rio Tinto Company was not penalised by the Spanish authorities for refusing to supply Germany. Franco's determination to pursue a strongly nationalistic economic strategy only constrained the activities of British companies in Spain at a later date.[83]

Historians tend to characterise French foreign policy in the late 1930s as being subservient to that of Britain; that at least France obeyed its 'English governess'. In this version France's invention of, and commitment to, non-intervention in Spain in August 1936 was a direct response to British pressure: without it French intervention would have been inevitable. By the same token the decision of the French government in June 1938 to close their frontier with Spain which had been open since March was purportedly a consequence of British pressure.[84] French policy towards the Spanish civil war tends to bear out Anthony Adamthwaite's view that 'in practice French policy was much more assertive and independent than supposed'.[85] Yvon Delbos and the Quai d'Orsay initiated the policy of non-intervention, then sought British support since otherwise, they feared, the more extreme elements in the Popular Front would succeed in forcing France to intervene in Spain. Accordingly, throughout August and September 1936 they covertly solicited British pressure, which admittedly the British authorities willingly provided.[86] Similarly, in June 1938 the British ambassador, Sir Eric Phipps, strongly advised the French government to close their frontier with Spain, but the French needed little persuasion. As Georges Bonnet, the foreign minister, later told Phipps, his government were convinced that if they did not close the frontier the risk of war would have been increased by 100 per cent because they had heard that a large shipment of war *matériel* had left or was about to leave the Soviet Union for Le Havre and Bordeaux for trans-shipment to Spain. Bonnet deplored 'Russia's renewed and unhealthy wish to fish in troubled Spanish waters far removed from her own territory, which would therefore be immune from the disturbances and damage she wished to cause others'.[87]

Earlier in the civil war, in October 1937, the French government had agreed to keep the Pyrenean frontier closed, partly in deference to British wishes but largely because apart from some Socialists there were few Frenchmen who wanted to open it. Senior officials at the Quai d'Orsay, notably Massigli and Léger, were opposed to opening the frontier because they believed 'it would be completely ineffective in so far as it was intended to help the Valencia government to free Spain from the Italian stranglehold'. As an alternative to opening the frontier the Quai d'Orsay favoured the occupation of Minorca as a *gage*.[88] The French authorities also demonstrated their independence by refusing to follow London's lead in exchanging agents with the Nationalist authorities in Spain. For their part the British government were often irritated by French attempts to disregard non-intervention. Early in September 1936, for example, Britain strongly reprimanded France for allowing several hundred Republican militiamen, who had fled from Irun into France, to return rearmed in special trains to the Pyrenean frontier where they were able to rejoin the Catalan anarchists. When, in October 1937, the French suggested a temporary authorisation of the transit of arms to the Spanish government unless the Italians desisted from further armed intervention in Spain, the British cabinet rejected the suggestion out of hand, deploring it for 'casting doubts on Italian pledges and good faith'.[89] While in these cases the British view tended to prevail it can hardly be claimed that the French were passive or supine camp followers.

Most probably during the late 1930s the greatest divergence in the respective policies of France and Britain occurred in respect of their relations with Italy. The Spanish civil war contributed significantly to the deterioration in Franco–Italian relations, to the chagrin of British authorities who, since the summer of 1936, had made strenuous efforts to repair their relations with Mussolini. Neville Chamberlain acknowledged the civil war as a major obstacle to the appeasement of Italy when he informed George VI that Spain was the 'nigger in the woodpile' and that 'unless and until that affair is settled there will always be the danger of an open quarrel with France and always the road to appeasement will be blocked'.[90] Unfortunately for Chamberlain, the end of the Spanish conflict did not herald an improvement in Franco–Italian relations. While Daladier was prepared, eventually, to make some concessions to Franco's Spain, he was not prepared, despite the urgings of Chamberlain, Halifax and even Bonnet, to do the same for Mussolini's Italy before September 1939.[91]

The deterioration of Franco – Italian relations was not matched by an improvement in Franco – Soviet relations even though the Soviet Union had intervened on the side of the Spanish Republic. During 1937 the French authorities refused to consider military conversations as a means of strengthening and consolidating the Franco – Soviet pact of 1935. Like their British counterparts they saw no virtue in the pact other than as a means of preventing a Nazi – Soviet *rapprochement*, and the purges in the Red Army during the middle of 1937 ended any lingering thought that conversations might be possible or desirable.[92] The Soviet failure to win over Britain and France to collective security through Spain and Czechoslovakia reinforced Moscow's isolationism after September 1938 and increased fear and suspicion that the western powers intended to direct Germany eastwards. In view of these apprehensions, made worse in November 1938 by Moscow's awareness that German – Japanese – Italian negotiations for a tripartite pact had progressed to a new and active stage after Munich, it was clearly prudent for the Soviet authorities to withdraw completely from their involvement in Spain.[93]

By the time the Soviet Union revealed a renewed interest in collective security, in the form of Stalin's offer of a tripartite alliance to Britain and France in April 1939, the Spanish Republic had passed into history and the civil war could no longer be utilised as a catalyst for an Anglo – French – Soviet *rapprochement*. In view of the refusal of the British authorities to take advantage of the opportunity provided by the Spanish conflict for such a *rapprochement* it is surely ironic that the chiefs of staff should have advised in May 1939 that 'the possibility of antagonising Franco's Spain should not from the military point of view be allowed to stand in the way of the conclusion of a pact with Soviet Russia'.[94] The pact with Soviet Russia was not to materialise until more than two years later in the context of a much greater conflagration than the civil war in Spain. Those powers who had fought war almost by proxy in Spain between 1936 and 1939 were then engaged in a titanic contest which resulted in the demise of European Fascism and which paved the way for the Bolshevisation of eastern Europe and the democratisation of western and central Europe. The exception to these trends was the Iberian Peninsula which survived for 30 years longer as the last redoubt of the authoritarian right in Europe.

NOTES AND REFERENCES

1. For the origins of the Spanish Civil War see H. Thomas, *The Spanish Civil War* (3rd edition London, 1977); P. Preston, *The Coming of the Spanish Civil War: Reform, Reaction and Revolution in the Second Republic 1931–1936* (London, 1978); R.A.H. Robinson, *The Origins of Franco Spain: The Right, the Republic and Revolution 1931–1936* (Newton Abbot, 1970); G. Jackson, *The Spanish Republic and the Civil War 1931–1939* (Princeton, 1965); and E. Malefakis, *Agrarian Reform and Peasant Revolution in Spain: Origins of the Civil War* (London, 1970).

2. For the airlift see R.L. Proctor, *Hitler's Luftwaffe in the Spanish Civil War* (Westport, 1983), pp. 3–37; J.F. Coverdale, *Italian Intervention in the Spanish Civil War* (Princeton, 1975), pp. 85–87; and Thomas, *The Spanish Civil War*, pp. 939–940. For Soviet intervention in October and November and the arrival of the International Brigades see Thomas, pp. 439–497; D.T. Cattell, *Soviet Diplomacy and the Spanish Civil War* (Berkeley, 1957), pp. 32–37; E.H. Carr, *The Comintern and the Spanish Civil War* (London, 1984), pp. 19–28; and J. Haslam, *The Soviet Union and the Struggle for Collective Security in Europe 1933–1939* (London, 1984), pp. 114–120.

3. For details see Coverdale, *Italian Intervention*, pp. 69–74.

4. For details see Proctor, *Hitler's Luftwaffe*, pp. 10–19; G.L. Weinberg, *The Foreign Policy of Hitler's Germany: Diplomatic Revolution in Europe 1933–1936* (Chicago, 1970), pp. 288–289; H. Abendroth, *Hitler in der spanischen Arena* (Paderborn, 1973), pp. 23–39; M. Merkes, *Die Deutsche Politik im spanischen Bürgerkrieg 1936–1939* (2nd edition Bonn, 1969), pp. 23–30; A. Viñas, *La Alemania nazi y el 18 de julio* (Madrid, 1977), pp. 335–344; and G.T. Harper, *German Economic Policy in Spain during the Spanish Civil War* (The Hague, 1967), pp. 11–20.

5. For details see Thomas, *The Spanish Civil War*, pp. 977–979; Coverdale, *Italian Intervention*, pp. 393, 418–419; and Merkes, *Die Deutsche Politik im spanischen Bürgerkrieg*, ch. 3.

6. *Documents on German Foreign Policy 1918–1945, (D), vol. III* (London, 1951), Doc. 783, pp. 892–894. Hereafter *DGFP*. Coverdale, *Italian Intervention*, pp. 392–393; C.E. Harvey, *The Rio Tinto Company: An Economic History of a Leading International Mining Concern 1873–1954* (Penzance, 1981), n. 59, p. 289; and R.H. Whealey, 'Foreign Intervention in the Spanish Civil War', in R. Carr (ed), *The Republic and the Civil War in Spain* (London, 1971), p. 219.

7. See P. Broué and E. Témime, *The Revolution and the Civil War in Spain* (London, 1972), p. 346 and D. Mack Smith, *Mussolini's Roman Empire* (London, 1976), p. 100.

8. Coverdale, *Italian Intervention*, pp. 78–83, 399–404 and Thomas, *The*

Spanish Civil War, p. 353. For the Farinacci mission see H. Fornari, *Mussolini's Gadfly: Roberto Farinacci* (Nashville, 1971), pp. 162–164.

9. Speech to Nazi Party officials, 29 April 1937. D. Smyth, 'Reflex Reaction: Germany and the Onset of the Spanish Civil War' in P. Preston (ed), *Revolution and War in Spain 1931–1939* (London, 1984), p. 244. See also G.L. Weinberg, *The Foreign Policy of Hitler's Germany: Starting World War II, 1937–1939* (Chicago, 1980), pp. 155–156.

10. Thomas, *The Spanish Civil War*, p. 356.

11. 'A Busman's Holiday', 10 September 1936. *Documents on British Foreign Policy 1919–1939, (2), vol. XVII* (London, 1979), App. I, p. 760. Hereafter *DBFP*.

12. Thomas, *The Spanish Civil War*, p. 356 and Smyth, 'Reflex Reaction', pp. 253, 257.

13. For Hitler's extension of military conscription see *DGFP*, (D), vol. III, Doc. 55, pp. 56–57.

14. Smyth, 'Reflex Reaction', p. 251.

15. *DBFP*, (2), vol. XVII, App. I, p. 761, 'A Busman's Holiday', 10 September 1936.

16. Smyth, 'Reflex Reaction'. p. 252.

17. Ibid., pp. 254–255.

18. Abendroth, *Hitler in der spanischen Arena*, pp. 35–36. For the debate on Hitler's ultimate objectives including discussion of the so called *Stufenplan* see K. Hildebrand, *The Foreign Policy of the Third Reich* (London, 1973); M. Michaelis, 'World Power Status or World Dominion? A Survey of the Literature on Hitler's 'Plan of World Dominion (1937–1970)', *Historical Journal*, vol. XV (2–1972); A. Hillgruber, 'England's Place in Hitler's Plan for World Dominion', *Journal of Contemporary History*, vol. IX (1–1974); M. Hauner, 'Did Hitler want a World Dominion?', *Journal of Contemporary History*, vol XII (1–1978); and E.M. Robertson, 'Hitler's Planning for War and the Response of the Great Powers (1938– early 1939)', in H.W. Koch, *Aspects of the Third Reich* (London, 1985).

19. CAB24/277, CP 163(38) 'German Attitudes towards Events in Spain and Portugal: Memorandum by Lord Halifax', 7 July 1938. See also the *News Chronicle*, 12 July 1938. For strategic issues see D.C. Watt, 'German Strategic Planning and Spain 1938–1939', *Army Quarterly*, 1960, pp. 220–227. For the strategic significance of the Portuguese Alliance for Britain at this time see G.A. Stone, 'The Official British Attitude to the Anglo–Portuguese Alliance, 1910–1945', *Journal of Contemporary History*, vol. X (4–1975), pp. 738–740. For German naval planning see J. Dülffer, *Weimar, Hitler und die Marine: Reichspolitik und Flottenbau 1920 bis 1939* (Düsseldorf, 1973).

20. For details see the author's unpublished Ph. D thesis, *The Oldest Ally: Britain and the Portuguese Connection 1936–1941*, pp. 91–94, University of London, 1986.

21. Coverdale, *Italian Intervention*, pp. 40–41, 389. It is Coverdale's contention that it was principally concern over Italy's position in the western Mediterranean *vis-à-vis* France which influenced Mussolini to provide arms and money to army and monarchist conspirators before 1936. Ibid., p. 65.

22. *Ibid.*, pp. 50–53, 76.

23. Ibid., pp. 76–77. J. Edwards, *The British Government and the Spanish Civil War 1936–1939* (London, 1979), pp. 138–142.

24. Coverdale, *Italian Intervention*, pp. 76-77 and Cattell, *Soviet Diplomacy and the Spanish Civil War*, pp. 2–3.

25. R.G. Colodny, *Spain: the Glory and the Tragedy* (New York, 1970), p. 32 and Thomas, *The Spanish Civil War*, p. 951.

26. CAB24/277, CP 163(38). Weinberg, *The Foreign Policy of Hitler's Germany 1937–1939*, pp. 164-165; Thomas, *The Spanish Civil War*, pp. 940–941, 977–979; Coverdale, *Italian Intervention*, pp. 394–398; Proctor, *Hitler's Luftwaffe*, pp. 253–265; and M. Cooper, *The German Air Force 1933–1945: An Anatomy of Failure* (London, 1981), pp. 58–60.

27. Proctor, *Hitler's Luftwaffe*, pp. 258–259 and Coverdale, *Italian Intervention*, pp. 408–410.

28. For the internal position in Italy for 1936 see Coverdale, *Italian Intervention*, pp. 19–23.

29. *Ibid.*, p. 390 and Weinberg, *The Foreign Policy of Hitler's Germany 1933–1936*, pp. 295–296.

30. For the view that economic considerations were a by-product of German intervention see H. Abendroth, 'Deutschlands Rolle im spanischen Bürgerkrieg', in M. Funke (ed), *Hitler, Deutschland und die Mächte: Materialen zur Aussenpolitik des Dritten Reichs* (Düsseldorf, 1978), p. 480. Abendroth's view is shared to a large extent by Smyth, 'Reflex Reaction', pp. 256–257.

31. Weinberg, *The Foreign Policy of Hitler's Germany 1937–1939*, pp. 146–149; Harvey, *The Rio Tinto Company*, pp. 271–273; A. Viñas, 'The Financing of the Spanish Civil War' in Preston (ed), *Revolution and War in Spain*, pp. 277–278. For the significance of German intervention for the Four Year Plan see W. Schieder, 'Spanischen Bürgerkrieg und Vierjahresplan' in W. Schieder and C. Dipper (eds), *Der spanische Bürgerkrieg in der internationalen Politik, 1936-1939* (München, 1976), pp. 162–190.

32. Weinberg, *The Foreign Policy of Hitler's Germany 1937-1939*, *pp.* 152–154, 158–169; Harvey, *The Rio Tinto Company*, pp. 275, 282–284; and Viñas, 'Financing the Spanish Civil War', pp. 278–279.

33. Viñas, 'Financing the Spanish Civil War', pp. 273–277. *DGFP*, (D), vol. VII, Doc. 329, p. 325.

34. Haslam, *The Soviet Union and the Struggle for Collective Security*, pp. 108–111; Carr, *The Comintern and the Spanish Civil War*, p. 15; and Thomas, *The Spanish Civil War*, pp. 360–361.

35. Haslam, *The Soviet Union and the Struggle for Collective Security*, pp. 111–120; Carr, *The Comintern and the Spanish Civil War*, pp. 23–25; and Thomas, *The Spanish Civil War*, pp. 392–394, 440–443.

36. Thomas, *The Spanish Civil War*, pp. 940–941, 943, 980–984 and Broué and Témime, *The Revolution and the Civil War in Spain*, pp. 372–373. For NKVD activity in Spain see D.T. Cattell, *Communism and the Spanish Civil War* (New York, 1965), pp. 116–119; Haslam, *The Soviet Union and the Struggle for Collective Security*, pp. 116, 133–134; and Carr, *The Comintern and the Spanish Civil War*, pp. 35–44.

37. Carr, *The Comintern and the Spanish Civil War*, pp. 28–29 and Cattell, *Communism and the Spanish Civil War*, pp. 98–115.

38. Haslam, *The Soviet Union and the Struggle for Collective Security*, pp. 1–3. The Soviet collaboration with Weimar Germany under the Rapallo arrangements was certainly consistent with this approach since it sought to drive a wedge between the defeated and victorious imperialist powers of World War One. *Ibid.,* p. 3.

39. Ibid., pp. 6–51. See also J.A. Large, 'The Origins of Soviet Collective Security Policy 1930–1932', *Soviet Studies*, vol. XXX (2–1978).

40. For the origins and adoption of the popular front strategy of Comintern see Haslam, *The Soviet Union and the Struggle for Collective Security*, pp. 52–59. E.H. Carr, *Twilight of Comintern* (London, 1982), pp. 143–155, 405–417; J. Degras (ed), *The Communist International 1919–1943. Documents : vol. III 1929–1943* (London, 1971), pp. 355–365; and J. Haslam, 'The Comintern and the Origins of the Popular Front 1934–1935', *Historical Journal*, vol. XXII (3–1979).

41. Haslam, *The Soviet Union and the Struggle for Collective Security*, pp. 107–120; Carr, *The Comintern and the Spanish Civil War*, pp. 12–28; and Cattell, *Spanish Diplomacy and the Spanish Civil War*, pp. 14–52.

42. For the reorganisation of the Republican military forces in late 1936 and early 1937 see Carr, *The Comintern and the Spanish Civil War*, pp. 29–30; Cattell, *Soviet Diplomacy and the Spanish Civil War*, pp. 111–115; and Thomas, *The Spanish Civil War*, pp. 542–550. For the need to neutralise *bourgeois* opposition and to end the revolutionary phase of the civil war see Stalin to Largo Caballero (Spanish Prime Minister), 21 December 1936 and Caballero to Stalin, 12 January 1937 in Carr, *The Comintern and the Spanish Civil War*, pp. 86–88. See also Degras (ed), *The Communist International*, pp. 396–400. For the destruction of the Spanish revolution see Cattell, *Communism and the Spanish Civil War*, pp. 120–163; Carr, *The Comintern and the Spanish Civil War*, pp. 37–44; and Broué and Témime, *The Revolution and the Civil War in Spain*, pp. 265–295.

43. Haslam, *The Soviet Union and the Struggle for Collective Security*, pp. 125–128, 142–157.

44. Soviet assistance to Nationalist China in 1937 was predicated on the same assumptions as those influencing their intervention in Spain. In this

connection *Le Journal de Moscou*, in an editorial during August 1937, re-emphasised the indivisibility of peace and referred to the close 'interdependence' of 'the events which are taking place in China and Spain'. *Ibid.*, p. 143.

45. Carr, *The Comintern and the Spanish Civil War*, p. 71.
46. Thomas, *The Spanish Civil War*, pp. 943–945, 952–953; J. Erickson, *The Soviet High Command* (London, 1962), pp. 429–431, 455–456; A. Boyd, *The Soviet Air Force since 1918* (London, 1977), pp. 74–83; and Colodny, *The Glory and the Tragedy*, pp. 32–33.
47. For an illuminating discussion of the issue of the Spanish gold see A. Viñas, 'Gold, the Soviet Union, and the Spanish Civil War', *European Studies Review*, vol. IX (1–1979), pp. 105–128.
48. Thomas, *The Spanish Civil War*, pp. 943, 981–983 and Viñas, 'Financing the Spanish Civil War', pp. 268–270.
49. For a discussion of the economic issues as they affected Britain see Harvey, *The Rio Tinto Company*, pp. 270–289 and Edwards, *The British Government and the Spanish Civil War*, pp. 64–100. See also C.E. Harvey, 'Politics and Pyrites during the Spanish Civil War', *Economic History Review*, Second Series, vol. XXXI (1–1978).
50. For a discussion of the domestic considerations see R.J. Young, *In Command of France: French Foreign Policy and Military Planning, 1933–1940* (Harvard, 1978), pp. 139–141; J.E. Dreifort, *Yvon Delbos at the Quai d'Orsay: French Foreign Policy during the Popular Front 1936–1938*, (Kansas, 1973), pp. 38–43; and D. Carlton, 'Eden, Blum, and the Origins of Non-Intervention', *Journal of Contemporary History*, vol. VI (3–1971), pp. 46–47.
51. For a full discussion of Britain's rôle in the context of the French decision to adopt a policy of non-intervention see Edwards, *The British Government and the Spanish Civil War*, pp. 1–37; Dreifort, *Yvon Delbos at the Quai d'Orsay*, pp. 35–38, 43–54; Carlton, 'Eden, Blum and the Origins of Non–Intervention', pp. 40–55; G.A. Stone, 'Britain, Non-Intervention and the Spanish Civil War', *European Studies Review*, vol. IX (1–1979), pp. 129–149; and G. Warner, 'France and Non-Intervention in Spain, July–August 1936', *International Affairs*, vol. XXXVIII (2–1962), pp. 204–205, 212–215, 218–220.
52. Stone, 'Britain, Non-Intervention and the Spanish Civil War', pp. 139–145.
53. *Ibid.*, pp. 136–137 and D. Little, *Malevolent Neutrality: The United States, Great Britain and the Origins of the Spanish Civil War* (Cornell, 1985), pp. 222–245.
54. *Chatfield Papers* CHT/3/1 and *Simon Papers* MSS.7 diary entry, 5 February 1938, L. Pratt, *East of Malta, West of Suez: Britain's Mediterranean Crisis 1936–1939* (London, 1975), n.35, p. 43; S. Roskill, *Naval Policy Between the Wars II: the Period of Reluctant Rearmament 1930–1939* (London, 1976), p. 374; and Thomas, *The Spanish Civil War*, p. 258.

55. Stone, 'Britain, Non-Intervention and the Spanish Civil War', pp. 131–132.
56. *Ibid.,* pp. 139–141 and Little, *Malevolent Neutrality,* pp. 244–245.
57. Dreifort, *Yvon Delbos at the Quai d'Orsay,* pp. 52–53. For the impact of Blum's speech see *The Times,* 4, 5 and 7 September 1936.
58. For the Foreign Office view see minutes by Sir Orme Sargent, Cadogan and Mounsey, 12–13 August 1936. *DBFP,* (2), vol. XVII, Doc. 84 and n.1, pp. 90–91. For Eden's view see his conversation with Arthur Greenwood, Deputy Leader of the Labour Party, 19 August 1936. FO371/20534 W9331/62/41. See also Lord Avon, *The Eden Memoirs: Facing the Dictators* (London, 1962), p. 463 and Lord Halifax, *Fulness of Days* (London, 1957), p. 192.
59. Franco–British efforts to reach a general settlement between March and August 1936 are well documented in W.N. Medlicott, *Britain and Germany: The Search for Agreement 1930–1937* (London, 1969), pp. 25–30.
60. British efforts to appease Germany and Italy, and especially the latter, in the context of the Spanish civil war provide the theme of the author's unpublished MA dissertation, *Britain and the Spanish Civil War: A Study in Appeasement,* University of Sussex, 1971.
61. CAB24/264 CP 234(36) CID 1259–B (COS 509) 'Western Mediterranean – Situation Arising from the Spanish Civil War', 24 August 1936. See also *DBFP,* (2), vol. XVII, Doc. 126, pp. 151–158. CAB5/9 478–C (Also CID 1457–B and COS 750) 'The Spanish Civil War: Position in the Straits of Gibraltar', 20 July 1938. CAB53/45 COS 843 'European Appreciation, 1939–1940', 20 February 1939.
62. See memorandum by Lord Cranborne and minutes by Eden and Mounsey, 21 July 1937. FO371/21298 W14857/1/41. See also Edwards, *The British Government and the Spanish Civil War,* pp. 190–191.
63. Young, *In Command of France,* pp. 136–139 and nn. 22 and 25, p. 286.
64. Eleventh session of the Comité Permanent de la Défense Nationale, 15 March 1938 in A. Adamthwaite (ed), *The Making of the Second World War* (London, 1977), Doc. 46, p. 182.
65. Stone, 'Britain, Non-Intervention and the Spanish Civil War', pp. 138, 144.
66. *Ibid.,* p. 136.
67. *Ciano's Diary 1937–1938* (London, 1952), 29 October 1937, p. 26.
68. Robertson, 'Hitler's Planning for War', p. 206.
69. For the impact of Franco's declaration of neutrality see *DGFP,* (D), Vol. II, Docs. 622, 638, 641 and 659, pp. 950–951, 969–970, 972–973, 991. See also Merkes, *Die Deutsche Politik im spanischen Bürgerkrieg,* pp. 328–329.
70. For Portugal's neutrality in September 1939 and Britain's response see CAB53/54 COS 973 'The Role of Portugal in the Event of War', 1 September 1939.
71. For details of the submarine bases see C. Burdick, '"Moro": the Re-

supply of German submarines in Spain, 1939–1942', *Central European History*, vol. III, 3(1970), pp. 256–283. For details of the Z Plan see Robertson, 'Hitler's Planning for War', pp. 208–211.

72. Harvey, *The Rio Tinto Company*, pp. 285–286 and Weinberg, *The Foreign Policy of Hitler's Germany 1937–1939*, pp. 153–154, 165–166.

73. For the origins of the Italo–German *rapprochement* see E.M. Robertson, *Mussolini as Empire Builder: Europe and Africa 1932–1936* (London, 1977), pp. 181–183, 186–188. For the impact of the Spanish civil war on the development of an official anti-semitic policy see M. Michaelis, *Mussolini and the Jews: German–Italian Relations and the Jewish Question in Italy 1922–1945* (Oxford, 1978), pp. 93, 102.

74. Weinberg, *The Foreign Policy of Hitler's Germany 1937–1939*, pp. 143–144, 163.

75. Smyth, 'Reflex Reaction', pp. 258–260.

76. For the Bérard-Jordana agreement see A. Adamthwaite, *France and the Coming of the Second World War* (London, 1977), pp. 261–262. General Francisco Jordana y Sousa was Franco's foreign minister. Léon Bérard was a member of the French Senate and a friend of Pierre Laval. Later he became Vichy ambassador to the Vatican.

77. Edwards, *The British Government and the Spanish Civil War*, pp. 208–209. For the Labour's party's attitude concerning the civil war in Spain see J.F. Naylor, *Labour's International Policy – the Labour Party in the 1930s* (London, 1969), pp. 161–168, 181–189, and C. Fleay and M.L. Saunders, 'The Labour Spain Committee: Labour Party Policy and the Spanish Civil War', *Historical Journal*, vol. XXVIII (1–1985), pp. 187–197.

78. CAB55/15 AFC(39)1 JP 379 'Anglo-French Staff Conversations 1939: British Strategical Memorandum', 14 March 1939.

79. P.N. Buckley, E.B. Haslam and W.B.R. Neave-Hill, 'Anglo–French Staff Conversations 1938–1939' and P. Le Goyet, 'Les Relations Economiques Franco–Britanniques à la Veille de la Deuxième Guerre Mondiale', in Centre National de la Recherche Scientifique, *Les Relations Franco-Britanniques de 1935 à 1939* (Paris, 1975), pp. 114, 198–199.

80. *Documents Diplomatiques Français 1932–1939, (2), vol. XV* (Paris, 1981), Docs. 37, 38, 83, 172, 472, and 492, pp. 51–53, 54–55, 115–116, 234–236, 772–774, 807–808.

81. For details of British and Portuguese efforts to persuade France to take a more conciliatory line *vis-à-vis* Franco see Stone, *The Oldest Ally*, pp. 223–230.

82. For Britain's success in countering the Axis in Portugal see *ibid.*, pp. 90–177.

83. Harvey, *The Rio Tinto Company*, pp. 285–286.

84. Edwards, *The British Government and the Spanish Civil War*, pp. 15–39, 172–175; Thomas, *The Spanish Civil War*, pp. 344–345, 387–389, 825; Dreifort, *Yvon Delbos and the Quai d'Orsay*, pp. 37–54; and D. Smyth,

Diplomacy and Strategy of Survival: British Policy and Franco's Spain 1940–1941 (Cambridge, 1986), pp. 12–13.

85. A. Adamthwaite, 'France and the Coming of the Second World War', in W.J. Mommsen and L. Kettenacker (eds), *The Fascist Challenge and the Policy of Appeasement* (London, 1983), p. 250.

86. Stone, 'Britain, Non-Intervention and the Spanish Civil War', pp. 139–141.

87. Phipps to Halifax, 16 July 1938. *Phipps Papers* PHPP 1/20. *Cecil of Chelwood Papers* MSS 51084. Note of interview with Lord Halifax at the Foreign Office, 29 July 1938.

88. Minute Orme Sargent of his meeting with Roger Cambon, French *Chargé d'Affaires* in London, 12 October 1937. *Phipps Papers* PHPP 1/19. The idea of using Minorca as a *gage* was revived momentarily in January 1939. See P. Stafford, 'The Chamberlain–Halifax Visit to Rome – a reappraisal', *English Historical Review*, vol. XCVII, 386, January 1983, p. 93.

89. Stone, 'Britain, Non-Intervention and the Spanish Civil War', p. 135.

90. Stafford, 'The Chamberlain–Halifax Visit to Rome', p. 91.

91. D.C. Watt, 'Britain, France and the Italian problem 1937–1939', in *Les Relations Franco–Britanniques de 1935 à 1939,* pp. 287–290 and R. Girault, 'La décision gouvernementale en politique extérieure', in R. Rémond and J. Bourdin, *Edouard Daladier: chef de gouvernement avril 1938–septembre 1939* (Paris, 1977), pp. 213–214, 220.

92. J.E. Dreifort, 'The French Popular Front and the Franco–Soviet Pact 1936–1937: A Dilemma in French Foreign Policy', *Journal of Contemporary History*, vol. XI (2 and 3–1976), pp. 217–236. For official British attitudes to the Franco–Soviet Pact see R. Manne, 'The Foreign Office and the Failure of Anglo–Soviet *Rapprochement*', *Journal of Contemporary History*, vol. XVI (4–1981), pp. 727–730, 737–742.

93. See D.C. Watt, 'The Initiation of the Negotiations Leading to the Nazi–Soviet Pact: A Historical Problem', in C. Abramsky (ed), *Essays in Honour of E.H. Carr* (London, 1974), p. 155.

94. CAB27/625 FP(36) 47th meeting, 16 May 1939.

7. 'Guilty Men': The Case of Neville Chamberlain

SIDNEY ASTER

'History . . . is often simpler than the historians make it'. Sean O'Faolain, *The Irish* (London, 1947)

I. GUILTY MEN[1]

On Friday morning, 31 May 1940, three London journalists gathered, as was their habit before the local pub opened, on the roof of Lord Beaverbrook's *Evening Standard*. The topic of conversation was the unmitigated military catastrophe that had enveloped the British Expeditionary Force on the beaches of Dunkirk. Accounts of the first interviews with rescued survivors had just reached Fleet Street. The former Prime Minister, Neville Chamberlain, already knew of the 'terrible tales . . . of ships full of troops torpedoed or bombed . . . of thousands of men hiding in the dunes waiting to be taken off, and parched with thirst'.[2] By nightfall on 2 June, almost a quarter million British and over 100 000 French troops would be evacuated. As the three journalists discussed the disaster, the idea for a book emerged. One chose the title, *Guilty Men* – inspired by an episode in J.B. Morton's *Saint-Just* (1939), a biography of the French revolutionary leader. Another was dispatched to find a publisher, who was to be 'a slightly hesitant' Victor Gollancz. The task of writing the book was divided among the three. It was drafted in the course of that

233

weekend, eight chapters from each author. The book was finished by Tuesday, 4 June and published on 5 July, the first in a new series of Left Book Club 'Victory Books'. It bore the pseudonym 'Cato' because Cato had cleaned out the sewers of Rome.[3]

The identity of 'Cato' was a mystery. Some guessed that he was Duff Cooper or Aneurin Bevan. Others pointed to Randolph Churchill, H.G. Wells, Leslie Hore-Belisha or even Lord Beaverbrook.[4] In fact, the authors were a less lofty, though quite a brilliant trio of radical journalists. They included Michael Foot whom Lord Beaverbrook had wooed away from the socialist *Tribune* in 1938 to the *Evening Standard*. Foot would become its editor in 1942; later he would return in various capacities to *Tribune* and the Labour *Daily Herald*, before leading the Labour party from 1980 to 1983. In 1940 he was the author of *Armistice, 1918–1939*, a scathing critique of foreign policy in the inter-war years. Frank Owen, a turbulent, hard-drinking Welshman, served his apprenticeship on the *Daily Express* before becoming editor of the *Evening Standard* in 1938. The youngest member of the 1929–1931 Parliament, and a die-hard Lloyd George Liberal, he too contributed to the foreign policy debate in *The Three Dictators* (1940), and subsequently wrote a doting biography of Lloyd George, *Tempestuous Journey* (1954). Peter Howard, one of the principal leader writers for *Express* newspapers since 1933, was an accomplished athlete, farmer and playwright. He became a fervent convert to, and prolific propagandist for, the Oxford Group, – the British component of the Moral Rearmament movement of Dr Frank Buchman.[5]

What bound the three journalists together, besides their devotion to the same boss, Lord Beaverbrook, was an impassioned contempt for Neville Chamberlain's appeasement diplomacy. They were sensitive to the shift in public opinion after Dunkirk, and believed that if given firm leadership the British people were prepared for the supreme sacrifice in the 'people's war' against Nazism.

Such was the talent which produced *Guilty Men*, described in 1983 by the BBC commentator, Robin Day, as 'the most famous polemic in British political history'.[6] The book was certainly popular. In time it was to be famous, and to this day it is influential. It was reprinted 22 times before October 1940 and eventually sold, in the words of one of its authors, 'like a pornographic classic'.[7] Sales reached 217 432, despite the refusal of four major distributors – W.H. Smith, Wymans, Simpkin Marshall and Boots' Libraries – to handle it. [8] As late as 1945 the trade unionist, Clive Jenkins, recalled his visits to the local library, where still 'you had to put your name down on the waiting list for your copy of *Guilty Men*'.[9]

The instant success of the book was hardly due to its erratic structure, hinting at a collaborative effort. Written in 'pseudo-Beaverbrook jargon',[10] the book listed a 'cast' of 15, including three Prime Ministers, ten ministers, an advisor and the government Chief Whip in the House of Commons. The contents were 24 brief chapters dedicated to savage character assassination. Sarcastic chapter titles such as 'The Navy that Sam Built' (Sir Manuel Hoare), 'Umbrella Man' and 'Missing the Bus' (Neville Chamberlain), 'Caligula's Race Horse' (Sir Thomas Inskip), 'The Man with the Snow Suit' (Leslie Burgin), and 'Portfolio without a Minister' (Lord Stamp) enticed the reader.

The popularity of the book was not surprising. National disasters and their attendant shock need scapegoats – *Guilty Men* helped to explain the Dunkirk débâcle and assuaged the shock of defeat. Its preface of two short quotations clearly spoke to a public looking for answers. One was a quote by Winston Churchill who had stated in 1936: 'The use of recriminating about the past is to enforce effective action at the present'. The other described an angry crowd which beseiged the French Convention in 1793 searching for 'a dozen guilty men'. In 1940, 'Cato found more than a dozen guilty men, and the sentence was merciless:

> The nation is united to a man in its desire to prosecute the war in total form: there must be a similar unity in the national confidence. Let the guilty men retire, then, of their own volition, and so make an essential contribution to the victory upon which all are implacably resolved.[11]

In the course of the war, under the leadership of Winston Churchill, the guilty men were either retired or scattered to world wide postings. Neville Chamberlain himself did not live to see their dispersal. He died on 9 November 1940, soon after the publication of *Guilty Men*.

Guilty Men enshrined the disillusion of a generation which had experienced the depression, appeasement diplomacy in the 1930s, and Dunkirk. It set the tone of debate for the study of appeasement for 20 years after the war. 'Cato's' verdict was endorsed by anti-appeasement, right wing historians as well as liberal and left wing internationalists. Proponents of the former included Winston Churchill, Lewis Namier and John Wheeler-Bennett. Prominent among the latter were Elizabeth Wiskemann and A.L. Rowse. Sympathy with the 'guilty men' thesis never in fact died with this pre-war generation. It continues to reverberate in the writings, for example, of A.L. Rowse. In *A Man of the Thirties* (1979), he reprinted with relish a poem he first published in 1937:

A day will come when there shall descend on them
From the skies they do not observe, some stratagem

Of fate to search and sear their flesh with fire,
Seal the eyes that are stupid with desire. . . .

For these are they who, warned of what's to come,
Walk blindly on to their appointed doom.

Rowse reiterated that condemnation in his numerous volumes of memoirs and, most pointedly, in *All Souls and Appeasement* (1961). In the latter, appeasement was derided as the foreign policy of 'a class in decadence' who 'well-nigh ruined their country and reduced it to a second-rate place in the world'.[12] It has also been consistently reaffirmed by such historians as Martin Gilbert and Richard Gott, Telford Taylor, Anthony Adamthwaite, J.A.S. Grenville, Larry William Fuchser and Williamson Murray.[13]

By the mid-1960s the 'orthodox consensus' inspired by *Guilty Men* was under attack. First, Max Beloff in several book reviews, then A.J.P. Taylor in *The Origins of the Second World War* (1961), and W.N. Medlicott's *The Coming of War in 1939* (1963) and *British Foreign Policy Since Versailles* (1968) challenged the 'guilty men' thesis. Secondly, research which went beyond the few published volumes of British and German diplomatic documents, memoirs and parliamentary debates was propelled by historic legislation passed in May 1967. The British Parliament reduced the period of secrecy for most state documents from 50 to 30 years. The floodgates of revisionism were opened.

There followed a period of 20 years of frenetic research. The question of guilt was put aside while the evidence was re-examined, some would argue for the first time, and a revisionist interpretation emerged. It was now suggested that appeasement was too contentious a word, too misunderstood to belong to the vocabulary of a diplomatic historian. Instead, research was diverted towards uncovering the strategic, economic, imperial and political factors which motivated appeasement. Military policy, apparently, had been dictated by inadequate resources and over-extended global commitments. Public opinion, it was alleged, had been too pacifist to consider a policy of 'standing up to Hitler'. There was a sound financial rationale, one was told, for the Treasury's arguments against unlimited rearmament. The Dominions, it appeared, played an active role in support of appeasement. More recently, we have been urged to accept the view that domestic-political factors (*Primat der Innenpolitik*) were as vital in determining the course of appeasement as external events (*Primat der Aussenpolitik*). Finally, it has been argued that appeasement was not unique to the inter-war years, but had respectable antecedents in the nineteenth century. Every accusation laid down by 'Cato', the revisionist historian has dismissed on the basis of new evidence or mitigating circumstances.[14]

The result of revisionist investigation, therefore, has been a widespread condemnation of the 'guilty men' thesis. Historians have generally concluded that *Guilty Men* was 'unbalanced and unfair'. Of the few Chamberlain cabinet ministers to address the verdict directly, former air minister Lord Swinton observed that 'it is totally unjust to pillory them as guilty men'.[15]

But is that the case? Have 'Cato's' accusations been adequately considered? Of those original charges, which can be confirmed and which can now be dismissed? Can they be buried, once and for all, to linger only in the memories of the dwindling survivors of the 1930s? If not, then can one return to the 'guilty men' indictment and be done with the appeasement debate – for it is over.

II. GUILTY OF WHAT?

'Cato' began his slim volume with a chapter titled 'The Beaches of Dunkirk'. Quoting the evacuees, it described how 'hungry, bandaged, thirsty, soaked in oil, salt water and blood the unbeaten Army returned to the shores of England'. The causes of this disaster were the subject of *Guilty Men*. Unfortunately, the book is erratic, lurching from subject to subject, without chronological or structural coherence. To understand 'the origins and monstrous growth of this régime of little men', 'Cato' began by analysing the 'MacDonald–Baldwin ascendancy'. Both Prime Ministers were condemned because they 'took over a great empire, supreme in arms and secure in liberty. They conducted it to the edge of national annihilation'. There followed a litany of alleged miscalculations, deceptions, myopic foreign and defence policy decisions, and outright incompetence.

MacDonald was regarded as having been 'blind to the purposes of the criminal new Nazi war power arising in the heart of Europe', dismissing it 'as a manifestation of exhuberant German youth', and for 'leaving us more defenceless at the end of four years' office than he found us'. Baldwin was condemned for having overseen 'the reduction of British air power to fifth in world rank'. He was also chastised for his confession that he could not have won the 1935 election on a rearmament platform. Sir Samuel Hoare was labelled the 'clever fumbler', who in his handling of the Anglo–German naval agreement of 1935 and the Abyssinian crisis was described as having 'passed from experience to experience, like Boccaccio's virgin, without discernible effect upon his condition'. Commenting upon Baldwin's retirement in 1937, 'Cato' wrote 'that he and his colleagues had let their country's defences fall into such disrepair that, being challenged, they dare not risk a war even against a second-rate bully like Mussolini'. Both Prime Ministers were blamed for having 'fumbled or funked' major foreign policy questions, while their huge parliamentary majorities 'yessed the government through every situation'.[16]

'Cato' acknowledged that Neville Chamberlain was 'a tough old businessman, of great vitality and fibre' who, until he became Prime Minister in 1937, had been an advocate of the 'urgent need' to rearm. Once taking power, Chamberlain began to admit that progress in this area was slower than anticipated. Nonetheless, he made numerous optimistic statements on the rate of British rearmament. Such assurances did nothing to deter Hitler during the course of the Czech crisis. Nor did they prevent the German occupation of Czechoslovakia in March 1939 or the outbreak of war on 3 September 1939. 'Cato' pointed out that Chamberlain was then exhorted from all quarters to make 'the most terrific exertions to equip the nation for war in every department'.[17] Dunkirk confirmed 'Cato's' argument that this advice had fallen on deaf ears.

The narrative was then interrupted by several chapters dedicated to character assassinations of some leading ministers and advisors. Baldwin's announcement on 13 March 1936 that the long-awaited post of minister for the co-ordination of defence was to be filled by Sir Thomas Inskip evoked the remark: 'It is a clerical error . . . . there has been no similar appointment since the Roman Emperor Caligula made his horse a Consul'. The four year opposition campaign to create a ministry of supply was accorded the same criticism. Only after the Chamberlain government had been 'slapped and kicked and cursed' did it yield. On 29 April 1939 the announcement of the new minister, Leslie Burgin, was greeted with 'astonishment'. The next target for 'Cato's' invective was Sir Horace Wilson, chief industrial advisor to the government. His 'was the policy, his the philosophy of life, his the ideology' which mesmerised Chamberlain. Finally, the government Chief Whip, Captain David Margesson, was credited with manipulating Parliament and quelling discontent among Tory backbenchers.[18]

The final portion of *Guilty Men* was concerned with the period of the 'phoney war', when Chamberlain would have been expected to commit the entire resources of the country to remedying past deficiencies. Instead, 'Cato' asserted, Chamberlain 'preferred to continue with the peacetime methods' of rearmament in a 'leisurely manner', because 'our rulers were still unaware of the meaning of total war'. The government 'did not exert itself to any great extent in the arming of our country, even after we had clashed into war with the most tremendous military power of all times'. For that reason alone, if not for the pre-war record, 'Cato' urged: 'Let the guilty men retire'.[19]

What do all the accusations and invective amount to? The fundamental argument is that the MacDonald–Baldwin–Chamberlain administrations failed in their duties to rearm Britain adequately to meet clear threats of aggression in Europe, the Mediterranean and the Far East. They deceived public opinion with optimistic accounts of military preparedness. Secondly, the foreign policy of appeasement was condemned as blind to the aggressive ambitions of Nazism and one which made damaging and unnecessary concessions in the vain hope of preserving peace. Thirdly, the large Conservative majorities gained in the 1931 and 1935 elections were used to enforce parliamentary compliance with government policies, even when these were unpopular. The political apparatus blurred the sharp edges of issues, deliberately smeared the reputations of opposition critics, and ignored the talented in favour of the incompetent and the subservient.

It would be foolhardy outside a full scale book to assess the findings of revisionist history relating to the 'guilty men' thesis. This essay will attempt a more circumscribed contribution. The charges in *Guilty Men* will be examined in relation to the prime ministerial career of Neville Chamberlain. There are sufficient and compelling reasons to concentrate on him. In *Loyalists and Loners* (1986) Michael Foot observed that 'pride of place as Guilty Man Number One must surely always be allotted to Neville Chamberlain'.[20] One need not concur with this view to concede that for 'Cato', as in popular conceptions and as a focus for historians, Chamberlain's career was most closely associated with appeasement, the origins of the war and the military disasters of 1940. More than half of the 125 pages of *Guilty Men* concentrated on his term as Prime Minister. In addition, it would require separate essays, each devoted to the 14 co-accused, to assess properly the 'guilty men' thesis.

There is a more urgent reason for focussing on Chamberlain. Much of the evidence used by revisionist historians from the late 1960s to the mid-1980s has been drawn from the same source – the documents in the Public Record Office – and it is running dry. Furthermore, history written from official papers tends towards a pro-Conservative interpretation. This may be due simply to the British generation gap, the charitable nature of historians or, more likely, because official documents present evidence that alternatives were not feasible.[21] Whatever the reason, revisionism has attempted to transform Chamberlain from a myopic appeaser to a tough practitioner of *Realpolitik*. Such was the situation until 22 July 1975, when a unique archive was opened to historical investigation. Chamberlain's private papers, deposited in the University of Birmingham Library, proved to be a vital addition to a more complete understanding of the man.[22]

Alternating between his two spinster sisters, Hilda and Ida, Chamberlain developed the habit of writing long confessional letters on a weekly basis. In this manner, he wrote almost 80 000 words a year, each letter running to eight or ten sheets of notepaper, 'penned with a steel nib in a slightly sloping script with hardly a correction'. Chamberlain trusted the recipients of his outpourings and valued their 'sympathy' and 'understanding approval' in times of crisis.[23]

State secrets notwithstanding, this correspondence spelled out Chamberlain's policies and reactions to personalities and events. The letters are acerbic in their assessment of individuals, painstaking in their exposition of views, and poignant, often to the point of embarrassment, in their emotional honesty. Buttressed by occasional diaries which he kept in small hardcover notebooks, they offer extraordinary insight into his mind and emotions. They reveal a personality with marked traits of inferiority that were only assuaged by a litany of repeated compliments and congratulations. This hunger for flattery nourished a growing vanity and self-righteousness. Chamberlain began to believe he was irreplacable as Prime Minister and exulted in the powers of his office. He wrote with confidence of his abilities and policies, yet admitted to bouts of severe depression and sleepless nights only curtailed with sleeping pills. The correspondence portrays a man with an obsessive sense of mission, making predictions which were invariably optimistic and invariably wrong. In foreign affairs and politics his letters reveal a disregard for the aggressive dynamics of totalitarian states, his physical and moral repugnance for war – made all the stronger by the loss of one of his cousins – his conviction that there were no alternatives to appeasement, and his implacable opposition to unlimited rearmament. There is abundant evidence of his hatred for his parliamentary critics whose comments he always took as a personal insult. He was obsessed with out-manoeuvring political opponents such as Winston Churchill and David Lloyd George and, most surprisingly of all, expressed undisguised contempt for members of his own cabinet, particularly the 'wets'. For all of them he reserved the Victorian gentleman's escatology of 'cur', 'insufferable' and 'blackguard'.[24] In essence, the letters confirm that the accusations spelled out by 'Cato' in 1940 were in fact largely justified.

III. THE GUILT OF NEVILLE CHAMBERLAIN

Neville Chamberlain was 68 years old when he succeeded Stanley Baldwin as Prime Minister on 28 May 1937. It was an office for which he was destined never to fight an election. He brought to it the approval of political colleagues and 'quasi-prime ministerial experience'.[25] First elected to Parliament in 1918, he served as postmaster-general (1922-23), minister of health (1923, 1924-29, 1931), and Chancellor of the Exchequer, briefly in 1923-24 and more significantly from 1931 to 1937. It was in this latter capacity that Chamberlain steered Britain through the depression along the road towards economic recovery.

At this time, while being groomed as Baldwin's successor, Chamberlain became increasingly critical of the Prime Minister and more confident of his own abilities and priorities in the area of foreign affairs. As Britain embarked on the rearmament programme announced in the major defence White Paper of 1935, and as the country weathered the Italian invasion of Ethiopia, the reoccupation of the Rhineland and the outbreak of the Spanish civil war, Chamberlain's diary recorded a constant lament: the country was 'drifting

without a policy'.[26] When he finally became Prime Minister, he
brought to the office as clearly formulated a set of priorities as any
twentieth century British Prime Minister, which he described as 'the
double policy of rearmament and better relations with Germany and
Italy'. These derived from a conviction that Hitler's Germany was
'the bully of Europe', 'utterly untrustworthy and dishonest', and that
Italy must be weaned away from too close association with the Nazis.
Believing that 'fear of force is the only remedy' and that legitimate
grievances were capable of peaceful solution, Chamberlain embarked on a policy of deterrence and appeasement. Nothing would
distract him from his stubborn quest to find 'decency even in dictators'. Such an approach, he was convinced, would produce the
'*détente* which would then lead to an Anglo–German *entente* – the
mission of his leadership.[27]

This search for *détente* was derived from principles to which Chamberlain adhered with singleminded determination. War he regarded
as the ultimate absurdity, which 'wins nothing, cures nothing, ends
nothing'. He never accepted the view that at some point war might
indeed be inevitable. On several occasions, his private letters suggested
that 'the ultimate decision of war' would be one which he would be
too intimidated to make. He saw the task of making 'gentle the life of
the world' as the noblest ambition of an English statesman.[28]

Such passionate hatred of war bordered on pacifism, but in the
final analysis Chamberlain believed in the idea of the 'vital cause'. He
defined this as 'a cause that transcends all the human values, a cause
to which you can point, if some day you win the victory, and say,
"that cause is safe"'. For this Chamberlain would go to war, although
he was less forthcoming with regard to a definition. He suggested that
he would fight either to resist 'a claim by one state to dominate others
by force', or 'for the preservation of democracy'.[29] He believed that
Europe was perilously close to being divided into 'two opposing *blocs*
or camps', along ideological lines. Such a development he regarded
as 'dangerous', 'stupid' and to be avoided at all costs.[30]

Chamberlain's assertion that Britain was 'a very rich and a very
vulnerable Empire' supported this view. He regarded the League of
Nations as incapable of providing collective security without the
membership of several major powers. He held France and its statesmen in near contempt. 'She (sic) never can keep a secret for more
than half an hour, nor a government for more than nine months', he
observed in January 1938. Of particular concern were French economic and industrial troubles which hindered its rearmament pro-

grammes. His attitude to the United States was equally reserved. He never neglected to pay the usual homage to the 'special relationship', but his opinion of Anglo–American relations was that 'it is always best and safest to count on *nothing* from the Americans except words'. With regard to the Soviet Union, he was always quick to refute any allegations of ideological antipathy: 'I have no bias in favour of Nazism, Fascism, or Bolshevism'. Nonetheless, his private letters indicate that he had no faith in Soviet military capabilities and considered the Russians untrustworthy as a potential ally. Soviet intelligence activities abroad and in Britain also increased his suspicions.[31] Consequently, Britain could only look to its own resources for protection, having no reliable allies.

Chamberlain was convinced that 'you should never menace unless you are in a position to carry out your threats'. An effective foreign policy, involving the threat of resistance, depended on the ability to deploy military power. Until Britain was adequately armed 'we must adjust our foreign policy to our circumstances', he wrote, 'and even bear with patience and good humour actions which we would like to treat in very different fashion'.[32]

These principles all pointed to appeasement – conciliation and pacification of the dictators. This was not a cause and effect sequence for Chamberlain. He genuinely believed that the Versailles Treaty of 1919 had given the Germans 'good cause to ask for consideration of their grievances'.[33] His policy would enable discontents to be assuaged, grievances to be remedied and potential danger spots to be defused.

In sharp contrast were the objections to these principles which were inherent in *Guilty Men*. Abhorrence of war was a cloud that hung over the entire inter-war generation. However, the responsibilities of power included the option to declare war, as well as the pursuit of peace. A 'vital cause' was certainly fundamental, but it was a subjective judgement. The problem, as dramatised by 'Cato', was the point at which such a cause was at stake. Why had it not been in 1936 during the reoccupation of the Rhineland, or the 1938 *Anschluss* between Germany and Austria? In September 1938, Britain could also have drawn the line at the height of the Czech crisis. Why then should it have been in March 1939 that Britain gave a guarantee of the independence of Poland, which 'Cato' derided as a 'bastard caricature of collective security'.[34] The polarisation of Europe was not a concern for the authors of *Guilty Men*. In their view, Europe was already ideologically at war, split between a democratic *bloc* and a totalitarian one. On the subject of allies, there was some common ground between Chamberlain and 'Cato'. For the latter, beggars could not be choosers and Britain's vulnerability was all the more reason to make friends and influence people. There was deep disagreement on the need to buy time in order to rearm. For 'Cato', the time gained through the sacrifice of Czechoslovakia and during the phoney war was criminally squandered. Finally, 'Cato' regarded the appeasement of Hitler as futile. Hitler's ambition was not the legitimate redress of grievances but continental domination. The gulf which separated Chamberlain's principles and 'Cato's' perspective was unbridgeable.

'If only we could get on terms with the Germans', Chamberlain wrote to his sister, Ida, on 4 July 1937, 'I would not care a rap about Musso'. Chamberlain would spend his honeymoon period as Prime Minister chasing the indifferent Germans and being stranded with the equally indifferent Italians. From May 1937 to March 1938 he embarked on a diplomatic offensive in search of *détente* with the dictators. Privately he wrote 'of the far reaching plans which I have in mind for the appeasement of Europe and Asia and for the ultimate check to the mad armament race, which if allowed to continue must involve us all in ruin'.[35]

Feelers were put out to both the Italian and German governments to explore the ground for a settlement of outstanding differences. Acting on his own initiative, Chamberlain personally met with the Italian ambassador in London, Count Dino Grandi, engaged in direct correspondence with Mussolini, and used his sister-in-law, Ivy Chamberlain, as a private intermediary. Chamberlain was determined to grant *de jure* recognition of the Italian conquest of Ethiopia as a prelude to opening Anglo – Italian talks. He by-passed the Foreign Office, which he accused of having 'no imagination and no courage'. The issue had nothing in fact to do with either. Rather it centered on the real degree of trust which could be accorded to Mussolini. 'The FO persist in seeing Musso only as a sort of Machiavelli putting on a false mask of friendship in order to further nefarious ambitions', Chamberlain wrote on 2 September. He believed that the only alternative would be an armaments race in the Mediterranean, and was determined to divide the Axis powers at its weakest link.[36]

Anglo – German relations proved even more contentious. 'The Germans and the Italians are as exasperating as they can be', Chamberlain complained, yet he missed no opportunity to seek an opening. That finally came in the autumn of 1937. Lord Halifax, Lord

President of the Council, accepted an invitation to visit Berlin and Berchtesgaden. This went ahead and included meetings with senior Nazi officials and Hitler. On 26 November Chamberlain wrote that the visit had been 'a great success' because it created the atmosphere in which Anglo – German differences could be discussed. He then added not the first of his many inaccurate estimates of the dictators: 'Both Hitler and Goering said repeatedly and emphatically that they had no desire or intention of making war and I think we may take this as correct at any rate for the present'.[37]

What Chamberlain described as the 'new impetus' he had given to British foreign relations had been achieved largely by ignoring the Foreign Office. At the least he was determined 'to stir it up with a long pole' and ended up with a new foreign secretary. Anthony Eden may not have been as anti-appeasement as he later contended in his memoirs, but he felt his authority as foreign minister being undermined. The sticking point proved to be Anglo – Italian relations. Eden wanted to have charge of the negotiations with Italy and, as 'Cato' put it, require that 'old agreements with Mussolini should be carried out before new ones were made'.[38] Chamberlain saw this rather as obstruction. On 20 February 1938 Eden resigned, to be replaced by Lord Halifax.

In seeking an explanation of his colleague's actions, Chamberlain observed: 'I have gradually arrived at the conclusion that at bottom Anthony did not want to talk either with Hitler or Mussolini and as I did he was right to go'. Chamberlain found Eden's departure an enormous relief. It also served more crucial purposes. Having also replaced Sir Robert Vansittart with a permanent under-secretary of state of his own choosing, Sir Alec Cadogan, Chamberlain was now in control of foreign affairs, with compliant personnel to assist him. His delight with this turn of events was unbounded. 'I feel that things are moving in the right direction in Rome, Washington and Tokio (*sic*),' he noted, 'so unless Berlin gives us another unpleasant surprise we should see a gradual improvement during the next few months'.[39] He would shortly find that he had no gift for prophecy, only a *penchant* for unwarranted optimism.

The German occupation of Austria on 12 March 1938, the *Anschluss*, came as no surprise to Chamberlain. His only objection was to 'German methods' and his hope that violence might be excluded.[40] The Austrian *coup*, however, ushered in an 18 month period when crisis followed crisis. Significantly, each crisis put appeasement to the test, evoking further resolves for additional but limited rearmament and the pursuit of appeasement. Each crisis found Chamberlain's policies in ruins, yet with his principles unshaken. He readily described the *Anschluss* as 'very disheartening and discouraging', and admitted 'that force is the only argument Germany understands'. Although collective security was quite dead, he contemplated reviving alliance diplomacy and showing 'some increase or acceleration in rearmament'. He acknowledged that conversations with Germany must be temporarily abandoned, while those with Italy would be steadily pursued. On the other hand, he blithely observed that 'I am not going to take the situation too tragically'. Never one to dwell on the past, he turned to the next danger spot on the European map and offered this sanguine prospect: 'If we can avoid another violent *coup* in Czechoslovakia, which ought to be feasible, it may be possible for Europe to settle down again, and some day for us to start peace talks again with the Germans'.

It was clear in Chamberlain's mind, and his military advisors later concurred, that no combination of powers could save Czechoslovakia from a German attack. Czechoslovakia 'would simply be a pretext for going to war with Germany. . . .[and] that we could not think of unless we had a reasonable prospect of being able to beat her to her knees in a reasonable time, and of that I see no sign'. Consequently, he dismissed as impractical the Churchillian alternative of a 'grand alliance' against the dictators. As for the problem of Anglo – German relations, Chamberlain wrote on 20 March that, having recovered his 'spirits and confidence', he had formulated a design for peace in Europe.

> My idea at present is that we should again approach Hitler following up our Halifax – Henderson conversations and say something like this. '. . . it is no use crying over spilt milk and what we have to do now is to consider how we can restore the confidence you have shattered. Everyone is thinking that you are going to repeat the Austrian *coup* in Czecho-Slovakia. I know you say you aren't, but nobody believes you. The best thing you can do is to tell us exactly what you want for your Sudeten *Deutsch*. If it is reasonable we will urge the Czechs to accept it and if they do you must give us assurances that you will let them alone in future'. I am not sure that in such circumstances I might not be willing to join in some joint guarantee *with Germany* of Czech independence.[41]

The scenario was in fact played out as the Czech crisis came to a head in September 1938. In the interim, the military option was rejected and plans were set afoot for reopening Anglo – German negotiations at an appropriate moment.

The conciliation part of the programme was secure. 'But what about rearmament?' 'Cato' had asked. Chamberlain's priorities were clearly set. His over-riding principle, articulated as early as 1934 while he was Chancellor of the Exchequer, was that Britain's best defence policy 'would be the existence of a deterrent force so powerful as to render success in attack too doubtful to be worthwhile'. As he wrote on 9 February 1936, in practical terms this meant 'our resources will be more profitably employed in the air, and on the sea, than in building up great armies'.[42] Nothing, including the outbreak of war with Germany in 1939, ever changed his view on this subject. Given this strategy, his priorities were to maintain fiscal stability, providing for home and imperial defence, and absolute opposition to Britain ever again committing itself to raising a 1914-style continental army.

As Prime Minister, Chamberlain was in a position to impose his version of rearmament.[43] In December 1937 the cabinet decided that neither the Territorial Army nor the Field Force should be equipped for military intervention on the continent but that the production of fighters should be accelerated. In February 1938 the Field Force was relegated to two infantry and one mobile division which, as a last resort only, would be given a continental role. Finally, under the impact of the *Anschluss* a further increase was authorised in defensive air protection. This was done, but at the expense of the army whose estimates were cut.

However little of this was known to 'Cato', government statements led 'Cato' to conclude˙ that the British public had been deceived. Chamberlain was quoted at various times as having said that 'production has begun in earnest', the 'country is strong' and, in March 1938, that 'the almost terrifying power that Britain is building up has a sobering effect on the opinion of the world'.[44] As far as 'Cato' was concerned, the man least impressed by this 'terrifying power' was Hitler.

Chamberlain spared no effort to negotiate a solution to the crisis precipitated by Hitler's campaign to achieve self-determination for the Sudeten Germans. The one success he enjoyed, but on a different front, was to oversee the signature of the Anglo – Italian agreement on 16 April. This pledged Mussolini to withdraw his volunteers from Spain, and committed Britain to seek League of Nations recognition of the Italian conquest of Ethiopia. Nevertheless, the road to Berlin remained blocked. Chamberlain foresaw the reopening of Anglo – German talks as soon as the Czechs were forced 'to face up to realities and settle their minority problem'.[45] The French agreed to follow the persuasive lead of the British Prime Minister, who was to be entrusted the task of satisfying Hitler's demands.

Despite the 'weekend crisis' in mid-May 1938, when it was rumoured that Germany was poised to attack Czechoslovakia, Chamberlain remained confident. He was sometimes discouraged by what he called 'cranks' who denigrated him 'as a Fascist, an enemy of the League and a materialist'. Yet he consoled himself with the view that the 'country wants peace and appreciates the fact that this Govt. is delivering the goods'. He was convinced that 'we shall pull through without a disaster'. By June, for the first time though not the last, he exulted in the thought that the Germans 'have missed the bus and may never again have such a favourable chance of asserting their domination over Central and Eastern Europe'. 'I am completely convinced that the course I am taking is right', he wrote, adding that he would allow nothing to stand in the way of appeasement.[46]

This exuberant determination infused Chamberlain's letters throughout July and August despite the lack of progress. As late as 6 September he professed optimism. 'I have a feeling that things have gone in such a way', he observed, 'as to make it more and more difficult for him [Hitler] to use force'. Five days later it was crisis once again: 'It has been a pretty awful week – enough to send most people off their heads, if their heads were not as firmly screwed on as mine'. Negotiations between Germany and Czechoslovakia had reached an *impasse*, despite the efforts of the British mediator, Lord Runciman, to bring the protagonists together. As a result, on 13 September Chamberlain implemented what he called his 'unprecedented step'. He proposed a summit meeting to Hitler. It was as daring as it was foolhardy. The initiative committed the British Prime Minister, in effect, to imposing a negotiated settlement upon the Czech government. In his view this was not a situation where 'really the great issues' were at stake.[47]

Chamberlain and Hitler met three times, first at Berchtesgaden, then at Godesberg, and finally at Munich on 30 September which resulted in the agreement to partition Czechoslovakia. This shuttle diplomacy and the Munich accords have been the subject of debate for almost half a century. Criticised and maligned, explained and rationalised, they have preoccupied historians bedevilled by their significance and lessons. Nor is this surprising. The events of September 1938 involve issues which concern the ultimates of war and peace, morality, and expediency versus principle. No definitive resolution likely will be possible, though the perimeters of the debate have been well established.

In defence of the Munich agreement, several arguments have proven most enduring. British public opinion was isolationist and would not have condoned a war in defence of Czechoslovakia. Certainly Chamberlain had no enthusiasm for getting involved in what he myopically described as 'a quarrel in a far-away country between people of whom we know nothing'.[48] Dominion opinion, as relayed by the High Commissioners in London, pressed consistently for a peaceful resolution (see Chapter 8). War might have divided the empire, and in September 1938 Britain had no reliable allies. The problem was further compounded by the nightmare of a three front war. In November 1935 the chiefs of staffs had warned that Britain was dangerously over-extended, without the resources to defend its empire against simultaneous threats. The warning was repeated in 1938: 'War against Japan, Germany and Italy simultaneously in 1938 is a commitment which neither the present nor the projected strength of our defence forces is designed to meet, even if we were in alliance with France and Russia'.[49] It has also been argued that the strongest defence of the Munich agreement was the parlous state of British rearmament. Munich bought Britain an additional year in which to accelerate the rearmament programme.

Unfortunately, none of these considerations counted for much in Chamberlain's mind at the time. His approach to foreign policy had been elaborated before he became Prime Minister. Munich was its logical culmination. War had been averted, and what he termed 'a stable future for Czecho-Slovakia (*sic*) and the sterilisation of another danger spot' had been achieved. Moreover, the Munich accords were designed to insure the self-determination of three and a half million Sudeten Germans, a principle which they had been denied in the peace settlement in 1919. The demand for its application in September 1938 was the strength of Hitler's case. To have ignored it would have meant war against a cause which no western statesman could oppose. Besides, as Chamberlain had confided on 19 September to his sister, Ida, 'on principle I didn't care two hoots whether the Sudetens were in the Reich or out of it according to their own wishes'.[50] That still left a question mark over the morality of this act. Peace in Europe may have been secured in the short term, as 'Cato' contended, or the long term as Chamberlain hoped, but this was pacification which was bought at the expense of a third nation. For that reason alone there can be no defence of the Munich agreement.

Equally, there can be no defence based on the contention that Chamberlain was never 'taken in' by Hitler. 'Cato' made the case that Chamberlain 'was convinced that Hitler meant to play ball. He felt sure that the German *Führer* would never go to war against Britain now'. Support for these allegations derived from Chamberlain's comments on the Munich agreement as well as his views on rearmament. On his return from Munich he had stated that the Anglo – German declaration signed by himself and Hitler was 'only a prelude to a larger settlement in which all Europe may find peace'. From 10 Downing Street he spoke to cheering crowds of 'peace with honour' and 'peace for our time'. He later told parliament that 'when I signed the document I meant what was in the document. I am convinced that *Herr* Hitler meant it too when he signed it'. In his private papers he observed, 'I got the impression that here was a man who could be relied upon when he had given his word'. And in conversation with a former member of his cabinet, Chamberlain expostulated, 'but I have made peace'. In the Commons Chamberlain ascribed such comments to euphoria and fatigue. Yet he repeated in the same breath: 'I do indeed believe that we may yet secure peace for our time'.[51]

Apologists for Munich have argued that British defence weaknesses and the need to buy time for the rearmament programme dictated foreign policy. Unfortunately, nowhere in Chamberlain's public utterances nor in his private correspondence is there a shred of supporting evidence.[52] Time was certainly a crucial factor for the Prime Minister, but what he had in mind was the time needed to avoid war, or that Hitler would conveniently die and thus peace would be secured. Keith Feiling, the first biographer to study Chamberlain's private papers – and his most perspicacious – observed: 'to gain time to arm against an inevitable war. . . . was never his first motive, which was plain enough, simply the rightness of peace and the wrongness of war'. Horace Wilson, Chamberlain's confidant and 'Cato's' *bête noire*, likewise commented that 'our policy was never designed just to postpone war, or enable us to enter war more united. The aim of appeasement was to avoid war altogether, for all time'.[53] If this is kept in mind the issue of rearmament in the post-Munich period becomes understandable.

The September crisis provided its own focus for 'Cato's' invective.

The cession of the Sudetenland to Germany was described as having 'been crammed down the reluctant gullet of the Czech rulers and eventually, with many a groan and retch, swallowed into their stomachs'. In the post-Munich parliamentary debate, 'MPs vied with each other', according to 'Cato', 'in their exertions to lick the hand of the Premier'. On one question only was unanimity achieved. The entire House was 'soothed and silenced by the expressed resolve of the Government now to set about the rearmament of Britain with energy'. Chamberlain promised Parliament 'further steps . . . to make good our deficiencies in the shortest possible time'. But he was determined to restore confidence so that the armaments race could be throttled. To his sister, Ida, he explained on 22 October: 'A lot of people seem to me to be losing their heads and talking and thinking as though Munich had made war more instead of less imminent. . . . though there are gaps to fill up we need not believe that we have got to make huge additions to the programmes now being put into operation'. He was also at pains to emphasise that 'the conciliation part of the policy is just as important as the rearming'.[54]

For such reasons Chamberlain balked at reconstructing his government to include Labour party members, or taking Eden back into the cabinet. He feared that this 'would sooner or later wreck the policy with which I am identified'. He resisted the temptation to call a post-Munich election to secure a mandate for his policies, although he did not entirely rule this out. Likewise he rejected suggestions that it was time for Britain to have ministers of supply and National Service. Should the need lessen, the government would have difficulty disbanding them. Chamberlain also admitted that the only reason he hesitated to make further overtures to Hitler was his fear that such a move might precipitate other resignations from his cabinet.[55]

Indeed, Chamberlain's private correspondence reveals for the first time the widespread, post-Munich disaffection which existed both in cabinet and party ranks. The resignation of the First Lord of the Admiralty, Duff Cooper, came close to being emulated by an additional minister, Oliver Stanley, and two junior ministers, Harry Crookshank and Robert Bernays. Chamberlain had nothing but contempt for these 'weaker breathren' and 'weak kneed colleagues'. Only reassurances that he would press on with rearmament staved off this potential damage to cabinet unity and appeasement. On other occasions in the autumn, unnamed 'followers' warned the Prime Minister of the low esteem in which his cabinet was held. Chamberlain was not unmindful of this disaffection. 'The material available is meagre in the extreme', he wrote in his own defence, 'I don't remember any time when there was so little promise among the younger men in the Government and on the back benches'. Many of the former he dismissed as individuals 'whose judgement I cannot trust and who are always a source of trouble in difficult times'. The minor cabinet reshuffle which followed early in 1939 did nothing to change Chamberlain's conviction of his own indispensability and that he was surrounded, as so vividly dramatised in *Guilty Men*, by incompetence.[56]

'It has struck me today', Chamberlain wrote on 6 November, 'that my policy is summed up in the old trinity of Faith Hope and Charity'. It was out of this trinity, as 'Cato' commented, that 'the Golden Age was born'. For the next five months, 'British politicians spent their time telling us that all was well, that Hitler was tamed, that the tiger had been transmogrified into a tabby by that old wizard of Number 10 Downing Street'. The Golden Age was not without setbacks. Chamberlain was repulsed by *Kristallnacht*, when on 10 November violent attacks were made against German Jews and their property. He condemned it as a pretext for Nazi 'barbarities'. Nevertheless, he remained as committed as ever. 'The only thing I care about', he noted on 4 December, 'is to be able to carry out the policy I believe, indeed *know* to be right'. He was buoyed by the results of his January visit to Rome, proud that Mussolini liked him. By mid-February his optimism was unbounded. 'All the information I get seems to point in the direction of peace', he observed, 'and I repeat once more that we have at last got on top of the dictators'.[57]

The 'Golden Age of confidence' shattered on 15 March 1939 when German troops over-ran the post-Munich frontiers of Czechoslovakia and occupied Prague. Chamberlain was shocked by Hitler's action which mocked the spirit and letter of Munich. In his private correspondence he labelled Hitler a 'fanatic', capable of a surprise attack against London and confessed, 'I *cannot* feel safe with Hitler'. Even more, 'such faith as I ever had in the assurances of dictators', he wrote, 'is rapidly being whittled away'.[58] Nothing would alter his abhorrence of war, his belief in appeasement and defensive rearmament and commitment to *détente*. But his tactics were to change under the impact of the March crisis.

'As always I want to gain time', Chamberlain wrote on 19 March, not to rearm it must be noted, but because 'I never accept the view that war is inevitable'. A week later, he expanded on his reactions, albeit still without a riposte to the Prague *coup*:

> I see nothing for us to do unless we are prepared ourselves to hand Germany an ultimatum. We are not strong enough ourselves and we cannot command sufficient strength elsewhere to present Germany with an overwhelming force. Our ultimatum would therefore mean war and I would never be responsible for presenting it. We shall just have to go on rearming and collecting what help we can from the outside in the hope that something would happen to break the spell, either Hitler's death or a realisation that the defence was too strong to make attack feasible.[59]

A definite response finally came on 31 March. Chamberlain announced in the House of Commons that the British government had guaranteed Poland. The guarantee had resulted from reports of an imminent German attack against Poland. It was one of the most disastrous decisions ever taken as a result of what proved to be faulty intelligence (this issue is discussed in Introduction). The authors of *Guilty Men* interpreted the guarantee as signifying that 'appeasement was pronounced dead', and that Britain would at last seek allies against German aggression. 'With or without Russia', 'Cato' wrote, 'we were committed to war against Nazi-ism at any moment when the Polish Government believed their independence threatened'. Such an undertaking could only be justified 'if we pledged our all to the most terrific exertions to equip the nation for war in every department'.[60]

'Cato' was labouring under several misconceptions. For Chamberlain, the guarantee was of Polish independence, not its existing boundaries. Moreover, he intended the guarantee to be not a declaration of war, but a signal to Hitler: 'a definite check which will enormously affect his prestige'. Nor did it mark the return of alliance diplomacy. As he later informed the House of Commons, his was 'not a policy of lining up opposing *blocs* of Powers in Europe . . . and accepting the view that war is inevitable'. Nonetheless, Chamberlain doubled the size of the Territorial Army, without providing for an equipment increase. He also established, finally, a ministry of supply, although the office was not set up until August and was restricted to supplying the army. A conscription bill was introduced on 26 April, but it was to remain in force for only three years and limited training to a six months' period. Such measures hardly fulfilled the pledge which Chamberlain had given on 17 March to spare no effort to insure the nation's safety.[61]

What remained of Chamberlain's dual approach of appeasement and rearmament? His first calculation was the odd fixation that he would survive Hitler. 'I did say when I returned from Munich that I could not imagine Hitler living to be an old man', he confided to his sister, Hilda, 'and I have often heard since that he himself does not expect to live long'. In the event, Hitler outlived him. His second calculation was that deterrence, backed by the guarantee to Poland and similar ones given shortly after to Rumania, Greece and Turkey, would prove effective. This assumed that Hitler would be impressed, and credible military sanctions and material resources could be deployed. Both assumptions proved equally faulty. Chamberlain was left, therefore, with a short term expectation that the deterrent front would succeed and a long term conviction that there were no alternatives to appeasement.

From April to August 1939, Chamberlain walked a mental and physical tightrope in what he described as 'the war of nerves'. Mussolini's seizure of Albania on 7 April forced him to acknowledge that *rapprochement* with Italy was blocked. Likewise he had to admit that further Anglo – German conversations would command no support in Britain. Yet his faith in his mission remained undented, and by the end of April he was pointing to a relaxation of tension. 'I believe every month that passes without war makes war more unlikely and although I expect to have more periods of acute anxiety yet in cold blood I cannot see Hitler starting a world war for Danzig'. In May he was positively exultant, declaring 'I myself still believe Hitler missed the bus last September and that his generals won't let him risk a major war now'. He then added gratuitously and without elaboration, 'but I can't see how the *détente* is to come about as long as the Jews obstinately go on refusing to shoot Hitler!'[62]

Despite the fact that Danzig was clearly marked as the next flashpoint, by early July Chamberlain's optimism became self-reinforcing. He reckoned a solution was possible and was already working on the details, conscious though he was that 'it is difficult to proceed when there are so many ready to cry "*Nous sommes trahis*"'. On 23 July he outlined privately the *vade mecum* which sustained him:

> One thing is I think clear, namely that Hitler has concluded that we mean business and that the time is not ripe for the major war. Therein he is fulfilling my expectations. Unlike some of my critics I go further

and say the longer the war is put off the less likely it is to come at all as
we go on perfecting our defences, and building up the defences of our
allies. . . . You don't need offensive forces sufficient to win a smash-
ing victory. What you want are defensive forces sufficiently strong to
make it impossible for the other side to win except at such a cost as to
make it not worth while. That is what we are doing and though at
present the German feeling is it is not worth while yet, they will
presently come to realise that it never *will* be worth while. Then we
can talk. . . . Meanwhile there is I think a definite *détente*.

Chamberlain was convinced by 30 July that Hitler had decided 'to put
Danzig into cold storage'. As a result, he encouraged any form of
contact, preferably discreet, to maintain an open line to Berlin. He
considered this an important way to encourage German moderates.
It was also desirable from the point of convincing Germany that it
'has a chance of getting fair and reasonable consideration and treatment from us and others', provided that it gave up the idea of
forcible solutions.[63]
  'Phew! What a week', Chamberlain wrote on 27 August, 'I feel like
a man driving a clumsy coach over a narrow cracked road along the
face of a precipice'. The war of nerves with Germany had heated up
with the signature on 24 August of the Nazi – Soviet pact of non-
aggression. When German terms for a Polish settlement were then
followed by an ultimatum for a Polish emissary to be dispatched to
Berlin, the British refused to press the issue in Warsaw (see Chapter
7). 'I count every hour that passes without a catastrophe', Chamberlain observed on 27 August, 'as adding its mite to the slowly accumulating anti-war forces'. On 1 September time ran out as Germany
launched its *Blitzkrieg* against Poland. Chamberlain was then confronted by militant cabinet ministers anxious to have Britain immediately fulfill its guarantee to Poland. The Prime Minister quelled this
'sort of mutiny' and dismissed the episode as having been precipitated by 'those who always behave badly when there is trouble
about'.[64] It was only on 3 September that Britain declared war against
Germany.
  Appeasement, deterrence, *détente* and *entente* – everything with
which Chamberlain was personally identified – were destroyed with
the outbreak of war. His failure was pervasive and personal. This was
a fact that he was forced to acknowledge not just once. As soon as the
British ultimatum to Germany to quit Poland had expired, Chamberlain spoke to the House of Commons. 'Everything that I have

worked for, everything that I have hoped for, everything that I have
believed in during my public life,' he confessed, 'has crashed into
ruins'. Eight months later, after his resignation as wartime Prime
Minister, Chamberlain again had to admit: 'All my world has
tumbled to bits in a moment'.[65]

Such massive failure invites the question as to Chamberlain's competence as a wartime Prime Minister. His private correspondence
indicates that he contemplated resignation shortly after the outbreak
of the war. 'While war was still averted', he wrote on 10 September,
'I felt I was indispensable, for no one else could carry out my policy.
Today the position has changed. Half a dozen people could take my
place while war is in progress'. He decided to cling to office because,
'the war was so different from what I expected that I found the strain
bearable'.[66] Unfortunately, he was the wrong man to lead a country
at war. His leadership had been debilitated by his hatred of war.
From September 1939 it was coupled with an abhorrence of the
deadly results of wartime decision-making. He readily admitted to an
'agony of mind . . . to give directions that would bring death and
mutilation and misery to so many'. After the battleship *Royal Oak*
was sunk in Scapa Flow, he confessed: 'How I hate and loathe this
war. I was never meant to be a war minister'. On a December tour of
the western front in France he was 'sickened . . . to see the barbed
wire and pill boxes and guns and anti-tank obstacles remembering
what they meant in the last war'.[67] There was much about Chamberlain therefore that detracted from an aggressive prosecution of total
war with its bloody consequences.

What emerged as a result was Chamberlain's obsession with the
chances of negotiating a peaceful settlement. His letters indicate that
he would make no peace with Hitler, but all other alternatives to end
the state of war were eagerly explored. It was the one area where he
believed he would have a vital role to play. In September he was
heartened by the 'stop the war' advocates. Throughout October and
November he monitored the peace proposals emanating from inter-
mediaries, but by 3 December he had to admit disconsolately that
'the underground peace movements . . . have dried up'. By that time
it was clear that the only peace would be based on Hitler's retention
of his conquests, and in December that was out of the question. In
May 1940 Chamberlain showed a temporary loss of nerve. If France
collapsed, he noted in his diary on 16 May, Britain's only chance for
survival would be if the United States appealed to Germany for an
armistice.[68]

Chamberlain's concern with the possibility of a negotiated end to the war was related to his conception of war strategy. This can best be summed up in the two epithets which recur in his private correspondence: 'a waiting war' and a 'war of wills'. This approach was largely determined by his peacetime experience with Germany. It was predicated on a rational approach to international affairs which had already proved so remarkably unsuccessful. He argued that in 'a waiting war' the British could outlast the Germans. As a result he intended to increase munitions production, maintain the blockade and take no offensive initiative. 'I do not believe that holocausts are required to gain victory', he wrote on 23 September, 'while they are certainly liable to lose us the peace'. He was fortified by the assumption that Hitler, too, would avoid a major confrontation with heavy casualties and concentrate on inflicting economic damage against Britain. On 8 October he observed that 'if we are allowed to carry on this policy we shall have won the war by the Spring'.[69]

Such were the bases of Chamberlain's war. In war, as in peacetime, his confidence left no room for doubt: 'I shall do as I always have done, go for what I believe to be the right course and risk the consequences'. He derived enormous satisfaction from assessing British radar as 'remarkably efficient', the food situation as 'improved', the shipping problem 'fairly gripped', and economic warfare as 'being waged with remarkable efficiency'. With regard to the air factor, he was convinced that 'in personnel, and in material, though not in numbers, we are superior to the Germans'. Not surprisingly, in view of these glowing assessments, his letters harked back to the Czech crisis, repeating the refrain that 'Hitler missed the bus in September 1938', for he 'could have dealt France and ourselves a terrible, perhaps a mortal blow then'. By 13 January 1940, Chamberlain declared himself satisfied: 'we have done all we can to be ready for it if it does come'.[70]

The activities which gave Chamberlain such satisfaction gave the authors of *Guilty Men* paroxysms of anger, for Chamberlain's wartime strategy divided public opinion as profoundly as had his peacetime policies. 'Cato' charged that the Chamberlain government failed to take advantage of Britain's 'last chance'. The Nazi invasion of Poland demonstrated Germany's capacity to launch a 'devastating, overwhelming' war machine, which left 'no excuse for inaction'. 'Cato' continued: 'Henceforth the rulers of Britain, if they knew their job, would summon all the resources of their empire to meet the assault. This was elementary responsibility. How did they discharge it?'

The reply offered in *Guilty Men* was designed to indict Chamberlain's mobilisation for war as a 'half-baked, unco-ordinated scheme' in the hands of the incompetent. Rather than a supreme economic minister, Chamberlain appointed a part-time advisor, Lord Stamp. Ernest Brown, the employment minister, could still find no work in May 1940 for more than a million unemployed. The agriculture ministers, William Morrison and his successor Sir Reginald Dorman-Smith, were both taken to task for failing to provide adequate food supplies. Lord Stanhope, First Lord of the Admiralty, was blamed for the disastrous sinking of the *Royal Oak*. His appointment, 'Cato' charged, was based on his friendship with Chamberlain. Sir Kingsley Wood, the air minister, was held responsible for the 'criminal' delays in aircraft production. His replacement on 3 April 1940 by Sir Samuel Hoare, who had held the portfolio twice before, for once left 'Cato' speechless. The Chancellor of the Exchequer, Sir John Simon, 'reinforced by the Banks, representing Big Business', was accused of having refused to sacrifice peacetime production for the rearmament programme. 'Millions of tons of raw materials which could have been converted into instruments of war were manufactured into perambulators'. Finally, the government and its military advisors were condemned for misleading public opinion about Britain's war preparations. Chamberlain's declaration of 3 April 1940 that the first months of the war had enabled Britain 'to make good and remove our weaknesses' was dismissed as 'futile boasts and foolish brags'.[71] Britain's last chance had been squandered.

Chamberlain's optimism prompted him once again to play prophet. From October 1939 until April 1940 he wrote with monotonous regularity of his 'scepticism' about a major attack on the western front. On 20 April 1940 he positively crowed to his sister, Hilda, 'Well, you see the great offensive hasn't come off . . . though we are still told it is going to'.[72] On 10 May, faced with Germany's offensive on the western front and a loss of support in the House, he resigned. Chamberlain's 'waiting war' had been replaced by Hitler's total war.

IV. EX-PRIME MINISTER CHAMBERLAIN

In June 1940 the shattered remains of the British Expeditionary Force lay huddled on the beaches at Dunkirk waiting for evacuation. 'How was it', 'Cato' demanded, 'that the bravest sons of Britain ever came to be placed in such jeopardy?' What had pitted 'marching men against unceasing bombers' and 'flesh against steel?' The reply was offered: 'It is a story of an Army doomed *before* they took the field'.[73]

Charges of unpreparedness and equipment deficiencies surfaced even before the publication of *Guilty Men*. Winston Churchill, who had succeeded Chamberlain as Prime Minister, was determined to insure Conservative party solidarity, and ruled out 'a purge of the "guilty men"'.[74] Chamberlain was retained in the cabinet as Lord President of the Council. Freed from the responsibilities as Prime Minister, Chamberlain again began to keep a diary. Therein, and in his weekly letters, were recorded his fears that Britain might not survive a Nazi onslaught, or that the Expeditionary Force might perish in its entirety. Therein too may be found Chamberlain's reactions to the 'guilty men' controversy.

On 1 June the ex-Prime Minister received information about a group of MPs who met nightly at the Reform Club, under the chairmanship of 'that treacherous Welshman' Clement Davies. Chamberlain was pained 'that the people who have been building up a "hate" against me have not in any way given it up'. Over the following days he monitored both the parliamentary opposition group and what soon amounted to a press campaign against him. On 4 June he noted that 'Clement Davies and Labour men are making efforts to whip up opinion against me on the ground that I let down the BEF by under-equipping them'. Chamberlain argued that the Labour and Liberal leaders of the opposition 'ought to be held responsible for this fight', and secondly that the French were guilty of military incompetence. Neither explanation really comforted him as he witnessed the 'growing crescendo' of criticism from the press and his 'political enemies' in Parliament.[75]

Faced with this vendetta, Chamberlain feared that an upcoming secret session of the House of Commons would debate the question. He would be unable to defend himself without criticising the newly formed coalition government. Chamberlain enlisted the help of Churchill, who replied that 'we must stand or fall together', and offered to argue the case 'that in our deadly peril this was no time for raking up the past or seeking scapegoats'. He also undertook to use his influence to stop the press campaign. It was silenced at once, like 'turning off a tap', Chamberlain wrote on 8 June. The debate in the Commons on 20 June passed without incident, and Chamberlain afterwards noted that 'the heresy hunt has at last been scotched'.[76] Within a month *Guilty Men* took up the cudgels laid down by Clement Davies and Fleet Street.

There is no direct evidence that Chamberlain read *Guilty Men*. However, he was fully apprised of its contents and the controversy surrounding its publication, as the following letter of 20 July indicates:

> By the way does it occur to you when you read of the 'Men of Munich who brought us into this mess' that the exploits of the Navy, RAF and BEF must have been made possible by the 'Men of Munich'? For no one can suppose that our equipment has all been turned out in the last six weeks. However, it would be foolish to expect from these blind partisans either reason or logic since those things are not allowed to interfere with their emotions.

Three months later Walter S. Liddall, a Conservative MP, banker and journalist, urged the former Prime Minister to respond in book form to the charges and thereby clear his 'reputation and actions'. Chamberlain replied on 21 September:

> As for 'Guilty Men', I have myself no intention of sponsoring any reply to these scurrilous personal attacks and I should hesitate to encourage anyone to waste either his time or his talents in doing so. Of course rubbish of this kind always sells, not because it convinces the public but because it amuses by its malice. An answer only encourages the libel because it draws attention to it and induces many to buy it just to see what all the noise is about. . . . Believe me, I am deeply touched by your solicitude for my good name. I am however convinced that it will survive all the mud that has been thrown upon it.[77]

Chamberlain's *penchant* for prophecy failed him yet again and for the last time. On 3 October ill health forced him to resign his cabinet position. He died soon afterwards on 9 November. Among his last letters was one to Stanley Baldwin, defending his foreign policy. Chamberlain concluded: 'So I regret nothing in the past'.[78]

V. WERE THE GUILTY MEN TRULY GUILTY?

'Were the Guilty Men truly guilty?' Michael Foot, the last surviving member of the 'Cato' triumvirate, asked in 1986. His conviction on the subject remains as firmly rooted as in 1940. He still described Dunkirk as 'the most dangerous moment in British history since 1066'. He noted that his original interpretation had been reinforced by the endorsement from Churchill in his account of the Second World War.

Churchill had indicated that the 1930s showed 'how the English-speaking peoples through their unwisdom, carelessness and good nature allowed the wicked to rearm'. This confirmed Foot's opinion that 'those who wish to know what actually happened in the 1930s, how the nation was so nearly led to its doom, had better stick to rough-and-ready guides like *Guilty Men*'.[79]

Throughout the 1960s and the 1970s this advice was ignored by many historians. Instead, research was directed to the limitations imposed on foreign policy and the constraints which precluded any alternative to appeasement: global commitments versus limited military resources, rearmament versus fiscal stability, and limited liability versus a continental commitment. While the motives of the appeasers were being rationalised, the 'guilty men' thesis was condemned as untenable, misleading and malicious.

The pendulum of appeasement historiography, with the necessary refinements, must now return closer to the position first trumpeted by 'Cato'. In hot pursuit of documentary evidence in cabinet, committee and departmental files, historians have put aside as irrelevant issues of morality and the dimension of personality. But inherent in the moral fervour of anti-appeasers as 'Cato' was a belief in such Gladstonian notions as 'maintaining the principles of European law and peace', and that 'however deplorable wars may be . . . there are times when justice, when faith, when the welfare of mankind, require a man not to shrink from the responsibility of undertaking them'.[80] Throughout 1938 and 1939 Chamberlain's critics were increasingly united by the conviction that Hitler had returned European inter-state relations to the law of the jungle. It was recognised even more widely after the occupation of Czechoslovakia that peace with Nazi Germany could only be purchased at the expense of other nations. The immorality of such a policy is what forced the Chamberlain cabinet to declare war against Germany in September 1939. And it was that moral outrage, culminating in the Dunkirk disaster, which consumed the authors of *Guilty Men* and impelled them to indict the Chamberlain government with such passion. To ignore this dimension in favour of official government documentation is to turn a blind eye to the divisiveness of appeasement. To return to *Guilty Men* is to admit that moral judgements cannot be ignored as 'Cato' realised in 1940.

What further compels this move is the evidence contained in the private papers of Neville Chamberlain. An examination of this archive should remind historians how far afield they have strayed from Chamberlain's reality in the 1930s. Chamberlain's papers also confirm many of the original accusations popularised by 'Cato'. The charges with regard to rearmament appear to be appropriate. This is not to support the view, never maintained by 'Cato', that the British government failed to rearm. Rather that deterrence in peace, and defensive rearmament in war, neither deterred nor defended. They certainly failed to meet the requirements of Hitler's *Blitzkrieg*. In that context, Dunkirk was an appropriate outcome to an inappropriate policy.

Closely related is the evidence with regard to the management of public opinion on the issue of military preparedness. Chamberlain's concern was to insure adequate defensive forces to constitute a credible military deterrent to Germany. His confidence in his foreign policy, and its prospects for success, was bolstered by the limited measures of rearmament achieved while he was Prime Minister, and so he informed public opinion on numerous occasions. Self-deception, therefore, rather than the wilful deceit suggested by 'Cato', is a more accurate charge, for which there is adequate support.

In the area of foreign policy, denunciation of appeasement permeates every page of *Guilty Men*. What emerges from the evidence in the Chamberlain papers is misplaced trust, unwarranted optimism and erroneous judgements. Confidence in the ultimate success of appeasement or the chances of a negotiated end to the war hindered Chamberlain's assessment of alternatives. On 20 July 1940, after considering reports of a speech by Hitler, Chamberlain accused the *Führer* of 'self-deception' and 'thinking in blinkers'. The same charge of tunnel vision, inherent in *Guilty Men*, equally applied to the British Prime Minister.

Finally, there is abundant evidence that Chamberlain despaired of the political talent at his disposal either in the cabinet or among younger Conservative members of parliament. Ironically, in that he differed little from 'Cato'. The lack of political talent served to consolidate the Chamberlain one-man-band approach to foreign policy. It strengthened Chamberlain's convictions as to the appropriateness of his policies and his indispensability. For these reasons he could never contemplate the prospect of failure with equanimity.

Foreign policy, in the final analysis, is judged equally by justice and success. Appeasement, which was intended to conciliate, failed to pacify. Rearmament, which was meant to deter, failed to do so. War, which it was hoped to avoid, broke out on 3 September 1939, and the British Expeditionary Force proved inadequate for its task. As

Michael Foot observed, 'often the guilty men have seemed to offer evidence against themselves'.[81]

NOTES AND REFERENCES

1. I am grateful to the Humanities and Social Sciences Committee of the University of Toronto Research Board for funding to examine the papers of Neville Chamberlain at the Library, the University of Birmingham; the help there offered by Dr B.S. Benedikz, Sub-Librarian, Special Collections; and the valuable comments of Helen Hatton. Quotations from the Neville Chamberlain papers are by permission of the Library, the University of Birmingham.

2. Neville Chamberlain [NC] Diary, 28 May 1940, NC2/24A.

3. On the genesis of *Guilty Men* see Michael Foot, *Debts of Honour* (London, 1980) pp. 96–8; his *Loyalists and Loners* (London, 1986) pp. 172–5, 180–1; the introduction by Philip Wittenberg to the American edition of *Guilty Men* (New York, 1940) pp. v-xii; and Anne Wolrige Gordon, *Peter Howard: Life and Letters* (London, 1969) pp. 104–5; for additional information see Paul Addison, *The Road to 1945: British Politics and the Second World War* (London, 1975) pp. 110–12; John Lewis, *The Left Book Club: An Historical Record* (London, 1970); William Harrington and Peter Young, *The 1945 Revolution* (London, 1978) pp. 55–67; Simon Hoggart and David Leigh, *Michael Foot: A Portrait* (London, 1981) pp. 79–83; and Ruth Dudley Edwards, *Victor Gollancz: A Biography* (London, 1987) p. 317.

4. Michael Foot, *Aneurin Bevan: A Biography*, vol. 1, *1897–1945* (London, 1962) p. 319; *Time*, 30 Sept. 36(1940) p. 76; according to A.J.P. Taylor, *Beaverbrook* (London, 1972) p. 435, 'Inspiration from Beaverbrook himself had not been lacking'.

5. Information about the authors of 'Cato' was derived from Foot, *Loyalists and Loners*, p. 157; David Farrer, *G-For God Almighty: A Personal Memoir of Lord Beaverbrook* (London, 1969) pp. 28–9, 103; Foot, *Bevan*, pp. 181–2; Arthur Baker, *The House is Sitting* (London, 1958) pp. 98–101, 155–6, 219; and Gordon, *Howard, passim*; Michael Foot under the pseudonym, 'Cassius', contributed *The Trial of Mussolini* (London, 1943) to the Left Book Club; Frank Owen's critique of foreign affairs in the inter-war period can be followed in *The Three Dictators: Mussolini, Stalin, Hitler* (London, 1940); Peter Howard's views on Lord Beaverbrook are in *Men on Trial* (London, 1945) pp. 27–32; and *Beaverbrook: A Study of Max the Unknown* (London, 1964); his conversion to Moral Rearmament in *Innocent Men* (London, 1941); his repudiation that the Oxford Group was pro-Nazi in *Fighters Ever* (London, 1942); he refers obliquely to *Guilty Men* in *Fighters Ever*, p. 7; and *Ideas Have Legs* (London, 1945) p. 62.

6. Quoted in Michael Foot, *Another Heart and Other Pulses: The Alternative to the Thatcher Society* (London, 1984) p. 198.

7. Foot, *Bevan*, p. 319.

8. Sales figures supplied in letter, Victor Gollancz Ltd to the author, 16 July 1986; in the House of Commons, the Minister of Information, Duff Cooper, affirmed 'that no steps have been taken by the Government in any way to prevent the circulation of this book in this country'. *House of Commons Debates*, 5th Series [*HC Debs.*], vol. 364, 7 Aug. 1940, col. 197.

9. Quoted in Harrington and Young, *1945*, p. 66.

10. Foot, *Debts of Honour*, p. 96.

11. 'Cato', *Guilty Men*, pp. 5, 125; the episode in 1793, taken from J.B. Morton, *Saint-Just* (London, 1939) p. 88, speaks of 'twenty-two guilty men'; according to Foot, *Debts of Honour*, p. 97, Victor Gollancz 'insisted, with good reason, on a softening of the final pages'; according to Gordon, *Howard*, p. 104 these were written by Howard and Gollancz feared a libel suit.

12. A.L. Rowse, *A Man of the Thirties* (London, 1979) p. 20; and *All Souls and Appeasement: A Contribution to Contemporary History* (London, 1961) p. 117; see also his *The End of an Epoch* (London, 1947) pp. 24–89; *Portraits and Views: Literary and Historical* (London, 1979) pp. 186–9; *Memories of Men and Women* (London, 1980) pp. 35–9; and *Glimpses of the Great* (London, 1985) pp. 15–98.

13. Martin Gilbert and Richard Gott, *The Appeasers* (London, 1963); A.P. Adamthwaite, *The Making of the Second World War* (London, 1977); and his 'War Origins Again', *Journal of Modern History*, 56(1984) 100–15; Telford Taylor, *Munich* (New York, 1979); J.A.S. Grenville, 'Contemporary Trends in the Study of the British "Appeasement" Policies of the 1930's', *Internationales Jahrbuch für Geschicts– und Geographie – Unterricht*, 17(1976) 236–47; Larry William Fuchser, *Neville Chamberlain and Appeasement: A Study in the Politics of History* (New York, 1982); and Williamson Murray, *The Change in the European Balance of Power, 1938–1939: The Path to Ruin* (Princeton, NJ, 1984).

14. Max Beloff, 'Professor Namier and the Prelude to War', *Fortnightly*, 167(1950) 235–42; and 'Historians in a Revolutionary Age', *Foreign Affairs*, 299(1951) 248–62; as the literature on appeasement is now too vast for summary citation, the student should consult relevant bibliographies such as Sidney Aster, *British Foreign Policy, 1918–1945: A Guide to Research and Research Materials* (Wilmington, DE, 1984).

15. Paul Kennedy, 'Appeasement', in Gordon Martel, ed., *The Origins of the Second World War Reconsidered: The A.J.P. Taylor Debate after Twenty-Five Years* (London, 1986) p. 154; Lord Swinton, *Sixty Years of Power: Some Memories of the Men Who Wielded It* (London, 1966) p. 122.

16. 'Cato', *Guilty Men*, pp. 13, 19–20, 26, 29, 40–2; the attack on Baldwin

and Hoare was taken up again in Howard, *Beaverbrook*, pp. 105–14, 120–1.

17. 'Cato', *Guilty Men*, pp. 44–5, 60, 72.
18. 'Cato', *Guilty Men*, pp. 76, 83, 85–6, 91–2; Howard, *Beaverbrook*, p. 109 attributes the comment on Inskip to Winston Churchill and quoted it somewhat differently.
19. 'Cato', *Guilty Men*, pp. 99, 101, 113, 125.
20. Foot, *Loyalists and Loners*, p. 180.
21. Compare Robert Skidelsky, 'Going to War with Germany: Between Revisionism and Orthodoxy', *Encounter*, 39(1972) 56–62; and D.C. Watt, 'The Historiography of Appeasement', in Alan Sked and Chris Cook, eds., *Crisis and Controversy: Essays in Honour of A.J.P. Taylor* (London, 1976) pp. 115–21.
22. On the Chamberlain archive see B.S. Benedikz, *Guide to the Chamberlain Collection* (Birmingham, 1978).
23. David Dilks, *Neville Chamberlain*, vol. 1, *Pioneering and Reform, 1869–1929* (London, 1984) p. 165; NC to Hilda Chamberlain [HC], 18 May 1936, NC18/1/961; NC to Ida Chamberlain [IC], 10 Sept. 1939, NC18/1/1116; on Neville Chamberlain's relationship with his sisters see Dilks, *Chamberlain*, vol. 1, pp. 57, 109, 119, 165, 258, 390.
24. NC to HC, 15 Apr. 1939, NC18/1/1094; NC to HC, 30 July 1939, NC18/1/1110; NC to HC, 27 Feb. 1938, NC18/1/1040.
25. Alan Beattie, 'Neville Chamberlain', in John P. Mackintosh, ed., *British Prime Ministers of the Twentieth Century*, vol. 1, *Balfour to Chamberlain* (London, 1977) p. 221.
26. NC Diary, 17 June 1936, NC2/23A.
27. Quoted in Keith Feiling, *The Life of Neville Chamberlain* (London, 1946) pp. 319, 256; NC to IC, 28 May 1938, NC18/1/1054; NC to HC, 6 Nov. 1937, NC18/1/1027; quoted in Feiling, *Chamberlain*, p. 252; Feiling, *Chamberlain*, p. 365; NC to IC, 26 Sept. 1937, NC18/1/1022.
28. Neville Chamberlain, *The Struggle for Peace* (London, 1939) pp. 434, 177; NC to HC, 19 Mar. 1939, NC18/1/1090; NC to IC, 26 Mar. 1939, NC18/1/1091; NC to HC, 2 Apr. 1939, NC18/1/1092.
29. Quoted in Feiling, *Chamberlain*, p. 321; Chamberlain, *Struggle for Peace*, pp. 6, 117, 319.
30. Chamberlain, *Struggle for Peace*, pp. 164–5, 171, 347.
31. Quoted in Feiling, *Chamberlain*, p. 323; Chamberlain, *Struggle for Peace*, pp. 100–1, 140–2, 173; NC to IC, 1 May 1938, NC18/1/1049; NC to HC, 6 Nov. 1938, NC18/1/1075; NC Diary, 19 Feb. 1938, NC2/24A; NC to HC, 17 Dec. 1937, NC18/1/1032; Chamberlain, *Struggle for Peace*, p. 116; NC to IC, 20 Mar. 1938, NC18/1/1042 and the numerous letters of April to July 1939 to his sisters for his attitude to the Russians, NC18/1/1093–1107.
32. NC to IC, 11 Sept. 1938, NC18/1/1067; quoted in Feiling, *Chamberlain*, p. 324.

33. NC to HC, 19 Feb. 1939, NC18/1/1086.
34. 'Cato', *Guilty Men*, p. 70.
35. NC to IC, 4 July 1937, NC18/1/1010; NC to IC, 30 Oct. 1937, NC18/1/1026.
36. See Neville Chamberlain – Ivy Chamberlain correspondence, 16 Dec. 1937 to 11 Mar. 1938, NC1/17/5–10; NC to HC, 12 Sept. 1937, NC18/1/1020.
37. NC to IC, 4 July 1937, NC18/1/1010; NC to IC, 26 Nov. 1937, NC/18/1/1030.
38. NC to HC, 5 Dec. 1937, NC18/1/1030a; NC to HC, 24 Oct. 1937, NC18/1/1025; 'Cato', *Guilty Men*, p. 45.
39. NC to HC, 27 Feb. 1938, NC18/1/1040; NC Diary, 19 Feb. 1938, NC2/24A; NC to HC, 6 Feb. 1938, NC18/1/1038; see also NC to Ivy Chamberlain, 3 Mar. 1938, NC1/17/9; until September 1938 Chamberlain was quite enamoured with Halifax, praising him as a 'comfort' and 'calm and unruffled'; thereafter Chamberlain's letters largely grow silent on the subject until June 1940 when Halifax is described as 'innocent and doesn't read the papers'; NC to IC, 20 Mar. 1938, NC18/1/1042; NC to HC, 9 July 1938, NC18/1/1059; NC Diary, 5 June 1940, NC2/24A.
40. NC to HC, 13 Mar. 1938, NC18/1/1041.
41. NC to HC, 13 Mar. 1938, NC18/1/1041; NC to IC, 20 Mar. 1938, NC18/1/1042.
42. Quoted in Michael Howard, *The Continental Commitment* (London, 1972) p. 110; quoted in Feiling, *Chamberlain*, p. 314.
43. See N.H. Gibbs, *Grand Strategy*, vol. 1, *Rearmament Policy* (London, 1976) pp. 441–86.
44. 'Cato', *Guilty Men*, pp. 45, 46; the last quote is accurately given in Chamberlain, *Struggle for Peace*, p. 116.
45. NC to HC, 9 Apr. 1938, NC18/1/1046; NC to IC, 16 Apr. 1938, NC18/1/1047; NC to HC, 24 Apr. 1938, NC18/1/1048.
46. NC to IC, 1 May, 1938, NC18/1/1049; NC to HC, 8 May, 1938, NC18/1/1050; NC to HC, 22 May 1938, NC18/1/1053; NC to IC, 18 June 1938, NC18/1/1056; NC to HC, 25 June 1938, NC18/1/1057.
47. NC to HC, 6 Sept. 1938, NC/18/1/1067; NC to IC, 11 Sept. 1938, NC/18/1/1068; Chamberlain, *Struggle for Peace*, p. 276.
48. Chamberlain, *Struggle for Peace*, p. 275.
49. Quoted in Howard, *Continental Commitment*, p. 124.
50. NC to IC, 28 May 1938, NC18/1/1054; NC to IC, 19 Sept. 1938, NC18/1/1069.
51. 'Cato', *Guilty Men*, p. 61; Chamberlain, *Struggle for Peace*, pp. 302–3, 325, 346; NC to IC, 19 Sept. 1938, NC/18/1/1069; Swinton, *Sixty Years of Power*, p. 120; reference to 'peace with honour' was repeated in NC to HC, 2 Oct. 1938, NC18/1/1070; see also NC to Mary Endicott Chamberlain, 5 Nov. 1938, NC1/20/1/186; and Lord Croft, *My Life of Strife* (London, 1948) p. 289.
52. It was only after he resigned as Prime Minister that Chamberlain ob-

served for the first time that 'I realised from the beginning our military weakness, and did my best to postpone, if not to avert the war'. NC to IC, 25 May 1940, NC18/1/1158.

53. Feiling, *Chamberlain*, p. 359; quoted in Martin Gilbert, 'Horace Wilson: Man of Munich?' *History Today*, 32(1982) 6.

54. 'Cato', *Guilty Men*, pp. 50–1, 54, 56–7; Chamberlain, *Struggle for Peace*, p. 326; NC to IC, 22 Oct. 1938, NC18/1/1074; NC to HC, 15 Oct. 1938, NC18/1/1072.

55. NC to HC, 15 Oct. 1938, NC18/1/1072; NC to IC, 22 Oct. 1938, NC18/1074; see also Lord Halifax to NC, 11 Oct. 1938, NC11/31/124a.

56. NC to IC, 9 Oct. 1938, NC18/1/1071; NC to HC, 27 Mar. 1938, NC18/1/1043; NC to HC, 11 Dec. 1938, NC18/1/1079; NC to IC, 17 Dec. 1938, NC18/1/1080; see also NC to IC, 28 Jan. 1939, NC18/1/1083; NC to HC, 5 Mar. 1939, NC/18/1/1088; the ministers who were criticised, and Chamberlain's correspondence indicates he largely agreed, were Lord Runciman, Leslie Hore-Belisha, Walter Elliot, Lord De La Warr, and Lord Winterton, NC to IC, 17 Dec. 1938, NC18/1/1080; other ministers whom Chamberlain criticised at some point were Duff Cooper ('desperately lazy' and 'a failure', NC to HC, 1 June 1936, NC18/1/963); Lord Chatfield ('rather disappointing', NC to HC, 10 Mar. 1940, NC18/1/1146); Lord Hankey ('not . . . a very forceful personality', NC to HC, 10 Mar. 1938, NC18/1/1146); Robert Hudson ('a disloyal colleague', NC to IC, 23 July 1939, NC18/1/1108); Sir Samuel Hoare ('ruthless ambition', NC to HC, 30 May 1937, NC18/1/1006); and Lord Macmillan ('a failure', NC to IC, 22 Oct. 1939, NC 18/1/1126).

57. NC to HC, 6 Nov. 1938, NC18/1/1075; 'Cato', *Guilty Men*, p. 61; NC to IC, 13 Nov. 1938, NC18/1/1076; NC to IC, 4 Dec. 1938, NC18/1/1078; NC to HC, 15 Jan. 1939, NC18/1/1082; NC to HC, 19 Feb. 1939, NC18/1/1086.

58. 'Cato', *Guilty Men*, p. 63; NC to IC, 26 Mar. 1939, NC18/1/1091; NC to IC, 9 Apr. 1939, NC18/1/1093.

59. NC to HC, 19 Mar. 1939, NC18/1/1090; NC to IC, 26 Mar. 1939, NC18/1/1091.

60. 'Cato', *Guilty Men*, pp. 71–2.

61. NC to HC, 2 Apr. 1939, NC18/1/1092; *HC Debs.*, vol. 347, 19 May 1939, col. 1833; Chamberlain, *Struggle for Peace*, p. 419.

62. NC to HC, 30 July 1939, NC18/1/1110; NC to HC, 29 Apr. 1939, NC18/1/1096; NC to HC, 28 May 1939, NC18/1/1101; Chamberlain's correspondence, while indicating some sympathy with the plight of German Jewry, also contains such disparaging comments as 'No doubt Jews aren't a lovable people; I don't care about them myself', NC to HC, 30 July 1939, NC18/1/1110; see also NC to IC, 4 Dec. 1938, NC18/1/1078.

63. NC to HC, 2 July 1939, NC18/1/1105; NC to IC, 23 July 1939, NC18/1/1108; NC to HC, 30 July 1939, NC18/1/1110.

64. NC to HC, 27 Aug. 1939, NC18/1/1115; John Simon to NC, 1 Sept. 1939, NC7/11/32/231; NC to IC, 10 Sept. 1939, NC18/1/1116.

65. *HC Debs.*, vol. 351, 3 Sept. 1939, cols. 291–2; NC to HC, 17 May 1940, NC18/1/1156.
66. NC to IC, 10 Sept. 1939, NC18/1/1116; NC to HC, 17 May 1940, NC18/1/1156; see also NC to Mary Endicott Chamberlain, 11 May 1940, NC1/20/1/198.
67. NC to HC, 17 May 1940, NC18/1/1156; NC to HC, 15 Oct. 1939, NC18/1/1125; NC to HC, 10 Dec. 1939, NC18/1/1134.
68. NC to IC, 23 Sept. 1939, NC18/1/1122; NC to HC, 1 Oct. 1939, NC18/1/1123; NC to IC, 8 Oct., 1939, NC18/1/1124; NC to IC, 22 Oct. 1939, NC18/1/1126; NC to IC, 3 Dec. 1939, NC18/1/1122a; NC Diary, 16 May 1940, NC2/24A.
69. NC to IC, 23 Sept. 1939, NC18/1/1122; NC to IC, 30 Mar. 1940, NC18/1/1148; NC to IC, 8 Oct. 1939, NC18/1/1124.
70. NC to IC, 23 Sept. 1939, NC18/1/1122; NC to IC, 27 Jan. 1940, NC18/1/1140; NC to IC, 8 Oct. 1939, NC18/1/1124; NC to HC, 30 Dec. 1939, NC18/1/1136.
71. 'Cato', *Guilty Men*, pp. 98–116.
72. NC to HC, 15 Oct. 1939, NC18/1/1125; NC to IC, 5 Nov. 1939, NC18/1/1129; NC to IC, 16 Mar. 1940, NC18/1/1147; NC to HC, 6 Apr. 1940, NC18/1/1149; NC to HC, 20 Apr. 1940, NC18/1/1151.
73. 'Cato', *Guilty Men*, pp. 14, 16.
74. Winston S. Churchill, *The Second World War*, vol. 2, *Their Finest Hour* (London, 1949) p. 9.
75. NC to HC, 1 June 1940, NC18/1/1159; NC Diary, 4 June 1940, NC2/24A; NC to IC, 25 May 1940, NC18/1/1158; NC to IC, 8 June 1940, NC18/1/1160.
76. NC Diary, 5 June 1940, NC2/24A; NC to IC, 8 June 1940, NC18/1/1160; NC to IC, 21 June 1940, NC18/1/1162.
77. NC to IC, 20 July 1940, NC18/1/1166; Liddall to NC, 18 Sept. 1940, NC8/34/70; NC to Liddall, 21 Sept. 1940, NC8/34/68; see also Joseph Ball to NC, n.d., NC7/11/33/19.
78. Quoted in Feiling, *Chamberlain*, p. 456; the shadow of *Guilty Men* also clouded Baldwin's reputation, see Keith Middlemas and John Barnes, *Baldwin* (London, 1969) pp. 1055–61; Baker, *House is Sitting*, pp. 40–3; and Howard, *Beaverbrook*, pp. 114–15.
79. Foot, *Loyalists and Loners*, pp. 180–1.
80. W.E. Gladstone, *Political Speeches in Scotland, March and April 1880* (Edinburgh, rev. ed., 1880) pp. 30–1, 33.
81. NC to IC, 20 July 1940, NC18/1/1166; Foot, *Loyalists and Loners*, p. 180.

8. Why the British Dominions Declared War

RITCHIE OVENDALE

The decision of the 'old' Dominions in September 1939 to fight at Britain's side may be seen as an instance of the power of sentiment in politics. Possibly, in the end, what counted most were ties of kith and kin and a patriotic allegiance to the mother country. Viewed from the standpoint of the Dominions, this sentiment found expression mainly through the actions of certain Dominion statesmen who accepted the need for Commonwealth solidarity.[1] But an examination of British records confirms that British statesmen were constantly alive to the importance of a united front and skilfully shaped their policy in order to ensure the evolution of Dominion sentiment.

I

With the rise of Hitler and Mussolini in Europe successive British governments, conscious of their imperial and world responsibilities, had to weigh carefully the opinion of the Dominions. Britain was more than just a European power. The issue of information for, or consultation with the Dominions was important. On 22 March 1934 the British cabinet discussed the direction of foreign affairs. A policy designed to keep Britain out of all war in Europe and the Far East was rejected as being too inhibiting. Britain could not restore international peace and confidence by 'backing out of Europe and

269

leaving others to take the consequences'. But the cabinet was reminded of the attitude of the Dominions at the time of the Locarno
Treaty in 1925 which guaranteed Germany's western frontier and the
demilitarised zone. The Dominions and India were not bound by this
treaty. As foreign secretary, Sir Austen Chamberlain had told the
House of Commons that Britain needed to act on its own and could
not wait for a common policy for the empire. The Dominions approved, and after that most of them had strongly opposed any further
empire commitments. Indeed, following Lloyd George's appeal in
September 1922 for Dominion support over the Chanak crisis, W.L.
Mackenzie King, the Canadian Prime Minister, had contended that
only the parliament of a Dominion could decide whether that country
was at peace or war, and this was accepted by the British government
with the passing of the Statute of Westminster in 1931. After that, in
practice, the Dominions were not only self-governing, but also fully
autonomous states, equal and in no way subordinate to Britain. The
British government could not, and did not, dispute the right of a
Dominion parliament to conduct its own external affairs, make its
own defence arrangements, and declare its right of neutrality in any
future war in which Britain might be involved. It was only within the
Dominion parliaments that there were wrangles on these issues. The
interests of the individual Dominions diverged, and British statesmen
had to contend with the reality that a common Commonwealth
policy, even in times of grave danger, could no longer be assumed,
and had to be patiently sought after. By the end of 1934 it looked as if
the British government was anxious to avoid a repetition of its action
over Locarno, and care was taken to inform the Dominions of the
conversations with the Japanese and American delegations to the
naval conference. The British stand was endorsed by the Dominion
High Commissioners in London.[2]

II

With rearmament under way the British government thought it
necessary to encourage the Dominions to accelerate their defence
programmes and to sound out the possibility of defence co-operation.
Accordingly, Sir Maurice Hankey, the secretary to the cabinet and to
the committee of Imperial Defence, visited South Africa, Australia and New Zealand in the second half of 1934. Each Dominion had
to be considered individually. South Africa with its policies of racial

discrimination against blacks, presented an especially difficult case, particularly as Oswald Pirow, the South African minister of defence, envisaged his country playing a crucial role in the defence of the whole continent.

Hankey saw the South African Prime Minister, J.B.M. Hertzog, on 6 September. Warned in advance of Hertzog's German sympathies, Hankey emphasised Hitler's unpleasant activities and Germany's intention to rearm. Britain, he assured Hertzog, was not contemplating any new commitment, but it needed to be sure that it could intervene to preserve its own security. Hertzog did not dissent from this policy: even South Africa, far away from the danger zone, was taking steps to rearm. But he was critical of British policy towards France which 'had not always been sufficiently firm'; France, after all, had been responsible for the repression of Germany which lay at the root of existing difficulties. Hertzog hoped that Britain would never allow itself to be drawn into a war in Europe unless that were 'absolutely essential to its own security'. In the interests of co-operation within the Commonwealth, Britain should not 'get involved on the continent'. The deputy Prime Minister, Jan Christian Smuts, was, however, more enthusiastic about Britain's programme of rearmament. His main sources of concern were Japanese ambitions in Mozambique and Ethiopia. Should Singapore fall, South Africa would be in the front line. For him the British navy was the shield of the whole empire, and its strength should be maintained. Hankey's visit to Australia in October and November 1934 coincided with two changes in the Commonwealth's government. He was, however, welcomed as a 'brother in arms' by the chiefs of staff: co-operation between Australia and Britain on defence seemed promising, but Australia's defence arrangements all hinged on the maintenance of a British naval presence in the Far East. Similarly in New Zealand the new British policy was received warmly and even the attempt to improve relations with Japan was endorsed.[3]

III

On the occasion of King George V's Silver Jubilee in the spring of 1935 the Dominion Prime Ministers met in London and were briefed on the deteriorating international situation by Ramsay MacDonald. The British Prime Minister emphasised, however, that Britain 'must not allow itself to be pushed into a position of entering into a system of military alliances for the defence of Europe'. The Canadian delegate, R.B. Bennett, was exercised over the extent to which British foreign policy had affected the dominions, but he was assured by MacDonald that Britain had kept faithfully to the 1930 agreement on the conduct of foreign policy by the members of the British Commonwealth. Unless a Dominion objected to British policy its agreement would be assumed. R.G. Menzies of Australia was especially concerned about the dispute between Italy and Ethiopia and the difficulties that this would create for the League of Nations.[4] The methods of consultation established between Britain and the Dominions during the subsequent Ethiopian crisis created the precedent for the remaining years leading up to the outbreak of the Second World War.

An important aspect of this consultation was the meetings between the Dominion High Commissioners in London and British officials. This was so effective that on 2 December 1935, before the Hoare – Laval Plan had been drawn up, the cabinet was reminded of the 'remarkable unanimity' between the Dominions and the mother country on the question of sanctions against Italy. So intimate was this consultation that on occasion soundings were taken from the High Commissioners as to the likely reaction of their governments to proposals even before these went to the British cabinet. In a note on the Italo – Ethiopian dispute, the Foreign Office asserted that if Britain were to go to war in defence of international order, the 'practically unanimous' assent of the British people would be essential. The Foreign Office drew particular attention to Dominion concern over the racial aspects of the war, which Mussolini portrayed as being one between blacks and whites. Repercussions were expected not only from 'native opinion' in Africa but also from 'other races' in the Far East.[5]

The Dominion High Commissioners in London also headed their countries' delegations to Geneva and similar consultation took place there. Some were even anxious to take the initiative. Before leaving for Geneva Stanley Bruce of Australia, who was convinced that economic sanctions against Italy should not be enforced unless they could be made effective, suggested a 'deliberately dramatic' declaration by Britain and the Dominions to the effect that they had 'decided upon a large increase in their armed forces to serve as a factor towards the stability of the world'. At a meeting with Dominion representatives at Geneva the South African delegate, Charles te Water, supported by Bruce, outlined a scheme of 'tutelage' for

Ethiopia on the grounds that this could pre-empt German claims for colonies in Africa.[6] The Dominions, however, seemed anxious for close co-operation with Britain. On 3 September 1935 the Canadian government indicated its willingness to help to secure a peaceful settlement. A month later, Bennett, the Canadian Prime Minister, expressed the view that if Britain were attacked, a wave of sentiment would carry Canada to the side of the mother country.[7] The Australian government, though it felt that sanctions were impracticable and could lead to a general war, indicated its willingness to co-operate with Britain and the Dominions 'in any action that will be conducive to upholding the principles of the League but most of all of their desire to ensure the unity and safety of the Empire'.[8] South Africa opposed any compromise by the League. At Geneva Hoare found the co-operation of the Dominion delegates 'whole hearted'. This was at a time when Neville Chamberlain confided to his sister, 'People are scared of another war in Europe, but I believe we can keep clear of that, for the French are determined not to fight and we are not going to act without them'.[9]

The High Commissioners were informed on 5 December 1935 that the British cabinet had decided to support the proposal that the export of oil to Italy should be prohibited. Both Bruce and te Water favoured a postponement of the decision to fix a date for this action, though the latter emphasised the need to avoid any appearance of weakening. Vincent Massey, speaking for the newly elected Liberal administration in Canada under Mackenzie King, said it would loyally observe any sanctions but emphasised that there should be no repetition of an earlier incident which had given the impression that Canada was taking the lead in this matter.[10] A socialist government had been returned in New Zealand. Sir James Parr, the High Commissioner, thought, however, that it would be equally forthcoming in its support of the League.

This qualified endorsement of British policy by the Dominions was shaken by the proposed concessions of Italy in the negotiations leading up to the Hoare-Laval Plan. On 10 December the secretary of state for the Dominions, Malcolm MacDonald, was warned of te Water's fears that the League could find itself in the position of condoning the original aggressor. Parr felt that the proposals went further than anything the League had in mind. Massey was worried about the effect on public opinion in Canada. The following day the cabinet learnt from MacDonald that the High Commissioners, apart from Bruce, were alarmed at the probable effect of the peace proposals on public opinion in their respective dominions. Te Water in particular was worried about the prospect that blacks might be armed. MacDonald hoped for modification in the details to meet these Dominion fears. Consequently, just before he left for Geneva, Anthony Eden was instructed to bear in mind the High Commissioners' criticism of proposals for an Italian zone of economic expansion and colonisation in Ethiopia: Eden should be 'on his guard against acquiescing in any modification of the proposals in favour of Italy such as M. Laval might be expected to suggest'. In line with the suggestion of the High Commissioners, there should be no date fixed for the imposition of oil sanctions. The South African government let Britain know in rather 'violent' language that it disapproved of the Hoare-Laval peace proposals that emerged from Paris. New Zealand couched its censure in more friendly terms, but the Irish Free State and Canada said nothing. The British War Book based its arrangements on the assumption that the Dominions were prepared fully to co-operate with Britain the event of war. But at a meeting on 20 December 1935, two days after the Hoare-Laval Plan had been disowned in London, te Water suggested that if Britain were attacked it could not be assumed that the Dominions would be involved automatically.

Following Hoare's resignation the High Commissioners endorsed Eden's policy of taking stock rather than proceeding immediately to consideration of the oil sanction. New Zealand was prepared to support any country that was attacked for applying sanctions, but Massey advised that, with memories of the Chanak incident still very much alive in Canada, any such appeal for assistance should come from the League rather than Britain. Australia, with its cruisers in the Mediterranean, was likely to be involved anyway, and te Water thought the time had come for League members to face up to the implication of sanctions. When, at the end of February 1936, the British cabinet once again decided to impose the oil sanctions, the High Commissioners did not demur. Indeed, early in March, despite reservations over the complications of any South African participation, the British government, prompted by Bruce and a sudden New Zealand interest in air defences, again raised the possibility of Dominion co-operation over defence.[11]

IV

No sooner was a common front achieved with the Dominions over Ethiopia than it was challenged by Hitler's reoccupation of the Rhineland. On 12 March Neville Chamberlain recorded in his diary that the 'mad dictator' was in 'a state of fanatical frenzy'.[12] The same day, the cabinet was exercised by the difficulties of conducting conversations under the Locarno Treaty on the question. Although the Dominions were not a party to this treaty, te Water had asked whether representatives of the Dominions could act as observers at the Locarno talks. The difficulty was that the governments of the Irish Free State and Canada were likely to reject any such invitation. The cabinet decided to turn down te Water's request on the grounds that acceptance of it might lead to anyone being able to attend.[13] In any case Hertzog warned immediately that the South African government felt the European atmosphere was poisoned by the unequal terms imposed on Germany by the Treaty of Versailles, together with the French preoccupation with security and the consequent fear and distrust of Germany: European appeasement could only be secured by the negotiation of a new settlement.

South Africa considered the proposal to purchase the co-operation of Italy against Germany by abandoning the League's policy of sanctions as subversive of the whole League system and a condemnation of French policy'. Furthermore, it regarded Germany's offer of a 25 year non-aggression pact as a sounder basis for peace than Locarno. Two days later Hertzog was even more explicit: there was a danger that the Commonwealth could be shaken to its foundations. Not only might South Africa have to withhold its support but also condemn Britain's participation in a war. After the German offer any country imposing sanctions against Germany or invading its territory would be the real aggressor: should France declare war against Germany on the grounds that Germany had militarily occupied territory otherwise under its full sovereignty, South Africa would consider France's act 'one of inexcusable aggression'. The Australian government, though it could not agree that Britain was supporting France unduly, did advise that war would find little support in Australia. Australia wholeheartedly supported the British attempt to find a formula acceptable to Germany, pending negotiations for a general settlement with the German proposals as a basis for discussion.[14] Malcolm MacDonald impressed on the British cabinet that 'it was extremely important as negotiations proceeded to bear the position of the Dominions in mind'. Their representatives in London did not agree with the French attitude, and MacDonald therefore hoped that under any new arrangement Britain would not be committed to action unless an actual invasion of French of Belgian territory took place. Eden assured the cabinet that this would be the case.[15]

In April it became evident that Mussolini's army was rapidly defeating the Ethiopians. On 6 May Bruce's arguments for lifting sanctions against Italy swayed Massey, but Hertzog remained opposed to such action, as Eden learned on 8 May, when he explained Mussolini's desire for *détente* with Britain to the Dominion High Commissioners. Indeed, on 22 May te Water insisted that sanctions should be continued indefinitely, or at least until Mussolini agreed to a scheme which acknowledged that Ethiopia, as a barbarous country, should never have been admitted to the League, and hence should be administered by Italy as a mandate with the specific provision that the natives should not be armed.[16]

MacDonald told the cabinet of South Africa's attitude on 27 May, explaining at the same time that while the High Commissioners of Canada, Australia and New Zealand favoured the lifting of sanctions they did not know their countries' attitudes. The line taken by the Irish Free State was likely to be similar to that of South Africa.[17] Pirow repeated the South African mandatory scheme to MacDonald and Eden. In response to the British suggestion that sanctions be lifted, he repeated South Africa's opposition. Hertzog and Smuts felt strongly on the subject, as did the South African press which was inclined to be more liberal than public opinion, although South Africans as a whole were not really interested.[18]

V

Following the isolationist and even pro-German views offered by some of the Dominions during the Ethiopian crisis, the preparations by the British government for the imperial conference of 1937 were of considerable importance. At the end of February 1937, the British chiefs of staff drew up a review of imperial defence outlining schemes to facilitate co-operation amongst members of the Commonwealth. A basic premise of this report was that the Commonwealth could not survive a British defeat. Dominion assistance, at least in the form of munitions, was anticipated in the event of a war against Germany.

The ability of a Dominion to help, however, was not construed as a commitment for that Dominion.[19]

Foreign policy was a more complex issue. Mackenzie King, the Prime Minister of Canada, was as ardent an isolationist as some of his United States friends. Hertzog in South Africa favoured his country's neurality and had debated for seven years on this issue with Smuts. J.A. Lyons in Australia was faced by a vociferous and influential Labour opposition pledged to fight any commitments outside Australia. Only M.J. Savage of New Zealand was happy to come to Britain's assistance in time of war, but that Dominion still clung to the ideal of the League of Nations and openly criticised any British deviation from the covenant. For the Dominions, Eden's Leamington speech in November 1936 had offered assurance that Britain would only become entangled in a European conflict if it seemed that its vital interests were at stake. It was, however, no longer possible to generalise about the Commonwealth as a whole. Each dominion had to be considered individually.[20]

Internal conditions in South Africa were such that, of all the Dominions, it was the one least likely to give even qualified support to British involvement in Europe. Hertzog and Smuts headed the fusion government. They had agreed to differ on the issue of the divisibility of the crown. The minority Nationalist opposition party, headed by Dr. D.F. Malan, which had the avowed aim of establishing a republic, encouraged a policy of neutrality for South Africa and was not averse to closer relations with Germany. On these issues the Nationalists did not lack sympathisers in the government party. The small but vociferous Dominion party, headed by Colonel C.F. Stallard, deplored any recognition of the Statute of Westminster, and anxiously watched the severing of the links of empire. The South African government was prepared to co-operate with Britain on certain matters of defence, but these were limited to technical assistance and use of the Simonstown base. The visit to Britain of Pirow, the minister of defence, in 1936 had not changed that. Indeed, the parliamentary debates of 1937 suggest that Hertzog's attitude to neutrality did not differ markedly from that of the republican Malan.

South African attitudes tended to crystallise around the opinions attributed to Smuts and Hertzog. Hertzog was the more consistent: a man who even before 1914 had rejected conciliation, he was in many respects the father of Afrikanerdom and had distinctly anti-British traits. His attitude to Germany should be seen in the light of this. Hertzog's traditional roots were not in a liberal British democracy, but rather in the Boer republican ideal of the strong individual leader. The South African Prime Minister expected great things from Hitler, and hoped that the *Führer* would stop the advance of Russia. Smuts's attitude was neither consistent nor easy to analyse. In public he stated one thing, in private he wrote another. His over-riding motive seems to have been not to lose favour with anyone. Sir Keith Hancock argues that by the middle of 1936 Smuts had discovered that appeasement had come to mean a policy of propitiation pursued by the weaker party towards the stronger. In April 1937 Smuts wrote privately about colonial concessions to Germany, the inevitability of the *Anschluss*, of Danzig and Memel as being passing makeshifts, and of the need for economic and financial concessions to Germany. Smuts assured Lord Lothian:

> Our South African representatives at the Imperial Conference will go all out for some way of arriving at a European settlement and will be extremely averse to South Africa or the British Commonwealth being involved in any European conflict.[21]

Canada did not differ markedly from South Africa on imperial defence commitments and neutrality. In March 1937 Mackenzie King visited President Roosevelt in Washington. There he spoke to Sir Ronald Lindsay, the British ambassador, and launched into what Lindsay described as:

> a diatribe . . . against sanctions . . . He said that Canada was resolved to maintain neutrality in any war at any price, and that on no account would she be dragged into any hostilities. His attitude corresponded very closely to that generally adopted in America.

A section of Canadians tended to be anti-British and against any commitment by their government to foreign wars. The French Canadians had made their stand on this point clear during the 1914–8 war, and the following two decades had not mollified their rancour. Public concern in Canada was increasing, but reaction to the defence debate in early 1937 forestalled any commitment to imperial defence as far as Canada was concerned. The attitude of the Canadian delegates to the imperial conference was given by T.A. Crerar, the veteran liberal politician, in April 1937:

> Whatever we do, I feel certain that Canada will keep out of that net of a common Empire foreign policy . . . the more I see of the whole thing, the more I am certain that our destiny is on the North American continent.[22]

Australia and New Zealand, on the other hand, were both countries with a largely homogeneous population which had its roots in Britain. Sentimental ties were strong. Strategically, too, Australia and New Zealand were more vulnerable. An aggressive Japan, if unrestrained, might have disastrous consequences for the Pacific dominions.

In Australia, because of the domestic situation, the government could only pursue a policy which the British considered weak. While the government felt that Australia could not conveniently detach itself from Britain and British commitments, the opposition Labour party condemned expenditure on imperialist wars and argued in favour of a defence policy which provided for Australian defence only. But the Australian delegates to the imperial conference sought to secure imperial co-operation on defence.[23]

New Zealand differed from Britain on principles of foreign policy and still had a trusting faith in the League, but the leaders of New Zealand in 1937 saw their country's future linked with that of the Commonwealth. Although not prepared blindly to follow Britain's lead, they were less likely to place obstacles in the way of imperial defence than Canada and South Africa.

On matters of foreign policy and defence the Commonwealth was divided, and colonial compensation for Germany was equally a prickly subject. W. Ormsby-Gore, the secretary of state for colonies, suggested there should be no more instances of Dominion statesmen irresponsibly advocating the return of another country's mandates, but not of their own. This was all that the Dominions were prepared to do.[24]

VI

The imperial conference met in London in May 1937 amidst the patriotic fervour of King George VI's coronation. From the British point of view the opening discussions were not propitious. Eden's survey of foreign policy was met by an isolationist response from Mackenzie King; Savage of New Zealand was polite but gave 'a sermon on the immorality of British foreign policy'; Hertzog considered the British attitude towards the French too warm, and towards the Germans too cold; the Australian delegate attacked British opposition to the *Anschluss*. Eden's persuasions did not win over the delegates. Except for New Zealand they remained opposed to European commitments, and the final *communiqué* was so full of reservations that it could hardly be said to represent a common front.

Dominion response to the question of colonial concessions to Germany was equally discouraging. The only concession came from Hertzog: if the restitution of Tanganyika could bring peace to Europe, South Africa would not stand in the way.

British efforts to secure a joint defence scheme for the Commonwealth were also unsuccessful. Mackenzie King objected vociferously, and had his way. Although the Dominions, in line with British rearmament and the worsening international situation, were willing to increase their defence expenditure in their own interests, there were obstacles in the way of any imperial defence scheme.

MacDonald was being rather optimistic when he reported to the cabinet that the policies of the members of the Commonwealth were closer than they had been before the conference. When the Prime Ministers returned to their various Dominions it seemed that little had changed. On 28 September 1937 Hertzog championed isolation: it was not for South Africa to become involved in righteous crusades, or to go to the assistance of any part of the empire, unless its own vital interests were at stake. Pirow, in October, spoke of his disapproval of democracy, and of his preference for Fascism to Communism, the only other alternatives. Mackenzie King called on Hitler and apparently warned him of Dominion support for Britain in any war against Germany, but the British High Commissioner in Canada reported that Mackenzie King had been 'completely hypnotised' by his reception in Germany and he doubted even whether Hitler had been warned. For Mackenzie King, the conference had been crucial in winning him over to Chamberlain's policy of the appeasement in Europe. He urged Chamberlain to keep the Commonwealth out of war 'at all costs'. Hitler's enchantment lasted. Lyons returned to Australia to face a barrage of criticism from the opposition Labour party, but in October he fought and won a general election on a non-isolationist platform. The New Zealand government reaffirmed, with the support of the opposition, its attachmemt to the principles of the covenant and of collective security.[25]

VII

Direct influence of Dominion opinion on British policy at this time is difficult to discern. Professor Cameron Watt has argued that Dominion determination to keep out of Europe was a decisive factor in encouraging Chamberlain to pursue his policy of the appeasement of Europe,[26] but this policy had been decided on before the imperial conference. Probably the statements of several of the delegates to the imperial conference helped to confirm Chamberlain in a course of action that he had already decided upon. There is no record in the Foreign Office papers of any of these moves being taken because of Dominion pressure. The imperial conference convinced Chamberlain that his policy of preserving peace in Europe was the right one, but to say that it caused him to embark upon it is probably an exaggeration.

During the Sino – Japanese dispute which flared up in the second half of 1937 the Dominions were able to influence British policy in the direction that Britain wanted. As Gladwyn Jebb, a Foreign Office official, minuted:

> Generally speaking, we seem to have put ourselves in the excellent position of allowing the Dominions to torpedo a 'sanctions' policy in advance before definitely committing ourselves one way or the other.[27]

Chamberlain, in his renewed attempts to reach an agreement with Germany and Italy, at the beginning of 1938, was partially limited by Dominion opinion on the colonial issue. The Prime Minister, in drawing up his scheme of colonial development, had to consider South Africa's longstanding refusal to hand over South West Africa, and its sensitivity about Tanganyika. The Dominions were not informed of the scheme, and, in any case, the matter was dropped as Hitler said that the colonial settlement could be allowed to wait. The German – Austrian *Anschluss* on 18 March 1938 evoked little response from the Dominions and, with the exception of New Zealand, they approved the Anglo – Italian agreement of April 1938.[28]

After the *Anschlusss* the British government considered how to prevent 'an occurrence of similar events in Czechoslovakia'. On 18 March MacDonald warned the cabinet committee on foreign policy of the peculiar dangers attending a new commitment to Europe by guaranteeing Czechoslovakian independence. He assured his colleagues that he had never favoured a particular foreign policy simply in order to please the Dominions, but in present circumstances, where a commitment to Czechoslovakia might involve Britain in a war to prevent Germans in the Sudentenland joining with Germany, his colleagues must realise the wider consequences:

> On this issue the British Commonwealth might well break in pieces. Australia and New Zealand would almost certainly follow our lead.

Eire [formerly the Irish Free State] would no doubt take the same line partly because she would feel that on an issue of this kind she could not take a line different from our own, but South Africa and Canada would see no reason whatever why they should join in a war to prevent certain Germans from rejoining their fatherland.[29]

Two principal obstacles emerged in the cabinet and the cabinet committee on foreign policy to a guarantee of Czechoslovakia: such a move might mean the end of the Commonwealth; and, in any case, it would be logistically impossible to save Czechoslovakia.[30] The attitude of the Dominions was considered, and was a factor militating against any British guarantee to Czechoslovakia.

The Dominions did react. Lyons wired that his government felt that 'no definite commitment should be undertaken with regard to Czechoslovakia'; Savage felt generally that 'we were so far away out here that you on the spot were far better able to judge the best course to pursue'.[31] Hertzog initially supported the German case over Czechoslovakia. He was emphatic that 'the Union has no interest whatever in political questions affecting Czechoslovakia or any other Eastern European Power, and that it cannot be expected that the Union would deem herself in any way concerned in any form of warlike hostilities which may arise from such political questions'.[32] Mackenzie King wrote to MacDonald on 2 April of his admiration for the way in which Chamberlain had performed his task:

I approve wholeheartedly of the course he has adopted, particularly his determination to get in touch with Italy and Germany . . . I am more convinced than ever that to keep the British Empire out of a European war, is the one means of saving the Empire.[33]

VIII

The committee of imperial defence and the cabinet, in considering the defence preparations which followed on Hitler's moves against Austria, were careful to take the position of the Dominions into account. The debate on building aircraft in Canada suggested that this should be done largely in an attempt to overcome isolationist sentiment in Canada and involve it in imperial defence. Increased aircraft production meant, in effect, that the new standard fleet proposals had to be discarded, and jeopardised the chances of sending a fleet to the Far East in an emergency. At the imperial conference the Dominions had been told that this could be done. Attempts had to be made to conceal the true position from Australia and New Zealand.[34]

On 30 August 1938 British policy was discussed at a meeting of ministers. Halifax pointed out that the only effective deterrent against Hitler would be to declare that if Germany invaded Czechoslovakia Britain would declare war, but he accepted that such a move would divide opinion in Britain and the Commonwealth. Chamberlain was particularly concerned about South Africa's reaction and warned that a verbal challenge to Germany 'might well result in disunity, in this country, and in the Empire'. Lord Maugham, the Lord Chancellor, similarly warned that it 'might lead to the break up of the empire'. MacDonald was equally pessimistic. From the purely British point of view, military weakness and the opposition of a large minority, perhaps eventually a majority, of the population argued against going to war over Czechoslovakia. From the Dominions's point of view, Britain could not properly threaten to go to war without consulting them, since some might be considered bound to go to war alongside Britain. 'The result of consultation with the Dominions . . . would probably, therefore, be that we should not be in a position to utter the threat. If, nevertheless, we made the threat, we should put a great strain on the loyalty of the Dominions and might break up the Commonwealth. The British Commonwealth of Nations and the United States of America together were the only force which could eventually check the progress of dictatorship; one day this combination might have to fight to defeat the growing evil. His Majesty's Government should not take a step now which would break the Commonwealth.'

In the end, the arguments of Chamberlain, Halifax and MacDonald were conceded;[35] it would have been unwise for the British government to guarantee Czechoslovakia at that time, as such a step might have broken up the Commonwealth. MacDonald duly warned the cabinet on 12 September of the need to avoid a decision 'without allowing time for what the Dominions would regard as reasonable consultation in the circumstances'.[36]

IX

From 12 September to 1 October care was taken to keep the Dominions informed of British policy. MacDonald even claimed that the Dominions had more information at their disposal than members of the cabinet. It could be said that during these weeks the High Commissioners in London formulated what was close to a common Commonwealth foreign policy, and were more effective in influencing British policy than the individual Dominion leaders.

From 22 September, when it seemed that Hitler's insistence at Godesberg on the immediate occupation of the Sudetenland by German troops was 'a challenge to the whole principle of peaceful negotiations', the Dominion High Commissioners became particularly active. Only Bruce of Australia supported a stand on the basis of principle. Te Water doubted whether the occupation of the Sudeten areas by German troops should be regarded as a question of principle, and suggested a compromise on methods. Chamberlain took special note of te Water's view. Dulanty, representing the Irish Republic, and Massey agreed with te Water. At a meeting of the inner cabinet of Halifax, Simon, and Templewood – which for the previous week had discussed policy though not necessarily decided it – MacDonald explained the High Commissioners' views. Commonwealth support would be less likely over Czechoslovakia than if the issue were French security. These opinions seemed to influence Chamberlain. On 25 September he told the cabinet:

> It was clear that a position had arisen in which we might before long be involved in war. If that happened, it was essential that we should enter war united, both as a country and as an Empire. It was of the utmost importance, therefore, that whatever steps we took, we should try to bring the whole country and Empire along with us, and should allow public opinion to realise that all possible steps had been taken to avoid a conflict.

Chamberlain planned to send Sir Horace Wilson to see Hitler with a message suggesting an international commission to put into effect proposals already accepted by the Czechoslovak government. This move might 'also help to rally the Dominions to our side'.

That day Massey was horrified that there might be war over the method of transfer of the Sudeten territory which was already ceded. He effectively banded the High Commissioners together with the view that failure to improve on the terms of the German memorandum should on no account involve the Commonwealth in a war. Bruce, representing the High Commissioners, put this view to the inner cabinet on 27 September. Chamberlain spoke to the cabinet at 9.30 pm that day. He had reports that Czechoslovakia would offer a feeble resistance, but 'more disturbing than this was the fact that the Dominions were far from happy about the situation'. Chamberlain read messages from Lyons and Hertzog to this effect. The High Commissioners had also visited Downing Street that afternoon and urged that pressure should be put upon the Czechoslovak government to accept Hitler's terms. 'The situation *vis-à-vis* the Dominions was thus very delicate'. MacDonald elaborated the position: in his view, 'all the Dominions would sooner or later come in with us, but it was clear that they would come in only after making a number of reservations half-heartedly and with mental reservations about our policy'. MacDonald ceded that it was difficult to be certain about public opinion in the Dominions, and mentioned the telegram from the acting High Commissioner in Australia which had contradicted Lyons's message. There was no doubt, however, about the unanimity of the High Commissioners.

MacDonald met the High Commissioners immediately after the cabinet meeting. Massey, te Water and Bruce warned of the dangerous reaction in the Commonwealth if Britain went to war over the issue of how Hitler was to take possession of territory already ceded to him in principle. The effect of war in such circumstances 'must be most seriously to endanger the future unity and cohesion of the Commonwealth'. Massey feared that 'the minority of Canadians who were not favourably disposed towards the British connexion would, long after the war was over, continue to use the fact that Canada had become involved in it to reinforce their view'. Te Water similarly agreed that 'South Africa would be most unwilling to fight on this issue and that the result of becoming involved in war would be to strengthen enormously the position of those hostile to the British connexion'. Dulantly took the same view.

An examination of opinion in the Dominions at this time does not altogether support the views of the High Commissioners expressed on the night of 27 September, but then the High Commissioners were speaking of the long term consequences of becoming involved in war. In South Africa on 28 September, at Hertzog's instigation, the full cabinet accepted the declaration of benevolent neutrality agreed on earlier by the inner cabinet – the British did not know of this. In Australia Labour was divided and, probably as a consequence of the government's policy of avoiding discussion, a large group of Australians had no formulated attitude. F.H. Cleobury of the Foreign Office assessed tha position on 30 September: 'My own impression is that *before* an outbreak of war Australia would be for peace at almost any price – but after the outbreak she would do all that we could reasonably expect'. New Zealand's position had always been clear: it would support Britain's position 'right or wrong'. It seems that Mackenzie King was prepared to recommend that Canada should fight. Massey did not know of this decision, nor did Britain.

The British government did consider the issue of Dominion neutrality, and on 26 September sent a telegram to its representatives in Canada, Australia and South Africa hoping that the Dominion governments would accept the doctrine of common belligerency. Britain wanted the Dominions to take such measures of co-operation as were envisaged in the War Book scheme, even though a particular Dominion might wish to make it clear that active participation was a matter for parliament to decide. The Dominions were implicated in War Book measures, and there was trouble in South Africa and Canada over these. Australia and New Zealand took full naval measures as well as various army and air force preparations. Canada took some steps, but no action was taken in South Africa, nor as far as was known, in Eire.

Chamberlain was probably confirmed in his decision to use Mussolini as a mediator by a telegram from Lyons. When the Prime Minister left for Munich he knew that the Dominions were totally opposed to war over Czechoslovakia. He disliked war, and feared the suffering that air raids would bring to Britain (see Chapter 8). But it was the attitude of the Dominions which weighed most heavily in the account that he had given of the situation to the cabinet on 27 September.

Chamberlain and most of the cabinet still believed in the Commonwealth. It seemed clear that a war over Czechoslovakia would endanger the continued existence of that body. If war had to come, as Chamberlain had often said, it would be best if Britain and the empire could face it with a united front. On 29 September this did not seem probable, and even if the Dominions did eventually join in, it seemed that repercussions within these countries, in the long run, might lead to the dissolution of the Commonwealth. On the crucial day of 27 September he and the majority of the cabinet seem to have been swayed by this consideration. At the very least he used it to reinforce a policy which he had already decided upon, but he made it clear to the cabinet that if the majority thought otherwise he was prepared to abandon conciliation. The majority did not – the Commonwealth still counted.[37]

X

After Munich British policy was, in Chamberlain's words, 'to drive two hoses abreast: conciliation and rearmament'. Australia, New Zealand and Canada helped Britain to increase production capacity. The Dominions were informed rather than consulted about the bringing into effect of the Anglo – Italian treaty. There is little evidence of Dominion views having a decisive influence on British statesmen, but the stand by Lyons and Hertzog bolstered Chamberlain's case, and probably helped the Prime Minister to secure a favourable reception for his policy. On the whole the Dominions favoured the British policy of conciliation and rearmament and assisted the British government where they could, but were careful to maintain freedom of choice in their hands. The attitude of South African ministers forced Britain to reconsider the colonial question, and unfavourable United States opinion brought the refugee issue, which had become all the more urgent after the *Kristalnacht* of 9–10 November, to the fore. Pirow, on a visit to Britain to obtain assistance for South African defence, acted as a messenger of the British government on both these issues. But Pirow's visit to Hitler showed that no further steps in the direction of the appeasement of Europe could be expected from Germany. Britain had to prepare itself for the likelihood of war, and it was necessary to secure the support of the Dominions for co-operation in defence.[38]

From January to April 1939 the views of the Dominions were considered, but they did not decisively influence policy. Possibly the Dominions would not have wished for more: they were informed rather than consulted, and thus Canada and South Africa could feel that they were not committed by British policy. Inskip, the new secretary of state for the Dominions, told the High Commissioners on 30 March of the pending British guarantee to Poland: time did not allow consultation with their governments. Inskip felt sure that the Dominions 'would not have wished that the United Kingdom should invite them to share responsibility for the decision'. Massey and te Water agreed. The other High Commissioners did not comment.[39] It was the views of the Dominion High Commissioners in London that probably had most influence on the cabinet.

The Dominions did not always receive full information, and that which was circulated deliberately presented a serious picture of the situation in Europe. The Dominions were neither consulted nor informed about the changed defence plans which affected their interests directly. The committee of imperial defence even controlled some cabinet information that went to the Dominions, such as the conclusion that Japan could embarrass Britain 'by making a strategic disposition of her forces which would constitute a severe threat to Australia and New Zealand'.[40]

By the time of Hitler's occupation of Prague education of opinion in the Dominions had progressed considerably. Hitler, with his anti-semitic purges and broken promises probably played as large a part in this as any efforts by Chamberlain or the Dominion leaders. The euphoria of Munich did not last, and from December 1938 the Dominions made decisive moves towards rearmament, military preparedness and even conscription.

XI

After Hitler's occupation of Prague, Australia and New Zealand were, in reality, committed to British policy, but in South Africa Hertzog would not be drawn, and Smuts offered no lead. Mackenzie King, from internal considerations, and possibly personal convictions, would try to stand outside European affairs till the last moment. The Commonwealth was still not united after Prague.[41]

At the time of the Russian negotiations in June 1939 attention shifted to the Far East. Japanese intransigence and maltreatment of British subjects in the Tientsin concession during the first month of 1939 meant that for a time it seemed as if war would start in the Far East, not in Europe. This meant a serious rethinking of British contingency planning. If war did start in the Far East, it was unlikely that Germany and Italy would be able to resist the temptation to move in Europe. Britain might have to fight on three fronts simultaneously. The dispatch of a fleet to the Far East already committed to the Mediterranean after the guarantees to Greece and Rumania had to be questioned seriously, with obvious ramifications for Australia and New Zealand. Australia was especially concerned. On 24 June Menzies, the new Prime Minister, asked for confirmation that Australia be entitled to assume 'that in the event of war with Japan the United Kingdom Government would send a fleet to Singapore within appropriate time capable of containing Japanese fleet to a degree sufficient to prevent a major act of aggression against Australia'. The British could not give satisfactory assurances, and the Australians were able to infer that the sending of a fleet to Singapore might not be a top priority in this new situation.[42] On 16 April, following promptings from Lord Halifax, Roosevelt announced that the American fleet would be moved from the Atlantic to its 'normal operating areas' in the Pacific. And in August the British government confronted the question of a defence pact with the Soviet Union and accepted its advisability. The decision on a new British policy towards Russia was a cabinet decision: Chamberlain had to give way under pressure from his colleagues. The cabinet and the foreign policy committee did consider the views of the Dominions although they were not a crucial factor.[43]

In assessing the influence of the Dominions during these months it is important to consider the role of the High Commissioners in London. Their suggestions again came close to a collective Commonwealth foreign policy. At times their influence was more decisive than that of the official telegrams from the various Dominion governments. Te Water, Massey and Bruce were particularly active, but they all, in various degrees, continued to favour the appeasement of Europe to the end. In this they reflected the attitude of their respective governments. Even Australia, though prepared to fight at the end of August, urged restraint on Poland. During this period some Dominions even offered advice as to what British policy should be. This was the first time that this had happened.[44]

XII

Until May 1939 British contingency planning for possible war was based on the assumption that the Dominions would fight. It was not until then that the committee of imperial defence tailored its plans to fit the possible contingency of a Dominion opting for neutrality.[45] Eire, however, was in practice not considered a Dominion, and precautions were taken to prevent leakage of intelligence material through that country.

There is evidence to suggest that the relay of information between the Dominions Office, the Foreign Office, and the various Dominion goverments, was not always as efficient as it might have been,[46] but Inskip, as secretary of state for the Dominions, seemed to sympathise with the Dominions' position, and to place their case fairly to his cabinet colleagues. During the last few days of peace he was particularly evident in this role. The British government was prepared to give careful consideration to the views of the Dominion High Commissioners in particular, but would not significantly alter policy because of them.

XIII

When war came Britain did have the support of four Dominions. The months between Hitler's occupation of Prague and the march into Poland were crucial in bringing this about.

In South Africa, which was of utmost strategic importance, the position was uncertain until the day war was declared and rested on the stand that Smuts would take. By a narrow majority of 13 votes South Africa went to war as a divided country. The Governor General, Patrick Duncan, and the British High Commissioner, W.H. Clark, both played their part in this. Clark confirmed Duncan in his decision to refuse Hertzog a dissolution of Parliament, and at a crucial stage in the debate leaked this information to a member who had come to see him on behalf of Smuts. Hertzog's supporters were spreading the rumour that if Hertzog were defeated, Duncan would grant him a dissolution and a general election. It was thought that some of Smuts's would-be supporters were hesitating because of this.[47] English-speaking South Africa, for reasons of sentiment and ties of kin, probably always was willing to fight for Britain, but it was in the minority. The vote was carried by those Afrikaners who still believed in the Smuts – Botha ideal of conciliation. Smuts's position is enigmatic. It is difficult to see what caused him to oppose neutrality in September 1939 when he had agreed to it a year previously. His personal correspondence suggests little enthusiasm for British foreign policy, but by the end of August a feeling that a stand had to be taken is discernible. His political speeches were ambiguous: he told English-speaking South Africa what it wanted to hear without giving any firm pledge. In Parliament he was silent. Perhaps Hertzog's complaint of Smuts's duplicity would have had some foundation had Smuts changed his mind earlier than September 1939 on the neutrality issue, but the only firm evidence for such a change is discernible at the end of August. Perhaps his actions were governed by his desire to become Prime Minister. His lack of enthusiasm for Chamberlain's policy after Prague suggests that he was not influenced by the British Prime Minister. The decision was Smuts's own, and on the available evidence it is difficult to assess his motivation. The only danger in the European situation for South Africa derived from possible German ambitions in South West Africa.

South Africa declared war, but as R.H. Hadow minuted, it was 'torn asunder on social lines'. If Smuts could not heal the breach South Africa might react to a peace move by Hitler. That would be 'Hertzog's oppurtunity – or Malan's – for revenge'.[48] 20 years later Pirow wrote that the cabinet meeting of 3 September made it a certainty 'that when the policial pendulum swung back again, as it was bound to do, Malan's extremists would take over and the English-speaking South Africans would become *bywoners* (aliens) in their own country'.[49]

Chamberlain's tactics of exploring every avenue of peace probably helped to convince the Australians of the need for solidarity with Britain. In July the Australian press was sceptical of the campaign to include Churchill in the government. But by August even Menzies, so impressed by Germany during his visit in 1938, had tempered his praise. Menzies insisted that he favoured the British policy of keeping the door open for an international conference till the last moment. The threats of the Labour opposition did not, however, disturb him as they had his predecessor. Curtin, a Labour spokesman, said that it would be a bold man who 'committed the lives of Australians as pawns in the fate of Poland. The safety of the Australian people impelled us to recognise our inability to send Australians overseas to take part in a European war'. A few minutes after Chamberlain announced that Britain was at war with Germany, Menzies broadcast: 'Britain is at war therefore Australia is at war'. The Federal Parliament was not summoned on this issue as the government felt that no separate declaration of war by Australia was required. Australia fought for King and country. Menzies, despite his insecure position, ignored Labour criticism, and did not even concede that Australia had the constitutional right to make a separate declaration of war.

Although there had never been any question of New Zealand's loyalty, that country had proved awkward with its insistent belief in the ideals of the League of Nations, and because of the pacifist convictions of its Prime Minister. During the months following the German occupation of Prague, both these obstacles fell away. The Pacific defence conference in Wellington in April convinced Savage of the need for an efficient army. On 28 June, Viscount Galway, the Governor General, in his speech from the throne affirmed that, 'in the circumstances of to-day my Advisers (*sic*) have most reluctantly been forced to recognise the fact that a full and effective application of the Covenant is for the time being, impracticable'. On 23 August Mr Hamilton, the leader of the opposition, assured the government of its unanimous backing. New Zealand on 28 August expressly approved the British decision to stand by the Polish guarantee and just before midnight on 3 September the cabinet decided to go to war. In this Dominion sentiment and ties of kinship were paramount, and defence considerations were only a factor. A united country was prepared to stand and fight by Britain's side.[50]

In Canada the key figure, Mackenzie King, is difficult to evaluate. His confidence in Chamberlain and the conviction that the British Prime Minister had done all that was possible to preserve peace probably helped to convince him that he should lead his country into war. What cannot be assessed is the influence of spiritualism upon his decisions. Canada did participate in closer defence co-ordination with Britain. It did not declare war until 10 September, as the declaration had to go through Parliament, but in effect it was at war as soon as Britain, for all war measures were in full operation.

It seems strange that Canada fought on the Polish issue, particularly in the light of views frequently expressed about the dangers of becoming involved in British quarrels in Europe, and the possible internal repercussions within Canada. There was no strategic reason for Canada's fighting: Roosevelt had guaranteed Canada's security in his Kingston speech in September 1938. The economic arguments are not convincing and were not raised. More important was the fact that the British element was large and strongly patriotic. The royal visit in the spring of 1939 possibly played its part in consolidating public opinion. By May Quebec was reported to be not unfavourably inclined towards fighting. In late August a crowd of 20 000 in Toronto spontaneously sang *Land of Hope and Glory* at the end of the royal tour film. At the time of Munich it had been forecast that Canada would be divided if the cabinet recommended that it should fight. A year later this danger had largely disappeared. Perhaps Chamberlain's repeated efforts to find a peaceful solution helped to convince Canada of the justice of the British cause. Canada did not fight for a vague concept of collective security, but for the values of the Commonwealth. As the High Commissioner, Gerald Campbell, wrote:

While it would be untrue to suggest that Canada guards her independence one whit less jealously to-day than she did a year ago the visit of their Majesties earlier this year and the ordeal which now faces the democracies of the world have served to show, if the lesson were needed as I think it was, in some quarters here that equality of status is not incompatible with co-operation in common aims, loyalty to a common allegiance, and the defence of common principles.[51]

XIV

Chamberlain was particularly conscious of the need to educate the Dominions to the realities of the European situation. Far away from the European theatre the Dominions could not always understand Britain's concern with the dictators. But Britain was still an imperial power, and the Dominions had to be carried along somehow. The Dominions were not, however, bound by British policy decisions, and they were informed rather than consulted. That – with the exception of the Irish Republic which was hardly a Dominion anyway – they fought, was little short of a miracle, since apart from New Zealand the Dominions favoured the policy of the appeasement of Europe. They were not responsible for it: Dominion opinion only confirmed Chamberlain on a course of action on which he had already decided. Over Czechoslovakia Chamberlain probably saw the reluctance of the Dominions to fight, and the consequent break up of the Commonwealth, as decisive. This was the view he put to the cabinet. As the European situation became more serious with Hitler's occupation of Prague, Dominion influence diminished. Their opinions were considered, and weighed against other factors, but care was taken to sift information on the European situation going to the Dominions. In January 1937, before he became Prime Minister, Chamberlain was worried lest too gloomy a picture be painted for the Dominions. In March 1939 the worry was that the Dominions would have too optimistic an impression, and information was selected accordingly. The personal trust that some Dominion leaders placed in Chamberlain after the imperial conference probably helped to secure Dominion participation in the war. Another important factor was Chamberlain's demonstration that every means to preserve peace had been tried. This was essential as some Dominions continued to favour the appeasement of Europe until the day war was declared.

NOTES AND REFERENCES

1. See R. Ovendale, *The English-Speaking Alliance. Britain, the United States, the Dominions and the Cold War 1945–1951* (London, 1985), *passim*, for the later significance of this.
2. R. Ovendale, 'Britain, the Dominions and the Coming of the Second World War, 1933–9', in W.J. Mommsen and L. Kettenacker (eds), *The Fascist Challenge and the Policy of Appeasement* (London, 1983), pp. 323–38 at pp. 323–4; *'Appeasement' and the Englih Speaking World. Britain, the United States, the Dominions, and the Policy of 'Appeasement', 1937–1939* (Cardiff, 1975), pp. 20–35; R.F. Holland, *Britain and the Commonwealth Alliance 1918–1939* (London, 1981) pp. 1–126.
3. Public Record Office, London, PREM 1/174.
4. *Documents on Canadian External Relations*, 5, pp. 107–16.
5. Public Record Office (PRO) London, CAB 23/82, fo. 350, CM 50(35)2, 2 December 1935; DO 114/66, fo. 3, 6109/A/111A, Meeting with Dominion High Commissioners, 29 July 1935.
6. DO 114/66, fos 9–12, 6109A/11S, Meeting with Dominion High Commissioners, 21 August 1935; fos 12–13, 6109A/334S, Meeting with Dominion Representatives at Geneva, 9 September 1935.
7. DO 114/67, fos 6–7, A/270, Canadian Government to Dominions Office, Telegram No. 62, 3 September 1935; fo. 16, 6109A/314, Office of the High Commissioner of Australia to Foreign Office, 2 September 1935.
8. DO 114/67, fo 9, 6109A/3/2, High Commissioner in Canada to Dominions Office, Telegram No. 234, 19 October 1935.
9. Birmingham University Library, Neville Chamberlain Papers, NC 18/1/1935, Neville Chamberlain to Ida Chamberlain, 5 October 1935.
10. See Holland, *Britain and the Commonwealth Alliance*, pp. 180–6 for an account of the development of policy within the dominions.
11. Ovendale, 'Britain, the Dominions and the Coming of the Second World War', pp. 324–7; D. Carlton, 'The Dominions and British Policy in the Abyssinian Crisis', *Journal of Imperial and Commonwealth History*, I (1972–3), pp. 59–78; R. Meyers, 'Britain, Europe and the Dominions in the 1930s: Some aspects of British, European and Commonwealth Policies', *Australian Journal of Politics and History*, XXII (1976), pp. 36–50; P.N.S. Mansergh, *The Commonwealth Experience*, vol. II 2nd ed., (London, 1982), pp. 74–5.
12. Neville Chamberlain Papers, NC2/23A, Diary, 12 March 1936.
13. CAB 23/83, fos 298–300. CM 19(36)1, 12 March 1936.
14. PREM 1/194, te Water to Malcolm MacDonald, 12 March 1936 enclosing Hertzog to te Water, Telegram No. 321, 12 March 1936; Hertzog to te Water, Telegram No. 323, 14 March 1936; Bruce to Malcolm MacDonald, 17 March 1936.
15. CAB 23/83, fo. 313, CM 20(36)3, 16 March 1936.

16. See DO 114/68, fos 15–27.
17. CAB 23/84, fo. 216, CM 39(36)8, 27 May 1936.
18. See DO 114/67, fos 26–8; DO 114/68, fos 27–31.
19. CAB 24/268, CP73(37), Memorandum by Inskip, 26 February 1937.
20. For internal developments within the dominions see P.N.S. Mansergh, *Survey of British Commonwealth Affairs. Problems of External Policy 1931–1939* (Oxford, 1952).
21. Ovendale, *'Appeasement and the English Speaking World*, pp. 23–7. For the situation in South Africa see O. Pirow, *James Barry Munnik Hertzog* (Cape Town, 1958); C.M. van den Heever, *General J.B.M. Hertzog* (Johannesburg, 1944); *General J.B.M. Hertzog* (Johannesburg, 1946); W.K. Hancock, *Smuts, The Fields of Force, 1919–1950* (Cambridge, 1968).
22. Ovendale, *'Appeasement and the English Speaking World*, pp. 27–31. For the situation in Canada see J. Eayrs, *In Defence of Canada. Appeasement and Rearmament* (Toronto, 1965); V. Massey, *What's Past is Prologue* (London, 1963); L.B. Pearson, *Mike. The Memoirs of the Rt. Hon Lester B. Pearson*, vol. I, *1897–1948* (Toronto, 1972); J.L. Granatstein and R. Bothwell, '"A Self-Evident National Duty"': Canadian Foreign Policy, 1935–1939', *Journal of Imperial and Commonwealth History*, III (1974–5), pp. 212–33.
23. Ovendale, *'Appeasement' and the English Speaking World*, pp. 31–3. For the situation in Australia see P. Hasluck, *The Government and the People 1939–1941 (Canberra, 1952); E.M. Andrews, Isolationism and Appeasement in Australia. Reactions to the European Crises, 1035–1939* (Canberra, 1970); R. Menzies, *Afternoon Light* (London, 1967).
24. Ovendale, *'Appeasement' and the English Speaking World*, pp. 33–5. For the situation in New Zealand see F.L.W. Wood, *The New Zealand People at War. Political and External Affairs. Official History of New Zealand in the Second World War 1939–45* (Wellington, 1958); A. McIntosh *et al.*, *New Zealand in World Affairs*, I (Wellington, 1977).
25. Ovendale, *'Appeasement' and the English Speaking World*, pp. 38–63; see also R. Tamchina, 'In Search of Common Causes: The Imperial Conference of 1937', *Journal of Imperial and Commonwealth History,* I (1972), pp. 79–105.
26. D. Cameron Watt, *Personalities and Policies* (London, 1965), pp. 156, 165; see also R. Meyers, 'British Imperial Interests and the Policy of Appeasement', in Mommsen and Kettenacker (eds), *The Fascist Challenge*, pp. 339–51; M. Beloff, 'The Imperial Factor in Appeasement', in *Mélanges en l'honneur de Charles Morazé. Culture science et développement. Contribution à une histoire de l'homme* (Toulouse, 1979), pp. 419–32.
27. Ovendale, *'Appeasement' and the English Speaking World*, pp. 77–9. On the Dominions and the Far East see also W.R.Louis, 'The Road to

Singapore: British Imperialism in the Far East, 1932–42', in Mommsen and Kettenacker (eds), *The Fascist Challenge*, pp. 352–88.
28. Ovendale, *'Appeasement' and the English Speaking World*, pp. 107–8, 113–15.
29. CAB 27/623(2), fos 1–27, FP(36)26, Lock and Key, 18 March 1938.
30. CAB 23/93, fos 1–10, CM 15(38), 22 March 1938.
31. Public Record Office, London, FO 800/310, fos 8–9; fos 1–2.
32. DO 114/94, fo. 14, Aide Memoire of a Message from Hertzog, 25 March 1938; fos 13–4, Aide Memoire of a Message from Hertzog, 23 March 1938.
33. FO 800/310, fos 10–11, Mackenzie King to MacDonald, 2 April 1938.
34. Ovendale, *'Appeasement' and the English Speaking World*, pp. 125–9.
35. CAB 23/94, fos 1–33, Notes of a Meeting of Ministers, 30 August 1938.
36. CAB 23/95, fos 9–35, CM 37(38), 12 September 1938.
37. Ovendale, *'Appeasement' and the English Speaking World*, pp. 146–80; *Documents on Australian Foreign Policy 1937–49*, 1, pp. 484–97, Bruce to Lyons, 7 October 1938.
38. *Ibid.*, pp. 182–203.
39. PRO, FO 371/22969, fos 13–5, C5265/15/18, Hankinson to Harvey, 6 April 1939, transmitting Notes of Meeting between Inskip and Dominion High Commissioners, 30 April 1939.
40. Ovendale, *'Appeasement' and the English Speaking World*, pp. 209–13. Also FO 371/21/2191, C14096/13564/18; CAB 23/96, CM/55(38) 13 November 1938.
41. Ovendale 'Appeasement', pp. 240–5.
42. CAB 2/9, fo 32, Menzies to Chamberlain, Telegram, 24 June 1939; fos 33–9, Record of Meeting between Chamberlain, Inskip, Nash and Bruce, 28 June 1939; fos 40–5, Record of Meeting with Bruce, 11 July 1939.
43. CAB 23/99, fos 275–80, CM 30(39)1, 24 May 1939.
44. Ovendale, *'Appeasement' and the English Speaking World*, pp. 267–75.
45. CAB 16/183A, DPP(P)54, Memorandum by Inskip on the Position of the Dominions in the event of War, Lock and Key, 5 May 1939.
46. FO 371/22975, fos 127–30, C10767/15/18, Minute by R.H. Hadow, 24 May 1939.
47. DO 114/98, fo 47, High Commissioner in South Africa to Dominions Office, 13 September 1939.
48. Ovendale, *'Appeasement' and the English Speaking World*, pp. 300–6.
49. Pirow *Hertzog*, p. 246.
50. Ovendale, *'Appeasement' and the English Speaking World*, pp. 306–10.
51. *Ibid.*, 310–14; DO 114/98, fo 43, High Commissioner in Canada to Dominions Office, 20 September 1939.

9. Deterrent Diplomacy: Roosevelt and the Containment of Germany, 1938–1940

CALLUM MACDONALD

INTRODUCTION

The Munich conference produced not an era of negotiation but a new period of tension. A European settlement was blocked by Hitler's attacks on British rearmament and the *Kristallnacht* pogrom. It was rumoured that extremists were dominant in Berlin and that Hitler planned to solve German problems by force. Nor was Germany the only source of tension. At the end of the year Mussolini provoked a crisis in the Mediterranean with a series of demands on France. In the Far East the Japanese continued to advance into southern China. In November 1939 Tokyo proclaimed a 'New Order' in Asia. Washington viewed these developments as part of a single global crisis. In the autumn of 1938 President Franklin D. Roosevelt rapidly abandoned the illusion that Munich would pave the way to a stable world order. He assumed that the totalitarian powers had co-ordinated their plans

of aggression and that their ultimate target was the western hemisphere. These suspicions were confirmed by German attempts in
1938 and 1939 to convert the triangular anti-Comintern pact of 1937
into a tripartite military alliance between Berlin, Rome and Tokyo
(see Chapter 10). Hitler was no longer regarded as a traditional
German statesman concerned only to correct the injustices of Versailles. He was seen instead as an extremist with indefinite ambitions,
an image confirmed by the Czech *coup* in March 1939. Thus Nazi
Germany was defined as the moving force in a global conspiracy
against the Americas.

In this situation the frontiers of the United States lay on the Rhine
and the Yangtse. Roosevelt, however, was reluctant to envisage
direct intervention in Europe or Asia. He hoped instead to contain
the Axis threat by methods short of war. The target of his new policy
was Germany. Hitler, so Roosevelt thought, was to be deterred by
the deployment of US economic resources behind an anti-Nazi coalition. US industry would be mobilized in support of British and
French rearmament, redressing the European balance of power
particularly in the air. The German people would rapidly lose their
taste for aggression when faced with the threat of bombing by a
powerful alliance backed by the United States. Hitler would have the
choice of negotiation or a political crisis which would destroy his
regime. The German problem would be solved without war or a fresh
surrender to Nazi demands.

THE AFTERMATH OF MUNICH

The Roosevelt administration was divided over the meaning of
Munich. One group believed that the settlement had secured no
more than a pause in the Nazi drive to dominate Europe. These
officials had always seen Hitler as an extremist, dedicated to armed
expansion. They believed that the German – Japanese anti-Comintern
pact of November 1936, which was joined by Italy in December of the
following year, was a totalitarian alliance, a league of aggressor
states hostile to the international *status quo*. They suspected Hitler of
organizing a Fascist international, a 'Nazitern' with territorial designs
upon the Americas. The pact was his instrument for eliminating
Britain and France, the only barrier between Nazi Germany and the
western hemisphere.[1] In this situation the anti-appeasers favoured
some kind of united front with Britain and France to contain and

isolate Hitler. Before Munich, however, they were unable to produce a coherent programme or to exercise a decisive influence on US policy.[2] At home the President was unwilling to go beyond rhetoric in expressing American concern about Axis expansion. Public opinion was isolationist and anxious to avoid involvement in war, a sentiment reflected in the Neutrality Act of 1937, banning the export of arms and munitions to belligerents.[3] Abroad the leaders of Britain and France seemed determined to compound with Hitler while the United States stood on the sidelines.

The anti-appeasers condemned Munich as a bloodless Nazi victory which would not divert Hitler from his goal of world power. On 29 September, George S. Messersmith, the assistant secretary of state and a longstanding critic of the Nazi regime, warned against exaggerated notions of permanent peace in Europe. His experiences as Consul-General in Berlin during the Roehm purge and as minister to Austria when Dollfuss was murdered had convinced him that the Nazis were gangsters with whom no deal was possible.[4] He had been preaching the German danger ever since. According to Messersmith, the nature of Hitler and his movement had not changed: 'If, in the desire to avoid the war with which Hitler is threatening . . . the world, too far-reaching concessions are made, we will find that instead of arranging peace a war has been made inevitable'. Messersmith was particularly worried that Munich would be followed by a British loan to prop up the German economy, German economic problems would have to be solved but not while the Nazi regime remained in power. In his judgment, 'The Germany with which certain arrangements could have been made under Stresemann and Brüning is a different Germany from the one with which we have to deal today . . .' Hitler would use financial assistance to strengthen his capacity to arm and threaten. Messersmith had always believed that Hitler should be left to stew in his own juice in the hope that a domestic economic crisis would provoke a military *coup* and the overthrow of the Nazi government.[5]

Cordell Hull, the secretary of state, was also apprehensive about the future. Although less outspoken than his subordinate, Hull believed that Munich had settled nothing. At most it had gained a breathing space before a new round of Nazi demands.[6] Henry Morgenthau Jr., the secretary of the Treasury wished to pre-empt this development by waging economic warfare against Hitler's regime. At the beginning of October he ordered Treasury lawyers to prepare a brief justifying discrimination against German exports to the United States.[7] Although such duties would be imposed as an anti-dumping measure, they would amount to concealed economic warfare against the Third Reich. Bilateral trade would be restricted and German purchases of American raw materials such as cotton, which were incorporated in the rearmament programme, would be curtailed.

The official US response to Munich, however, was dominated by a different group which was unconvinced that Hitler had indefinite aims and regarded him as a traditional German statesman. The most prominent members of the appeasement circle at the State Department were Sumner Welles, the under-secretary of state, his assistant Adolf Berle, and Joseph P. Kennedy, the US ambassador to London. These officials traced Nazi radicalism to the political and economic injustices of Versailles, a settlement which they regarded as indefensible. They were sceptical about the ideological solidarity of the anti-Comintern powers and believed that it would be possible to detach Germany and Italy from Japan by a policy of judicious concessions.[8] In January 1938, Welles prepared an American appeasement plan designed to parallel Chamberlain's attempt to conclude political settlements with Berlin and Rome. This would incorporate British efforts into a new world economic order which guaranteed international stability by offering justice for all. In such a liberal economic system, American trade could expand and flourish.[9] The scheme was never launched because of Chamberlain's icy response and the *Anschluss* of March 1938 which raised doubts about the reception of such an offer in Berlin. Throughout the Czech crisis, however, it was held in reserve by Welles and Berle. If Chamberlain succeeded in averting war and Hitler proved satisfied with German domination of central Europe, it might yet prove possible for Washington to summon a new 'Congress of Berlin,' co-opting the Reich into a liberal – capitalist economic order dominated by the United States. Meanwhile, as Berle noted, the United States must await the results of British efforts to 'sell' the Czechs.[10]

The appeasers supposed that Munich opened the way to a new era in world affairs and were prepared to bring forward the plan delayed in the spring. In a conversation with the French ambassador on 1 October 1938, Welles was in an optimistic mood. He hoped that the European powers would proceed to solve their remaining political problems such as colonies and the Spanish civil war. While Washington could take no part in such political negotiations, it was prepared to assume a role in the area of disarmament and the revision of the world financial and economic structure. According to Welles, such a general settlement would isolate Japan and force Tokyo to conclude a just peace with China. He repeated this view of the future in a radio broadcast on 3 October in which he claimed that an opportunity existed to create a new international order based on justice and law.[11] His forecast was echoed by Kennedy who had supported Chamberlain throughout the Munich crisis. On 20 October Kennedy called for co-operation between dictatorships and democracies to guarantee peace and end the arms race. Significantly his speech had been cleared by Welles although it annoyed Hull who was less convinced about the prospects of a lasting settlement.[12]

Roosevelt's response to Munich seemed to reflect the optimism of the appeasers rather than the pessimism of their opponents. If there was to be a general settlement as a result of Chamberlain's efforts, he was plainly anxious to secure a US role. In the weeks after Munich he even tried to assume some of the credit for the peaceful outcome of the crisis.[13] This, however, reflected opportunism rather than conviction. Roosevelt had long been concerned about Nazi Germany and aware of the potential threat of Hitler to the western hemisphere. In December 1937 he described the triangular anti-Comintern pact concluded the previous month as a global conspiracy of the Axis powers and suspected that the Japanese invasion of China, the *Anschluss* and the Czech crisis had been co-ordinated between Berlin, Rome and Tokyo. He was doubtful about the prospects of appeasement but reluctant to confront the isolationists and pursue a more active US foreign policy. As the European situation deteriorated in 1938, he chose to stand on the sidelines and let Chamberlain make the running. If the Prime Minister succeeded in buying Hitler off, the US could build on his efforts, asserting American interests within a new international order. If British efforts failed, German intentions would be clear and Roosevelt could pursue a less isolationist policy, including Neutrality Act revision, with greater public support.[14] The prospects of such a policy were improved by the Anglo – Irish Agreement of April 1938 which meant that Roosevelt had less to fear from the Irish lobby in the event of war.[15]

At the height of the Munich crisis Roosevelt preferred appeasement to war even at the cost of the 'terrible remorseless sacrifice' forced on Czechoslovakia. As he informed the British ambassador on 20 September, if Chamberlain succeeded he would be 'the first to cheer'.[16] At the same time he had no doubt that if Hitler proved insatiable, American interests lay in supporting Britain and France.

In the event of war Roosevelt planned to adopt a policy of forward defence, throwing US industrial resources behind the democracies. He would give no promise to revise the Neutrality Act but hoped that Britain and France would solve this difficulty by establishing factories in Canada to assemble items like aircraft, with parts purchased from the United States. These ideas were part of a general strategy which relied on economic strength and productive capacity rather than bloody land offensives to contain and exhaust Nazi Germany. According to Roosevelt, Hitler must be starved out by a tight blockade with which the United States would co-operate. This would be accompanied by a bombing offensive which would complete the erosion of the German will to fight. The American role in such a war would be to act as the arsenal of democracy, providing the allies with the means to continue the struggle and exhaust Germany. The result would be a quick victory without the horrific casuality lists of the First World War. According to Roosevelt, Britain and France could pay for American goods by liquidating their assets in the United States, avoiding the need to confront Congress over the Johnson Act of 1934 which forbade loans and credits to countries which had defaulted on their war debts.[17] Such an approach offered the administration the maximum benefits at the smallest possible cost. It would increase allied dependence on the United States and guarantee Roosevelt a seat at any peace conference without American participation in the fighting. Moreover it would stimulate the domestic economy and solve the persistent problem of unemployment before the Presidential election of 1940, a consideration which was not overlooked by key advisers such as Harry Hopkins.[18] The President was to return to the central role of American industry in a broad strategy of containment in the months after Munich.

Whatever the future prospects in Europe, the Munich crisis proved to Roosevelt the dangers of dealing with Hitler from a position of military weakness. His dreams of a bombing offensive which would bring Germany to its knees were undermined by revelations about allied inferiority in the air. The French were particularly impressed with German air power and argued that the correlation of forces left them little choice but capitulation to Hitler's demands (see Chapter 4)[19] They had been preoccupied with this problem ever since December 1937 when the chief of the air staff warned that France lacked sufficient modern aircraft to fight Germany and Italy simultaneously. It did not even posses the resources to stand on the defensive against

Hitler whilst launching a knock-out blow against the Italians which would clear the Mediterranean and relieve the threat to the French Empire in north Africa. This situation could not be easily remedied since France faced a critical shortage of skilled labour and machine tools.[20] At the beginning of 1938 the French approached the United States in an attempt to remedy these deficiencies. The purchase of American aircraft would circumvent the bottleneck in French industry. It might also restrain Berlin by raising the spectre of US intervention in the event of a European war. In January 1938 a purchasing mission, headed by Baron Amaury de la Grange, arrived in Washington. At meetings with US officials he emphasised the importance of matching German aircraft production and explained that what he had in mind was to 'harness American industry to the French war machine.'[21] The results were more modest. In the spring of 1938 France ordered 100 Curtiss fighters. There was no assurance, however, that these would be delivered in the event of war since, despite French pressure, Washington would give no undertaking to suspend or revise the Neutrality Act.[22]

The French air position had not improved when the Munich crisis erupted. It was erroneously supposed that Hitler had the ability to level the capitals of Europe. According to Colonel Charles Lindbergh, the American aircraft expert, 'Germany now has the means of destroying London, Paris, and Praha (*sic*) . . . England and France together have not enough modern war planes for effective defense or counter attack'.[23] This report echoed general assumptions about Nazi air strength then prevalent in Europe. It much exaggerated the disparity which existed. While the *Luftwaffe* was the strongest air force, there was a shortfall of 20 per cent on German production plans by 1938. This was complicated by an in-commission rate of 57 per cent in August 1938 and marked deficiencies in crew strength and training (see Chapter 3). As one authority concludes, although the *Luftwaffe* 'had a major impact on British and French diplomacy' at Munich, it was 'not prepared to face a military confrontation over Czechoslovakia'.[24] Exaggerated estimates of German air strength were used by the French Foreign Minister, Georges Bonnet, as an excuse for capitulation to Hitler's demands. William C. Bullitt, the US ambassador to Paris, drew a different moral. As he reported to Roosevelt on 20 September: 'If you have enough airplanes you don't have to go to Berchtesgaden',[25] The President was prepared to act on this lesson in October 1938, seeking for the first time a military deterrent to back up his diplomacy. Whatever the prospects of a permanent settlement with Hitler, he wanted to rearm in the air and to encourage Britain and France to follow suit.

As early as 12 September, Roosevelt had ordered Harry Hopkins, his closest advisor, to investigate the productive capacity of the US aircraft inductry in the light of the European situation.[26] Despite the Munich agreement he continued to emphasise the importance of air power. In early October he approved a French plan to buy more American aircraft and to establish Canadian factories, assembling US parts, as a means of circumventing the Neutrality Act.[27] The Canadian scheme was later dropped in favour of direct purchases from the United States. On 21 October he urged Britain to adopt a similar scheme. At a meeting with Colonel Arthur Murray, a British friend, he stated that his object in the event of war would be to assist Britain and France gain air superiority. He was prepared to export partly finished raw materials, not covered by the Neutrality Act, to Canadian aircraft factories. He urged London to appoint a liaison officer who could discuss the technical details of this plan. Roosevelt wanted Chamberlain to feel that he had 'the industrial resources of the American nation behind him in the event of war with the dictatorships'. While the Prime Minister should not state this publicly, he might say that 'Great Britain, in the event of war, could rely upon obtaining raw materials from the democracies of the world'. The President argued that public opinion was becoming less isolationist and more aware of the Axis threat to the Americas. At this stage, however, he remained unwilling to request the modification of the Neutrality Act.[28]

In the weeks after Munich, Roosevelt also took the first steps towards American air rearmament. At a meeting in the White House on 20 October he talked about developing the capacity to produce 15 000 aircraft a year. Part of this total would be available to Britain and France. The remainder could be used to defend the western hemisphere and to back up American diplomacy. The decision to rearm 'in drastic fashion' pleased anti-appeasers who regarded it as the first step in a firmer line towards Germany.[29] While Roosevelt himself remained undecided about the implications of Munich, rearmament seemed a wise precaution. As the journalist Anne McCormick commented on 29 October 1938: 'Nobody in Washington is quite sure whether we are at the beginning of another Napoleonic era or of a period of appeasement. They are taking no chances . . . the watchword is . . . arm.'[30]

METHODS SHORT OF WAR - NOVEMBER 1938–MARCH 1939

By November 1938 German actions had resolved American doubts and tipped US policy towards containment. It soon became clear that Hitler did not regard Munich as the basis for a permanent settlement. Instead at Saarbrücken he launched a bitter attack on British rearmament which left US diplomats under no illusion that 'the Munich accord has established all these conditions . . . necessary for a lasting peace'.[31] Tension in Europe was accompanied by reports of German attempts to strengthen the anti-Comintern pact and revelations about supposed Nazi designs on Latin America. On 12 October Joseph C. Grew, the US ambassador to Japan, reported that the Germans were putting pressure on Tokyo to conclude a firm military alliance with Berlin and Rome. Washington had always disliked an arrangement which linked the totalitarian powers and accorded the anti-Comintern pact a greater significance than it deserved. This fresh revelation of Nazi intrigue with Japan merely confirmed suspicions that the pact was the vehicle of a world conspiracy with ultimate designs on the western hemisphere (see Chapter 12).[32] Washington had long been sensitive to German activities in the Americas. After 1933, German trade with the Latin American states expanded rapidly, threatening US hemegony in key areas such as Brazil. Since the Nazi trade drive was accompanied by attempts to organise German immigrants and to influence Latin American armies it was easy to regard Hitler as a menace to the Monroe Doctrine. When Brazilian Fascists launched an unsuccessful *coup* in May 1938, the US saw the hand of Berlin in the affair. At the beginning of November 1938 there was a fresh scare over Brazil with the uncovering of a plot based on the secession of four provinces and the establishment of a puppet state under Nazi influence.[33]

This incident was regarded as an example of what Washington might expect if Hitler and his allies were allowed to dominate Europe and Asia. While there is no evidence that Hitler drew up plans to bring the Latin American states into the German orbit, he was interested in acquiring African colonies and in building a fleet capable of taking on Britain and perhaps the USA at some stage after 1944. The Z-Plan of January 1939 gave priority to naval rearmament and called for the creation of a balanced modern fleet by 1945, including ten superbattleships and four aircraft carriers.[34] The aim was to prepare for conflict with the 'strong naval powers', which can

only have included the United States. Robertson concludes 'that the
Z-programme(*sic*) was imposed on reluctant service chiefs late in
1938 and in January 1939, precisely at a time when not only Britain
but also the USA had become a target of bitter German propaganda
is significant. It indicates that the great racial war which lay ahead
might have to be fought not only against Bolshevik and Jewish-
infested Russia but also the USA whose President had made himself
"the mouthpiece of Judah and the instrument of the Comintern"'.[35]
Despite his strong interest in naval affairs, Roosevelt does not seem
to have known about the Z-Plan. The work of Dülffer and others,
however, suggests that he was correct in suspecting that German
domination of Europe would be followed by a drive for global
supremacy. Roosevelt was correct about the Nazi threat to the
Americas but apparently based his conclusions on faulty evidence.

The final blow to appeasement was the *Kristallnacht* pogrom of 9
November. Nazi savagery against the Jews confirmed the impression
of a radical regime, based on repression at home and expansion
abroad. As Kennedy informed Lord Halifax, the British foreign
secretary, on 15 November, *Kristallnacht* had led to a violent reaction
against appeasement in the United States.[36] Even officials such as
Welles concluded that it was impossible to deal with the Nazis and
embraced a policy of containment. Only Kennedy remained to argue
the appeasement case and he was increasingly isolated from
Washington. In the wake of the pogrom, Hugh Wilson, the US
ambassador, was recalled from Berlin and Hans Dieckhoff, the
German ambassador, left the United States. At a press conference
Roosevelt strongly condemned Nazi excesses. He was motivated not
only by genuine horror that such events could occur in a civilised
country but also by a desire to mobilise the public behind a more
active anti-Nazi policy.[37] After *Kristallnacht* the President felt freer
to support the European democracies and was even prepared to
envisage the revision of the Neutrality Act. By his flagrant disregard
for the rules of civilised conduct, Hitler had cleared the way for this
development. Since his conduct after Munich had also alarmed
Britain and France, he was creating the outlines of a coalition which
might contain the Rome – Berlin – Tokyo axis and end his dreams of
world power.

In November 1938 links between Britain, France and the United
States tightened as each sought insurance against the threat of German power. The Daladier government had been courting Washington since early 1938, seeking to create an appearance of solidarity

which might deter Hitler. French aircraft orders were intended to have this effect and to draw the US deeper into the affairs of Europe. Daladier later argued that he had selected Georges Bonnet as foreign minister as part of this strategy. Bonnet had served as ambassador to Washington and had good contacts in the Roosevelt administration. French efforts were redoubled after Munich. According to Bonnet, it was imperative that the United States should rearm and openly support France.[38] Britain had been more circumspect following the resignation of Anthony Eden, the foreign secretary, in March 1938. Eden was identified with an American strategy similar to that pursued by Daladier. Chamberlain, however, was impressed by American isolationism. While the Prime Minister could see a possible US role in restraining Hitler, he was unwilling to make sacrifices to secure American friendship. In the spring of 1938 he believed that peace could best be secured by offering Germany justice rather than by pursuing the chimera of a democratic *bloc* with France and the United States.[39]

As Hitler continued to arm and threaten in the weeks after Munich, Chamberlain became more anxious to appease the United States. *Kristallnacht* was the final blow to British hopes of a general European settlement. As Oliver Harvey, Halifax's private secretary, remarked on 16 November: 'At Cabinet Committee on Monday it was decided . . . that owing to the Jewish persecutions it was no good trying to attempt further progress with Munich settlement and any question of making an offer of colonies must be set aside'.[40] In such a tense atmosphere an appearance of Anglo – American solidarity might restrain Nazi extremism and deter Japan from an open challenge to the British position in Asia.[41] A symbol of this new willingness to cultivate Washington was the Anglo – American trade treaty of 15 November 1938. It had been delayed for over a year by commercial considerations, but the unsettled situation after Munich made London ready to accept economic sacrifices to secure political benefits. As Herbert von Dirksen, the German ambassador in London, argued, Hitler's intransigence forced British concessions to the United States which might not otherwise have been considered.[42] Chamberlain emphasised the importance of the trade agreement because the Germans imagined that it contained secret political clauses. The possibility of American intervention in Europe might deter the German generals, if not their *Führer*, from risking war in any future crisis.[43]

Chamberlain therefore welcomed Roosevelt's pledge of industrial support when it was delivered by Colonel Murray on 14 December 1938. According to the Prime Minister, the message was 'most important'. There was 'no question . . . but that in certain circumstances a statement which really brought it home that the vast resources of the United States would be behind Great Britain might have a properly deterrent effect'.[44] He did not respond, however, by placing huge aircraft orders in the United States. He disagreed with Roosevelt's exaggerated estimate of German air strength and wished to preserve British financial stability and the balance of payments. Nor did he desire to concede to the President the political leverage which would follow British dependence on American supplies. Not until March 1940 did he authorise a course which involved such harsh political and economic consequences for Britain. Instead he invoked the appearance of Anglo – American solidarity to encourage uncertainty in Berlin. For Chamberlain the United States was thus valuable as a psychological deterrent rather than as an arsenal or as a possible military ally. He continued to believe, rightly, that in the event of war the USA would remain at best a benevolent neutral.[45]

It was in the new atmosphere of co-operation after *Kristallnacht* that Roosevelt elaborated his policy of deterrence. Economic strength was the central element in his strategy. Britain and France, backed by the United States, could outproduce the Axis powers which were experiencing economic strains during 1938, and Roosevelt hoped to use this fact to contain and exhaust Germany. If economic strength could be translated into military power, particularly air power, Hitler would not risk war. The balance would tip decisively against the Reich which would be forced to terms by economic exhaustion. American industry would play a key role in this process. In the weeks after *Kristallnacht* the President elaborated his ideas on air armaments. At a White House meeting on 14 November he called for the creation of a 20,000 plane air force and an industry capable of producing 24,000 aircraft a year. As a first step the War Department was to develop a programme for 10,000 modern planes. He related his demands to the threat posed by: 'The recrudescence of German power at Munich . . . for the first time since the Holy Alliance . . . the United States now faced the possibility of an attack on the Atlantic side in both the Northern and Southern Hemispheres'. In contrast to his attitude in early October the President admitted shame at his association with the Munich agreement:

> I am not sure now that I am proud of what I wrote to Hitler in urging that he sit down around a table and make peace. That may have saved

many, many lives now, but that may ultimately result in the loss of many, many times that number later. Had we this summer 5,000 planes and the capacity immediately to produce 10,000 per year even though I might have had to ask Congress for authority to sell or lend them to the countries of Europe, Hitler would not have dared to take the stand he did.[46]

The President encountered problems with his scheme for air rearmament and industrial mobilisation. He regarded aircraft as a political weapon and emphasised the value of numbers to impress Hitler. The US army, however, demanded a balanced programme which did not neglect the requirements of the ground forces. As for the air component, it stressed rearmament in depth rather than breadth, concentrating on airfield construction, pilot training and research and development into new types. According to the army chief of staff, General Malin Craig: 'A vast air force with a huge reserve of planes [was] prohibitively expensive because of rapid obsolescence, costly storage requirements and costly maintenance even for reserve planes'.[47] Roosevelt was forced to take the arguments of the professionals into account. Moreover he had to consider what Congress was likely to accept in the military budget. In January 1939 he bowed to the e realities, requesting funds for the development of a 3,000 plane air force, a drastic reduction from the figure of 10,000 which he had demanded in November.[49] In the end the President chose to rely on allied rather than US orders to expand the American aircraft industry. He refused to consider anything like economic mobilisation or a War Production Board.

There were flaws in this strategy. The British kept their orders to a minimum. The French never realised their ambition of harnessing American industry to the French war machine. The plan was hampered by financial problems and the low initial capacity of US aircraft plants. Although Roosevelt over-ruled War Department objections to allow France access to secret prototypes, this decision did not make large numbers of modern aircraft instantly available. By the end of 1938 the French had discovered that the US could supply only 555 aircraft by October 1939, half of them trainers, although the situation would improve by 1940.[49] Paris hoped to keep this modest figure secret. As Daladier explained in Febrary 1939: 'The impression produced . . . by the idea that France could obtain an unlimited number of planes in the United States has been so valuable a deterrent . . . that it should not be disturbed by actual figures of moderate dimensions.'[50] Thus the French, like the British, finally emphasised the value of the United States as a psychological deterrent rather than a real source of supply. This situation lasted into the Phoney War. It was not until March 1940 – alas too late – that the allies placed massive aircraft orders in the United States.[51]

Roosevelt believed that deterring Hitler depended on more than helping the French rearm. If the Germans were to take the United States seriously something would have to be done about the Neutrality Act. As the French emphasised, the US must provide firm evidence of its readiness to aid the European democracies in case of war. The question had been under consideration since October 1938. Outright repeal of the Neutrality Act was regarded as impossible. An alternative was the introduction of a cash and carry provision which lifted the arms embargo and allowed belligerents to purchase war material if they transported it in their own ships. Since Britain and France controlled the seas, this revision would discrimate against Germany. It was decided to adopt an indirect approach to secure new legislation since an administration bill might be blocked by a coalition of isolationists and conservatives hostile to the New Deal. In January 1939 the matter was placed in the hands of Key Pittman, chairman of the Senate Foreign Relations Committee.[52] Although the President thus chose to remain in the background, neutrality reform had been placed on the political agenda for 1939.

Morgenthau wished to go further towards containing the Third Reich. He pressed for the imposition of countervailing duties on German exports to the US, a course he had favoured since Munich as a means of hindering German rearmament and increasing the strains on the Nazi economy.[53] His programme was opposed by the State Department which resented Treasury interference in foreign affairs. Hull hesitated to move too far ahead of public opinion and he was sensitive to the possible reaction of southern Congressmen to any interference with American cotton exports. Welles was reluctant to cut all ties with Germany and argued that economic warfare would complicate the problem of dealing with Germany on the emigration of Jewish refugees. Although the President called Morgenthau's ideas 'bully', he showed no signs of over-ruling the State Department as he had over-ruled the War Department over French aircraft orders. Indeed he ordered the Justice Department to suspend a ruling on whether German exports were subsidised and thus liable to countervailing duties.[54] Roosevelt was thinking about the domestic situation. An attempt to move too openly against Hitler might give the isolationists a propaganda weapon and hinder the chances of a revision of the Neutrality Act. Morgenthau's approach was not adopted until the Nazi seizure of Czechoslovakia in March 1939.[55]

Morgenthau had more success in the Far East. In October 1938 he advocated a programme of financial aid to China which had been resisting Japanese aggression since July 1937. US aid would keep Chinese forces in the field and tie down the Japanese. By the autumn of 1938 the situation in Asia was serious. After the fall of Canton and Hankow in November 1938 the Chinese had been driven far into the interior and Tokyo proclaimed a 'New Order' in the Far East to which the western powers would have to adapt. There was talk of a peace of exhaustion and Japanese domination of China (see Chapter 12). In this situation Morgenthau argued that the US must act. The Chinese were 'busted' and could no longer endure the economic strain of the war. 'By risking little more than the cost of one battleship', Washington could 'give renewed vitality and effectiveness to the Chinese', averting a totalitarian victory in the Far East which would rival Munich.[56] Once again Morgenthau faced opposition from the State Department. Hull believed that financial support for China would enrage the Japanese and might lead to war. On this occasion, however, Roosevelt decided in favour of the Treasury and on 14 December 1938 a $26 million loan was announced.[57] This was followed by a British loan in March 1939. The two powers also discussed a programme of joint sanctions against Japan but dismissed the idea as too provocative. It was merely hinted in Tokyo that such measures were under consideration in order to make the Japanese think twice about further anti-western measures or a full military alliance with Germany.[58]

If Germany and Japan were to be contained by the employment of American economic strength, the third Axis partner, Italy, was to be tempted out of the totalitarian coalition altogether. The defection of Italy would ease the threat to the British and French in the Mediterranean and might make the Japanese think twice about concluding a military alliance with Germany (see Chapter 11). Rome was therefore regarded as the key to a diplomatic revolution which would isolate Hitler. These hopes were kindled by memories of Italy's defection to the highest bidder in the First World War and by Mussolini's mediating role at Munich. Washington intended to extend a financial carrot to Rome while demonstrating that a powerful coalition was developing against the Axis. Mussolini might then choose to loosen his ties with Berlin and Tokyo.[57] The Italians were experiencing difficulties in developing their new Ethiopian empire because of revolts and a shortage of capital. Roosevelt hoped to interest them in a scheme to settle Jewish refugees 'in part of Ethiopia and surrounding colonies' with American economic assistance.[60] This initiative was designed to drive a wedge between the dictators. It was also intended to support British efforts to play on Mussolini's supposed moderation. The US offer was extended to Rome on 3 January 1939, eight days before Chamberlain and Halifax were due to visit Italy.[61]

Anglo – American attempts to cultivate Mussolini ended in failure. He had already decided to sign a military pact with Hitler. As the Italian foreign minister, Count Galeazzo Ciano, remarked on 1 January 1939, Mussolini considered 'a clash with the Western democracies more and more inevitable, and therefore he wished to effect a military alliance in advance'. Roosevelt's initiative was thus rejected and Ciano exchanged jokes with the German ambassador about 'American lack of political sense'.[62] In approaching Mussolini Roosevelt ignored recent Italian demands for the annexation of Tunisia, Nice, Corsica and Savoy – at this stage the French did not take these claims seriously. On 6 December Bonnet concluded an agreement with Ribbentrop which guaranteed the Franco – German border and pledged consultation in the event of future disagreements. He therefore chose to believe that Mussolini's demands would not be supported by Berlin.[63] The situation was to change dramatically in January 1939 when French alarm drew American attention to the developing Mediterranean crisis.

In his state of the union message on 4 January 1939 Roosevelt attempted to make deterrent diplomacy credible by emphasising that the USA was moving away from isolationism. He called for strong national defence and warned that potential aggressors should not ignore American economic power: 'Words may be futile, but war is not the only means of commanding a decent respect for the opinions of mankind. There are many methods short of war but stronger and more effective than mere words, of bringing home to aggressor governments the aggregate sentiments of our own people'. He went on to recommend revision of the Neutrality Act.[64] The speech was welcomed in Britain, France and Poland as a symbol of US support which might deter Germany. Roosevelt thought that he had seized the initiative from the dictators. On 15 January he boasted to his cabinet that he had been 'doing some straight talking to Hitler'.[65]

Within days, however, the President found himself facing a new series of crises which coincided with a domestic debate about the foreign policy of his administration. On 23 January plans to supply arms to France were revealed when a bomber, being tested in secret, crashed in California with French officers aboard. That day, when Roosevelt faced the political repercussions of this event, a report reached London from Carl Goerdeler of the German opposition that Hitler planned to solve German economic problems by breaking loose in the west. He intended to mobilise on the Dutch and Swiss borders in order to terrorise Britain and France into conceding his demands for financial assistance. This was the first step in a broader strategy to eliminate France. It would be followed by co-ordinated action with Italy and Spain to dominate the Mediterranean and conquer Africa. This information was passed on to Washington where it was taken seriously.[66] Roosevelt expressed fears about the repercussions of a new Nazi *coup* in Latin America and the Far East. He informed his cabinet on 27 January, 'Hitler will not have to control all of Europe . . . in order to make it difficult for us economically. For instance, the Argentine now exports 80 per cent of her products to Germany and other European countries. If Hitler can dominate the major part of Europe, he can serve notice on the Argentine that unless it accepts Fascist principles and yields to Fascistic economic domination, all of her exports to Europe will be cut off . . . And the same situation would exist with respect to other South American countries. They would be turned against us and we . . . would be powerless to do anything except to retire within our own territory, there to get along as best we could'.[67] Roosevelt also suspected that Hitler would demand the Dutch East Indies and, having secured the islands, cede them to the Japanese to secure Tokyo's agreement to the tripartite military pact. Despite his alarm he felt powerless to act. Congress was already raising questions about aircraft sales to the French and the isolationists were 'full of fight'. A false step could lose any chance of Neutrality Act revision.[68]

Matters were not improved by Hitler's *Reichstag* speech of 30 January. Chamberlain seized on the *Führer's* statement that Germany must 'trade or die' as evidence that deterrence had worked. Hitler, according to Chamberlain, had been impressed by British rearmament and American firmness, and was now seeking a negotiated solution to German problems. In the following weeks the Prime Minister initiated a series of economic contacts designed to promote the trend towards moderation which he incorrectly detected in Berlin.[69] The French, however, chose to put greater emphasis on Hitler's pledge, also made on 30 January, to march with Italy in the event of war. In contrast to their earlier attitude, they became almost hysterical in their predictions of a Mediterranean crisis, an attitude which they communicated to Washington. As Berle remarked on 7 March: 'The French have been scaring Bullitt almost to death, talking of war at any moment and of the certainty that the American embassy will be bombed'.[70] Mussolini's rejection of Roosevelt's offers to Italy encouraged the White House to take a grim view of the future. American fears that a new international crisis was imminent were further aroused by events in the Far East. On 12 February the Japanese seized the Chinese island of Hainan, an action which put them in a position to threaten French Indochina. On 17 February Welles expressed his apprehension of the role which this played 'in the timing between Italy, Germany and Japan'.[71]

Roosevelt's problems with Congress precluded any bold warning. On 31 January the President met members of the Senate Military Affairs Committee and justified the sale of aircraft to France on the grounds that a strong France was vital to US security. This leaked to the press as a statement that America's frontiers were 'on the Rhine' and caused a new political storm.[72] Although Roosevelt believed that the affair had deterred the dictators, he had to move carefully to avoid giving a further handle to the isolationists. In these circumstances he could only complain that Chamberlain seemed 'wilfully blind to reality' and raise questions about the economic contacts between London and Berlin.[73] There was little doubt in Washington that the Axis planned a *coup* in the spring, either in Europe or Asia, and that a fresh surrender to force would confirm the ascendancy of the totalitarian powers.[74]

In the event the expected crisis occurred neither in the Mediterranean nor the Far East but in central Europe. On 15 March Hitler tore up the Munich agreement and marched into Prague. This action made it difficult for political opponents to condemn Roosevelt as an alarmist and cleared the way for new measures which he now felt would be acceptable to the American public. Countervailing duties were imposed on German goods and the US – Czech trade treaty was suspended to prevent the Nazis from benefiting by its terms. On 17 March Roosevelt renewed the call for Neutrality Act revision and expressed the hope that Congress would produce satisfactory legislation. On 20 March, under pressure from the administration, Pittman introduced his 'Peace Act' repealing the arms embargo and placing all trade on a cash and carry basis.[75] As the neutrality debate began at home, the President attempted to use his influence abroad to encourage the formation of an anti-Nazi coalition which would contain German expansion and end the global threat of the tripartite Axis.

THE US AND THE GUARANTEE SYSTEM

The Prague *coup* was followed by the creation of an Anglo – French security system in eastern Europe, beginning with the guarantee to Poland on 31 March (see Chapter 6). On 17 April negotiations were initiated for a military alliance with the Soviet Union.

The Chamberlain government now assumed that Hitler's aims were unlimited, a suspicion which had been growing since the January crisis, and that it was 'impossible to continue to negotiate on the old basis with the Nazi regime'. Britain must now show its determination to resist further aggression and mobilise international support. A firm stand might yet deter Hitler short of war.[76] The United States was an important factor behind this strategy. American sympathy in the shape of Neutrality Act revision would add weight to the peace front. Moreover if Britain were to face Hitler in Europe, it would require US naval assistance in the Far East both to deter Japan and to reassure Australia and New Zealand (see Chapter 10). Halifax believed that the American public was more likely to support such moves if Britain took a principled stand in the wake of the Prague *coup* rather than waiting until Poland or Rumania had also fallen victim to Nazi aggression. This impression was confirmed by Kennedy in an interview on 18 March.[77] The effect of Hitler's action was thus to increase US influence on British policy.

The Prague *coup* confirmed Roosevelt's belief that Hitler was the moving force in a world conspiracy. If he were allowed to dominate Europe his next step would be the western hemisphere. This was reinforced by secret information which reached William Bullitt, the US ambassador in Paris, on the eve of the Czech *coup*. According to Bullitt's source, Otto von Habsburg, the Austrian pretender, Hitler held a meeting at Berchtesgaden on 8 March at which he emphasised that German survival depended upon seizing sources of raw materials and eliminating the enemies of the Reich, named by Hitler as the Jews and the democracies. As the first step, Prague would be occupied before Easter 1939. Poland, Hungary and Rumania would be forced into the Nazi orbit by the end of summer. In 1940, employing the vast resources of *Mitteleuropa*, he would crush France, 'the hereditary enemy', and dominate Britain. He would then be free to

launch the 'greatest operation in all history', an attack on the United
States. Germany would no longer have to suffer insults from
Roosevelt: 'We will settle accounts with the Jews of the dollar . . .
We will exterminate the Jewish democracy and Jewish blood will mix
itself with the dollars.'[78]

There is no German record of this conference and the account
given to Bullitt may have been compiled from a variety of sources
with the assistance of the *Deuxième Bureau*. What he passed on to
the White House, however, proved to be a chillingly accurate forecast of Hitler's plans for Europe and for the Jews. It reflected the
revenge theme which dominated Hitler's thoughts after Munich and
reiterated several other ideas expressed by the *Führer* between
Munich and Prague. After *Kristallnacht* it was evident that Hitler
regarded Roosevelt as the tool of the Jews, conspiring to encircle and
stifle the Nazi Reich. In his speech of 30 January he pledged that if
international Jewry succeeded in plunging Europe into war it would
mean the 'extermination of the Jewish race in Europe.'[79] Moreover
the strategy outlined in Bullitt's account accords with what many
historians regard as a plan to achieve world hegemony by stages. In
the first phase Hitler would dominate Europe and expel Britain from
the continent. In the second he would confront the USA, employing
the navy created for this purpose by the Z-Plan. Whatever its real
origin, Roosevelt treated Bullitt's information with the utmost seri-
ousness, emphasising on several occasions that he had received
warnings about Nazi plans from sources 'very close indeed to
Hitler'.[80] He thus stressed the need for early action. The Nazis must
be stopped before they could create an autarkic *Mitteleuropa* as the
basis for an attack on the west.

Britain was the key to an anti-Nazi coalition. If Britain were to
take a firm stand in Europe, however, it would require US support in
the Far East. The British government was committed to defend
Australia and New Zealand but lacked the naval resources both to
fight in Europe and restrain the Japanese. In the wake of the Czech
coup, Halifax approached the Americans and asked if the US fleet,
which had completed manoeuvres in the Caribbean, could be moved
to the Pacific in case of need. He also requested the resumption of
secret staff talks, initiated in January 1938 following the sinking of the
USS Panay on the Yangtse by Japanese aircraft.[81] Roosevelt did not
reject these approaches but took no action, despite the British
guarantee to Poland on 31 March. The redeployment of the US navy
was delayed until after the Italian seizure of Albania on 7 April.

Although Chamberlain was prepared to guarantee Greece in the wake of the Italian invasion, he did not believe that Mussolini had co-ordinated the *coup* with Hitler and wished to keep Rome in play.[82] The French viewed the situation with greater alarm and conveyed their misgivings to Washington. In Paris the Italian move was regarded as the prelude to a combined Axis assault on the French position in the Mediterranean, coupled with a German *coup* against Poland and a Japanese attack on Singapore. In this event the British would send their fleet to the Far East leaving France to fight the European dictators alone. Daladier warned Washington that if this happened he 'would have nothing more to do with resistance in central and eastern Europe'.[83]

French panic was misplaced and based on a complete misunderstanding of British intentions. Nevertheless Roosevelt responded by ordering the US fleet to the west coast to reassure Daladier, to ease the strain on British naval power, and to save the emerging guarantee system from collapse.[84] When the transfer of the fleet was announced on 15 April, Roosevelt retained several units in the Atlantic. He planned to deploy them on a neutrality patrol which would protect US waters from Axis raiders and allow allied warships to concentrate on more vital strategic areas.[85] At secret staff talks in mid-June the US representative, Admiral William Leahy, revealed this scheme to the British and stated that in the event of a war in which the USA was neutral, the main American fleet would be moved to Hawaii to deter a Japanese move southwards against Malaya and Indochina. Leahy was more cautious about the possibility of US intervention on the side of Britain and France but stated as his own opinion that the USA would concentrate its naval effort in the Pacific whilst Britain and France handled the Atlantic and the Mediterranean.[86] The result of Hitler's Prague *coup* was thus the creation of an informal Anglo – US strategic alignment.

Roosevelt expected something in return from Britain following the transfer of the US fleet: in particular he wanted London to introduce conscription as a sign of British determination to uphold the guarantee system. The French were desperate for this British commitment, regarding it as a key in deterring Hitler. When their efforts failed in London they turned to Washington to put pressure on the Chamberlain government. The Prime Minister was reluctant to introduce national service because it would disrupt normal trade and cause political problems with the trade unions.[87] At a meeting with Sir Eric Phipps, the British ambassador to Paris, on 19 April, Bullitt reported

Roosevelt's view that it was 'absolutely essential' for Britain to introduce conscription at once. Bullitt implied that the President expected such a move in return for sending the fleet to the Pacific. Simultaneously Roosevelt asked Léon Blum, the former Popular Front Prime Minister of France, to use his influence with the British Labour party and the Trades Union Congress to overcome their opposition to compulsory national service.[88] US intervention in support of French appeals proved decisive, and on 22 April Chamberlain informed the cabinet that conscription was to be introduced.[89]

While encouraging the emergence of the guarantee system, Roosevelt attempted to isolate Germany from its Axis partners. The movement of the US fleet was intended as a veiled warning to Tokyo where opinion was divided on the merits of a military alliance with Germany and Italy (see Chapter 12). At informal meetings with Japanese officials Joseph C. Grew, the ambassador, took the line that if Germany and Italy went to war against the European democracies it would be impossible for the United States to remain uninvolved. 'If Japan were then tied up in the German camp in a general military alliance, it would be almost impossible for the United States to remain at peace with Japan'. The democracies, backed by the inexhaustible resources of America, would win in the long run.[90] A similar approach was adopted towards Italy. When the new Italian ambassador, Prince Colonna, presented his credentials at the White House on 22 March the President read to the astonished diplomat a lecture on the world situation. According to Roosevelt the economic power of the United States would be mobilised behind Britain and France in the event of war. He went on to warn that 'Europe could not contain two overlords at the same time . . . Hitler would undoubtedly throw over Mussolini at any time that seemed to him expedient'. When Italy failed to heed these words and signed a military alliance with Germany on 22 May, countervailing duties were imposed on Italian goods.[91]

The President combined these efforts with an assault on the German home front designed to weaken the position of the Nazi regime. He had long been convinced that German morale was weak and would collapse in the face of Anglo – French determination to fight. As he emphasised on 25 March, Hitler must not be allowed a monopoly on intimidation.[92] In April 1939 he attempted to couple the impact of the guarantee system with an initiative which offered the German people an escape from war. The original idea seems to have come from Carl Goerdeler, a leading member of the German opposition, who on 16 March drew up a plan of action to capitalise on the Prague *coup*. For the first time, Goerdeler argued, Hitler had gone beyond Versailles grievances by annexing non-German territory. The issue was no longer revision but aggression. This might be brought home to the German people if the democracies proposed a conference to discuss legitimate German claims. As part of such an offer they should insist on firm guarantees against further military action, a demand which Hitler was bound to resist. He would thus be branded as an aggressor with profound effects on the German home front. The Nazi extremists would be repudiated by the people and Hitler forced to co-operate with the generals who opposed war. To avoid distortion by Nazi propaganda, Goerdeler advised that the appeal should be broadcast to the Reich in German, particularly by US radio stations which were trusted by the German people. The Pope should also be invited to endorse the initiative.[93]

These recommendations were brought to the attention of Messersmith by Goerdeler's British contact, the businessman Arthur Young, on 24 March. Ostensibly Young was in the USA to attend an industrial conference but his real purpose was to influence US policy. In this he was wholly successful. Messersmith immediately grasped the importance of the Goerdeler memorandum and forwarded it to Hull, emphasising that it came from 'the best informed man on the situation in Germany and one who has contacts in high places . . . particularly in the army and industrial and financial circles.' Hull studied the material with 'much interest' and it appears to have formed the basis of Roosevelt's appeal of 14 April.[94] On that date the President broadcast a message asking Hitler to guarantee his neighbours against German aggression. In return the USA offered to sponsor a world conference on disarmament and equal access to raw materials. Roosevelt emphasised that the peoples of the world longed for peace and would hold their leaders responsible in the event of war. The administration ensured that the appeal was translated and broadcast directly to Germany. Simultaneously an attempt was made through the American hierarchy to persuade the Pope to endorse the initiative.[95] Roosevelt regarded his plan as a means of both dividing the German people from Hitler and mobilising the American people behind Neutrality Act revision. If the *Führer* rejected the appeal he would weaken his position at home and brand himself as an aggressor in the eyes of the world. The President was attempting to regain the initiative and to force Hitler onto the defensive. It was to be his last dramatic intervention before the outbreak of a European war over Poland in September 1939.

Roosevelt's initiative enraged Hitler whose irritation with the President had been growing since the beginning of the year. On 7 January the Polish Prime Minister, Josef Beck, found Hitler 'not only furious but also extremely worried' by Roosevelt's state of the union message. On 21 January the *Führer* informed the Czech foreign minister that the President was encouraging 'all those who are agitating abroad against Germany'. Roosevelt was increasingly identified, along with international Jewry, as the leading enemy of the Reich. In the spring of 1939 Nazi propaganda attempted to hinder attempts at Neutrality Act revision by condemning the President as an alarmist and a warmonger.[96] Hitler's reply to the peace appeal was designed to silence the White House once and for all. In a speech to the *Reichstag* on 28 April he announced that none of the countries named by Roosevelt had asked for a guarantee from Germany. He also recalled that the German people had been offered justice by US Presidents in the past. Woodrow Wilson's 14 Points had been a fraud which led to the humiliation of Versailles. It was a masterly performance which attained its aim of preserving national unity. As the former German Chancellor Heinrich Brüning ruefully remarked, 'the linking . . . of Roosevelt with Wilson and his 14 Points had been almost entirely successful'.[97] Moreover by denying that Germany had any designs on the Americas, an idea with its origins 'in a stupid imagination', and by calling attention to Roosevelt's failure to solve domestic problems, Hitler appealed to the political opposition in the United States. As William Shirer, the CBS correspondent, remarked: 'His answer to the President was rather shrewd . . . in that it was designed to play on the sympathies of appeasers and anti-New Dealers at home . . . ' The German embassy in Washington tried to maximise this effect by distributing thousands of copies of the speech.[98]

Despite the failure of his peace initiative Roosevelt continued to believe that war could be avoided if the balance of power was tipped decisively against Germany. Such an outcome depended on the revision of the Neutrality Act and the conclusion of an alliance between Britain, France and the Soviet Union which would face Hitler with the threat of war on two fronts. Confronted with a powerful international coalition, backed by the industrial resources of the United States, he would eventually be compelled to negotiate on the basis of Roosevelt's April offer or face the collapse of the German economy.[99] As European tension mounted over German claims on Poland, which were made noisily late in May (see Chapter 10), the administration redoubled its efforts to secure repeal of the arms embargo. For the first time Roosevelt placed his political influence directly behind new legislation. This belated intervention proved fruitless. On 14 July a combination of isolationists and anti-New Dealers blocked revision. A direct appeal by the President to Senate leaders on 18 July failed to reverse this decision. Roosevelt was furious and argued that the result encouraged German aggression. As he complained to Morgenthau, statues of the guilty Senators ought to be erected in Berlin 'with a swastika on them'.[100] Congress had repudiated deterrent diplomacy and left him impotent in the event of crisis.

The debate had already paralysed US diplomacy and forced Roosevelt to adopt a less strident role. When the Japanese began a blockade of the British concession at Tientsin in China on 14 July, an action which the Americans believed had been co-ordinated with German plans for Poland, the President chose to remain silent because of the possible repercussions in Congress.[101] Only after Neutrality Act revision had failed did he feel free to act in the Far East. On 26 July Washington gave notice that it would not renew the US – Japanese trade treaty of 1911 when it expired at the end of the year. This was intended to raise the possibility of sanctions and to warn Tokyo against placing its faith in isolationism following the Senate decision to maintain the arms embargo.[102] On 31 August he revealed that he had two more methods of pressure 'in the locker' if Japan continued to threaten the Western position in Asia. One was to send aircraft carriers and bombers to the Aleutian islands; the second was to move the US fleet to Hawaii. This confirmed the tacit agreement of the spring by which the United States assumed the main responsibility for restraining Japan.[103] Washington thus took the first steps towards a strategy based on sanctions backed by the threat of force which was ultimately to lead to Pearl Harbor.

In contrast to the Far East, the President was little more than an observer of the European scene. Forced onto the sidelines by Congress, he made a final effort to preserve the deterrent front by an appeal to Stalin. Although Washington had recognised the Soviet Union in 1933 relations had neither been close nor cordial. The atmosphere was soured by the dispute over the Kerensky debt and US reaction to the great purges.[104] An influential group at the State

Department regarded the Communists as a greater menace to peace than the Nazis, a perspective which only changed as the result of events after Munich.[104] Roosevelt himself was always interested in the possibility of using the Russians to contain Germany and Japan. He sympathised when the Russians attempted to purchase a super-battleship from the US in 1936–38 which they intended to base at Vladivostok. He hesitated, however, to over-rule the navy which objected to the transfer of advanced technology to a foreign power.[105] By 1939 Roosevelt had come to believe that he had a special influence with Stalin, who regarded him as a disinterested figure unlike Chamberlain or Daladier whom the Russian leader distrusted, and this myth was encouraged by Joseph Davies, the former US ambassador to Moscow.[106] In July 1939, as neutrality revision bogged down and rumours circulated of secret Nazi – Soviet exchanges, the President intervened and drew upon his supposed moral capital with Stalin. The Soviet ambassador, Oumansky, preparing to return to Moscow, was interviewed by Roosevelt and asked 'to tell Stalin that if his government joined up with Hitler, it was as certain that night followed day that as soon as Hitler had conquered France, he would turn on Russia, and that it would be the Soviets turn next'. As Oumansky reported on 2 July, there could be no doubt of Roosevelt's personal interest in a favourable conclusion to Anglo – French negotiations for a military alliance with the Soviet Union.[107]

At the beginning of August staff talks were still bogged down while evidence accumulated from a secret source that Berlin was seeking a deal with Moscow.[108] This would relieve Germany of the threat of war on two fronts and further weaken the guarantee system following the failure of neutrality revision. On 4 August Roosevelt intervened directly with the Kremlin to preserve the balance of power. In a personal message to Stalin he argued that the Axis threatened Soviet security not only in Europe but also in Asia where an undeclared war was raging with Japan at Nomonhan. According to the President, Russian interests demanded an Anglo – French alliance.[109] This appeal lacked credibility. Roosevelt was asking the Russians to place themselves in the front line, a risk which the United States itself had no intention of taking. In the event of war over Poland, the Soviet Union would find itself fighting Germany and exposed to the threat of Japanese aggression in the Far East. On 24 August Stalin rejected Roosevelt's advice and concluded a non-aggression pact with Hitler. This symbolised German readiness to abandon Japan; Soviet forces, in conflict with the Japanese in Manchuria, brought the Nomonhan incident to a successful conclusion on 31 August.[110]

In the final days of peace Roosevelt was unable to do more than maintain a death watch over Europe. There was a sense of impotence in Washington which reduced some officials to despair.[111] The President could only seek consolation in the effects of the Nazi – Soviet pact on Japan and the reluctance of the Italians to fight alongside Germany. Despite the outbreak of war over Poland, Roosevelt continued to hope that Hitler could be contained by methods short of war. He believed that Germany, abandoned by Italy and Japan, might yet be forced to terms without the destruction of European civilisation. In November 1939 Congress repealed the arms embargo, thereby placing US industry at the disposal of Britain and France. He wanted the allies to exploit this concession to the full, in order to tilt the balance against Hitler and convince the Germans that they could not win. On 14 December he talked about exploiting such a situation by a peace appeal to Germany along the lines of his April initiative. He would overcome fears of a new Versailles by offering justice in return for guarantees against aggression.[112] In February 1940 Welles was dispatched to Europe to investigate the prospects of such an offer which might divide the German people from the Nazi regime or at least preserve Italian neutrality and gain time for allied rearmament to benefit from American supply.[113] Roosevelt's hopes of isolating Hitler were only finally destroyed by the successful German offensive in the west which ended with the fall of France in June 1940. This transformed the situation by isolating Britain, bringing Italy into the war and stimulating new Japanese moves in the Far East. Fears of an Axis conspiracy were confirmed by the tripartite Pact of 27 September 1940, a German – Italian – Japanese alliance aimed at the United States. In these circumstances Roosevelt was forced to consider more than the limited American role he had assumed since Munich. Until Pearl Harbor, however, he remained reluctant to envisage US participation in a European land war, seeking instead a solution through Lend-Lease and the deployment of naval power to protect the supply line to Britain. Hitler was to be defeated by the commitment of US industrial resources, not American lives.[114]

CONCLUSIONS

Although Hitler dismissed the United States as a mongrel nation in 1938–39, there is evidence that he took note of the new turn in US policy after Munich. As long as he planned to fight a big war with Britain and France for continental supremacy, he was bound to take the US factor into account even if only as a psychological stimulus to Anglo – French resistance. Certainly he was anxious to counter Roosevelt's encouragement of a firmer stand against Nazi expansion. As his attention switched after May 1939 to a short campaign against Poland, from which he believed Britain and France would stand aside, he ignored Roosevelt and pursued a pact with Stalin which would guarantee a quick victory in the east. The failure of Neutrality Act revision in July 1939 possibly encouraged this dismissal of the United States.[115] After 1939 Hitler concentrated on destroying his enemies by a series of short campaigns while avoiding a direct challenge to the United States. A final reckoning with the 'mouthpiece of Judah' was to await the achievement of continental supremacy. Despite this caution, however, Hitler consistently underestimated American industrial and military potential, writing off the United States as 'a feeble country with a big mouth.' He refused to face reality even after Pearl Harbor, gratuitously declaring war and clearing the way to the full deployment of American resources against his regime.[116] US power was always more evident to his opponents. As Churchill remarked when Japan brought the United States into the conflict, whatever the future setbacks to the allied cause, the Axis had lost: 'Hitler's fate was sealed. Mussolini's fate was sealed. As for the Japanese, they would be ground to powder. All the rest was merely the proper application of overwhelming force'.[117]

NOTES AND REFERENCES

1. W. Carr, *Poland to Pearl Harbor* (London, 1985), pp. 44, 45, 50–1; DGFP, ser D.I. Dieckhoff to Weizsäcker, 20 December 1937.
2. C.A.MacDonald, *The United States, Britain and Appeasement 1936–1939* (London, 1981), pp. 83–9.
3. J.B. Duroselle, *From Wilson To Roosevelt* (London, 1964), pp. 240–4.
4. MacDonald, *The United States, Britain and Appeasement*, p. 6.
5. FRUS, 1938, I, Memorandum by Messersmith, 29 September 1938; MacDonald, *The United States, Britain and Appeasement*, p. 6.
6. C. Hull, *The Memoirs of Cordell Hull*, vol. 1 (London, 1948), p. 595.
7. J.M. Blum, *From the Morgenthau Diaries. Years of Crisis 1928–1939* (Boston, 1959), pp. 523–4.
8. FRUS, 1937, I, Memorandum by Welles, 26 October 1937; Franklin D. Roosevelt Library (hereafter FDRL) Berle Papers, Box 210, Adolf Berle Diary, 11 October 1937.
9. A.A. Offner, *American Appeasement* (Cambridge, Mass., 1969) pp.

216–26; MacDonald, *The United States, Britain and Appeasement*, pp. 63–4.

10. FDRL, Berle Diary, 16 March 1938; A.A. Berle and T.B. Jacobs (eds.), *Navigating the Rapids, 1918–1971. From the Paper of Adolf A. Berle* (New York, 1973), pp. 183–5.

11. *Documents diplomatiques français*, 2e série , tome 9, pp. 753–4, St. Quentin to Bonnet, 1 October 1938; *New York Times*, 4 October 1938.

12. R.J. Whalen, *The Founding Father* (New York, 1968), p. 248; N.H. Hooker *The Moffat Papers* (Cambridge, Mass., 1956), pp. 220–1.

13. D.C. Watt, 'Roosevelt and Neville Chamberlain: Two Appeasers', *International Journal*, vol. 28 (1973), p. 202.

14. H.L. Ickes, *The Secret Diary of Harold L. Ickes* (London, 1955) vol. 2, pp. 275–8; D. Reynolds, *The Creation of the Anglo – American Alliance 1937–1941* (London, 1981), pp. 40–1; MacDonald *The United States, Britain and Appeasement*, p. 88.

15. R. Fisk, *In Time of War Ireland, Ulster and the Price of Neutrality* (London, 1983), pp. 40–1.

16. DBFP, ser. 3, VII, Lindsay to Halifax, 20 September 1938.

17. Ickes, *Secret Diary*, vol. 2, pp. 467–70.

18. J.M. Haight, *American Aid to France* (New York, 1970), p. 53; R.E. Sherwood, *The White House Papers of Harry L. Hopkins*, vol. 1 (London, 1949), pp. 97–8.

19. Ickes, *Secret Diary*, vol. 2, p. 474; FRUS, 1938, I, Bullitt to Hull, 9 May 1938; C.A. Lindbergh, *The Wartime Journals of Charles A. Lindbergh* (New York, 1976), p. 70.

20. France, Comite permanant de la défense nationale, Assemblée Nationale, *Rapport fait au nom de la commission chargée d'enquêter sur les événements survenus en France de 1933 à 1945* (hereafter *Rapport*) (Paris, 1951–2), 250–1; Guy Chapman, *Why France Collapsed* (London, 1968), pp. 31–4.

21. FRUS, 1938, II, Memo by Green, 18 January 1938.

22. *Ibid*, Hull to Bullitt, 18 May 1938; *Ibid*, Memo by Green, 31 May 1938.

23. FRUS, 1938, I, Kennedy to Hull, 22 September 1938; Lindbergh, *Wartime Journals*, p. 70.

24. R.Overy, 'The German Pre-War Aircraft Production Plans: November 1936–April 1939', *English Historical Review*, 1975, pp. 781–2; W.Murray, *Luftwaffe* (London, 1985), pp. 18–19.

25. FRUS, 1938, II, Bullitt to Roosevelt, 20 September 1938.

26. Sherwood, *The White House Papers of Harry L. Hopkins*, vol. 1, p. 97.

27. Haight, *American Aid to France*, pp. 25–33; Reynolds, *The Creation of the Anglo – American Alliance*, pp. 42–3.

28. National Library of Scotland (hereafter NLS), Elibank Papers, File 8809, Conversation with Colonel Murray, 21 October 1938.

29. J.M. Blum, *From the Morgenthau Diaries. Vol. 2, Years of Urgency 1938–41* (Boston, 1965), p. 46.

30. *New York Times*, 29 October 1938.

31. National Archives of the United States (hereafter USNA), 76OF. 62/1617, State Department memorandum, 9 October 1938.
32. FRUS, 1938, III, Grew to Hull, 12 October 1938, Reynolds, *The Creation of the Anglo – American Alliance*, p. 41; MacDonald, *The United States, Britain and Appeasement*, pp. 106–24.
33. M. Grow, *The Good Neighbor Policy and Authoritarianism in Paraguay. United States Economic Expansion and Great Power Rivalry in Latin American during World War 2* (Lawrence, Kansas, 1981), pp. 25–51; Hull, *Memoirs*, vol. 1, pp. 495–6, 601; FRUS, 1938, V, Scotten to Hull, 2 November 1938; PSF State Department, FDRL, Long to Roosevelt, 18 November 1938.
34. J. Dülffer, *Weimar, Hitler und die Marine. Reichspolitik und Flottenbau 1920 bis 1939* (Düsseldorf, 1973), pp. 488–505; H.H. Herwig, *Politics of Frustration: The United States in German Naval Planning, 1889–1941* (Boston, 1976), pp. 188–95; M. Hauner, 'Did Hitler Want a World Dominion?', *Journal of Contemporary History*, 1978, 23–9.
35. E.M. Robertson, 'Hitler's Planning for War and the Response of the Great Powers' in H.W. Koch (ed), *Aspects of the Third Reich* (London, 1985), pp. 208–11.
36. J. Harvey (ed), *The Diplomatic Diaries of Oliver Harvey* (London, 1970), p. 219.
37. MacDonald, *The United States, Britain and Appeasement*, p. 113; Hull, *Memoirs*, vol. 1, p. 599.
38. France *Rapport*, pp. 2888, 2646–7.
39. D. Carlton, *Anthony Eden. A Biography* (London, 1981), pp. 120–1; MacDonald *The United States, Britain and Appeasement*, pp. 43–67.
40. Harvey, *Diplomatic Diaries*, pp. 220.
41. FRUS, 1938, I, Kennedy to Hull, 12 October 1938; PRO, FO, 371/21659. Cl444/42/18, minute by Cadogan, 14 October 1938.
42. DGFP, ser D, IV, Dirksen to Ribbentrop, 3 January 1938.
43. University of Birmingham Library, Neville Chamberlain Papers, NC18/1/1583, Chamberlain to Ida Chamberlain, 28 January 1938; NLS, Elibank Papers, Murray to Roosevelt, 13 December 1938.
44. *Ibid.*
45. Reynolds, *The Creation of the Anglo – American Alliance*, pp. 50–3.
46. Blum, *Morgenthau Diaries*, vol. 2, pp. 48–9.
47. Haight, *American Aid to France*, pp. 50–1.
48. DGFP, ser D, IV, Chargé in Washington to Foreign Ministry, 13 January 1939.
49. Blum, *Morgenthau Diaries*, vol. 2, pp. 70–1; Haight, *American Aid to France*, p. 69.
50. FDRL, PSF Bullitt, Bullitt to Hull, 3 February 1939.
51. R. Dallek, *Franklin D. Roosevelt and American Foreign Policy 1932–1945* (New York, 1979), pp. 212–13; Reynolds, *The Creation of the Anglo – American Alliance*, pp. 90–1.

52. Hooker, *Moffat Papers*, Hull, *Memoirs*, vol. 1, p. 613.
53. Blum, *Morgenthau Diaries*, vol. 2, p. 79.
54. FDRL, Book 151, Morgenthau Diary, 19 November 1938; *Ibid*, Book 155, 7 December 1938; Blum *Morgenthau Diaries*, vol. 2, p. 81.
55. Blum, *Morgenthau Diaries*, vol. 2, p. 82.
56. *Ibid*, pp. 58–9; Dallek, *Franklin D. Roosevelt and American Foreign Policy*, p. 193.
57. Blum, *Morgenthau Diaries*, vol. 2, pp. 60–3.
58. P. Lowe, *Great Britain and the Origins of the Pacific War* (Oxford 1977), pp. 56–62; PRO, FO371/23436, F1285/44/10, Craigie to Halifax, 8 February 1939.
59. Houghton Library, Harvard (hereafter HLH), Moffat Papers, vol. 41, Moffat Diary, 5 December 1938.
60. Muggeridge (ed), *Ciano's Diary, 1939–1943* (London, 1947), p. 4.
61. HLH, Phillips Papers, vol. 18, Phillips Diary, 3 January 1939.
62. Muggeridge, *Ciano's Diary*, pp. 2–5.
63. FDRL, PSF Confidential France, Bullitt to Hull, 15 December 1938.
64. Dallek, *Franklin D. Roosevelt and American Foreign Policy*, p. 179.
65. Ickes, *Secret Diary*, vol. 2, p. 558.
66. I. Colvin, *The Chamberlain Cabinet* (London, 1971), pp. 180–1; A.P. Young, *The X Documents* (London, 1974), pp. 156–62; DBFP, ser 3, IV, Halifax to Mallet, 24 January 1939.
67. Ickes, *Secret Diaries*, vol. 2, pp. 569–70.
68. DBFP, ser 3, IV, Mallet to Halifax, 27 and 30 January 1939.
69. MacDonald, *The United States, Britain and Appeasement*, pp. 128–34.
70. FDRL, Berle Diary, 7 March 1939.
71. HLH, Moffat Diary, 17 February 1939.
72. Dallek, *Franklin D. Roosevelt and American Foreign Policy*, pp. 181–2.
73. MacDonald, *The United States, Britain and Appeasement*, pp. 135–7.
74. HLH, Moffat Diary, 2 and 4 March 1939.
75. Blum, *Morgenthau Diaries*, vol. 2, p. 82; Dallek, *Franklin D. Roosevelt and American Foreign Policy*, p. 183.
76. Colvin, *The Chamberlain Cabinet*, p. 188.
77. S. Aster, *1939: The Making of the Second World War* (London 1973), pp. 33–4; MacDonald *The United States, Britain and Appeasement*, pp. 142–3; DBFP, ser. 3, IV, Halifax to Lindsay, 18 March 1939.
78. FDRL, PSF Bullitt, Bullitt to Roosevelt, 12 March 1939.
79. Robertson, 'Hitler's Planning . . .', pp. 202–3; Lucy Davidowicz, *The War Against the Jews, 1939–1945* (London 1983), pp. 142–3.
80. Ickes, *Secret Diaries*, vol. 2, pp. 609–10.
81. J.R. Leutze, *Bargaining for Supremacy, 1937–1941* (Chapel Hill, NC, 1977), pp. 18–25, 34–5; FRUS, 1939, I, Kennedy to Hull, 22 March 1939.
82. Aster, *1939*, pp. 131–4.
83. USNA, 740.00/770, Bullitt to Roosevelt, 11 April 1939.

84. Hull, *Memoirs*, vol. 1, p. 630.
85. Blum, *Morgenthau Diaries*, vol. 1, p. 91.
86. Leutze, *Bargaining for Supremacy*, pp. 37–8.
87. Aster, *1939*, pp. 88–9.
88. DBFP, ser, 3, V, Phipps to Halifax, 20 April 1939; Dalton, *The Fateful Years* (London 1957), p. 252.
89. MacDonald, *The United States, Britain and Appeasement*, p. 152.
90. J.C. Grew, *Ten Years in Japan* (London, 1944), p. 247.
91. FRUS, 1939, II, Memorandum of Conversation, 22 March 1939; Blum, *Morgenthau Diaries*, vol. 2, p. 86.
92. PRO, FO 371/22829, A2907/1292/45, Memorandum by Sir Arthur Willert, 25/26 March 1939.
93. University of Delaware Library, George S. Messersmith Papers, file 1172, Memorandum by Goerdeler, 16 March 1939; *Ibid*, file 1178, Leiper to Messersmith, 24 March 1939.
94. *Ibid*, File 1178, Messersmith to Hull, 25 March 1939; Columbia University Library, Butler Papers, Hull to Nicholas Murray Butler, 3 April 1939.
95. Berle and Jacobs, *Navigating the Rapids*, p. 210; PRO, FO 371/22969, C5468/15/18, Lindsay to Halifax, 17 April 1939.
96. FDRL, PSF Poland, Biddle to Roosevelt, 13 January 1939; DGFP, ser D,IV, Memorandum of conversation, 21 January 1939; S. Friedländer, *Prelude to Downfall* (London, 1967) pp. 10–11.
97. W.L. Shirer, *Berlin Diary* (London, 1977), pp. 132–3; PRO, FO 371/23008, C8027/53/18, Foreign Office minute, 6 June 1939.
98. Shirer, *Berlin Diary*, p. 133; Friedländer, *Prelude to Downfall*, p. 14.
99. Ickes, *Secret Diaries*, vol. 2, pp. 634–5.
100. R.A. Divine, *The Illusion of Neutrality* (Chicago, 1968), pp. 267–82; Dallek, *Franklin D. Roosevelt and American Foreign Policy*, p. 191.
101. FDRL, Berle Diary, 17 June 1939, PRO, FO 371/22814, A4279/98/45, Lindsay to Halifax, 20 June 1939.
102. Dallek, *Franklin D. Roosevelt and American Foreign Policy,* pp. 195–6.
103. DBFP, ser, 3, VII, Lothian to Halifax, 31 August 1939.
104. J.L. Gaddis, *Russia, the Soviet Union and the United States* (New York, 1978), pp. 124–33.
105. *Ibid*, p. 136.
106. J.P. Davies, *Mission to Moscow*, (London, 1942), p. 287; T.R. Maddox, 'Watching Stalin Maneuver between Hitler and the West: American Diplomats and Soviet Diplomacy', *Diplomatic History* (1981), pp. 140–154.
107. Davies, *Mission to Moscow*, p. 287; Aster, *1939*, p. 315.
108. Charles E. Bohlen, *Witness to History* (New York, 1973), pp. 67–82.
109. FRUS, 1939, I, Roosevelt to Steinhardt, 4 August 1939.
110. Carr, *Poland to Pearl Harbor*, pp. 62–5.

111. Dallek, *Franklin D. Roosevelt and American Foreign Policy*, pp. 197–8.
112. Reynolds, *The Creation of the Anglo – American Alliance*, pp. 55–7. PRO, FO 800/347, Lothian to Halifax, 14 December 1939.
113. PRO, FO 371/24417, C1839/285/18, Lothian to Halifax, 2 February 1940; PRO, 371/24407, C5073/89/18, Lothian to Halifax, 3 April 1940. See Also Stanley Hilton, 'The Welles Mission to Europe, February–March 1940: Illusion or Realism?', *Journal of American History*, June 1971, pp. 93–120, and A.A. Offner, 'Appeasement Revisited: The United States, Great Britain and Germany 1933–1940', *Journal of American History*, September 1977, pp. 384–93.
114. Dallek, *Franklin D. Roosevelt and American Foreign Policy*, pp. 292–3.
115. Friedländer, *Prelude to Downfall*, pp. 9–26.
116. G.L. Weinberg, 'Hitler's Image of the United States', *American Historical Review*, vol. 69, 1963/4, pp. 1017–9.
117. W.S. Churchill, *The Second World War*, vol. 3, *The Grand Alliance* (London, 1950), p. 539.

10. German Mobilisation Preparations and the Treaties Between Germany and the Soviet Union of August and September 1939[1]

ESMONDE M. ROBERTSON

Although the German – Soviet negotiations which led to the non-aggression pact of 23 August 1939 have been dealt with admirably in several accounts of the origins of the Second World War,[2] there is still uncertainty about what Hitler primarily hoped to achieve. Was his first consideration to deter Britain and France from intervention on Poland's behalf, or to threaten Poland from the east? Did he hope to use the non-aggression pact and subsequent treaty of 28 September in order to create conditions which would render it easier for Italy, whose power he greatly over-rated, to go to war? Did he consider plausible an alternative to a deal with Russia such as agreement with Britain? Could he sell the idea of a deal with Russia and war to his own people? No definite answer to these questions is possible until more is known about the military intelligence of the main participants.[3] A short review of German mobilisation plans and operational intentions helps to clarify some of the issues.

On 3 and 11 April, 1939, when Hitler and the German armed forces high command ordered that contingency plans for 'Operation White' should be drawn up for a possible invasion of Poland,[4] several issues likely to disturb German – Soviet relations had not yet been resolved. One was Ukrainian nationalism. Although the Soviets were relieved that the Carpatho – Ukraine had not been granted independence on 15 March but had been annexed to Hungary which would not tolerate Ukrainian nationalism,[5] fear of Ukrainian nationalism had become something of an obsession with sections of the Communist party in Moscow.[6] Hence Hitler's changing attitude towards the Ukraine has a direct bearing on German – Soviet relations. On 25 March he had told General Walter von Brauchitsch, commander-in-chief of the army, that he did not intend a German occupation of the Ukraine and that he would leave open the question of whether an independent Ukraine should be established at a later date.[7] This pro-Ukrainian course was favoured by Alfred Rosenberg, the self-styled party expert on Soviet Russia, as well as by Admiral Canaris, head of the armed forces intelligence (*Abwehr*).[8] The Kremlin was also anxious on account of the German – Rumanian commercial treaty of 23 March, for if this agreement were extended to political matters Rumania might become a virtual German protectorate. As a result Russia would be denied a chance to recover its lost – and the much coveted – province of Bessarabia, which was inhabited by Ukrainian, German and Hungarian minorities.[9]

More dangerous from the Soviet point of view was the German threat to the Baltic which came to the forefront after the German seizure of Memel on 23 March. With Finland in control of the northern coast of the narrow sea route to Kronstadt, and the southern coast controlled by Estonia and Latvia, Leningrad stood in the jaws of a vice. Maintenance of good relations with Finland and the extension of German influence over the three Baltic states had been the aim of German policy in eastern Europe after Munich. There was no knowing, as Hans Booms maintains, when Hitler would stake his claim for *Lebensraum* over parts of this area, where there was strong anti-Soviet feeling.[10] For the present Hitler kept his options open. He informed his generals in the April directives for a possible invasion of Poland that it might be necessary to annex the areas of the old Courland, which comprised all of Lithuania and southern Latvia, including Riga. Military necessity (or preponderance) would alone determine future German frontiers in the north.[11] No wonder that in their negotiations with Britain and France the Soviets vehemently insisted that the independence of the Baltic states should be guaranteed not only against direct military action but 'indirect' aggression.[12]

After the occupation of Albania by Italy on 7 April, it seemed for a time that Greece was threatened. In order to secure British communications in the eastern Mediterranean the cabinet in London were anxious to guarantee that country, and for reasons which have not been fully explained, the French also insisted, even after rumours of a German invasion of Rumania had died down, that a guarantee should be given to Greece.[13] One strategic consideration might have influenced French policy – Britain would be more committed to the defence of the continent provided that the guarantee to Poland was extended to other countries. The French Prime Minister, Daladier, was backed by President Roosevelt in insisting that Britain should take a strong stand which included the introduction of conscription.[14]

After the guarantees of Greece and Rumania on 13 April two courses were pursued simultaneously from Moscow. It has been claimed that about this time Stalin had learnt from a Soviet agent that Hitler's aim was first to conquer Poland and then to turn on the west. Having defeated France and Britain the German armies would finally be hurled against the Soviet Union.[15] Not only the authenticity of this report needs to be checked but also the credibility of its major premise. There are strong reasons for believing that Stalin in 1939 still thought highly of the French army and its ability to tie down perhaps 40 German divisions facing the Maginot line.[16] Provided that the British and French felt that an alliance with Russia was a valid option, the greater would be their resolve to resist German military expansion in the east. Hence, on 17 April the Kremlin declared that negotiations with the western powers for a triple alliance should begin. Stalin, however, was aware that, having guaranteed Poland and Rumania against German aggression, the British and French were not likely to allow the Russians to reclaim eastern Poland, Bessarabia and the Baltic States. Britain and France also realised that neither Poland nor Rumania would in any circumstances accept a

Soviet guarantee, for this might mean that Soviet troops could enter their territory. For its part, Rumania did not feel obliged under existing commitments to render Poland military assistance against Germany. For these reasons the Allies found it impossible to establish an effective eastern front against Germany in Europe.[17] Although Britain was involved in a serious crisis with Japan over the Tientsin incident in June and July, which might have brought it closer to Russia, the British were almost as apprehensive of Soviet as of Japanese influence in China.[18] Above all, the deep-rooted suspicion of the Soviet Union rendered it especially difficult for Chamberlain personally, and most of his cabinet, to reach an accommodation with Russia.(see chapter 8)[9]

While Hitler had something substantial to offer the Soviet Union, even at an exorbitant price, Stalin had every reason to be ruffled by the unequal treatment accorded him by Britain and France. If the western powers became involved in war with Germany, resulting from their obligations to Poland and Rumania, Russia would be required to back them. But if Russia first became involved in war, because of Poland and Rumania, the western powers would not be obliged to reciprocate. From the Soviet point of view the Allied terms were one-sided. It thus seems to have been Stalin's aim to pursue an alternative policy to that of a treaty of alliance with the west.[20] The first official step towards this goal was taken on 17 April, the same day as the proposal of a triple alliance with the west had been made, in a discussion between Merekalov, the Soviet ambassador in Berlin, and Ernst von Weizsäcker, the state secretary of the German foreign ministry. Soon Stalin himself wished to determine Soviet foreign policy, and on 3 May Molotov, his henchman, was appointed commissar for foreign affairs in the place of Litvinov, who had favoured collective security in co-operation with the western powers.[21]

Hitler does not seem to have been unduly ruffled by the prospect of an alliance between Russia and the west and he was in no hurry to follow up 'feelers' from Moscow. Indeed, he evidently still believed that the Red Army had not recovered from the purges. True, after Poland had refused to join the anti-Comintern pact, under which it might have been persuaded to contain units of the Red Army in the event of war with the west, Germany could exert less leverage over Russia in Europe. Japan on the other hand could – so Hitler told his generals on 23 May – be persuaded to threaten Russia in the Far East.[22] Since Japan was already involved in a border battle with

Russia after 10 May, which was later to escalate, Russo – Japanese antagonism could be taken for granted.[23] The most important factor which spoke in favour of improved relations with Russia, however, was Hitler's belief, also expressed at the meeting with his generals on 23 May, that Russia was not 'disinterested in the destruction of Poland'.[24] But this would only apply if an invasion of Poland, and not war with the west, was the first priority of German policy and if it involved the full mobilisation of the German army.

According to the original directive for 'Operation White' of 11 April, German armaments for war against the west were given priority over the current needs of the army.[25] This meant that the Z-Plan, providing for the construction of a giant battle fleet as well as a separate plan for a large air force, was still to be completed by 1944–45. Instead of going into the 'bottomless pit' of the army, German raw materials and manpower were to be channelled into the junior branches of the armed forces (see Chapter 3).[26] War against Poland was to be regarded as an extension of the scope of war with the west. Even while the Polish campaign was still in progress, troops engaged in the east might, Hitler thought, have to be withdrawn for an occupation of northern Holland. Hitler still believed that the real war would be fought after the occupation of the Low Countries and the defeat of France, when Italy would be an active ally against the west. The enemy would then be Britain who, as a result of the guarantee to Poland and the re-introduction of conscription, was trying to deprive Germany of its *Lebensraum* – this war would be a 'life and death struggle' lasting many years. Significantly, on this occasion Hitler mentioned neither the United States as Britain's potential ally, nor President Roosevelt's latent hostility to Germany which had been so marked from January to April 1939.(see chapter 9)[27] Despite his bombastic talk, Hitler had to provide Germany with maximum security against a French attack. Hence work on the West Wall, first started in earnest late in May 1938, was accelerated in the spring of 1939. Hitler was so proud of the progress already made that he seemed to be suffering from 'fortress mania', but there was a contradiction in his thinking. If the West Wall,which lacked inter-connecting tunnels and trenches, could prevent a French attack on Germany, why could not the technically superior Maginot line prevent a German attack on France?[28] It will be seen later how Hitler believed that while Germany, despite the risks involved, had the will to attack France, the French lacked the will to attack Germany.

After Brauchitsch issued a general directive for an attack on

Poland on 26–27 April, a working party under General von Rundstedt drew up operational plans.[29] The military possibilities open to Poland as a result of a German attack were first considered, though owing to a lack of reliable information on the Polish army, the German planners relied largely on conjecture.[30] The Poles, they believed, were acting on the assumption that war with Germany could only be prosecuted with success if outside aid was forthcoming. Hence they had some reason to take encouragement from a military offer made to Poland by the French high command on 19 May in accordance with which it was open to the French to launch an all out offensive in the west with 35 to 38 divisions approximately 15 days after mobilisation. Even though the French were not committed by the proposal, Hitler himself evidently took it seriously into account. Otherwise, it is difficult to explain why he ordered work on the West Wall to be extended along Germany's frontiers with Holland and Belgium. Provided that the West Wall acted as an adequate deterrent, the industrial area of the Ruhr would remain secure. If the west took no action or remained on the defensive, Hitler had little reason to fear an alliance with Russia directed against Germany.[31]

Rundstedt and his staff assumed that although the Poles would only reluctantly evacuate the industrial areas of their country, which lay mainly in the western areas, the possibility remained that after heavy frontier battles they would have no choice but to withdraw behind the Narew, Vistula and San rivers which divide Poland , and provided they could count on Russian aid in the form of war material reaching them, they hoped to continue waging war from behind this river barrier until western intervention achieved success. The intention of German operations was therefore to prevent the Poles from taking such action. Concentric attacks were to be made on them with two army groups: The first operating from East Prussia and Pomerania with two armies; the second, from Silesia, with three armies. The Polish army was to be destroyed by a surprise blow with mechanised forces west of the Vistula, San and Narew rivers before it had time to mobilise. Both army groups were to be supported by strong air force formations.[32] Swift action would have the additional advantage of proving to the British that intervention on Poland's behalf would prove futile. The conclusion to be drawn was that, provided a military victory could be achieved speedily, it would be enough if the Russians were mere spectators of a German *fait accompli*. Thus their active participation for war against Poland was not yet required.

Although the Rundstedt plan was adopted and formed the basis of a second directive issued by Brauchitsch on 15 June, provision had to be made for unexpected developments. For instance if the Poles, in reacting to growing political tension, were better prepared than was foreseen, then the initial attack could not be made with a small number of mainly armoured and mobile formations, but only after sufficient forces of all arms were available.[33] After the first plans for operations against Poland were drawn up a contradiction between Hitler's military and political intentions becomes apparent. In the summer of 1938 he had realised that there was no popular enthusiasm for war:[34] still in 1939 he needed to whip up a warlike spirit among his own people. Plans for a propaganda campaign against Poland had been drawn up by the foreign ministry on 17 April but, probably because they would have alerted the Poles to the German threat, they were not implemented until mid-May. The aim was to foment trouble over Danzig, so as to provide Germany with a good case for taking action. In June and July, as a result of German agitation, the Poles threatened to retaliate to the threat of a militarisation of Danzig.[35] It was these circumstances that first confronted Britain with the practical possibility of having to honour obligations to Poland under the treaty of 6 April. In spite of the military problems involved, Chamberlain, following the lead given by Lord Halifax, told the House of Commons on 10 July that a seizure of Danzig, organised by surreptitious methods, could not be regarded as a local matter but as a threat to Poland's independence. He drew his listeners' attention to the British guarantee which, he said, his government was determined to fulfill.[36] The danger that Germany might 'slither' into war with Britain over Poland, which Hitler expressed on 23 May, could no longer be dismissed.[37]

The impact of Britain's assurances to Poland was however undermined by an appalling diplomatic blunder on the part of Chamberlain's government. On 22 July the *News Chronicle* revealed facts about negotiations at a whaling conference in London between Helmuth Wohltat, an intimate of Georing, and Robert Hudson, of the department of overseas trade, together with Sir Horace Wilson, chief industrial advisor to the British government and a confidant of Chamberlain. It was proposed that there should be a joint Anglo–German declaration not to use aggression. In Wilson's opinion, such a declaration would render superfluous Britain's guarantees to Poland and Rumania.[38] In so far as the proposals might provide Britain with a pretext for leaving Poland in the lurch, Hitler had good cause to welcome them – but there was a snag. If negotiations for an Anglo – German agreement were continued on an official level they might enable the British to play the same role they had done on the eve of Munich and come forward with a credible compromise plan for the future of Poland. A compromise, leading to a second Munich, would deprive Hitler of his 'little war' and could not be tolerated.[39] Nevertheless, throughout the crisis of the summer of 1939 Hitler regarded a German – British understanding, coming into force after German claims on Poland had been met, as a genuine option and he frequently referred to it not only on the eve of the war but even after its outbreak.

Even before knowledge of these talks reached the press the Russians felt that the British could hardly be trusted.[40] Hence, Stalin again turned to Berlin, and it was announced in the press on 22 July that economic negotiations between the two countries should start, but the German foreign ministry knew that Stalin had an alternative and it evidently reacted to the announcement, made on the 25th, that an Anglo–French military mission was preparing for negotiations in Moscow. On 2 August, Ribbentrop informed Astakhov, the Soviet *Chargé-d'Affaires* in Berlin, that all outstanding problems between the two countries could be resolved. There was, he said, 'room for the two of us in the Baltic', a vital interest to both countries. Ribbentrop dropped a 'gentle hint' that 'an agreement could be reached on the fate of Poland'.[41] Weizsäcker was not so sanguine as Ribbentrop in thinking that Stalin would opt for an understanding with Germany rather than the west, and he noted on the 29 July that the issue of war and peace depended on decisions reached in Moscow. If the western powers failed to come to an agreement with Russia, however, the depression there would be so great 'that we could do what we liked with Poland'.[42] Weizsäcker was later to revise his attitude radically. As for Hitler himself, he reiterated on several occasions the reasons why he believed Britain would not go to war on behalf of Poland. He viewed Britain as a rich country with an over-extended and unruly empire which, under pressure from Italy and Japan as well as internal discontent, would break up if the mother country were involved in war in Europe. The British leaders, some of whom he met at Munich, were at best 'small – fry' who were utterly incapable of performing heroic acts. Hitler also claimed that the British navy would not be ready for war until 1941–42, although he admitted that the RAF was formidable. In fact, Britain would have two additional battleships after September 1939, and the

German navy was so weak in the summer of 1939 that the German admirals shuddered at the thought of war with Britain.[43]

Hitler also realised that Italy, whose military aid was badly needed to pin down some 15 French divisions, was more likely to enter a conflict, the reward of which might be chunks of Croatia and Dalmatia, and perhaps Greece, provided that it had nothing to fear from Turkey and Rumania. The prospect of an agreement with Russia would virtually neutralise those countries.[44] During negotiations with Ciano – the Italian foreign minister – at Salzburg on 12 August, which proved to be a fiasco, Hitler informed his guest that he had just learned that the Kremlin was prepared for negotiations with Germany which should be held in Moscow. He added that the question whether the German ambassador or a special envoy should conduct these talks remained open.[45] It is difficult to establish which political development prompted Stalin to take this important step. Probably he wanted to establish where the Germans stood as regards the Soviet Union, before the belated arrival of the Anglo–French military mission. In the second week of August, the political reasons from the German point of view for coming to an agreement became all the more imperative. On the 14th, Polish custom officials were informed that they would be obstructed in carrying out their duties, and this resulted in a vehemently hostile exchange of notes and a general escalation of the crisis. According to Nevile Henderson, British ambassador in Berlin, German propaganda which had previously concentrated on British encirclement as an object of attack, turned full blast on Polish atrocities.[46] Hitler was now determined to strike, but he was not free to take military decisions solely in the light of political developments. Germany's military needs were soon to set the pace of political action, not *vice-versa*.

Hitler had every reason to be satisfied with the conclusions of a situation report, drawn up by the high command's foreign armies section on 12 August, and which was evidently quoted by him after that date. According to the report, General Ironside's visit to Poland on 19 July proved that the British were not in a position to render the Poles military aid, and an agreement of 2 August under which the Poles were to receive £8,163,300 was much less than that originally envisaged by the press. Had the Poles been sure of British backing, they would, according to Hitler, have been more 'cheeky'. There were distinct signs that the French were not in a position to stand by their proposal of 19 May and launch a fullscale attack on the Reich within 15 days, nor according to the report were units of the French air force expected to operate from Polish soil. One development was viewed with special gratification. Far from expecting material support from the Soviet Union, the Poles even had to send two badly needed army corps to their Eastern frontier, in order to resist a possible Soviet attack. Although it cannot yet be established what the Soviet aim was for reinforcing their western frontier, the Russians were already rendering a useful service to Germany.[47]

The German planners were also labouring under difficulties. According to a timetable drawn up by the high command on 12 August, the campaign had to be over by early October, before the autumn rains fell.[48] Thus a postponement of the attack to a date later than 2 September entailed too many risks. Nor, for logistical reasons, could the date of the attack be put forward. German rolling stock had not only to move troops in unprecedented numbers over widely dispersed assembly areas, but to carry men and raw materials for work on the West Wall – approximately one to one and a half million tons of coal were needed for the assembly. This task had to be continued until 25 August, the date which the high command considered to be the most favourable for operations to begin. According to Gercke, chief of army transport: 'Germany is not at present ready for war'. It was necessary to know well in advance the exact date for action.[49] Assuming that 26 August would be the first day of full mobilisation without public announcement as well as for the attack, Hitler's generals were most anxious to know by the 15th whether an army manoeuvre on the Weser should be cancelled. The same applied to the annual party rally which imposed a strain on rail and motor transport. At the very latest the decision to go ahead would have to be taken on the 23rd with confirmation 24 hours later. At a meeting with his staffs of 14 August, Hitler declared that, because political developments could not be foreseen with certainty, he would withhold the decision to attack until 48 hours in advance, namely until 23 August. Important decisions were taken in other respects: a military convention was concluded with Slovakia, the party rally was cancelled, disturbances were instigated in Upper Silesia, and German ships in enemy or neutral ports were put to sea.[50]

One highly unwelcome development, which might have upset the German timetable, had to be considered. Because of the hostile German propaganda, German intelligence reported, concealed mobilisation had been introduced in Poland on 25 July; the early age groups were due to be called up by 15 August and preliminary mobilisation completed by the 27th. To keep abreast, Germany would have to start preliminary mobilisation on the 21st. On the 15th General Franz Halder, chief of the army general staff, reviewed the changed situation. While the objectives laid down in the assembly order remained unchanged, it was now no longer considered possible to disrupt enemy mobilisation and to defeat them west of the river barrier on which such emphasis had previously been laid.[51] This had serious political implications. It was no longer desirable that the Soviet Union should just keep out of the war with Poland: its active assistance would be an advantage in order to cut off a retreat by the Poles to the area behind their river barriers.

Late on 14 August, after conferring with his generals who were anxious that he should reach a decision as soon as possible on whether preparations for 'Operation White' should go ahead, Hitler decided that Ribbentrop and not a less prominent person should go to Moscow and conclude a non-aggression pact. He was now determined on an agreement with the Soviet Union. But Hitler had two irons in the fire – also on 14 August he told his generals that he had hinted to the British that after the Polish question was solved he would make them a generous offer.[52] The ramifications of this dual policy will be considered presently. In his dispatch arranging for this visit, Ribbentrop reminded Molotov, through Count Werner von der Shulenberg, German ambassador in Moscow, that if an agreement were not reached soon matters might take a turn which would deprive both governments of the possibility of 'restoring German – Soviet friendship and clearing up jointly the territorial questions of eastern Europe'. This meant that if the Soviet Union did not sign on the dotted line Germany might occupy the whole of Poland and thus gain a vantage point from which to threaten Russia's western frontier. Speed was again emphasised by Ribbentrop on the 16th and 18th. The last thing that Stalin wanted was to be hustled, and although he allowed members of the Anglo – French military delegation in Moscow to form the impression that he might enter a treaty with the west, he received no satisfactory answer to the question, abruptly posed on 15 August, whether Soviet troops could enter Poland and Rumania to defend those countries from German aggression. Hence the negotiations were deadlocked.[53]

There was another issue. Could the Soviet Union gain more from German or British friendship in the Far East? By 10 August the Soviets were on the offensive against the Japanese at Nomonhan on the borders between Outer Mongolia and Manchuria, and troops were being dispatched to the east. Stalin was determined to win this battle. Despite appalling logistical problems, an army corps of the best units of the Red Army, under General Zhukov, attacked the Japanese on 20 August. Before the offensive had made progress Molotov could not have known what the outcome of this battle would be, and he upbraided the Germans for encouraging Japanese aggression. He and Stalin must have realised that an agreement with Germany would remove the danger of a war on two fronts which the Soviet high comand for the last three or four years had regarded as axiomatic.[54] It was realised in Berlin that from the Soviet point of view nothing could be more favourable to the Soviet Union than a treaty with Germany, for this would nullify the anti-Comintern pact and enable the Soviet Union to concentrate against Japan – in fact at that time an estimated 600,000 troops, one-third of the Red Army, were deployed east of Lake Baikal. After Soviet forces had driven the Japanese from the heights near Nomonhan at the end of August, Stalin could dispense with the good offices of Germany and conclude a bilateral agreement with Japan whose leaders had by now a healthy respect for the Red Army. This strengthened his (Stalin's) position *vis-à-vis* Germany in Europe. Nevertheless Germany was more valuable to the Soviet Union as a neutral, which ensured that the Soviets need no longer fear a war on two fronts, than having Britain as an ally.[55]

While Hitler was pressing Stalin to act as quickly as possible, Stalin could use the Red Army in Europe as a lever against Germany. On 18–19 August reports from diverse sources reached German intelligence to the effect that the Soviets and Poles had composed at least some of their differences, and that approximately 250,000 Russian troops had been withdrawn from Poland's eastern frontier, enabling the Poles to concentrate against Germany. Such rumours were at least partly confirmed in a situation report of 21 August.[56] The easing of military pressure on Poland's eastern frontier was so serious that it later had to be brought to the attention of Molotov. Because most of the Soviet archives are inaccessible it is impossible to establish precisely what Stalin's intentions were. He certainly did not wish to take any action against Poland which could be used by that country's allies as a pretext for non-intervention. He might have tried to galvanise the Poles into putting up stiff resistance by making offers of Soviet aid. Probably he assumed that, provided the western powers were committed to fighting Germany and could keep an army in being, the Soviet Union was immune from an immediate German attack. On the 19th Stalin gave way to German pressure and agreed to receive Ribbentrop, but he suggested that in order to make the necessary preparations for the visit it should take place on the 26 or 27 August. These dates were too late for Germany: the deal had to be clinched and its less sinister clauses made public before, not after, the day of attack which was still to be 26 August. That Hitler accepted a Soviet draft treaty, the territorial clauses of which were highly favourable to the Soviet Union, without reservations on the 20th, is an indication of the price he was prepared to pay for Soviet co-operation. Stalin agreed on the 21st to accept Ribbentrop on the 23rd – subsequently the treaty was signed at 2 am on the 24th, and backdated to the 23rd.[57]

Even after the conclusion of the non-aggression pact friction with Moscow did not abate. The Soviet Union continued for a few days to negotiate with the west. They delayed ratification of the treaty with Germany as well as the dispatch of a new ambassador and a team of military experts to Berlin until the end of August. Far more serious was the continued lack of Soviet military activity in Europe, referred to previously. On 25 August the *Neue Züricher Zeitung* published an article revealing that the Allies had recently obtained a guarantee from Moscow to the effect that if Poland was at war with Germany it would not be attacked from the east.[58] Hence 250,000 Soviet troops were withdrawn from areas of easy access to the Polish frontier. The article seems to have been taken at its face value in Berlin, for on 27 August Weizsäcker ordered Schulenburg to discover whether Soviet troops had been withdrawn. He added ominously: 'Any appearance of Poland's being threatened from the Russian side too would naturally contribute to easing the situation in the west and might even, in the end, bring about a remarkable reduction in their readiness to help Poland'.[59] Certainly Stalin had by now every reason to withdraw his troops. For if Poland were threatened in the east and put under maximum pressure from Germany it might succumb to German demands and become a German satellite, in which event France and Britain would not intervene. Only on 30–31 August was greater Soviet military activity observed for a time near the Polish frontier. Hence on the eve of hostilities the Poles had to send additional troops to the east as well as to their frontier with Lithuania. In these circumstances Halder even believed that the Soviet Union would march on the day of the German invasion. The Soviets also agreed to a German request to keep Turkey neutral.[60]

If the treaty with the Soviet Union at first failed to relieve Germany from having to fight the bulk of the Polish army, its effect as a deterrent against intervention by the western powers was almost disastrous. Until 23 August Hitler believed that in the event of a German war with Poland Britain might sever diplomatic relations with Germany and furnish Poland with economic aid, and that it might impose a commercial embargo on the Reich – but that it would not declare war or even resort to a tight blockade for fear that this might lead to an incident precipitating war.[61] News that the non-aggression pact was about to be signed was made known on the 21st, and A.J.P. Taylor has demonstrated admirably how, because of this treaty, all parties in the House of Commons were united in favour of Britain's fulfilling its obligations to Poland.[62] At 1 pm on the 23rd, after it was learnt that a non-aggression pact was soon to be signed, Hitler received from Henderson a letter from Chamberlain in which he was warned that no greater mistake could be made than to believe that, because of the German – Soviet treaty, 'intervention by Great Britain on behalf of Poland is no longer a contingency that need be reckoned with'. In Ribbentrop's absence in Moscow, Weizsäcker, who was present at this meeting and who was also in private consultation with Hitler, formed the impression that Hitler's aim was to intimidate the British by brutal threats from fulfilling their obligations: 'Thereby the *Führer* calculates that on 24 [August] under the impact of our *coup* in Moscow, Chamberlain would be overthrown and the idea of a guarantee dropped'. During the interview, Hitler sharply reminded Henderson that Britain had given Poland a blank cheque to commit acts of terrorism.[63] But the British were not to be brow-beaten – on the 23rd, mobilisation was reported to have started in Britain, and increased military activity was also – at least for a time – observed in both Britain and France. At 3 pm on the 24th, Chamberlain re-affirmed in the House of Commons the assurances given to Poland. Hitler could hardly ignore the more rigid stand that the British government was now taking. For one thing 650 German ships, totalling three million tons, were still on the high seas and, if war broke out, they would most certainly fall as prizes to the British admiralty. At 5.30 pm on the 24th R. Schmundt, Hitler's adjutant, informed Gerneral Jodl, chief of the operational section of the armed forces high command, that 'the *Führer* was not quite certain whether Britain was in earnest this time. But he does not want war with England'. On the same day, Weizsäcker was also of the opinion that the prospect of war with the west was more painful for Hitler than it had been on the previous day. Hitler told him that he had doubts on whether Italy would intervene on Germany's side.[64]

23 August was a turning point and Hitler soon struck a different note on his policy towards both Poland and Britain. He now thought that the Poles might 'give in' and that there could be a solution reached in stages which he was to define more clearly later. After the first stage the British would 'drop' the Poles. In contrast to Hitler, Weizsäcker felt certain that Chamberlain's talk of war would win acclamation in favour of intervention in the House of Commons.[65] Because British intervention could no longer be ruled out, Hitler, contrary to his previous policy of rejecting negotiations for a compromise set about devising a cunning stratagem by lowering his demands on Poland with the aim of detaching Britain from that country. Meanwhile another unforeseen development threatened to upset Hitler's entire timetable.

Perhaps of equal significance to Hitler as Britain's attitude was the immediate reaction in Italy to the news of the non-aggression pact. The reactions of both Britain and Italy to the abrupt changes taking place in Berlin and elsewhere must be seen in conjunction with each other. Even if Hitler greatly over-rated Italy as a power factor, it was pinning down 15 badly needed French divisions for the defence of the north-east of France. Although Hitler, when addressing his staff on 22 August, felt that the Italians had no interest in a major war at least for the next few years, they were at least led by a man who might – like himself – be shot by a lunatic. He felt that Mussolini would not let him down. Early on the 25th, Ribbentrop, exaggerating the favourable repercussions of the pact, contacted Ciano on the need for Italian intervention. At first Mussolini felt that he was bound by honour to stand by Hitler, but under pressure from Ciano and the King the *Duce* later changed his mind.[66] But before the negative Italian reply reached Berlin late on the 25th, Hitler again met Henderson and his changed attitude, alluded to above, became noticeable. After the Polish problem was solved, he would approach Britain with a 'generous and a comprehensive offer'. He would not only respect the British empire, but even help Britain to defend it. On 25 August, before leaving for London, Henderson informed Ribbentrop that his government might decide to mediate between Germany and Poland, and also stated that he would not play to gain time.[67] Later that afternoon news reached Berlin that the Anglo–Polish Treaty of 6 April was about to be ratified, but this was not entirely unexpected. The order for the attack on Poland, which was to take effect at dawn on the 26th, still stood. The negative Italian reply was received at 6 pm: Italy could not intervene immediately unless supplied with raw materials. Hitler was shattered by this news, and he even believed that Ciano had treacherously informed the British of Italy's reluctance to go to war. As a result Brauchitsch told Hitler that Germany was not ready for war with the west, and the order for the attack was postponed. For the next few days Hitler showed signs of psychological stress, which indicates that he was losing control over events.[68]

The treaty with the Soviet Union affected Italy in one vital respect. The Japanese were so infuriated with Germany because of its new policy towards the Soviet Union, that the new government in Tokyo adopted a more pro-western policy. This meant that the Japanese fleet would no longer be used to force the British to keep a large naval force in the Far East, which again came up for discussion during the Tientsin crisis of June and July. The British navy could now concentrate their forces against Italy in the Mediterranean. The presence of US aircraft carriers, bombers and warships near the Aleutian Islands might also have restrained Japan.[69]

The postponement had one serious consequence. It has been seen how the German high command believed that if the operation were called off at the last minute it would no longer prove possible to disguise the feverish military activity already undertaken after the 25th as part of routine manoeuvres, for mobilisation without proclamation would take effect at the moment the attack began. Surprise was now out of the question. Since the British knew not only of the original date of action but that Hitler was 'wobbling',[70] resolute military measures by them and the French might still force Hitler to withhold the attack for just those 48 hours which would mean that the defeat of Poland could not, because of the weather, be accomplished in 1939. Everything depended on what positive action the Allies would take to back up their paper promises and on how Hitler and his generals assessed their military capability and aims.

In this connection it should be stressed that the balance of strength in August and September 1939 was gradually being tilted in Germany's favour. By the summer of 1939 Czech weapons, captured after 15 March, were already distributed to German units or were being used to buy vital raw materials. Germany was, therefore, better prepared for war than in 1938. There was also much less apprehension that war would mean *finis Germaniae* as there had been during the Czech crisis when Ludwig Beck was chief of staff.[71] But the term 'balance of strength' can mean several things. Hitler's generals weighed each contingency against the other: possession of strategic frontiers, the number of trained reserves, industrial output, the superiority of certain weapons and military organisation all formed part of the equation. Hitler, on the other hand, weighed each contingency in light of the most favourable conditions, which for him meant speed and surprise. Obsessed by the efficacy of fortifications, he was convinced that the West Wall would act as a deterrent against France – nor in his mind could there be any doubt about the outcome of war in the east. The Poles possessed few tanks, no fortifications, virtually no armoured formations and no effective anti-aircraft guns. Hence a *Blitzkreig*, fully backed by the *Luftwaffe*, would carry the day. But a psychological element, perhaps of wishful thinking, can be discerned in Hitler's thinking – for him it was a fixed principle in time of peace and war that a quick blow against an enemy would prove devastating. The idea of a *Blitzkreig*, and the taking of risks, appealed to him psychologically. On 23 May, 1939, Hitler personally believed that with Italian help the Maginot line could be pierced.[72]

Although Hitler devoted the greater part of his addresses to the generals on the 14 and 22 August to the British reluctance to go to war, and the fact that it was leading France in tow, neither he nor his generals could ignore a possible French attack. According to the German general staff, the balance of strength was still decidedly in favour of the French. At the start of operations 41 to 44 French divisions, out of a grand total of 86, faced 31 German divisions. The French also had a vast superiority in armour and artillery on the western front. It was expected that as a precautionary measure the French would occupy Luxembourg by the third day of hostilities. German fortifications on the French and Dutch frontiers were not yet complete. Hence, on 14 August the Dutch and Belgian military *attachés* were to be told that, because the French were not expected to respect the neutrality of their respective countries, military preparations were necessary on the German side of the frontier.[73]

If Belgium territory were occupied, seven to nine French divisions might reach the German frontier on the sixth day of mobilisation. Operations from this area were evidently expected, not as a prelude to a full scale attack against the Reich, but as a means to secure a more favourable defensive base for possible operations against a German attack. A larger force with an offensive aim might reach the German – Belgian frontier in about two weeks, and the German – Dutch frontier in the third week of mobilisation. The German evidence points to the conclusion that the French could not relieve pressure on Poland unless that country was capable of holding up a

German offensive until well into October, but the possibility of a French attack could not be ignored. Even as late as 24 August the military staffs in Berlin still feared that the French might invade the Low Countries so as to strike the Ruhr in an area where fortifications were not yet complete.[74]

The most vulnerable sector of the German line was the German – Dutch frontier, for with bases in Holland the French could operate on the German side of the Maas and the Rhine rivers. On 28 May, 1938, and again on 23 May, 1939, Hitler spoke about a pre-emptive strike against Holland, the aim being the extension of the German coast for war at sea. There was another problem which involved the army. The Maas, north of the Maastricht salient, which was of great strategic value, runs parallel to but inside the Dutch frontier. Since the Germans were short of anti-tank artillery, they considered it desirable to push forward their line to this water obstacle, but Hitler and his staffs felt relatively assured that the Dutch would not allow the Allies to enter their territory, since for one thing war in Holland itself might mean a Japanese occupation of the Dutch East Indies.[75]

Whether the Belgians would allow the Allies entry to their territory was less certain. The area south of a line between Lille and Liège, through which the main Allied thrust could be made, was inhabited mainly by Walloons who, on the whole, were pro-French. The Walloons were also strongly represented in the Belgian government. Hitler himself expressed reservations on Belgian policy on account of the alleged influence of Jews in the government, but on 24 August it was announced in Brussels that Belgium would defend its neutrality at all costs. The next day the German foreign ministry announced that it would respect that neutrality, but that it still feared a French invasion.[76] The Allies were left with no alternative but to follow suit. Despite protests from Gamelin, the French commander-in-chief, they too informed the Belgians on the 28th that their neutrality would be respected. The decision was crucial for it acted as an assurance to Germany that at least during the Polish campaign the Allies, who had failed to concentrate their forces near the Belgian frontier, would take no effective military action. Later the Germans were to give the dubious assurance to the Belgians that, if they felt threatened by France, they could count on German 'help'.[77]

There were other indications that the Allies were 'soft' on the issue of war. Hitler personally laid great stress on the fact that whereas in the frontier zones in Germany civilians had to be evacuated compulsorily, in France evacuation was voluntary. Nor did the French close

their frontier with Germany. After Britain had ratified its treaty with
Poland on 25 August, it was reported to have started mobilisation of
the fleet and parts of the regular army. Within a few days, however,
British mobilisation was discontinued, and there was no evidence
that the British forces allocated to France had disembarked, as
Daladier, the French Prime Minister, had requested.[78] This passivity
on the part of the Allies might have led Hitler to the conclusion, 'The
opportunities they have missed we will take'. The French were also
short of aircraft which they hoped would arrive from the united
States (See Chapter 9).

In contrast to their allies, the Poles at first took bold steps to
defend their country from an attack by Germany. After 25 August
two additional divisions were located in the Corridor and one in
Polish Silesia. Equally, the equivalent of general mobilisation was to
be announced by the Polish government on 29 August. But because
the British and French governments, contrary to Gamelin's objections, believed that such a step would increase the likelihood of war,
it was delayed until 30 August, and only came into full effect on the
31st. It has been calculated that as a result of Polish compliance, a
quarter of the Polish army never reached the front. Hence the Poles
were badly prepared to meet the German onslaught.[79]

By the end of August, Hitler was reasonably assured that even if
the western powers intervened, there would only be a 'qualitatively
limited' war. He told Brauchitsch that, 'if the worst came to the worst',
he would fight a war on two fronts. One development alone might
transform the whole scenario: an Italian public declaration of neutrality. After Mussolini had informed Hitler that Italy could not enter
the war unless it was furnished with vast quantities of arms and raw
materials, news was eagerly awaited in Berlin on what Mussolini's
precise demands would be. On the morning of the 26th the shopping
list was prepared. 'It is enough to kill a bull', noted Ciano, 'if a bull
could read it'.[80] Goering and Brauchitsch insisted that in no circumstances could Germany meet the Italy's exorbitant requirements – at
all costs Mussolini had to be persuaded to continue to play his part as
a friend of Germany. Hitler implored the *Duce* not to let the outside
world know that Italy would not intervene. He requested Mussolini
to provide Germany with additional workers, and by propaganda and
the movement of troops to pin down French forces. For a time Hitler
had cause for satisfaction. Italy had brought its army of the Po up to
full strength on 24 August (See Chapter 11). On 1 September Hitler
informed Brauchitsch that the concentration of Italian troops, es-

pecially on the Egyptian frontier of Libya, would reduce the likelihood of a general conflagration and exercise a restraining influence on Britain and France.[81] However, Italy's defection of 1915 had never been forgotten nor forgiven, and Hitler had cause for anxiety. On 30 August London severed all telecommunications with Rome. Fearing that in the event of war the Allies would do nothing against Germany but instead throw all their forces in an attack on Italy, Ciano, with the *Duce's* approval, committed an 'indiscretion'. He frankly asked Sir Percy Lorraine, the British ambassador, 'Can't you understand that we will never start a war against you and the French?'[82] Italian non-belligerency was declared on 1 September. While Ciano's indiscretion came too late to enable the French, had they so wished, to withdraw their troops from the Alps and north Africa to their north-east frontier, it did enhance Mussolini's image both in London and above all in Paris. Mussolini was now prepared to play the role of honest broker in persuading both sides to accept a compromise at Poland's expense. Indeed, Hitler himself was now fully committed to this idea. For this and other reasons Italy's role as a non-belligerent was welcomed in Berlin.[83]

It has been seen how Hitler intended driving a wedge between Britain and Poland. He distinguished between his 'minimum demands', which included the return of Danzig and a piecemeal solution of the Corridor as well as the return of Polish Silesia, and the 'maximum demands' which depended on the military situation. If the 'minimum demands' were not satisfied there would be war. In these circumstances there was much to-ing and fro-ing between London and Berlin.[84] Chamberlain no less than Hitler was prepared to compromise. On 28 August Henderson returned to Berlin with his instructions from Chamberlain. The British government would honour its obligations to Poland if Germany resorted to war, but it believed that a compromise between Germany and Poland was possible and advocated direct negotiations between the two parties. Chamberlain even went so far as to suggest that an exchange of populations might prove possible. 'If agreement were reached' the way would then be open for 'negotiations of that wider and more complete understanding between Germany and Britain'. Hitler expressed his appreciation of Chamberlain's efforts to bring about a solution, but added a *caveat*: no further settlement in eastern Europe was possible without the participation of the Soviet Union.[85]

On the 29th Hitler, jubilant over Chamberlain's letter, declared to his generals that he would act in accordance with the principles of self-determination. Within six months international troops, including the Soviet Union, could supervise a plebiscite in Poland in accordance with which Germans and Poles, as in the Saar plebiscite in January 1935, would have equal rights. The British, Hitler boasted, would pressure the Poles to send a representative to Berlin to negotiate on this plan. The Polish negotiator would arrive in Berlin on the 30th. The British would accept the terms but not the Poles – hence negotiations would break down on the 31st. The following day, Germany would attack Poland which would then be isolated.[86] Once more Hitler indicated his belief that Britain would not fight.

If Chamberlain and Hitler were prepared to do a deal over Poland, they had to persuade a very different person than Beneš to accept a plan imposed by others on his country. Beck rejected a virtual ultimatum to send a negotiator to Berlin by 30 August, and it was believed in Berlin that the British were encouraging him to stand fast. Henderson told Hitler that it was beyond the power of his government to force the Poles to accept an ultimatum. Had the British given way the Poles would most probably have fought, and Hitler would have had his 'little war' which he was determined to fight with outright savagery. The war would be a 'testing of the tool' for bigger things ahead. It would also enable Germany to overcome its economic problems. At 6.30 pm on the 31st, Hitler released the order that the German army must take up its position for the attack, and the next day at dawn – on 1 September – German troops invaded Poland.[87]

If Hitler's central aim was to kill off the Poles and obliterate their national identity as well as that of the Jews in Poland, why did he tell Brauchitsch on 2 September that Posen, and perhaps the industrial areas of Upper Silesia, must be occupied as soon as possible, unless he wanted peace on the principle of *uti possidetis?* That day contact was in fact made between Horace Wilson and a certain Dr. Fritz Hesse, Ribbentrop's man in London. It emerged from their discussion that whereas Chamberlain might have been prepared to allow Germany slices of Polish territory after German troops were withdrawn, Ribbentrop and Hitler were determined to cling to their conquests and to use them to force a compromise on the British and Poles.[88] One consideration might have influenced Hitler to compromise. The aim of the non-aggression pact with Russia was twofold: to deter the British from intervention, and to exert military pressure on Poland from the east. In both respects the pact had manifestly failed. This again raises the question whether Hitler was pursuing an alternative policy to the one which would have made the Soviet Union a neighbour of Germany.

According to the secret articles of the non-aggression pact of 23 August, as amended on the 25th, the Pissa, Narew, Vistula and San rivers were, in the event of a territorial adjustment, to divide Poland into spheres of influence. Whether the existence of a truncated Polish state should be tolerated would be decided jointly by both parties. The Baltic States were, apart from Lithuania, which was to acquire Vilna from Poland, to belong to the Soviet sphere. Germany also recognised Soviet political interests in Bessarabia and expressed its own 'désintéressement' in this territory, although the ambiguity of the language used on this subject was to give rise to complications in the summer of 1940. The terms of the treaty meant that even if Hitler chose to moderate his demands on Poland in order to create more favourable conditions for a negotiated settlement with the west, he could no longer ignore Soviet wishes. He had conferred on the Soviet Union membership of the 'Concert of Europe'.[89]

The last thing that Stalin can conceivably have wanted was a negotiated peace between Germany and the west. This would not only bring the German frontier nearer the vital strategic areas of the Soviet Union but it might even mean that, if the Soviet Union were next on Hitler's list, it would get no support from the west. But the Soviet leadership, no less than Hitler himself, were surprised by the speed of the German advance, and hence, Germany's need to implement the agreement in case France attacked in the west, became all the more urgent.

On 3 September Ribbentrop instructed Schulenburg to urge the Soviets to move their troops into Poland. Molotov replied on the 5th that the time for action was not ripe.[90] So long as the Red Army remained inactive Hitler was not committed to partition, and he told his military staff on the 7th that if the Poles wished to negotiate, Germany was prepared to do so. He did not believe that the Soviet Union would march. As for Poland, it would be required to sever its ties with Britain and France, in return for which it would be allowed to retain the area behind the Narew – Vistula line (already allocated to the Soviet Union as well as certain areas around Warsaw and Cracow except for the industrial areas which were reserved for Germany, while in the south a western Ukrainian state would be established. But Hitler went on to say that should the Soviet Union stake its claims, or should Germany be attacked by the west, which again caused apprehension after France declared war on the 3rd, then the Narew – Vistula line would be the frontier.[91]

That Hitler was thinking of an alternative to his Ostpolitik stands out again in a conversation he had with Brauchitsch on the 12th, and because the Soviet Union was unlikely to march, Germany should now try to establish an independent Ukraine. A proposal of this kind would find favour with the French. He also raised the question of limiting his demands to Polish Upper Silesia and the Corridor and he even believed that the Poles were prepared to accept an armistice. As soon as German troops had crossed into the intended Soviet zone of Poland, in some cases to a distance of 200 kilometres, it was more than likely that Stalin, who always dreaded a German–Polish alignment, grew anxious, although when the possibility of a German–Polish armistice was raised in Berlin by the Soviet *Chargé d'Affaires*, Ribbentrop denied flatly that this was true.[92] On 17 September, two days after the Soviet Union had concluded an armistice with Japan, which brought to an end the fighting at Nomonhan, the Red Army unexpectedly invaded Poland inflicting heavy casualties. According to General Nicholas von Vormann, liaison officer between Hitler and the general staff, news of the Russian advance stunned the senior generals. This occurred because Hitler and the foreign ministry had failed to inform them either that a demarcation line had been agreed to, or if so, where it was to run. Although the back of Polish resistance was broken, Warsaw had not fallen and a large part of the German army was still involved in heavy fighting in areas allocated to Russia, so that an immediate retreat behind the line agreed to on 23 August was impossible. After much confusion the time limit for the German withdrawal had to be extended.[93]

Stalin for his part feared that the Germans would ignore the demarcation line or that there might be a deal between Germany and the west over Poland. This is evident from a conversation between Molotov and Schulenburg on the 19th. Contrary to the original inclination to permit the existence of a rump Poland, the country should, Molotov stressed, be partitioned. From the Soviet point of view this action, which would result in the territorial destruction of Poland, would have the advantage of ruling out a compromise between Germany and the west. Hitler deferred to Molotov's proposals. If there was to be peace with the west the subject of Poland had in future to be excluded from discussion.[94]

Despite the low morale of the German rank and file during the

Polish campaign, the *Blitzkrieg* had been such a tearing success that Hitler and some of his generals were soon to come round to the view that the same tactics might be employed against the west. On the 27 – 28 September Brauchitsch and Halder were aghast to learn from Hitler that he intended to begin an offensive in the west almost immediately in October 1939, and this explains why Hitler talked so much about withdrawing troops and bringing the bloodshed in the east to an end as soon as possible. Hitler gave two reasons for taking this sudden decision: first, time was on the side of Germany's enemies. Even within six months Britain and France would be better prepared to halt a German attack than now. Second, despite euphoria over the German victory in Poland, the population would soon become sick of the war. Hitler even implied that the treaty with Russia would prove unpopular. In order to render the war more popular he needed a new spectacular success. But because weather late in the year might impede operations by the *Luftwaffe* and because of the logistic problems entailed, Hitler was eventually persuaded to wait until the spring of 1940 before attacking the west.[95]

Hilter's obsession with war in the west, which again came to the forefront after the capture of Warsaw on 27 September, had a direct bearing on why he was prepared to make such far-reaching concessions to Russia in the second treaty of 28 September. Virtually all of Lithuania, previously a vital German interest, was to pass to the Soviet sphere of influence. The two remaining Baltic states, and even Finland, were to be included in the Soviet sphere. Bialystok in northern Poland, which was valued for its timber as well as the oil wells east of the San in the south, together with the town of Lemberg, which had a strong German minority, were to be handed over to the Russians. In return most of the provinces of Warsaw and Lublin in central Poland, where there were many Poles and Jews but fewer ethnic Germans, were allocated to the Reich. The two powers also agreed to quell Polish nationalism. That the Soviet Union should have a free gift of territory conquered for it by the German army and in which Germany had either cultural or economic interests, was regarded as preposterous by the opponents of the regime.[96]

The total partition of Poland not only put paid to the idea of an immediate negotiated settlement with the west, which Hitler proposed on 6 October, but tied Germany to a country whose regime had hitherto been pilloried as the negation of everything for which National Socialist Germany represented. Hitler therefore had to justify it to the party leaders as well as the officer corps. On 27 August he told a group of senior party officials that it was necessary to drive out Beelzebub with Beelzebub – which in *Mein Kampf* he had claimed, was an impossibility. Some of his listeners must have been aware of this contradiction. As Hassell observed, 'He worshipped what he burnt and burnt what he worshipped'. He also claimed that the Soviet Union had ceased to be a Bolshevik state and that it was assuming a military and authoritarian character. Nor did Hitler conceal his personal admiration for Stalin. Here was a man who had no time for Jews and knew how to put truculent generals in their place – never again would they stab *him* in the back.[97] The generals, who had the invidious task of ordering German troops to withdraw from areas already allocated to the Soviets, regarded Hitler's concessions to the Soviets as 'shameful',[98] but Hitler knew how to overcome their scruples about the future of German – Soviet relations. On 27 September he told Brauchitsch and Halder that, as a true disciple of Bismarck, he realised that treaties need no longer be observed after they had served their purpose. Did this not mean that one day he might go to war with Russia?[99] Suppose the Soviets moved into the areas allocated to them at a time when the German armed forces were fully engaged in war with the west, the result would be, as Hitler later observed, that he would have to decide whether the two countries should stand 'side by side' or 'face to face'.[100] The realisation of the terms of the treaty of 28 September would in fact prove its own undoing (See Chapter 11).

There can be little doubt that for the immediate future Stalin seemed to have gained more from the treaty than Hitler. He could now strengthen the Soviet Union's military economy and raise the striking power of the Red Army. The additional territories in the west moreover made it possible for him, had he deemed it necessary, to adopt a strategy of defence in depth. His failure to do so was to cause his country devastating losses after the German attack of 22 June 1941.[101] But Soviet action also had long term repercussions of a serious kind. That the Red Army, in collusion with the Germans, massacred and deported Poles caused outrage in the west. Stalin and Hitler wanted to destroy the Polish nation. Considered in conjunction with the later attack on Finland, the Soviet invasion of Poland might be regarded as a significant stepping stone to the Cold War. It must be admitted, however, that Stalin would not have acted on his own initiative: he had been goaded into action by his brother dictator.

Hitler believed that if the war in the west proved longer than expected, submarines and aircraft would have to be deployed against Britain, but that this would take a year or two to prove effective. There was not the slightest hint of an invasion, but Hitler had already given priority in the Z-Plan of January 1939 to the construction of battleships over submarines and cruisers for a war to be fought against Britain, and perhaps the USA, in 1944. Significantly his obsession with possessing 'the most powerful navy in the world' was also shared by Stalin early in 1938. World power seems to have had an irresistible attraction for these dictators,[102] but because of the need to expand the army for war against Poland, the Z-Plan had to be postponed but not cancelled. Hitler now had to calculate on war with Britain at a much earlier date than in 1944. This meant that his armaments programme had to be brought into line with the changing goals of his foreign policy, not *vice-versa*. Not surprisingly the construction of long range JU 88 bombers, which had sufficient range to attack targets in Britain, was to be doubled after 31 August 1939. There were also plans to construct planes of sufficient range to attack the USA[103] (See Chapter 3).

There is one explanation for Hitler's abrupt fits of friendship and antagonism to Britain, expressed so often during the Polish crisis. According to Weizsäcker and other officials and party chiefs, Hitler acted under the influence of Ribbentrop, and that whenever proposals were made by other persons that he should seek an agreement with Britain, Ribbentrop 'nipped them in the bud'. It must be admitted that in the absence of Ribbentrop in Moscow on 23 and 24 August, Weizsäcker persuaded Hitler to change tactics in his dealings with Britain and Poland. In contrast to Ribbentrop, however, Hitler did not wish to smash the British empire by building up a closely knit coalition of Germany, Italy, Japan and, latterly, the Soviet Union. The British empire stood for the supremacy of the Aryan race. Its demise would lead to the augmentation of the power of other nations who might one day be ranged against Germany.[104] It must be added that Chamberlain and his cabinet regarded Hitler's racial theories as a positive threat to the stability of the empire. The Africans were now becoming politically conscious, and after the pogrom against the Jews on 9–10 November 1938 all discussion on the possible return of colonies to Germany by Britain was ruled out.[105] If Hitler intended to fight the British it was solely in order to prevent them from thwarting his aims on the continent. Hitler had, through his own provocative action involved Germany in the wrong war at the wrong time with the wrong weapons. It was a war it could not win,[106] and Ribbentrop was not responsible for this. The possibility of his having to fight Britain, and the disadvantages which this would entail, partly explains Hitler's hesitation about reaching the accord with Russia which was so strongly advocated by Ribbentrop.

Can it still be contended that it was through a miscalculation on the part of Hitler, as well as provocation arising from the British government's rash policy towards Poland, that war broke out?[107] Whatever might be said about the events leading immediately to the outbreak of hostilities, late in 1938 and early 1939 Hitler repeatedly declared to his generals and party leaders that the next war would be a great 'racial and ideological' confrontation, which would provide Germany first with control of the continent and later world power. Hitler's mind thereafter was set on two things: world domination by the Aryan race, and the annihilation of the Jews. On 30 January 1939 Hitler declared to the *Reichstag* that if world Jewry were to involve the nations in war, this would not lead to Bolshevik domination of the earth and victory for the Jews, but to 'the annihilation of the Jews as a race in Europe'. In the course of the war Hitler and Himmler constantly referred back to this 'prophetic utterance', although they brought forward the date on which it was made to a second speech to the *Reichstag* of 1 September 1939, the day Germany went to war against Poland.[108]

Lastly, can the war which broke out in September 1939 be described as Hitler's war or a German war? Was there a consensus between Hitler, the ruling élites and the population at large about the necessity of war with Poland? (This subject is also discussed in Chapter 3). For emotional reasons certain senior army officers were far less opposed to fighting the Poles than they had been against the Czechs in 1938. In their eyes war with Poland was popular, war with Czechoslovakia merely necessary. Indeed, some of them had been born in what was now Polish territory. But officers of all three branches of the armed forces were opposed to war with Poland if this were to lead to war with the west. Certain senior diplomats, such as Weizsäcker, while vehemently hostile to Poland, were appalled by the territorial concessions made to the Soviet Union. Leaders of the SS such as Himmler, who strove to become minister of the interior on the eve of the war, and Heydrich, actively intrigued to augment their powers.[109] Yet even the leader of the SS might not have been all that keen on an additional task which was imposed on them after the Soviet Union had staked its territorial claims. The SS now had to supervise the extradition and resettlement of Germans from their ancestral homelands in the Baltic States and from Bessarabia. This might explain the estrangement which was to develop between Himmler and Ribbentrop on account of Germany's policy towards the Soviet Union.[110] Rosenberg and other party leaders might have mistrusted Hitler's justification of his treaties with Russia, but they issued muted protests at the most. The population of eastern Germany were probably pleased, as Weizsäcker claimed, to see Posen and West Prussia reincorporated in the Reich,[111] but it cannot be claimed that there was a consensus between the population as a whole and the regime on the question of war. In 1939, as in 1938, there were no associations of landless farmers or of village craftsmen clamouring for *Lebensraum* in the east, as advocated by Himmler and others. Nor did navy leagues spring into existence and start drumming up enthusiasm for Hitler's programme to construct a giant fleet. Anti-semitism admittedly had its roots deep in German society, but this did not mean that the program of 9–10 November 1938, let alone the extermination camps which followed, met with enthusiasm. News of the outbreak of the war itself was received, from all accounts, with none of the jingoistic patriotism that had been so marked in 1914, and even Hitler could not deny that the German infantry lacked the fighting spirit of the men who had fought in the First World War. There was much apathy and even despondency among civilians, who dreaded the prospect of food shortages and whose lives were dislocated by mobilisation.[112] Nonetheless, with the exception of members of the opposition, the citizens of Hitler's Reich had already abdicated political responsibility and were more than ready to participate and rejoice in their *Führer's* triumphs. Later they were to fight with the resolution of despair. Had Hitler not been head of the Nazi state there might have been no war in September 1939. But where else could Hitler have come to power except in the Germany of the 1930s? 'Better than the truth from the lips of the liar is the lie itself'.[113] Dietrich Bonhoeffer's words are highly apposite to the *terrible simplificateur* , who in order to deceive others knows how to make himself plausible.

NOTES AND REFERENCES

1. The author first became interested in Russo – German relations for the period 1939–1941 when he worked on a monograph at the Cabinet Office Historical Section, *Barbarossa: The Origins and Development of*

Hitler's Plan to Attack Russia on 22 June 1941 (EDS Appreciation 5 1952). Work was continued in the original unpublished text of *Hitler's Pre-War Policy and Military Plans* (London, 1955). This is considerably longer than the book with the same title (London, 1963). References to the original documents, used therein, are given below. Most of them can be found in xeroxes in the Imperial War Museum (*IWM*).

2. C. Thorne, *The Approach of War 1938–39* (London, 1967) and W.J. Hofer, *War Premeditated* (London, 1954) remain of interest to the general reader. So too are the articles in W.J. Mommsen and L. Kettenacker (eds). *The Fascist Challenge and the Policy of Appeasement* (London, 1983), and in R. Douglas (ed.), *1939, a Retrospect Forty Years After* (London, 1983). For an excellent survey of the literature on the origins of the war, see A. Adamthwaite, 'War Origins Again', in *Journal of Modern History* (March 1984). Among the earlier accounts of German – Soviet relations in 1939 those of P.W. Fabry, *Der Hitler – Stalin – Pakt 1941* (Darmstadt 1962) and G.L.Weinberg, *Germany and the Soviet Union 1939–1941* (Leyden, 1954 and 1971) have withstood the test of time. Weinberg has developed his ideas in, *The Foreign Policy of Hitler's Germany, vol. II, Starting World War II, 1937–1939* (Chicago, 1980). This detailed and scholarly work is indispensable. For a succinct analysis of historical interpretations of the German – Soviet Pact, see D.C. Watt, 'The Initiation of Negotiations Leading to the Nazi – Soviet Pact: A Historical Problem', in C. Abramsky (ed), *Essays in Honour of E.H. Carr* (Hamden Conn., 1974).

3. C. Andrew, *Secret Service. The Making of the British Security Community* (London 1985) has provided a stimulus to the study of military intelligence. See also F.H. Hinsley *British Intelligence in the Second World War. Its Influence on Strategy and Operations,* vol. I (London 1979)

4. *Documents on German Foreign Policy* (series D) abbr. DGFP (D) VI, nos. 149, 185, and Weinberg, *The Foreign Policy of Hitler's Germany*, vol. II, p. 560. See also M. Messerschmidt, 'Aussenpolitik und Kriegs-vorbereitung', viertel Teil, in W. Deist et al (eds), *Ursachen und Voraussetzungen der deutschen Kriegspolitik* (Stuttgart, 1979), pp. 187–201.

5. E.M. Robertson, 'Hitler's Planning for War and the Response of the Great Powers', in H.W. Koch (ed), *Aspects of the Third Reich* (London, 1985), pp. 196–234.

6. W. Kolarz, *Religion and the Soviet Union* (London, 1962), p. 113.

7. DGFP (D) VI, nos. 99, 185.

8. H.-G. Seraphim (ed), *Das politische Tagebuch Alfred Rosenbergs* (Munich, 1956), pp. 80–81 and 168–176, and H. Groscurth, *Tagebücher eines Abwehr-offiziers*, 1938–1940 (eds.) H. Krausnick and H.C. Deutsch (Stuttgart, 1970), 15 March 1939, p. 171.

9. DGFP (D) VI nos. 160, 227, 234 and 375. *Documents diplomatiques*

français 1932–1939 (2nd series) 1936–1939, vol. XV, no. 147, and Weinberg, *The Foreign Policy of Hitler's Germany*. vol. II, pp. 587–589.

10. H. Booms, 'Der Ursprung des Zweiten Weltkrieges – Revision oder Expansion?', in *Geschichte in Wissenschaft und Unterricht*, vol. 16, no. 6 (June 1965), pp. 329–353.

11. DGFP (D), VI, nos. 149 and 185.

12. J. Haslam, *The Soviet Union and Struggle for Collective Security in Europe 1933–1939* (London, 1984), pp. 207, 209, 219, and J. Herman, 'Soviet Peace Efforts on the Eve of World War II: A Review of Soviet Documents', *Journal of Contemporary History*, vol. 15, no. 3.

13. S. Aster, *1939, The Making of the Second World War* (London 1973), p. 128 *et seq.*, and A. Adamthwaite, *France and the Coming of the Second World War* (London, 1977), pp. 308, 316.

14. C.A. MacDonald, *The United States, Britain and Appeasement* (London 1981), ch. 10, and his, 'Britain, France and the April Crisis of 1939', in *European Studies Review*, no. 2 (London 1972).

15. Weinberg, *The Foreign Policy of Hitler's Germany*, vol. II, pp. 533–534.

16. DGFP (D) VII, 22 Aug. 1939, no. 192.

17. A. Prazmowska, 'The Eastern Front and the British Guarantee of Poland of March 1939', *European Historical Quarterly*, vol. 14, no. 2 (April 1984).

18. B.A. Lee, *Britain and the Sino – Japanese War, 1939–1939: A Study in the Dilemmas of British Decline* (California 1973), ch. 7.

19. Aster, *1939*, p. 89.

20. Haslam *The Soviet Union and the Struggle for Collective Security*, pp. 215–216, and A.B. Ulam, *Expansion and Coexistence: Soviet Foreign Policy 1917–73*, second edition (New York, 1974), p. 267 *et seq.*

21. DGFP (D) VI nos. 325 and 332, also Weinberg, pp. 568–570, and Haslam, p. 212.

22. Hitler's talk to his generals of 23 May 1939, DGFP (D) vol. VI, no. 433.

23. The military confrontation between the Soviet Union and Japan at Nomonhan on the border between Outer Mongolia and Manchuria is described in A. Sella, 'Khalk in-Gol: The Forgotten War', *Journal of Contemporary History*, vol. 18, no. 4 (October 1983); J. Erickson, *The Soviet High Command* (London, 1962), p. 532 *et seq.*, and J. Haslam, 'Soviet Aid to China and Japan's Place in Moscow's Foreign Policy 1937–1939', *Millennium Journal of International Studies*, vol. 11 (1982), pp. 35–58.

24. He expressed this view in a conference with his military commanders of 23 May 1939 (see note 22). A.J.P. Taylor, without giving a reference, calls into question the authenticity of this document. He maintains that of the nine people said to be present eight were not, see Taylor, 'The British View', in Douglas, *1939, a Retrospect*, p. 46. In fact 15 senior officers were present, M. Domarus (ed.), *Hitler Reden und Proklamationen 1932–1945* (Neustadt 1962), vol. II, pp. 1194–1199. R.

Schmundt, Hitler's adjutant, perhaps some months later, took notes on what Hitler said. He has not left a verbatim account. See also H.W. Koch, 'Hitler and the Origins of the Second World War: Second Thoughts on the Status of Some of the Documents', in *The Historical Journal* vol. XI, no. 1 (1968).

25. DGFP (D), vol VI, no. 185.

26. Hitler's talk with his generals of 23 May (Note 22) and J. Dülffer, 'Der Beginn des Krieges 1933–1939', in K.D. Bracher et al (eds.) *Nationalsozialistischer Diktatur. Eine Bilanz* (Düsseldorf, 1980).

27. On 9 May Thomsen, German *Chargé d'Affaires* in Washington, maintained that because of setbacks to his policy in Europe Roosevelt had reverted to isolationism, DGFP (D) VI, no. 348. See also MacDonald, *The United States, Britain and Appeasement*, ch. 10 and 11.

28. DGFP (D) VI, no. 185, p. 124 note 2, and Groscurth *Tagebüches*, p. 173 and his entry for 3 Aug. 1939, p. 179, and Domarus, *Hitler Reden Und Proklomationen* vol. II, pp. 1189–1191.

29. For a concise account of German plans for the invasion of Poland, see H. Rohde, 'Hitlers erster Blitzkrieg und seine Auswirkung auf Nordosteuropa', in A. Maier et al (eds.), *Die Errichtung der Hegemonie auf dem Europäischen Kontinent* (Stuttgart, 1979), p. 92 *et seq.* Also H. Roos, 'Die militärpolitische Lage und Planung Polens gegenüber Deutschland vor 1939. Die Operation des Heeres', in *Wehrwissenschaftliche Rundschau* vol. 7 no. 1 (1957), pp. 193–202 and N. von Vormann, *Der Feldzug 1939 in Polen* (Weissenburg, 1958), *passim.*

30. IWM, EDS, Box 113. AL 1449, Arbeitsstab Rundstedt, 20 May 1939, la, nr 1/39.

31. *Ibid.*

32. *Ibid.*

33. *IWM*, EDS, Box 113. AL 1448, 'Absicht des ObdH und Aufträge', nr 1750, 4200/39, 15 June 1939. See also W. Murray, *The Change in the European Balance of Power: The Path to Ruin* (Princeton, 1984), pp. 131–134.

34. See Robertson, 'Hitler's Planning for War', p. 203.

35. DGFP (D) VI, no. 367, of 11 May 1939 and 387 of the 15th. See also Weinberg, *The Foreign Policy of Hitler's Germany*, vol II, p. 562 and pp. 583–584.

36. Aster, *1939*, ch. 9, and L.B.Namier, *Diplomatic Prelude 1938–1939* (London, 1948), pp. 224–225 and pp. 236–237. Namier's work still contains many insights of value for historians working on the subject today. See also DGFP (D) VI, no. 645, 10 July, 1939.

37. The author is on the whole in agreement with J. Henke, *England in Hitlers politischen Kalkül 1935–1939* (Boppard, 1973), pp. 242–245 and pp. 255–258, that until late in May Hitler's enmity was turned mainly towards Britain rather than Poland.

38. DGFP (D) VI, no. 716 of 24 July. See also Aster, *1939*, pp. 245–249.
39. Generaloberst Franz Halder, *Kriegstagebuch*, (ed.) H.-A. Jacobsen (Stuttgart, 1962), vol. I, 14 Aug. 1939, p. 7.
40. Weinberg, *The Foreign Policy of Hitler's Germany*, vol. II, p. 605.
41. DGFP (D), VI, nos. 758 and 760.
42. L. Hill (ed.), *Die WeizsäckerPapiere, 1933–1950* (Frankfurt, 1974), 30 July, p. 157.
43. Hitler's lengthy arguments on why he supposed that Britain would not go to war are given in addresses to his staff of 14 and 22 Aug. 1939; Halder, *Kriegstagebuch*, pp. 8–15 and pp. 23–26; DGFP (D), VII, no. 192; Groscurth, *Tagebüches*, pp. 180–181 and Dülffer, 'Der Beginn'.
44. M. Knox, *Mussolini Unleashed 1939–1941. Politics and Strategy in Italy's Last War* (Cambridge, 1982), pp. 39–43, and R. Quatararo, *Roma tra Londra e Berlino: La politica estera fascista dal 1930 al 1940* (Rome, 1980), p. 465, *et seq.*
45. DGFP (D), VII, nos. 43 and 47 and G. Ciano, *Diplomatic Papers, 12 June 1936 – 30 April 1942*, (ed.) M. Muggeridge (London, 1947), pp. 298–304 and Ciano, *Diario* (Italy, 1947), pp 148–149.
46. N. Henderson, *Failure of a Mission, Berlin 1937–1939* (London, 1940), p. 250.
47. *IWM*, EDS, Box 113 GMDS, OKW/11, 62, nr. 1750/39, "Die militärische Lage in Polen am 12/8/39".
48. *IWM*, EDS, Box 113, PID doc no. 5, OKW, WFA 92/39 Zeittafel für Fall Weiss.
49. Nuremberg Documents: International Military Tribunal, no. 3787 – PS a report of a meeting of the National Defence Council of 23 June 1939 (Nuremberg, 1949), and Groscurth, *Tagebüches*, 20 June 1939, p. 177.
50. Jodl, *Diary* (fragments) January 1937 – August 1939, reproduced in, *Nuremberg Documents: International Military Tribunal* 1780 – PS (Nuremberg, 1948), and E.M. Robertson, *Hitler's Pre-War Policy*, pp. 178–179.
51. See above note 47 and Halder, *Kriegstagebuch*, 15 Aug. 1939 pp. 17 and 29. H. Roos 'Die militärpolitische age', p. 200, claims that German mobilisation was in advance of Polish mobilisation.
52. Halder, *Kriegstagebuch*, 14 Aug. 1939, pp. 8–15. See also U. von Hassell, *Vom Andern Deutschland* (Frankfurt, 1964), 15 Aug. 1939, p. 66. For Chamberlain's secret negotiations with B. Dahlerus, which Hitler was probably referring to on 14 Aug. 1939, see Aster, *1939*, pp. 240–241 and Haslam, p. 227.
53. DGFP (D), VII nos. 56, 61, 62, 70. See also, R. Manne, 'Some British Light on the Nazi – Soviet Pact', *European Studies Review*, vol. XII, no. 1 (1981), p. 94–95, Ulam, pp. 274 *et seq.*, and Herman, 'Soviet Peace Efforts'
54. See note 23 above and DGFP (D), VI no. 766 and VII nos. 61 and 79.

By 16 August the Germans were no longer accused of encouraging aggression by Japan but were requested to influence the Japanese government in Russia's favour, *ibid.*, no. 88.

55. See note 23 above and Hill (ed.), *Weizsäcker Papiere*, 20 Aug. 1939, p. 159 and DGFP (D), VII, no 186, which refers to Germany and Japan.

56. *IWM*, EDS, GMDS, OKW/469, 1/32/31, geh, Ausl/111a/b 'Zusammenstellung Wichtiger Militärischer Nachrichten', reports of 18, 19 and 21 August 1939.

57. DGFP (D) VII, nos. 111, 113, 132, 133, 140, 142, 143, 149, 157, 158 and 159.

58. DGFP (D) VII, no. 446, 30 Aug. and no. 285 of 25 Aug. 1939. Also nos. 347, 360, 381, 383, 387, 388, 413, 453.

59. Weizsäcker to Schulenberg, 27 Aug. 1939, *ibid.*, 360. See also nos. 381, 383, 387, 388, 413, 414, 425, all of which deal with alleged withdrawal of Soviet troops and the need for a new ambassador and a military mission to Germany.

60. IWM, EDS, GMDS, OKW, 469, nr 98, Aust/lll Lagebericht 31/8/39; Halder, *Kriegstagebuch*, 31 Aug. 1939, p. 49; and DGFP (D) VII no. 456 of 30 Aug. 1939, 480. For Soviet relations with Turkey, see DGFP (D) VII nos. 516 and 551.

61. Halder, *Kriegstagebuch*, 14 Aug. 1939, pp. 10–11 and p. 14; and Hitler's speech to his generals of 22 Aug. 1939 DGFP (D) nos. 192 and 193. See also Liebmann, Notes, *Vierteljahrshefte für Zeitgeschichte*, vol. 16, no. 2 (April 1968). For an account of Hitler's fluctuating policy towards Britain, see D. Aigner, *Das Ringen um England* (Munich, 1969), p. 359 *et seq.*

62. A.J.P. Taylor, *English History 1914–1945* (Oxford, 1965), p. 450.

63. DGFP (D) VII, nos. 200 and 201; *Documents on British Foreign Policy* (DBFP) (3), VII, nos. 149, 178 and 200. Also *Weizsäcker Papiere*, 23 Aug. 1939. p. 159 and Halder, *Kriegstagebuch*, 22 Aug. 1939, p. 25.

64. Jodl, *Diary*, 24 Aug. 1939, and *Weizsäcker Papiere*, 24 Aug. 1939 p. 160.

65. *Weizsäcker Papiere*, 23 Aug. 1939, pp. 159–160, and Hassell, *Von Andern Deutschland*, p. 67.

66. DGFP VII, nos. 192, 193, Halder, *Kriegstagebuch*, pp. 23–26; Groscurth, *Tagebüches*, p. 180. See also W. Baumgart, 'Zur Ansprache Hitlers vor den Führern der Wehrmacht am 22 August 1939', *Vierteljahrshefte für Zeitgeschichte*, vol. 16 (1968), pp. 16–48. For H.W. Koch's criticism of the evidence for this speech, see above, note 24. Also Ciano, *Diario*, 26 August 1939, pp. 149–150 and pp. 290–292.

67. DGFP (D) VII, nos 265 and 296, and DBFP (3) vol. VII, 284, 288 and 310, and no. 412, 28 Aug. 1939.

68. Halder, *Kriegstagebuch*, p. 34; DGFP (D) VII, no. 271; Vormann, *Der Feldzug 1939 in Polen*, p. 44. For a detailed account of the times decisions were taken, see H. Greiner, *Die Oberste Wehrmachtführung*

1939–1943 (Weisbaden, 1951), p. 44 *et seq;* for signs of strain on the part of Hitler, see Halder, *Kriegstagebuch*, 26 and 28 Aug. 1939, p. 34 and p. 38.

69. DGFP (D) VII, nos. 212, 246, 262, 329, 403, and Halder, *Kriegstagebuch*, p. 63. See also MacDonald, ch. 9 of this volume.
70. DBFP (3) VII, no. 397.
71. On captured Czech equipment, see Murray, *The Change in the European Balance of Power*, pp. 290–292, and W. Deist, *The Wehrmacht and German Rearmament* (London, 1981), pp. 88–89. For General Beck's view that war would result in the complete destruction of Germany, see H. Krausnick, 'Ludwig Beck', in R. Lill and H. Oberreuter (eds.), *20 Juli – Portraits des Widerstands* (Düsseldorf – Vienna 1984), pp. 73–86.
72. See note 22 above. On Hitler's readiness to take risks, see H.-A. Jacobsen, *1939–1945. Der Zweite Weltkrieg in Chronik und Dokumenten* (Darmstadt, 1961), nos. 1, 3, 6, 7, and 16, and Robertson, *Hitler's Pre-War Policy*, p. 134.
73. Halder, *Kriegstagebuch*, 14 Aug. 1939, p. 8.
74. Halder, *Kriegstagebuch*, pp. 8–15 and p. 26; and DGFP (D) VII, nos. 192, 193 and Groscurth, *Tagebüches*, pp. 182 and 186. For French military intentions, see B. Bond, *France and Belgium, 1939–1940* (London, 1974).
75. Robertson, 'Hitler's Planning for War', in Koch, *Aspects*, p. 299, and Halder, *Kriegstagebuch* 14 Aug. 1939, pp. 7, 8, 9 and 12.
76. DGFP (D) VII, nos. 257, 272, 279, 315, 404. For Hitler's views on Belgium, *ibid.*, no. 192.
77. IWM, EDS, GMDS, H2/608 Lageberichte West nr 13, 28/8/39 and nr 15. See also *Documents on International Affairs, 1939–1946* (London, 1951), vol. I, pp. 515–517, and DBFP (3) VII, nos. 393, 423 and Halder, *Kriegstagebuch* 29 Aug. 1939, p. 41 and 7 Sept. 1939, p. 65, esp.note 14.
78. *IWM*, EDS, GMDS, H2/608, Lageberichte West, nr 9 and 10, 27 and 29 Aug. 1939, and Halder, *Kriegstagebuch*, pp. 29, 30, 46, 48, 50, 52, 65.
79. DBFP (3), VII, nos. 517 and 553 and Roos, (note 29), pp. 200–202; see also Adamthwaite, *France and the Coming of the Second World War*, pp. 347–348, in which he quotes N. Bethell *The War Hitler Won* (London, 1972), p. 45.
80. See Hitler's conversation with Brauchitsch, Halder, *Kriegstagebuch*, 28 Aug. 1939, p. 40. For Italy's need for supplies, see DGFP (D) VII, no. 301 and Ciano, *Diario*, 26 August 1939, pp. 149–150.
81. DGFP (D) VII, nos. 307, 308 and 320 and E.von Rintelen, *Mussolini als Bundesgenosse. Erinnerungen des deutschen Militärattaché in Rom 1936–1943* (Tübingen, 1951), pp. 68–74. See also Jodl's *Diary*, 25 August 1939 and *IWM*, EDS, Box 113 GMDS H2/608, 'Anlage zum Lagebericht West', no. 9, 27/8/39. See also Halder, *Kriegstagebuch*, 31 Aug. 1939, p. 48 and 1 Sept. 1939, p. 50 and DGFP (D) vol VII nos, 349, 423.

82. Ciano, *Diario*, 31 August 1939, pp. 154–156.
83. DGFP (D) VII, nos. 535 and 565.
84 Halder, *Kriegstagebuch*, 26 Aug. 1939, p. 34. Hitler evidently discussed his plan for driving a wedge between Poland and Britain at a meeting with senior party members on 27 Aug. *Ibid*, p. 38. For an account of Dahlerus' mission to London on behalf of Göering, see Aster, *1939*, pp. 339–344.
85. DGFP (D) VII, nos. 384, 440 and DBFP (3) VII nos. 490, 493, 502 and 508.
86. Halder, *Kriegstagebuch*, 28 Aug. 1939 p. 40 and 29 Aug. p. 42 and p. 43.
87. DGFP (D) VII nos. 461, 466, 470, and DBFP (D) VII, nos. 570, 571, 574, 575, 579, 597. See also Halder, *Kriegstagebuch*, 12 Aug. 1939, pp. 25–26 and Groscurth, *Tagebücher*, 24 Aug. 1939, p. 180.
88. Halder's *Diary*, 2 Sept. 1939, p. 56; DGFP (D) VII, no. 558, also Ciano, *Diario*, 3 Sept. 1939, pp. 157–158.
89. DGFP (D) VII, nos. 228, 229 and 284 of 25 Aug. 1939, and Halder, *Kriegstagebuch*, p. 65. For the difficulties which the problem of Bessarabia was to cause, see H.W.Koch, 'Hitler's Programme and the Genesis of Barbarossa', in *Aspects*, pp. 293–295.
90. DGFP (D) VII no 567, VIII nos. 3 and 5, Halder, *Kriegstagebuch*, p. 65. For Germany's vulnerability to resist an attack by France even after the attack on Poland, see Vormann, *Der Feldzug 1939 in Polen*, pp. 71–72.
91. Halder, *Kriegstagebuch*, p. 65.
92. DGFP (D) VIII, nos. 44, 59 and 63.
93. Vormann, *Der Feldzug 1939 in Polen*, p. 153 *et seq*. According to Rohde, 'Hitler's erster Blitzkrieg', p. 133, the Poles suffered 70,000 casualties fighting the Germans; 50,000 against the Russians; 700,000 prisoners of war were taken by the Germans, 300,000 by the Russians, 200,000 escaped. These figures cannot be taken at their face value without corroborative evidence.
94. DGFP (D) VIII, no 104. See also Ulam, *Expansion and Coexistence*, p. 280 *et seq*. For a short account of military operations in Poland, see J.R. M. Butler, *Grand Strategy*, vol. II (London, 1957), pp. 57–59.
95. Halder, *Kriegstagebuch*, 27 Sept. 1939, p. 86, *et seq*. also 28 Sept. 1939, p. 91.
96. DGFP (D) VIII Nos 131, 152, 157, 158, 159 and 160.
97. Hassell, *Von Andern Deutschland*, 11 Oct. 1939, pp. 76–86 and 19 Oct. 1939, p. 80 *et seq*. *Mein Kampf*, Murphy edition (london, 1939), p. 539. See also DGFP (D) VII, 22 Aug. 1939, nos. 180 and 192. See also Groscurth, *Tagebüches* 29 Aug. 1939, p. 190.
98. Halder, *Kriegstagebuch* 20 Sept. 1939, p. 80.
99. *Ibid.*, p. 86. See also C.J. Burckhardt, *Meine Danziger Mission* (Mu-

nich, 1960), p. 348, in which Hitler discussed an eventual war with Russia.
100. Halder, *Kriegstagebuch*, vol. II, 16 Nov. 1940, p. 189.
101. V. Sorovov, 'Who was planning to attack whom in 1941, Hitler or Stalin?', *Royal United Services Institute for Defence*, vol. 130, no. 2 (June 1985). Sorovov's conclusions are not likely to gain general acceptance.
102. For the Z-Plan see note 26. For Stalin's attitude to the navy, see Erickson, *The Soviet High Command*, pp. 475–477.
103. E.L.Homze, *Arming the Luftwaffe: The Reich Air Ministry and the German Aircraft Industry* (Nebraska, 1976), and G.L. Weinberg, 'Hitler and England 1933–1945: Pretence and Reality', *German Studies Review*, vol. VII, no. 2 (May 1985), pp. 299–309.
104. *Weizsäcker Papiere*, 28 Aug. 1939, p. 158 and 160 and *ibid.*, note 83. See also Hassell, 30 Aug. 1939, pp. 72–73 and Henke, *England in Hitlers politische Kalkul*, pp. 294–296. For differences in foreign policy between Hitler and Ribbentrop, see W. Michalka, 'From the Anti-Comintern Pact to the Euro-Asiatic Bloc: Ribbentrop's Alternative Concept to Hitler's Foreign Policy Programme', in Koch, *Aspects*, pp. 267–284.
105. See *The Diplomatic Papers of Oliver Harvey 1937–1940* (ed.), O. Harvey (London, 1970), pp. 217–220.
106 Aigner in *Aspects*, pp. 251–266, and Robertson, *Hitler's Pre-War Policy*, p. 194.
107. A.J.P. Taylor, in '1939 Revisited', The, Annual Lecture of the German Historical Institute in London, has re-asserted the view that Hitler was provoked into war to an even greater extent than in his earlier works.
108. M. Domarus, *Hitler Reden und Proklamationen*, vol. 11, p. 1058. H.W. Koch in *Aspects*, p. 459, claims that the paragraph following Hitler's threat 'produces an entirely different connotation'. No unbiased reader can see how the next two paragraphs in any way mollify the severity of Hitler's threat. The whole speech is permeated with hatred and malice against the Jews and their religion.
109. *Weizsäcker Papiere*, 30 July 1939, p. 157. For the role of the SS see R. Runsheimer, 'Die Grenzzwischenfälle am Abend vor dem deutschen Angriff auf Polen', in *Sommer 1939: Die Grossmachte und der Europaische Krieg*, (eds.) J. Benz and H. Graml (Stuttgart, 1979).
110. See B. Wegner, 'The Aristocracy of National Socialism: The Role of the SS in National Socialist Germany', in *Aspects*, pp. 439–440. For Rosenberg's attitude to the Russo – German Pact, see Seraphim (ed.), *Das Politische Tagebuch Alfred Rosenbergs*, p. 93. Dissatisfaction on the part of the SS is also described in C.A. MacDonald, 'The Venlo Affair', *European Studies Review* vol. 8 (1978), pp. 443–464.
111. *Weizsäcker Papiere*, 30 July 1939, p. 157.

112. Count Wolf Helldorf, President of the Berlin police, believed that because of food shortages and the general inconvenience caused by mobilisation, there might be rioting in the city as soon as the blackout was imposed. He asked the army to put troops at his disposal. Halder rejected the request. Helldorf might have been planning a *coup* against the SS and even Hitler, see Groscurth *Tagebüches*, 25 Aug. 1939, p. 183, 379, 26 Aug. 1939, p. 186, 2 Sept. 1939, p. 197 and Halder, *Kriegstagebuch*, p. 33.
113. Dietrich Bonhoeffer, *Ethik* (Munich, 1953), p. 11.

11. Hitler Turns from the West to Russia May-December 1940

ESMONDE M. ROBERTSON

For Hitler, all treaties remained valid only for so long as expediency required. On 28 September 1939 he concluded a treaty with the Soviet Union settling the new German – Soviet frontier amidst the ruins of Poland, but as early as 23 November 1939 he was indicating to his military staffs that he would secure his objectives in the west, then turn on the Soviet Union before it too constituted a military threat. For the present he regarded the Soviet Union as weak because of the recent purges of senior Red Army officers,[1] and later still he said that the Russian problem could even be disposed of by his successors.[2] However, within a year he had altered his views once more and decided to embark upon a full scale attack on the Soviet Union in 1941.

The decision was an error of historic proportions. Germany again became involved in a two front war which stretched its resources to the limit. As will be seen, the explanation lies partly with Hitler's low opinion of Soviet military strength, and partly with his increased confidence in his own invincibility. Largely, however, it marked an extension of, rather than break with, earlier plans, which were dominated to a remarkable extent by his interest in Britain and an eventual showdown with the United States.

Shortly before the armistice with France took effect on 25 June 1940, Hitler decided that the German infantry should be reduced by one sixth of its present strength. This would provide Germany with additional skilled workers for the armaments industry, so that the air force, navy and armoured formations for the army could be expanded. At that time Hitler and the foreign ministry believed that the policy of Lord Halifax, the foreign secretary, allegedly in favour of peace with Germany, might prevail against Churchill's clarion calls to fight on. Britain, so Hitler thought, would rather have peace with Germany than surrender its naval supremacy to the United States.[3] On paper the terms Hitler planned to offer Britain seemed not unreasonable. Britain would be required to recognise German lordship over the continent, and in return could retain its empire except for those areas which had formerly belonged to Germany. But even before Halifax himself rejected Hitler's terms on 22 July 1940 Hitler had come to believe that Britain might after all continue the war. He and his generals, as will be seen, formed the opinion by late June that a further military action against Britain would be necessary. General Alfred Jodl of the armed forces high command (OKW) proposed on the 30 June that not only should attacks on British communications and ports be intensified, but that preparations should be made for an invasion. On 16 July Hitler issued OKW the directive for 'Operation Sea Lion' – for the invasion of Britain. That same day Jodl also called for attacks on the British empire.[4] By now Goering's *Luftwaffe* was intensifying its daytime bombing raids, and in August the Battle of Britain got under way in earnest.

Although originally pessimistic about the outcome of an invasion, German army leaders were more hopeful by the middle of July, certainly more so more than the naval high command on whom the main responsibility for the success of the operation lay. Admiral Raeder went so far as to inform the army high command (OKH) that every unit of the German army used in the operation might be lost.[5] Germany, he insisted, did not enjoy sufficient supremacy in the air to ward off attacks from the British navy and the RAF. The German war economy, according to Raeder, would also suffer if virtually all ocean-going ships, trawlers and barges were requisitioned.[6] The naval high command as well as Jodl and Ribbentrop therefore advocated a war against the periphery of British empire, which would call for the co-operation of Italy, Japan, the Soviet Union and Spain in a great continental *bloc*. The navy also laid great stress on the capture of Gibraltar.

Hitler fully recognised the force of Raeder's arguments on the technical difficulties in carrying out 'Operation Sea Lion' – it would be no river crossing – but rather than abandon it he chose to give it absolute priority over all others.[7] One consideration might have influenced Hitler to favour it. The break up of the British empire was not in Germany's interest and ran contrary to his belief in world domination by the Aryan race (See Chapter 6). Better than allowing other nations, such as Russia, Japan, and the USA, to pluck at the limbs of the empire and thus acquire territory for themselves, Germany, he seems to have believed, should swiftly occupy London so that the empire could be controlled but allowed to retain its unity. As Ronald Wheatley contends, Hitler was serious in his intention to carry out 'Sea Lion', provided that Britain was first pulverised by air attacks.[8] Towards the end of July it became progressively more evident that the earliest date by which 'Sea Lion' could be launched would have to be after 15 September. Later in the autumn, weather conditions would hinder operations by the German army. Still worse would be a postponement to May 1941, which Raeder by the end of July considered a distinct possibility. Hitler was fully aware that the longer he had to wait the greater would be the resistance by the British army, and he sought some other means for bringing Britain to its knees.[9]

II

There was one course of action other than 'Sea Lion' or attacks on the strategic points of the British empire which was open to Hitler. Britain, he told his generals on 13 July – and they concurred with him – was continuing the war because it was pinning its hopes on eventual intervention by the Soviet Union.[10] The army high command for its part was also becoming increasingly apprehensive of that country.[11] At the time of the attack in the west on 10 May not more than ten divisions were retained in the east. By the end of June the outlook had become distinctly unnerving. The Baltic States, 70 per cent of whose exports went to Germany and which were marked out for German expansion, were now occupied by approximately 20 divisions of the Red Army. By the end of July they were incorporated into the Soviet Union. A further 20 divisions were deployed in the

Russian annexed areas in Poland. Worse still, at the end of June Russian troops had not only occupied Bessarabia, which had been allocated to the Soviet Union, albeit in ambiguous language under the treaty of 23 August 1939, but also northern Bukovina which had previously formed part of the Hungarian half of the Habsburg Empire; in both areas there were German minorities. With the town of Czernowicz in Soviet hands certain imports from Rumania could be cut.[12] As a result of Soviet troop concentrations, General Jodl noted, 'the position in the East is becoming threatening'.[13] Countermeasures were necessary. These, according to General Halder, chief of the army general staff, should take the form of a build-up of German troops in the east to 24 divisions facing 100 Russian divisions. According to Halder, the aim should be to deliver a 'military shock (*Schlag*)' to the Russians, and by the word *Schlag* Halder meant a demonstration of German strength, not a warlike enterprise.[14]

H.W. Koch and B.A. Leach contend that there is evidence that without instructions from Hitler, late in June and early in July 1940 the army high command started to plan for a Russian campaign and that Hitler only later gave it his attention. According to Koch, 'it was not Hitler's eyes that were turned eastwards, but those of Halder.'[15] This contention can only be accepted with qualifications. On 30 June Ernst von Weizsäcker, state secretary of the foreign ministry, informed Halder of Hitler's views. The success of the French campaign could only be secured by force which Weizsäcker believed would prove too burdensome. German eyes, according to Weizsäcker's account of what Hitler said, 'were firmly directed towards the east'. As far as could be foreseen, Britain would probably need 'a further demonstration of our military power before she gives in'. This would 'secure our rear for the East'.[16] The implication is that Hitler was alive to the Soviet problem and that he and the general staff were thinking simultaneously of possible future military action against the Soviet Union. Hitler, however, expressed satisfaction that Soviet action against Rumania was restricted in its scope, by which he probably meant that it did not lead to war in the Balkans.[17] Hitler also had to pay attention to the United States. But in July he and his generals took comfort in the isolationist trend which was still evident in that country.[18] For their part the generals had reasons for favouring preparations for an emergency in the east. Despite the promotions and decorations lavishly bestowed on them they were none too keen on the idea that the army should be reduced in size. Besides, they had always hated the treaty with the Soviet Union of 28 September 1939 (see Chapter 10). After the defeat of France, boredom was evident amongst those generals even of the most exalted rank. They no longer regarded Hitler as a jumped-up corporal who would involve Germany in a disastrous war: he was now a sort of Lord of Hosts *Feldherr*, whom they could count on to safeguard their country's destiny.[19]. But the situation was becoming acute on account of the deterioration of German – Russian relations. Instead of Germany threatening British positions in the area of the Persian Gulf, which seemed possible earlier in the year, it now seemed that Britain and the Soviet Union might carve Iran up into spheres of influence in the same way as they had done in 1907. Out of this an alliance might emerge between 'the whale and the bear'.[20]

The greatest danger, however, lay in the Balkans. The Soviets might continue their thrust from Bessarabia to the rest of the Danubian estuary, and were also encouraging Hungary and Bulgaria to stake their claims against Rumania. Threatened on all sides, Rumania might destroy the Ploesti oil fields, on which the German war economy was largely dependent: nor were the Germans only dependent on oil from the Balkans. Chrome, manganese, copper, lead, nickel, tin and aluminium were also imported from the area. Some of these raw materials were either obtained from Yugoslavia or reached the Reich by rail or roads through that country.[21] Yugoslavia presented a serious problem.

From May to late July 1940 Mussolini was itching to invade either Greece or Yugoslavia, his aim in the latter being to convert Croatia into a satellite of Italy. For their assault on Yugoslavia Italian troops would, however, have to operate from Carinthia and Styria in Austria and this necessitated German permission. Having at first held out false hopes, Hitler resolutely vetoed Mussolini's plan. It would precipitate a free-for-all in the Balkans where the Germans for economic reasons favoured peace.[22] The Yugoslavs did not want to be too dependent on their covetous neighbour on their northern frontier, and having lost France as their ally, they turned to the Soviet Union, a country with which, mainly for ideological reasons, they had always been on bad terms. (The Yugoslavs contacted Moscow through the intermediary of Turkish diplomats whose government was now prepared to revise the Montreux convention of 1936 governing the passage of ships through the Straits in Russia's favour.) Diplomatic relations were established between Belgrade and Moscow on 24 June.[23]

Later in July Mussolini struck upon a 'brilliant' stratagem for winning Germany's tacit consent for an Italian invasion of Yugoslavia. He sent to Berlin extracts of intercepted conversations between the recently appointed Yugoslav ambassador Gavrilovic and Soviet leaders as well as with other diplomats.[24] As this intelligence revealed, Gavrilovic was given a warm welcome by President Kalinin when he presented his credentials on 17th July. Having cast aspersions on Germany's sharp practices in her commercial relations with Yugoslavia, Kalinin went on to say: 'In this way the Germans would not secure peace . . . No, you must struggle against it; you must be vigilant – you must stand together'.[25] Halder was persuaded that Russia's real attitude was to be discerned in its relations with Yugoslavia, which had to be persuaded to resist the Germans, rather than with Britain whose newly appointed ambassador, Sir Stafford Cripps, was given a much colder reception in Moscow than Gavrilovic.[26] Molotov was even more outspoken in his censure of German policy. Having referred to the German occupation of the Ukraine in the First World War, he gleefully declared: 'But our army was once in Berlin'. Gavrilovic also met Sir Stafford Cripps, who allegedly told a member of the diplomatic *corps* in Moscow that Russia would enter the war on Britain's side within a year and that Britain was making immense headway in reforming its army. Cripps prophetically added that while Hitler would prefer to attack the Soviet Union in the autumn of 1940, he would have to wait until the spring of 1941, by which time Russia would be vastly stronger.[27] Gavrilovic was also in contact with the Turkish ambassador, Heydar Aklay, who was not only outspoken against Germany but described in deferential terms recent reforms in the Red Army.[28] Even if Gavrilovic, and more specially Cripps, did not subsequently achieve noteworthy success in influencing the Soviet Union to adopt a more forward policy against Germany the intercepted conversations were interpreted in Berlin as evidence of a Russo–Yugoslav–Turkish conspiracy against Germany to the advantage of Britain. Gavrilovic also learned that the Soviet Union was willing to give some backing to Bulgaria, and this again was to aggravate Russo – German relations. While they did not convert Hitler to the idea that Italy should have a free hand against Yugoslavia, he quoted the conversations as evidence of Russian bad faith.

III

At a conference with Field Marshal von Brauchitsch, commander in chief of the German army, on 21 July, Hitler still believed that 'England's situation is hopeless', for he went on to say, 'England sees the following possibilities: to cause unrest in the Balkans through Russia in order to deprive us of our fuel resources and to paralyse our air force'. He therefore stressed the idea of a peripheral war in conjunction with Spain and Italy and paradoxically with Russia herself.[28] Russia was at this stage regarded both as a potential ally and as a potential enemy. Hitler continued, 'Stalin is coquetting with Britain to keep her in the struggle. . . .*He has an interest in not letting Germany become too powerful*, but there are no indications of any Russian activity against us'.[29] He next described his plans for an invasion of Russia. The assembly of German troops could take four to six weeks. This meant that the operation could still take place in the autumn of 1940. Sufficient territory had to be occupied to secure Berlin and the industrial areas of Silesia as well as the Rumanian oil fields from air attacks. The political aim was to establish an independent Ukrainian state, a confederation of Baltic states and an augmented Finland.[30]

Significantly Hitler did not mention the necessity of a seizure of the oil fields of the Caucasus or of the raw materials in the Donetz basin, but this does not mean that he gave no thought to such things. On 23 November 1939 he had declared: 'Today we fight for oil fields, rubber, mineral wealth'. Also in this talk he spoke of the 'racial struggle',[31] but the need to establish German colonies in the Soviet Union and to liquidate the Jews only became practical issues later. The primary object of the war, as envisaged in the summer of 1940, was to secure Germany strategically, not to launch a crusade against Bolshevism. Germany, according to Hitler, would commit 80 to 100 divisions against 50 to 75 good Soviet divisions. At this meeting Hitler also told Brauchitsch that Britain could not expect positive help from the United States where isolationism was strong – but within a few days there had been a change. The government of the United States welcomed the British navy's recent attack on the French fleet and strongly supported the British declaration of 22 July to continue the war.[32]

IV

The first occasion on which Hitler discussed at length with his closest military advisors his decision to prepare for an invasion of the Soviet Union was at the Berghof conference of 31 July 1940.[33] Surveying the technical problems connected with 'Operation Sea Lion', he spelt out his plans if an invasion of Britain could not be launched. 'The English, who were down and out, have now taken heart.' Germany must dash all its hopes for continuing the war, which derived primarily from the help it expected from the Soviet Union and the United States. These two countries were frequently to change places in Hitler's orders of priorities and there was a connection between the issues they posed. The destruction of the Soviet Union would not only deny Britain the possibility of a continental ally, it would mean an enormous augmentation of the power of Japan which, relieved from the danger of attack by the Red Army, would fully occupy the attention of Britain and the United States in the Pacific.

It should be added that a pro–Axis government had recently been established in Tokyo, but neither on this occasion nor at a later date did Hitler mention the need for Japanese help against the Soviet Union: Germany with its own resources was strong enough to conquer that country. (Ribbentrop did however later try to persuade the Japanese to attack Russia.)[34] After the defeat of the Soviet Union, Germany would be master of the Balkans and Europe, but Russia had to be liquidated in the spring of 1941 and operations involving 120 German divisions would last five months. 60 divisions were to be retained in the west, a very large force. Significantly Hitler did not say what he intended to do after eliminating Russia – almost certainly, as will be seen, his aim was world power.

While the generals might have persuaded Hitler to launch the attack against Russia in the spring of 1941, instead of in the autumn of 1940, Brauchitsch and Halder were also fully aware of the military threat constituted by the Red Army, and they were not in agreement with the position Hitler had now adopted. Previously both he and the generals had agreed that Britain must first be defeated before Germany could deal with the Soviet Union, but Hitler was not virtually saying, 'Britain should be defeated in the Soviet Union'. For the generals this meant a two front war, and in order to avoid it they deemed a visit by Stalin to be desirable. He might well be persuaded that Soviet expansion should be diverted to the Persian Gulf and the Straits: 'In the Balkans, which economically falls in our zone, we can keep out of each other's way'.[35] But for reasons already mentioned, the generals did not try and impose their alternative strategy on Hitler.

Several important developments resulted from the Berghof conference. Instead of reducing the size of the German army from 159 to 120 infantry divisions, it was to be raised to 180 divisions; communications in the east were also improved, air fields constructed, the number of troops on the Soviet border was increased and intelligence data collected. On Hitler's verbal orders plans were drawn up for an invasion of Russia separately by both the armed forces (OKW) and army high command (OKH). Exports to the Soviet Union were to stop by May 1941.[36] But was Hitler committed to an eastern offensive? Could not his attention be diverted to other lucrative enterprises?

Certainly in August and September Russo–German relations continued to deteriorate. Germany permitted Bulgaria, not the Soviet Union, to seize most of the Dobrudja area on the mouth of the Danube. By the Second Vienna Award of 30 August Hungary obtained northern Transylvania, and what was left of Rumania was guaranteed by Germany, a guarantee that could only have been directed against Russia. Later the Germans were to send a military mission to Rumania. The measures the Germans took to secure their supplies of nickel from Petsamo in northern Finland and the ostentatious use they made of Finnish railways for sending troops to Norway also caused serious apprehension in Moscow.[37] By the end of September no solution had been found to the outstanding differences between the two countries. The treaties of August and September 1939 were now emptied of meaning.[38]

V

In spite of the deterioration of German–Soviet relations an invasion of Russia lay in the future. War with Britain engaged the immediate attention of Hitler and the high command. Although preparations for 'Sea Lion' were continued until the middle of October the unexpected German failure to win air supremacy during the Battle of Britain meant that 'Sea Lion' had by the middle of September become less feasible, and because of developments outside Europe additional emphasis was given to the peripheral strategy.[39] In August the United States and Canada were co-ordinating plans for mutual defence. On 2 September Britain and the United States reached an agreement whereby Britain was to receive 50 out-dated destroyers in return for ceding islands in the Caribbean as bases to the USA.[40] Raeder was now coming round to the view that Germany should prepare for the inevitable war against the USA. On 9 September he discussed with Hitler the possibility of Spanish intervention and the seizure of Gibraltar. The idea appealed to Hitler who had hoped to secure air bases for Germany in Morocco and to establish colonies in central Africa at the expense of France and Belgium. There is thus evidence that Hitler was pursuing two simultaneous aims: the peripheral strategy against the British empire and a bid to secure bases for world power directed mainly against the United States. Although the two aims overlapped, they were not synonymous.

A further event stimulated Hitler's interest in the Atlantic. On 23–25 September the government of Vichy France in west Africa warded off an attempt by British and Free French forces to seize Dakar. Having conferred with Raeder on 26 September Hitler believed that the attempt would be made again, next time by British and American forces which would also try to seize the Azores, Madeira, the Canary and Cape Verde islands.[41] Germany would have to act first by occupying these islands, and Hitler was especially interested in the Azores: not only would they provide Germany with bases to attack British sea communications with the Americas and the Middle East, (via the Cape) but they would provide Germany with bases to attack targets in the United States with new long range bombers not yet under construction.

Raeder did not think that Germany had naval forces adequate for the supply of all these islands. Instead, having captured Gibraltar and the Canary Islands, a drive should be made towards Suez and into Palestine and Syria. The army favoured similar Raeder plans, but also studied the possibility of a move towards Turkey from the north. According to Raeder, if the Soviet Union could be threatened from the Middle East it would be forced to toe the German line which would mean that plans to attack could be cancelled. For a time Raeder might have caused Hitler to have second thoughts on the absolute priority of attacking Russia,[42] but one thing became completely clear – as soon as the Atlantic and the Mediterranean were at the forefront of German strategy, co-operation with Japan became vital. This in itself marks a turning point in Hitler's strategy.

VI

While the navy was concerned with the strategic implications of closer relations with Japan, Ribbentrop was preparing the ground for a continental *bloc* on the diplomatic level. Under the terms of the tripartite pact between the three Axis Powers of 27 September 1940, Germany would have to go to war with the United States if that country intervened in the Sino–Japanese War, while Japan would have to go to war with the United States if it intervened in the war in Europe, though *casus foederis* would only arise if the US acted first. Far from acting as a deterrent, which was the intention of the signatories, the tripartite pact confirmed Roosevelt in his conviction that there was a world–wide Fascist conspiracy. (See also Chapter 9.) The alliance was not overtly directed against the Soviet Union: in fact it was to be invited to join it.[44] It was hoped that Italy would play at least a subsidiary role in the peripheral war – in the Indian Ocean according to Raeder.

At first the German army intended to reinforce the Italians in their offensive against Egypt. But Marshall Badoglio in the summer of 1940 opposed the idea: the Italian army was strong enough, so he supposed, to defeat the British in Egypt on its own resources. By mid-September Italy was making such slow progress that other options seemed preferable.[45] In July and August the German aim of an occupation of parts of the Greek mainland and islands, especially Crete, was still intended, according to Martin van Creveld, to prevent the British, who had a strong fleet in the Eastern Mediterranean, from establishing air bases for attacks on the Ploesti oil fields in Rumania. By late September the emphasis had changed. The aim was now to use Greece and the islands as a springboard for an offensive against the British empire. Hitler was therefore not in principle opposed to an Italian attack on Greece as was the case with an attack on Yugoslavia, but he did hold that an Italian invasion of the whole of Greece should take place only after a decisive Italian success against the British in Egypt had been secured. He also tried to stop Mussolini from making exorbitant demands on Vichy France, whose co-operation after the Dakar incident promised more to Germany than Spanish or Italian co-operation: but Mussolini had become frustrated by Hitler's one-sided exploitation of his victories, and not least in expanding German influence in the Balkans through Rumania and Bulgaria. Having abandoned all idea of an attack on Yugoslavia, Mussolini attacked Greece in October. On 12 November, when it was apparent that the Italians were making no headway in Greece, Hitler signed the first directive for a German invasion of Greece.[46]

At that time two events of major importance occurred. On 11 November British torpedo planes attacked and put out of action three battleships and two cruisers at Taranto, thereby reducing the Italian fleet by a half. This served to remind Franco that Britain had not lost the war, and ruled out the German plan to seize Gibraltar, (Operation Felix) until after further German successes. Also from 11 to 13 November Molotov visited Berlin to negotiate the removal of outstanding differences between Germany and the Soviet Union. Although the talks were inconclusive, Molotov proved that he was a tough negotiator. After his departure Russia was also invited to join the tripartite treaty, and the Soviet reply was given on 25 November and reached Berlin the next day. The Soviet Union could only adhere to the treaty on certain conditions: if German troops evacuated Finland; if Russia concluded an alliance with Bulgaria and obtained naval bases to secure its interests in the Straits, and if Japan ceded to Russia its oil and coal concessions in northern Sakhalin. Because the Soviet documents are unavailable it is impossible to establish how decisions were reached in Moscow, but the reply had the character of a stern warning which was what Hitler wanted. Hence, as Van Creveld and Koch rightly contend, it was only after 26 November 1940 that Hitler finally decided to invade Russia. He discussed his plans with his generals on 5 December, and Operation 18, 'Barbarossa', for an invasion of Russia was signed on 21 December. From now on the conquest of Russia was no longer a means of defeating Britain but an end in itself.[47]

VII

Just before Hitler reached this momentous decision the Italian army was thrust back to the Albanian border by Greek forces. To add to his difficulties, on 9 December General Wavell's forces in Egypt began an offensive that ended in February 1941 with Italian troops swept completely out of western Egypt and Cyrenaica. Hitler had no choice but to prevent an Italian collapse, which necessitated German attacks on the British empire. Having failed to mediate between Greece and Italy, Hitler again issued a directive for operations against Greece on 13 December (Operation Marita). German aircraft were also assembled for attacks on Malta and preparations were made for a small expeditionary force under the command of General Erwin Rommel to be sent to Tripoli. Because of the logistical and political problems connected with the entry of German troops into Bulgaria, operations for the conquest of Greece and later Yugoslavia were delayed. This in turn meant that the attack on Russia had to be postponed from the middle of May to 22 June 1941.[48]

VIII

Hitler, who still had to deal with the United States, adopted a paradoxical policy. While urging the Japanese to take action in the Pacific, for instance by stopping supplies from the USA reaching Vladivostok after the attack on Russia, he restrained Raeder from ordering attacks on US ships on their way to British ports until after Pearl Harbor. Raeder was especially worried by the US military presence in Iceland and advocated war against the United States, not Russia.[49] The subsequent German declaration of war on the USA on 11 December 1941 has puzzled historians, although admittedly, Germany could only win world power after America's defeat. What has been less well understood has been the importance Hitler attached to the Z-Plan for a monster fleet in January 1939 and the Atlantic thrust of his policy in September 1940 and again in July 1941. This renders his decision to go to war with the USA intelligible, provided that his armies were successful in Russia. That some of the troops which saved Moscow had recently been transferred from the Far East is proof that he was a victim of his own policy. He was certainly aware that the battle of the Atlantic had forced Germany and the USA onto a collision course.[50] Did he not wish for 'honour's' sake to deny Roosevelt's administration the privilege of declaring war on Germany by a seizure of the initiative himself? 'Better to go down with honour than to betray your cause through cowardly compromise' was a fixed principle behind his policy. His aims late in 1941 were to establish a continental base, make a bid for world power and destroy European Jewry – no longer in stages but simultaneously. It is more than a coincidence that Japanese militarists took a similar stand. One of their number declared: 'If there is war, the country may be ruined. Nevertheless, a nation which does not fight in this plight has lost its spirit and is a doomed country. Only if we fight to the last soldier will it be possible to find a way out of this situation'.[50] Both in Hitler's

Germany and in Imperial Japan courage to the point of self-destruction took pride of place over the compromises necessary for survival. The two powers were partners in the dance of death.

NOTES AND REFERENCES

1. Documents on German Foreign Policy (DGFP), D, vol. viii, no. 384. See H.W. Koch, 'Hitler's "Programme" and the Genesis of Operation Barbarossa', in *Aspects of the Third Reich* (ed.) H.W. Koch (London, 1985). Koch refers to many German works on 'Barbarossa'. See also B.A. Leach, *German Strategy against Russia 1939–1941* (Oxford, 1973) and Robert Cecil, *Hitler's Decision to invade Russia* (London, 1975).
2. Koch, 'Hitler's "Programme"', p. 291.
3. Generaloberst F. Halder, *Kriegstagebuch* (Stuttgart, 1962), vol. I, 15 June 1940, p. 35, also vol. II, 22 July, p. 30. See also General Thomas, *Grundlagen der deutschen Wehr- und Rustungswirtschaft*, pp. 320–321, 406 and 413–416; Leach (note 1), pp. 48–50. See Jodl's Diary Fragments, Nuremberg Documents ND, International Military Tribunal (IMT) 1809 PS; Halder (note 3), 30 June, 9 July. Koch (note 9), p. 292, esp. note 34.
4. R. Wheatley, *Operation Sea Lion: German Plans for the Invasion of England 1939–1942* (Oxford, 1958), p. 15 and Karl Klee, *Das Unternehmen Seelowe. Die gelante deutsche Landung in England, 1940* (Gottingen, 1958). Halder (note 3), 30 June, p. 375. For Jodl's directive, IMT vol. xxviii 1776-PS, 'Die Weiterfuhrung des Krieges gegen England', 30 June 1940.
5. Wheatley, *Operation Sea Lion*, p. 41.
6. *Ibid.* pp. 44–5.
7. *Ibid.*
8. *Ibid*, pp. 48–9. Also Halder, *Kriegstagebuch*, 13 July, p. 21 and G. Ciano, *Diaries* 1 Jan. 1939, 23 Dec. 1943, (ed.) Malcolm Muggeridge (London, 1947), pp. 266–7.
9. For the problems connected with 'Sea Lion' see Halder (note 3), 30 July vol. II, p. 45.
10. Halder *Kriegstagebuch*, vol. II, 13 July 1940, p. 21.
11. L.E. Hill (ed.), *Die Weizsäcker Papiere 1933–1950* (Berlin, 1979) p. 204 and Halder *Kriegstagebuch*, 30 June 1940, vol. I, p. 375 and 3 July vol. II, esp. note 'zu 3.7, 1940'.
12. Leach *German Strategy against Russia*, p. 187 *et seq.*
13. Jodl's Diary *Nuremburg Documents*.
14. Halder vol. I, 25, 26, 27 June 1940, pp. 372–374 and vol. II, 6 July, p. 12. See also H. Groscurth, *Tagebuch eines Abwehroffizieres 1938–1941* (Stuttgart, 1970), pp. 489–490.
15. Koch 'Hitler's "Programme"', pp. 291–292 and Leach, *German Strategy against Russia*, pp. 55–56.

16. Halder vol. I, 30 June 1940, pp. 374–375 and vol. II, 3 July editorial note in which it is stated that Brauchitsch and Halder started to study plans for a campaign against Russia after Halder's meeting with Weizsäcker who described Hitler's views on 30 June.

17. Halder vol. II, 1 July, p. 19 and 22 July, p. 30. See also W. Carr, *Poland to Pearl Harbor: The Making of the Second World War* (London, 1985), pp. 101–102.

18. Halder, vol. I, 26 June, p. 373 and 28 June p. 374. Also Leach, *German Strategy against Russia*, pp. 52–53.

19. Halder, 9 and 11 July. According to Etzdorf, liaison officer between the army and foreign ministry, these rumours could not be proved, see E.M. Robertson's monograph, 'Barbarossa: The Origins and Development of Hitler's Plan to attack Russia' (March 1952), a copy of which is in the Imperial War Museum.

20. Koch, 'Hitler's "Programme"', pp. 293–295 and Martin L. van Creveld, *Hitler's Strategy 1940–1941. The Balkan Clue* (Cambridge, 1973), p. 4.

21. Creveld, *Hitler's Strategy*, p. 7 *et seq*, and Macgregor Knox, *Mussolini Unleashed 1939–1941. Politics and Strategy in Fascist Italy's Last War* (Cambridge, 1982), p. 139 *et seq*.

22. Creveld *Hitler's Strategy*, pp. 9ff.

23. V.Ph. Fabry, *Der Hitler–Stalin–Pakt* (Darmstadt, 1962), p. 257 *et seq*. The intercepts are studied at some length in Robertson (note 19), pp. 58–63. For Mussolini's continued hostility to Yugoslavia, see DGFP (D) X no. 232 of 26 July.

24. Robertson 'Barbarossa', p. 59 and *passim*.

25. Halder, 22 July, pp. 33–34. See also Etzdorf's papers for the same period, and Robertson, 'Barbarossa', pp. 58 and 59.

26. DGFP (D) X no. 238 dispatch of 26 July 1940.

27. Robertson, 'Barbarossa', p. 60.

28. Halder's record of a conversation between Hitler and Brauchitsch, 22 July, *Kriegstagebuch*, vol. II, pp. 30–34.

29. *Ibid*.

30. DGFP (D) VIII no. 384.

31. Carr, *Poland to Pearl Harbor*, p. 102 *et seq*.

32. Halder, *Kriegstagebuch*, vol. II 31 July 1940, pp. 46–50.

33. James V. Compton, *The Swastika and the Eagle: Hitler, the United States and the Origins of the Second World War* (London, 1968), pp. 210–11. See also Carr (note 17), p. 150.

34. Halder, *Kriegstagebuch*, vol. II 30 August 1940, p. 46.

35. *Das Deutsche Reich und der Zweiten Weltkrieg*. Die Errichtung der Hegemonie auf dem Europaischen Kontinent, p. 368.

36. Koch 'Hitler's "Programme"', pp. 303–304 and Leach *German Strategy against Russia*, pp. 187–88.

37. Carr *Poland to Pearl Harbor*, p. 137. 115 *et seq*.

38. Koch 'Hitler's "Programme"', pp. 304–305; A. Hillgruber, *Hitlers*

Strategie und Kriegsfuhrung 1940–1941 (Frankfurt, 1971), pp. 188–192. See also *Das Deutsche Reich und der Zweiten Weltkrieg* (note 34), IV, *Die Rucker zu einer indirekten Strategie gegen England* by Klaus A. Maier, pp. 409–419.

39. Carr *Poland to Pearl Harbor*, p. 107.
40. *Ibid.*
41. For details see C.B. Burdick, *Germany's Military Strategy in Spain in the Second World War* and H.H. Herwig, 'Prelude to Weltblitzkrieg': Germany's Naval Policy towards the United States of America 1939–1941', *Journal of Modern History* 4 (1971), p. 657. These works have been used in Dr Glyn Stone's doctoral thesis:'Britain's Oldest Ally, Anglo–Portuguese Relations'.
42. Creveld, *Hitler's Strategy*, pp. 28–29.
43. 'The Tripartite Pact of 1940: Japan, Germany and Italy', *International Studies* 1984/111, London School of Economics, papers by Jost Dülffer, John Chapman, Ernest Bramsted, (ed.) Ian Nish.
44. Creveld, *Hitler's Strategy*, pp. 52–55.
45. *Ibid.*, pp. 17–18, 22–31, 36–37 and 59.
46. DGFP (D) vol xi no. 405 and Koch (note 2).
47. Creveld, *Hitler's Strategy*, pp. 85–91, pp. 92–109 and conclusions, pp. 179–183.
48. Compton *The Swastika and the Eagle*, chs. X, XI and XIV.
49. Carr *Poland to Pearl Harbor*, ch. 5 esp. 140 *et seq.*
50. *Ibid.*, p. 149.

12. The Japanese Decision to Move South(1939–1941)

SUMIO HATANO AND SADAO ASADA

This paper attempts to re-examine, mainly on the basis of unpublished military sources,[1] Japan's decision to move into South-East Asia, which became a crucial turning point on Japan's road to war with the United States, Britain and the Netherlands.

What were the principal motives that shaped this fateful decision?[2] Should we interpret Japan's southward advance as part of its efforts to terminate the Sino–Japanese War by cutting off the most vital supply line to Chiang Kai-shek? Or was it primarily Japan's response to the outbreak of the European war: an attempt to take advantage of Germany's *Blitzkrieg* to control the French, Dutch and British colonial possessions in South-East Asia? How was it related to Japan's wish to create a self-sufficient economic *bloc* by capturing strategic resources there? How was the policy of southward expansion affected by inter-service rivalry and differences between the army and the navy?

Japan's decision to move south was a highly complex one, involving all of the above-mentioned and other factors.

I

It was not until the middle of the 1930s that the Japanese government began to formulate a policy of advancing into South-East Asia.

383

However, this southern policy, so-called, differed from Japan's continental (and northern) policy, led by the army, which had already taken the form of armed expansionism. Having brought about the Manchurian Incident in 1931 and created Manchukuo the following year, the army was increasingly hostile towards the Soviet Union. On the other hand, the navy envisaged southward expansion through peaceful means.

The reason for the proposed southern strategy was essentially two-fold. Partly it was the navy's desire to contend with the army for an increased share of armaments and budgetary appropriations. With the expiry in 1935 and 1936 of the London and Washington treaties on naval limitation, the navy became haunted by a deepening sense of crisis. It greatly feared a naval race with the United States – its traditional 'hypothetical enemy Number One.' (It should also be noted that in 1936 Britain was included among Japan's potential enemies for the first time.) In this sense, the southern strategy was little more than a budgetary strategy, conceived in order to rationalise and win support for a naval arms build-up, and turned against the army, which wished to build up its own forces *vis-à-vis* the Soviet threat in the north.[3]

There was also an economic reasoning behind the southern strategy. For a while an arrangement seemed possible as the Japanese government did not consider it urgent to control such strategic resources as petroleum, rubber and scarce metals (tin, nickel, copper) in South-East Asia. These resources could be obtained from the United States and the western colonial powers through the medium of peaceful trade. The petroleum problem came to the fore, however, with the navy's mounting concern over the shortage of petroleum for its fleets and of aviation fuel for its air force. To conduct research on the oil question, vital for Japan's 'national defence', in July 1935 the navy established a committee to investigate southern policy, with the vice-chief of the navy general staff serving as its chairman. It was staffed by key officers of middle-rank both in the navy ministry and the navy general staff.[4] Thus, for the first time, the navy began in 1935–36 to make systematic investigations of petroleum resources in South-East Asia.

The upshot of the army-navy differences over the direction of Japan's expansion – which were never resolved – was the formulation and adoption of the now famous 'Fundamentals of National Policy' in August 1936. Although this policy paper totally failed to integrate Japan's national policies and strategies, it was of decisive significance in placing a southward advance on a par with continental expansion at the centre of Japanese foreign policy. According to the 'Fundamentals of National Policy', however, the means for southward expansion were to be confined to gradual, peaceful procedures in line with the conclusions of the committee to investigate southern policy.

In the mid-1930s the radical advocates of drastic military action in South-East Asia were a group of middle-rank naval officers represented by Captain Nakahara Yoshimasa and Commanders Ishikawa Shingo and Chūdō Kan'ei[5]. Formulation of the 'Fundamentals of National Policy' was partly meant to constrain the militant arguments and actions of these officers. Their arguments were to revive with the outbreak of the European war, and proved of decisive influence within the Japanese navy from late 1940 onward. For the moment the adoption of the 'Fundamentals of National Policy' seemed to give equal priority to the navy's southern policy and the army's continental policy. Still, the Sino–Japanese war, which broke out in July 1937, soon escalated into full-scale hostilities, so that policy towards South-East Asia came once again to be subordinated to the continental programme. The navy's policy of 'northern defence and southern advance', could no longer function as a restraint on continental expansionism. For a while, therefore, the navy followed a highly opportunistic course, taking advantage of the China war to control the South China coast and islands in the South China Sea. In February 1939 it brought under occupation Hainan – rich in high-grade iron and strategically located for further moves southward – and a month later took the Spratley Islands.

II

The outbreak of the European war in September 1939 attenuated the hold that the preoccupied western powers maintained over colonial possessions in South-East Asia. This opened up a magnificent vista for Japan for aggressive expansion into the southern areas. Suddenly it seemed quite within the bounds of possibility to conquer the Dutch East Indies, French Indochina, British Malaya and Singapore. Captain Nakahara Yoshimasa – the foremost exponent of a southward advance – wrote in his diary:

> Japan as a nation must be reoriented as a sea power, concentrating her efforts on naval expansion. In this way, Japan can establish once and

for all the New Order in East Asia and really settle the China incident. (To attain this purpose, Japan should not hesitate even to fight Britain and the United States.)[6]

But such a change in national policy, advocated by middle rank officers, could hardly win support of the more cautious naval leaders. In fact, at the outset, the navy's policy (as agreed upon in October 1939) was based on the premise that Japan must not ever become involved in the European war. It gave priority to the speedy settlement of the China war, emphasising that Japan's central aim was to make third parties stop their assistance to the Chinese Nationalists. In this respect, leaders of the navy did not differ much from those of the army and the foreign ministry. This policy of non-involvement in the European war was endorsed by the foreign, army, and navy ministers in late December 1939.[7] It prevailed over a dissenting view that 'the South Seas regions must become a part of our Empire's self-sufficient economic sphere'. In short, Japan's non-intervention was a two-fold policy: Japan would refrain from intervening in the European war, but would not tolerate any interference in the Sino–Japanese war by third parties.

What were the international conditions that prevented Japan from strongly committing itself to a particular power or powers at this time? Two factors which had crystallised Japanese policy into one of non-intervention were the conclusion of the Nazi–Soviet non-aggression pact (August 1939) and Japan's severe defeat in the Nomonhan incident, the Russo–Japanese border clash of May–September 1939. The Nazi–Soviet pact at one stroke caused the breakdown of Japanese–German negotiations for an alliance directed against the Soviet Union, making closer ties with Germany momentarily impossible. Japan's defeat at Nomonhan had forced a conciliatory policy towards the Soviet Union. Another important problem facing the Japanese government was the need to improve relations with the United States after it gave notice (July 1939) that it would abrogate the US–Japanese treaty of commerce and navigation after one year.

In the early summer of 1940, Japan's policy of non-intervention in the European war and giving the highest priority to a bilateral settlement of the China war underwent a reversal. German successes in the west during May–June had so dazzled Japanese officials as to generate a feverish clamour for an opportunistic southern advance that would take advantage of an apparently imminent German victory. 'Don't miss the bus' was the catch-phrase of the day.

Significantly, the initiative in translating this mood into national policy was taken by the army – the traditional advocate of the policy of 'northern advance and southern defence'. Of course, the army's new southern policy had little in common with the navy's policy; the latter regarded expansion into the South Seas as distinct and separate from the China war. The army tended to subsume South-East Asia under the programme to construct the 'Greater East Asia Co-prosperity Sphere'. The solution the army eventually offered was to end the war with China by linking it with a southward advance that, in turn, would involve Japan in the European war.

Counting on an early German invasion of the British Isles, a handful of middle-rank officers in the operations section of the army general staff hastened to draw up a blueprint for a forceful southern advance centering on the capture of Britain's colonial possessions in the Far East. The essence of the army's first draft of a national policy paper (3 July) was that Japan should first conclude the China war and then strike southward, but it could also be construed that, if presented with a favourable opportunity, Japan might immediately attack Britain's Far Eastern possessions without awaiting an end to the China war. The army planners expected the German invasion of Britain to take place in late August.

This army draft was forwarded to the navy on 4 July. As the traditional exponent of the strategy of 'defend the north, advance to the south', the navy accepted the army draft 'in its general outline', but pointed out that the draft's greatest weakness was that it 'did not consider seriously enough' relations with the United States. The army took the position that Japan would be able to start a war with Britain without incurring US entry; thus military operations would be 'restricted insofar as possible to Britain alone'. The navy, convinced of the 'inseparable connections between Britain and the United States', stressed that any attack on Britain's Far Eastern possessions would lead to war with the United States. Here was the central difference between the army and the navy.[8]

The most prominent feature of the navy's stance in these interservice deliberations was the special emphasis it placed on the risk of war with the United States. Its counterdraft stressed that 'since war with the United States might become unavoidable, sufficient preparations must be made for this eventuality'. In reality, how serious was the navy's concern with war with the United States at this time? Bureaucratic factors go far to explain the navy's alarmist stand: the navy saw a great threat in the succession of huge building plans the United States had recently announced – the second and third Vinson plans (May 1938 and June 1940 respectively). Desperately caught in the straits of an ever-escalating arms race, it was contending with the army for a larger share of resources for its arms build-up. If only as a rationale, the navy needed to stress the threat of war with the United States.[9]

Another difficulty with the army draft was that it could mean that Japan would move southward even if the China war remained unsettled. The army, committed to the China war far more deeply than the navy, had been making agonising efforts in search of an early settlement – by early 1940 the army leaders had come round to the conclusion that it would be impossible to defeat Chiang Kai-shek by military means.

Since the autumn of 1938, the army had been focussing on a settlement of the China war through political plots and machinations. This aim was to be attained in two different ways: establishment of a puppet regime under the pro-Japanese Wang Ching-wei[10]; and direct negotiations with the Chungking government. The army's hopes for collaboration with Wang gradually faded as the weakness of his support became increasingly apparent. By late 1939 the army came to believe that the only chance for a negotiated settlement was simultaneously to deal with Chiang. Progress was made by early 1940, and in February negotiations with Chungking, known as the Kiri Project, were approved by army authorities in Tokyo.

Clandestine peace negotiations speedily progressed: preliminary talks were held in March 1940 between the representatives of the China Expeditionary Army and Chungking delegates. From May to June negotiations with representatives of Chungking dealt with conditions for a cease-fire. Japanese army leaders placed great hope on the success of the Kiri Project. While it lasted it gave promise of a cease-fire, and this expectation, in turn, became an important factor which attracted army planners to a southern advance policy.[11]

While peace negotiations in China set the stage, the more important idea that triggered the army's decision for southward expansion was the assumption that Japan would be able to settle the China war by linking it with a southern strategy. The army leaders had now abandoned their initial fear of becoming involved in the European war. Since the spring of 1940, Sawada Shigeru, vice-chief of the army general staff, had been voicing his conviction that 'the fate of the China Incident is inseparably connected with that of the European war. Will not the execution of southern operations be a possible way to favourably settle the China Incident?'[12] With the fall of France in June 1940 and the rising expectation of a speedy invasion of Britain, Sawada's argument gained influence among the army general staff.

It was against such a background that agreement was reached on a basic national policy set out in a document bearing the ponderous title, 'Outline of the Main Principles for Coping with the Changing World Situation'. It was based on the army draft of 3 July, with revisions proposed by the navy. Approved by top army and navy officers, it was sanctioned on 27 July at the Imperial Headquarters Cabinet Liaison Conference, the second highest policy organ, which consisted of cabinet representatives and the supreme command.[13] However, as it was based on highly wishful assumptions about the European war and Anglo–American relations, the 'Outline of the Main Principles' amounted to little more than a verbal expression of strength, a product of fertile imaginations. The only substantial stipulation it contained was the following passage: 'If French Indo-china should refuse our demands through diplomatic channels, we might resort to force of arms'. Japan's objective in the intermittent diplomatic negotiations with France since 1939 had been to block off the supply route via Indochina to the Chiang regime. This policy stemmed from the conviction, shared by the Japanese government and the military, that the greatest obstacle to an early settlement of the China war was British and French assistance to Chiang.

With the outbreak of the European war, the Japanese army had dispatched troops to the Indochinese border to bring pressure upon both Chiang and the French. The French Indochina authorities, counting on Britain and the United States, showed no sign of accepting Japanese demands. The French surrender to Germany, however, undermined the position of the Governor-General, Georges Catroux, who acceded to Japanese demands and closed the border between China and Indochina. By this time, however, such a move could no longer satisfy middle-rank officers in the army general staff (especially the operations division) and the South China army; in late June they began to clamour for a military invasion of Indochina.

The Japanese objective in the negotiations, conducted in Tokyo in August 1940, was to force the French authorities in Indochina to permit the passage of Japanese troops through their territory and the use of air bases there. Negotiations between foreign minister Matsuoka Yōsuke and French ambassador Charles Arsene-Henry dragged on, but on 31 August the latter was finally pressed into accepting Japanese terms. Details concerning the passage of troops were to be worked out later. Meanwhile, middle-rank officers in the army general staff and the South China army, in defiance of superiors, schemed for a military invasion with a view to obtaining a springboard for further advances in South-East Asia. Their activities, as one navy observer noted, revealed 'an aggressive southern policy aimed at future acquisition of bases for further expansion to the south. There is a strong tendency for our local troops to take the initiative, leaving the Tokyo authorities to approve the *fait accompli*'.[14] In mid-September the operations divisions of both the army and the navy were pressing for action in Indochina.

III

The southward advance policy, as stipulated in the 'Outline of the Main Principles', depended to a large extent on an improvement of relations with Germany and the Soviet Union. As for Germany, Japanese leaders (especially in the army) desired to strengthen ties with the Nazis through a military alliance, in order to establish the 'New Order' in the Far East and dominate South-East Asia. At the same time they feared that the sweeping German conquest of the Netherlands and France might tempt the Germans to control South-East Asia – the central question was the extent to which Japan was willing to offer military assistance to the war against Britain. Army and navy staff officers advocated an attack on Singapore. The army's policy paper of 27 July went so far as to state that, when requested to enter the war by Germany, Japan should 'in principle be ready to comply'.[15] However, the final draft treaty, agreed among the foreign, army and navy ministries on 6 August, stipulated that Japan would retain the right to decide 'independently' when to enter the war.

Initially seen as a military alliance against Britain, the Japanese–German pact was transformed into an instrument to deter the United States, when foreign minister Matsuoka revised the draft to include the United States. He argued that expansion to the south would inevitably lead to war with the United States, and that only by aligning with Germany could Japan prevent it. Although Matsuoka repeatedly emphasised that a tripartite pact was aimed at preventing a Japanese–American war by enabling Japan to act from a position of strength, it was to result in provoking the United States.

The army's plan for a tripartite pact (27 July) contained the prototype of a grand design to bring in the Soviet Union. Such a four-power 'combination', the army expected, would bring pressure to bear upon the United States. The foreign ministry, concerned about the aggravation of German–Soviet relations, rejected any such plan. However, the idea of a four-power combination was soon to be taken over by the foreign minister, Matsuoka.

The principal requisite for southward expansion was the removal of the threat from the north. The army general staff had been pursuing a policy of reconciliation with the Soviet Union since the settlement of the Nomonhan incident; its aim was an early end to the China war. The intelligence division hoped to shut down Soviet assistance to Chungking. With the rising clamour for southern expansion in the summer of 1940, policy turned to assuring security in the north in order to protect the southern advance. Negotiations with the Russians began in August to enable Japan to redeploy forces in Manchuria and northern China to central and southern China.[16]

These diplomatic efforts, beset with difficulties, were doomed. The Japanese – especially the army – desired close ties with the Soviet Union, comparable to the Nazi–Soviet non-aggression pact of 1939, but could not offer the Russians anything tangible as an inducement. When the Japanese proposed a neutrality pact, the Soviets demanded retrocession of oil and coal mining rights in northern Sakhalin – the navy in particular opposed the Soviet demand, because it refused to give up the high-grade oil in this area.

IV

Japanese troops began marching into northern Indochina on 22 September 1940. The United States responded with a new loan to China, and on 26 September President Franklin D. Roosevelt signed an executive order placing aviation gasoline, high-grade iron and steel scrap under export licensing. To keep in step with United States policy, the British soon reopened the Burma Road. Having survived the Battle of Britain, they were moving closer an alliance with the United States.

Soon after the Japanese thrust into northern Indochina and conclusion of the tripartite pact (signed on 27 September), the Kiri Project (peace negotiations with Chunking) collapsed, leaving Japan no choice but to abandon a bilateral settlement of the China war and recognise the Wang Ching-wei regime. From this time onwards the army became convinced that the only positive means left for terminating the China war had to be sought in the European war. The army draft memorandum (4 November) stated that to conclude the China war and overcome economic dependence on the Anglo–American powers, Japan must 'seize an opportunity to take military actions (*sic*) in southern areas'.[17] Settlement of the China war was to depend on an armed southern advance.

In late 1940 army planners began to spell out the circumstances under which Japan would undertake military operations in the south. The programme of southward advance was still predicated on an early German invasion of Britain, which would become the signal for Japanese attacks on Britain's Far Eastern colonies. According to the army general staff's estimate in September–October 1940, Hitler's delay in attacking Britain was merely 'tactical' and did 'not mean any change in determination to invade'. The cross-Channel invasion would take place by the spring of 1941 at the latest.[18] Such wishful thinking was belied by the fact that in mid-September Hitler issued an order indefinitely postponing – in effect, abandoning – the cross-Channel operation. Such a development undermined Japan's programme for a southward advance. The premise underlying the army's opportunistic policy (as set out in the 'Outline of the Main Principles') was becoming increasingly untenable.

Meanwhile army planners made rapid progress in working out the southern strategy. By mid-July they had prepared an operational programme, according to which construction of air bases in southern Indochina was the pre-requisite for attacks on the British colonies and the Dutch East Indies.

Before the strategists could make much more headway, the border dispute between Indochina and Thailand intensified. With the collapse of Thai–Indochinese negotiations in October, the Japanese army became anxious to intervene. As the condition for its mediating efforts, the army demanded military agreements whereby Japan would obtain the right to construct air bases in southern Indochina and supply bases in Thailand.

When in January 1941 this border dispute escalated into an armed conflict, the Japanese government feared that Thailand might seek British support. The liaison conference decided to prepare for coercive action – the army by reinforcing troops in northern Indochina and the navy by manoeuvres off the Indochina peninsula.

It is worth noting that in inter-service deliberations the navy, hitherto content with a passive stance, was beginning to take the initiative in a hardline southern policy. Especially important in this process, from a bureaucratic viewpoint, was the establishment of the First Committee in December 1940.[19] This was part of a broader institutional reorganisation in the navy designed to gain a greater voice in national policy. Composed of energetic strategists at the section-chief level, the First Committee was led by the chief of the operations division of the naval general staff and the chief of the newly established second section of the naval affairs bureau, whose duty it was to specialise in foreign and defense policy and conduct liaison with the army. Members of the First Committee, impatient with the 'passive' and 'vacillating' stand of senior officers, showed willingness to risk war with the United States.

Although some Japanese historians have questioned the importance of this committee, there is no doubt that its members were determined to assert their leadership over the navy's policy toward South-East Asia.[20] In January 1941 the navy suddenly began to take an extremely tough position. The navy's policy towards the Thai–Indochina dispute was so bellicose that it surprised even the army general staff.

One possible reason for the navy's sudden militancy at this time may have been a recently revealed incident in intelligence warfare – the 'Automedon affair' of December 1940[21]. Under extraordinary circumstances the Japanese navy had come into possession of a copy of the British war cabinet minutes of 8 August 1940, portraying an extremely pessimistic outlook on the Far Eastern situation. The top secret chiefs of staff report attached to the minutes emphasised that since Britain was 'unable to send the fleet to the Far East', it 'must avoid [an] open clash' with Japan:

> In current situation, we would put up with Japanese attack on Siam or Indochina without going to war. In [the] event of Japanese attack on the Dutch, and they offered no resistance, no war between us and Japan. But if the Dutch resist, then they would have our full military support.[22]

Upon receiving this information from the German naval *attaché*, Paul Wennecker, vice-admiral Kondō Nobutake, vice-chief of the navy general staff, remarked that 'such a significant weakening of the

British Empire could not have been identified by outside appearances'.

There is some evidence that Japanese naval leaders regarded this information as confirming not only Britain's capabilities but also its intentions. At the liaison conference of 27 December 1940, navy minister Oikawa Koshirō stated: 'According to our intelligence document, it is estimated that Britain would not go to war as long as Japan confines itself to advancing into French Indochina, but war would become inevitable if Japan should advance into the Dutch East Indies'.[23] Given such an estimate, the Japanese naval leaders must have been all the more emboldened to launch military operations in southern Indochina.

On 30 January the liaison conference approved the 'Outline of Policy toward French Indochina and Thailand', which envisioned strengthening Japan's control over French Indochina and Thailand[24]. However, foreign minister Matsuoka opposed the demands of the navy and the army for military action on the grounds that it would lead to war with Britain and the United States. Instead, he succeeded in mediating the Thai–Indochinese dispute. As a navy general staff officer complained, the mediation was virtually 'an unremunerated labour', since Japan's military demands in southern Indochina were 'simply shelved'.[25]

The navy had been engaged in manoeuvres off Saigon and Bangkok, and was keenly aware of the alarmist reactions of the British who were vociferous about 'a crisis in the Far East'.[26] Commander Fujii Shigeru, a member of the First Committee, wrote in his diary that navy manoeuvres had triggered a crisis fraught with danger of war with the US. He held that these actions strengthened 'the oppressive anti-Japanese front' led by the United States. 'As long as such a drift toward mutual provocations goes unchecked', he wrote, 'a Japanese–American war is conceived to be inevitable'.[27]

Such a view again showed the navy's conviction that Britain and the United States were inseparable, and that a further armed advance southward would lead directly to war with the United States. The judgment of senior navy leaders was that even if Germany should defeat Britain, this would not provide an opportunity for southward expansion.

In late March 1941 the navy presented a scenario of southern policy that supposed war with the United States.
1. For the moment Japan should continue negotiations to construct bases in Indochina and Thailand.

2. Japan must resort to force only when the United States, alone or in co-operation with Britain and the Netherlands, imposed total embargoes, or when the United States applied military pressures on Japan.
3. Resources in the Dutch East Indies must be obtained only by diplomatic negotiations.[28] In short, unless Japan was prepared and determined to fight the United States, military action in Thailand and Indochina would be impossible.

By the end of March the army, struck by the hostile reactions of the Anglo–American powers to Japanese mediation of the Thai–Indochina dispute, had come to agree with the navy that Britain and the United States were 'inseparable'. From January to March the army had made a reappraisal of Japan's national strength, especially strategic resources, in case of war. The conclusion was that shortage of liquid fuel made protracted war impossible; for the moment Japan should avoid further provocation, attempting to secure strategic resources through negotiations with the Dutch East Indies.

As a result of these basic reconsiderations it became necessary to scrap the opportunistic southern policy of July 1940 (the 'Outline of the Main Principles') and to formulate a new policy in accord with the international situation. Adopted by the army and navy on 17 April, 1941, the new policy paper (the 'Outline of Policy towards the South')[29] stated that Japan should expand southward by diplomatic means, unless resort to military measures became imperative for 'the empire's self-existence and self-defense'.

A disgruntled Commander Fujii wrote in his diary that the new policy could be interpreted as 'avoidance of the use of force in the southern regions'.[30] Looked at the other way, however, it could also be argued that the navy had determined to take action in the south and open hostilities with the United States if and when Japan faced an all-out US embargo. For this reason, some Japanese historians argue that this policy constituted a further step toward Japan's military advance southward.

VI

On 18 April, the day on which the army and navy agreed on a new southern policy, Tokyo received from ambassador Nomura Kichisaburō in Washington the draft understanding between the United States and Japan, which had been informally worked out by the unofficial American advisers on foreign policy, the John Doe

Associates.[31] This draft understanding, although demanding that Japan not enter the war on the side of the Axis, contained conditions favourable to Japan: normalisation of US–Japanese commercial relations; US co-operation for procurement of resources in South-East Asia; and mediation of the Sino–Japanese War. Such conditions led the Japanese government to see the possibility of further concessions from the United States.

In sending the draft understanding, ambassador Nomura took care to emphasise that 'not to use military means for southern expansion is the very foundation of this entire draft understanding'.[32] Contrary to such caution, however, an optimistic view prevailed among middle-rank army and navy officers who believed that an armed southern advance was compatible with adjustment of relations with the United States. Such optimism was shared by Japanese leaders. It stemmed from the feeling that the southward advance would not bring a war because the United States did not possess vital interests in southern regions, with the exception of the Philippines.

Japanese–American negotiations, commenced through informal channels, met with strong objection from the foreign minister, Matsuoka, who had just returned from a tour of Europe. He suspected that the US aims in these negotiations were to restrain Japanese advances to the south and gain time to extend all-out assistance to Britain. Besides, Japanese–American negotiations were incompatible with his policy of what a later generation would call 'brinkmanship'. Having lived in the United States in his formative years, he was convinced that a position of strength was necessary in dealing with the United States.[33]

Matsuoka had been planning a four-power pact that would bring the Soviet Union into the existing tripartite pact. He wished to start negotiations with the United States, but had counted on browbeating them by confronting them with a Japanese–German–Italian–Soviet pact. However, Matsuoka's proposal to expand the tripartite pact to a 'four-power alliance' was rejected by Hitler, who had decided to attack the Soviet Union. In Moscow Matsuoka succeeded in concluding a neutrality pact on 13 April. During his tour of Europe and Russia, he had obtained information about the aggravation of German–Soviet relations, although there is no evidence that he took it seriously.[34]

Another expectation that Matsuoka held in concluding the neutrality pact with the Soviet Union was that it would expedite the settlement of problems in the south. The issue that confronted

Matsuoka upon his return was economic negotiations with the Netherlands. The Dutch authorities, backed by Britain and the United States, resisted Japanese demands; in late May the negotiations with the Dutch were suspended and in early June the Japanese government decided to call them off. The failure of the Dutch–Japanese negotiations did much to renew the clamour for a military advance into southern Indochina.

Middle-rank navy officers in particular had become increasingly dissatisfied with what they saw as weak leadership on the matter of a southern advance. Echoing this discontent, on 5 June the First Committee presented a notable paper which urged that the navy 'immediately make clear its determination for war' with the United States and Britain, and 'lead' the higher echelons in the government and the army in this direction. Japan must carry out 'without a day's delay' an armed advance into Indochina and Thailand – the key to a strategic position in the Far East. Such expansion was justified by the need to secure strategic resources upon which the 'self-existence of the Japanese Empire' was said to depend.[35]

Commander Fujii, who drafted this paper, noted in his diary that it 'seems to have greatly shocked the top leadership from the navy minister down; it has had a considerable effect in crystallising the determination for war'.[36]

About this time, 5 June, Tokyo received information from ambassador Ōshima Hiroshi in Berlin that a German–Soviet war was imminent. Since April the rumours of German–Soviet hostilities had been conveyed by *attachés* in European capitals, but could not be substantiated. On 3 June, Ōshima was told about Operation Barbarossa directly by Hitler and his foreign minister, Joachim von Ribbentrop.[37] The First Committee at once demanded a policy of non-intervention. It also redoubled its demand for the construction of bases and stationing of troops in southern Indochina and Thailand. The navy's high echelon leaders were reluctant to station troops there, but were forced to fall in line because of the collapse of economic negotiations with the Dutch East Indies.

The army general staff was also prompted by the rupture of these negotiations to take a stiffer policy on southern expansion, and news of the outbreak of the German–Soviet war supported this move. On 10 July the joint conference of the army and navy bureau chiefs and Operations Division chiefs reached an agreement that the stationing of troops and construction of air bases in southern Indochina must be carried out as soon as possible.

On the basis of this agreement the First Committee drafted a new policy paper, presented by chief of the naval general staff Nagano Osami to the liaison conference on 12 June. It stipulated that Japan should demand bases and the stationing of troops, and if this demand should meet resistance, it should use force. Despite Matsuoka's strenuous opposition, the policy was approved by the liaison conference on 25 June.

The great obstacle here was Matsuoka: Soviet–German hostilities being imminent, he reversed his earlier stand and now opposed a southern advance, insisting on an attack on the Soviet Union even at the cost of shelving the southern policy. Army and navy leaders, who had regarded Matsuoka as a proponent of a southern advance, were at a loss to understand his intentions. Years after the Pacific War, Matsuoka testified that he had objected to armed action in Indochina for fear of provoking war with the United States and Britain, but this explanation remains to be confirmed. Evidently he also attached great importance to the tripartite pact, in the conclusion of which he had played a crucial role.

Whatever the case, the army and navy repeatedly attempted to persuade Matsuoka to drop his opposition. Captain Ishikawa Shingo, a leading member of the First Committee and personally close to Matsuoka, appealed to him in a letter on 19 June.[38] He emphasised that the liaison conference decision of 12 June had unequivocally turned national policy towards southward advance, and time was ripe for striking southward since the threat from the north would lessen with German–Soviet hostilities. Finally Matsuoka came around to endorsing an advance into southern Indochina.

Meanwhile, the army and the navy had drafted a paper explaining the need in detail. Japan's influence in South-East Asia – its 'lifeline' – was being eroded because of the ABCD (American–British–Chinese–Dutch) encirclement. Japan must set itself free and consolidate its strategic position in French Indochina against the Anglo–American powers. Stationing troops in southern Indochina would be a great shock to the Chungking government, contributing to a settlement of the China war; it would also help reopen Japanese–Dutch negotiations.[39]

It is to be noted that the Japanese government and the military made no serious study of how the 'ABCD powers' would react to Japan's entry into southern Indochina, nor was any thought given to the threat that Japan's military actions in the south would pose to Britain and the United States.

The German attack on the Soviet Union of 22 June shattered Matsuoka's grand design for a four-power pact and drove the Soviet Union into the arms of Britain and the United States. Yet this development did not tempt the Japanese leaders to demand abrogation of the tripartite pact; they chose to continue supporting the pact. They predicted that the Soviet–German war would end in an overwhelming German victory and believed it would provide a chance to remove the threat from the north, not to mention an opportunity to strike south. Ever since it received ambassador Ōshima's dispatch of 5 June, the army had been formulating a new policy; its conclusion was that Japan should station troops in southern Indochina, while preparing for war against the north (the Soviet Union) in case the situation should turn out to be 'extremely advantageous'. The navy opposed a war against the Soviet Union, but it acquiesced in the army policy on condition that 'preparations against the United States and Britain would not be compromised'. This new agreement was sanctioned at the Imperial Conference of 2 July, 1941,[40] and on the following day orders were issued to mobilise. The army and the navy prepared for both peaceful and armed advances, and on 28 July 40,000 Japanese troops marched 'peacefully' into southern Indochina.

The United States was already aware of Japanese actions through 'MAGIC', the technique for decoding secret Japanese telegrams, and a presidential order froze all Japanese assets in the United States on 25 July. The British government immediately followed suit and enforced a complete embargo against Japan. Although the British had contemplated a more limited form of economic retaliation, the war cabinet decided to give whole-hearted support to the United States in order to sustain the development of Anglo–American co-operation.[41] This decision placed the initiative and leadership of policy in the hands of the United States. What had worried London was that it could not obtain a commitment from the United States to give military support in the event of a Japanese attack on British or Dutch possessions, and British leaders now hoped this weakness could be solved by closer co-operation. On 1 August a total oil embargo went into effect, and this confronted Japan with a shortage of petroleum – the lifeblood of its fleet.[42]

Had Japanese leaders calculated the risk of such a sharp reprisal? Already in August 1940 the operations section of the naval general staff had drawn a scenario of mutual escalation leading to hostilities. It was characterised by peculiarly circular reasoning: to prepare for hostilities with the Anglo–American powers, Japan would have to march into Indochina to obtain raw materials; the United States would counter by imposing an economic embargo; this in turn would compel Japan to seize the Dutch East Indies to secure essential oil, a step that would lead to hostilities with the United States.[43]

However, most Japanese leaders held to an optimistic belief that the southward drive would not invite a full embargo. Some members of the First Committee did not expect Washington to respond in such a drastic way because they felt American leaders would surely wish to avoid provoking Japan into war at a time when the United States was not prepared for a two-ocean war. From this perspective, it is not surprising that when the embargo did materialise, Japanese strategists took it as unmistakable proof that the United States was ready to go to war.[44]

VII

Immediately after the United States had placed an embargo on exports, the Japanese navy ministry made a new assessment of the supply of, and demand for, petroleum. If the oil embargo by the United States and the Netherlands were to continue, total consumption of petroleum (5,400,000 kl per year) would far exceed supply (800,000 kl) in the first year, and during the second year oil in storage would be exhausted. For this reason the navy needed to secure oil fields in South-East Asia as soon as possible, even at the risk of war with the United States and Britain. Such an estimate underlay the navy's demand for speedy preparations and a 'determination' for war.[45]

On 3 August the navy's First Committee drafted a paper stating that diplomatic negotiations and war preparations should be pursued in parallel until late October.[46] If a compromise with the United States should fail then, Japan must open hostilities.

Meanwhile the army ministry, which had been making its own estimate of Japan's resources, came to the conclusion that it was impossible, if only on account of the limited petroleum supply, both to enter the war against the Soviet Union and conduct operations in the south. On the basis of this assessment on 9 August the army general staff decided to abandon the idea of war with the Soviet Union and to give priority to war with the United States and Britain.

After the Japanese advance into southern Indochina, the army and the navy – especially their strategists – intensified their demand that the government determine to open hostilities so that preparations for war with Britain and the United States could be completed. Vehemently insisting on this course of action, the army brought great pressure not only on navy leaders but also on the government authorities. The Imperial Conference of 6 September adopted a new national policy based on the demands of the First Committee set out on 3 August. War preparations were to be complete by late October and a determination for war should be made if a diplomatic settlement could not be reached by early October.[47] This decision did not necessarily mean a final commitment to embark upon war with the United States, but it was difficult to reject the argument that war preparations could not be completed unless there was a consensus regarding determination for war. The army's intention was revealed by an ambiguous passage, inserted in the national policy of 6 September 1941, that Japan would strike 'with full determination not to hesitate to go to war with the United States, Britain, and the Netherlands'. Meanwhile the Konoe Cabinet was ready to make concessions to Washington on key issues regarding the tripartite pact and Japanese withdrawal of troops from China.

The United States now stiffened its policy. This was based upon a miscalculation: Washington considered that by taking a strong position it could deter the Japanese from a further southward thrust, which threatened Britain's colonial empire in the Far East. The decision to institute a full embargo was part of the same miscalculation.[48]

As shown by the first summit meeting between President Roosevelt and Winston Churchill, the British Prime Minister, at Placentia Bay, Newfoundland in August 1941,[49] American attention focussed on all-out aid to Britain, while Britain desired America's entry into the war against Hitler. Preoccupied with developments in the Atlantic, Roosevelt hoped to defer a war in the Pacific for as long as he could.

The last desperate means proposed by Prime Minister Konoe to bring about a breakthrough was to hold a summit meeting with Roosevelt. Konoe's idea was to offer the United States drastic concessions without regard to the policy of Japan's military and naval leaders, reach a peaceful settlement and immediately obtain the sanction of the Emperor, who would order army minister Tōjō Hideki to avoid war.[50] In early October the summit meeting plan was rejected by Cordell Hull, Roosevelt's inflexible secretary of state, who insisted on an advance agreement concerning basic principles. Japanese historians have speculated whether war with the United States could have been prevented, had Washington accepted Konoe's proposal. According to one authority, if Konoe had succeeded in gaining time by some *modus vivendi* with Roosevelt, weather conditions would have made it nearly impossible to launch a surprise attack on Pearl Harbor.[51]

The failure of the proposal for a summit meeting further increased army pressure to terminate negotiations. In mid-October the Konoe Cabinet resigned, and General Tōjō became Prime Minister while concurrently serving as army minister.

In any war with the United States the navy would play a major role, and conceivably could have restrained the army by unequivocally stating that it was in no position to fight the United States. In fact, at the Five Ministers' Conference in 1938, navy minister Yonai Mitsumasa had declared flatly that there was no chance of Japan's winning a conflict of this nature – the Japanese navy was 'simply not designed to fight a war with America and Britain'.[52] The dilemma the navy leaders faced in the autumn of 1941 was that the navy had meanwhile increased its armaments by emphatically calling the United States its 'hypothetical enemy' and advocating a southward expansion. Since the autumn of 1940 the navy had demanded and obtained budget priority in allocation of *matériel*, and it was now impossible to declare itself unprepared to fight the United States without jeopardising its position *vis-à-vis* the army. As navy minister Oikawa Koshirō later apologetically explained, 'after so many years of clamouring about its "invincible fleet", the navy was hardly in a position to say it was not prepared for war with the United States.[53]

By October 1941 some navy leaders had become determined to fight the United States. Oka Takasumi, chief of the naval affairs bureau, wrote in his diary (14 October): 'The navy is confident about success in the first phase of the operations against the United States'. The new navy minister, Shimada Shigetarō, was even more bellicose: 'Unless hostilities are commenced immediately', he wrote in his diary of 30 October, 'we shall lose the opportunity to strike'. On the same day Shimada gathered the high-ranking navy leaders and informed them of his determination to start a war. The Imperial Conference of 5 November adopted a final national policy: hostilities must be commenced if diplomatic negotiations did not produce a peaceful settlement by the end of November.[55] No army or naval officers of consequence had any illusion about a successful diplomatic adjustment. Already on 6 September, immediately after the Imperial Conference of that day, Commander Fujii – an ardent advocate of southward expansion – had drunk a toast with his colleague in the First Committee, Commander Shiba Katsuo[56]

> On this very day two years ago [Fujii wrote in his diary], we made a decision not to interfere in the European War. Today, we made a new decision [for hostilities with the United States, with a time limit]. We gave ourselves up to deep emotion.[54]

Neither officer, it seems, was prepared to consider the possibility that what they thought was an occasion for celebration would turn out to be a prelude to the catastrophes of war and defeat.

NOTES AND REFERENCES

1. Most of these archival and manuscript materials are deposited in the War History Department, Japanese Self Defence Agency (hereafter abbreviated as JDA Archives).
2. James William Morley (ed.), *The Fateful Choice: Japan's Advance into Southeast Asia, 1939–1941* (New York, 1980). This volume is a selective translation of Nihon Kokusai Seiji Gakkai ([The Japan Association of International Relations] (ed.), *Taiheiyō sensō no michi: kaisen gaikō shi* (The road to the Pacific War: A diplomatic history of the origins of the war (Tokyo, 1963), vols. 6 and 7. (Hereafter abbreviated as *TSM*.) To this date, this work remains the most detailed and authoritative study of the subject. In addition, see Akira Iriye, 'The Failure of Military Expansionism' in James W. Morley (ed.), *Dilemmas of Growth in Prewar Japan* (Princeton, 1971), pp. 107–38. This article presents a lucid analysis of the gaps between Japanese leaders' perception and international realities. The most recent monograph is Murakami Sachiko's Ph.D. dissertation, 'Japan's Thrust into French–Indochina, 1940–1945, submitted to City University of New York. (It was privately published in Japanese translation as *Futu-In shinchū* in 1984.) It makes extensive use of hitherto unused French materials.
3. Sadao Asada, 'The Japanese Navy and the United States', in Dorothy Borg and Shumpei Okamoto (eds.), *Pearl Harbor as History: Japanese–American Relations, 1931–1941* (New York, 1973), p. 235. Hereafter cited as Asada, 'The Japanese Navy'.
4. The creation of this committee was prompted by middle-echelon officers (like Captain Nakahara Yoshimasa and Commander Chūdō Kan'ei) who advocated an aggressive southern policy. The primary task of this committee was to study the strategic importance of South-East Asia and the means for Japan's advance into that area. The results of this study

became the basis for preparing the navy's draft of the 'Fundamentals of National Policy'. For details, see Hatano Sumio, 'Nihon kaigun to "nanshin"' (The Japanese navy and southward advance', in Shimizu Hajime (ed.), *Ryō taisenkan ki Nihon–Tōnan Ajia kankei no shosō* (Aspects of relations between Japan and South-East Asia in the inter-war period). (Tokyo, 1986), pp. 217–20. Ōkubo Tatsumasa et al (eds.), *Shōwa shakai keizai shiryō shūsei, Kaigunshō shiryō* (Collection of materials relating to the social and economic history of the Shōwa period: Documents of the Navy Minstry) (Tokyo, Tōyō kenkyūjo), vol. 2 (1978), 282–305, 343; vol. 3 (1978), pp. (1)–(3). (Hereafter cited as Ōkubo, *Kaigunshō shiryō.*)

5. In accordance with Japanese usage, Japanese names are given with the surname first (with the exception of the co-authors of this essay and Akira Iriye).

6. Diary of Rear Admiral Nakahara Yoshimasa, 15 January 1940, JDA.

7. This description of Japan's reaction to the outbreak of the war in Europe is based on the Japanese Foreign Ministry Archives (hereafter abbreviated as JFM Archives). A. 1.1. 0. 30 'Shina jihen shori ni kansuru seisaku' (Policy relating to the settlement of the China Incident), 3 vols.; and A. 1.0.0.6 'Teikoku tai-nanpō seisaku kankei ikken' (File relating to the Japanese Empire's policy toward the south).

8. *TSM: Bekkan shiryō-hen* (Supplementary volume: Documents), 99, 315–16; Japanese Monograph no. 146, published as *War in Asia and the Pacific, Vol. 2: Political Background of the War* (New York and London, 1980), pp. 13–20.

9. Asada, 'The Japanese Navy', p. 251.

10. For these peace manoeuvres, see John Hunter Boyle, *China and Japan at War, 1937–1945: The Politics of Collaboration* (Stanford, 1972), *passim*.

11. For details on the relationship between the Kiri Project and the decision to move south, see Hatano Sumio, 'Nanshin e no senkai, 1940' (Switching to a policy of advancing south, 1940), *Ajia keizai*, IIVI, no. 5 (May 1985), pp. 30–33.

12. Morimatsu Toshio (ed.), *Sanbō jichō Sawada Shigeru kaisōroku* (Recollections of Vice-Chief of the Army General Staff Sawada Shigeru (Tokyo, 1982), pp. 172–73.

13. For a detailed account tracing the formulation of the 'Outline of the Main Principles for Coping with the Changing World Situation', see Hata Ikuhiko, in Morley (ed.), *The Fateful Choice*, pp. 247–49, 250–53.

14. Telegram from the chief of staff, 2nd China Fleet, to vice-chief of the navy general staff, 19 June 1940 (contained in navy general staff, ed., 'Futsu-In mondai keii' (Circumstances relating to the French Indochina question), vol. 1, JDA Archives.

15. Ōkubo, *Kaigunshō shiryō* (1985), X, pp. 300–306.

16. The unpublished recollections of Major General Tsuchihashi Yūichi,

chief of the information division, army general staff, JDA; Lieutenant Colonel Kōtani Etsuo, a staff member of its Russian Section gives his account in his own article, 'Rekishi to tomo ni ayunde' (The path I followed in the course of history), *Gunji shigaku*, II, No. 4 (March 1967), pp. 91–93.

17. Navy general staff, 'Shōwa 15-nen Shina jihen shori yōkō tsuzuri' (Files relating to settlement of the China Incident, 1940), Part I, JDA Archives.

18. Army general staff, 'Kokusai jōhō geppō' (Monthly report on the international situation), no. 20 (25 September 1940); no. 21 (25 October 1940).

19. The first study to emphasise the role of the First Committee is Tsunoda Jun, 'Nihon no tai-Bei kaisen, 1940–1941' (Japan's decision for war with the United States, 1940–41) in *TSM*, vol. 7. According to Tsunoda, it was the pro-Axis, anti-American members of the First Committee who pressed for an armed southern advance with the realisation that it would lead to war with the United States. See also Asada, 'The Japanese Navy', pp. 233–34. Official naval historians, most notably Nomura Minoru, minimise the influence of the First Committee on the navy's decision-making process. Nomura regards this committee merely as a niche for Captain Ishikawa Shingo who led it with his bellicose self-assertations. Bōeichō Senshishitsu, *Senshi sōsho, Daihen'ei kaigunbu: Rengō kantai, I: kaisen made* (War History Series: Imperial Headquarters, Navy: The Combined Fleet, vol. I: Up to the outbreak of the war) (Tokyo, 1976) pp. 495–96. See also Ikeda Kiyoshi, 'The Japanese View of the Royal Navy', in Ian Nish (ed.), *International Studies* 1985/3: *Anglo–Japanese Naval Relations*, pp. 1–9.

21. On 11 November 1940 the British steamer *Automedon* was intercepted by the German raider *Atlantis* off the Nicobar Islands in the Indian Ocean. Among the 60 packages of mail seized was a copy of the War Cabinet minutes for 8 August 1940, including the highly secret chiefs of staff report, which was being sent to the commander-in-chief Far East, Robert Brooke-Popham. After having sunk the *Automedon*, the *Atlantis* reached Kobe on 4 December. James Rusbridger, 'The Sinking of the "Automedon", the Capture of "Nankin"', *Encounter* LIV (May 1985) p. 10. For the background of the War Cabinet minutes, see Peter Lowe, *Great Britain and the Origins of the Pacific War: A Study of British Policy in East Asia 1937–1941* (Oxford, 1977), pp. 160–65.

22. John W.M. Chapman, edited and translated, *The Price of Admiralty: The War Diary of the German Naval Attaché in Japan, 1939–1943*, vols. II & III (East Sussex, 1984), pp. 333–34.

23. The first Japanese scholar to write on the '*Automedon* affair' and its impact on Japan's southern policy is Ikeda Kiyoshi, 'Aru jōhōsen: Wennekā senji nisshi o yonde' (An episode in intelligence warfare: On

the wartime journal of Paul Wennecker), Nihon Bunka Kaigi (ed.), *Bunka kaigi* (March 1986) pp. 14–19. Sanbō Honbu (ed.), *Sugiyama memo*, (Tokyo, 1967), vol. 1, p. 157.

24. Morley (ed.), *Fateful Choice*, pp. 227–32; Arthur J. Marder, *Old Friends, New Enemies: The Royal Navy and the Imperial Japanese Navy, 1936–1941* (Oxford, 1981), pp.156–57.

25. Diary of Fujii Shigeru, 25 June 1941, p. 127, JDA.

26. Marder, pp. 185–87.

27. Diary of Fujii, p. 180.

28. Sanbō Honbu Sensō Shidōhan (war guidance section, the army general staff), 'Kimitsu sensō nisshi' (Secret war journal), 5 April 1941, JDA.

29. The English translation is printed in Morley (ed.), *Fateful Choice*, pp. 303–304. For a good analysis, see James Crowley, 'Japan's Military Foreign Policies', in James W. Morley (ed.), *Japan's Foreign Policy, 1868–1941: A Research Guide* (New York, 1974), pp. 91–93.

30. Diary of Fujii, p. 125.

31. Robert J.C. Butow, *The John Doe Associates: Backdoor Diplomacy for Peace, 1941* (Stanford, 1974).

32. Gaimushō (Japanese Foreign Ministry) (ed.), *Nichi–Bei kōshō shiryō* (Documents on Japanese–American Negotiations, 1941) (Tokyo, 1979), p. 26; Diary of Fujii, pp. 71–73.

33. The best treatment of the way in which Matsuoka's attitude toward the United States was shaped by his personal experiences in Oregon is Hosoya Chihiro, 'Matsuoka Yōsuke', in Hayashi Shigeru (ed.), *Jinbutsu Nihon no rekishi* (Japanese history through personalities), vol. 14 (Tokyo, 1966), pp. 176–211; see also Hosoya, 'The Tripartite Pact', in James W. Morley (ed.), *Deterrent Diplomacy: Japan, Germany, and the USSR, 1935–1940* (New York, 1976), pp. 191–257, *passim*.

34. The most detailed treatment of Matsuoka's 'grand design' for a four-power pact is contained in Hosoya, 'The Japanese–Soviet Neutrality Pact', in Morley (ed.), *The Fateful Choice*, pp. 3–114, *passim*.

35. Asada, 'The Japanese Navy', p. 253.

36. Diary of Fujii, p. 188.

37. Ambassador Ōshima to Foreign Minister Matsuoka, no. 636 (sent on 4 June 1941); nos. 638, 639 (sent on 5 June). (Contained in the papers of Konoe Fumimaro, at Yōmei Bunko, Kyoto).

38. The content of this letter to Matsuoka is confirmed by the diary of Ishikawa Shingo, 19 June 1941, JDA.

39. Asada, 'The Japanese Navy', p. 253.

40. Nobutaka Ike (translated, edited, with an introduction), *Japan's Decision for War: Records of the 1941 Policy Conferences* (Stanford, 1967), pp. 77–90.

41. 'Documents Relating to the Outbreak of War with Japan', p. 46, Foreign Office Archives, Public Record Office; Peter Lowe, *Great Britain and the Origins of the Pacific War: A Study of British Policy in East Asia,*

1937–1941 (Oxford, 1971), pp. 236–40; Lowe, 'Great Britain and the Coming of the Pacific War', *Transactions of the Royal Historical Society*, 5th Series, vol. 24, 1974, p. 57.

42. From the Burma Road Crisis to Pearl Harbor', memorandum by the Far Eastern Department, FO 371/35957, F 26–21 S21/G, p. 46, PRO. A recent study reveals that President Roosevelt had not intended the freeze to result in a total embargo, because he was aware that it might compel Japan to attack the Dutch East Indies or even United States territories. It was the 'hawks' in the foreign policy bureaucracy who converted a rather limited measure into an all-out oil embargo. Jonathan G. Utley, *Going to War with Japan* (Knoxville, Tennessee, 1985) pp. 151–56. See also: Irvine H. Anderson, Jr., *The Standard–Vacuum Oil Company and United States East Asian Policy, 1933–1941* (Princeton, 1975), pp. 158–200.

43. Asada, 'The Japanese Navy', p. 253.

44. *Ibid*, p. 154.

45. Nomura Minoru, 'Japan's Plans for World War II, *Revue Internationale d'Historire Militaire*, no. 38 (1978), pp. 210–11.

46. Diary of Fujii, pp. 243–44.

47. Ike, *Japan's Decision*, pp. 133–63.

48. Hosoya Chihiro, 'Miscalculation in Deterrent Policy: Japanese-U.S. Relations, 1938–1941', *Journal of Peace Research*, no. 2 (1968), pp. 97–115.

49. Theodore A. Wilson, *The First Summit: Roosevelt and Churchill at Placentia Bay, 1941* (Boston, 1969).

50. Hosoya Chihiro, *et al*. (eds.), *Nichi–Bei kankeishi: Kaisen ni itaru 10–nen (1931–41)* (Japanese–American relations: Ten years prior to the war, 1931–41) (Tokyo, 1971), vol. 1, pp. 298–99.

51. Hosoya Chihiro, 'Taiheiyō sensō wa sakeraretaka?' (Could the Pacific War be avoided?), *Rekishi to jinbutsu* (July 1973), pp. 30–47.

52. Quoted in Asada, 'The Japanese Navy', p. 247.

53. *Ibid*, pp. 249, 255.

54. Diary of Fujii, p. 260.

Bibliography

The following select list, with a few exceptions, is restricted to books published since 1970 and is intended simply as an aid to further study.

GENERAL

Adamthwaite, Anthony. *The Making of the Second World War* (London, 1977)

Aster, Sidney. *1939: The Making of the Second World War* (London, 1973)

Bariéty, Jacques. *Les relations franco–allemandes après la première guerre mondiale* (Paris, 1977)

Baumont, Maurice. *The Origins of the Second World War* (New Haven CN, 1978)

Carr, William. *Poland to Pearl Harbor. The Making of the Second World War* (London, 1985)

Douglas, Roy. *The Advent of War, 1939–1940* (London, 1978)

— , ed. *1939: A Retrospective Forty Years After* (London, 1983)

Forstmeier, Friedrich and Hans-Erich Volkmann, eds. *Wirtschaft und Rüstung am Vorabend des Zweiten Weltkrieges* (Düsseldorf, 1975)

Gatzke, Hans W., ed. *European Diplomacy between Two Wars, 1919–1939* (Chicago, 1972)

Hauser, Oswald, ed. *Weltpolitik 1933–1939: 13 Vorträge* (Göttingen, 1973)

Jacobson, Jon. *Locarno Diplomacy: Germany and the West, 1925–1929* (Princeton, 1972)

Louis,William Roger, ed. *The Origins of the Second World War: A.J.P.Taylor and his Critics* (New York, 1972)

McDougall, Walter A. *France's Rhineland Diplomacy, 1914–1924: The Last Bid for a Balance of Power in Europe* (Princeton, 1978)

Martel, Gordon, ed. *The Origins of the Second World War Reconsidered The A.J.P. Taylor debate after twenty-five years* (London, 1986).

Mommsen, Wolfgang and Lothar Kettenacker, eds. *The Fascist Challenge and the Policy of Appeasement* (London, 1983)

Remak, Joachim. *The Origins of the Second World War* (Englewood Cliffs, NJ, 1976)

Robertson, Esmonde M., ed. *The Origins of the Second World War: Historical Interpretations* (London, 1971)

Sked, Alan, and Chris Cook, eds. *Crisis and Controversy: Essays in Honour of A.J.P. Taylor* (London, 1976)

Taylor, A.J.P. *The Origins of the Second World War*, 2nd ed. (New York, 1966)

THE EUROPEAN CRISIS

Adamthwaite, Anthony. *The Lost Peace. International Relations in Europe, 1918–1939* (London, 1980)

Baer, George W. *Test Case: Italy, Ethiopia, and the League of Nations* (Stanford, 1977)

Bell, P.M.H. *The Origins of the Second World War in Europe* (London, 1986)

Benz, Wolfgang and Hermann Graml, ed. *Sommer 1939: Die Grossmächte und der Europaische Krieg* (Stuttgart, 1979)

Bond, Brian. *France and Belgium, 1939–1940* (London, 1975)

Bruegel, J.W. *Czechoslovakia before Munich: The Germany Minority Problem and British Appeasement Policy* (Cambridge, 1973)

Brundu, Olla P. *L'equilibrio difficile:Gran Bretagna, Italia e Francia nel Mediterraneo 1930–1937* (Milan, 1980)

Emmerson, James T. *The Rhineland Crisis of 7 March 1936: A Study in Multilateral Diplomacy* (London, 1977)

Funke, Manfred. *Sanktionen und Kanonen: Hitler, Mussolini und der Abessinienkonflikt 1934–1936* (Düsseldorf, 1970)

Girault, René and Robert Frank, eds. *La Puissance en Europe, 1938–1940* (Paris, 1984)

Haraszti, Eva H. *Treaty-Breakers or 'Realpolitiker'? The Anglo–German Naval Agreement of June 1935*, trans. by S. Simon (Boppard-am-Rhein, 1973)

Hardie, Frank M. *The Abyssinian Crisis* (London, 1974)

Kaiser, David E. *Economic Diplomacy and the Origins of the Second World War: Germany, Britain, France, and Eastern Europe, 1930–1939* (Princeton, 1980)

Kieft, David O. *Belgium's Return to Neutrality* (London, 1972)

Little, Douglas, *Malevolent Neutrality: The United States, Great Britain, and the Origins of the Spanish Civil War* (Ithaca NY, 1985)

Lowe, Alfred D. *The Anschluss Movement, 1931–1938, and the Great Powers* (London, 1985)

Lukacs, John A. *The Last European War: September 1939–December 1941* (London, 1976)

Munch-Petersen, Thomas. *The Strategy of Phoney War: Britain, Sweden and the Iron Ore Question, 1939–1940* (Stockholm, 1980)

Riekoff, Harald von. *German–Polish Relations, 1918–1933* (Baltimore, 1971)

Rostow, Nicholas. *Anglo–French Relations, 1934–1936* (London, 1984)

Taylor, Telford. *Munich: The Price of Peace* (London, 1979)

THE FAR EASTERN CRISIS

Borg, Dorothy, and Shumpei Okamoto, eds. *Pearl Harbor as History: Japanese–American Relations, 1931–1941* (New York, 1973)

Boyle, John H. *Japan and China at War: The Politics of Collaboration* (Stanford, 1972)

Bunker, Gerald E. *The Peace Conspiracy: Wang Ching-Wei and the China War, 1937–1941* (Cambridge MA, 1972)

Butow, Robert J.C. *The John Doe Associates: Backdoor Diplomacy for Peace, 1941* (Stanford, 1974)

Fox, John P. *Germany and the Far Eastern Crisis, 1931–1938. A Study in Diplomacy and Ideology* (Oxford, 1982)

Herzog, James H. *Closing the Open Door: American–Japanese Diplomatic Negotiations, 1936–1941* (Annapolis MD, 1973)

Iriye, Akira. *The Origins of the Second World War in Asia and the Pacific* (London, 1986)

Issraeljan, V. and L. Kutakov. *Diplomacy of Aggression: Berlin–Rome–Tokyo Axis. Its Rise and Fall* (Moscow, 1970)

Marder, Arthur J. *Old Friends, New Enemies: The Royal Navy and the Imperial Japanese Navy: Strategic Illusions, 1936–1941* (Oxford, 1981)

Morley, James William, ed. *Deterrent Diplomacy: Japan, Germany, and the USSR. 1935–1940* (New York, 1976)

Nish, Ian, ed., *Anglo-Japanese Alienation, 1919–1952* (Cambridge, 1982)

Shai, Aron. *The Origin of the War in the East: Britain, China and Japan, 1937–1941* (London, 1976)

Thorne, Christopher. *The Limits of Foreign Policy: The West, the League and the Far Eastern Crisis of 1931–1933* (London, 1972)

MILITARY AND INTELLIGENCE, GENERAL

Andrew, Christopher and David Dilks, eds. *The Missing Dimension. Governments and Intelligence Communities in the Twentieth Century* (London, 1984)

May, Ernest R., ed. *Knowing One's Enemies: Intelligence Assessment before the Two World Wars* (Princeton, 1984)

Murray, Williamson. *The Change in the European Balance of Power, 1938–1939. The Path to Ruin* (Princeton NJ, 1984)

Posen, B.R. *The Sources of Military Doctrine: France, Britain and Germany between the World Wars* (Ithaca NY, 1985)

Preston, Adrian, ed. *General Staffs and Diplomacy before the Second World War* (London, 1974)

Watt, Donald Cameron. *Too Serious a Business: European Armed Forces and the Approach to the Second World War* (London, 1975)

BRITAIN AND THE BRITISH EMPIRE

Andrew, Christopher. *Secret Service. The Making of the British Intelligence Community* (London, 1985)

Barnett, Correlli. *The Collapse of British Power* (London, 1972)

Bialer, Uri. *The Shadow of the Bomber: The Fear of Air Attack and British Politics, 1932–1939* (London, 1980)

Bond, Brian. *British Military Policy between the Two World Wars* (Oxford, 1980)

Boyce, Robert W.D. *British Capitalism at the Crossroads, 1919–1932. A Study in Politics, Economics and International Relations* (Cambridge, 1987)

Carlton, David. *Anthony Eden, a Biography* (London, 1981)

Cowling, Maurice. *The Impact of Hitler: British Politics and British Strategy, 1933–1940* (London, 1975)

Dennis, Peter. *Decision by Default: Peacetime Conscription and British Defense. 1919–1939* (London, 1972)

Dilks, David, ed. *Retreat from Power: Studies in Britain's Foreign Policy of the Twentieth Century*, vol. 1, *1906–1939* (London, 1981)

Edwards, Jill. *The British Government and the Spanish Civil War, 1936–1939* (London, 1979)

Gannon, Franklin R. *The British Press and Germany, 1936–1939* (Oxford, 1971)

Gibbs, Norman H. *Grand Strategy*, vol. 1: Rearmament Policy (London, 1976)

Haggie, Paul. *Britannia at Bay: The Defence of the British Empire against Japan, 1931–1941* (Oxford, 1981)

Hillmer, Norman and Robert Bothwell, eds. *The In-Between Time: Canadian External Policy in the 1930s* (Toronto, 1975)

Hinsley, F.H. et al. *British Intelligence in the Second World War*, vol. 1 (London, 1979)

Howard, Michael. *The Continental Commitment: The Dilemma of British Defence Policy in the Era of the Two World Wars* (London, 1972)

Kennedy, Paul. *The Realities Behind Diplomacy. Background Influences on British External Policy, 1865–1980* (London, 1981)

Lee, Bradford A. *Britain and the Sino–Japanese War, 1937–1939: A Study in the Dilemmas of British Decline* (Stanford, 1973)

Louis, William Roger. *British Strategy in the Far East, 1919–1939* (Oxford, 1971)

Lowe, Peter. *Great Britain and the Origins of the Pacific War: A Study of British Policy in East Asia, 1937–1941* (Oxford, 1977)

McIntyre, W.D. *The Rise and Fall of the Singapore Naval Base* (London, 1979)

Meyers, Reinhard. *Britische Sicherheitspolitik 1934–1938* (Düsseldorf, 1976)

Middlemas, Keith. *Diplomacy of Illusion: The British Government and Germany, 1937–39* (London, 1972)

Neidpath, James. *The Singapore Naval Base and the Defence of Britain's Eastern Empire, 1919–1941* (Oxford, 1981)

Newmann, Simon K. *March 1939: The British Guarantee to Poland – A Study in the Continuity of British Policy* (Oxford, 1976)

Ovendale, Ritchie. *'Appeasement' and the English Speaking World. Britain, the United States, the Dominions, and the Policy of 'Appeasement' 1937–1939* (Cardiff, 1975).

Peden, George C. *British Rearmament and the Treasury, 1932–1939* (Edinburgh, 1979)

Peters, A.R. *Anthony Eden at the Foreign Office, 1931–1938* (Aldershot, 1986)

Powers, Barry. *Strategy without Slide-Rule: British Air Strategy, 1914–1939* (London, 1976)

Pratt, Lawrence R. *East of Malta, West of Suez: Britain's Mediterranean Crisis, 1936–1939* (Cambridge, 1975)

Pritchard, R. John. *Far Eastern Influences upon British Strategy towards the Great Powers, 1937–1939* (New York, 1986)

Roskill, Stephen. *Naval Policy between the Wars*, 2 vols. (London, 1968, 1976)

— , *Hankey, Man of Secrets*, vol. 3 (London, 1974)

Schmidt, Gustav. *The Politics and Economics of Appeasement: British Foreign Policy in the 1930s* (London, 1986)

Shay, Robert P. Jr. *British Rearmament in the Thirties: Politics and Profits* (Princeton, 1977)

Smith, Malcolm S. *British Air Strategy between the Wars* (Oxford, 1984)

Stacey, C.P. *Canada and the Age of Conflict*, vol. 2, *1919–1941* (Toronto, 1981)

Thompson, Neville. *The Anti-Appeasers. Conservative Opposition to Appeasement in the 1930s* (Oxford, 1971)

Trotter, Anne. *Britain and East Asia, 1933–1937* (Cambridge, 1975)

Waley, Daniel P. *British Public Opinion and the Abyssinian War, 1935–1936* (London, 1975)

Wark, Wesley K. *The Ultimate Enemy: British Intelligence and Nazi Germany, 1933–1939* (London, 1985)

Wendt, Berndt Jürgen. *Economic Appeasement: Handel und Finanzen in der britischen Deutschlandspolitik 1933–1939* (Düsseldorf, 1971)

FRANCE

Adamthwaite, Anthony. *France and the Coming of the Second World War, 1936–1939* (London, 1977)

Duroselle, Jean-Baptiste. *La politique étrangère de la France: La décadence, 1932–1939* (Paris, 1979)

Dreifort, John E. *Yvon Delbos at the Quai d'Orsay: French Foreign Policy during the Popular Front, 1936–38* (Lawrence, 1973)

Frankenstein, Robert. *Le prix du réarmement français 1935–1939* (Paris, 1982)

Gates, Eleanor M. *End of the Affair: The Collapse of the Anglo–French Alliance, 1939–1940* (Berkeley, 1980)

Gunsberg, Jeffrey A. *Divided and Conquered: The French High Command and the Defeat of the West, 1940* (Westport CN, 1979)

Néré, J. *The Foreign Policy of France from 1914 to 1945* (London, 1975)

Paillole, Paul. *Services Spéciaux, 1935–1945* (Paris, 1975)

Rémond, René and Jean Bourdin, eds. *Edouard Daladier, chef de gouvernement (avril 1938–septembre 1939* (Paris, 1977)

Vaisse, Maurice. *Sécurité d'abord. La politique française en matière de désarmement, 9 décembre 1930–17 avril 1934* (Paris, 1981)

Young, Robert J. *In Command of France: French Foreign Policy and Military Planning, 1933–1940* (Cambridge MA, 1978)

GERMANY

Burleigh, Michael. *Germany Turns Eastwards: A Study of Ostforschung in theThird Reich* (Cambridge, 1988)

Carr, William. *Arms, Autarky, and Aggression: A Study in German Foreign Policy, 1933–1939*, 2nd ed. (London, 1979)

— . *Hitler. A Study in Personality and Politics* (London, 1978)

Deist, Wilhelm. *The Wehrmacht and German Rearmament* (London, 1981)

— , Manfred Messerschmidt, Hans-Erich Volkmann, and Wolfram Wette (eds.) *Das Deutsche Reich und der Zweite Weltkrieg.* vol. 1 (Stuttgart, 1979)

Deutsch, Carl. *Hitler and his Generals: The Hidden Crisis, January–June 1938* (Minneapolis, 1974)

Dülffer, Jost. *Weimar, Hitler und die Marine: Reichspolitik und Flottenbau 1920–1939* (Düsseldorf, 1973)

Forstmeier, F. and H.E. Volkmann, eds. *Wirtschaft und Rustung am Vorabend des Zweiten Weltkrieges* (Düsseldorf, 1975)

Funke, Manfred, ed. *Hitler, Deutschland und die Mächte: Materialien zur Aussenpolitik des Dritten Reiches* (Düsseldorf, 1976)

Heineman, John L. *Hitler's First Foreign Minister: Constantin von Neurath* (Berkeley, 1980)

Henke, Josef. *England in Hitlers politischen Kalkül 1935–1939* (Boppard-am-Rhein, 1973)

Herwig, Holger H. *The Politics of Frustration: The United States in German Naval Planning, 1889–1941* (Boston, 1976)

Hiden, John. *Germany and Europe, 1919–1939* (London, 1979)

Hildebrand, Klaus. *The Foreign Policy of the Third Reich*, trans. by Anthony Fothergill (London, 1973)

Hillgruber, Andreas. *Germany and the Two World Wars*, trans. by William C. Kirby (London, 1981)

Hirschfeld, Gerhard and Lothar Kettenacker, eds. *The 'Fuhrer State': Myth and Reality* (Stuttgart, 1981)

Hoffmann, Peter. *The History of the German Resistance, 1933–1945*, trans. by Richard Barry (London, 1977)

Homze, Edward L. *Arming the Luftwaffe. The Reich Air Ministry and the German Aircraft Industry, 1919–39* (Lincoln NB, 1976)

Jäckel, Eberhard. *Hitler's Weltanschauung. A Blueprint for Power*, trans. by Herbert Arnold (Middletown CN, 1972)

Jacobsen, Hans-Adolf. *National-sozialistische Aussenpolitik 1933–1939* (Frankfort-am-Main, 1968)

Kershaw, Ian. *The Nazi Dictatorship. Problems and Perspectives of Interpretation* (London, 1985)

Kuhn, Axel. *Hitlers aussenpolitisches Programm: Entstehung und Entwicklung 1919–1939* (Stuttgart, 1970)

Leach, Barry A. *German Strategy against Russia, 1939–1941* (Oxford, 1973)

Michalka, Wolfgang, *Ribbentrop und die deutsche Weltpolitik 1933–1940* (Münster, 1980)

— ed. *Nationalsozialistischen Aussenpolitik* (Darmstadt, 1978)

Milward, Alan. *The German Economy at War* (London, 1965)

Overy, Richard. *Goering: the 'Iron Man'* (London, 1984)

Petersen, Jens. *Hitler–Mussolini: Der Entstehung der Achse Berlin–Rom 1933–1936* (Tübingen, 1973)

Rich, Norman. *Hitler's War Aims: Ideology, the Nazi State, and the Course of Expansion*, 2 vols. (London, 1973, 1974)

Seaton, Albert. *The German Army, 1933–1945* (London, 1982)

Schroder, Hans-Jürgen. *Deutschland und die Vereinigten Staaten 1933–1939: Wirtschaft und Politik in der Entwicklung des deutsch–amerikanischen Gegensatzes* (Wiesbaden, 1970)

Smelser, Ronald M. *The Sudeten Problem 1933–1938: Volkstumspolitik and the Formulation of Nazi Foreign Policy* (Folkestone, 1975)

Van Creveld, Martin L. *Hitler's Strategy, 1940–1941: The Balkan Clue* (London, 1973)

Weinberg, Gerhard L. *The Foreign Policy of Hitler's Germany*, Vol. 1, *Diplomatic Revolution in Europe, 1933–1936*; Vol. 2, *Starting World War Two, 1937–1939* (London, 1970, 1980)

ITALY

Brundu Olla, Paola. *L'equilibrio difficile: Gran Bretagna, Italia, e Francia nel Mediterraneo 1930–1937* (Milan, 1980)

Ciano, Galeazzo. *Diario, 1937–1943* (Milan, 1980)

Coverdale, John F. *Italian Intervention in the Spanish Civil War* (Princeton, 1976)

Felice, Renzo de. *Mussolini il Duce*, 2 vols., Vol. 1, *Gli anni del consenso*

1929–1936; Vol. 2, *La Stato totalitario 1936–1940* (Turin, 1974, 1981)

Ferretti, Valdo. *Il Giappone e la politica estera italiana 1935–41* (Rome, 1983)

Giordano, G. *Il Patto a Quattro nella politica estera di Mussolini* (Bologna, 1976)

Guerri, Giordano B. *Galeazzo Ciano, una vita 1903–1944* (Milan, 1979)

Knox, Bernard MacGregor. *Mussolini Unleashed, 1939–1941: Politics and Strategy in Fascist Italy's Last War* (Cambridge MA, 1982)

Lowe, Cedric J. and Frank Marzari. *Italian Foreign Policy, 1870–1940* (London, 1975)

Mack Smith, Denis. *Mussolini's Roman Empire* (London, 1976)

— . *Mussolini* (London, 1981)

Mazzetti, Massimo. *La politica militare italiana fra le due guerre mondiali (1918–1940)* (Salerno, 1974)

Michaelis, Meir. *Mussolini and the Jews: German–Italian Relations and the Jewish Question in Italy, 1922–1945* (Oxford, 1978)

Mori, Renato. *Mussolini e la conquista dell'Etiopia* (Florence, 1978)

Quartarero, Rosaria. *Roma tra Londra e Berlino: Politica estera fascista dal 1930 al 1940* (Rome, 1980)

Robertson, Esmonde M. *Mussolini as Empire-Builder: Europe and Africa, 1932–1936* (London, 1977)

Sarti, Roland. *The Ax Within. Italian Fascism in Action* (New York, 1974)

Toscano, Mario. *The Origins of the Pact of Steel*, 2nd ed. (Baltimore, 1967)

JAPAN

Barnhart, Michael A. *Japan Prepares for Total War: The Search for Economic Security, 1919–1941* (London, 1987)

Bergamini, David. *Japan's Imperial Conspiracy: How Emperor Hirohito Led Japan into War against the West* (New York, 1971)

Chapman, J.W.M., R. Drifte and I.T.M. Gow. *Japan's Quest for Comprehensive Security: Defence, Diplomacy, Dependence* (London, 1983)

Ienaga, Saburo. *Japan's Last War* (London, 1979)

Jones, F.C. *Japan's New Order in the Far East, 1919–1939* (Oxford, 1971)

Kyozo, Sato. *Japan and Britain at the Crossroads, 1939–1941: A Study in the Dilemmas of Japanese Diplomacy* (Tokyo, 1986)

Kutakov, Leonid N. *Japanese Foreign Policy on the Eve of the Pacific War: A Soviet View* (Florida, 1972)

Minear, Richard. *Victor's Justice: The Tokyo War Crimes Trial* (Princeton, 1971)

Morley, James W., ed. *Dilemmas of Growth in Pre-war Japan* (Princeton, 1971)

— , ed. *The China Quagmire: Japan's Expansion on the Asian Continent* (New York, 1974)

— , ed. *The Fateful Choice: Japan's Advance into Southeast Asia, 1939–1941* (New York, 1980)

Nish, Ian. *Japanese Foreign Policy, 1869–1942: Kasumigaseki to Miyakezaka* (London, 1977)

Peattie, Mark R. *Ishiwara Kanji and Japan's Confrontation with the West* (Princeton, 1975)

Shillony, Ben-Ami. *Revolt in Japan: The Young Officers and the February 26, 1936 Incident* (Princeton, 1973)

Storry, Richard. *Japan and the Decline of the West in Asia, 1894–1943* (London, 1979)

Titus, David A. *Palace and Politics in Pre-war Japan* (New York, 1974)

Toland, John. *The Rising Sun: The Decline and Fall of the Japanese Empire, 1936–1945* (New York, 1970)

POLAND

Ciencala, Anna Maria. *Poland and the Western Powers, 1938–1939: A Study in the Interdependence of Eastern and Western Europe* (London, 1968)

Korczynski, Alexander and Tadeusz Swietochowski, eds. Poland between Germany and Russia, 1926–1939: The Theory of Two Enemies (New York, 1975)

Lipski, Jozef. *Diplomat in Berlin, 1933–1939: Papers and Memoirs of Jozef Lipski, Ambassador of Poland* (New York, 1968)

Lukasiewicz, Juliusz. *Diplomat in Paris 1936–1939: Memoirs of Juliusz Lukasiewicz, Ambassador of Poland* (New York, 1970)

Biddle, A.J. Drexel Jr. *Poland and the Coming of the Second World War: The Diplomatic Papers of A.J. Drexel Biddle Jr., United States Ambassador to Poland, 1937–1939*, eds. Philip V. Cannistraro, Edward D. Wynot Jr., and Theodore P. Kovaleff (Columbus, 1976)

Polonsky, Antony. *Politics in Independent Poland, 1921–1939* (London, 1972)

SOVIET UNION

Erickson, John. *The Soviet High Command. A Military–Political History, 1918–1941* (London, 1962)

— . *The Road to Stalingrad: Stalin's War with Germany*, vol. 1 (London, 1975)

Falin, V.M. et al, eds. *Soviet Peace Efforts on the Eve of World War II(September 1938–August 1939): Documents and Records*, 2 vols. (Moscow, 1973)

Haslam, Jonathan. *Soviet Foreign Policy, 1930–1933: The Impact of the Depression* (London, 1983)

— . *The Soviet Union and the Struggle for Collective Security in Europe, 1933–1939* (London, 1984)

Ponomaryov, B.N., A.A. Gromyko, and V. Khvostov, eds. *History of Soviet Foreign Policy 1917–45* (Moscow, 1969)

Ulam, Adam B. *Expansion and Coexistence: The History of Soviet Foreign Policy, 1917–1967* (New York, 1968)

UNITED STATES

Barron, Gloria J. *Leadership in Crisis: FDR and the Path to Intervention* (Port Washington NY, 1973)

Cole,Wayne S. *Charles A. Lindbergh and the Battle against American Intervention in World War II* (New York, 1974)

— . *Roosevelt and the Isolationists, 1932–45* (Lincoln NB, 1983)

Dallek, Robert. *Franklin D. Roosevelt and American Foreign Policy, 1932–1945* (New York, 1979)

Divine, Robert. *The Reluctant Belligerent: American Entry into World War II* (New York, 1965)

Gardner, Lloyd C. *Economic Aspects of New Deal Diplomacy* (Madison, WN, 1974)

Hearden, Patrick J. *Roosevelt Confronts Hitler: America's Entry into World War II* (Dakalb IL, 1987)

Kinsella, William E. *Leadership in Isolation: FDR and the Origins of the Second World War* (Cambridge MA, 1978)

Lash, Joseph P. *Roosevelt and Churchill, 1939–1941: The Partnership that Saved the West* (New York, 1976)

Leigh, Michael. *Mobilizing Consent: Public Opinion and American Foreign Policy, 1937–1947* (Westport CN, 1976)

Leutze, James R. *Bargaining for Supremacy: Anglo–American Naval Collaboration, 1937–1941* (Chapel Hill NC, 1977)

MacDonald, Callum A. *The United States, Britain and Appeasement, 1936–1939* (London, 1981)

Marks, Frederick W. *Wind over Sand: The Diplomacy of Franklin Roosevelt* (Athens GA and London, 1988)

Offner, Arnold A. *American Appeasement. United States Foreign Policy and Germany, 1933–1938* (Cambridge MA, 1969)

— . *The Origins of the Second World War: American Foreign Policy and World Politics, 1917–1941* (New York, 1975)

Reynolds, David. *The Creation of the Anglo–American Alliance: A Study in Competitive Co-operation* (London, 1981)

Russett, Bruce M. *No Clear and Present Danger. A Skeptical View of the US Entry into World War II* (New York, 1972)

Toland, John. *Infamy: Pearl Harbor and its Aftermath* (New York, 1982)

Notes on Contributors

SIDNEY ASTER, formerly Lecturer in the University of Glascow and a freelance historian, is currently Associate Professor at the Erindale campus of the University of Toronto. He is the author of *1939, The Making of the Second World War* (1973), *Anthony Eden* (1976), *British Foreign Policy: A Guide to Research and Research Materials* (1984), and editor of A.P. Young, *The 'X' Documents: The Secret History of Foreign Office Contacts with the German Resistance, 1937–1939* (1974), and *The Second World War as a National Experience* (1981).

ROBERT BOYCE teaches international history at the London School of Economics. He is the author of *British Capitalism at the Crossroads, 1919–1932: A Study in Politics, Economics, and International Relations* (1987), and a forthcoming book on the politics of the world depression.

SUMIO HATANO is Associate Professor of Diplomatic History at the Institute of Social Sciences, University of Tsukuba, Ibaragi, Japan.

SADAO ASADA is Professor of International History at Doshisha University, Kyoto, Japan. His most recent English-language publication is *Japan and the World, 1854–1952: A Bibliographical Guide to Recent Japanese Scholarship in Foreign Relations* (1988), which he edited and co-authored.

MICHAEL HOWARD is Regius Professor of Modern History at Oxford. His works include *The Franco–Prussian War* (1960), *The Continental Commitment* (1973), *War and the Liberal Conscience* (1978), *War in European Society* (1976), and a translation with Peter Paret of Clausewitz *On War* (1976).

NICOLE JORDAN received her PhD from the London School of Economics where she studied with Esmonde Robertson. She is now Assistant Professor of History at the University of Illinois at Chicago, and is preparing a study of the breakdown of the French alliance system in Central Europe, 1933–1939.

CALLUM MACDONALD is Senior Lecturer in the Joint School of Comparative American Studies at the University of Warwick. He has written *The United States, Britain and Appeasement, 1936–1939* (1981), *Korea, the*

418

War before Vietnam (1986), and *Operation Anthropoid. The Assassination of SS Obergruppenführer Reinhard Heydrich* (forthcoming).

STEVEN MOREWOOD studied at Bristol Polytechnic and the University of Bristol where he received his PhD in 1985, with Esmonde Robertson as his external examiner. He is currently teaching European history at the University of Warwick.

RITCHIE OVENDALE is Reader in the Department of International Politics, University College of Wales, Aberystwyth. His publications include *'Appeasement' and the English Speaking World: Britain, the United States, the Dominions and the Policy of 'Appeasement', 1937–1939* (1975); *The Origins of the Arab-Israeli Wars* (1984), *The English-Speaking Alliance: Britain, the United States, the Dominions, and the Cold War, 1945–51* (1985); and has edited *The Foreign Policy of the British Labour Government, 1945–1951* (1984).

RICHARD OVERY is Reader in History at King's College, University of London. His many books include *William Morris, Viscount Nuffield* (1976), *The Air War, 1939–1945* (1980), *Goering: the 'Iron Man'* (1985), and *The Nazi Economic Recovery, 1932–38* (1982).

ESMONDE M. ROBERTSON taught international history at the London School of Economics until his death in January 1987. Among his books are *Hitler's Pre-War Policy and Military Plans* (1963), *Mussolini as Empire-Builder* (1977), and as editor, the first volume in this series on *The Origins of the Second World War* (1971).

GLYN STONE studied at the Universities of Lancaster and Sussex, and obtained his PhD from the London School of Economics under the supervision of Esmonde Robertson. He is Principal Lecturer in International History at Bristol Polytechnic and the author of several articles on the Anglo–Portuguese Alliance and on British non-intervention in the Spanish civil war.

Index